Scarecrow Professional Intelligence Education Series
Series Editor: Jan Goldman

In this post–September 11, 2001 era, there has been rapid growth in the number of professional intelligence training and educational programs across the United States and abroad. Colleges and universities, as well as high schools, are developing programs and courses in homeland security, intelligence analysis, and law enforcement, in support of national security.

The Scarecrow Professional Intelligence Education Series (SPIES) was first designed for individuals studying for careers in intelligence and to help improve the skills of those already in the profession; however, it was also developed to educate the public in how intelligence work is conducted and should be conducted in this important and vital profession.

1. *Communicating with Intelligence: Writing and Briefing in the Intelligence and National Security Communities*, by James S. Major. 2008.
2. *A Spy's Résumé: Confessions of a Maverick Intelligence Professional and Misadventure Capitalist*, by Marc Anthony Viola. 2008.
3. *An Introduction to Intelligence Research and Analysis*, by Jerome Clauser, revised and edited by Jan Goldman. 2008.
4. *Writing Classified and Unclassified Papers for National Security: A Scarecrow Professional Intelligence Educational Series Manual*, by James S. Major. 2009.
5. *Strategic Intelligence: A Handbook for Practitioners, Managers, and Users*, revised edition by Don McDowell. 2009.
6. *Partly Cloudy: Ethics in War, Espionage, Covert Action, and Interrogation*, by David L. Perry. 2009.
7. *Tokyo Rose / An American Patriot: A Dual Biography*, by Frederick P. Close. 2010.
8. *Ethics of Spying: A Reader for the Intelligence Professional*, edited by Jan Goldman. 2006.
9. *Ethics of Spying: A Reader for the Intelligence Professional*, Volume 2, edited by Jan Goldman. 2010.

TOKYO ROSE / AN AMERICAN PATRIOT

A Dual Biography

Frederick P. Close

Scarecrow Professional Intelligence Education Series, No. 7

THE SCARECROW PRESS, INC.
Lanham • Toronto • Plymouth, UK
2010

Published by Scarecrow Press, Inc.
A wholly owned subsidary of The Rowman & Littlefield Publishing Group, Inc.
4501 Forbes Boulevard, Suite 200, Lanham, Maryland 20706
http://www.scarecrowpress.com

Estover Road, Plymouth PL6 7PY, United Kingdom

British Library Cataloguing in Publication Information Available

Library of Congress Cataloging-in-Publication Data

Close, Frederick Phelps, 1943-
 Tokyo Rose/an American patriot : a dual biography / Frederick P. Close.
  p. cm. — (Scarecrow professional intelligence education series ; no. 7)
 Includes bibliographical references.
 ISBN 978-0-8108-6777-2 (hardcover : alk. paper) — ISBN 978-0-8108-7025-3
(ebook)
 1. Tokyo Rose, 1916-2006. 2. Japanese Americans—Biography. 3. World
War, 1939-1945—Japan. 4. World War, 1939-1945--Propaganda. 5. World
War, 1939-1945—Radio broadcasting and the war. 6. World War, 1939-1945—
Collaborationists—Biography. 7. Trials (Treason)—California—San Francisco. I.
Title. CT275.T717C567 2010
940.54'252092--dc22
 [B]
                                                                 2009028243

∞™ The paper used in this publication meets the minimum requirements of
American National Standard for Information Sciences—Permanence of Paper for
Printed Library Materials, ANSI/NISO Z39.48-1992.

Printed in the United States of America

Contents

Editor's Foreword by Jan Goldman   vii

Acknowledgments   ix

Introduction   xiii

1   Baseball Paths and Two-Lane Blacktops:
Youth at Full Speed (1916–1940)   1

2   A Fateful Letter in Failing Light (1940–1941)   27

3   Tokyo Rose: Origins of the Legend (Prewar)   41

4   Collision with Japan: Before Pearl Harbor (1941)   67

5   At War and on Her Own (1942)   83

6   The Toguris Back Home: Internment (1942–1945)   107

7   Barely Surviving: A Typist at Radio Tokyo (1943)   133

8   A New Career in Broadcasting: *Zero Hour*
(1943–1944)   155

9 Tokyo Rose: The Legend of the Radio Siren
   (Wartime)   181

10 Black Marketeer: The Destruction of Imperial
    Japan (1944)   215

11 War's End (1945)   241

12 The Scoop (1945)   255

13 CIC and FBI Investigations: Exoneration and
    Release (1946–1947)   275

14 Into the Cold War: A Furor Grows (1947–1948)   297

15 The Perjurors: The FBI at Work (1948–1949)   321

16 The Prosecution: *United States v. Tokyo Rose* (1949)   357

17 The Defense: *Iva Toguri v. Tokyo Rose* (1949)   391

18 The Verdict: *United States v. Iva Toguri* (1949)   437

19 Alderson Federal Reformatory: Failed
    Appeals (1950–1959)   447

20 The Quest for a Pardon (1960–2006)   479

Epilogue   505

Appendix: The Indictment   509

Bibliography   511

Index   515

About the Author   521

Editor's Foreword

The words "intelligence" and "information" are sometimes incorrectly interchangeable. Particularly for the intelligence professional, the differences between these two words should be clearly understood. "Intelligence" is the result of a process that includes the collection and analysis of data or material, and it is perceived to have some value, whereas "information" can be raw data or material that may or could have some value or no value at all. To extract meaningful information, which can be turned into intelligence is the job of the analyst. The purposeful use of information to deceive, mislead, or conceal intelligence is called "disinformation." Unlike propaganda techniques, which are designed to engage at an emotional response, disinformation is designed to manipulate the audience in their decision making. No person has become more famous or better embodied the terms "disinformation" or "propaganda" than the individual known as "Tokyo Rose."

Previous books in this series have focused on the skills required to become an intelligence professional. However, with this book, the series takes a different approach.

This book goes beyond the concepts of intelligence, information, disinformation, and propaganda. This book discusses the life of a person who has come to embody these concepts.

This series is extremely fortunate to include the first extensive and definitive biography of someone who has become part myth and part legend in the annals of propaganda. Fred Close has done a remarkable job of discussing the tactics and consequences of the role of disinformation and propaganda during war. However, this book is much more than that . . . the author describes the impact an individual can have on the world stage, while also telling a great story.

Jan Goldman, Ed.D.
SPIES Editor
Washington, D.C.

Acknowledgments

I first wish to thank those who read the manuscript's drafts. Most especially, I thank Dr. Aida Barrera, an ethnic-American studies scholar, who carefully scrutinized every chapter and made dozens of suggestions for improvements that caused the book to be far better than it otherwise would have been. I am also grateful to Dr. William Stott, Professor Emeritus of American Studies at the University of Texas at Austin, whose support through thirty years and whose recommendations helped make the book publishable. Dr. David L. Perry, Professor of Ethics, General Maxwell Taylor Chair of the Profession of Arms, U.S. Army War College, not only read the manuscript but first recommended it to Scarecrow Press. Finally, Lydia Schindler and her husband Greg Akins kindly provided me with free room and board for visit after visit to the National Archives in Maryland, and Lydia also read the book, provided counsel, and assisted me in doing research.

In addition, I should acknowledge several individuals and institutions whose help and support I can mention only briefly: The Rev. Frank Eiji Sugeno accompanied me when I first met Iva Toguri, when she first came to visit in Texas, and discussed on many occasions Japanese culture and the characters of the Japanese proverb on the book's back cover. Dr. Clifford Uyeda also was present at Iva's and my first meeting; in addition, he graciously served on a board of advisors for a PBS television project my company was producing and eventually recommended to Iva that she cooperate with me in my work. Louis Barbash explained the legal context of the case and recommended Thomas D. Morgan of George Washington University School of Law, author of the seminal text *Legal Ethics*. He and his colleague Stephen A. Saltzburg, Wallace and Beverley University Professor of Law, unraveled the mystery of why Wayne Collins could not call hostile witnesses. Military historian Alan Carey devoted considerable effort to research on the Apamama battle. Newspaperman Bill Boldenweck took time to share his memories of the *San Francisco Examiner*. I discussed the case with biographer Masayo Duus and her husband, Peter, and have had a number of conversations over the years with journalist Russell Warren Howe.

National Archives civilian records specialist Daniel Rooney and military records specialist Eric van Slander helped me find materials I otherwise would have missed entirely. David Kessler and Erica Nordmeier of the Bancroft Library at the University of California at Berkeley and Jennifer Broomhead and Jim Andrighetti of the Mitchell Library, State Library of New South Wales, Australia helped me locate photographs and gave me permission to use them without charge. I am especially grateful for the gratis permission to use two unique items: the Milton Caniff drawing of the GIs' imaginary Tokyo Rose, provided by Harry Guyton for the Estate of Milton Caniff; and the autographed yen note, provided by J. Richard Eisenhart, who also gave me an interview.

Finally, I must thank June and Iva Toguri. June and her husband allowed me to stay in their condo in Chicago during my formal interviews with Iva and herself. Iva Toguri not only participated in those interviews, but discussed every aspect of the case without reservation during years of friendship. She graciously provided me with dozens of family pictures for use in the book, along with handwritten notes identifying subjects she recognized and the circumstances of the photograph. She also provided me with many personal documents for use in research, signed a letter stating she was cooperating with me, and wrote dozens of letters in her own hand encouraging this project. Here is one of my favorite passages, from September 1999:

My dear Frederick:

It was more than just a pleasure to see you here in Chicago. You made my day, my month, you always do. When did I fly to Austin and add a most pleasant chapter to my life? [Iva first visited me in 1980.] Much water has passed under the bridge of life and I am so fortunate that you, Frederick, have always been there and here for me. There are so few members of the human race who can claim the wonderful delightful years of friendship we have experienced. I don't know about you, Fred, but I have been blessed and have thoroughly enjoyed these many years you have been such a comforting and fun person to know.

Much love and affection, Iva

I found Iva Toguri an inspiration. Although in this book I have criticized some of her decisions and come to conclusions she might not have desired, I tried above all else to tell the truth. I believe she would have wanted nothing less.

Introduction

The ancient biographer Plutarch wrote a series of studies titled *Parallel Lives of the Noble Greeks and Romans* in which he paired two individuals and compared their life stories. Included among these *Lives* were mythical figures such as the founders of Athens and Rome.

I have modeled the present work on Plutarch's *Lives*. *Tokyo Rose / An American Patriot: A Dual Biography*[1] compares the parallel life stories of Tokyo Rose and an American patriot named Iva Toguri. Both individuals are real, though real in different ways. Tokyo Rose is a legend. Iva Toguri was a young Japanese American woman trapped in Japan by the events of World War II. Tokyo Rose was purportedly an English-speaking radio propagandist for the Japanese during the war. American servicemen believed she infallibly predicted Allied military movements and drove their fellow soldiers and sailors to suicide with tales of unfaithful wives and girlfriends back home. Iva Toguri, forced to survive as an enemy alien without ration coupons, found a job at Radio Tokyo as a typist and then as one of several English-speaking disk jockeys used by the Japanese military. Toguri proved her patriotism in many ways, for example, by smuggling food and medicine to Allied POWs in Tokyo's notorious Bunka Camp. The legend and the human being had little in common. However, in the course of history, their lives intersected.

Sailors claimed to have heard Tokyo Rose taunting them a few days after the attack on Pearl Harbor. She addressed servicemen by name, and tormented them with soft music and salacious come-ons. The Japanese temptress had spies everywhere who supplied her with U.S. military secrets. In addition to being well informed, she was seductive, subversive, cunning, deceitful, and duplicitous. Tokyo Rose became famous throughout the Pacific and eventually back in the United States as the *New York Times*, *Time* magazine, and other news organizations speculated about her identity.

The U.S. government also wanted to identify this woman, to discover how she knew our military plans and could announce them over the radio. It covertly launched an investigation. U.S. military authorities determined that almost all such broadcasts were myths, and that of the women (some American, some not) who broadcast for Japan, not one ever called herself Tokyo Rose.

Nonetheless, news coverage back in the States made Tokyo Rose such a celebrity that gaining an interview with her was the first priority of Allied journalists entering Japan after the surrender. When they learned what the Army Counter-Intelligence Corps (CIC) already knew, that there was no Tokyo Rose, reporters faced a difficult decision: inform their readership that our servicemen had been duped by their own imaginations, or find someone to cast in the role. They found Iva Toguri.

Although post-war investigations in Japan by both the CIC and the Department of Justice (DoJ) determined that Iva Toguri was not the fabled Tokyo Rose, the U.S. government did little to publicize this fact. When Toguri attempted to return to her native country, many Americans, convinced that Tokyo Rose must be guilty of treason, expressed outrage that the U.S. government would allow the famous traitor to return without punishment. The Truman administration, facing a close election, capitulated to public demand and political expediency. The United States convicted and imprisoned Tokyo Rose. Iva Toguri did the time.

The legend of Tokyo Rose has remained vibrant in American culture. Movies from *Destination Tokyo* in 1943 to *Flags of Our Fathers* in 2006 feature scenes of servicemen gathered around a radio listening to broadcasts of Tokyo Rose propaganda. In 2005, Secretary of Defense Donald Rumsfeld compared those reporters who criticized the war in Iraq to Tokyo Rose. His reference, now a familiar part of the American popular lexicon, needed no explanation. An Internet search of the name returns hundreds of thousands of hits, most of which concern current political controversies. Tokyo Rose lives today as a symbol of the enemy within. She is the turncoat who sells out her country, besmirches its honor, denigrates its resolve, and subjects the nation's true patriots to scorn and derision.

⟿

To write a biography of an actual human being is a fairly straightforward undertaking. In the case of Iva Toguri, the facts of her life are largely a matter of public record. Through conversations with her, I also know personal information that is not available publicly but that has contributed to a comprehensive portrait of this largely misunderstood figure in American history. But how does one create a biography of Tokyo Rose? Tokyo Rose had no parents, no youth, no bad breaks, no declining years, and she cannot die. She is an ageless and abiding phenomenon of the imagination, not an existing human being.

Plutarch faced such a problem when he wrote the life of Theseus, the founder of Athens. Plutarch's contemporaries had heard of Theseus. They knew Theseus had a human father as well as a divine father, and that during his life he slew the Minotaur, a creature that was part man and part bull. When Plutarch researched the life of Theseus, he did not limit his inquiry to credible historical events. Instead, comparing himself to geographers confronted with empty spaces on the edges of their maps, Plutarch left the familiar ground of empirical evidence and set off to explore the terra incognita of "fables and tragic stories, the province of poets."[2] He took it as his task to sort out fact from fiction, serious mythology from silly tales, and reasonable speculations from credulous conjectures.

I have approached the "biography" of Tokyo Rose in a similar fashion. Most Americans today have heard of Tokyo Rose. She appeared at the outset of World War II as a voice on radio, the imagination-intensive medium she required for her particular seductions. The elements of her legend were remarkably uniform for American military personnel across the length and breadth of the Pacific theater and have remained so. The many and various Japanese broadcasters did not provide that uniformity, so the explanation for it must be found in the minds of her hearers. The particular characteristics of her persona in 1941–1945 derived from what her listeners shared: the common culture of ordinary American men as they marched off to war and their common experiences in fighting that war.

Plutarch would have likely viewed the parallel lives of Tokyo Rose and Iva Toguri in terms of fate. Given their needs, their prejudices, their fears, American servicemen seemed fated to create Tokyo Rose in their imaginations and to believe she lived in the real world. Conversely, Iva Toguri herself believed that she was fated to be identified with Tokyo Rose. "Who else could it have been?" was one way she put it. She meant by this that of the many women who were on-air personalities at Radio Tokyo, only she had refused to renounce her U.S. citizenship. The other women either had renounced or were not American. Therefore, only she could be charged with treason and convicted under U.S. law.

However, the fact that she was the only woman technically available for prosecution seems to me of small importance. Americans were adamant about punishing Tokyo Rose after the war concluded. Since she didn't exist, this meant some innocent would have to pay for her crimes. These conditions and many others—the loss of our atomic secrets to spies shortly after World War II, the fixation on ferreting out communists in the late 1940s, the demand for loyalty oaths, voters' view of Truman as soft on traitors—all contributed to the prosecution of Iva Toguri as Tokyo Rose.

On a more personal level, Iva's own character partly sealed her fate. During her youth, she developed entrepreneurial interests and ambitions modeled after those of her father, whom she adored. Had she lived in the United States during peacetime, she probably would have succeeded handsomely in business. Caught in wartime Japan, she made the most of her resources and survived against terrible odds. However, when she was offered the opportunity for fame and fortune as the human embodiment of the legendary Tokyo Rose, her ambition led her into tragic mistakes that also contributed to her prosecution.

~

In the early 1980s, a new game called *Trivial Pursuit* became all the rage.[3] As I played one evening, a friend read the question, "By what name is Iva Toguri better known?" I replied, "I spoke with Iva last weekend . . . , " and everybody laughed at how clever I was. But I was telling the truth; I really had telephoned her. I knew Iva Toguri for more than 25 years.

My interest in the Tokyo Rose story spans a period of three decades. It began with my association with Clifford Uyeda, a former national president of the Japanese American Citizens League, who led the fight for Toguri's pardon. He introduced me to Iva Toguri in 1980. Over the years, Iva and I had numerous conversations, and I got to know her well. In addition, I conducted more than 50 hours of formal interviews with Iva and her sister June. The casual conversations we shared during week-long visits have allowed me to infuse this biography with personal insights and anecdotes not available in any public record.

I also examined approximately 10,000 pages of archival material in Federal Bureau of Investigation (FBI), DoJ, Army CIC, and Federal Broadcasting Intelligence Service files. Many of these records have only recently been declassified and have never been cited previously. I analyzed the 6,000 pages of trial transcripts from 1949. I also investigated newspaper and magazine reports, immigration records, prison documents, military and civilian records in Australia, historical texts, archival film footage, and oral histories. I collected dozens of photographs to illustrate the text. This research grounded the opinions expressed in the work that follows.

The fact that I considered Iva a friend has not influenced my commitment to tell her story as accurately as possible. I found that her memories could not be trusted. She misremembered people and events in a way that indicated her experience of prosecution and imprisonment had distorted her recollections of what actually happened. At times, she intentionally misled me and knowingly failed to tell the whole truth. I also believe that her inability to avail herself of the defense of duress forced her to tell falsehoods at her trial. This book will considerably revise earlier accounts of her life story.

However, I do not wish to give the impression that I think Iva Toguri was a villain or a traitor, as the U.S. government alleged. I merely suggest that Iva was a flawed human being, not a saint. The fact that she was an ordinary person, with the normal strengths and weaknesses we all share, only makes her story more interesting and compelling.

Notes

1. The punctuation mark in the title, *Tokyo Rose / An American Patriot*, is a slash. The slash separates the compound alternative items "Tokyo Rose" and "An American Patriot." *A Dual Biography* is the subtitle of the work and therefore is separated from the title by a colon.

2. Christopher Pelling. *Plutarch and History: Eighteen Studies* (New York: D. Brown Book Co., 2002), 171. Translation of *Theseus*, opening paragraph.

3. *Trivial Pursuit* is a registered trademark of Hasbro, Inc.

Figure 1.1.   A young Iva Toguri holds tightly to her bag of candy.

1

Baseball Paths and Two-Lane Blacktops

Youth at Full Speed

It has been said that no authentic human life is possible without irony.[1] Iva Toguri, who will be identified forever with the infamous traitor Tokyo Rose, was born on the Fourth of July.[2]

Iva's earliest childhood memories were of the fabulous parties her father threw to celebrate both her own birthday and the birthday of the United States. Like many immigrants, her father Jun (rhymes with "gun") Toguri delighted in his status as a new American. When his first daughter was born on July 4, as Iva put it, "He was so proud of it! He wouldn't let me forget it! You'd think that he had won the lottery!"[3]

Iva Ikuko Toguri (Iva believed Ikuko, which her father selected for her, derived from a Chinese character that meant "pacific" or "floating"[4]) was born in Los Angeles in 1916, but the birthday parties she remembered took place in the small town of Calexico, where her family moved when she was three. Calexico is a town on the California–Mexico border with a mix of ethnic groups, and her father invited the whole neighborhood to a huge outdoor barbeque to celebrate the Fourth.

Iva's sister June remembered that her mother often remarked that Iva, even as a child, "was a little different."[5] The other three Toguri children, Fred, June, and Inez, were shy and quiet, like their mother. Iva was an extrovert who made friends easily among the Caucasians and their families. She also had a temper and talked back, even to their father. Jun Toguri had the demeanor one would expect of a male who grew up in Japanese society in the late nineteenth century. He was a traditional patriarch who dominated his wife and children. They accepted his word as law and followed his edicts without question—except for Iva, who was cut from his same cloth. She bucked him constantly. Jun enrolled her in preschool as soon as they arrived in Calexico. "My father told me, 'I put you in this preschool. You were three years old. You were driving me crazy at home.'" Iva promptly took over. "By the time I was five, I was a pro! In fact, I was teaching kindergarten because I'd been there forever. I knew the routine."

June remembered that Iva was a little different in another way. "I think maybe she should have been born a boy instead of a girl." Iva didn't take to being girlish. She had no love of cooking or dresses. Iva explored the world of greater Calexico on her bicycle, and her great passion was baseball.

She preferred first base, but she would play any position. She liked to compete. The only Toguri child to love sports, Iva wore out more pairs of shoes than the other three put together. Her father would drive her to games in small towns like El Centro and Brawley, where the children would play hard in the heat and then pile into their parents' cars for the drive home. Iva, soaked with perspiration, sat in the breeze of the open car window. As if to prove the old adage "sit in a draft and catch your death," she caught pneumonia several times. While her mother tended to the other children, her father made steam to help her breathe and stayed up night after night nursing his tomboy daughter back to health.

Over and over, as a child and as an adult, Iva Toguri displayed her love of action. She was not a contemplative. Hers was an exterior rather than an interior life. She preferred doing over thinking or talking, working over sitting or relaxing. Given a choice between board games and tree climbing, the youthful Iva picked the tree every time.

Iva's father had enrolled Iva in the preschool of the local Congregationalist church.[6] When the preschool held a ten-year reunion, the principal asked Iva to address the assembly. Her mother made a beautiful turquoise-blue dress especially for the occasion, and her father drove the whole family through a ferocious rainstorm to attend. Iva, eager to rally the troops of preschoolers and deliver her first important speech, basked in her celebrity. Even at age 70, she could still hear the sound of rain falling on the old tin roof of the schoolhouse, still could recall that new dress her mother had sewn just for her, still could remember her father's proud look as the family entered. "The reason I can remember is that I had to go outside the building for some reason, and I fell in the mud. I fell in the mud, and I created something terrible. I don't remember anything after that, but I remember falling in the mud and my father had a fit!"

When Iva recounted such stories from her childhood and youth, most of her memories centered around her father, not her mother. June noticed that their two personalities—those of Jun and his daughter Iva—were strikingly similar. However, if Jun noticed this similarity, neither Iva nor June recalled him giving any indication of it. Because Iva was a girl, he seems not to have even considered the possibility.

~

Jun Mamoru Toguri[7] was born March 25, 1881 or 1882[8] in the silkworm and grape district of Japan's Yamanashi Prefecture. (Japan is divided into prefectures in the same way that the United States is divided into states.) While still a teenager, he left his native country for the United States. His father, Renzaburo Toguri, a civil engineer, bought him a ticket on the ship *Riojun Maru*, and he arrived in Seattle on October 25, 1899. Immigration records show he was a small man, 5 feet 3 inches tall, with brown eyes, black hair, a small mole on his face, and a physique described as "stout."[9]

Emigration by Japanese in those days was rare. By 1900, fewer than 30,000 Japanese had entered the United States. In comparison, about 250,000 Chinese had been admitted by 1882. That year, responding to outcries by influential Californians against the "Yellow Peril," the U.S. Congress passed the Chinese Exclusion Act to prevent further immigration. This legislation singled out the Chinese by nationality, making them the first group to be legally banned from entering the United States. However, it left the door open for Japanese and other Asians.

Jun's reasons for leaving Japan, he told his children, were to be on his own, to make decisions for himself, and to become a commercial success. This no doubt had some truth to it, but late in his life, when her father was nearly 90 years old, Iva discovered a deeper, more compelling explanation. Jun Toguri had a secret. When he was a boy, his mother abandoned him. She divorced his father and moved away to the great city of Tokyo, where she remarried, started a new family, and forgot about him. His father remarried and had two sons by his new wife, so Jun grew up as an only child reared by his paternal grandmother. In Japan, ancestry matters profoundly, and the neighborhood kids taunted him. As a result, Jun Toguri developed a tough-minded, independent personality. He was proud in the way shamed children can be. He got into fights even though his grandmother warned him against it. He did not fit in, and as soon as he could, he left Japan to start a new life.

Jun Toguri chose the United States because a Seattle businessman, Kakuzo Kawakami, offered him a job. Kawakami oversaw the import–export business of the Furuya Company,[10] and the young Jun Toguri lived in Seattle from 1899 to 1904, then in Vancouver, Canada for a year before returning to the United States in April 1905. He described his job as "manager" to immigration officials. He learned the business, built the Furuya chain by opening new branch stores in Portland, Tacoma, and Vancouver, and put away savings.

Thanks to this industry, Jun soon possessed the financial resources to start a family. His boss had a young lady in mind for his valuable manager, but Jun Toguri feared an entangling alliance. To maintain his independence without insulting his employer, he searched for a wife on his own. Since only 2 percent of first-generation Japanese immigrants (*Issei*) married non-Japanese in those days, and the ratio of Japanese males to females entering the U.S. was 24 to 1, Jun sought a bride in Japan during one of several trips he made on behalf of the business.[11]

He selected Fumi Iimuro, the youngest of nine sisters.[12] Fumi resembled the women in traditional Japanese woodcuts—long hair, long nose, small eyes, small mouth, round face. Iva inferred that her father found her mother beautiful because late in his life, decades after Fumi had died, Iva overheard him remark on the beauty of a woman who resembled her mother. But she never heard him express such an opinion directly. "Oh no, no, nooo! Not the Japanese man. He might have told her in private, but he certainly wouldn't have told her in front of us."

A child's character is partially developed through pa
ing her stories of ancestors who can serve as family heroes and role
models. Iva remembered that her mother—a quiet, refined, and
exquisitely gentle woman—knitted as she told her about her grandfather. Fumi's father was a samurai, an expert horseman selected
to drive the Emperor. As a result, he had entered the Imperial palace. For an ordinary Japanese to have seen the emperor was quite
something, but to have seen both the emperor and the interior of the
palace was extraordinary. He was, however, illiterate, and when the
samurai were disbanded in 1876, he taught himself to read and write
by studying with little children in school. He discovered he had an
aptitude for mathematics and the abacus, and eventually became an
architect. Iva's maternal grandmother was also a fighter. Diagnosed
with tuberculosis (often a fatal disease in the nineteenth century),
she cured herself through bathing in ice cold water and by taking up
archery. She built her strength, and became an expert with a 6-foot
bow even though she was only 4 feet 10 inches tall herself.

In 1907,[13] Jun Toguri married Fumi Iimuro in an arranged marriage—arranged by himself, that is. On their honeymoon, with the
help of a guide, they climbed Mt. Fuji, the Japanese equivalent of
a trip to Niagara Falls. For the first six years of their marriage, Jun
traveled between his business interests in North America and his
romantic interests in Japan. On the first day of November 1910,
their first child, a son, was born in Japan. Jun Toguri named him
Fred; Iva has no idea why he chose this particular American name.
Jun extracted himself from Kawakami and Furuya and opened an
import store of his own in Los Angeles, as well as a cotton business
in Imperial County on the Mexico border. On October 22, 1913,
Fumi and Fred arrived in San Francisco.[14] Three years later, Iva
appeared on the scene, and Jun also gave her an American name.
This time, however, we know the namesake. She was a childless
French woman who lived next door, and she was so delighted
when the Toguris agreed to name their daughter after her that she
took over all the expenses associated with the newborn. The elder
Iva bought the baby Iva's clothing, shoes, and toys. In 1919, Jun
closed his Los Angeles business and moved his family to Calexico.
Almost as soon as they arrived, Iva had a little sister, June, and five
years later, with the birth of Inez, the Toguri family was complete
(Figures 1.2, 1.3, 1.4, 1.5).[15]

Figure 1.2. Iva on Fumi's lap; Jun and Fred standing.

Figure 1.3. Fred and Iva.

Figure 1.4. Iva (middle, left), Fred (back, right).

Figure 1.5. Fumi, Inez, June, and Iva.

Iva Toguri remembered growing up in a small town wistfully, as a time that would not only never come to her again, but that has never existed for most Americans living today. No one locked their doors, bikes and skates left in the yard would be there the next morning, and the thought that the world might be a dangerous place of crime and war remained alien to Iva's childhood mind. She and Fred had the run of their dusty little Eden, and the Toguri family worked and played together. The children did chores and homework on weekdays, but Friday night was "freedom night" when the family played games and had fun.

On one of those Friday evenings, Iva's father brought home a special treat. He had acquired some records of traditional Japanese music, and he was anxious to introduce his young children to his native culture. June remembered the children wanted to learn about their heritage: "except for Iva. She couldn't care less; she just wanted to be an average American." The four children sat dutifully as their father grandly put on the first record. Fred, June, and Inez listened, smiled, and nodded their appreciation. Iva, a fan of the Big Band sound of the Swing Era, did not. "I can remember saying, 'What is that awwwful music?' And out the door I went."

June noticed her older sister's independent streak. Iva recalled, "My sister remarked to me one time that I had a tendency to shoot off my mouth. I said, 'June, if I believe that isn't the way to go, I think I should say it. Not that Dad's going to do it the way I want, but at least he'll know what I'm thinking, that I'm not just a puppet.' She was a very obedient child. I wasn't that obedient. My father used to tell me, 'I think you deliberately go around looking for trouble!' In fact I didn't. It was on my lap."

June believed her father and mother's favorite was their eldest, Fred. Iva agreed: "I'm sure my mother loved my brother much more than she loved me. I guess she had an inner sense that I was going to make it some way. With my brother, she believed he needed her." The affection mother and son felt for each other was natural; the two were very much alike. Fred possessed his mother's sweet disposition. He was gentle and considerate. As an adult, his friends praised his unstinting charity and helpfulness. But his generosity meant Fred was not a natural businessman. He hated to reprimand and chasten workers; he did not hunger to increase volume, decrease costs, and make more money. As heir apparent to the family business, he served his father diligently, but he never challenged him. "I used to say, 'Fred, you're just too damn good. You let people run all over you.' And sometimes he'd bring up my case, and he'd say, 'You know, if you'd kept your mouth shut, maybe you wouldn't have had this problem.' Words to that effect. Because he would have kept his mouth shut. This was the difference in our personalities."

~

In the seventh grade, Iva's school required female students to take a cooking class. Iva ruined one casserole after another. For the final exam, the teacher decided the class should put together a meal for the administration. She needed a volunteer to set up and decorate the table. Here, Iva saw her opportunity, and she quickly petitioned for the job. "So I talked my father into getting all kinds of things from the shop, unusual decorations, fans, little parasols, and I made up a terrific table. Boy, the principal thought that was the best thing he had ever seen, and the teacher was in her glory, and guess who got an A. Yours truly. And I couldn't cook! I couldn't open a can of beans!"

Later, when her mother became ill, her father said, "You know there are three female children in this house. We ought to take turns cooking. One day Iva will cook and June will do the dishes and Inez will set the table, and then the reverse will take place and so forth." Iva completed the story: "That was about the time I was starting to read about microbes and undercooked pork and trichinosis. So, as luck would have it, my night was pork chops. Well! I knew that I had to cook the pork very well, so I put them in the fry pan and really cooked them and after that I stuck them in the oven so they'd be well done, right? They were like—they stood up on their own! My father said, 'I think we'll just eliminate you in the cooking. You can do the pots and pans.' I said, 'Thank you.' I was terrible in the kitchen!"

Iva showed even more deviousness in her school's sewing class. Her sister June, an excellent seamstress, won awards for her work, but Iva couldn't sew a stitch. So, she smuggled her assigned project out of school and brought it home for her mother to work on. She shrewdly had her mother do only a little at a time so that the slow progress appeared to be Iva's own diligent work. The teacher never caught on.

Thus, while her sisters dutifully mastered the traditional feminine crafts, Iva subverted standards of achievement to her own ends. She was not exactly a delinquent; she merely became adept at figuring out how to overcome a difficult situation by seizing whatever opportunities presented themselves. Iva learned something valuable in cooking class and sewing class, but not how to cook or sew. However, Jun Toguri was determined that his little infielder master at least one feminine art. So he bought a piano and hired a teacher, Mildred Rex. (Iva remembered Rex dolefully. "She got married and had a child. A few years later, there's this sensational murder. Her husband murders her and her child. We couldn't believe it."[16]) Iva sat at the keyboard, kept still as best she could, and dreamed of fly balls and tag outs while she practiced. Her interest often flagged, but Iva persevered to please her father and learned the basics.

She learned something else from her father. Every year Jun provided his children with a small, inexpensive gift for their teachers. He did not intend the gift as a bribe. It was his way of showing, as was typical of Japanese, his respect for teachers. He asked for nothing in return. "We took this gift on the first day of school, and we welcomed the teacher. Of course, you know, they were so unaccustomed to it they just fell over. So the teacher remembered me from Day One. She had no problem with my name or me." Later, Iva would make use of her father's technique for smoothing the rails.

$\sim$

On May 7, 1900, shortly after Jun Toguri's arrival in the United States, Stanford Professor of Sociology Edward Alsworth Ross addressed the first anti-Japanese mass meeting in San Francisco. Ross opined that the Japanese were so undemocratic, so poor, and so unassimilable that the United States should "turn our guns on every vessel bringing Japanese to our shores rather than to permit them to land."[17] At about the same time, the *San Francisco Chronicle* launched an anti-Japanese campaign with articles titled "The Yellow Peril—How Japanese Crowd out the White Race," "Brown [Japanese] Men an Evil in the Public Schools," "Japanese American

Menace to American Women," and "Brown Artisans Steal Brains of Whites," adding that "Every one of these immigrants is a Japanese spy."[18] Following these provocations, the California legislature on March 1, 1905, passed a resolution asking Congress to exclude the Japanese from the United States. The vote was 28–0 in the California Senate and 70–0 in the Assembly. The Japanese Exclusion League formed in San Francisco shortly thereafter, and within a year the organization had a membership of almost 80,000, 75 percent of whom resided in the Bay area. The Japanese replaced the Chinese as the Yellow Peril to worry about. Opined the *Chronicle*, "The Chinese are faithful laborers and do not buy land. The Japanese are unfaithful laborers and do buy land."[19]

In Southern California, Japanese Americans had formed a close-knit community in Los Angeles and, by the 1920s, they supported more than 350 organizations. Japanese immigrants in general were model citizens. Crime was almost nonexistent in their communities; they paid their debts, took care of their own indigents, conducted campaigns to improve their homes, and adopted American clothes and habits. They were also aligned with white business associations such as the Merchants and Manufacturing Association, were strongly anti-labor and profoundly anti-communist, and voted overwhelmingly Republican.[20] Iva herself, when she came of voting age, registered as a Republican.[21]

As Iva grew into a teenager, anti-Japanese agitation relaxed somewhat for the simple reason that the white supremacists had won. Led by the Native Sons of the Golden West, whose motto was "California must remain what it has always been and God Himself intended it shall always be—the White Man's Paradise," the group experienced one success after another.[22] The 1906 Gentlemen's Agreement between the United States and Japan had limited the number of Japanese males entering America. The Agreement did not include women, specifically "picture brides," whose numbers grew exponentially until the Japanese government stopped their emigration in 1920. In 1913, the Alien Land Act prevented Japanese from owning land, although they could lease it. The Issei circumvented the law by putting the land either in the name of their American-born children or of corporations. In 1920, these loopholes were closed. Every county in California voted in favor of preventing Japanese from owning or leasing land, or being corporation shareholders or guardians of minor children who owned or leased land. The same law passed in surrounding states and as far away as Texas and Delaware. The resourceful Issei evaded these laws as well by having whites purchase farmland for them or by working as "managers" for their children or for more distant relatives. The worst indignation occurred on November 13, 1922, when the U.S. Supreme Court finally settled the controversial question of citizenship; the Court found the Japanese were not "free white persons" and were therefore ineligible to be U.S. citizens.[23] Senator Henry Cabot Lodge led the fight to adopt the 1924 Exclusion Act in the U.S. Congress, which effectively ended Japanese immigration until after World War II. In response, the Japanese in 1924 elected to their parliament, the Diet, candidates pledged to retaliate against the United States.

In the United States in the late 1930s, Togo Tanaka, the editor of the *Japanese Daily News*, started a column in English called the "Nisei Business Bureau." In this column, he exposed the common practice of restrictive racial covenants in deeds in southern California that limited occupancy to "persons of the Caucasian race. In practice we were told we could buy it, but couldn't live in it."[24] Jun Toguri knew such bigotry from personal experience. He recognized that many neighborhoods were closed to Japanese, and he took some pride in opening them up. Iva's sister June recalled that although the family lived in white neighborhoods, they did not mix with Caucasians, although she added that this described herself more than Iva.

Assessing Iva's personal experience with racial prejudice is difficult. Whatever the local situation in culturally mixed Calexico, it is hard to imagine a child of Asian descent would escape nasty remarks or social snubs in cities like San Diego and Los Angeles, where Iva spent her young adulthood. However, in her interviews with me in 1987, she claimed that she could not remember a single instance of bigotry. June, in her separate interview, also failed to recall any such experiences. Iva adamantly denied that anyone pulled their eyes back at her or called her a "Jap" or jeered at her to "go home." She had not experienced a failure of memory many years after the fact. Iva told the *San Francisco Chronicle* the same story in 1949, even going so far as to say, "I was never aware of the existence of [racial prejudice]."[25] Certainly, at that time, just before her trial for treason, she had no reason to lie. On the contrary, she might have garnered sympathy by portraying herself as a victim of racism. But she did not.

Iva and June's failure to recall evidence of racism may be symptomatic of the attitudes of many Nisei (children of original immigrants) of their generation, which historian John Modell has described as "considerable bravery, mixed sometimes with despair but more often with self delusion." Modell quotes as typical the remarks of a Los Angeles Nisei unable to find a job: "Frankly, the time-worn 'emotion rouser'—racial discrimination—is very distasteful to me. The word is promiscuously applied to every situation which may seem repugnant to an individual of Japanese ancestry. Too often, it is used to excuse oneself for his own shortcomings."[26] When the labor union consortium the Congress of Industrial Organizations tried to end discrimination at Lockheed Aircraft in 1940, the Nisei attacked the CIO. "It is just a matter of company policy. To make a big hullaballoo and fuss would be merely to build the wall still higher. We shall probably see the day soon when a deserving and especially capable American citizen of Japanese ancestry will secure employment at Lockheed."[27]

The 1939 holiday edition of the San Francisco-based *Japanese American News*, written in English by Nisei, summed up their positive attitudes. Championing the need to "burn a few of our bridges behind us" (i.e., to stop trying to be a bridge between Japan and America, between their parents and general American society), the writers proclaimed that the Nisei realizes,

> that his true cultural background is not one of Japanese art and music and literature but is essentially the culture of middle-class America. The young Nisei listens to Bob Hope and Fred Allen; he sings the songs made famous by Bing Crosby; he reads *Collier's* and the *Satevepost* [sic] and the *American Magazine*; he likes swing, the Sunday funnies, and Myrna Loy.[28]

Such interests were certainly typical of Iva Toguri.

In the end, however, positive attitudes did not matter. As Aiji Tashiro lamented in 1934, "the Jablioskis, Idovitches, and Johannsmanns streaming over from Europe slip unobtrusively into the clothes of 'dyed-in-the-wool' Americans by the simple expedient of dropping their guttural speech and changing their names to Jones, Brown, or Smith." Tashiro could not. Even though he was born in New England and spoke perfect English, "average Americans" easily recognized his foreign ancestry because, in his words, "[I] possessed the marked characteristics of the race . . . flat nose, almond eyes, black hair."[29]

Iva too was marked. American in her heart, she still looked like a "Jap." As a result, she could not, and did not, escape racial prejudice. Despite her denials, we know this for a fact. Iva wrote a letter from Japan in 1941 warning her brother, sisters, and friends to stay in America. "No matter how bad things get and how much you have to take in the form of racial criticisms and no matter how hard you have to work, by all means remain in the country you learn to appreciate more after you leave it."[30] Clearly she realized there were "racial criticisms" to be endured.

~

When the bottom fell out of the cotton market, Jun Toguri abandoned his Calexico brokerage business and, in 1925, moved his family to San Diego. Here he became a broker of produce, acting as a middle man between growers in the valley and wholesalers in the city. This business also failed to prosper, and he soon returned to what he knew best: retail and imports. He managed a store in Los Angeles on Broadway, across the street from the Orpheum Theater, and auctioned goods on a pier in Long Beach. For a while he commuted weekly from San Diego, and Iva remembered a new side of her father uncovered by the separation. "I recall how gentle he was when he wanted to say goodbye to us in San Diego and go back to his work in Los Angeles. He was a different person. He'd hug all of us kids, give us a peck, and he always said, 'Be good. Behave yourselves.' Sometime he'd have to take the night train, and we'd be in bed, and he'd come and hug us all and tell us, 'Soon we'll all be together. I'll call you guys from Los Angeles.' I remember that sweetness. The rest of the time he was, well . . ."—not sweet. The idea of a Japanese father hugging and kissing his children would come as a shock to any Japanese of Iva's generation and to many even today. Iva's Japanese friends simply did not believe her when she told them, saying they could not imagine their fathers acting in such a way.

He gave his children affection but not compliments. "I mean, we could excel, we could perform out of this world, and it would be, 'You did satisfactory.' Nothing like, 'You were great, kid!' Like when my sister graduated from this sewing and designing school. For her presentation, she made a tailored coat. It was gorgeous. She got wool material that was very difficult, with embossed lines going through it, and to match those lines! It was sensational, the hit of the show. My father went to the graduation. I said, 'Boy, that is some coat!' Everybody just went wild about it. He says, 'Not bad.' And I thought to myself, 'Well, that's it, you know.' I have never, ever heard my father praise. And he admitted it. He said, 'I have never praised my children in any way whatsoever.'"

The sometimes open affection Jun Toguri displayed toward his children did not extend to Iva's mother. He did not hug or kiss his wife in front of his children, nor did he ever pay her a compliment. "My father was a true patriarchal individual. His wife was second in command. Her part in this world was to raise us, maintain the household, keep us fed, and that was her duty. She did not have to be praised or complimented to get any work out of her, I guess."

As a young woman, Iva Toguri was as careful with her emotions as her father was with compliments. She admired her father tremendously just as he admired June's coat. But neither let on. In her maturity, she was more open. "My father was a fantastic person. You could never knock him down, he was always coming up. God rest his soul, he was a grand old man."

Part of his appeal for Iva was that he could do everything. For example, he built from scratch an entire room on the side of the house for Iva and her sisters. How he learned the skills of carpentry she does not know. He repaired all sorts of gadgets and machines, but he never studied mechanics. He farmed the side yard, providing the family with an abundance of vegetables and fruits.

He also possessed a passion for the beautiful. He filled his garden with flowers, and he would sit and admire them, especially his favorites. He loved roses, tree roses in particular. Iva was less enthusiastic. "To me they looked artificial.

"One morning, I remember there was a yell you would have never forgotten. We all jumped out of bed, ran over to my father's room, and my father was cussing, cussing to beat the band. We said, 'Dad, what's the matter?' He said, 'Look out that window!'

We looked out. Somebody in the night had come in and dug up his roses." Her father immediately drove to a nursery, bought replacements, and planted them again. "Then he went out and bought a dog!" Iva laughed as she recalled the events. "He goes out and buys a dog! It was a black-tongued chow dog. You know, they're like one-owner dogs, terrific watchdogs. Then he immediately started to plant a hedge of boysenberries around the entire house, and they grew like weeds. Before you knew it, the whole house was fenced in, plus he had this dog. He and my father, they took to each other very well. I don't know how he trained him, but the dog knew his own territory and if you put one foot inside the property, off went your leg."

Her father did not call the police. Jun Toguri preferred to solve the problem himself. He went around channels, not through them. Whenever the authorities could not be avoided, such as teachers in school, he dealt with them as people, not officeholders. Iva watched her father and learned, learned an approach to institutions that works best when public scrutiny doesn't harden an official's position.

In his personal life, when he himself was in charge, he employed the same technique and went around himself. He loved fresh fish, fresh sardines in particular. But in a house without exhaust fans, cooking fish in the kitchen could leave the house smelling for weeks. Fumi couldn't stand the odor, but "my mother was very gentle. She wouldn't directly say, 'You have to do it outside.' But he understood. So, he gets himself some bricks and he makes a barbecue pit with the grates and everything and cooked his dog-gone fish outside, and brings it inside and enjoys it. The pit was humongous! Where he learned to build it, I don't know. He wasn't a bricklayer. He was something else."

In 1927, the Toguri family returned to Los Angeles, where they would reside until their internment in 1942. For most of this period, they lived on Bandera Avenue, just one block from Jun Toguri's Wilmington Avenue Market where he sold groceries and imported goods.

Iva attended McKinley Junior High and Compton High School.[31] Her friends were about equally divided between Asians and non-Asians. In our interview, she only reluctantly discussed them because she felt so many had abandoned her when she needed them.

They represented bad memories for Iva Toguri, but perhaps few youthful acquaintances could have stood firm in the firestorm that would have engulfed anyone who defended "Tokyo Rose." Before the war, however, Iva's life was far from lonely. She dated, as did most young people at that time, in a group rather than individually. She liked one Japanese boy because of the car he owned. However, although many of her friends were white, she did not date any of them because her father would have disapproved of such a relationship (and perhaps because their own families would have also disapproved). Jun Toguri's reservations were typical of Japanese in the United States. Only 4 percent of Nisei intermarried with whites, in part due to pressure from their parents to stay within the community.[32] (By contrast, in 1920, 22 percent of second-generation Mexican American women and 30 percent of men intermarried.[33]) Even these few Nisei marriages had to slip past California's anti-miscegenation laws, in effect from 1905 to 1948. Ralph Newman, a white minister, defended the need for such laws in 1913: "Near my home is an eighty-acre tract of as fine land as there is in California. On that tract lives a Japanese. With that Japanese lives a white woman. In that woman's arms is a baby. What is that baby? It isn't white. It isn't Japanese. It is a germ of the mightiest problem that ever faced this state; a problem that will make the black problem of the South look white."[34]

The young lady soon to be identified with one of history's most notorious sirens was not particularly active in matters romantic. Perhaps the sports competitor who ran with abandon through baseball infields proved too full a hand for most young men, especially Japanese Americans used to a more traditional female personality. Also, Iva, by her own estimation, was not especially attractive. She considered herself "average, just average." She wore her hair long, like the woman her father had married, but she did not resemble her mother in any other way. "See, my brother and both of my sisters were fair. My mother had milky white skin almost, unusual for a Japanese—very clear, very light skin. Whereas my father was darker. I thought he was darker because he was outside all the time. Mother always used to say, 'Boy, you took after your dad in more ways than one, even the color of your skin.' I guess she resented the fact that I was not fair like the rest of them. But it didn't bother me."

In 1933, Iva graduated from high school. She had skipped a grade and attended Compton Junior College to take additional classes to prepare for full-time college work. With four children to support and having recently purchased his own grocery store, Jun Toguri lacked funds to fully underwrite his daughter's education. This narrowed the choice of schools. Iva chose the University of California at Los Angeles (UCLA) because tuition was only $54 a year and she could live at home. Her father encouraged her frugality with an offer: if she attended UCLA, he would buy her a car. But she had to support it. Iva accepted, and launched her career as a capitalist.

Jun bought his daughter a 1934 olive-green Chrysler Royal four-door sedan. Iva immediately placed an ad for passengers in the UCLA newspaper, the *Daily Bruin*. She maxed out at five, and with plenty more to take their place, she demanded each pay for a week whether they rode in the car or not. If they were sick, that was their bad luck. With gas wars common in Southern California, and gas often available at 9 cents a gallon, "you could fill up for a dollar." She made money and friends of her riders; soon they socialized together as well as car pooled.

Iva Toguri developed into a businesslike and practical young adult. She focused on the circle around her, people she knew. She lived in the realm of facts. At UCLA, she started out as a music major, then switched to pre-med, and finally settled on zoology, which requires a strong memory for detailed, empirical knowledge. She still hoped to use this course of study as a springboard to medical school. Her mother's eldest sister had four or five sons who became doctors in different cities in Japan. "My mother always was interested in medicine, and she thought it would be something for me to go into. She kept on talking about so many doctors in her family." Iva added with some disdain, "When I was in college, women were all going to be nurses. It's strange, but I wanted to be a doctor." To become a doctor would have been a tremendous accomplishment for any American woman in the 1930s, and especially for a woman of Japanese ancestry. In college, Iva proved to be a good student but not brilliant.

During her years at UCLA, Iva belonged to Chi Alpha Delta, the nation's first Asian American sorority, but her heart belonged to the science fraternity, Lambda Sigma. She often joined her

Lambda Sigma colleagues on field trips, driving other students in her car. One of her professors remembered that Iva "associated for the most part with Caucasian students, was well liked, a good mixer, and any crowd she was in was always aware of her presence. Her voice was loud, and she used a great deal of slang and joked a lot with fellow students."[35] She loved to camp out for several days and "dig." She once discovered the remains of a Miocene horse. She fearlessly handled snakes and, despite her professor's warning, picked them up and put them in bags. She liked to go into the desert to shoot her rifle and target practice, especially at night with the illumination from her car's headlights. She switched from baseball to tennis, coached by May Bundy (Wimbledon champion in 1905 and 1907). With her grandmother in mind, she tried archery. "It was a disaster! Utter disaster! My mother was very disappointed."

In November 1934, Iva suffered a ruptured appendix. Needing several months to recuperate from her operation, she decided to drop out of school and work at the Wilmington Avenue Market. During that stint, her father made it clear to Iva that Fred would take over his business. He told her bluntly that "women didn't belong in business." To what extent this closed door preyed on the mind of the young woman trying to win favor in her father's eyes cannot be known. But Iva knew in her heart the traditional role of Japanese women did not suit her. She had no particular interest in marriage and motherhood. "You know, it's strange, but I never could picture myself [in that role]. And that's the way it ended up."

~

The Great Depression drove the Furuya Company into bankruptcy and Kawakami, Jun Toguri's old boss, asked Jun to fly to Seattle to help him start anew. Jun Toguri felt he owed this man his loyalty, and he stood ready to help. But duty has its limits, and piercing the clouds on the dubious assumption that airplanes were capable of sustained flight was beyond the call. So, Jun lassoed his maverick daughter and asked her to drive him in her new Chrysler. Some children, full of comrades and sports and school projects, might have found it a chore. Not Iva. For Iva Toguri, no memories were as sweet as those of the long excursions she took with her father.

They made two trips a year for three years. They took an inland route on U.S. 99 from California to Seattle and Vancouver, and on the way back they'd take the coast highway, U.S. 101. They drove straight through from Los Angeles to Seattle without stopping. Thanks to these many hours alone together, they got to know each other well. Iva discovered her father's unusual tastes in food. He enjoyed all sorts of cheeses, various internal organs, tongue, frog's legs, pig's feet, and he liked his steaks very rare. Iva, who preferred simple foods, felt queasy when she watched him eat. They hassled each other, he complaining that her choices were predictable and she retorting that he didn't so much eat as commit slaughter.

In contrast to his adventurous eating habits, Jun was a cautious driver. Iva loved speed. At that time, a state like Oregon had mostly country highways without speed limits. Iva pushed the accelerator to the floor. "Many times, I'd race the bus. The bus drivers—you know, they were crazy. Couple of times my father said, 'I'm going to sleep because I can't stand it. I'm going to have a heart attack, between you and the Greyhound Bus!' 'Well, go to sleep then!'"

They talked, but she couldn't remember what about. Nothing very personal. Her father was a religious iconoclast, neither Christian nor Buddhist. He once explained he had his own religion and his own God, to which Iva muttered under her breath, "Oh, brother." It is not hard to sense the mood between the two. Cruising beside the Pacific, the windows of the big Chrysler open wide, Iva and Jun bickered and bantered almost as equals.

After the trips with her father ended, Iva faced the fundamental decision that plagues all young people: what to do with her life. She was, in her words, "open to possibilities." Possibilities were soon on her lap.

Notes

For texts cited only once in this book, I have included complete reference information in notes at the end of each chapter. For texts cited more than once in the book, only a brief citation—author, title, and page number—appears in the chapter endnotes. The Bibliography contains complete reference information for such works.

The abbreviation NARA refers to the National Archives and Record Administration. Documents in the National Archives are classified by record group. If a record group is cited only once in the book, complete reference information is included in the chapter endnotes. The Bibliography contains reference information for record groups cited more than once.

NARA counsels authors not to cite box numbers within record groups because box numbers may change. Nevertheless, where possible, I have done so as an aid to contemporary researchers. Finding individual documents in these voluminous files without a box number is an arduous task.

1. Soren Kierkegaard, *The Concept of Irony*, trans. by Lee Capel (Bloomington, Ind.: Indiana University Press, 1965), 338.

2. Certificate no. 4112; vol. 123. Name: Ikuko Toguri. Born (at home) at 947 Denver Avenue, Los Angeles. Midwife: Toune Ausai. NARA 1, Box 43.

3. Quotations of Iva Toguri throughout the book are, as stated in the Introduction, taken from interviews I conducted with her primarily in 1987.

4. I do not know whether Iva developed this idea on her own or if it came from her father. In Japanese, *Iku* means to bring up or nourish; *ko* means child, and is a traditional ending for a girl's name. Therefore, *Ikuko* roughly translates as "raised child," "child nourisher," or "homemaker."

5. I also conducted a separate interview with June Toguri on June 8, 1987, from which her recollections are taken. Future quotations attributed to June are from this interview.

6. I rely on Iva for this information. Her mother Fumi attended a Methodist mission school in Japan, and Iva said that she grew up Methodist. Apparently her father picked this preschool because it was run by Japanese.

7. I have never seen his name in this form. I base my judgment that Jun's middle name was Mamoru on conforming birthday information from immigration records. See note 8 below. Mamoru Toguri, when he "first" entered the United States in 1906, claimed he was born in 1881, a manager for the Furuya Co., and stated he had resided in the United States from 1899 to 1904. All were true of Jun. No records of Mamoru entering the United States before 1904 are extant. Based on these overlapping facts, I believe Mamoru had to be Jun traveling under his middle name.

8. Early in life, Jun Toguri claimed he was born in 1881; later in life, 1882. I do not know which is true.

When Jun Toguri filled out the form in Japan on October 10, 1899, for a voyage to Seattle, he stated his age was "18 years, 8 months" old, thus making his birthday March 1881. When Mamoru Toguri arrived by rail from Canada on April 4, 1905, he stated his age was 24, thus making his birthday compatible with March 1881. When Mamoru filled out the form in Japan on September 6, 1906, for a voyage to Seattle, he stated his age was "25 years, 6 months" old, thus making his birthday March 1881. When Jun filled out a different form on May 24, 1911, for another voyage to Seattle, he stated his age was 30 (no months), thus making his birthday compatible with March 1881.

On June 5, 1918, Jun registered for the World War I draft. (All males in the United States, eligible or not, had to register; see chapter 6.) He first told the registrar he was 37. He next stated his birthday was "March 25, 1882." The registrar apparently did a quick calculation, and informed him if that were his birth date, he was only 36. Jun accepted this, and the registrar wrote 36 over the 37. (I have examined the original document. The order of questions and writeover is obvious.) Henceforth, Jun's records show his birth year as 1882. His Social Security records, including his death record, use the 1882 date.

(The one exception is the 1930 U.S. Census taken on April 9, 1930, in Los Angeles. Jun stated his age was 47, which would mean he was born in March 1883. But this contradicts other information in the same document: namely, that Fumi was 43, but 5 years younger than Jun when they married. Thus, his correct age on April 9, 1930, would have been 48, assuming he was born March 25, 1882.)

The family celebrated Jun's birthday as 1882, including the significant birthdays of ages 60, 77, and 88. Jun journeyed to Japan to receive a medal from the Emperor (Iva claimed he went in 1969 in connection with his 88th birthday), and one must assume the emperor had the wherewithal to check Jun's birth record. If 1882 is accurate, why did Jun initially lie about being one year older?

9. Jun as Mamoru also arrived in Seattle from Japan aboard the *Kaga Maru* on September 20, 1906, and as Jun aboard the *Kamakura Maru* on June 8, 1911. "Passenger and Crew Lists of Vessels Arriving at Seattle, Washington, 1890–1957," Record Group 85, Micropublication M1383. NARA, Washington, D.C.

10. "In 1892, Masajiro Furuya founds the Furuya Company, which becomes the largest and most successful business in Seattle's Nihonmachi (Japantown), now called the International District. It is a one-stop, multipurpose business that provides services in real estate, construction, mailing, printing, and banking. The firm thrived for many years. But in the fall of 1931, during the Great Depression, it went bankrupt, and many of Seattle's Japanese lost their life savings, businesses, and land." David Takami, *Executive Order 9066: 50 Years before and 50 Years after: A History of Japanese Americans in Seattle* (Seattle: Wing Luke Museum, 1992), 16.

11. O'Brien, and Fugita. *The Japanese American Experience*, 84, 32.

12. For reasons I cannot explain, Fumi's California death certificate states that her mother's maiden name was Torii and her father's surname was Senichiro. *California Death Index*, 1940–1997, State of California Department of Health Services, Center for Health Statistics, Sacramento. However, Iva was quite clear about her mother's name and even spelled it for me. She knew her mother's family history and lived with her mother's sister in Japan. Therefore I have used Iimuro, not Torii or Senichiro.

13. The 1907 date is based on the 1930 U.S. Census for which Jun stated he was 25 at the time of their marriage and Fumi, that she was 20. However, Iva said about one of the pictures she gave me (the daughter of one of her father's friends had sent it to her in early 1987), "I couldn't get over the fact that here is my mother and my father and a young guide, and they had just come back or were going up Mt. Fuji." This photo is clearly marked "1904." The year is not in Iva's hand, but she never disavowed this dating, neither in the interview nor in her handwritten descriptions of her photos. However, Jun Toguri told authorities he lived in the United States from 1899 to 1904, and then in Vancouver, so he could not have married Fumi in 1904. I myself am not convinced the couple in the photo are Jun and Fumi, although Iva stated she recalled seeing the photo as a child before the family lost it during the internment. She also said that her parents had told her many times about the honeymoon climb, her mother remarking on how she was repulsed by the trash strewn along the mountain paths.

Masayo Duus states, "On June 8, 1907, at a ceremony in Yokohama, [Jun] married nineteen-year-old Fumi Iimuro (Duus, *Orphan of the Pacific*, 41)." Iva understood they married in Yamanashi. It seems odd that two people from Yamanashi would journey to Yokohama to marry only to return to Yamanashi for their honeymoon. (The most popular route up the mountain, the Yoshidaguchi Trail, leads from the Kawaguchiko Fifth Station to the summit. Kawaguchiko Station is in Yamanashi Prefecture.) However, Duus's marriage date is extraordinarily specific. Duus, a native of Japan and fluent in Japanese, may have found a civil record in Japan. On the other hand, if Fumi, born February 14, 1887, married on June 8, 1907, she would have been 20, not 19 as Duus states. See in this regard, chapter 6, note 27.

14. They were aboard the *Shinyo Maru*; Fred traveled under his middle name Koichiro. Passenger Lists of Vessels Arriving at San Francisco, 1893–1953; Records of the Immigration and Naturalization Service. Record Group 85, Microfilm Publication M1410.

15. Some confusion exists about the date and place of the other Toguri children's birth. According to the Federal Bureau of Investigation (FBI)'s summary, introduced as Exhibit XX at Iva's trial, Fred Koichiro Toguri was born November 1, 1910, in Tokyo; June Mizue Toguri was born November 8, 1919, in Calexico; and, Inez (misspelled "Mez") Hisako Toguri was born January 26, 1925, in Calexico. Duus (*Orphan of the Pacific*, 41) claims Inez was born in San Diego.

California birth records show the FBI's information was correct concerning Inez; she was born in Calexico. However, June was born December 8, 1919. Not only is this public record, June told me so herself. How the FBI came up with the date of November 8 is a mystery. The Toguris also had a son, William, coincidentally also born December 8 in 1921, who died shortly after birth. Fred named his first son William, and William Toguri now manages J. Toguri Mercantile in Chicago.

16. I assumed from her statement that Rex was murdered when Iva knew her (i.e., before the war). But then I noticed an FBI interview with June Toguri in 1945 in which she listed among Iva's friends, "Mildred Rex, now Mrs. Thornton . . . Iva's music teacher." FBI Report, "Neighborhood Investigation," November 23, 1945. NARA 1, Box 39. So I looked into it.

Mildred Scott Rex (b. May 14, 1906, in Virginia) married Joseph Cole Thoburn—not Thornton—in the early 1940s. Thoburn (b. November 8, 1897, in Tennessee) never knew his father and lived with his mother, sisters, and grandfather in Indiana as a child. About 1930, Joseph and his mother Nora moved to Inglewood, California, where they lived together until he was in his 40s. Nora died October 19, 1942, and about this time Joseph married Mildred. Their daughter Jennetta was born July 11, 1950.

On July 3, 1956, Joseph strangled or smothered Mildred and Jennetta, wrote a long suicide note, and hanged himself in his garage. He claimed he faced financial ruin and didn't want to leave them in poverty. But his bills were paid, he had $2,660 in savings (about $20,000 today), and was about to collect on the successful sale of his business. The story hit the newspapers on July 4, while Iva celebrated her first birthday outside of prison. *Los Angeles Times*, July 4, 1956, 3.

17. *San Francisco Call*, May 8, 1900.

18. *San Francisco Chronicle*, February 23–28, 1905.

19. *San Francisco Chronicle*, March 1905.

20. To cite one example, a poll in the Imperial Valley in 1936 found 90 percent of all ethnic Japanese favored Republican Alf Landon. From McWilliams, *Prejudice*, 103.

21. Iva registered July 14, 1940, in Los Angeles County (registration number C406113). NARA 3, Box 1.

22. Issues of the organization's magazine, the *Grizzly Bear*, from the 1910s and 1920s state this philosophy explicitly, but for a larger perspective on how the Native Sons impacted Japanese Americans, see Mark Weber, "The Japanese Camps in California," *Journal of Historical Review* 2, no. 1 (Spring 1980).

23. *Takao Ozawa v. United States*, 260 U.S. 178, 194; 43 S.Ct. 65, 67. Japanese nationals were not allowed to become U.S. citizens until the passage of the McCarran-Walter Act of 1952, which revised previous laws and regulations regarding immigration, naturalization, and nationality into one statute.

24. This and other of Tanaka's memories are recorded at http://content.cdlib.org/xtf/view?docId=ft358003z1&doc.view=content&chunk.id=d0e20788&toc.depth=1&brand=oac&anchor.id=0.

25. *San Francisco Chronicle*, July 5, 1949, 2.

26. Modell, *The Economics and Politics of Racial Accommodation: The Japanese of Los Angeles, 1900–1942*, 128.

27. *Japanese Daily News*, March 19, 1940.

28. Smith, *Americans from Japan*, 245–246.

29. Aiji Tashiro, "The Rising Son of the Rising Sun," *New Outlook* 164, no. 3 (September 1934): 36, 39.

30. October 31, 1941, letter home. Iva gave me a copy; I regret to admit I did not research where others might access it, although I'm confident it is in the public records.

31. The FBI's summary of Iva's education, also part of Exhibit XX, is even more confused than its birth summary (note 13 above). The Bureau apparently accepted at face value Iva's statement to the Counter-Intelligence Corps (CIC) of December 21, 1945, in which she claimed she attended Calexico Grammar School (1923–1925), Lincoln Heights Grammar School in Los Angeles (1925–1928), McKinley Junior High School in Los Angeles (1928–1931), Compton Union High School in Los Angeles (1931–1933), and UCLA; 1936–1941). Had the Bureau read its own field reports, it should have realized her recollections were incomplete and muddled.

If Iva entered the public schools at the normal age of six, she attended Calexico Grammar School from September 1922 to June 1925. Iva would have attended elementary school in San Diego from September 1925 to June 1927. After that, the records for the Los Angeles City Schools apply. These records show she entered Vernon Avenue Grammar School on September 26, 1927, and left February 3, 1928, at the end of her first semester as a sixth grader. At the time, she lived at 1610 East 38th Street in Los Angeles. (Iva testified at trial that she lived in San Diego in 1927 and moved to Wilmington Street in Los Angeles in 1928; she apparently forgot her first home on 38th. See Trial Transcript, vol. XLVI, 5165.)

She entered McKinley Junior High (renamed Carver Junior High by 1948) in February 1928, as a second-semester seventh grader, thus skipping a grade. She graduated in January 1931. On January 26, 1931, Iva entered Compton Union High School. She graduated June 22, 1933, at the age of 16.

According to Eleanor B. Doig, Secretary to the Registrar at UCLA in 1948, Iva first applied for admission to UCLA on August 12, 1933. On her application she stated she was 17 and hoped to be admitted in September 1933. Doig noted, "She was notified that she would be required to do additional work in certain high school subjects before she would become eligible for admission." Iva attended Compton Junior College from September 18, 1933 to February 3, 1934 to complete this additional work. On February 17, 1934, Iva filed a second application and was admitted to UCLA on February 26, 1934. She took a break due to a ruptured appendix and the need to work, and eventually graduated on January 31, 1940. See Los Angeles Field Report, LA 61–614, 3–5. NARA 3, Box 1.

32. O'Brien and Fugita, *The Japanese American Experience*, 84.

33. Elizabeth Wildsmith, Myron P. Gutmann, and Brian Gratton, "Assimilation and Intermarriage for U.S. Immigrant Groups, 1880–1990" (Austin, Tex.: Population Research Center, University of Texas), 27–28. See http://www.hss.caltech.edu/Events/Archives/EPP/intermar.pdf

34. Paul R. Spickard, *Mixed Blood: Intermarriage and Ethnic Identity in Twentieth Century America* (Madison: University of Wisconsin Press, 1989), 25.

35. Dr. Raymond B. Cowles, FBI Report LA 61–614, 7. NARA 3, Box 1.

2

A Fateful Letter in Failing Light

Iva Toguri graduated from the University of California at Los Angeles (UCLA) with a bachelor's degree in zoology on January 31, 1940. She was 23. Her job prospects were dim. About 40 percent of Nisei women in Los Angeles in 1940 helped their parents for no pay. Most of the remainder worked for other Japanese in clerical jobs. Only 5 percent of Nisei, male or female, worked in white-owned businesses. The second most common job for Nisei women was domestic or maid. As a college graduate, Iva might have hoped to teach, but not one Nisei, male or female, was a public school teacher in the city of Los Angeles in 1940.[1] Iva was trapped. She had no professional career possibilities, she could hardly become a maid, she could not desert her father to work for another employer, and the one job she wanted and could get had no future since her father was grooming Fred, not her, to take over the family business.

Iva's marriage prospects, if she were to follow her father's wishes and marry within the Japanese community, were equally dim. "They were in the same shoe as me, the ones that graduated from college. At that time, all the doors weren't open. It was a short time after the Depression. A lot of the kids with college degrees, they ended up working in fruit and produce markets and went and helped their families on the farm. I didn't picture myself as a farm wife. I had a couple of dates with fellows whose families owned grocery stores but—well—they were just not my type, let's put it that way." Policies against hiring "Orientals" were widespread at the time and even prestigious universities could not find positions for their graduates. The University of California at Berkeley judged its placement of Asian graduates to be "most unsatisfactory," as did Stanford: "It is almost impossible to place a Chinese or Japanese of either the first or second generation in any kind of position, engineering, manufacturing, or business."[2] Even civil service jobs were difficult to obtain. In addition to having no Nisei teachers, Los Angeles also employed no fire fighters, police, or mail carriers of Japanese descent.[3] Nonfamily jobs for Nisei males were concentrated in a few "Japanese"-specific categories: gardener, truck farmer, contract fisherman, and fruit stand operator. In the words of one college graduate, "I would much rather [be a] doctor or lawyer . . . but my aspirations were frustrated long ago, and I am only what I am, a professional carrot washer."[4] Since Iva's own aspirations were equally thwarted, she enrolled in graduate courses and helped out at the store while she searched for an opening that might offer her the opportunity to become an economic success like her father.

Many Americans, not just Iva Toguri, experienced the future as especially uncertain. The dawn of the 1940s found Europe and Asia at war and the United States in an uneasy peace. Most Americans focused on Germany's blitzkrieg conquests of its neighbors, but they also watched Japan's pitiless war against China with growing revulsion. A popular ad in magazines showed a Chinese father on a war-torn landscape holding his dead, emaciated child; the caption, referring to U.S. sales of steel to Japan, read, "Did you help pay for this bomb?" The roots of Japan's war with China lay in the beginning of the twentieth century, when Japan had forced the local Chinese warlord in charge of Manchuria to grant it extensive privileges in the territory. In an incident in 1931, officers of the Japanese Army attacked their own railway and claimed the Chinese were responsible. The Army kept this subterfuge secret from the Japanese public until 1946 and used the Chinese "attack" as an excuse to annex Manchuria into the Japanese empire. The poorly armed Chinese initially had to accept Japanese control, but in 1937 they fought back against further incursions, and the war began in earnest. The superiority of Japanese weaponry led to massive

Chinese losses, and this apparent unfairness, coupled with Japanese atrocities against Chinese civilians, especially women, created such sympathy in the United States for China that polls showed 90 percent of Americans were in favor of cutting off shipments to Japan of all war materiel, as well as boycotting Japanese imports.[5] Posters in California read, "Ladies, don't spend your husband's hard-earned money on Japanese junk."[6]

Because of Japan's continuing brutality toward China, on July 26, 1939, U.S. Secretary of State Cordell Hull denounced (a technical term meaning to serve notice of termination) the 1911 commerce and navigation treaty with Japan, and exactly six months later, at midnight on January 26, 1940, treaty obligations ended. By itself, the treaty's expiration did not restrict trade between the two nations, but the United States hoped the realization that it possessed the power to strangle Japan's war machine would cause Japanese militarists to rethink their policies. It did, but in the opposite direction from what Washington anticipated. The United States and Japan steamed at each other like two locomotives on the same track. Each expected the other to switch course. Misunderstandings and national ego fueled their inevitable collision. What one nation considered reasonable response, the other took as provocation.

For its part, the United States did not recognize Japan as a world power. Japan had one-half the U.S. population but only one-ninth its industrial output. More important, Japan possessed no natural resources. It imported almost all of its oil, iron ore, scrap metal, bauxite (for aluminum), rubber, tin, and other war necessities. A simple blockade could incapacitate it. In addition, Americans lacked respect for Japanese in general. Cartoons portrayed them as buck-toothed, bespectacled little men. They were likened to flocks of geese, with no individual initiative. As one commentator put it, "Nothing is much stupider than one Japanese, and nothing much brighter than two."[7] Japanese children supposedly never played with mechanical toys, so as adults they were poor engineers. Military experts determined that the Japanese were inferior pilots. They believed the Japanese as a people suffered from congenital inner ear defects that limited them to only the most basic flying. (Later, when Japanese pilots ripped apart Far East British defenses, often strafing while flying upside down, experts speculated the pilots must be German.[8]) Finally, the American military considered the

U.S. mainland too distant for the Japanese to attack and the facilities at Hawaii impregnable. General Marshall counseled President Franklin D. Roosevelt in May 1941:

> The Island of Oahu, due to its fortification, its garrison, and its physical characteristics, is believed to be the strongest fortress in the world. Hawaii will be defended by 35 of our most modern flying fortresses, 35 medium range bombers, 13 light bombers, 150 pursuit aircraft of which 105 are our most modern type. Enemy carriers, naval escorts, and transports will begin to come under air attack at a distance of approximately 750 miles. With this force available, a major attack against Oahu is considered impracticable.[9]

Major George Fielding Eliot put it more succinctly: "A Japanese attack upon Hawaii is a strategical impossibility."[10]

Poor news coverage of Japan clouded America's view. U.S. correspondents in Japan tended to be young and inexperienced, and most had only recently arrived in the country. The *New York Times* and the *London Times* sent experienced reporter Otto Tolischus early in 1941, but he had transferred from Germany and had few contacts. In addition, Japanese censors tightly controlled reporters. Tolischus initially stayed at the Imperial Hotel, but omnipresent surveillance prevented him from moving freely to report. Clerks recorded the exact minute he left his room and the minute he returned to it. At his office, he discovered the police had secretly rifled the contents of his wastepaper basket. Censors required him to provide the text of his telephone conversations and cable dispatches beforehand. They examined each sentence, and either passed or refused to allow their transmission.[11] In 1940, the police jailed reporter James Young for three months, relentlessly questioned him, prosecuted him for espionage, and threw him out of the country. However, Class of 1938 Duke University graduate James J. Halsema, attending the 1940 Japan America Student Conference with several Nisei friends, claimed that "according to the old-timers who hang around the Imperial Hotel lobby, Jimmy Young deserved what he got."[12] Young's treatment, deserved or not, was far from an isolated case. Police also jailed Joseph Dynan of the Associated Press and Reuters correspondent Melville James Cox. Cox fell to his death from a fifth-floor window in a Tokyo military prison. The Japanese claimed he committed suicide. News reporters knew better and tried to avoid confrontations with the authorities. As a result, the quality and quantity of news coming from Japan suffered.[13]

For their part, the Japanese resented American disrespect. They believed their war needs could be met from sources nearby. Malaya and the Dutch East Indies were rich in oil, rubber, and tin; northern China, in coal and iron ore; Southeast Asia, in bauxite for aluminum. The Imperial Navy guaranteed a steady flow of supplies; blockade would be impossible. Whereas the Americans had three carriers in the Pacific, Japan's navy had ten, two of which displaced twice the tonnage of the largest American vessel. Japan owned the world's best fighter and had 1,500 trained and experienced aviators to fly it. The American Asiatic and Pacific fleets had eight battleships compared to the Imperial Navy's ten, but the two Yamato-class battleships dwarfed their American counterparts. At sea in 1940, the *Yamato* was the largest battleship ever built (and still is); its 18-inch guns (American ships had only 14-inch batteries) could fire a 3,200-pound shell 26 miles. Imperial Navy planners anticipated the *Yamato* could destroy an entire American fleet before it could maneuver within firing range. Given that the Japanese Navy had more capital ships in the Pacific than the navies of all the Allied powers combined, planners considered an attack upon Japan impossible. Washington's demands to come to heel only antagonized Japanese authorities.

On June 24, 1940, the Japanese government demanded that Great Britain close the Burma Road to stop war materiel from reaching China. The British were fighting for their very existence against the Nazis and had little choice. Three weeks later they agreed to close the road for three months. In June 1940, Japan significantly increased its iron and steel imports from the United States, and on June 29, Japanese Foreign Minister Hachiro Arita[14] announced Japan's interest in expanding southward when he advocated the inclusion of "South Seas areas" in the "New Order for East Asia." This policy became the blueprint for what Japan called the Great East Asia Co-Prosperity Sphere. The Japanese intended to establish military bases, isolate the Chinese from their supply sources, dominate the embattled British in key areas, and pave the road for their own self-sufficiency were events to interrupt trade with the United States. The Japanese viewed themselves as surrounded by what they called the ABCD Powers (Americans, British, Chinese, Dutch). They hoped that by expanding their reach, they could effectively overcome their lack of natural resources. The United States warned Japan against further aggression but in fact other nations, chiefly Great Britain, France, and the Netherlands, controlled the territories in jeopardy. The only U.S. territory of significance, the Philippines, was militarily indefensible and scheduled for independence.

In July 1940, Yosuke Matsuoka became Japanese Foreign Minister. Matsuoka was gruff, blunt, and a nonstop talker. Many in Japan viewed him as more American than Japanese. He had traveled to the United States in 1893, a starving 13-year-old. When his brother deserted him, an American woman took him in and reared him with her own son as though they were brothers. Matsuoka graduated from Oakland High School in the same class as writer Jack London and later graduated from the University of Oregon. He claimed never to have experienced discrimination while in America. After graduation, he returned to Japan and joined the foreign service, where he became an advocate for Japanese militarist policies. In 1933, he withdrew Japan from the League of Nations, vowing "We're not coming back" after a report criticized Japan's actions in Manchuria. After his walkout, he returned to America to dedicate a tombstone to his surrogate mother. Despite Matsuoka's association with the United States, he moved quickly to put the militarists' policy of southward expansion into effect when he became Foreign Minister.

In 1940, the *danse macabre* between the United States and Japan began in earnest. On July 2, 1940, Roosevelt signed into law "An Act to Expedite the Strengthening of National Defense" or the Export Control Act. The law established a requirement that exporters obtain a license to export arms, ammunition, certain chemicals, aircraft parts, machine tools, and other materials. The Act did not create an embargo on trade with Japan, only the need for a license, but the Japanese understood its significance. Trade could be stopped, and Japan's access to what it needed to survive depended on the U.S. government.

On July 20, Roosevelt signed into law the Two-Ocean Navy Expansion Act, which authorized an immediate expenditure of

$1 billion for construction of warships. At the same time, the U.S. Army announced it would seek $4 billion for additional tanks, airplanes, and other equipment. On July 25, Roosevelt added oil and scrap metal to the list of items requiring an export license. On July 31, Roosevelt first used his powers under the Act, banning the exportation of aviation fuel outside the Western hemisphere.

The next day, August 1, 1940, Foreign Minister Matsuoka "requested" that the Vichy government (the regime of Nazi-controlled France) give Japanese troops the right to pass through French Indochina (now Vietnam, Laos, and Cambodia) and permit the use of airfields and ports. Vichy, which had only existed three weeks, stalled. The Japanese warned the French that they would occupy with or without permission on September 22. On that day, local French officials in Indochina signed an agreement allowing 6,000 Japanese troops to be garrisoned there. But communications failed and the Nakamura Division crossed over from China and made a frontal attack on French troops at Lang Son.

Four days later, on September 26, Roosevelt ordered a complete embargo of scrap metal and scrap iron to Japan. The Japanese imported 91 percent of its scrap needs from the United States.[15] FDR had previously, on September 16, signed into law the Selective Training and Service Act, the first peacetime draft in American history.

On September 27, 1940, Matsuoka's negotiations with German Foreign Minister von Ribbentrop culminated in Japan's signing the Tripartite Pact with Germany and Italy, creating what came to be called the Axis Powers.

～

During the years of the late 1930s and early 1940s, in which the United States moved inexorably toward war, Iva's mother, Fumi Toguri, became increasingly ill. All but one of her sisters had died young, and now the family history had come to her. She had a stroke, then another. She was wheelchair bound, often bedridden, and the family gathered around her. "We had this magnet that held us together, and that was my mother's frail physical condition. That had a lot to do with the family's playing together, working together, eating together, so that we could be around my mother, and everyone looked after her comfort. My father set the example."

In a time before air-conditioning, Jun devised a method of placing hundred-pound blocks of ice in wash tubs around his wife's bed and setting up fans to blow across the ice. It cooled the room on hot California nights and made Fumi's bed rest more agreeable. When asked if she believed her father truly loved her mother, Iva responded with typical candor. "That I can't say for sure. I know my father was very good to my mother. They certainly respected each other. During her illness, he was so concerned for her."

About 1940, Jun bought a big console shortwave radio and put up a tall antenna in the yard so that he and his wife could listen to programs from Japan. Iva and the other children also tried to listen but "we definitely couldn't understand it." As Fumi Toguri weakened, "She went back to Japanese. I noticed that." Asked how she was able to communicate with her mother during this period, Iva replied, "Well I couldn't talk to her in Japanese because mine was very poor. I could understand most of what she was saying, because we didn't talk philosophy. Just daily routine. The nouns were just common nouns, so it was not hard."

Iva's recollections were at variance with those of her sister June. June remembered, "My mother understood English but didn't speak it much. She spoke in Japanese. We had to speak Japanese once we got into the house. We tried not to speak English in the house."[16] At another point, however, June said her father did sometimes converse in English.

Iva's ability, or lack thereof, to understand and speak Japanese at any given point in her life will become an important aspect of her defense against the postwar charge of colluding with the enemy. Although it is impossible to be confident about this subject, the differences between Iva's and June's memories need not be viewed as contradictions. Iva and her father were extroverts who regularly dealt with Caucasians in the outside world. June and her mother were homebodies who did not. June spoke more often with her mother in Japanese, and Iva more often with her father in English. Both parents no doubt simplified and slowed their Japanese whenever they spoke it to the children. Thus, it is likely that when Iva heard the rapid-fire delivery of native speakers either on the radio or when she encountered them personally in Japan, she struggled to understand what they were saying even though her ear had grown accustomed to the language's cadences and inflections from hearing her mother at home.[17]

~

In June 1941, amidst wars and rumors of wars, a letter arrived at the Toguri household. Iva's mother received news that her only living sister was gravely ill. Fumi could not physically withstand a sea voyage to Japan to visit her sister. Fred helped manage the store and could not be spared. Iva, however, had few commitments.

Jun and Fumi Toguri discussed the matter with some seriousness. They worried about the length of the trip, but Iva had proven herself an adept traveler. Iva also had a friend, Chiyeko Ito,[18] who could travel with her. In the end, they decided Iva should represent her mother. As a side benefit, Iva could carry onboard ship many items such as textiles and sugar currently rationed in Japan. Her father asked her to make the journey, suggesting that she might find a niche in Japan. Iva herself considered the possibility of attending medical school there. In any case, she thought a trip to Japan would be interesting and educational. She agreed to go.

~

Those inclined to view Iva Toguri as a traitor introduce their brief against her with this decision. Why, given the tensions between Japan and the United States, would she travel to the enemy homeland if not for nefarious purposes? The short answer is that the Toguris, like many other Americans, never saw Pearl Harbor coming. Iva did not recall any discussion of the atmosphere of U.S.–Japanese relations before her trip. "My father was very optimistic. He never suspected there would be a war between the countries. Had that been in their minds, they would never have let me go."

The Toguris were in good company. Two weeks before Iva left, Roosevelt halted the export of oil from the East Coast to relieve shortages in New York and other eastern cities. The *Washington Post* noted positively, "The new restrictions were doubly designed to relieve Japan sorely in need of American oil."[19] In late August 1941, nationally syndicated columnist Walter Lippmann wrote: "Whereas a year ago we felt constrained to buy time, we are able now to talk with Tokyo on the basis of a new situation. It is so much better that the opportunity now exists to make sure that Japan will not, because she cannot, stab us in the back."[20] On the very same day, United Press International (UPI) correspondent Miles Vaughn assured his readers that "most observers believe that Japan under no condition will declare war on either Britain or the U.S."[21] Matsuo Kato had attended U.S. schools and, in 1937, had become a Japanese newspaper reporter in Washington, D.C. He, like Iva, traveled to Japan in July 1941. Later he remembered "the thought of war breaking out seemed no more than a fantastic possibility."[22] In October 1941, Winston Churchill told his cabinet that Japan would not risk war with the United States and Britain.[23] Just four days before Pearl Harbor, Churchill dismissed war with Japan as a "remote possibility."[24] Conspiracy theories notwithstanding, Roosevelt did not foresee the attack. The Japanese apparently surprised the U.S. government and military as much as they did the Toguris.

~

Iva made ready to embark on her long voyage. The first step was to secure a passport, but even though she brought her birth certificate, passport officials were oddly reluctant to issue one. "They pointed out that times were uncertain, that people shouldn't be leaving this country for Japan." It seems unlikely that Los Angeles passport officials would have possessed knowledge of foreign policy contingencies, but for whatever reason they were suspicious of Iva's and Chiyeko's intentions. Jun learned from other Japanese Americans that an affidavit would allow travelers to reenter the United States without difficulty. In fact, most Americans in 1940 did not bother about passports when they went overseas. So Iva obtained a "Certificate of Identification to Facilitate Return to the United States of America,"[25] valid for six months, and she and Chiyeko left the country without passports.

The celebration of Iva's twenty-fifth birthday that Fourth of July was bittersweet. When she said good-bye to her mother at the house, they cried a little because they would be apart. But the Toguris were not an emotional family, and everyone expected Iva would be home in a few months. Iva kissed her mother good-bye, both unaware they would never see each other again.

Iva packed her own belongings plus innumerable goods for her aunt. She sailed with 41 boxes and pieces of luggage.[26] At the last minute, her father brought two crates of honeydew melons, a fruit unknown in Japan. He told her, "They should survive the trip. Give one to the relatives. And the other crate, give to the purser." Iva didn't understand why but she made sure to inform the purser once they were underway.

The Japanese passenger ship *Arabia Maru* left San Pedro, California on July 5, 1941, bound for Yokohama, Japan. Since few single women were onboard, Iva and Chiyeko were popular with the young officers. They chatted with the two girls and practiced their English while Iva practiced her Japanese. As the ship neared the harbor at Yokohama, the purser waived freight charges on Iva's belongings because she had been so helpful in keeping up morale.

On July 25, 1941, the tomboy first baseman who raced with Greyhounds stepped onto Japanese soil and into a new life.[27] Iva Toguri now began a quest to find herself in the distant land of her ancestors. Her quest would ultimately bear fruit. The unexpected, dreadful events that followed developed her character and brought forward her true identity in ways no one who knew her, including Iva herself, could have foreseen.

Notes

1. Statistics from Modell, *The Economics and Politics of Racial Accommodation*, 131–33.

2. Eliot Grinnell Mears, *Resident Orientals on the American Pacific Coast* (New York: Arno Press, 1978), 199–200.

3. Modell, *The Economics and Politics of Racial Accommodation*, 133. Some Nisei were listed as county and city employees in 1941 before Pearl.

4. Taishi Matsumoto, "The Protest of a Professional Carrot Washer," *Kashu Mainichi*, April 4, 1937, cited in John Modell, "Class or Ethnic Solidarity: The Japanese American Company Union," *Pacific Historical Review* 38 (1969), 192–206.

5. The *Gallup Poll*, Survey #213–K, Question #5, published October 20, 1940, 246. "Do you think our Government should forbid the sale of arms, airplanes, gasoline, and other war materials to Japan?" Of those expressing an opinion (8 percent did not), 90 percent answered Yes.

6. *Asahi Shimbum* staff. *The Pacific Rivals*, 72.

7. Fletcher Pratt, *Sea Power and Today's War* (New York: Harrison-Hilton, 1939), 178–79.

8. S. W. Kirby, *The War against Japan* (London: H. M. Stationery Off, 1957), vol. 1, 184.

9. *Hearings before the Joint Committee on the Investigation of the Pearl Harbor Attack*, Pt. 15, 1635.

10. *American Mercury*, September 1938, 19.

11. Tolishcus, *Tokyo Record*, 88, 229.

12. See his memoirs at http://www.ceas.ku.edu/Images/EPP/Halsema%20Diary/jasc3.html.

13. See Relman Morin, *Circuit of Conquest* (New York: A. A. Knopf, 1943), 60–65; Wilfrid Fleisher, *Volcanic Isle* (Garden City, N.Y.: Doubleday, Doran & Co., 1941), 307–9; Joseph Newman, *Goodbye Japan* (New York: L. B. Fischer, 1942), 167, 253–54; James R. Young, *Behind the Rising Sun* (Garden City, N.Y.: Doubleday, Doran & Co., 1941), 284–90.

14. In Japan, the family name comes first and the given name follows. America's Jun Toguri is Japan's Toguri Jun. Some historians and some Japanese, when writing in English, reverse this order to conform to Western usage. To avoid confusion, I have also reversed Japanese names in this manner. Please be aware that other texts may conform to proper Japanese style, referring to Foreign Minister Arita as Arita Hachiro and war Premier Tojo by his Japanese name Tojo Hideki.

15. *Washington Post*, September 16, 1940, referencing statistics for 1939.

16. Internment records for the Toguri family state that Fred and June could read, write, and speak Japanese, and that Inez could speak Japanese. This bolsters June's claim that the Japanese language was pervasive in their home. NARA, Record Group 210, Japanese-American Internee Data File, 1942–1946.

17. In our interviews, Iva herself drew this distinction, claiming she could understand the daily conversation at home within a month or so of her arrival but not, for example, understand a train conductor's speech.

18. Iva and some documents use the modern spelling of this name, which is "Chieko." However, Ito's California birth certificate of January 10, 1923, has "Chiyeko" and I have adopted that spelling.

19. *Washington Post*, June 21, 1941, 3.

20. *Washington Post*, August, 28, 1941, 15.

21. *Washington Post*, August 28, 1941, 15.

22. Kato, *The Lost War*, 18.

23. Quoted in Thorne, *Allies of a Kind*, 56. See CAB (Records of the Cabinet), 69/8.

24. Quoted in Thorne, *Allies of a Kind*, 4. See CAB (Records of the Cabinet), 69/2.

25. Signed "Ikuko Toguri," July 1, 1941. Introduced as Exhibit IV at Iva's trial. NARA 1, Box 40.

26. "Custom officials had examined her baggage for possible violations of the Neutrality Act, but had found no exceptions. . . . According to their records, Iva Toguri had forty-one pieces of baggage." FBI Report, December 29, 1945, Russell A. Williams, Asst. Collector of Customs. NARA 2, Box 1.

27. Iva's ship arrived on July 24, 1941, but she had to stay onboard ship an extra day. The harbor police office was closed, and she couldn't disembark unless they issued her a residence permit.

3

Tokyo Rose:
Origins of the Legend

Tokyo Rose, in the view of Allied servicemen, was a seductive, cunning, and deceitful woman who broadcast on shortwave radio for the Japanese. She knew American military secrets. She had spies everywhere, and addressed GIs by name and rank, warned them of attacks, and accurately predicted their maneuvers before even they had received their orders. She tormented them with tales of their wives and girlfriends playing around on them back home. Rumors tore through ships and island camps that some anonymous soldier had committed suicide after she informed him of his unfaithful wife. Tokyo Rose became famous throughout the Pacific, and eventually back in the United States as the *New York Times*, *Time* magazine, and other news organizations speculated about her identity.

We know that Americans believed in Tokyo Rose very early in the war. On March 4, 1942—less than three months after the attack on Pearl Harbor—Robert J. Casey of the *Chicago Daily News* Foreign Service filed a report from the Pacific fleet titled "Hard Pushed Japs Lie to Save Face." He remarked on listening to Japanese radio broadcasts dismissing the effectiveness of the U.S. Navy:

> With things as they are and with full cognizance of the imperfections pointed out by Tokyo Rose—the female Lord Haw Haw[1] of

41

the Son of Heaven—it would seem the time had arrived for an inventory of the poltergeist activities of ours. . . .

It has been encouraging to one grown weary of communiques where, when and if found, to listen to Tokyo broadcasts. Save for Rose, who rumor identifies as a music student in Hawaii, voices of commentators are mostly midwestern in accent, thoroughly American in pronunciation and use of phrase. You are tempted almost to believe these boys. . . .[2]

However, despite this press release, despite dozens of other similar press releases as the war progressed, despite the testimony of hundreds of thousands of American soldiers and sailors who swore they heard Tokyo Rose broadcast the vile propaganda attributed to her, one fact is now certain: Tokyo Rose did not exist. The Federal Broadcasting Intelligence Service (FBIS), with listening posts in Portland, Oregon and Vancouver, British Columbia, recorded and transcribed every Japanese broadcast in English.[3] We still possess many of these records. As will be detailed in chapter 9, what they show is that between the attack on Pearl Harbor on December 7, 1941 and March 4, 1942, only one nameless woman broadcast via shortwave from Tokyo. She spoke for a total of 30 minutes. She did not call herself Tokyo Rose, and her two brief broadcasts contained nothing like the material associated with Tokyo Rose. All other English-language broadcasts were by men. They reported the news and now and then in commentaries bragged about Japanese military success. These male announcers did not predict attacks, address units by name, or discuss wives back home. The entire Tokyo Rose phenomenon derived from the imaginations of American military service personnel.[4]

This conclusion is not mine alone. The U.S. government, worried about enemy agents, wanted to find out how Tokyo Rose had learned closely held military information. It covertly launched an investigation. Shortly before the war with Japan ended, the U.S. Office of War Information publicly announced the results of the government's research:

There is no Tokyo Rose; the name is strictly a G.I. invention. Government monitors listening in twenty-four hours a day have never heard the words "Tokyo Rose" over a Japanese-controlled Far Eastern Radio.[5]

However, although I believe it is an established and indisputable fact that no actual woman performed the feats attributed to Tokyo Rose, I also believe it would be a mistake to discount Tokyo Rose's reality. Denying Tokyo Rose broadcast is like denying Kilroy[6] really was there: it is to misunderstand. Although the U.S. government correctly determined that Tokyo Rose did not exist, the men who swore they heard her did not lie. Tokyo Rose was real. The challenge is to unveil the special nature of her reality. This means, and should have meant, not organizing a witch hunt, at least not with the hope of locating for prosecution a flesh-and-blood witch. Instead, one must seek out Tokyo Rose without assumptions, and accept her reality as soldiers and sailors in the Pacific experienced it: a siren's voice from across the waters, a feminine presence whose identity remained in darkness, then and still today, lost within the subconscious needs and desires of those who heard her.

The archetype of the femme fatale, the irresistible but deadly female, has fascinated humankind since the beginning of recorded history. She has manifested herself throughout human history in literature, in mythology, and in a few actual women. The details of the myth vary with time and place. The legend of Tokyo Rose, therefore, did not represent a novel phenomenon. She was simply World War II's incarnation of this famous archetype. American servicemen supplied the "facts" that fleshed out their particular temptress. One of the most significant aspects of the Tokyo Rose mythology is that during World War II, the dominant means of mass communication was radio. Radio, an imagination-intensive medium, helped define her legendary exploits.

Because she was a legend, we can learn almost nothing about Tokyo Rose from actual Japanese broadcasts. Tokyo Rose should be studied as a work of art in terms of sources and influences. She lacked biological parents, but we can trace her provenance in the literal sense.[7] No single artist created her; instead her persona sprang from the imaginations of thousands of GIs. We can gain insight into these regular Joes by perusing the articles, photos, cartoons, and advertisements that popular media developed in 1940–1941 to enchant and entertain the American public. The artifacts from this period provided the content of the future servicemen's shared prewar experiences. This common culture led them, within a few days

of the entry of the United States into World War II, to create sub-
liminally a larger-than-life feminine adversary whose broadcasts
originated not from radio transmitters but from the wellsprings of
their own minds.

~

Americans in 1940 worried that
the strife destroying the rest of
the world would eventually engulf
them as well. The United States, in
the view of its citizens, was behind
the eight ball (Figure 3.1).[8] The situation filled them with anxiety about
their future. Cartoonists expressed
these common fears through humor (Figures 3.2 and 3.3).[9]

Popular magazines of the time
mirrored the tension between war
and peace that troubled the minds

Figure 3.1. Cover, January 25, 1941.

Figure 3.3. "Don't get so upset, Ruth. Remember, it's only a newsreel."

Figure 3.2. "Oh, relax, Edith—we
all have to go sometime."

of everyday people by placing side by side the most incongruous material. On a page in *Life*—the most popular and influential magazine of the time—a girl blushes prettily as she discusses a love secret she recently learned; in the column immediately beside her is an explanation of bomber formations.[10] A vacation advertisement for "Fun-times in Phoenix" and an ad for "Dean's Ornamented Cakes" bracket a poem about fighter planes flying low while "sea gulls scream their terror to the sky."[11] In another issue, a smiling bathing beauty heading for a swim seeks help from an armed soldier because the barbed wire from beach defenses has snagged her suit (Figure 3.4).[12]

Americans focused their fear of war on Europe. Japan had initiated a grinding, full-scale war with China in 1937, but in the interests of U.S. citizens, this conflict took a distant second place to the military triumphs of Nazi Germany. German tanks had defeated Polish horse cavalry in about two weeks in September 1939, using a style of attack known as *blitzkrieg* or "lightning

Figure 3.4.

war." Afterward, Germany had failed to prosecute its war efforts for seven months in the so-called sitzkrieg. Then, in May 1940, the Nazis attacked France through Belgium, and World War II began in earnest, triggering daily news coverage that gave Americans a sense of inevitability about the United States being pulled into the fighting just as it had into World War I.

However, the tremendous volume of popular articles on Nazism, fascism, Hitler, panzer divisions, the Luftwaffe, and other aspects of the war in Europe did not seed American culture with the source material for a mysterious, all-knowing German radio temptress. Yet a Nazi radio propagandist actually existed. Servicemen in Europe nicknamed an American woman who broadcast for the Germans, "Axis Sally."[13] She offered opinions about German invincibility and Roosevelt's "kike boyfriends."[14] Her vocal delivery was unequivocal, pedantic, and without any obvious sex appeal. Allied listeners dismissed her as an anti-Semitic Nazi mouthpiece. They did not dream of having sex with her, and no rumors circulated about GIs who had killed themselves as a result of her broadcasts. When in 1946 the U.S. arrested Axis Sally, whose real name was Mildred Gillars, she surprised Americans when she "cut a theatrical figure in tight-fitting black dresses . . . scarlet lips and nails . . . and long silver hair [worn] in the manner of Rita Hayworth."[15] The American public had expected a querulous crone in jackboots.[16]

Tokyo Rose was different. Throughout the war, the elements of Tokyo Rose's legend showed remarkable uniformity among American military personnel across the length and breadth of the Pacific. The various and sundry Japanese broadcasters, who later in the war included females, did not provide that uniformity. American servicemen had entered the war subconsciously prepared to hear an Asian temptress. One key aspect of the different reactions to Axis Sally and Tokyo Rose lies in the treatment of Japanese as opposed to Europeans, such as Germans, in the press, movies, and other organs of popular American culture.

~

American magazines in the pre-war period usually portrayed the Japanese as a malevolent combination of deviousness, immorality, and lunacy. The *New Yorker*, with tongue in cheek, listed "Some Expressions of a Highly Spiritual Nature Recently Reported from across the Pacific Indicating That Even War Cannot Tarnish the Tender Soul of Nippon." Japanese tourism ads touting "twenty-six centuries of Japan's colorful history" that "unfold in spectacular celebration marked by fascinating festivals . . . brilliant pageantry . . . enthralling ceremonies . . . medieval splendor" may have inspired the article.[17] In any case, the lampooned celebrations and ceremonies from the "Realm of Pageantry" included Tokyo legislators setting aside a day to honor rabbits who had died providing fur to the Japanese Army, mulberry farmers making a pilgrimage to honor silkworms who had died for the cause, and Shinto priests praying over 600 pieces of straw rope to be sent to the troops in China "to inspire them to greater efforts in showing the enemy the virtues of the Sun Goddess in preserving calm."[18] The *New Yorker* also reprinted strange news bulletins from the Japanese newspaper *Asahi Shimbun*. This item is typical: "There are many insincere skiers who ski purely for enjoyment and there are some who go to resorts and do not ski at all. When they appear at mountain resorts and do not ski earnestly, they will be presented with handbills saying 'Let us remember to keep these mountains and so enjoy skiing.'"[19] Americans found Japan's resolutely purposeful skiing risible.

Figure 3.5. "You can never tell what they're thinking, can you?"

Weird celebrations of the Japanese war effort only added to the generic stereotype of the Japanese as inscrutable. The inability to comprehend their thoughts angered one matron and inspired fear in the other in the cartoon in Figure 3.5. [20] Other pre-war cartoons pictured Japanese tourists busy photographing everything from U.S. port facilities to Civil War cannons. In one, a returned traveler proudly shows a group of Japanese military officers his vacation snapshots: "And here's the new Curtiss-Wright propeller plant, slightly to the left of Mrs. Togomatsu and the children."[21]

Were bizarre behavior and spying not bad enough, *Collier's* carried an article on widespread prostitution in Japan. It featured an illustration of an elderly man presenting a young woman to a geisha with the caption, "No one but a girl's real father may sell her into prostitution, and only for 'proper' reasons such as buying a government bond."[22] No wonder readers of the *Saturday Evening Post* thought nothing of this title (Figure 3.6).[23] Even though Americans widely feared Hitler and the German

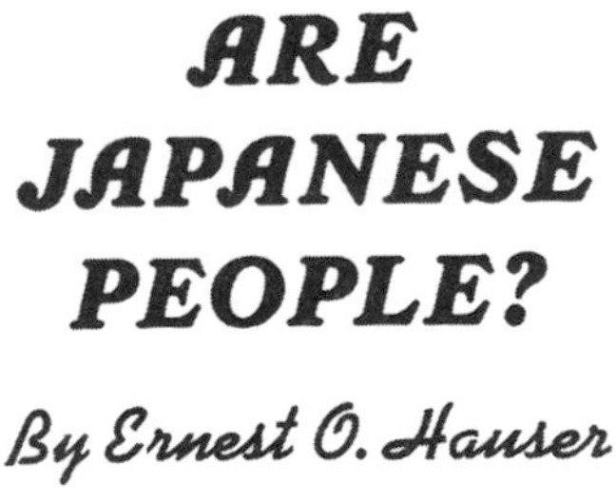

ARE JAPANESE PEOPLE?

By Ernest O. Hauser

Figure 3.6.

military, it is difficult to imagine a similar article titled "Are Germans People?" The sheer ignorance of Japanese culture in general combined with the widespread belief that their thought processes were an enigma promoted a racism in which they were portrayed as subhuman, or "monkey-men" in a popular expression of the time. Perversely, this supposed opacity of the Japanese to rational understanding later provided fuel for the legend of Tokyo Rose, whose ability to see and know everything was also viewed as not quite human.

Such coverage of Japan in magazines added up to a portrait of a nation that could not be trusted. This perception of duplicity and treachery applied with particular virulence to the Japanese now resident in America's heartland; that is, Japanese immigrants, the Issei, and their children, the Nisei.[24]

Figure 3.7.

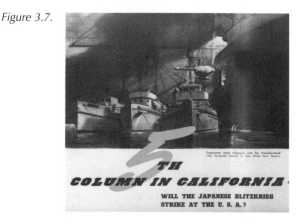

Figure 3.8.

Notice how the photographer included the oil wells in his shot.

The Nisei, editorialized *Liberty* publisher Bernarr MacFadden, resulted from a scheme to take over California. The Japanese "send one of their countrymen there with a wife. She would have four children, go back to Japan, and another wife would be sent to her husband. How many times this was repeated I was not informed."[25] *Life* captioned a picture of kimono-clad Nisei marching in a parade, "Though they carry American flags, Californians do not like it." The article showed a Nisei dancer creating "sinuous Oriental evolutions." "Japanese voices seldom please U.S. ears, but Nisei girls dance as ably as they play tennis," *Life* informed readers.[26]

~

Before the war began for the United States, Americans celebrated two conspicuous precursors of Tokyo Rose in their popular culture. The first was detective Charlie Chan. Chan appeared as the hero of more than 20 movies in the 1920s and 1930s, and starred in 4 additional films in 1940 alone. As both Chinese and male, Charlie Chan would seem an unlikely inspiration for the Japanese and female Tokyo Rose, but he possessed two characteristics that would later inform her legend. The first was intelligence. Charlie Chan was always the smartest guy in the movie. Smarter than the society swells who hired him, smarter than the perpetrator of the crime, way smarter than the police, Chan displayed a shrewdness and an ability to ferret out secrets that Tokyo Rose would similarly manifest during the war. Second, Charlie Chan spoke in an elevated Pidgin English[27] whose syntax Americans came to associate exclusively with intelligent Asians. No ordinary American parents addressed their eldest child "Number One Son" as Charlie Chan did. No other foreigners began sentences, "Honorable ancestors say. . . . " His article-free, pronoun-free, fortune cookie aphorisms were movie highlights. The following, all taken from 1940, seem in retrospect especially relevant to the wartime mistakes of Iva Toguri and her post-war prosecution for the broadcasts of Tokyo Rose:

Dividing line between folly and wisdom very faint in dark tomb. (*Charlie Chan in Panama*; March 1940)
   One cloud not make storm, nor one falsehood criminal. (*Charlie Chan's Murder Cruise*; June 1940)

> Conviction of most dangerous public enemy bring more peaceful sleep. (*Charlie Chan at the Wax Museum*; September 1940)
>
> Eye easily deceived. Same leopard can hide beneath different spots. (*Murder over New York*; December 1940)[28]

GIs during the war and reporters after it would attribute similarly flawed English to Tokyo Rose. (See the discussion in chapter 16 of correspondent Clark Lee's revision of Iva's own speech to make it sound more "Oriental.") The pidginizing of Tokyo Rose's broadcasts continues to the present time. (See the quotations attributed to the Tokyo Rose-inspired "Orphan Ann" in *Flags of Our Fathers*, discussed in chapter 20.)

More than 30 million Americans encountered another unmistakable prototype for Tokyo Rose every day in the newspaper.[29] Milton Caniff named his Asian seductress the Dragon Lady (Figure 3.9), and she schemed against clean-cut American boys in his "Terry and the Pirates," a densely drawn and immensely popular cartoon strip set in the Far East. "Terry and the Pirates" first appeared in 1934, and the powerful Dragon Lady was the central villain from the outset.[30] The strip was so popular that it became a radio series in 1937 and a movie serial in 1940. Whereas the Japanese later purportedly employed Tokyo Rose as part of their effort to defeat the United States, Caniff left the larger purposes of the Dragon Lady obscure. The shrewdness and duplicity of the two women derived from their ethnicity but also from the simple fact that they were female.

Figure 3.9. Dragon Lady.
Courtesy of Nantier Beall Minoustchine Publishing.

Figure 3.10. *"Generals don't know anything—see what you can get out of some of these radio commentators."*

Figure 3.11. *"See here, if you're trying to steal our defense plans, you'll have to pay closer attention."*

Figure 3.12. *"I think we have a leak around here. The Army seems to be getting their plans before we get them."*

Figure 3.13. *"Now here's where she gets the military secrets."*

Finally, another exemplar of the duplicitous female during the pre-war period helped inspire the Tokyo Rose legend, though not as conspicuously as the Dragon Lady. These eight cartoons share a common subject not often explored today: female spies (Figures 3.10 through 3.17).[31]

Figure 3.15. "Well, to begin with, Major Fleecy's wife is interested in a young lieutenant and her hair really isn't blonde . . ."

Figure 3.14. "You're making a grave mistake, Miss Loesch. We scoutmasters are not entrusted with military secrets."

Figure 3.16. "Operator U-6, I fear the American lieutenant let you carry away an exaggerated idea of the value of these diagrams."

Figure 3.17. "That's Q37, in her day one of the most effective agents this country ever had."

Spy images inundated U.S. popular culture before the war. An analysis of these cartoons suggests that, in the eyes of American men, only beautiful women could qualify as spies—the exception in the last cartoon was retired—because such operatives had to obtain military secrets through sex and seduction. Later, American servicemen dreamed that Tokyo Rose would try to obtain their secrets through similar means. In their imaginations, Tokyo Rose broadcast wearing her sexiest, low-cut dresses, much as the spies above reported to their superiors wearing similar outfits. (In Milton Caniff's re-creation of the average GI's mental image of Tokyo Rose—it begins chapter 9—she wears next to nothing as she broadcasts, and her female servants wear even less.) The cartoons also illustrate another common view of the period: namely, that treacherous women always had long black hair.

~

Untrustworthy females, whether they manifest themselves as spies or in more benign incarnations, are nothing new, and American magazines of the pre-war period did not limit their numbers to Asians or Japanese or even dark-haired women. America's popular media regularly demeaned women's intelligence while affirming their craftiness, ridiculed their lack of economic good sense while declaring them venal in romance, and portrayed them as lazy and self-centered yet also ambitious in finding a husband/meal ticket.

This denigration of women is extremely important in the current context. The mythology of Tokyo Rose pitted the evil foreign seductress against the "girl back home." But as will be obvious from what follows, the future GIs were ambivalent about the virtue and purity of heart of their wives and girlfriends back in the States. As a result, the post-war attack on the prevarications of Tokyo Rose may have been ferocious precisely because she purportedly said out loud ideas about the behavior of these women that many Americans wanted kept quiet.

No reputable magazine today would dare publish some of the images of women common in 1940–1941. For example, a ubiquitous ad for Pep-O-Mint Life Savers displayed a college girl "working for her M.R.S (better known as Mrs.)" degree in cap and very short gown while sitting on a professor's lap. The text explained she "should watch her b-r-e-a-t-h" in order to "keep romance warm."[32] This ad worked for those who assumed women went to college to meet men and get married. For those women who lagged in the pursuit of this all-consuming goal, *Good Housekeeping* ran an article featuring a young woman with a huge shadow behind her under the title "What does one do with the *Unmarried Daughter*?" Among the subtitles: "You're not getting any younger," "How much money does he earn?" and "Don't be so choosy."[33]

Cartoons of romantically successful women included a beauty in a strapless evening gown reclining among furs and jewelry: "Ah, Marie! It's *good* to be in love."[34] Love and marriage in such cartoons were mercenary activities. In another, a blonde in a fur coat on the arm of her older husband tells a sidewalk Santa, "Don't bother with anything but diamonds."[35] As her suitor waits on bended knee before her, yet another curvaceous beauty counsels, "Try to be patient. I'll give you my answer in a moment." Behind her a jeweler with an eyepiece examines the boyfriend's recently offered engagement ring.[36] A new bride so leggy that she towers over the groom strides down the aisle following their wedding and inquires, "How does it feel to be my first husband?"[37]

Even for those women interested in a career, sexual allure was a key attribute and marriage always a hidden option. Thus, a female job applicant presents a framed photo of her glamorous self as she announces, "Here's my card."[38] Still another cartoon beauty confesses to a startled employer, "No, sir. No experience at all. If you hire me, you will be my first job."[39] A harried officer worker, desk piled high with papers, calls her savior: "Charlie, do you still want to marry me?"[40] A foxy young mom points to her older husband and tells her young son, "Darling, this is your new daddy—mother got tired of working."[41]

Magazine stories provided men a remedy for such women: a good spanking. Realistic drawings of husbands with upraised hands over the bottoms of squirming wives held across their knees illustrated stories in *Collier's* and other popular publications (Figure 3.18).[42]

It would be a mistake, however, to believe these negative images of treacherous, deceitful, and materialistic women predominated. American culture and the future GIs who bore it were more schizophrenic than misogynistic. Favorable images of women, chiefly in the roles of wife and mother, had equal if not greater currency. Whereas cartoons tended to contain critical portrayals, advertisements usually displayed more positive representations, even though they too sometimes suffered from the chauvinism of

Figure 3.18.

the times. A Kellogg's ad for Pep cereal showed a wife bringing her husband his pipe and slippers. She complained "Look what I married," but gave him vitamin-filled Pep so he could regain his old "snap and sparkle."[43] Fletcher's Castoria (a sugary laxative for children) ran a series of multi-photograph ads featuring a mother hugging her crying child as she stood up to her hairbrush-wielding husband. With titles such as "You ought to *hate* yourself for spanking that child!" and "This is the last time he spanks that child!" the ads told the story of the wife's refusal to allow her husband to punish their son (never their daughter) because the boy wouldn't swallow a competitor's bad-tasting product.[44] Instead, she forcefully demanded her husband buy Castoria. Other images of women contrasted with such audacity. For example, *Collier's* complimented Mrs. Cordell Hull (Hull was Secretary of State) for being "one of the most self-effacing . . . wives in Washington."[45]

Two themes concerning good women that would be paramount to the Tokyo Rose phenomenon appeared before the war. The first portrayed faithful girlfriends, as in the cartoon below of

Figure 3.19. "I'll be waiting for you, Edward."

children about to be separated by summer camp (Figure 3.19).[46] Second, the cosmetics giant Revlon ran a series of ads aimed at women who wanted to "do something to help." Revlon dedicated its campaign to beauty salons, presumably to encourage women to visit more often in order to keep men's spirits up. Although the model in the advertisements changed, the caption always remained the same (Figure 3.20). It would become the defining theme of the Tokyo Rose legal case.[47]

MORALE IS A WOMAN'S BUSINESS

Figure 3.20. Revlon ad campaign.

The women who dealt with sparkle-free husbands and crying kids, with Pep cereal and Fletcher's Castoria, relieved the tedium of their everyday lives by reading about *le beau monde*, the world of high society and high fashion. *Vogue* and *Harper's Bazaar* were its house organs in America, conveying a sense of the leading edge of fashion to the interested public. These magazines featured models chosen by their editors and photographers as representing the epitome of feminine beauty and style. The selection process was not then and is not now an academic enterprise. If the photos and ads do not drive the magazine's female readers to exclaim, "Isn't she attractive! I want to walk into a room and create exactly the same effect, be just as ravishing," then they won't buy the clothes, accessories, and cosmetics upon which the magazine's survival depends. For fashion magazine editors, sensing and slightly anticipating society's taste is everything.

In 1940–1941, something peculiar happened in the pages of *Vogue* and *Harper's Bazaar*. These prestigious fashion magazines became fascinated with an Asian look. [48] Not with Asians exactly, but with an Asian look. Editors selected for their covers and interior layouts the same sort of models they always had: American/ European (i.e., white) women. Then, barely conscious of what they were doing, photographers consistently made up their models' eyes to resemble those of the women of the Far East. Nor was that the extent of the fascination. Sometimes the models used their fingers to pull back the corners of their eyes, and then stared into the mirror to contemplate the effect of such a change in race. Even mannequins appeared to be Asian. In the selections that follow, one photograph of a woman pondering records could have served a year later as a wartime portrait of Tokyo Rose. Yet, to state again what will be obvious, all these models were Caucasian (Figures 3.21 through 3.29). [49]

The images of women in pre-war publications were as multifaceted as they are today. The models in high fashion magazines always have and probably always will look different from the women who appear in advertisements for toothpaste and vacuum cleaners. In contemporary times, however, the predominance of beautifully made-up movie stars, television stars, and supermodels in endorsed product ads and featured essays has blurred this difference. For this reason, modern readers flipping through popular

Figure 3.21. Cover, May 1940.

Figure 3.22. Cover, July 1, 1940.

Figure 3.23. Cover, December 1941.

Figure 3.24. Cover, May 1, 1941.

Figure 3.25. Model with records; military map on wall.

Figure 3.26.

Figure 3.27. Mannequins.

Figure 3.28.

Figure 3.29.

magazines of 1940–1941 will be struck by the contrast between the glamorous models in fashion magazines and everyone else. *Saturday Evening Post, Collier's, Good Housekeeping,* and *Redbook* invariably featured "all-American girls," often blondes. The models that populated *Vogue* and *Harper's Bazaar* routinely appeared to look Asian, and were often brunettes. As the United States wavered between war and peace, American popular culture drew a distinction between two kinds of women. The distinction was not sharply drawn, but in retrospect it seems clear enough. Looking "Oriental" meant being exotic, extravagantly fashionable, alluring, and, to judge from many of the poses—staring into mirrors, gazing into space, sidelong glances—self-absorbed, perhaps devious. In contrast, the all-American types came across as unpretentious, sensible, economical, and, indirectly, honest.

Two images from the *Saturday Evening Post* illustrate this distinction. The first was filler material from inside the magazine; the second, a *Post* cover. Neither had a caption. Together they summarize the yin and yang of the Tokyo Rose phenomenon. On one side was the enchantress herself; on the other, the women about whom she spoke. These two drawings perfectly illustrate the two views of women that would later occupy the center of the debate in the Department of Justice, the media, the jury room, and among ordinary citizens concerning the legal and moral case against Iva Toguri. Yet both images appeared before the war, before anyone had ever imagined a female enemy named Tokyo Rose.

Figure 3.30,[50] from April 1941, illustrates a particular vision of a mermaid. First and most interestingly, she, like Tokyo Rose, is Asian. She has long black hair, darkened skin, and her eyes are almond-shaped. However, unlike the eyes of the other creatures around her, hers have no pupils. Their blankness makes it impossible to tell if she is simply reading, or secretly watching us. The cover of her reading material is also blank, so we cannot be sure what it is—a report, a communiqué, a dispatch? Within a few months, Tokyo Rose would also read battlefield reports and military dispatches over the radio while secretly studying her American adversaries. The mermaid appears to be an extension and in the control of a larger, darker power represented by the octopus, just as Tokyo Rose would be an extension and in the control of the Japanese military. The corners of her full lips turn up in a sly smile, suggesting her allure, but many other elements of the drawing make her an object of dread. Her fingers are like a crab's claws and her tail forks like a serpent's tongue. Her body twists into a parody of a bow of submission, but despite the slightly lowered head, those eyes never leave us. The shadows that darken her body also sprout up like devil's horns from the seabed around her. Despite the grinning fish, the mood of the drawing is menacing, portentous. This mermaid is a sinister presence lying in wait at the bottom of the sea.

Figure 3.30.

On December 7, 1940, one year to the day before the attack on Pearl Harbor, rain assaulted the windshield of a woman alone on the cover of the *Saturday Evening Post* (Figure 3.31).[51] Unlike the sea siren, this woman is clearly American. Readers of the *Post* would recognize her as a sister, daughter, girlfriend, wife, or mother. For the moment, she is dry, safe from the rain. As the wiper clears the glass, we see that she too is beautiful like the siren, but her beauty is fresh and wholesome. She looks directly and honestly at us. Her eyes are large and open; she hides nothing. Her gloves betoken a woman of propriety. The menacing presence one senses in the drawing is the storm. American popular culture of the time consistently portrayed people caught in storms because that is how Americans felt. The entire world was at war, and we were soon to be caught in the downpour. Here, the mood of the drawing emphasizes the contrast between the lit safety of the car's interior and the wet darkness of the outside world. The car protects the woman for now but she is vulnerable. When the United States enters the war, she will be "the girl back home" for whom GIs fight and die. Tokyo Rose will demean her in broadcasts, painting her as a promiscuous tramp.

Because she is one of us, not one of them, Americans will resolutely defend her. The American public will not forgive Tokyo Rose for her impudence, and will mete out to her the justice she deserves.

Figure 3.31.

Notes

1. Allied service personnel in Europe dubbed various male propagandists for Germany "Lord Haw Haw," of whom the most prominent was the American-born William Joyce.

2. *Los Angeles Times*, March 29, 1942, 3. Note that Rose is an exception to the rule that Tokyo's propagandists are "thoroughly American in pronunciation and use of phrase." This implies she spoke with an accent; listeners would later claim she was English. Reporter Clark Lee also claimed he first heard the name "Tokyo Rose" in 1942. Trial Transcript, vol. VII, 512.

3. FBIS was renamed the Foreign Broadcast Information Service on November 1, 1946, and then the Foreign Broadcast Information Branch on December 31, 1946. The government reshuffled it within agencies over the years, and this continues to the present day. As of this writing, FBIS is part of the CIA but by the time of publication it may be incorporated into Homeland Security. I have decided not to trouble readers with these name changes and refer to the unit as the FBIS throughout the book.

4. Does this discovery, that Tokyo Rose was famous before any women broadcast, mean that her entire history as we know it has been backward, that the cause was the effect and vice versa? That is, is it possible that the Tokyo Rose phenomenon among American troops is what caused the Japanese to install women who broadcast in a Tokyo Rose style?

My answer in this book is no. I argue that it is unclear that any woman at any time broadcast Tokyo Rose-like material over Japanese radio. (See the section on Manila Rose in chapter 7.) The evidence also shows that the Japanese did not learn of the fascination of American servicemen with Tokyo Rose until 1944. (See chapter 10.) But new evidence arises regularly in this fascinating case, and the idea that fantasies created Tokyo Rose rather than the other way round has a certain logic to it.

5. *New York Times*, August 8, 1945.

6. American troops chalked "Kilroy was here" everywhere they went, thus creating the legend of a Super GI who had been everywhere and done everything, including areas and actions off-limit. Many explanations of the source of the legend have appeared over the years. The most popular claims James J. Kilroy, a shipyard inspector, chalked the words on bulkheads to show that he had inspected the riveting in the newly constructed ship. The notation baffled troops on those ships who jokingly reproduced the graffiti around the world. Stalin purportedly emerged from a brand-new outhouse specially built for him at the Potsdam Conference asking, "Who is Kilroy?"

7. Provenance, from the French *provenir*, "to come from," literally refers to the origin or source of something. The term now technically denotes the chain of ownership of a work of art, which is not my meaning here.

8. Figure 3.1, *Saturday Evening Post*, January 25, 1941.

9. Figure 3.2, *Collier's*, July 12, 1941, 72. Figure 3.3, *Collier's*, March 22, 1941, 48. The magazine was originally *Collier's Weekly*, but the name was abbreviated in popular reference and eventually abridged officially to the somewhat ungrammatical *Collier's*.

10. *Life*, September 9, 1940, 42.

11. *New Yorker*, November 16, 1940, 80.

12. Figure 3.4, *Life*, September 2, 1940, 64.

13. Mildred Gillars, born Mildred Elizabeth Sisk, referred to herself on the air as "Midge at the mike." For a short biography, see http://womens history.about.com/library/prm/blaxissally1.htm, or http://www.history net.com/mildred-elizabeth-sisk-american-born-axis-sally.htm

14. This particular broadcast at http://www.earthstation1.com/WWII Audio/Axis_Sally_02c.wav

15. Obituary, *New York Times*, July 2, 1988. Gillars died in obscurity in Columbus, Ohio, at age 87.

16. See chapter 19 for more about Mildred Gillars, whom Iva later met in prison.

17. *Vogue*, June 15, 1940, 5, among many publications.

18. *New Yorker*, October 4, 1941, 56.

19. *New Yorker*, December 28, 1940, 56.

20. Figure 3.5, *Life*, October 13, 1941, 9.

21. *New Yorker*, July 26, 1941, 10.

22. *Collier's*, June 21, 1941, 17.

23. Figure 3.6, *Saturday Evening Post*, November 16, 1940, 12.

24. Figure 3.7, *Liberty*, August 10, 1940, 13. Figure 3.8, *Life*, October 14, 1940, 75.

25. Bernarr MacFadden, *Liberty*, June 1, 1940, 4.

26. *Life*, October 14, 1940, 82.

27. Pidgin English originated as a means of intercommunication between Europeans and Chinese at Chinese seaports. Although the definition of pidgin has since expanded, white Americans in the 1940s routinely employed the jargon as a derogation of all Asians. A popular joke from the period after the war may illustrate:

The son of a socially prominent New York family, who was a soldier in the U.S. Army of Occupation in Tokyo, cabled his parents that he had fallen in love with a Japanese girl and intended to marry her. They cabled back that he shouldn't be too hasty. He responded, "Don't worry. She is lovely and she's a Republican." "How do you know?" cabled his father.

"Because," responded the son, "every time I ask her for a kiss, she says, 'Me know Dewey.'"

Few people today will get the joke. First, they won't remember Republican New York governor Thomas E. Dewey. Second, they've probably never encountered the lower forms of Pidgin English ("me likee flied lice") because no modern comedian dares make fun of Asians by using it. Finally, they can't imagine a girl wouldn't kiss her fiancé. That, of course, misses the point entirely. In the less sexually explicit culture of the 1940s, the joke's hearers understood kissing was merely a polite way to reference what the girl really would "no do-ee."

28. For a list of several hundred such aphorisms, see http://charlie chanfamily.tripod.com/id6.html.

29. "Terry and the Pirates," at 31 million (31M) readers in 1944, was the fifth most popular comic strip during the war, behind "Joe Palooka" (40M), "Blondie" (35M), "Li'l Abner" (32M), and "Orphan Annie" (32M). See Goodman, *While You Were Gone*, 495.

30. The comic strip "Terry and the Pirates" debuted on October 22, 1934; the Dragon Lady first appeared in it on December 13, 1934. Her real name was Lai Choi San, which means "Mountain of Wealth." She was either Chinese or Eurasian, but I assume most readers viewed her as just another treacherous Oriental. See http://www.tanjaycity.org/ Gerry%20Gil/SAMPLES/DRAGON.htm.

31. Female spy cartoons: Figure 3.10, *Saturday Evening Post*, May 3, 1941, 32; Figure 3.11, *Collier's*, June 15, 1940, 80; Figure 3.12, *Collier's*, November 8, 1941, 36; Figure 3.13, *New Yorker*, July 13, 1940, 25; Figure 3.14, *New Yorker*, July 27, 1940, 18; Figure 3.15, *New Yorker*, November 16, 1940, 28; Figure 3.16, *Esquire*, January 1940, 85; Figure 3.18, *New Yorker*, August 17, 1940, 14.

32. *Saturday Evening Post*, November 23, 1940, 47, among many publications.

33. *Good Housekeeping*, July 1941, 34.

34. *Esquire*, January 1940, 84.

35. *Esquire*, January 1941, 32.

36. *Saturday Evening Post*, March 23, 1941, 28.

37. *Collier's*, March 29, 1941, 52.

38. *Collier's*, March 23, 1940, 63.

39. *Collier's*, June 29, 1940, 24.

40. *Saturday Evening Post*, November 29, 1941, 80.

41. *Esquire*, June 1941, 51.

42. Figure 3.18, *American Magazine*, September 1941, 22. See also December 1941, 136 and *Collier's*, February 10, 1940, 12

43. *Redbook*, February 1940, 89, among many publications.

44. *Redbook*, February 1940, 75, among many publications.

45. *Collier's*, May 4, 1940, 14.

46. Figure 3.19, *New Yorker*, June 28, 1941, 21.

47. Figure 3.20, *Harper's Bazaar*, November 1941, 38, among many publications.

48. I do not mean to suggest that *Vogue* and *Harper's Bazaar* never used photographs or drawings of Asian women prior to 1940. For example, various *Vogue* covers by Benito and George Lepape in 1926 and 1927 featured stylized drawings of Asian-looking women. See http://gatochy .blogspot.com/2007/10/vintage-magazine-covers.html. Earlier in the century "Orientalism" was an important fashion movement. My claim is that just before the war such treatments suddenly became both widespread and oddly inappropriate (i.e., Caucasian models were made up to *look* Asian).

49. *Harper's Bazaar* covers: Figure 3.21, May 1940; Figure 3.24, December 1941. *Vogue* covers: Figure 3.22, May 1, 1941; Figure 3.23, July 1, 1940. Second following page: Figure 3.25, *Vogue*, September 15, 1940, 102; Figure 3.26, *Vogue*, February 15, 1941, 58; Figure 3.27, *Harper's Bazaar*, October 1941, 53; Figure 3.28, *Vogue*, October 15, 1941, 58; Figure 3.29, *Harper's Bazaar*, June 1941, 74.

50. Figure 3.30, *Saturday Evening Post*, April 26, 1941, 101.

51. Figure 3.31, *Saturday Evening Post*, cover, December 7, 1940.

4

Collision with Japan

Before Pearl Harbor

The Hattori family—Iva's aunt, uncle, and two English-speaking cousins—made the 20-minute trip from Tokyo to Yokohama to meet Iva at the pier. Her aunt was tiny, less than 5 feet tall, frail but ambulatory; her uncle was also small but considerably more robust. Customs agents viewed with suspicion the quantity of goods Iva brought with her. They assumed she intended to sell them. Given that her uncle was a tailor and Iva brought along textiles, their attitude was not simple harassment. Iva and the Hattoris wrangled with the officials, who allowed her baggage to pass only after charging her exorbitant duties.

The Hattoris treated Iva to lunch at the Grand Hotel in downtown Yokohama. When asked to recall her initial reaction to Japan, Iva laughed. "You'll think I'm crazy but my first thought was, 'I have never seen so many Japanese in one place in all my life!'" Besides teeming with Japanese, Yokohama also teemed with mosquitoes that bred in the open sewer system. In Japanese cities, all waste except human excrement drained through open concrete runnels. Iva also noticed the absence of tall buildings, the narrow streets, lack of sidewalks, the dominance of bicycles, and the rarity of cars. She was pleased that she did not stand out because most young women wore Western dress, not kimonos.

Japan in 1941 was in many ways a severely underdeveloped country. Six months before Iva's arrival, Otto Tolischus, reporter for the *New York Times,* had arrived in Yokohama and thought it "looked shabby and dingy." He journeyed to Tokyo by car. "Throughout the twenty-odd-mile drive, the disappointing impression I had received of Yokohama deepened. Both sides of the road were lined with dirty, dilapidated, ramshackle wooden shops and shacks which had nothing in common with the pretty doll houses pictured in Japanese scenes at home. The people looked equally poverty-stricken. Most of them shuffled about in dirty kimonos or a bizarre array of Western dress, and most of them, though it was winter, walked about in bare feet shod in wooden clogs. Farmers, driving lumbering oxcarts, were completely in rags, sometimes covered with a raincoat made of straw."[1]

After making arrangements to truck her luggage to Tokyo, Iva and the Hattoris rode the streetcar back to her aunt and uncle's home in the Setagaya district.[2] Small by American standards, the house was roomy in comparison to most Japanese dwellings. The Hattori living room was eight mats in size or 144 square feet (12' × 12'), although the ceiling was less than 6 feet from the floor. When they arrived, Iva entered the home's entrance hall, slid open the sliding paper screen door or *shoji,* a door type she had never seen before, and stepped directly into the living room and onto the straw mats. Her aunt, behind her, gasped. Iva had not removed her shoes, thus soiling the mats. Iva quickly rectified the mistake. Once properly inside, Iva discovered the house had only a few items of furniture. A dressing table and an eating table, each about 15 inches off the floor, were the extent of it. The family sat on the floor or on cushions to talk. To eat, they folded their legs underneath their bodies, tucked them under the table, and rested their torsos on their ankles.

The long day and long voyage had exhausted Iva. She just wanted to use the toilet, take a bath, and then go to bed and get a good night's sleep. Nothing went well. Recalling her first night, Iva groaned, "It was a very traumatic experience." Her misery began when she first confronted a Japanese toilet. It consisted of an oval enamel fixture set flat against the floor over an open hole, like an American outhouse but with no seating. To use it, she had to squat over it. The refuse fell into a concrete or metal box on a lower level. Despite the fact that workers cleaned out the container every few days, the apparatus lent a certain atmosphere to the home. Japan lacked fertilizer, and human waste, what the Japanese called "night soil," was integral to farming and gardening throughout the nation.

Her leg muscles aching from stretching in ways they had never previously experienced, Iva looked forward to a bath. The family showed her to a tub of hot water, and Iva could scarcely contain her delight. She jumped right in and lathered up. "When my aunt saw the soap in the tub, she became hysterical. My uncle asked why she expected anything else since I had come from America. He said I needed to be instructed in how to bathe in Japan. They emptied the tub, washed it out, filled it again, and then reheated the whole tub."[3] This represented a costly undertaking. Charcoal had been rationed in December 1940, and ordinary Japanese either could not obtain coal or found it mixed with slate and charred wood. "They instructed me to use a little bucket to pour water over my body, then to soap myself and wash, and only when clean to get into the soaking tub. Everybody took turns."

Finally to bed—except there were no beds. Instead the family installed mosquito netting in the living (now sleeping) area and unrolled for Iva an exotic item called a *futon*. Widely known in the West today, the 1941 version in Iva's view was just a skimpy sleeping bag. The transition from a box spring and mattress to sleeping on a hard floor left her next morning with an aching back. Breakfast consisted of fermented soy bean soup, rice, Japanese-style pickles, and flavored seaweed. Dinner was the same, except with some vegetables from the garden. Meat and even fish were extremely rare. At most, the family might get three ounces of meat to flavor a vegetable dish. Her aunt could buy two eggs once every two or three weeks and a pint of cooking oil every three months. Everyday American staples, such as coffee, lettuce, butter, milk, cakes, and cookies, could not be obtained. Iva had brought with her some Hershey's Kisses to use as gifts but "I hoarded quite a bit after I realized I would want candy in the future."[4]

Iva wrote her father that she hated Japan and wanted to come home. Her legs hurt, her back hurt, mosquito bites covered any exposed skin, and some insect had bitten her arm, causing it to swell up "like Popeye's. I thought I was going to die." She also suffered from boils, "several humdingers, carbuncles of the severest degree." The doctor lanced her sores to drain the pus. Jun responded that she should tough it out and not give up on Japan so quickly.

Actually, she had little choice. Upon her arrival, Japanese authorities insisted that Iva obtain a passport from the American Consulate, and within a day or two she applied for one. American officials took her picture and gave no hint her application would be problematic, only that it would require processing in the United States. Still Iva worried. She wrote her family, "If I do not get the passport, then what? If things keep getting worse every week, lord help me and Chiyeko! We probably won't be permitted to remain over here. The police said that since the U.S. is making it bad for Nippon residents in America, the Japan government is doing the same for U.S. citizens."[5] Although she checked in with the consulate periodically, the U.S. government never issued the passport.

One day after Iva entered Japan, the United States and Great Britain froze Japanese assets in their countries.[6] Three days later, Japan froze American assets. American nationals tried to retrieve their money from Japanese banks, but it was too late. Japanese exporters knew the freeze would ruin their businesses because they settled their accounts with overseas partners in dollars in New York. The Tokyo Stock Exchange hit its lowest point since 1931; the Yokohama silk exchange shut down. Troops marched through the streets to maintain order. Within days, the United States halted all exports of oil to Japan, as did the Dutch and British. The ABCD powers (American, British, Chinese, Dutch), as they were known in Japan, controlled 90 percent of Japan's oil supply.[7] Without oil, Japan's military would grind to a halt, rendering the country impotent and defenseless.

Iva had expected her father to send her additional funds, but the new regulations made this problematic. However, although these financial maneuvers between the two nations hastened the onset of war, their timing was lucky for Iva because she hadn't yet created a bank account and deposited the $300 she brought with her.[8] As a result, she could cash in dollars for yen as she needed money. The process often took hours, and Japanese inefficiency amazed Iva. She would watch as her simple exchange request slowly circulated through the bank, going from one desk to the next. "Japan is a country of documents," she discovered, and Japanese documents moved at a snail's pace.

She reported to the Metropolitan Police every month for Foreigner Registration. This required a trip from her aunt's home on the train or electric car downtown to the main station near the Imperial Palace. Unfortunately for Iva, Japanese authorities had begun their attack on English as an "enemy" language and had removed English-language signs on public transportation. Unable to read the Japanese signs or understand the conductor, she counted stops. Once she unknowingly boarded an express train and wound up at the end of the line, completely lost. This caused her to be late for dinner, and her aunt scolded her for inconveniencing the family. Her uncle defended her and wrote out the characters for "express" so Iva could avoid trains so marked.[9] The Metro Police for their part were arrogant and dismissive. "People in government really gave me a hard time. Sometimes they would totally ignore me for hours" even though she only required a stamp on her card. She also noticed an anti-American tone and demeanor, which she attributed to the new embargoes.

The embargoes, and especially the war in China, put a stranglehold on the Japanese economy. In 1938, the government adopted the slogan "Extravagance is the enemy." A Ginza department store staged a battle between electrically driven Japanese, U.S., and British warships in a pool while spokesmen urged customers to restrain their spending. Authorities strictly rationed gasoline that year, and the first charcoal-burning cars appeared. Children displayed their patriotism by eating "rising sun box lunches," a pickled red plum on a bed of white rice.[10] By the end of the war, these children would remember this skimpy fare as a sumptuous meal. Telephones were rare because copper wire was too precious to use for anything other than war materiel. Almost no leather was available; whale, salmon, and shark skin substituted.[11]

In 1940, shortages everywhere increased. In June, the government rationed matches and sugar. Clothes made of tree bark and wood pulp appeared. The government brewed sake (rice wine) from sweet potatoes and acorns. The government plowed over many golf courses to create farmland, and limited golfers on the few remaining courses to two new balls per season. It did not allow caddies, considered a luxury. The government closed dance halls at the end of October, which was just as well because the new bamboo needles ruined the records. The government banned cosmetics and permanent waves, and restricted hair dressers to three curls per customer. Matrons on street corners admonished women not to focus on their looks. Apparently their efforts were ineffective. A 1940 survey by the Bureau of Municipal Social Education in Tokyo found in one hour at one intersection: 27 unseemly hair-dos, 183 instances of extravagant foreign clothes, 172 women dressed in overly expensive kimonos, 192 with elaborate accessories.[12] But where persuasion failed, the massive textile shortages soon succeeded.

By 1941, the list of nonessential goods not allowed to be manufactured ran into the hundreds. Nonessential items included can-openers, camera tripods, nutcrackers, cufflinks, and various cooking pans.[13] Mass transit authorities reduced the number of trains when the quantity of gasoline made from sardines proved insufficient. Coffee disappeared. Due to low fixed prices, more and more farmers sold to black (i.e., free) markets instead of shipping their produce to the cities. On October 29, Premier Tojo, who enjoyed riding around Tokyo on horseback, visited a fish market. The fishermen complained that the lack of fuel for their boats reduced their catch. "Gasoline!" Tojo shouted. "Why not get up earlier and work harder!"[14] Such was the logic that carried Japan into war.

Iva remembered a conversation about the wealth and resources of Japan versus those of the United States. The family and Iva agreed the vast differences made war unthinkable. Her uncle summed up the prospect. "It would be like a flea biting an elephant."

~

Iva's understanding of spoken Japanese was poor; her understanding of written Japanese, nonexistent. She decided she would enroll in a language school in September after she had spent the summer exploring Japan. She walked all over Tokyo and took any opportunity to go places with her two cousins, Mugio and his sister Rinko. The three were about the same age, and Iva formed a close friendship with them.

Mugio was "a brilliant, brilliant person. He was fluent in Russian, German, and English, a graduate of Moscow University, and a devout communist." This fact didn't bother Iva because he never tried to sell her on Marxist ideology. Being a communist in Japan was illegal, and by the time Iva met him, Mugio had already spent nine years in jail for the crime. The Special Security Police (*tokko*) had branches in every police precinct to enforce the Peace Preservation Law of 1925, which targeted Marxist thinking.

The Thought Section of the Justice Ministry prosecuted offenders, called "thought criminals," in special courts. Military Secret Police (*kempei*) also hunted down wrong-minded individuals. In the 1930s, communists adopted the slogan "Oppose Imperialistic War" and dared to challenge the militarists. As a result, the various "thought police" arrested, interrogated, and tortured communists with the stated intention of reforming their thinking. Many died in custody. After police arrested the entire staff of a newspaper mildly critical of the government, they warned its chief editor, "If you intend to be stubborn about this, we know how to handle you. We'll just set you up as a communist. We can kill communists. Our superiors will not mind."[15]

Authorities feared communism because they viewed the masses as passive conformists. They worried the people could easily become caught up in a revolution from above, led by the intellectuals, or a revolution from below, led by the lower and middle classes, who were much worse off as a result of the war in China. In any case, Japan at this time remained a largely feudal society with hereditary titles and job placement at birth. To the upper classes and to the military, for whom hierarchy was paramount to order, the communist dream of a classless society was an abomination. By the 1940s, militarist fears had reached hysteria. In February 1940, when a Diet member who represented a farming district criticized the "holy war" in China, the militarists forced his expulsion. In April, the Special Security Police announced that a two-year investigation had uncovered a large cell of communists in the Cabinet Planning Board. They arrested hundreds. On May 10, 1941, the State Secrets Defense Law went into effect, and authorities initiated an anti-spy campaign to warn people to be silent because spies could be anybody, not just Westerners. That summer, authorities disbanded the last of the political parties, as well as the Federation to Acquire the Vote for Women. They also silenced journalist Kiryu Yuyu, who had criticized the militarists and the war in China. Terminally ill, he wrote in his journal just before his death in September, "Contrary to what one might expect, I am joyful at the prospect of disappearing from the face of the globe, which is rapidly degenerating toward ultra-bestiality. My sole regret is that I will not be here to see the fulfillment of the dream I have cherished for so long, the demilitarization which will inevitably occur after the war."[16]

One day, Mugio asked Iva and Rinko if they would like to take a trip with him and a group of his communist friends to Oshima Island. The girls quickly accepted. They journeyed by ferry, leaving at midnight. The group of about a dozen spoke English, German, and Russian, as well as Japanese and played word games to pass the time. They asked about America and were surprised at Iva's ambitions for a career. Rinko predicted women would play a prominent role in Japan some day.[17] Upon their arrival at 4:00 AM, locals greeted them at the docks with candle lanterns in the dawning light. Oshima is famous for its camellias that cover the ground like a carpet—red, peppermint stripes, pink. The beautiful hair of the women enchanted Iva; she first thought they used some sort of lacquer on it. In fact, they applied camellia oil to create the sheen. The group of friends hiked to the local zoo, ducked into a barn during a brief rain, then rode the bus back and cooked peanuts on its charcoal engine. The excursion was one of Iva's few pleasant memories of Japan, although on the way home Mugio took her aside to warn her to be careful with what she said and to give her pointers on recognizing *kempei* agents.

In August 1941, the government published *The Way of Subjects*. Every subject of the emperor had to read it; every school, to teach it. It represented the new bible of the Japanese people. *The Way of Subjects* pressed for a war against the evils of European and American thought, which honored the ideals of "individualism, liberalism, utilitarianism, and materialism."[18] The next month, Mrs. Inouye, president of the Japan Women's University, caught the spirit of the *Way*: "Japanese women working at home as good mothers and good wives make happy homes in such a way as no foreign women, brought up on the ideas of liberalism and individualism, can appreciate."[19] *The Way of Subjects* further called for the establishment of a new world order. It stated Japan's divine mission: to fight against Western attempts to dominate the world, to allow all nations to seek their proper place under one roof, to prevent the United States from doing to the Asians what it had done to American Indians and African Negroes, and to free the nations of the East from "the shackles and bondage of Europe and America."[20] Or, as Mitsuru Toyama, head of the powerful Black Dragon Society, more colorfully announced, the "red-haired barbarians" must be expelled from East Asia.[21]

Iva entered the Matsumiya Japanese Cultural School that September because it accepted young people who knew very little Japanese. Students were generally diplomatic corps members and Christian missionaries. She attended daily, from nine to noon. Iva's teacher, a woman named Keiko, refused to speak any English to her and always dressed formally in a kimono. Iva described her as "fantastic." Decades after the war, her teacher returned the compliment, describing Iva in an interview as the most brilliant student she ever had. Iva doubted that, but admitted she studied diligently because she wanted to converse more freely with her new friends. Becoming fluent in Japanese proved to be a difficult task for Iva. Headmaster Matsumiya, an English speaker, privately tutored her for fifteen months.[22]

Winter came early that year. "Since I had never experienced cold, being born and raised in southern California, it never occurred to me to wear earmuffs. One day my ears started itching, so I scratched them, which aggravated the condition. Soon my ears were very red and swollen. My aunt said I had chilblains. In the back yard she picked some kind of leaf she called a name that, literally translated, meant 'under the frost.' She cooked it, and put it under my ears. It didn't help."[23] Iva again saw the doctor, who bandaged her ears. Shortly thereafter the edges of her feet became frostbit. The doctor lanced them to let out the dried blood and reduce the swelling. Eventually Iva learned to cover up against the bitter cold of Japan's winters.

During this season, Iva's aunt had to journey to Yamanashi to celebrate, as Buddhist tradition requires, the seventeenth year of the death of her elder sister. (Of the Iimuro sisters, Iva's mother was youngest and her aunt was second from the eldest.) She asked Iva to accompany her. In Yamanashi, Iva met her country cousins. "Gad, they looked ancient to me. I couldn't relate to them. The customs, the farmhouses were completely Japanese. And cold—I thought I would freeze to death! They had the ceremony in the temple. In the rural areas of Japan, they might not have heating and they might not have beautiful homes, but by God they had beautiful temples. It was huge! I bet you that temple seats 1,500 people." Later, Iva took the priest aside. "I told him that I'm from America and my father was born somewhere in this area and most of the ancestors are supposedly buried in this vicinity. He said, 'Oh, yes.' He took me out to the cemetery, and I saw rows and rows of Toguris. I don't know whether I would say it was a revelation, but suddenly I found myself connected with the past. Heretofore, I had never met anyone with the name Toguri." The priest remarked that he couldn't think of any living Toguri. Iva found none in Tokyo. She believed her family had the name exclusively in the United States, and the only other Toguris in the world that she knew about lived in Canada.[24]

In November, Iva decided to telephone her father.[25] Although she could not read Japanese-language newspapers or comprehend radio broadcasts, she understood enough to worry that Japanese–U.S. relations had worsened, and she wanted to come home. Her father remained optimistic and told her it would be a shame to return after less than six months. Shortly thereafter, Jun Toguri realized his mistake. He cabled Iva to leave Japan immediately on the *Tatsuta Maru*. Unfortunately, the cablegram took two days to reach Iva; she received it December 1, one day before the ship was set to sail. Iva rushed to the American embassy. They informed her that they had not finished processing her passport but they gave her a letter of identification. She and her uncle then hurried to the Ministry of Finance. This Ministry had to issue a clearance before she could board ship or even buy a ticket. Officials there explained they had to verify her expenditures while in the country to compare the amount with which she entered to the amount which she had now, and that the process would take two or three days. Iva cared nothing about the money she might leave behind, but the bureaucracy would not be moved. She and her uncle returned home. It would not have mattered. The *Tatsuta Maru* never completed her voyage. The ship returned to Japan following the attack on Pearl Harbor.

~

Japanese military intelligence focused on operations, not policy decisions. Nonetheless, in 1941, a group of military planners known as the 20th Group provided Army Chief of Staff Sugiyama with studies of the relative economic power of the United States and Japan. He discarded them. Sugiyama sent Hideo Iwakuro, the Army's representative in American–Japanese negotiations, to the United States in 1941 to speak with Japanese trading companies and to collect information on American economic power. When Iwakuro returned to Japan in August, he reported that the United States could produce ten times the war materiel that Japan could. Sugiyama removed him from central headquarters and assigned him to command an infantry regiment.[26]

On September 3, 1941, General Sugiyama met with the emperor. He assured Emperor Hirohito that a war with the United States would be over in three months. Hirohito reminded Sugiyama that he had previously promised that the war with China would take only one month. The general responded that China was too large a country to be easily conquered. The emperor replied: "If the interior of China is immense, is not the Pacific Ocean even bigger? How can you be sure that the war will end in three months?"[27]

The answer to this question was that the war *had* to be short, otherwise Japan would lose. Most Japanese military experts, especially those in the Imperial Navy, knew that Japan could fight at most for two years. However dismal this prospect, the other option—do nothing in the face of American embargoes—appeared worse. Premier Tojo summed up the essence of Japanese thinking at the Imperial Conference on November 5. "The first stage of the war will not be difficult. We have some uneasiness about a protracted war. But how can we let the U.S. continue to do as it pleases, even though there is some uneasiness? Two years from now we will have no petroleum for military use. Ships will stop moving. When I think about the strengthening of American defenses in the Southwest Pacific, the expansion of the American fleet, the unfinished China Incident, and so on, I see no end to difficulties. We can talk about austerity and suffering, but can our people endure such a life for a long time? I fear that we would become a third-class nation after two or three years if we just sat tight."[28]

The Japanese based their decision to attack the United States on hope. Admiral Yamamoto, who planned the Pearl Harbor strike, hoped that Americans would view the Japanese as suicidal lunatics whom it would not pay to fight.[29] Another admiral, Suetsugu, hoped the Navy could quickly seize enough territories in the South Seas to provide Japan with the resources it needed, as well as a series of island fortresses that could fend off any counterattack. Vice-Chief of Staff Tsukada hoped that Japan's advance might allow Germany and Italy to defeat England, and if England fell, the United States would withdraw from the fight.[30] Almost every Japanese believed the fighting spirit of Japan's soldiers would outweigh any material advantages American personnel might possess.

Emperor Hirohito was not a passive onlooker to the military's prosecution of the war but an active participant. He often recommended revisions in operations, engaged in top secret strategic planning, and received a detailed summary of the surprise attack on Pearl Harbor a month before its execution. With the emperor's endorsement, the plan proceeded.[31]

By the end of 1940, U.S. intelligence had noticed a pattern in the military signals of the Imperial Navy. Whenever Japanese aircraft carrier fleets were underway, radio traffic existed in only one direction, from headquarters to the fleet. The fleet itself maintained radio silence. Then in February 1941, radio traffic ceased in both directions. The U.S. Combat Intelligence Unit guessed the fleets were in home waters utilizing short-range transmissions that could only be received locally. This analysis proved correct. In July 1941, as Japan moved to occupy French Indochina, a similar blank condition obtained for Japanese carrier fleets. No messages emanated from the carriers, and none were sent to them. U.S. intelligence assumed they must again be in home waters using low-powered transmissions. This analysis proved correct. In early December 1941, another blank condition occurred. No messages emanated from the carriers, and the Imperial Navy sent out only one uncoded, open-language message: "Climb Mount Nitaka." Never used before, the phrase meant nothing to American listeners in Hawaii. U.S. intelligence assumed Japanese carrier fleets were again in home waters. This analysis proved to be mistaken.[32]

Notes

1. Tolischus, *Tokyo Record*, 5–6. In our conversations, Iva never said that she found the Japanese impoverished, although her description of the Hattori home suggested it.

2. The exact address was H. Hattori, 825 Unano-Michi, Setagaya-ku, Tokyo, according to Iva's September 18, 1941, application for a passport to return to the United States. For a complete list of Iva Toguri's addresses during her time in Japan, see chapter 10, note 8.

3. Toguri Memories of 2000. See Bibliography.

4. Letter, October 13, 1941.

5. Letter, October 13, 1941.

6. Dates present a quandary. Here are three facts: 1) Iva entered Japan on July 25, 1941. 2) The United States froze Japanese assets on July 25, 1941. 3) The United States froze assets one day after Iva entered Japan. The apparent contradiction results from the fact that Japan is on the other side of the International Date Line from the United States. As a result, events occur there a day later than they do here. Pearl Harbor Day is December 7 for Americans but December 8 for Japanese. For business people in Japan, America froze their assets on July 26. Hence my quandary. If I conform every date to American standards and claim that Iva left the ship on July 24, those familiar with the case will assume I am unaware of Iva's trial testimony (vol. XLIV, 4920) that she arrived on the 24th but remained onboard ship until the 25th. Or, they will suppose I have evidence that Iva made a mistake about when she arrived, which I do not. On the other hand, if I use Japanese dates and claim that the United States froze assets on July 26, historians will think me sloppy or uninformed. All I can do is try to limit the confusion. Other things being equal, I use the American date . . . unless I can't, as is the case here.

7. Tolishcus, *Tokyo Record*, 180.

8. In her interviews, Iva stated that her father had sent her additional money and that "the exchange rate was great." Whether Jun circumvented the new regulations is unclear.

9. This portrait of a spiteful aunt and generous uncle comes from my 1987 interviews. It contradicts her letter of October 13, 1941. "Auntie is very nice and treats me just like one of her daughters." "Uncle is not like Dad. He's not the kind to go out of his way to help others." Apparently the advent of war with the United States brought out different character traits.

10. For a discussion of this lunch box image and its connection with Japan's historical culture, see Elizabeth Schultz and Fumiko Yamamato, "Japan: Land of the Rising and Setting Sun: A Study of the Image of the Sun in Japanese Culture," *Journal of Popular Culture* 18, no. 2 (Fall 1984): 117–34.

11. Information about the Ginza department store and leather substitutes is from Havens, *Valley of Darkness*, 15–16.

12. Information in this paragraph is from Havens, *Valley of Darkness*, 49–52, 18.

13. Tolischus, *Tokyo Record*, 254–55.

14. Tolischus, *Tokyo Record*, 282.

15. Ienaga, *The Pacific War*, 113.

16. Ienaga, *The Pacific War*, 121.

17. At one point in our interviews Iva said Rinko was a graduate of Japanese Women's University; at another, that Rinko was less educated than herself.

18. *The Way of Subjects*, Preamble.

19. Tolischus, *Tokyo Record*, 256.

20. *The Way of Subjects*, Part 1, final paragraph.

21. Toyama was 85 years old when he made this statement. The Black Dragon Society, named after the Black Dragon River (the Chinese name of the Amur River), had as its goal driving the Russians from their territories in east Asia south of this river. The society was a descendant of the ultra-nationalist Genyosha, which Toyama founded in 1881 at age 26 from ex-samurai, assassins, and criminals. Toyama was so powerful he was known as the "Shadow Shogun" and the "Boss of Bosses." See Tolischus, *Tokyo Record*, 96, and http://www.nationmaster.com/encyclopedia/Toyama-Mitsuru.

22. Matsumiya was born in Japan but reared in the United States. He was a graduate of Columbia University and was the son of the founder/owner of the school.

23. Toguri Memories of 2000.

24. The Canadian Toguris are a large and quite prominent family. Tokizo Toguri emigrated from Japan to Canada, where he and his wife Tomiye (Yamamoto) Toguri reared Eizo, Sam, James Makoto, Etsuko, Maki, David, Grace, Miki, and Allan Toguri. These children include several doctors, a choreographer, and a professor of metallurgy. The name "James Makoto" caught my interest (see chapter 6), and I contacted Dr. Allan Toguri to inquire whether Tokizo might be related to Jun. I received no reply. In any case, thanks to these Canadians, the Toguri name seems certain to survive. They've had lots of children—Professor James Makoto alone had five sons—and many grandchildren.

25. In 1987, Iva told me that Chiyeko Ito's aunt worked at the national telephone company and she helped her make the call. In her pre-trial notes, Iva discusses the Itos and does not mention this fact. At trial, she testified that Chiyeko was with her for the call and that Chiyeko spoke to her (Chiyeko's) father as well. Trial Transcript, vol. XLIV, 4924.

26. 20th Group and Iwakuro information from Michael A. Barnhart, "Japanese Intelligence before the Second World War: 'Best Case' Analy-

sis" in *Knowing One's Enemies*, ed. Ernest R. May (Princeton, N.J.: Princeton University Press, 1984), 452.

27. Shillony, *Politics and Culture in Wartime Japan*, 41.

28. Akira Iriye, *Pearl Harbor and the Coming of the Pacific War* (New York: Bedford/St. Martin's, 1999), 37–38.

29. *Asahi Shimbum* staff. *The Pacific Rivals*, 84.

30. Thomas Shook, "The Submarine War in the Pacific: American Success or Japanese Failure?," *War Studies Journal* 21, no. 1 (Spring 1996).

31. See Peter Michael Wetzler, *Hirohito and War Imperial Tradition and Military Decision Making in Prewar Japan* (Honolulu: University of Hawaii Press, 1998), esp. 3–9.

32. David Kahn, *The Codebreakers: The Story of Secret Writing* (New York: Macmillan, 1967), 8–9.

5

At War and on Her Own

Iva was asleep when her cousin shook her awake to inform her Japan and the United States were at war. Iva's reaction was shock, then numbness. "I understood it, but I didn't believe it. I didn't want to believe it." She sat in a daze the rest of the day, imagining herself trapped in Japan with no job and no income.

The next morning, the police arrived to arrest Mugio, apparently as part of a general roundup of subversives; he would remain in prison until 1944.[1] Then they turned their attention to Iva. Iva remembered the officer's name was Fujiwara. She believed he belonged to the Thought Police, although he claimed to be head of the alien observation division of the Metropolitan Police.[2] That he wore a police uniform at least ensured that he did not belong to the fearsome military police, the *kempeitai*. (*Tai* means group; *kempei* means military police; thus, *kempeitai* means military police group. The terms are often interchangeable, but an individual is a *kempei* and the organization is the *kempeitai*.) A small, ordinary-looking man, Fujiwara did not frighten Iva as much as he did her aunt. He questioned Iva using her cousin Rinko as interpreter. He came every other day, always with the same recommendation: Iva should become a Japanese citizen and pledge allegiance to Japan. Iva refused, and asked to be arrested like the Caucasian Americans. Fujiwara responded that as a woman she couldn't do much; besides, imprisoning her would create another mouth to feed. It soon became a drill. Fujiwara arrived and asked if she had reconsidered; Iva said no, and asked if he had reconsidered; he refused to arrest her, promised to discuss the issue again, and left. Fujiwara never lost his temper or became agitated. "He had dealt with Western women before; he knew they were different." The police pressured Chiyeko, who lived with her own relatives, in the same relentless way, and Iva counseled her to hang tough and not renounce her U.S. citizenship. Neither did.

The constant police visits soon attracted the attention of the Neighborhood Association. Created by Home Ministry Order No. 17, issued September 11, 1941, Neighborhood Associations represented the fundamental national building blocks of wartime Japan. For modern Japanese of a certain age, mention of Neighborhood Associations is certain to conjure up memories of World War II. By the summer of 1942, such associations, which were under the control of the Imperial Rule Assistance Association, numbered 1,323,473, with many others in Taiwan and Korea.[3] A merchant or landlord, almost always male, who seldom had more than an elementary school education, captained each Association, which included ten to twelve households.

The power of the Neighborhood Associations derived from their control of rationing. Initially they distributed charcoal, rice, and sugar, but after the war with the United States began, the list of rationed goods expanded exponentially. In 1942, 35 separate ration coupon books controlled what families received. For example, a family received 100 points per year for clothing; a single coat was 50 points. Many items such as eggs could not be divided (e.g., 6 eggs for 11 families), while others, like vegetables, were perishable and of varying quality. The captain had to adjudicate this distribution. Naturally, friction and claims of favoritism strained the association, especially after the attack on Pearl when the ration even for rice fell below what could sustain a healthy adult. Distant relatives never seen in the neighborhood appeared on family ration lists, and although the government threatened imprisonment for cheating, these "ghosts" supported requests for more rations and made division easier for captains, so the problem persisted. Still, the rationing of any item, especially food, instantly created a black market. Urban Japanese needed black markets to survive. A common legend of the time concerned one Ichiro Ito (the Japanese equivalent of John

Doe) who decided his patriotic duty required him to live on rations alone. When he starved to death, his family had to buy his casket on the black market. This mordant story stung even more later in the war when caskets themselves became so scarce they had to be "rented" and used over and over for funerals.

The government mandated participation in Neighborhood Associations. To ensure conformity and to save paper, official agencies sent one copy of edicts to the Association, which the captain or a designate circulated. Circulators would pull open each family's door, slide the edict in, and the family had to read and stamp it before passing it back. As neighbors became more involved in each other's lives, the Neighborhood Associations became bastions of public patriotism. Neighbors celebrated draft notices with flag-waving, banzai-shouting ceremonies at which the honored draftee pledged to fight to the death and his family had to smile and appear joyful. One fourth grader, Hiroshi Kajikawa, noted the different private reality in his diary. "My mother sometimes kneels in front of my father's photograph and weeps."[4] Hiroshi's father never returned from the war.

As Fujiwara's visits continued, the neighborhood children began to refer to Iva as a spy or traitor, an extremely dangerous designation. Even Japanese citizens who suggested Japan might lose the war were subject to arrest and torture.[5] Mrs. Hattori's disposition soured further, and Iva's formerly friendly cousin Rinko stopped speaking to her. Her uncle took the situation in stride, reassuring his wife that it was not Iva's fault, and that the police ought to lock her up as she requested.

In February 1942, Iva read a notice in the English-language version of the *Daily Mainichi* newspaper that the Swiss were accepting U.S. citizens for a repatriation ship.[6] On March 30, 1942, she and Chiyeko submitted an "Application for Evacuation" at the Swiss Legation.[7] Swiss officials required proof of citizenship and, at Iva's expense, they telegraphed the U.S. State Department to confirm her status. For reasons not clear, State replied that it doubted both Iva's and Chiyeko's citizenship, so the Swiss refused to allow them to leave. The repatriation ship sailed without them.

That summer, the Swiss sent Iva a letter announcing a second repatriation ship for September, but when Iva again applied, she learned the cost of passage would be $425, which she could not afford.[8] The Swiss, in their capacity as representative of the interests of U.S. citizens, paid a woman Iva knew, Mary Esson, $200 a month for expenses. Iva solicited similar help but the Swiss refused, citing her lack of a passport. The Swiss did explain that her family could wire her the fare after she arrived in New York.[9] Iva asked advice from family friends, the Gunjis, whom Iva had known since childhood and who now lived in Japan. They had received a letter from a Mr. Matsumoto, a Japanese national who had recently returned on an exchange ship from the United States. "In this letter Matsumoto informed Gunji that my family had been removed to an internment camp, they had to leave all their possessions, sold the business to some colored people and had been expecting $50 a month as payment for the business but they had not received a cent. Matsumoto wrote the family could barely make both ends meet and they had lost everything."[10] Mr. Gunji advised Iva not to try to return without having paid the fare in advance. Iva decided to accept the fact that she was stuck in Japan for the duration and, on September 2, withdrew her application. In retrospect, she should have boarded the ship and let the shipping line figure out what to do with her in New York when she couldn't pay. But of course she had no idea what the future held for her.

Among those who did repatriate were Otto Tolischus and other reporters. The Japanese had arrested them at the onset of war. However, before authorities allowed them to leave, they "requested" that they record radio broadcasts stating how well they had been treated. Several agreed, knowing it was their only means to escape. The Japanese politely asked print reporters to write articles on their beneficent treatment. Two policemen shoved Tolischus into a room with a typewriter for such a purpose. When he declined, they replied that he must write or he could not go home. Having been previously imprisoned and beaten, Tolischus "knew what this meant, and what would follow if I did not comply." Others refused and paid the price. Police choked Robert Bellaire of *Collier's* until he agreed; they punched another reporter in the jaw so hard it broke his dental bridge. Tolischus summed up, "I knew now how some of the statements credited to American war prisoners in the Japanese press originated."[11]

The initial war news uniformly favored the Japanese. In December 1941, following Pearl Harbor, Japanese bombers sunk the new British battleship *Prince of Wales* and the heavy cruiser *Repulse*. The Imperial Japanese Army (IJA) occupied Hong Kong and invaded the Philippines, destroying MacArthur's air force in three days and occupying Manila on January 2, 1942. Japanese forces conquered Rabaul on January 23. In February, the Japanese also struck at Singapore, Great Britain's most important base in the Pacific. Its strong defenses to the sea made its 90,000 British, Australian, and Indian defenders as confident that it could not be assailed as Americans had been confident of the impregnability of Pearl Harbor. The Japanese shrewdly attacked it by land. A week after the IJA's offensive began, Singapore surrendered.

On February 15, Japanese paratroops landed in Sumatra, and three days later Imperial forces took control of the key Palembang oil fields. The Allies, desperate to prevent the complete takeover of the resource-rich Dutch East Indies (now Indonesia), fought the Japanese invasion fleet in the seven-hour Battle of the Java Sea. The Imperial Japanese Navy (IJN) soundly defeated the Allies, suffering only one damaged destroyer versus the Allied loss of five warships. The Japanese landed on Java on February 28 and occupied the capital of Batavia (now Jakarta) on March 5; on March 9, 20,000 Allied troops on Java surrendered. Control of Malaya and the Dutch East Indies provided Japan with oil, rubber, tin, and bauxite for aluminum. A Japanese newspaper photo after the takeover displayed a huge pile of tires over the caption, "Japan has become a have [as opposed to a have not] country."[12]

The drumbeat continued. Admiral Nagumo's carrier and battleship squadron, which had carried out the attack on Pearl, bombed Darwin, the capital and chief port of the Northern Territory, Australia. Nagumo swept through the Bay of Bengal, sinking every ship his squadron encountered, including a British carrier and two cruisers. The Imperial Army occupied Rangoon (now Yangon) on March 8 and held all of Burma (now Myanmar) by the end of May, thus effectively sealing off China. MacArthur had withdrawn his troops in the Philippines to the Bataan Peninsula and the tiny island of Corregidor at the mouth of Manila Bay. Bataan surrendered on April 9. From one of the many tunnels on Corregidor, Third Lieutenant Norman Reyes broadcast the radio message: "Bataan has fallen, but the spirit that made it stand—a beacon to all the liberty-loving peoples of the world—cannot fall!"[13] On May 6, Corregidor surrendered and Reyes became a prisoner of war (POW).

After such battles, the Japanese brutalized Allied soldiers who surrendered. The Japanese Army was despotically authoritarian, with higher ranks punishing lower through slaps, kicks, beatings, and humiliation. Japanese Army draftees were *issen gorin*, a one sen/five rin bronze coin (worth about a penny), which was the least valuable Japanese wartime monetary unit and the cost of mailing a postcard draft notice. Officers often treated privates worse than horses, which cost real money. Prisoners of war and civilians were beneath privates. In addition, the Japanese military viewed POWs as cowards. Japan's Field Service Code of 1941, authorized by Tojo, stated simply, "Do not be taken prisoner alive." The commentary cited the case of Major Kuga, who had lost consciousness and been taken captive by the Chinese, who later released him. The Code noted approvingly that Major Kuga had committed suicide to atone for his disgrace. The commentary concluded, "This act typifies the glorious spirit of the Imperial Army."[14]

Ordinary Japanese citizens shared this view as well. Makiko Bessho, an elementary school student, sent little care packages to soldiers with the message, "Please fight well and die a glorious death."[15] News reporter Ashihei Hino witnessed firsthand the captured Americans on Bataan and saw them as "people whose arrogant nation once tried to unlawfully treat our motherland with contempt. As I watch large numbers of the surrendered soldiers, I feel like I am watching filthy water running from the sewage of a nation which derives from impure origins and has lost its pride of race."[16]

~

Iva kept up with the war news through still-published English-language newspapers, such as the *Daily Mainichi* and *Nippon Times*, and found herself thoroughly depressed as a result. Then on April 18, she heard planes. In her 1987 interviews, she remembered being with Chiyeko "somewhere high. I think we went to the roof."[17] They watched as Doolittle's bombers flew across Tokyo hitting targets. "People might think that I'm relating to you my feelings after the fact, but I was never so happy to see anything in my life.

I felt like—it's like a baseball game when it's 8 to 1 and you think, what hope is there? Then all of sudden, the home team loads the bases, someone hits a home run, and you wake up and think, 'There's life in this ball game yet.'" At the same time, she feared being hit by bombs.[18] She told Chiyeko she doubted the war could last much longer. "I don't know where they're coming from, Chiyeko, but they must be able to get back. They can't just come and dump themselves here." In fact, Doolittle's pilots did not get back; they ditched their planes in China. Those in disabled aircraft parachuted into Japan; the furious Japanese captured, tried, convicted, and sentenced them to death. (They commuted several sentences.) When Americans learned the POWs were to be executed for attacking Japan in exactly the way Japan had attacked the United States, it caused great resentment.

In the spring of 1942, Iva received her first marriage proposal. A Japanese diplomatic student studying English at the Matsumiya Japanese Cultural School asked her to dinner and a show. Iva didn't consider it a date. Japanese never dated, only Nisei. Anyway, they were simply friends. Then one day he announced he had train tickets for Kyoto and asked her to accompany him to meet his parents. She thought it peculiar. Why, she asked, had he not asked her first and bought tickets later. His explanation stunned her; he wanted to marry her. He was tall, about 5 feet 10 inches, slender, and handsome, but Iva thought she would make a terrible wife for a diplomat since she could carry on only the most rudimentary conversations in Japanese. He countered that her English would suffice in a diplomatic context, but she demurred. "Many times, I think, what would have happened if I'd said yes? He wasn't unappealing, but I didn't want to spend the rest of my life in Japan."

Iva's money dwindled, and her relationship with her aunt slowly deteriorated. In June 1942, Iva decided to move.[19] "One thing I learned was, when push comes to shove, relatives are no damn good. Friends and even total strangers are so much more helpful, as far as my experience is concerned." Iva's vexation was somewhat understandable. The Hattoris had an obligation to house Iva, war or not. But they had already run afoul of the police. Not only had authorities again incarcerated Mugio as a communist, they had imprisoned Iva's uncle before the war for pacifism. Pressure from the neighborhood to remove the disloyal American must have been intense as well. Iva's language school helped find her a cheap room in the nearby Onarikin boarding house. Rent was the same amount her aunt charged her, 50 yen(¥) a month (about $12). The rental fee also included two meals a day, an important consideration since Iva's refusal to become a Japanese citizen made her ineligible for ration cards.[20] The Hattoris and Iva parted amicably. She pretended she was moving to save herself the transportation costs from their house to the school. Iva's aunt was happy to see her go, and Iva was happy to leave. She stayed in touch with her uncle for a time and provided him the real war news. Eventually her relationship with the Hattoris faded away. Rinko married shortly after Iva left and died in childbirth in 1944; Iva attended the funeral and the family did not welcome her.

Iva badly needed a job. A fellow Nisei at the school told her that the Domei News Agency, the Japanese equivalent of United Press, where he worked had set up a special monitoring station at Atago Hill for overseas news broadcasts, and the Agency needed English speakers to transcribe them. Iva was the only female among more than a hundred applicants for the position, almost all of them Nisei. Her typing and shorthand skills learned in high school landed her the job.[21] The United States broadcast general news via shortwave, often carrying presidential speeches in their entirety. The broadcasts contained about the same content that average American citizens would hear on commercial radio or read in the newspaper. Iva transcribed the U.S. news into written documents. Boys on bicycles would pick up her transcriptions and take them downtown to the main Domei offices, where she assumed the agency would elide any news unfavorable to Japan. Asked if she considered her work aiding the enemy, Iva responded, "Oh, good Lord, no! How could it help the war effort? The Army and Navy would have their own reports. They wouldn't want ordinary news."

The job paid ¥130 a month, less 20 percent tax (¥104). Iva calculated her expenses at ¥50 for room and board, ¥30 for tuition, and ¥40 for extra food (¥120). Obviously, her salary had to be supplemented or she would have to survive on her skimpy boarding house meals, a daunting prospect. She decided to quit the school, but Headmaster Matsumiya reduced tuition in exchange for her work on a simplified Japanese–English dictionary. The military needed it to deal with the many English-speaking countries they had conquered. Also, as luck would have it, the Matsumiya School was located in Shiba Ward, a ritzy section of Tokyo in which men of influence and wealth kept their concubines. The men visited their second families when possible and made sure they did not want materially. Iva, in cooperation with the school, taught piano to the children of these concubines. The pay was poor, about ¥25, but just enough for her to avoid starvation. The role of teacher is greatly respected in Japan and that, plus her exotic status as a speaker of English, caused Iva to receive social invitations, which she invariably accepted because they included a free meal. Iva felt sorry for her young students. "You could sense that there was confusion in the makeup of the children. They'd say, 'Tonight's the night my father comes to the house. He comes once in a while. We never see him on holidays. He's very good to me. He brings me a lot of presents.'" Iva understood what it was like to miss your father. When these music students, now middle-aged, visited Iva in the United States late in her life, they still referred to her as *sensei* or teacher. Jun's insistence that his daughter learn to play the piano paid off in a way neither could have imagined.

Iva initially worked various shifts at Atago Hill, from 5:00 PM to 10:30 PM and from 9:00 AM to 3:00 PM.[22] However, superiors soon noted her ability to type speeches in real time. They valued such a skill because sound recorders were scarce and used hard-to-replace media, such as wax cylinders or acetate (aluminum) records.[23] One day, they asked her to transcribe a Churchill speech to be carried live at 1:00 AM Tokyo time. She agreed because she lived only a short distance from the listening post, whereas most of the male transcribers lived in Yokohama. Her ability to transcribe speeches as she heard them led to a gradual shift in her schedule. Due to international time differences, she often had to work in the dead of night. This meant that she walked to Atago Hill in pitch blackness. Although she was the only woman out at these hours, Iva swore that she never feared a criminal attack at any time during her stay in Japan.

At Domei, Iva heard unfiltered news of the war for the first time. The Battle of Midway was fought the first week of June 1942, just before Iva took her new job. This battle, only months after Pearl Harbor, sealed Japan's fate. The Imperial Navy sent a massive fleet of 4 heavy and 3 light aircraft carriers, 2 seaplane carriers,

11 battleships, 15 cruisers, 44 destroyers, 15 submarines, and miscellaneous small vessels to invade Midway. The much smaller U.S. Pacific fleet could hardly contend against such a force except for one advantage: the United States had broken the Japanese codes and knew exactly what to expect. American bombers attacked the Japanese while they were still 500 miles away and on a single day, June 5, 1942, sunk the 4 heavy aircraft carriers. Although Japanese newspapers portrayed the battle as a victory, in fact it was a catastrophe. Rear Admiral Keizo Matsushima described the reaction in the Imperial Navy's press section: "No one spoke. These were people who were not trained for defeat. Everyone sat silently, with arms folded. Who would have thought that the *Akagi, Kaga, Soryu,* and *Hiryu* would be sunk! Who would have imagined that our first and second air units would be annihilated! 'The most important thing is to keep it secret,' said the chief of the First Section. 'If even a part of the truth should become known it would be difficult to control the nation.'"[24]

After the loss at Midway, the Japanese broadcasting service enlarged its Overseas Bureau to four sections—American, European, Asian (which included the regions of the South Pacific), and Editorial. The latter prepared commentaries based on Domei and military news sources, and propaganda broadcasting began in earnest. The U.S. Marines landed on Guadalcanal in August. Japanese troops, without food supplies, eventually withdrew after suffering huge casualties due as much to starvation as to military attacks. Radio Tokyo called it a strategic withdrawal. When the United States destroyed Japanese positions in the Solomon Islands the next month, Radio Tokyo announced, "By attacking the Solomons, America has played into Japanese hands and placed Japan in an advantageous position. In landing troops, America has presented Japan with a decoy to entice further U.S. forces, who will be needed to supply the landing parties. The decoy will be used as long as required, but will be annihilated when it no longer entices the enemy."[25]

Iva generally kept her jubilation at American successes to herself because the Nisei she encountered at the listening station were pro-Japanese. That summer, she met two brothers at Domei, Phil (Felipe) and Ted (Thaddeus) D'Aquino. Their Portuguese father had married a Japanese woman, but although his sons were born in Japan, they retained Portuguese citizenship. They had attended St. Joseph's Academy, a Catholic school run by American priests. The Portuguese were officially neutral, but Phil and Ted were decidedly pro-American and disinclined to hold their tongues. Phil especially had something of a temper and constantly got into scrapes. He looked out for Iva, often bringing her food from his mother. He was small, about 5 feet 6 inches, and younger than Iva by five years. He spoke Japanese poorly but was fluent in French, thanks to his education, and in English, thanks to his father. Iva appreciated his concern for her, trusted him, and initially thought of him as a friend, nothing more.

~

The police continued to harass Iva. Often they would come in the middle of the night to take her to the local police station or downtown for questioning. To wake up Iva, they first had to wake up the landlady, who was profoundly aggravated, not with Iva but with the police. Couldn't they do this during the day?, she fumed. They had their orders. "Every time I was called to the station I was ridiculed, insulted, and was embarrassed at the questions of my personal life. Each time a mention was made of my taking out Japanese papers, which was laughed off by me saying I could not become a Japanese as I didn't know their language."[26] Iva obviously knew some Japanese by this point, but she avoided antagonizing the police with affirmations of her unyielding allegiance to the United States.

One day, Iva's relationship with the police took a new turn. A high-level chief whom Iva had not previously met showed up at the school to chat. Iva knew he must be important because he drove a car and offered to take her to lunch at a nice restaurant. She quickly agreed. "I'm not ashamed to admit it. Any place I could get a free meal I took it because I was fragile." The chief wanted "a favor." The school had several students affiliated with the Soviet Embassy who resided in Japan as neutrals. They spoke English with Iva because their Japanese was even worse than hers. Would it be possible, inquired the policeman, for Iva to befriend them? Iva immediately caught the drift. "You want me to be a spy, in other words." "No, no, don't be so harsh. We simply want to know their activities. For example, are they going home or having their families come here? And if so, when exactly? Just social matters." Whether this man, likely a member of the thought police, had picked Iva out because of her relationship with Mugio cannot be known. In any event, Iva promised to think his offer over, cagily figuring that he might be good for more meals. A couple of luncheons later, after many pretended deliberations, she informed the chief that he needed to find someone more trustworthy, a true Japanese citizen, which she was not. The chief angrily replied that he thought she would be more cooperative, and Iva's antagonistic relationship with the police returned to normal.

The possibility of employing Iva as a spy when the Japanese suspected her to be a foreign agent represented in miniature the Japanese military government's internal contradictions. The government spied relentlessly on its own citizens, prohibited political assemblies, made spreading rumors against the law, arrested people for violating speech codes, and enforced the most draconian censorship on the news and the press. At the same time, the government proclaimed to the world and its own people that Japan sought foremost to free the oppressed. According to an official government publication titled *The Divine Mission of Nippon*, the Japanese labored "to transform the present-day lawless, chaotic world, where the weak are left to fall prey to the strong, into one large family community, . . . into one household and thus to enable all nations to secure their due places."[27]

The newly conquered territories initially cheered their liberation by Imperial forces. Indonesians, for example, eager to be free of Dutch control, welcomed the Japanese enthusiastically. They quickly discovered the nature of their "due place." The IJA first outlawed assemblies of any kind, and then in June 1942, outlawed all speeches and writing. It proscribed the Indonesian flag and national song, substituting the Japanese national anthem instead. Indonesians had to learn the Japanese language. In short, the independence they received turned out to be a sham.[28] Civilian Japanese bureaucrats who might have ameliorated the situation were under the control of the military, whose police ruled by fear, intimidation, violence, and torture. In the occupied territories of the Southeast Asia Co-Prosperity Sphere, the colonialism of the Americans, British, and Dutch appeared almost benign by comparison.

The internal contradictions between Japan's perception of itself and its actual behavior included the military and contributed to Japan's defeat. The overarching image of Japan, so relentlessly hyped by the government that it became a national slogan, was "one hundred million hearts beating as one." In reality, the Imperial Army did not trust the Imperial Navy and vice versa. Premier Tojo did not learn the outcome of the war-defining Battle of Midway until a month after the fact, and even then the Navy did not give him the details because he was an Army man.[29] The Army maintained its own shipyards and built its own cargo ships, whereas the Navy maintained its own vehicles for land transport. If the Army required a screw with a left thread for a machine, the Navy would demand a screw with a right thread for the same equipment. Army plane parts did not fit Navy planes. When the Navy asked for materials to meet an emergency, the Army would refuse to relinquish them. Throughout the war, Army and Navy factories competed for materials.[30] Occupied territories had to be divided between the services. No unified command existed during battles because of squabbling between the services. If all this were not bad enough, various branches of the same service were often jealous of each other and sought to undermine their rival's efficiency.[31]

~

The Japanese dramatically expanded the English-language program schedule of their radio stations on April 1, 1942.[32] As part of this effort, they forcibly transported English-speaking POWs with radio broadcast experience to Tokyo. Authorities correctly surmised that their own propaganda efforts were woeful, and they hoped the POWs' professionalism and knowledge of Western values and culture would serve their interests. Three such POWs— one Australian, one American, one Filipino—assembled at Radio Tokyo for the task that ordained Iva's future life as an announcer.

The Australian, Major Charles Cousens, was born in India of English parents and educated at Sandhurst, the British equivalent of West Point. He had a distinguished military career before resigning his commission to emigrate to Australia. His civilian career led him to the field of broadcasting, and he became a popular radio personality. When Great Britain declared war, Cousens enlisted in the Australian Imperial Forces (AIF). He informed his listeners,

"This will be my last broadcast until the war is over." A fellow broadcaster said, "Those who heard his words of good-bye to his many thousands of friends cannot doubt the sacrifice he is making in leaving radio to 'do his bit.'"[33] Cousens also bade good-bye to his wife and children and joined AIF's 2/19th Battalion, which defended Singapore. He survived the initial fighting and was among the 15,000 Australians captured by the Japanese.

When General Yamashita ("the tiger of Singapore") negotiated the AIF's surrender, he assured them they would be treated according to international standards for POWs. During negotiations, Yamashita's troops bayoneted 150 patients and staff of a recently captured military hospital. Not until after the Australians had given up their arms and were marched under Japanese control to forced labor did they observe the ruthlessness of the Imperial Army firsthand. Along the road, they saw women's heads mounted on sticks, as well as pregnant Chinese and Malay women, now dead, attached to walls with bayonets through their bellies. Cousens himself watched horrified as the Japanese mercilessly flogged one of the soldiers under his command. When eight prisoners attempted an escape, the Japanese, despite Cousens' plea for leniency, executed them with a shot to the head. A third of AIF troops captured at Singapore died in Japanese hands.[34]

Cousens worried his broadcast experience would be found out, and he tried to keep his skills a secret. A fellow officer later testified, "Then, lo and behold, our own administration nailed him by directing him to make this broadcast [about their POW status], so immediately he was identified as a radio man. This was a stupid thing for AIF headquarters to have done, because it put a label on Cousens."[35] The Japanese soon demanded Cousens begin to broadcast for them. When he refused, they slugged him and warned him of consequences. An intercepted and decoded Japanese telegram of May 26, 1942, ordered that Cousens be conveyed from Changi Fortress on Singapore to Tokyo "for purpose of employment in overseas propaganda."[36]

In July 1942, authorities at *kempeitai* headquarters in Tokyo again threatened to torture or kill him if he did not comply with military orders to broadcast, and again Cousens refused. At his next interrogation, they beat him in the head until he fell almost unconscious, kicked him in the stomach until he vomited, and crushed the knuckles of his hand. On August 1, 1942, he met Major Shigetsugu Tsuneishi, the Army officer in charge of Radio Tokyo, who ordered him to broadcast.[37] Cousens countered with a request for a pistol and one round of ammunition so he could kill himself. This impressed Tsuneishi, and he drank a toast to this POW who acted as a true Japanese warrior would. However, Tsuneishi had no intention of allowing this valuable asset to commit suicide, and after another officer slapped Cousens around a bit, Tsuneishi forced Cousens to bow as he shouted out a series of orders, concluding with "You will obey all orders of the Imperial Army, or you will be executed!" Cousens, weak from dysentery and starvation, reasonably believed that he would be tortured until he complied and that the Australian government would not expect him to resist further. He agreed to obey orders. Later that same day another Japanese superior, Ryo Namikawa, handed him his first broadcast, an attack on President Roosevelt's Pacific policy written by the Japanese. When Cousens, shocked at the content, refused to read it, Namikawa slapped his face and screamed that the *kempeitai* would work him over. Cousens, now thoroughly defeated, submitted.[38]

Cousens' capitulation led to a change in his relationship with his captors. The Japanese knew they could force him to broadcast but they also realized that his reciting words in a monotone hardly served their larger purposes. Any POW could do that. They wanted to take advantage of Cousens' experience and personality. So, they embarked on a campaign to balance threat and intimidation with conciliation. They billeted him at the Dai Ichi (Number One) Hotel, where the Imperial Navy controlled a section, part of which housed Nisei and other foreigners working for Radio Tokyo, and they paid Cousens the equivalent of a Japanese major's salary. The Japanese "requested" he stop wearing his uniform, which they claimed made others uneasy. Tsuneishi withdrew from immediate supervision, turning that task over to a woman, the attractive Foumy Saisho,[39] who addressed him by his nickname, Bill. A talented scriptwriter, Saisho affected a collegial rather than an adversarial relationship.

Cousens, for his part, also had to make nice. He intended to sabotage his captors' propaganda efforts, and he knew the Japanese had to trust him to some degree if he was to get away with it. He broadcast essays critical of United States' foreign policy. These were in about the same vein as a modern Democrat might criticize the foreign policy of George Bush. He viewed Saisho as a snake in the grass and possibly a *kempei* agent, but he addressed her as Foumy. Cousens' efforts bore fruit. Tokyo at the time reverberated with stories of outrageous acts of Japanese heroism. This example from December 1941, purports to be a memoir by a British soldier facing a Japanese beach invasion:

> Dripping wet, the Japanese soldiers climbed out from the sea and commenced a slow march. But only bayonets were sticking out of the sand. It was a strange sight of gleaming bayonets marching on the sand by themselves. Realizing that there was nothing to shield themselves with, those Japanese fighters had used their own fingers to dig the sand. Yes! The flesh of their five fingered hands. They had dug holes large enough to cover their entire bodies. That was the explanation of the gleaming bayonets marching through the sand. I saw a miracle. The ominous steel helmets continued their marching, pushing up sand from beneath. The Japanese had dug through the sand beneath our barbed wires, and were marching at us. Now they revealed their entire selves from the dark coverage of the sand, towering over us like so many giants out of the huge sky.[40]

In another legend, a Japanese fighter pilot destroyed an entire squad of U.S. fighters. As he gave chase to eliminate the last plane, he realized he had no more ammunition, so he downed the American fighter by throwing balls of rice he had taken from his lunch. Another tale featured a Japanese pilot landing his disabled aircraft by putting his feet through its fuselage and running on the ground until his fighter stopped. Cousens convinced his superiors to emphasize these ridiculous stories to prove Japan's invincibility. Thus, one broadcast told the story of ten Japanese scouts who had wiped out 400 American soldiers without any casualties.[41] Cousens also undercut editorials through careful writing and word emphasis, ending for example with "everyone knows the truth *lies here.*" He held classes for Japanese broadcasters, training them by pounding notes on the piano while they chanted in singsong from Gray's Elegy: "the PLOUGH man HOME ward PLODS his WEAry WAY. . . ."[42] When his students utilized this announcing style on the radio, the effect was laughable.

∼

Wallace Ellwell Ince, nicknamed "Ted," was born July 16, 1912, in Spokane, Washington.[43] He was educated at Washington State University and, in 1932, he enlisted in the 41st Division, Aviation, Washington National Guard, at Felts Field, Spokane, serving until 1934. In April 1936, he joined the regular Army at Fort McArthur, California and was almost immediately transferred to the Philippine Islands. Ince was handsome, 6 feet tall, with red hair and blue eyes. On January 16, 1937, he married Anne Martinez, a Filipina, and in 1939 they had a son, Wallace Ellwell Ince, Jr.[44] (They divorced after the war, on April 1, 1948, Ince charging his wife with "extreme cruelty.") Ince left the Army that same year, honorably discharged as a corporal attached to Sternberg General Hospital, with his character recorded as "excellent."

Ince had become interested in radio work and, while he was still in the Army, he had broadcast as "Ted Wallace" for KZRM, Manila. At KZRM he met Norman Reyes, a high school student also working as an announcer. (Reyes would broadcast Bataan's final message to the "liberty-loving peoples of the world.") After Ince's discharge, he lived and worked as the public relations manager for the Marco Polo Hotel and for another station, KZRH. On December 23, 1941, following the attack on Pearl Harbor, Ince reenlisted in the U.S. Army in the Far East as a first lieutenant. He took his Oath of Office as a captain at Fort Mills on April 11, 1942, where he worked on the staff of General Wainwright.

Norman Reyes was the son of an American mother and a Filipino father. He too tried to enlist after Pearl Harbor, but the U.S. military rejected him because he was only nineteen and had no training whatsoever.[45] Reyes joined the Philippine Army as a third lieutenant. The Japanese had begun their attack on the Philippines within hours of Pearl. Reyes helped destroy equipment after the Japanese invasion, and he snuck through enemy lines to support American troops in their retreat. He was arrested by the United States, but Ince heard about his apprehension, sent for him, and assigned him to the Voice of Freedom broadcasts.[46]

The Japanese captured Ince and Reyes on May 6, 1942, with the fall of Corregidor. The IJA, under instructions from Tokyo to round up broadcasters, asked Ince about Ted Wallace. Ince denied knowing him. Within a few days, however, they had figured out Ince and Wallace were the same. Ince, Reyes, and other captured radiomen were sent to Fort Santiago on May 29, where the Japanese kept them, along with two other broadcasters, in cell nine, "a narrow room with one window the size of a postcard" in Reyes' recollection.[47] During their incarceration, soldiers of the IJA regularly beat them with boots, fists, and rifle butts.[48] Ince and Reyes survived, but other men died from the abuse. A cellmate, fellow radio announcer PFC Charles W. Boyle, died from sickness despite their pleas for medical care.

Ince and Reyes eventually wound up at Bilibid Prison in Manila where, on September 11, an IJA captain gave them a choice: go to Japan and do radio propaganda work, or "go to Australia." The latter phrase, the captain explained, was shorthand for decapitation.[49] Ince asked for and was given permission to see his wife and son before he left. He also visited his priest, Father Turner, to give confession and to ask if he could commit suicide by jumping off the transport ship. Father Turner counseled Ince that he should go to Japan and see it through.

On the evening of October 8, 1942, the two starved and beaten soldiers from the Philippines, Ince and Reyes, arrived by train at the Shinagawa Camp in Tokyo. On the 12th, they met the staff at Radio Tokyo and Major Tsuneishi. The military housed them at the Dai Ichi Hotel, along with Cousens. Although watched over by *kempei* spies, the three POWs soon formed a secret alliance. They determined to undermine Japanese propaganda whenever possible. Initially, they worked separately. In 1942, Cousens broadcast POW messages, his own essays, and "news reports" so slanted in favor of the Japanese as to be almost fiction. Ince broadcast similar material on "From One American to Another." Reyes corrected English grammar in scripts.

These three men had not yet crossed paths with Iva Toguri, who worked across town as a Domei transcriber. They would first meet Iva in 1943. The three would be impressed by her support of their—the Allied—cause. She would become their friend and they, with the best of intentions, would start her down the path to infamy as Tokyo Rose.

Notes

1. In her Notes, Iva asserted that Mugio was tried and acquitted in 1944, after which time he went home. In 1987, she told me that the Japa-

nese government intentionally poisoned communist prisoners with the tuberculosis (TB) bacillus, and that Mugio and every one of his communist friends that she met had died in prison of TB. She told me several life histories and that she visited one of these men within days of his death. Because the Notes are closer in time to the actual events, I have used the earlier recollection.

2. Trial Transcript, vol. XLIV, 4932. Against Iva's assertion, at her trial she tended to embellish the threats against her, and observation by the *tokkotai* or Thought Police seems much scarier than by the Metro Police.

3. Havens, *Valley of Darkness*, 76.

4. Ienaga, *The Pacific War*, 126.

5. For names of people arrested and methods of torture used on them, see Shunsuke Tsurumi, *An Intellectual History of Wartime Japan, 1931–1945* (New York: Routledge & Kegan Paul, 1986), 90–93.

6. Trial Transcript, vol. XLIV, 4935.

7. Application in NARA 1, Box 40 and Nara 11, Box 1.

8. Iva testified at trial that she didn't have a dollar to her name at the time of this second repatriation (vol. XLIV, 4939, 4941). Technically this was true: after Pearl Harbor, Iva converted her $300 into yen, so she literally didn't have a dollar. Japanese banks converted at the rate of 1 to 4; her $300 became ¥1,200, which was fair given that the pre-war official exchange rate was 1 to 4.3. It is unlikely she was dead broke by the summer of 1942. However, she claimed on her Application for Evacuation on March 30 that she had only ¥250 left.

9. The Swiss were mistaken. The Trading with the Enemy Act barred her parents, even if they had the money, from advancing her the fare, as her lawyer, Wayne Collins, pointed out in her appeal.

10. Toguri Notes, no page numbers. See Bibliography.

11. Both quotations from Tolischus, *Tokyo Record*, 382–85.

12. Kato, *The Lost War*, 90.

13. Carlos Romulo, *I Saw the Fall of the Philippines* (Garden City, N.Y.: Doubleday, Doran & Company, 1942), 302.

14. For Japan's Field Service Code, see http://www.warbirdforum .com/bushido.htm.

15. Ienaga, *The Pacific War*, 108.

16. Original quotation from Batān Hantō Kōjōki, translated by Haruko Taya Cook, "Voices from the Front: Japanese War Literature, 1937–1945," Master's Thesis, University of California at Berkeley, 1984, 59–60.

17. I cannot be sure Chiyeko was present. It seems something of a coincidence—they did not live together—and to my knowledge Iva never mentioned her presence prior to 1987. However, Iva's additional recollection that they were up high might be evidence that she and Chiyeko were

on an outing, perhaps somewhere downtown. Her uncle's home had only one story, so even were she on the roof she would surely not remember that as "up high." The entire issue is complicated by the fact that Iva was confident in 1987 that she had moved out of her uncle's home by the time of the Doolittle raid, and therefore would have viewed the raid from her boarding house. This is incorrect. See note 19.

18. According to International News Service correspondent Clark Lee, Iva told him, "On the day of the raid when I saw American planes over Japan I had mixed feelings. I didn't want the anti-aircraft to hit them. I wanted them to get away, but at the same time I didn't want them to hit me. It was a mixed peculiar sensation." Lee, however, is untrustworthy. His transcript puts into Iva's mouth blatant falsehoods. (Examples will appear in subsequent chapters; Lee was a key prosecution witness at Iva's trial.) I have left out Lee's assertion that Iva had "mixed feelings" because it is misleading. Iva would have known the United States had to bomb Japan to win. However, Iva's concern that she not be hit by bombs seems to me a normal, prudent reaction and that I have left. Lee's transcript at NARA 1, Box 42.

19. The minor issue of the month Iva Toguri moved out of her aunt's house presents an opportunity to discuss some of the difficulties biographers of Iva Toguri face. Discrepancies between personal interviews and depositions, between human memories and written records, between recollections at one time and recollections at another, trouble this history and the legal case.

When I interviewed Iva in 1987, she asserted she had moved out of her aunt's house shortly after the attack on Pearl Harbor. Iva felt confident she was not living there at the time of the Doolittle raid (April 18, 1942) and was certain she had been gone "for months" before her employment at Domei (June 12, 1942). She had no reason to lie, her memories were clear and specific, and it made sense that her aunt would not have allowed an American "spy" constantly visited by the police to stay very long.

On April 30, 1946, FBI agent Frederick Tillman interviewed Iva Toguri at Sugamo Prison. His transcript of the interview, which Iva signed, initialing every page, states, "I lived with [my aunt and uncle] until June 1942." That would seem definitive, but this document is profoundly flawed. See chapter 13 for an analysis.

However, the move-out date of June 1942, is also backed up by her testimony at trial. Wayne Collins asked, "Mrs. D'Aquino, how long did you continue to live at your uncle's home in Tokyo?" and she answered, "Let's see, until about June of 1942" (vol. XLIV, 4931). But this too is not definitive. Sometimes witnesses conform trial testimony to their previous depositions to avoid being attacked as duplicitous upon cross-examination. So, the question remains: Did she move out shortly after Pearl Harbor, as she told me in 1987, or in June 1942, as she stated at her trial?

Fortunately we can be reasonably certain of the truth, at least in this instance. In her Notes, Iva states, "My uncle's family was getting a little afraid of me because of the strong anti-U.S. feeling in the country. The Police were constantly calling on my uncle. . . . Therefore in June of 1942 I moved away from the family and found a room located near the language school." These notes are consistent with more official documents. Her Application for Evacuation, submitted on March 30, 1942, contains her aunt and uncle's address as her home address. On May 26, 1947, Iva submitted a sworn statement to the American Consular Service, stating that she lived at her aunt's from "July 1941–June, 1942." See SF#61-590, 20. NARA 1.

Therefore, the June date must be correct, and her recollection in 1987 that she had moved by February or March must be mistaken.

20. In her 1987 interview, Iva said, "I never had a ration card in Japan. I got a bread ration before the war. I never had ration coupons." She explained the boarding house bought food, adding, "I did not have a foreigner's ration card." In her Notes, she wrote, "I registered with the Atsugi Police Station as soon as I got settled in Atsugi. I went through the same red tape, had pictures made, applied for Residence permit, *got new ration cards*, applied for a traveler's permit in order to commute to work" (italics mine). On direct questioning at her trial, Iva testified that she had a ration card when she arrived, but did not possess one from June to September 1942, after which the police issued her another one (see vol. XLV, 4960). The latter may provide the key to resolving the discrepancy. What Iva had, except for the summer of 1942, was a special ration for bread issued to foreigners. What she lacked was the standard ration card of ordinary Japanese citizens, or the ration card issued to foreigners such as diplomats. Of course it is possible that her 1987 memories were mistaken and she had managed to obtain ration cards.

21. In her Notes, she also credits her supervisor, Ian Mutsu, with getting her the job out of sympathy for her plight. She says she later left Domei in part because Mutsu had left.

22. At trial, Iva testified that for the first two or three months she first worked evenings, mornings, and early afternoon, and from January through June 1943, from 5:00 PM to 10:00 PM (vol. XLIV, 4944). She told me in 1987 that she often went in the middle of the night as she was needed.

23. Although Japanese engineers, along with American and German engineers, independently discovered the basics of magnetic tape recording in 1939, it was the Germans who perfected the magnetic tape recorder in 1941. However, they kept it a military secret. Transcribers in the United

States used dictation equipment (wax cylinders) or acetate (aluminum) records for recording broadcasts.

24. Rear Admiral, IJN, Keizo Matsushima, "The False Song of Victory—Thus the Navy Press Section Fooled a Nation," in *Salon*, Tokyo, 1949. Quoted in Meo, *Japan's Radio War on Australia*, 64–65. (In what is apparently a failure of proofreading, Jane Robbins attributes the quotation to "the actual Japanese defeat in the [Battle of the] Coral Sea." *Tokyo Calling*, 105.)

25. Broadcast, October 5, 1942. Meo, *Japan's Radio War on Australia*, 68.

26. This candid admission strikes me as more likely to be true than her other accounts, in which she steadfastly refuses to renounce her citizenship in the face of unremitting pressure.

27. Chikao Fujisawa, Part I, "A Prophecy of the Dawn of a New Age," in *The Great Shinto Purification Ritual and the Divine Mission of Nippon* (Tokyo: Imperial Rule Assistance Association, February 1942). Also printed in English for wide distribution.

28. Ienaga, *The Pacific War*, 176–77.

29. Mamoru Shigemitsu, *Japan and Her Destiny* (New York: Dutton, 1958), 271.

30. Kato, *The Lost War*, esp. 106, 167.

31. Masanobu Tsuji, *Singapore: The Japanese Version* (New York: St. Martin's Press, 1961), 166–68.

32. The Japanese announced the new schedule on March 24, 1942. It featured seven transmissions of news and commentary that fell just short of a 24-hour broadcast. For a detailed breakdown, see JVW transcript, March 24, 1942, 1. NARA 10, Box 635.

33. Remarks of journalist Goodie Reeve, cited in Chapman, *Tokyo Calling*, 41.

34. For the best account of the battle of Singapore, see Lionel Wigmore, *The Japanese Thrust* (Canberra: Australian War Memorial, 1957), part of *Australia in the War of 1939–1945*, Series I, vol. IV. For more on Japanese atrocities, see Sibylla Jane Flower, "Captors and Captives on the Burma–Thailand Railway" in *Prisoners of War and Their Captors in World War II*, ed. Bob Moore and Kent Fedorowich (Washington, D.C.: Berg, 1996).

35. Interview with Maurice Brennan, 1983, cited in Chapman, *Tokyo Calling*, 82.

36. Riku-A-Mitsu Telegram 522. NARA 9, Box 238.

37. Major Tsuneishi belonged to the 8th Section of IJA General Staff. This section was responsible for overseas propaganda and also controlled POWs.

38. This represents Cousens' best recollection of the event shortly after the war. When he first met Tsuneishi, the IJA officer told him, "You must

broadcast everything or you will be shot!" After that, Cousens asked for a gun and one bullet. Cousens, Tsuneishi, and an interpreter were the only people present at that meeting. Tsuneishi swore he never threatened Cousens. In 1988, Chapman located the interpreter in the hope that he would provide a definitive account, but the interpreter refused to speak to him. At a subsequent meeting at which several people were present, Tsuneishi told Cousens, "You will obey all orders of the Imperial Japanese Army, or you will be executed."

In deposition and testimony, various witnesses differed in the particulars of this confrontation. Foumy Saisho testified under oath in Australia that Tsuneishi never made this threat, only that "some fuss was made." Under cross-examination, she admitted Tsuneishi had used "a very strong tone of voice" as he read out IJA orders and that she could not remember whether he concluded with a threat of execution. She also testified disobeying an IJA order meant neither torture nor death. Ryo Namikawa said after the war that he witnessed the scene with Cousens and that Tsuneishi's order was, "If you do not want to do this, you must return to the prison camp. Think about it and decide." Everything was dignified, Namikawa added, and the POWs were "subjected to no force, either physically or mentally." Namikawa joined the international section of NHK in 1931 and served as a member of the Cabinet Information Bureau during World War II. See "Japanese Overseas Broadcasting: A Personal View," in Short, *Film & Radio Propaganda*, 323. I find neither witness credible. Every POW, not just Cousens, testified to cruelty. Namikawa relates how he himself was slapped by Metropolitan Police after he allowed the playing of an inappropriate piece of music following the death of an admiral in 1934; 319–20. Authorities surely slapped Cousens.

I have telescoped these two confrontations, as well as other events, because they are simply too numerous to detail in a biography of Iva Toguri. See Ivan Chapman's excellent and exhaustive biography of Charles Cousens, *Tokyo Calling*, 104–5, 238, 242.

39. Saisho has the same given name as Iva's mother, but her name is usually spelled "Foumy" in historical documents, whereas Iva's mother's name appears in the modern spelling, "Fumi."

40. FBIS transcript, JZJ Tokyo English language broadcast of December 28, 1941, 1. NARA 10, Box 633.

41. Broadcast on November 30, 1943. Joel V. Berreman, "Assumptions about America in Japan's War Propaganda to the United States," *American Journal of Sociology* (September 1948): 112–13.

42. According to Cousen's testimony at his inquest. The courtroom erupted in laughter upon hearing of this ruse. Chapman, *Tokyo Calling*,

275. Personally, I find it difficult to believe the Japanese fell for it. They had many employees at Radio Tokyo who spoke English fluently.

43. Unless otherwise noted, Ince's biographical and military records are taken from CIC, FBI, and U.S. Army documents at NARA 9, Box 237.

44. A War Department memo, dated November 7, 1942, but obviously written later, presumably after the war, has her name as possibly Anna Romero, but when Department of Justice attorney J. Roger Walters interviewed her in person in San Francisco in late 1948 (SF #61-601), she gave her name as Anne Martinez. Their divorce information is from this interview.

In a letter supplied by Iva, Cousens referred to Ince's "children," plural. The aforementioned War Department document states that Ince and his wife had two sons. Other documents, e.g., another War Department file correctly dated September 19, 1945, which is part of his CIC file, states that he has one son. Mrs. Ince only mentioned one son. No name for a second son is extant. NARA 9, Box 237.

45. Such was Reyes' opinion. Males older than 18 are usually allowed to serve, and the Army trains them. The military may in fact have rejected him because he was a first-year college student or for other reasons. *Honolulu Advertiser*, June 28, 1976, A-4.

46. According to the transcript of Ince's interview with the FBI in October 1948, which may or may not be accurate.

47. *Honolulu Advertiser*, June 28, 1976, A-4.

48. Reyes saw much worse atrocities committed against others. See his testimony, chapter 17.

49. The "go to Australia" phrase is not mentioned by Ince, but it apparently was used chiefly by Filipino guerilla fighters. This, plus some details of Reyes' life, are taken from a three-part series about Norman Reyes in the *Honolulu Advertiser*, June 27–29, 1976. In 1976, Reyes was an assistant vice president of the First Hawaiian Bank, a public relations executive, and a radio and television newscaster.

6

The Toguris Back Home

Internment

By 1941, the financial success of Japanese immigrants and their children in California was at an all-time high. Jun Toguri's grocery store was one of more than a thousand in Los Angeles, most catering exclusively to whites. Historian Carey McWilliams summed up their growing power in agriculture: "Although the Japanese operated only about 3.9% of the farm land in California, they produced 50–90% of the celery, peppers, strawberries, cucumbers, artichokes, cauliflower, spinach, and tomatoes."[1]

Unfortunately, their integrated wholesale and retail produce system, in which they supplied each other and sold in their own stores, brought them into conflict with the large grocery chains and rekindled earlier anti-Japanese sentiments among some residents. William Randolph Hearst used the *Los Angeles Examiner* to send a message to Secretary of the Navy Frank Knox: "Colonel Knox should come out to California and see the myriads of little Japs peacefully raising fruits and flowers and vegetables on California sunshine and saying hopefully and wistfully, 'Some day I come with Japanese army and take all this.'"[2] Hearst, however, was in the minority. Many West Coast newspapers wrote sympathetic articles on the Japanese. The goodwill increased when the Japanese American Citizens League met with the Los Angeles City Council and military intelligence for both the U.S. Army and Navy in March 1941, and promised to help the United States in any way it could.

This goodwill evaporated with the attack on Pearl Harbor. The announcement left the Japanese, especially the Nisei, stunned and horrified.

> I was in junior college, and it was so shocking. I felt like crawling under the seat. I just felt as if we were inferior and part of the enemy at that time.

> The day the war broke out, I was at a party for one of my Caucasian friends. I was the only Japanese present at the gathering. It was such a shock. Everything in the room went blank for me. I wanted the floor to open up and swallow me. I was scared to death. I dreaded the thought of war and the hatred it would arouse.[3]

Nisei fears were justified. The federal government moved quickly to address the threat of cadres of Japanese saboteurs and sympathizers. On February 19, 1942, President Roosevelt signed Executive Order 9066, which authorized the Secretary of War to designate local military commanders who in turn could designate "military areas" as "exclusion zones" from which "any or all persons may be excluded."[4] Although Order 9066 makes no mention of any specific ethnic group, and although the military areas would eventually include almost one-third of the country, including both coasts, the Japanese were the only minority significantly affected.[5] The German and Italian communities were larger, more geographically scattered—and represented much larger voting blocks. Roosevelt made a point of praising them for their loyalty.

Lieutenant General John L. DeWitt, a short, bald, almost comic figure sporting pince-nez eyeglasses, was California's designated local military commander. Although he foolishly claimed thirty Japanese planes had overflown San Francisco, even DeWitt thought rounding up 120,000 civilians was "damned nonsense."[6] But DeWitt changed his mind and on March 2, 1942, he issued a public proclamation to all people of Japanese ancestry that they would soon be excluded from "Military Area No. 1," that is, the entire West Coast. On May 3, General DeWitt issued Civilian Exclusion Order No. 346, commanding all persons of Japanese ancestry to report to assembly centers, where they would live until they could be permanently relocated in internment camps. He explained his actions to Congress, "A Jap's a Jap. I don't want any of them here. They are a dangerous element. There is no way to determine their loyalty. It makes no difference whether he is an American citizen, he is still a Japanese. We must worry about the Japanese all the time until he is wiped off the map."[7] DeWitt's sentiments were informed by discussions with two future Supreme Court justices who were among the most forceful advocates of internment: Assistant U.S. Attorney General Tom Clark, in charge of alien activities on the Pacific Coast, and California Attorney General Earl Warren. Warren testified to Congress, "The fact that there has been no sabotage or espionage on the part of the Japanese-Americans is proof that there is a conspiracy and they are just waiting for the right moment to strike."[8] If there had been sabotage or espionage, presumably that too would have been proof of a conspiracy.

Among those delighted to see the Japanese leave were white farmers. Austin E. Anson, managing secretary of the Salinas Vegetable Grower-Shipper Association, said,

> We're charged with wanting to get rid of the Japs for selfish reasons. We do. It's a question of whether the white man lives on the Pacific Coast or the brown men. They came into this valley to work, and they stayed to take over. They undersell the white man in the markets. They work their women and children while the white farmer has to pay wages for his help. If all the Japs were removed tomorrow, we'd never miss them in two weeks, because the white farmers can take over and produce everything the Jap grows. And we don't want them back when the war ends, either.[9]

Anson's prediction that white farmers could make up for the loss was not vindicated. In 1942, consumers in southern California received 10,000 fewer truckloads of perishable vegetables than in 1941, and paid 10 million dollars more for what they got.[10]

~

The Toguri family read the notice of evacuation in the newspaper. They had one month to prepare. They stored their furniture and other belongings in the back of the grocery store and handed the keys to Bernard Young, a black friend Jun knew and trusted. No money changed hands, and Young did not send them any of the profits he made from operating the store. The Toguris left with what Jun could pull together in savings.

The experience of the Toguri family mirrored that of the larger community. As 90,000 Japanese vacated houses and apartments in "Japantown," 150,000 African Americans moved in.[11] "Little Tokyo" in Los Angeles became "Bronzeville." Blacks stayed, but many Japanese did not return. The former Toguri store is located in what is now known as Watts.

The grave concern of the Toguris was wheelchair-bound Fumi. Given that her right side was paralyzed, she could have remained in a care facility, but authorities would not allow any family member to remain with her. The family decided to stay together. They boarded the train, each carrying the one suitcase allowed, and laid Fumi on a seat. No berth was available; sick evacuees received no special treatment.

Six Toguris—Jun, Fumi, Fred and his wife Miyeko (he had married the previous February), June, and Inez—left on May 6, 1942, for the Assembly Center located in Tulare, California, a small agricultural city in the San Joaquin Valley just south of Fresno. The Center was a converted county fairgrounds, and the Toguris stayed, along with hundreds of others, in areas previously occupied by livestock. The six lived together in a former horse stall about 10 feet by 20 feet and slept on cots. They had no window, no fans, no fresh air, and no privacy. The walls were so low everyone could hear the conversation of their neighbors. On the positive side, June recalled, "The smell was not too bad."[12] Fumi's health precipitously declined in these conditions. June accompanied her to Tulare County Hospital (authorities allowed only one person to go, and June had been her mother's primary caregiver) and was with her when she died on May 24. "She would have lived much longer if we had not relocated. It didn't take away her will to live; she was very religious and prayed. She was happy because we were all together. But the moving around caused it."

(Both Iva and June believed the number "24" was unlucky for the Toguris. Their father Jun also died on the 24th day of the month, as did one of his brothers.)

On September 2, 1942, the Toguris moved to their assigned camp, the Gila [pronounced *heeluh*] River Relocation Center. Located on the Gila River Indian Reservation about fifty miles southeast of Phoenix, the camp's hundreds of barracks were still under construction as internees flooded in. Intended to hold about 10,000 people, the barracks quickly overflowed and, by December 1942, the camp's population hovered near 14,000, making it Arizona's fourth largest city. The camp eventually featured mess halls, ironing rooms, laundry rooms, latrine and shower buildings, schools, and warehouses, as well as a shoe repair shop, sewing shop, barber shop, beauty shop, canteen, post office, garages, mimeograph buildings, police office, court, water filtration plant, refrigeration facilities, and gas station. Internees built most of these structures.

Despite the inevitable problems of an overcrowded facility created from scratch in the middle of the desert, Gila River is generally considered the most benign of the camps, and the Toguris were lucky to have drawn it. Other internment centers resembled concentration camps, with armed guards in towers looking down on fences of barbed wire. Gila River had only one tower and once authorities realized the internees were not so foolish as to try to escape into the Arizona desert, they removed the barbed wire. In fact, the camp developed such a reputation for ease of living that Eleanor Roosevelt made a surprise visit in order to assure Americans that the Japanese were being treated sternly.[13]

The federal government could not have selected a more loyal group for suspicion of disloyalty than Japanese Americans. They caused no trouble. Had they rebelled and refused to leave their homes and businesses, the U.S. Army would have poured untold resources into rounding them up and imprisoning them. Instead, the internees dutifully reported as ordered, went where they were told, built their own prisons, and managed them. They served as their own police and fire departments; provided their own doctors and nurses; grew their own food, cooked and served it, and cleaned up afterward.

Everyone in the camps worked, and the Toguris were no exception. Jun, sixty and contemplating retirement, agreed to a second career as a buyer for the canteen. Fred, who had given up his pursuit of a law degree when he realized that since he was born in Japan he could not become a U.S. citizen and therefore could not practice law, labored in the camps as a butcher. June worked as a seamstress and an instructor in pattern making; Inez, in the mess hall. Inez got $16 a month as nonprofessional labor; the rest, including Jun, were paid the professional rate of $19 a month. By comparison, a teacher in the U.S. at that time earned about $120 monthly.

~

Before the war, Nisei Fred Korematsu tried to enlist in the U.S. Armed Forces but he was found medically unfit. So, he studied welding and served his country at the Oakland shipyard. After the attack on Pearl Harbor, the yard fired Korematsu. Aware that being Japanese American was now profoundly problematic, he sought out a plastic surgeon and paid for an operation on his eyes in the hope he would appear less Asian. When the United States announced the evacuation orders, Korematsu refused to report as the Toguris and most Japanese had. Instead, he hid out with his Italian American girlfriend. But his surgery had not been successful, and on May 30, 1942, Korematsu was spotted and arrested. Headlines in Bay Area newspapers the next day read, "Jap Spy Arrested in San Leandro."[14] Frank J. Hennessy, U.S. Attorney for Northern California, filed an information against Korematsu on June 12. (An information is an accusation similar to an indictment, except that it is brought by a public officer instead of a grand jury.)

The American Civil Liberties Union decided to take up the case, and selected attorney Wayne M. Collins to represent Korematsu.[15] Collins helped found the Northern California American Civil Liberties Union chapter in 1934 and believed the forced evacuation of the Japanese was wrongheaded and legally unjustified. He argued against internment on one set of grounds in the Korematsu case—Korematsu refused to go willingly to the camps—and on an entirely different set in the related case of another Nisei, Mitsuye Endo; Endo entered camp willingly and then sued to get out.[16] Collins also developed separate legal attacks against curfews for Japanese Americans, exclusion (the forced evacuation), and detention in the camps.

The controlling precedent for both the Korematsu and Endo cases was an earlier decision against Gordon Hirabayashi, who was charged with violating curfew and found guilty in the Western District of Washington State.[17] His conviction had been appealed to the Supreme Court, where the famously liberal Justice William O. Douglas concurred with the majority and upheld the lower court's conviction:

We cannot sit in judgment on the military requirements of that hour [after Pearl]. When the orders under the present Act have some relation to "protection against espionage and against sabotage," our task is at an end.[18]

American society today actively debates the wisdom of the rulings in these interconnected cases, as well as Douglas' words concerning the power of the Executive branch to rescind the ordinary rights of citizens in time of war.

Korematsu's first lawyer, Clarence E. Rust, answered the information on June 20, 1942, with an astounding 70-point attack on the law.[19] By the time this reached Federal District Court, Rust had been joined by Collins. The lower court dismissed this laundry list of legal failures by the government almost out of hand. In appealing their decision, Collins abandoned this approach and substituted instead rhetoric, eloquence, and moral outrage. Collins declared before the Supreme Court:

Who is this DeWitt [the general in charge of relocation] to say who is and who is not an American and who shall and who shall not enjoy the rights of citizenship? Did he think he was a "leader" called to summon these, our people, to a Munich or Berchtesgaden? While he was toying with the notion of a military dictatorship over them and trifling with its dangerous paraphernalia, did he think he was acting the part of a savior? A messianic delusion is a dangerous thing in a military mind. Napoleon had it and brought Europe to ruin. Mussolini had it and brought Italy to ruin. Hitler has it and has brought Germany to ruin. General DeWitt let Terror out to plague those citizens but closed the lid on the Pandora box and left Hope to smother. It is your duty to raise the lid and revive Hope for these, our people, who have suffered at the hands of one of our servants. Do this speedily as the law commands you. History will not forget your opinion herein.[20]

The argument of the United States in favor of internment differed strikingly from Collins'. It offered a purely technical brief that recited authorities from the Constitution, statute, executive order, military orders, and proclamations by DeWitt, and affirmed that they were valid.

From the long view of history, Collins' outrage concerning the treatment of Japanese Americans was eminently justified, but in the view of the Court, his rhetoric was excessive. Collins' comparisons of internment camps to concentration camps and of DeWitt to Hitler offended Justice Hugo Black. On December 18, 1944, Black, writing for the majority, delivered the opinion of the Supreme Court:

> In the light of the principles we announced in the Hirabayashi case, we are unable to conclude that it was beyond the war power of Congress and the Executive to exclude those of Japanese ancestry from the West Coast war area at the time they did. Exclusion from a threatened area, no less than curfew, has a definite and close relationship to the prevention of espionage and sabotage. The military authorities, charged with the primary responsibility of defending our shores, concluded that curfew provided inadequate protection and ordered exclusion. They did so in accordance with Congressional authority to the military to say who should, and who should not, remain in the threatened areas.[21]

Wayne Collins argued two other important cases involving Japanese in America and won both. The first case involved Japanese whom the United States had imported from Peru to use in prisoner exchanges for our own troops captured by the Japanese. Their use as trading pawns proved unnecessary and, at the end of the war, the U.S. government attempted to deport them. Peru, however, did not want them back and the Japanese themselves, who had grown accustomed to living in America, didn't want to leave. Collins won for most of them the right to stay.

His second success involved "renunciants." About 6,000 Nisei internees had renounced their American citizenship while in internment camps, including many minor children. They did so out of fear. The military authorities allowed fanatical pro-Japanese gangs to operate in a few camps, most notably at Tule Lake, California. These gangs convinced Issei parents they would be deported, and their Nisei children renounced their citizenship in the belief that this would be the only way to keep their families together. The gangs also beat, murdered, and enslaved anyone who refused to renounce. After the war, President Truman signed an executive order to deport these renunciants to Japan. Collins filed suit to prevent the deportation. Typical of the evidence he offered to support his contention of duress was the deposition of Tetsujiro Nakamura, a former store owner, who testified, "I do not know of a single person who renounced of his own free will." On April 29, 1948, Judge Louis B. Goodman sided with Collins.

The government appealed. On January 17, 1951, the Ninth Circuit held that the adult renunciants had acted for "simple expediency and crass material considerations" because they knew Japan would lose the war. Each, therefore, would have to separately submit an affidavit that they acted under duress; otherwise they would be deported. This ruling provides a striking contrast to the treatment of the Nisei who renounced their American citizenship while in Japan. Some of them renounced under duress; many others, out of simple expediency and crass material considerations. Nonetheless, the United States allowed them to return without a similar affidavit. In a heroic undertaking, Wayne Collins processed individual affidavits for the U.S. renunciants, successfully winning restoration of citizenship for 4,987 of 5,409 applicants. In this effort, he outlasted eight attorneys general, submitting the last affidavit in 1968 to Ramsey Clark, the son of Tom Clark, to whom he had submitted the first.[22]

In the Korematsu case, Collins used passionate rhetoric to make an emotional appeal for fairness and decency. He lost. In the Peruvian Japanese and renunciants cases, he stuck to a careful and technical reading of the law. Using this strategy, he won.

~

Makoto Toguri is a mystery. The name does not appear in the books about this case by Masayo Duus and Russell Warren Howe. Rex Gunn and Stanley Kutler in their shorter treatments do not mention him. No current Tokyo Rose website references him. One could search, as I did, through the tens of thousands of pages of Federal Bureau of Investigation (FBI), Department of Justice (DoJ), and Army Counter-Intelligence Corps (CIC) files devoted to the Tokyo Rose investigation and prosecution, including 6,000 pages of trial transcripts, and never come across his name. I interviewed June Toguri extensively for this chapter, asking her about the Toguri family in America, both before Iva left for Japan and afterwards, when the United States locked up the Toguris in the camps, and she never mentioned Makoto. When I interviewed Iva in connection with this biography, she noted in passing that Jun's father had remarried and produced two sons. "One came to the United States. The other one went down to Brazil." When I inquired generally about her family history, she again casually remarked, "We never questioned my uncle, his name was Toguri. . . ." And that was it. In the decades that I knew her, Iva never spoke his name nor did she ever tell me anything about him. I would not have known about Makoto Toguri had I not noticed something suspicious as I examined two seemingly unrelated California registrations for the World War I draft.

During World War I, every man between the ages of 18 and 45 living in the United States, except for those already serving in the military, had to register for the draft. This included aliens, even though they were not subject to induction into the U.S. military.[23] Registration took place on three days. The first registration day, June 5, 1917, was for all men aged 21 to 31. Makoto Toguri registered that day in Calexico, California. He stated he had been born in Tokyo and was single. He seemed confused about his birthday; he originally gave a date in October but changed it to August 20, 1888. He listed his occupation as "Rancher." His work address was 143½ RFD (Rural Free Delivery) in Holtville, California. He affirmed that he had verified the above answers and that they were true, and signed "Makoto Toguri."[24]

The second registration day, June 5, 1918, covered men who had turned 21 the previous year. The third day, September 12, 1918, was for men aged 18 to 45 not previously registered. Registrars used a different form that did not ask place of birth but instead for nearest relative. Jun Toguri, Iva's father, registered for the third draft in Los Angeles. He gave his date of birth as March 25, 1882, and named "Mrs. Toguri" as his relative. He stated his occupation was "cotton grower (owner)." His work address was 143½ RFD in Holtville, California. He affirmed that he had verified the above answers and that they were true, and signed "J. Toguri."[25]

Figures 6.1 and 6.2 show the 1917 signature of Makoto Toguri and the 1918 signature of Jun Toguri.

To my untrained eye, the signature for "Toguri" appeared to be by the same hand. This possibility led me to ask: Did Jun register as Makoto? Was Makoto a false identity? To find out, I began to research Makoto Toguri and discovered the answer to the latter question at least was no.

Makoto Toguri was Jun's younger half-brother.[26] He was born August 20, 1889—not 1888—in Yamanashi Prefecture. He was liter-

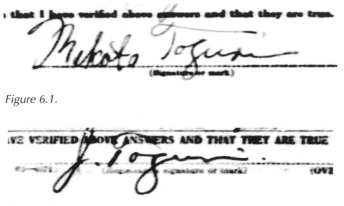

Figure 6.1.

Figure 6.2.

ate, possessing an elementary education. Makoto followed his big brother to America, first arriving at age fourteen in Seattle on February 28, 1904. He worked as a salesman for Furuya & Company, the same firm that employed Kakuzo Kawakami. However, Makoto became homesick. He returned to Japan in February 1907, married Kei Hasegawa on June 5 of that year, and quickly fathered two children, a girl, Suzuye and a boy, Taro.[27] He served in the Japanese Army for two years, from 1908 to 1910, but never saw combat and did not rise above the rank of private. After his discharge he worked as a clerk in Tokyo, and then for unknown reasons he decided to leave his wife and children and return to the United States, arriving April 15, 1914. He worked as a janitor in an apartment building for a year and as a salesman at Yamato Shoten (Japan Bookstore) in Los Angeles.[28] During this time he lived with Jun, Fumi, Fred, and in 1916, baby Iva.

In 1917, he moved to Calexico to operate a cotton business along with Jun. Jun and his family followed shortly thereafter, and the two brothers continued in this endeavor for five years. Makoto's wife died in Japan just after Christmas, 1920. He made provisions for his children but did not return to Japan. The cotton business failed, and the two brothers separated. Makoto worked as a truck driver for three years and then as a farm laborer for M. Hatta, often traveling to Mexico. In 1930, Makoto moved to Gardena, California, which at that time was south of Los Angeles, and the 1930 U.S. Census shows him living as a lodger in the household of Otozo Shintane, his wife, and their eight children. He remained in Gardena until the beginning of World War II. During this time, he joined the Imperial Military Friends Group (IMFG) so that, according to his later testimony to the FBI, he could go to a New Year's Eve party. This group had been infiltrated by the FBI because its stated purpose was "to show our friendship to our comrades at war, and to express the great spirit to build up the Japanese Empire. It is our duty to speed on towards our goal of a holy war."[29] Even though there is no record that he ever attended meetings and he denied doing so, Makoto's membership caused him to become the subject of FBI surveillance.

Within hours of the attack on Pearl Harbor, the FBI executed a search warrant on his lodgings. The only incriminating evidence agents found was a brochure from the IMFG. On December 11, 1941, Makoto was taken into custody. The general internment of Japanese Americans did not occur until May 1942. The FBI arrested only the most dangerous aliens immediately after the United States went to war. Makoto qualified as a potential saboteur because of his membership in IMFG, because he served in the Japanese Army, and because "Police Dept. files reflected negative information regarding subject's criminal record." This "criminal record" is not included in Makoto's FBI file, nor do FBI reports indicate the nature of this negative information. One assumes that had it been serious criminal conduct, the record surely would have been brought forward during Makoto's various parole hearings.

Makoto Toguri spent the war on a forced tour of America's internment camps. From Los Angeles the government sent him to Tuna Camp in Tujunga, California; then to Fort Missoula, Montana; to Fort Sill, Oklahoma; to Camp Livingston, Louisiana; to Santa Fe Camp, New Mexico; to Kooskia Camp, Idaho; and finally to Fort Stanton, New Mexico.

During this period, the family of Toyotaro Kato requested he be sent to Gila River Internment Camp to live with them because he was "not well enough to take care of himself." No such request from his brother Jun, also at Gila River, appears in the record. However, camp records indicate he functioned well at farm labor, so his health must have been reasonably good.

In the latter stages of the war, Makoto petitioned for release, explaining that he was no threat and had never tried to harm the United States. Officials interrogated him and found he would not agree to work in a munitions factory or as a dock worker loading munitions onto ships. He claimed he didn't understand such work, that he was a farmer. They considered his answers evasive, indicative of a lack of loyalty. Asked how and where he would live if released, he said he had a recent letter from Kawakami, the man Jun had worked for in Seattle, who promised to provide Makoto with start-up capital for a farm.

On December 29, 1945, four months after the defeat of Japan, the United States finally freed Makoto. Apparently nothing came of the Kawakami offer because he departed on January 12, 1946, "en route to Chicago," where "my elder brother and his family live and operate his business." Makoto worked for his brother for the remainder of his life, dying of a heart attack on November 25, 1956, ten months after Iva's return to Chicago from prison.[30]

The mystery of whether Jun registered as Makoto for the 1917 draft remains unsolved. Makoto signed documents as an internee. A witnessed 1945 signature (Figure 6.3) does not much resemble his 1917 signature. However, an unwitnessed 1942 signature in Louisiana (Figure 6.4) does.

But if Jun did not masquerade as Makoto in 1917, if Makoto himself registered for the draft, how could Makoto misremember his own birthday, giving 1888 instead of 1889? (The writing is perfectly legible; there is no confusion about the year.) Why would he say he was born in Tokyo, not Yamanashi? Why would he claim he was single when he was married with two children?

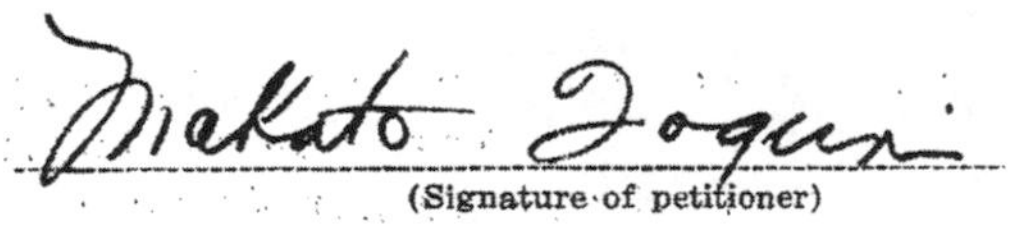

(Signature of petitioner)

Figure 6.3.

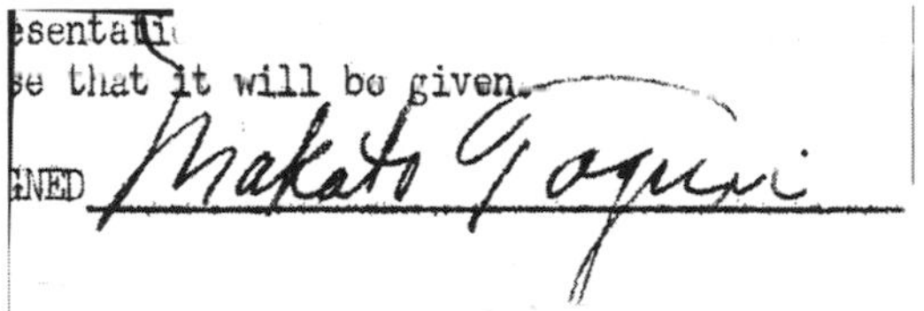

Figure 6.4.

The more significant mystery, however, is why Iva kept silent about her uncle Makoto. Iva and her family must have conversed about Makoto's interesting story and its surprising parallels with Iva's own. Both were accused of being spies, arrested, interrogated by the FBI, and imprisoned for years as adherents to the Japanese cause. Her deceptive reticence to share his story has caused me to wonder if certain photographs that Iva gave me in which she failed to recognize anyone other than her mother and father might in fact be pictures of Makoto. Figure 6.5 shows Makoto Toguri's mug shots taken by the U.S. government.

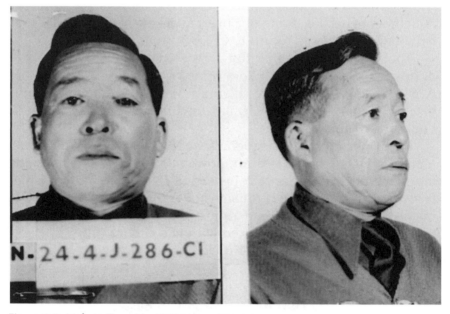

Figure 6.5. Makoto Toguri in 1942 at age 52.

In Figure 6.6, Iva identified only her seated father. Could the other two men be his half-brothers, with Makoto standing on the right?[31]

One reason why Iva might have failed to discuss her uncle is simple snobbery. Makoto was the poor relation. Jun made a fabulous success of himself in America. Makoto was a clerk, janitor, truck driver, and farmer. In 1945, when he was 56 years old, he still

Figure 6.6. Iva identified her father, Jun Toguri, as the seated man.

described his occupation as "laborer" and affirmed that he had no assets and no property.

Another, more likely, possibility is that Iva felt she had her hands full convincing people that she herself was not a traitor. She probably believed that it would not help her cause for anyone to learn that her father's brother was also investigated and arrested for anti-American activities. So Iva "forgot" about her uncle who had also suffered injustice, albeit on a smaller scale. She assumed I would not discover her indirect deception. Had her father's signature in 1917 not remarkably resembled Makoto's, she would have succeeded.

~

In 1942 and 1943, the U.S. war effort went into overdrive. The government set a 35-mph speed limit and limited gasoline purchases to three gallons a week for A ration cardholders. Initially many Americans lied to obtain the more generous B2, B3, and X cards, but public pressure soon shamed them into doing the right thing. In addition, the government banned driving for pleasure. As sports writer Paul Gallico recalled, "You could have fired a bazooka down any Main Street in the country without hitting a vehicle."[32] As a result, radio, already popular, became a mainstay of entertainment for families at home.

Ration books dominated daily life. The United States rationed sugar, meats, and cheeses, as well as innumerable other goods, such as shoes. The lack of sugar curtailed the manufacture of spirits, and the supply of good whiskey dwindled. The children's laxative, Fletcher's Castoria, turned sour and made kids sick. Leather goods, alarm clocks, cameras, binoculars, toys, and women's stockings disappeared from shelves because of new wartime priorities for manufacturers. The War Production Board banned hair curlers as part of the drive to preserve metal. To buy a tube of toothpaste, one had to turn in the empty. National scrap drives were organized for steel and rubber. Frequent blackouts caused by pressures on the electrical system created a new category of crime dubbed "muggings."[33] Women moved into factory work in significant numbers for the first time, but employers requested they not wear sweaters, halters, or other tight clothing lest they cause accidents.[34]

Young people also joined the workforce. By the spring of 1944, at least 3 million youth between the ages of 14 and 18 had jobs, about one in three, although actual employment was much higher because this number represented only those working legally with permits. High school enrollment hit a new low. The Boy Scouts took in 3 million books, 109 million pounds of rubber, and more than 370 million pounds of scrap metal. They planted 1.5 million trees, and they collected one half ton of paper for every Boy Scout in America.[35]

Americans of Japanese descent contributed to the war effort as well. More than 33,000 volunteered for the Armed Forces. The Nisei 442nd Regimental Combat Team, fighting in Europe, earned 21 Medals of Honor, 52 Distinguished Service Medals, 588 Silver Stars, 5,200 Bronze Stars, and sustained so many casualties it earned the nickname, the "Purple Heart Battalion."[36] In the Pacific theater, 5,000 Nisei working in intelligence translated documents, interrogated prisoners, convinced cornered Japanese soldiers to surrender, and broadcast propaganda. However, to protect national security, the U.S. military forbade them to speak of their service, so most Americans remained ignorant of their actions. MacArthur's Chief of Intelligence, General Charles Willoughby, estimated that "the Nisei saved a million lives and shortened the war by two years."[37]

Despite such contributions, most Americans gave the Nisei still in the States the back of their hand. During the evacuation, stores, filling stations, and eateries had refused to serve those heading for camps, posting signs such as, "This restaurant poisons both rats and Japs." Hunters' pickup trucks announced, "Open Season for Japs." Governor Chase Clark of Idaho opined, "The Japs live like rats, breed like rats, and act like rats. I don't want them coming into Idaho." But evacuees working in Idaho's fields harvested 915,000 tons of sugar beets, and according to Utah's *Deseret News*, "If it had not been for Japanese labor, much of the best crop in Utah and Idaho would have had to be plowed up." When evacuees in the Toguris' camp at Gila River requested that the University of Arizona send them some library books and perhaps allow faculty lectures, university President Alfred Atkinson denied the request. "We are at war and these people are our enemies." The Oregon School for the Deaf also denied a request to admit 12 hearing-impaired Nisei children. "This is no time to admit Japanese children, particularly in view of the war." Citizens who testified in favor of evacuees at the myriad government hearings on the subject were denounced as a "Jap lovers" and "Kiss-A-Jap-A-Day-Boys." On October 19, 1943, the *Los Angeles Times* headlined an article about what would happen after the war: "District Attorney Sees Bloodshed If Japs Return: Servicemen Vow to Kill Japs." A poll of its readers showed 94 percent favored "a constitutional amendment after the war for the deportation of all Japanese from this country, and forbidding further immigration."[38]

~

As war hysteria subsided, the United States allowed Nisei to leave the camps if they could find an outside job that wasn't on the West Coast. Inez was the first Toguri to leave permanently; she became a domestic servant to a family in Arizona. The government hired Jun as a buyer for the camps; in Chicago, he found a job for June as a domestic with a Chicago family, which allowed her to leave Gila River in the spring of 1943. Shortly thereafter, she became, with permission from the authorities, her father's secretary. Fred and his wife had a baby during their time in camp; they departed in September 1943. Jun Toguri traveled to St. Louis, Boston, New York, and the deep South as a buyer for canteens from Wyoming to Arkansas. However, since he always returned to camp, it is difficult to state exactly when he could be considered truly released. June put the date in as February 1944.[39] As they left, the U.S. provided internees $15 with which to start their lives over.

None could return to the West Coast. The government encouraged the Japanese to move to the East or Midwest and to avoid concentrating in so-called Japantowns. Jun Toguri had no problem following this advice. He'd lived among Caucasians and he very much liked Chicago. Although a group of angry Filipinos had assaulted some evacuees in 1943 over the atrocities of the Japanese Army in the Philippines, Chicago was generally a tolerant place. The two major newspapers, the *Tribune* and the *Sun*, had consistently supported Japanese Americans, and the many Americans of German and Italian descent living in the Chicago area knew that they could easily have been among those targeted for internment. As a result, historian Charlotte Brooks notes, "Chicago replaced the West Coast as the center of Japanese American life in the United States. Of the 60,000 internees who left camp by war's end, 20,000 settled in Chicago. Salt Lake City, the second most popular destination, attracted only 3,000. Yet despite this influx into a city with only 400 Japanese American residents before the war, Chicagoans demonstrated little active hostility toward their new neighbors. . . ."[40]

Jun Toguri played a tremendously important role in creating the community of almost 30,000 Japanese Americans that lives in

Chicago today.[41] When he arrived, housing in Chicago was tight and often discriminatory. To take one example, a Mrs. Haruye Masacka had five sons in the U.S. Army but no one would rent her an apartment.[42] Jun Toguri, working for the War Relocation Authority, rented entire tenement buildings on LaSalle Street and set up hostels in them for temporary accommodations until he could find freed evacuees permanent housing. He often found them employment. Iva remembered her father telling her about one white businessman whom Jun convinced to hire a few Japanese as an experiment. Shortly thereafter, the man asked, "Can you get me 600 more?" Jun helped create social and fraternal organizations and found capital for start-up businesses. He accomplished these feats even though the police constantly stopped him and demanded to see his papers. "My father was quite energetic. He could work twenty-two hours a day and sleep two hours and so what?" Jun Toguri became one of the most respected and beloved men in Chicago's Japanese American community.

~

When Fumi Toguri died, the family collected $1,000 on her life insurance policy. Because the United States paid for food and housing after the evacuation, Jun used this money and other savings to purchase a small apartment building to house his family and other renters. Just as the war ended, he opened a grocery/import store, which he and Fred managed (Figure 6.7).[43] As the premier store at which thousands of newly released evacuees could buy Japanese food and groceries, the business flourished. Jun bought rice in Arkansas and designed his own bags for its sale. He flew fresh tuna in from California by plane. He bought special machinery and made his own tofu at night after the store closed. He soon opened a separate store selling books and gifts. Later, he expanded his wares: "The GIs had gone over to Japan [for the Occupation], and when they came back, they wanted this music they had heard in the bars. My father imported records by the truckloads."[44]

With the war all but won, the U.S. allowed Japanese Americans of undisputed loyalty to return to the West Coast in early 1945. Because both he and Fred were busy managing his booming Chicago businesses, Jun abandoned his traditional prejudices and assigned his daughter June the onerous task of moving back to Los Angeles

Figure 6.7. Fred Toguri (left), June Toguri, and Masachi Hori, whom June would later marry, at the Toguri Food Shop, September 19, 1944. Courtesy of Bancroft Library, University of California at Berkeley.

and revitalizing the store they had abandoned. "I really didn't want to do it. I kept hoping someone would meet me at the train station, but of course no one did. I was very lonely." June found the place boarded up and the Youngs, the family to whom Jun had entrusted the store, operating a competing business across the street. The building had fallen into disrepair and was infested with rats. Someone had rifled their stored belongings, but June salvaged some china and pieces of memorabilia to ship back to Chicago. The Toguri experience was not unusual. A survey taken after the war indicated that 80 percent of goods stored by the Japanese were "rifled, stolen, or sold during absence."[45]

The quiet and unassuming June had more moxie than anyone realized. Within a short time, she had reopened the Los Angeles store and made it profitable. June married in 1948, had a daughter in 1950, and managed the store until 1956.[46] By that time, Jun had opened additional Chicago businesses, at one point operating at four different addresses, and needed June to help manage them. June sold their California property, and she and her family arrived in Chicago on Thanksgiving Day, 1956. In July 1969, Jun coalesced his various stores into J. Toguri Mercantile Company, which still operates in Chicago today.

∽

Jun helped June with the Los Angeles business whenever he could, and as luck would have it, he happened to be visiting her in early September 1945, when June decided to buy something at the store across the street. June recalled, "[Mrs. Young] said, 'Gee, you seem awfully happy. Did you see the paper?' I said, 'No, what's happening?' 'Your sister's been arrested for being a spy.' That's the first time I learned about it."[47]

June purchased a newspaper and ran back to her father. There on the front page was Iva's UCLA graduation photo. "Propagandist Tokyo Rose No. 5, one of the Japanese radio sirens who used to amuse Yanks with clumsy propaganda, was revealed today to be Iva Toguri D'Aquino, L.A. born."[48]

The story shocked both June and her father. Jun immediately doubted it could be true, and they decided to reserve judgment until they could speak with Iva herself. "Neither of us had ever heard of Tokyo Rose. I was petrified."

Notes

1. McWilliams, Prejudice, 87.

2. Editorial, *Los Angeles Examiner*, February 21, 1940.

3. Recollections from O'Brien, *The Japanese American Experience*, 44.

4. Text of 9066 at http://www.ourdocuments.gov/doc.php?flash =false&doc=74&page=transcript.

5. Others were affected. By February 16, 1942, the Justice Department had interned 1,393 Germans and 264 Italians in addition to 2,192 Japanese. These individuals, however, were alien nationals, not American citizens, and all were suspected of potential subterfuge.

6. Geoffrey Perrett, *Days of Sadness, Years of Triumph* (New York: Coward, McCann & Geoghegan, 1973), 216–30.

7. House Naval Affairs Subcommittee to Investigate Congested Areas, Part 3, 78th Congress, April 13, 1943, 739–40.

8. House Tolan Committee hearings on National Defense Migration, 77th Congress, February 1942, 11011–12. Or see Lewis H. Carlson and George A. Colburn, *In Their Place: White America Defines Her Minorities, 1850–1950* (New York: J. Wiley and Sons, 1972), 243.

9. *Saturday Evening Post*, May 9, 1942.

10. *Los Angeles Daily News*, February 17, 1943.

11. *San Francisco Examiner*, June 15, 18, 19, 1943.

12. June Toguri's recollections from my interview of June 8, 1987.

13. Eleanor Roosevelt's "A Challenge to American Sportsmanship" in 1943 is so sensible and fair-minded that one suspects had she been president instead of her husband, there would have been no internment. She wrote, "A Japanese-American may be no more Japanese than a German-American is German, or an Italian-American is Italian. All of these people, including the Japanese-Americans, have men who are fighting today for the preservation of the democratic way of life and the ideas around which our nation was built. Every citizen in this country has a right to our basic freedoms, to justice and to equality of opportunity. We retain the right to lead our individual lives as we please, but we can only do so if we grant to others the freedoms that we wish for ourselves." *Collier's*, October 16, 1943, 71.

14. Korematsu appealed his conviction in 1983 and it was overturned. President Clinton awarded him the Presidential Medal of Freedom in 1998. He died on March 30, 2005, at age 86. For a fuller treatment of his story, see Andrew Napolitano, *A Nation of Sheep* (Nashville, Tenn.: Thomas Nelson, 2007).

15. Wayne Mortimer Collins was born in Sacramento, California, on November 23, 1899.

16. Technically, Endo filed a petition for a writ of *habeas corpus*. Such writs function to release a person from unlawful imprisonment. *Endo*, 323 U.S. 283 (1944).

17. Collins did not represent Hirabayashi.

18. *Hirabayashi v. United States*, 320 U.S. 81, 106 (1943).

19. In legal language, Rust's answer is known as a *demurrer*. A demurrer admits the matters of fact alleged by the complaint (e.g., that Korematsu was Japanese American and living in the military zone) while disputing the sufficiency of the law under which the defendant is charged.

20. Petitioner's Opening Brief, *Korematsu v. United States*, 323 U.S. 214 (1944), 1–2, 98. Edited.

21. *Korematsu v. United States* (No. 22), 140 F.2d 289, affirmed. Opinion of the Supreme Court concerning 323 U.S. 214, *Korematsu v. United States*.

22. Facts in this paragraph from John Christgau, "Wayne Collins versus the World: The Fight to Restore Citizenship to Japanese American Renunciants of World War II," in *Pacific Historical Review* 54, no. 1 (February 1985): 1–31.

23. Almost 100 percent of men required to register did, about 24 million. See http://members.aol.com/Rayhbanks/bground.html.

24. Selective Service System, World War I Selective Service System Draft Registration Cards, 1917–1918. M1509, Roll 1530793. NARA: Washington, D.C.

25. Jun actually registered September 7, which was allowed for those who would be traveling on registration day. Selective Service System, World War I Selective Service System Draft Registration Cards, 1917–1918. M1509, Roll 1530897. NARA: Washington, D.C. Figures 6.1 and 6.2 are enlargements of the signatures from these cards.

26. According to his death certificate, Makoto's mother's name was Riyo Haito. Jun was alive at the time of Makoto's death and presumably knew. When Jun died, his mother's name was listed as "unavailable." The "informant" for the certificate was, I believe, someone in his widow's family. Renzaburo Toguri is listed as the father of both. State of Illinois Medical Certificate of Death, Bureau of Statistics, Illinois Department of Public Health; Makoto's is file number 82691 and Jun's, 617698.

Most of the information in this section, both official records and even such minor data as Makoto's becoming homesick, which is how he explained his return to Japan to U.S. authorities, comes from a single file, "Makoto Toguri," Record Group 60, Box 111. NARA, College Park, Md. Unless otherwise noted, citations for this section, as well as Figures 6.3 and 6.4, can be found in this file.

27. The marriage date, June 5, 1907, is from Makoto himself. Masayo Duus states that Jun married Fumi three days later, on June 8, 1907. This is a surprising coincidence and makes one wonder why they didn't marry at the same time. See chapter 1, note 13.

28. Jun might have owned Yamato Shoten. Iva remembered Jun's import/export store was at 9th and Broadway, across from the Orpheum Theater. Makoto told the FBI that Yamato Shoten was between 6th and 7th on Broadway. If Makoto or Iva misremembered the address, these could be the same business.

29. In its report of March 3, 1945, the FBI quotes a booklet prepared by the Nanka Teikoku Gunyu-Dan (IMFG) to commemorate the 2,600th anniversary of the founding of the empire.

30. "Makoto Toguri," State of Illinois Medical Certificate of Death, File Number 82691, Bureau of Statistics, Illinois Department of Public Health.

31. Figure 6.5 taken in Missoula, Montana, in early 1942, before he turned 53 in August. "Basic Personnel Record (Alien Enemy or Prisoner of War)," Record Group 389, Box 103. NARA, College Park, Md.

Figure 6.6 certainly has the appearance of a family photograph, with Jun the elder brother seated at the center. The man standing on the right looks to me like Makoto. I for some time believed the photo was taken in Japan, but I am now confident that is wrong. It had to be taken in a studio in Los Angeles. If readers will return to chapter 1 and look closely at Figure 1.2, they will see that the curtain and faux window in the background are the same as in Figure 6.6. That means for this to be a photo of Jun and his two half-brothers, the third brother had to stop in the United States to visit before continuing on to Brazil, if Iva is correct. However, I can find no record of another Toguri entering the United States around this time.

Japanese family records are tightly restricted to maintain family privacy. I have been unable to learn the name of Jun's other half-brother. Makoto, in dealing with U.S. authorities, told them in late 1941 that he had "two brothers and two sisters living in Japan"; on March 12, 1942, that he had "one brother living in Japan and no relatives in this country"; and, on March 3, 1945, that he had "one brother and one sister living in Japan" in addition to an elder brother in the United States. I cannot explain his confusion.

32. Paul Gallico, "What We Talked About," *While You Were Gone*, 43.

33. The term achieved widespread currency through the New York press in connection with a "Negro crime wave" in 1943. See Duane Robinson, "'Mugging' and the New York Press" in *Phylon* 6, no. 2 (Q2, 1945): 169–79.

34. Information in this paragraph from Gallico, *While You Were Gone*.

35. Anna W. M. Wolf, and Irma Simonton Black, "What Happened to the Younger People," in *While You Were Gone*, ed. Paul Gallico, 79.

36. This 442nd is also described as the most decorated unit in U.S. military history for its size and length of service. However, given the qualifications, the honorific has no clear meaning. Silver and bronze star totals include Oak Leaf Clusters, awarded in lieu of a second star. See http://www.njahs.org/research/442.html.

37. For more information about Nisei service, see Dan Nakatsu, "America's Secret Weapon of World War II," in *John Aiso and the M.S.S.: Japanese-American Soldiers in the Military Intelligence Service in World War II*, ed. T. Ichinokuchi (Los Angeles: Military Intelligence Service Club of Southern California, 1988), 76–84.

38. Paragraph quotations from McWilliams, *Prejudice*; Chase Clark, *Deseret News*, 164; Atkinson, 160; Jap lovers, *LA Times*, 263; poll, 264.

39. June told me in 1987 that Fred left in February 1944, and Jun left at the same time. However, the WRA photo, Figure 6.7, taken September 19, 1944, is accompanied by text that states that Fred left Gila River in September 1943. Since the text had to be written at about the time of the photo, I assume the text is more likely to be accurate than June's memory. So Jun may have been released in 1943 as well.

40. Charlotte Brooks, "In the Twilight Zone between Black and White: Japanese American Resettlement and Community in Chicago, 1942–1945," *Journal of American History* (March 2000): 1655.

41. For this and other information about Japanese Americans in the Chicago area, see Masako Osako, "Japanese Americans: Melting into the All-American Melting Pot," in *Ethnic Chicago: A Multicultural Portrait*, ed. Melvin G. Holli and Peter d'A. Jones (Grand Rapids, Mich.: William B. Eerdmans, 1995), 409–37.

42. McWilliams, *Prejudice*, 166.

43. The business was the Diamond Trading Company. By 1944, the War Relocation Authority listed the store, located at 1012 North Clark Street, as the Toguri Food Shop.

44. Figure 6.7, "War Relocation Authority Photographs of Japanese-American Evacuation and Resettlement," Series 13, vol. 51, section F, WRA # I-627, September 19, 1944, Bancroft Library Pictorial Collection, University of California.

45. Cited without reference by Michi Weglyn, *Years of Infamy: The Untold Story of America's Concentration Camps* (New York: William Morrow, 1976), 77.

46. As noted in the caption of Figure 6.7, June married Masachi Hori. When exactly he moved to Southern California to assist June in her management of the Los Angeles store I do not know. Their daughter, Patricia Ann Hatsue Hori, was born April 17, 1950.

47. June's best recollection in 1987 was that this was the first time she had heard anything from or about Iva since before the war. She did not remember the family receiving any letters after the war started. Iva gave letters to the Red Cross, but Iva's best recollection was that they were never delivered. However, the letter she gave to Danish diplomat Lars Tillitse in May 1945, was delivered. Fred told the FBI on January 24, 1946, that Red Cross letters addressed to June had been received in 1944. NARA 2, Box 1. When I asked Iva what the family had done with these letters, she replied, "Oh, we just threw them away. Who needs that old junk cluttering up the house?"

48. *Los Angeles Examiner*, September 1, 1945, 1. "No. 5" apparently indicates that in the view of the *Examiner*'s reporter, Clark Lee, there were at least four other Tokyo Roses.

7

Barely Surviving

A Typist at Radio Tokyo

In 1943, Iva Toguri and the nation of Japan began to starve. Iva and the Japanese people lacked food. Japan's military lacked the materiel to fight a war.

In preparing for war, the Imperial Navy had made a tremendous blunder. It had invested too many of its resources in offense. The Japanese possessed the largest and most potent capital ships of any nation, but their Navy had scrimped on defense. The Japanese should have produced more destroyers and other antisubmarine vessels to protect cargo, transport, and supply ships. Their Navy also failed initially to adopt defensive strategies, such as armaments for merchant ships, convoying, and zigzag maneuvers. The Japanese had assumed that because they directed their own submarines to attack military vessels, the Americans would behave the same way. Instead, American submarines relentlessly torpedoed the floating ducks of Japan's merchant marine.

Between Pearl Harbor and the end of 1942, the Japanese lost 74 fighting ships of the Imperial Navy and 241 merchant ships for a total of 2,589,433 tons sunk. Despite Herculean efforts at salvage, capture, and shipbuilding in yards not yet under attack, the Japanese replaced only a small percentage of these losses. By the start of 1943, the Allies were sinking ships ten times as fast as Japan could replace them, and through 1943 and 1944, the ratio of ships sunk to ships replaced worsened. America's submarine service accounted for 1.6 percent of U.S. naval personnel but sank 55 percent of Japanese ships. By war's end, the Japanese had lost a staggering 686 ships of the Imperial Navy (1,965,646 tons) and 2,346 merchant ships (8,618,609 tons).[1] The loss of life, including the women, children, and POWs sometimes aboard merchant ships, was dreadful. Unremitting submarine warfare decimated the Japanese economy, which depended upon imports even for food.

Unfortunately for Japanese civilians, military needs took precedence over theirs. The Navy diverted merchant shipping that might have imported Korean rice to other purposes. Mainland Japanese farmers found themselves under tremendous pressure to produce. "They tell us 'deliver, deliver!' Then they come and take away at a song the rice we sweated so hard to produce, to the point where it's hard for us to eat. Are they telling us to work without eating? Is it good if farmers die?" Another complained in early 1943, "When we farmers occasionally went to Tokyo, people would be gathered in a huge crowd in front of the kabuki theater trying to buy tickets. We could not bear the idea of sweating so hard to produce rice to be sent to city people who amused themselves like this."[2]

Still, farmers usually ate. City folk often did not. When families ran out of food, the mother would beg her Neighborhood Association leader for more. If he were a kind man, he would suggest she might be pregnant and give her the "expectant mother" supplemental ration, an extra 2.5 ounces of rice. People turned to the black market, so many in fact that the police gave up trying to enforce laws against it. But its prices were ruinous. In November 1943, black market rice cost 44 times the official price. In desperation, people went to the country to bargain directly with farmers for food. One Sunday in the summer of 1943, 10,000 residents of Tokyo journeyed to Funabashi for the chance to buy sweet potatoes.[3]

Iva Toguri did not escape these hardships, especially since she lacked the money to buy black market food. She received a meager breakfast and dinner at her boarding house, but she was the only resident not routinely supplementing her diet. Due to inflation in black market prices, her low salary at Domei did not allow additional purchases, so she often went hungry. In the Spring of 1943, Phil D'Aquino, her friend from Domei, also moved into the Onarikin boarding house, and his mother Maria sent the two of them food from her home in the rural city of Atsugi whenever she could.[4] One of Iva's music students, as well as the man in the next room at the boarding house, would bring her some vegetables from their families' farms. Iva's boarding house was owned by a woman with two daughters, one of whom, Kimi, functioned as the maid. Kimi diligently cleaned Iva's room, and they became friends. She was a young widow whose husband had died in Manchuria, leaving her with a little boy. The owner did not allow Iva in the boarding house kitchen, so whenever Iva got extra food from Phil's mother or some other source, she would give it to Kimi to cook and they would share it in Iva's room.

Despite such help, in the early summer of 1943, Iva contracted beriberi, a disease of the heart and nervous system caused by a deficiency of vitamin B_1. She could barely walk. Untreated, beriberi is fatal. Iva had suffered various maladies ever since she first arrived in Japan, and she had sought out an old friend of her father's, Dr. K. W. Amano. Amano had graduated from medical school in Pennsylvania, and his wife was a graduate of Yale School of Medicine. Both spoke perfect English. For that reason, the Amanos were the official doctors for the diplomatic corps and were expensive. In 1941, Iva had paid ¥100 for a visit. As the war had progressed, she could no longer afford his rates, but she had something to barter. "Because of his background, Dr. Amano was somewhat pro-American, interested in the progress made by the Allies. He wondered about the truth of the war reports put out by the Japanese. Since he knew I was with Domei, he'd ask [about Allied news reports] every time I saw him." Amano gave her rations from the clinic, including milk, which ordinary Japanese shunned. He prescribed liver, but "I'd rather die than eat liver," so Iva opted for liver shots, which she found extremely painful.

Later that same summer, Dr. Amano left for a resort area in the mountains to be near his affluent patients who traveled there to escape the Tokyo heat. He gave Iva a key to his clinic, so that she could continue receiving vitamins and milk. For these to be effective, however, she required rest. Her boss at Domei was Ian Mutsu. Mutsu was Eurasian: his father was Japanese, previously an attache to the Japanese embassy in London, and his mother was English. His grandfather, the nobleman Munemitsu Mutsu, had been a statesman during the Meiji Era (1868–1912). Unlike his grandfather, who became a conservative nationalist, Ian Mutsu sympathized with the plight of the Nisei and often took Iva to lunch just so he could feed her. When she contracted beriberi, Mutsu allowed her to stay at home and recuperate while he continued to pay her salary. Iva stated her gratitude simply: "I owe him my life."

Iva's other relationships at Domei were generally unfriendly. She claimed her efficiency and willingness to come at all hours made her the pet of managers, and that the male employees resented her because they lived too far away to return for a second shift at night. It may also be that they viewed her lunch dates with the boss as giving her unfair advantage. Her pro-American attitude rankled as well. "Anyone with any sense knew how the war was going, but the other Nisei were very slow to accept the fact that Japan was losing." After one battle, Iva voiced her belief that the Allied reports of Japanese ships sunk were true whereas the Japanese General Headquarters' claim of a Japanese victory was false. Her coworkers became so enraged, her friend Phil got into a fistfight protecting her.[5]

During this time, Iva came under scrutiny by the *kempeitai*. Once, when she was at work, three agents ransacked her room, pawing through her steamer trunks and throwing her books on the floor. Iva's friend, Kimi the maid, discovered them and asked what they wanted. They informed her they were searching for anti-Japanese materials in the English language. Finding none, they told Kimi to warn Iva that she better be careful because if they ever found antigovernment materials in her possession Iva would be in big trouble. After they left, Kimi straightened up the room. When Iva came home from work, Kimi recounted exactly what had happened. Although the Metro Police had routinely questioned Iva, she now realized that the dreaded *kempeitai* had her in view and therefore she had to be especially careful.[6]

$\sim$

The well-heeled investigator who had previously tried to convince Iva to spy on the Soviets was very likely a member of the *tokkotai* (Special Security Police). In January 1943, the *tokkotai* surveyed the Japanese public to determine the effectiveness of the government's internal propaganda efforts and found considerable discontent among the populace. To remedy the situation, they doubled their efforts to suppress expressions of discontent no matter how minor. They arrested thousands for negative thinking and spreading rumors. This crackdown led to anonymous graffiti scrawled on walls across Japan. To keep track of "sloganeering," which was a crime, the police in 1943 dutifully recorded such graffiti as:

2,000 yen to whoever lops off the emperor's head
  Ridiculous to be a soldier—35 sen [¢] a day
  For what purpose have you all been fighting for seven years?
  Three years without food. One after another, starvation. All the
strong have perished.
  Anglo-American victory, Japanese-German defeat
  Commoners die for the glory of a few
  Don't make the farmers weep. Kill the Minister of Agriculture.
  Kill Tojo
  Kill the dumb emperor[7]

In 1941, the Japanese had one of the most vibrant newspaper circulations in the world, with readership in the tens of millions. Large national papers published twice a day, seven days a week. But by 1943, government edicts and rigid controls on newsprint had shrunk the number of newspapers from 848 to 54. This allowed the government to more effectively censor their content. Publishers and editors pledged to lecture the Japanese public on the dangers of defeatist thought. One result of this concerted effort to inspire positive attitudes in the general populace was the appearance in the Japanese press of articles unimaginable in American papers. On August 24, 1943, news accounts claimed that "the deified souls of the heroes" had engaged in combat with American servicemen who "fought intensely and bitterly against this army of spirits over a period of three weeks."[8]

The government's campaign to control thought extended to the most innocuous items. In 1927, American charities sent 12,000 dolls to Japan to promote goodwill between the two nations. Children loved them because their eyes closed and they "went to sleep" when laid on their backs. Unfortunately, they had blond hair and blue eyes. In 1943, the *tokkotai* ordered them burned in order to guard children against "Western infection."[9]

Failing to defeat English-speakers on the seas, the government strove for final victory over the English language at home. This proved difficult because the Japanese populace had a longstanding love affair with English. They adored American movies. Girls cut their hair short like Jean Harlow, and those with sex appeal were said to have *Itto*, a reference to Clara Bow, the "It girl." The round glasses American cartoonists used to caricature Japanese were called "Lloyd glasses" in Japan because fashionable young men had adopted them in tribute to movie star Harold Lloyd. The Japanese also enjoyed American music, sometimes translated into Japanese and sometimes played in the original English. Far and away the most popular American import was baseball. A baseball manager, Junji Kanda, suggested one reason why. "Baseball is governed by rules more complicated than in any other sport. The Japanese, being passionate lovers of rules, find it very appealing." Osamu Miura, another manager, believed that whereas most sports require honesty, in baseball deception, coded signals, spying, and stealing play an important part in success. In his opinion, since the Japanese and Americans were honorable people who would not cheat or defraud in real life, the game offered an opportunity for vicarious thrills.[10]

The assault on English led to the banning of American movies and music. Authorities undertook a sustained effort to substitute pure Japanese words for those derived from English, and even went so far as to denounce children who called their parents *Mama* and *Papa*, names of affection that had been used in Japan since the end of the previous century.[11] Given the popularity of baseball, the government allowed it to continue, but altered its broadcast. Fans listening to games on the radio had no clue what was happening when the government replaced *boru* (ball) with *gaikyu* and *hitto endo ran* (hit and run) with *kyosoda*. Radio programs no longer had an *anaunsaa* (announcer) or *nyusu* (news).[12] Finally, in the spring of 1943, authorities banned baseball itself.

The government's attempt to eradicate English never fully attained its goal. The English-language newspaper *Japan Times* renamed itself *Nippon Times*, carried news of the government's crackdown on the alien language, and continued to publish in English throughout the war, as did the *Daily Mainishi*. Whenever Asian nations gathered to discuss ways to eliminate the invidious influence of American culture, the conferences had to be conducted in English because it was the only language the Asians shared. Tojo was mortified when, in December 1943, the Great East Asia Conference brought together leaders from throughout the empire—and English was the only language they had in common.

By 1943, the nation that envisioned itself as the older brother of the Great East Asia Co-Prosperity Sphere looked poor and shabby. Tokyo began to fall apart as the government collected scrap metal from every resource: wrought iron rails and fences, nails, screws, gongs, and bells. In the spring of 1943, because of a lack of fuel, electric-powered streetcars began to tow buses filled with passengers. The government cut back train service. The Japanese, renowned for their cleanliness, looked and actually were dirty. Families whitened laundry by putting white bird droppings in the wash water and scrubbed themselves with sacks in lieu of soap. Women were already hard at work in Japan, but the 1943 Factory Law Wartime Exemption overrode previous laws so that women and children could labor more than eleven hours a day. Authorities suspended their two days a month for rest. Still short of workers, the government pressed into service ever younger children, the elderly, and convicts, as well as what amounted to slave laborers—Koreans, Chinese, and Allied POWs.

Perhaps nothing captured the mood in Japan better than the baseball game between Keio and Waseda universities on October 16, 1943. Even though the government had earlier banned the American game, it made an exception for the university students, so many of whom had to enlist in the military and go to war. After the game, the students and their well-wishers met on the field, sang each other's school songs, wept, and said good-bye. The day ended as they sang the anthem of the Imperial Navy, *Umi Yukaba* ("Going to Sea"), which had become Japan's national song.[13]

"Going to Sea" was to Japan what "America the Beautiful" was to the United States. Both songs were slow elegies, evocative of religious values and nature, and both originated as poems. But the two songs reveal profoundly different national characters. The lyrics of the latter, familiar to every American, belonged to the dawn of the twentieth century.

O beautiful for spacious skies,
For amber waves of grain,

For purple mountain majesties
Above the fruited plain!
America! America!
God shed his grace on thee
And crown thy good with brotherhood
From sea to shining sea![14]

The lyrics of *Umi Yukaba* came from an ancient Japanese poem written in the eighth century. One cannot imagine an anthem like "Going to Sea" attaining popularity in America, but on that somber October day in 1943, 20,000 Japanese young people, filled with a love of their country, stood together and sang,

If I go away to sea,
I shall return a corpse awash;
If duty calls me to the mountain,
A verdant grassland will be my grave;
Thus for the sake of the Emperor
I will not die peacefully at home.[15]

Every meeting of the one and half million Neighborhood Associations in Japan opened with those in attendance singing *Umi Yukaba*. Before every flight of the kamikaze, the pilots sang this song.

~

In August 1943, a friend at Domei drew Iva's attention to a Help Wanted ad in the *Nippon Times* for a part-time typist at Radio Tokyo.[16] Iva's expertise at fast typing got her a job as *rinji shokutaku* (literally "temporary commission"), which supplemented her income from Domei.[17] At Radio Tokyo, she typed whatever her supervisors put before her, usually news items that someone else prepared. This second job brought in needed money but meant she no longer had time to attend language school. Thus her formal education in Japanese ended with Iva still inept at written Japanese but improving in speaking it. At Radio Tokyo, she typed in English on an English typewriter. Written Japanese at that time required knowledge of more than 4,000 characters, and attempts to simplify the language had to be put off until the end of the war.

Iva described her boss at Radio Tokyo, Shigechika Takano, as "one of the nicest guys" she met in Japan.[18] Over 6 feet tall, very handsome—"what a good-looking man!"—Takano was friendly and supportive. He admired Iva for clinging to her American citizenship, and he had access to the real news, so he understood the virtual certainty of an Allied victory. While in charge, he made Radio Tokyo a pleasant place for Iva to work. Takano would have been a superb witness for the defense at Iva's trial. Late in the war, the Japanese Army transferred him to the relative safety of Jun Toguri's birthplace, Yamanashi Prefecture, where he managed the radio station at the provincial capital of Kofu. As a province of farms and mountains, Yamanashi was a low-priority target for Allied bombers. Unfortunately, Takano died in the single air raid on Kofu.

At her new job, Iva saw for the first time the Allied POWs assigned to Radio Tokyo who would play such an important part in her life: Major Charles "Bill" Cousens, Captain Wallace "Ted" Ince, and Lieutenant Norman Reyes. The details of their first meeting are somewhat cloudy, but as Charles Cousens remembered it, Iva walked into the room, held out her hand, and said: "Keep your chins up!" The directness took him aback. He expected "Nips" (Cousens' derogatory word for Japanese) from America to ask how the Allies could justify fighting the war. When Iva left the room, he turned to the others and remarked that Iva's greeting certainly represented a new technique for *kempei* spies.[19]

Iva's clearest memory of their first meeting was how ill they looked. Both Cousens and Ince had become painfully thin, much of their hair had fallen out, and they had sores and missing teeth. Their rations at the Dai Ichi Hotel barely met subsistence level, but Japanese authorities had moved them to the even more austere Sanno Hotel on March 1, 1943, and would send them to the infamous POW Bunka Camp on December 18. Each transfer brought reduced rations.[20] Iva cultivated friendships with the POWs, whose situation she perceived to be even worse than her own.[21] She brought them uncensored news she had picked up from Allied sources while working at Domei. Cousens and Reyes warmed up to her quickly; Ince did not. "Ince was very arrogant. He said, 'I hate Japs. I don't give a hang whether you're Nisei, Issei, or whatever. I hate 'em all.'" Cousens, by contrast, was gentlemanly and cordial. "He had a clipped English accent. You could tell he was Sandhurst from head to toe [i.e., had a British military bearing]." Iva became his personal typist because only she could decipher his crabbed handwriting.

In October 1943, the Japanese created a puppet government known as the "Republic of the Philippines" and released Norman Reyes, a citizen of the new Republic, from POW status. However, he was not free to return to Manila. In fact his "freedom" really meant the Japanese no longer had to feed or house him. He had to continue to work, which he did. However, his pay must have increased with his new status. Iva remembered, "I do not know the exact salary he was receiving at the station but when we received our pay checks, he counted out hundred-yen bills whereas I counted out ten-yen bills."[22]

Enemy propaganda in time of war is seldom effective. Japanese radio propaganda during the World War II aimed at Allied audiences failed completely. The lack of success resulted from several causes.

Japanese propaganda was often ham-fisted. Broadcasts in 1943 disparaged Roosevelt as a paralytic cripple who suffered from a warped brain. No GI who heard such nonsense thought, "Gosh, that's so true. I guess I'll stop fighting."

The political messages often contradicted one another. On October 23, 1943, Australians received the message that "Japan has no intention of making war on Australia." As evidence of this pacific attitude, the propagandist offered the proof that "for a long time Australia was quite open to attack and Japan did not take any advantage of the fact." Australia, therefore, should have no qualms about now surrendering and placing itself "under the benign influence of Japan." Unfortunately, the gentle logic of this argument was undercut by the fact that earlier in the war the Japanese had deluged the people Down Under with myriad threats on the order of, "If Australia dares to resist, Japan has plans to annihilate the country."[23]

An infirm grasp of English converted much Japanese propaganda into an occasion for laughter. Japanese radio informed listeners, "With the exception of one dead, all on the exchange ship were in the best of spirits." Those dead exchangees do bring down a party. "The fact that Japan's air power will be increased 500 percent is fantastic!" announced its own falsity. For those inclined to worry, Radio Tokyo assured its audience that "Japanese men look furious but they are sweet inside." On July 24, 1943, Radio Tokyo asked, "What is it that makes the Japanese soldier so invincible in battle?" Not, it turned out, his sweet nougat center, but instead, "his immortal spirit of offensive."[24]

The Japanese interspersed their programs with POW messages to enhance listenership. They provided names, units, and messages from prisoners. Mainland Americans could not normally pick up the broadcasts, but families in such countries as Australia and New Zealand listened faithfully to these broadcasts in hopes of hearing some news of their loved ones. Programs ranged from 80 percent POW messages to just 10 percent. Between messages, propagandists tormented listeners with messages such as this, broadcast at the dinner hour:

> Australian mothers, wives! Any one of you may be the wife of the 15,000 men killed in the Gallipoli campaign [in Turkey, 1915–1916]. Then you cursed war with all your heart and soul, didn't you? Now for twenty years your son has been your all-enhancing love, the only keepsake of your dead husband. So you did all in your power to bring up your son with selfless devotion. There were no more precious moments for you than when you were sending him off to school and welcoming him home again. . . . Your country is at war again, and your son had to comply with enlistment orders. Where is he now? He may have met a violent death in Malaya or North Africa; or perhaps he is still fighting. You remember when casualty lists were made known, and many a wife, mother, fiancée, and sweetheart wept through the night, clasping to her heart a photo. . . . Restore peaceful relations with Japan.[25]

Propaganda depends on slanting the truth to one's own purposes, not making it up whole. Because military censorship held sway throughout the country, Japanese boasts of victory after victory were pure fiction, and Allied soldiers and sailors recognized it as such. This was perhaps the chief reason Japanese efforts failed. Their propagandists were the victims of propaganda themselves.

Only the military leadership knew the true course of the war. Everyone else, including the writers for the general radio broadcasts, was in the dark. The government had banned shortwave receivers; during the war, fewer than 500 sets could be found in the entire country of Japan.[26] No one had a way to check the truth of official announcements. Iva Toguri was among a tiny minority who knew the facts. Phil D'Aquino, who continued to work at Domei, had access to Allied news reports sent out by the U.S. State Department, as well as commercial broadcasts.[27]

A Japanese editor at Radio Tokyo admitted after the war that, by 1943, the morale of Radio Tokyo had been destroyed, first by understaffing and overwork, then by overstaffing, petty jealousy among coworkers, and indifference by superiors. Worse, the editor continued, the Japanese propagandists themselves no longer believed. They knew their broadcasts were lies.[28]

~

The announcers at Radio Tokyo, Radio Manila, Radio Batavia, Radio Singapore, and all the other Japanese stations lacked any knowledge of ongoing military operations, and yet Tokyo Rose—so GIs claimed—broadcast exact details of Allied ship and troop movements, as well as Japanese attacks on Allied positions. At Iva's trial, servicemen testified Tokyo Rose had predicted an attack on them at a certain hour and, sure enough, the Imperial Army or Navy had attacked them at just that time. Iva, speaking for herself but in truth for all civilians in Japan, asked in bewilderment, "Where would I get such information?"

The claim that Tokyo Rose broadcast news of upcoming Japanese attacks is, of course, ludicrous. No military in the world informs its enemies of its plans of attack and thereby gives them time to evacuate, hide in bunkers, or prepare defenses. The collateral information, knowledge of enemy positions and movements, is among the most closely guarded secrets in warfare. The United States knew Japanese positions and operations throughout the war. The U.S. military killed Admiral Yamamoto, the architect of Pearl Harbor, because it knew where his plane would be flying and when. However, at no time did the military divulge the fact that it possessed such knowledge, even to its own troops. Had the Japanese found out, they would have realized the Americans had broken their codes and would have changed them. The idea that Japanese military authorities would allow some woman to *broadcast over the radio* clear evidence that they knew which Allied units would move to what strategic position is beyond imagining. Despite the innumerable post-war recollections collected by the FBI, the U.S. government knew even before the war had concluded that such predictions never happened:

> "Tokyo Rose" is one of the great headaches, not because of her second-rate propaganda, but because of the false omniscience ascribed to her by men of the U.S. armed forces. The countless unfounded rumors attributed to her are frequently extremely detrimental to morale. It has been found more difficult to combat this unwitting propaganda originated by our own forces than real propaganda actually prepared and used by the Japanese.
>
> Japanese broadcasts have been monitored since before the outbreak of war [by] the Foreign Broadcast Intelligence Service. FBIS monitors not only Radio Tokyo but also [eight named stations broadcasting in nineteen named languages]. In all this monitored material, there has never been discovered one item resembling the general run of "Tokyo Rose" rumors. There is not a single instance of any Japanese-controlled radio announcing U.S. military movements prior to actual assault, or disclosing of the whereabouts of U.S. units.
>
> It is highly unlikely that the Japanese, even if they possessed such detailed information on U.S. military and naval matters, would prejudice their sources of information by revealing it in a broadcast.[29]

Japanese pre-war radio programs differed in style from American ones. They generally featured speeches, political analysis, war news, essays on American imperialism and injustice, and other "talk." On June 1, 1942, the Japanese ambassador to Iran, Hikotaro Ichikawa, returned to Japan and met with various officials at Radio Tokyo. He compared Japanese programming unfavorably to BBC and American productions, which contained more variety and music, and generally entertained rather than lectured.[30] Other Japanese repatriating from the United States echoed his views. Furthermore, Japanese propaganda at the beginning of the war had extolled the ferocity of the nation's ever-victorious military. Radio announcers sounded belligerent and threatening as they warned against resistance to Japanese hegemony. By mid-war, this message lacked credibility among Allied listeners. The sense that Japanese programs were failing to serve the nation's larger purposes percolated through the staff and eventually led to a twenty-minute program of jazz music hosted by Norman Reyes called *Zero Hour*.[31]

Zero Hour first broadcast on March 20, 1943, from 7:25 to 7:45 PM Tokyo time.[32] It became the vanguard of the transition from hard to soft propaganda. Japanese authorities allowed Reyes, a POW, to personally select the music from the station's collection of 10,000 RCA Victor and Columbia records[33] and to write his own patter. This made the program stand out from the standard fare produced by the Japanese, whose weak grasp of spoken English, amateurish broadcasting skills, and slowness in producing censor-certified scripts undermined whatever propaganda value their programs might have had. Soon officials decided to expand the length of *Zero Hour* to an hour and to keep the program mostly entertainment in order to build an audience. They no doubt hoped that hearing lyrics and music from more peaceful times back home would convert GIs from focused, unfeeling killing machines into emotionally sensitive, morally ambivalent human beings. To ensure their efforts were not compromised by their own lack of understanding of this foreign culture, they allowed *Zero Hour* to become their only show that POWs planned, scripted, and broadcast. As a result, *Zero Hour* was Radio Tokyo's best program.[34]

George Mitsushio[35] oversaw *Zero Hour* for the Japanese.[36] Born in San Francisco, he had grown up in America, graduated from Sacramento High School, and briefly attended the University of California at Berkeley and Columbia in New York. Kenkichi Oki assisted Mitsushio in his management. Oki was born in Sacramento and attended New York University. The two men were among the 10,000 Nisei who had returned to Japan because they could not find work in America.[37] Although they never formally renounced their U.S. citizenship, both disliked the United States, now considered themselves Japanese, and openly supported Japan's war efforts.[38]

In the fall of 1943, Mitsushio informed Cousens and Ince that they, along with Reyes, would oversee the expanded *Zero Hour*.

When Cousens protested, Mitsushio replied, "There's no escape I'm afraid. This is from Imperial Army H.Q. Apparently they've got an idea from a program that somebody's been doing in the South."[39]

The three POWs, who by now knew and trusted one another, immediately discussed how they could subvert Japanese intentions. Uncertain exactly what the Japanese had planned, they decided to break the broadcast into segments, so that any propaganda could be isolated and thus more easily identified as such by listeners. As a result, *Zero Hour* contained popular and classical music, banter, comic skits, POW messages, and censored news. They assumed the news portion of the program would be the most likely vehicle for Japanese propaganda, so they appropriated early war Japanese broadcast practice for their own purposes by datelining their news broadcasts "Japan" or "Germany" to signal Allied listeners it was not really news but misinformation.[40] Ince agreed to read the news bulletins with such speed that no one could really understand them. Cousens also convinced his superiors that POW messages would build an audience, and the Imperial Army allowed him to broadcast short recorded messages to loved ones back home.[41] Last, they adopted "Strike Up the Band!" as the *Zero Hour* theme song. They didn't dare use the song itself, only the instrumental version, but Cousens wrote scripts imploring listeners to sing along. GIs knew the words, and the Japanese had no clue their enemies gleefully chanted along:

> There is work to be done, to be done
> There's a war to be won, to be won
> Come, you son of a son of a gun,
> Take your stand!

Up to this point, Norman Reyes had kept the nostalgia content of his 15-minute *Zero Hour* to a minimum, but the Japanese wanted to create longing and homesickness in Allied servicemen, so they insisted on a female announcer for the soft music portion of the program. Cousens thought hard about how to undermine their purposes. He couldn't refuse the Army's demands, but he hoped to find an announcer he could trust enough to enlist in his cause and whose voice would not sound sexy or romantic and remind listeners of their wives or girlfriends.

He wanted Margaret Kato for the job. Kato had grown up in London, attended the Royal College of Music, and spoke with a perfect upper-class English accent. He and Kato had worked together previously, and Cousens had no doubts about where her loyalties lay. Kato described herself as "English to the core who would never do anything to betray my country."[42] She had a boyfriend waiting in England to whom she expected to return, and she and Cousens felt great personal warmth toward each other. However, Japanese authorities had caught on to Cousens' and Kato's subterfuge in undermining their broadcasts. Suspicions had reached official channels, and managers began a formal investigation. Several staff members at Radio Tokyo warned Kato that she should avoid further contact with Cousens, that he might be removed and executed. In September 1943, Kato quarreled with superiors, who demanded her resignation. Fearful that they might get rid of Cousens instead, she quickly agreed.[43]

Kato's departure left Cousens without viable options for a female announcer who might aid the POWs' efforts at subversion. Then he remembered, as he would later write,

> the girl with the gin-fog voice from the Accounts Dept. who had been down to see us a number of times and of whom we had been extremely wary. But she had made no attempt to ask us any of the stock questions (What do you think of Japanese culture? Why does America fight the Japanese?) which all the Kempei agents got around to eventually. And she was flat-footed in her expression of contempt and dislike for the Nip militarists. She spoke of "back home" with that little smile in the eyes that you can't fake, especially in those hard, brown eyes of a Jap which she has. And by "back home" she meant California, and her only topic of conversation was California and how soon she could get back. So we decided to trust her. Iva Toguri was her name.[44]

Notes

1. Estimates of vessels and tonnage sunk vary widely from one source to the next. I have used the figures of the United States Joint Army Navy Assessment Committee, *Japanese Naval and Merchant Shipping Losses During World War II By All Causes* (Washington, D.C.: U.S. Government Print-

ing Office, 1947). This report lists the names, weights, purpose, and means sunk for every ship. The Committee's estimates are higher than others, in part because they include ships sunk by running aground and other nonmilitary causes. Since I am considering the effects on Japan, the cause of the loss is irrelevant.

2. Farmers' memories from Havens, *Valley of Darkness*, 90, 99.

3. Havens, *Valley of Darkness*, 94–95, 124.

4. Phil's testimony, Trial Transcript, vol. XLIII, 4745.

5. The details of this incident are murky. At Iva's trial, Phil (Felipe) D'Aquino testified that the argument was about the Battle of the Coral Sea. Trial Transcript, vol. XLIII, 4749–52. Prosecutor DeWolfe did not attack this testimony but D'Aquino was likely confused. The Battle of the Coral Sea occurred May 4–8, 1942, more than a month before Iva arrived at Domei. The fistfight, therefore, was likely about another conflict. Furthermore, in his testimony, Phil claimed Iva was present (4752) and Iva agreed (4795). In her interviews with me, however, Iva said she was not there but heard about the fight later.

6. This paragraph represents my own reconstruction of events and contradicts Iva's trial testimony. In chapter 17, I explain why I believe my account is more accurate than hers.

7. Dower, *Japan in War and Peace* (New York: New Press, 1993), 126–28.

8. Shillony, *Politics and Culture in Wartime Japan*, 136.

9. Havens, *Valley of Darkness*, 149.

10. Both baseball quotes from the staff of *Asahi Shimbun (Daily Asahi)*, *The Pacific Rivals*, 98.

11. Snapshots of Japanese culture from *Asahi Shimbum* staff. *The Pacific Rivals*, 77–79.

12. Havens, *Valley of Darkness*, 31.

13. Havens makes the claim that "Going to Sea" was Japan's official national song. I have not found this in other sources. See *Valley of Darkness*, 85. For university story, see *Asahi Shimbun* staff, *The Pacific Rivals*, 97–98.

14. Katharine Lee Bates (1859–1929), an instructor at Wellesley College, Massachusetts, wrote the lyrics in 1893 as a poem; it first appeared in print in "The Congregationalist," on July 4, 1895. In 1910, the words were published together with "Materna," the tune composed by Samuel A. Ward in 1882 that we associate with the anthem today. See http://kids .niehs.nih.gov/lyrics/america.htm.

15. Roger Pineau, *The Divine Wind: Japan's Kamikaze Force in World War II*, trans. Rikihei Inoguchi and Tadashi Nakajima (Westport, Conn.: Greenwood Press, 1978), 61. I have taken the liberty of changing the somewhat archaic "sward" and "pall" to "grassland" and "grave," respectively.

16. At her trial, Iva said she responded to an ad in *Nippon Times*. She wrote the same in her Notes. In our interviews she denied this, asserting that the one and only job she ever got via a newspaper ad was at the Danish legation. In a statement of September 20, 1973, one of her lawyers, Ted Tamba, remarked that she heard about the job from a fellow Nisei at Domei, which is the same account that she gave me in 1987. However, the Tamba statement is flawed; it states she had this conversation after being discharged from Domei. We know this to be false. She got the Radio Tokyo typing job in June and left Domei in December. I have partially accepted both versions here.

17. Letter from Isamu Yamazaki, Liaison Office, Broadcasting Corp. of Japan, February 14, 1947. Nara 11, Box 1.

18. Iva described Takano as head of the Business Office in her Pre-trial Notes. Ruth Hayakawa said he was head of employment at Radio Tokyo. Deposition, NARA 2, Box 9. Mitsushio testified Takano was so much his superior that he never spoke with him. Trial Transcript, vol. XI, 1084, A.

19. Iva at her trial testified, "I asked Miss Hayakawa to see whether I could meet [the POWs] and she asked me why. And I said, 'It is just a natural instinct with me. I would like to meet with them and talk with them if I can.' She said, 'Why do you say that?' I said, 'I just feel sorry for them.' She said, "Don't you ever say that at Radio Tokyo because there are too many plainclothes *kempeis* in here.'" Iva went on to explain that the next day Hayakawa made up some excuse for them to bring papers to the POWs, and Iva met them. "I asked Major Cousens how long he would have to stay at Radio Tokyo, and he said so far as he knew, army orders would keep him there until the Allies won. I was surprised that he would say that directly to me. I told him, "It won't be too long the way things look now." And he said, "Thank you for saying that." (Trial Transcript, vol. XLV, 4979–80.)

Ivan Chapman, a dogged researcher, does not use this story. He says, "Toguri's first role at Radio Tokyo was that of a courier. Part of her routine job was to type resumes of overseas news, already vetted by the military censors, and take them to Cousens for use in news items and commentaries." (Chapman, *Tokyo Calling*, 152). Chapman apparently relies on various depositions of Cousens, as well as a 1986 letter from Iva.

Toguri Notes state, "Ruth was one of the first persons I met in Radio Tokyo, and she introduced me to the POWs at Radio Tokyo. The POWs, although they were kept in custody, did wander around the station, collecting material for their programs, records, news, etc. This was how I was able to meet them, talked with them several times before I actually started to work with them."

In her 1987 interviews with me, Iva expressly denied more than once that Ruth Hayakawa had any role in her meeting the POWs. I read to Iva the 1973 statement of her attorney, Ted Tamba: "One day while Ruth and Iva were conversing, three bedraggled Caucasians passed them in the hallway. Iva wanted to know who they were. She was told by Ruth that they were POWs. Iva insisted on meeting them." Iva responded, "I don't know when Tamba got that information from Hayakawa." I replied, "I assumed he got that information from you." Iva fell silent and finally admitted, "I don't have a clear memory."

I selected the Cousens' version because to me it rings truer than Iva's trial testimony. Cousens constantly dealt with turncoat Nisei and with Foumy Saisho, whom he profoundly mistrusted and with good reason. I doubt he would have been so honest with Iva at their first meeting. Needless to say, this is not evidence that Iva deliberately lied at her trial, only that, like most of us when we remember, she conflated several events into one.

20. Timeline is testimony of Wallace Ince. Trial Transcript, vol. XXXI, 3464. Ince also swore their rations at the Dai Ichi were only 50 to 75 percent of the rations at Bunka. "We actually had more in Bunka than we had at the Dai Ichi" (3561). I suspect this was hyperbole intended to counter prosecution suggestions that the POWs were living it up at the hotels. Ince weighed 175 pounds at the time of his capture, 128 at liberation.

21. Iva testified she first saw Cousens on August 24, 1943. Trial Transcript, vol. XLVI, 5096. She described his sickly condition (5095), and said that Ince looked even worse (5098).

22. Toguri Notes.

23. Radio broadcast quotations from Meo, *Japan's Radio War on Australia*, 102, 147.

24. Radio broadcast quotations from Meo, *Japan's Radio War on Australia*, 265, 99.

25. Meo, *Radio Japan's War on Australia*, 121.

26. John Morris, *Traveller From Tokyo* (London: Cresset Press, 1943), 94.

27. Toguri Notes.

28. From Hiroshi Saito, "Japan's Strategic Broadcasts" in *Chuo-Koron (Central Review)*, April, 1950. *Chuo-Koron* is a Japanese-language source quoted in Meo, *Japan's Radio War on Australia*, 46.

29. Memorandum for Op-23D42 Files. The memo is dated January 7, 1946, although the unknown writer's concerns about stopping rumor-mongering by American GIs suggests he wrote it during wartime. NARA 1, Box 40. I myself went through hundreds of transcripts and never found

any predictions of troop movements or similar Tokyo Rose-style material.

30. I am indebted to Robbins (*Tokyo Calling*, 142) for this story. She found it in Setsuro Kitayama, *Radio Tokyo: The Road to Greater East Asia* (Tokyo: Tabata Shoten, 1988), 178–79, a Japanese-language source.

31. At trial, Mitsushio testified that "zero hour" is the moment of attack. Trial Transcript, vol. X, 917. I doubt GI listeners got the reference. What jazz music has to do with a military attack, I have no idea.

32. Ryō Namikawa wrote, "According to my data, *Zero Hour* was broadcast from 7:25 to 7:45 PM. In August 1943, it was broadcast from 6:40 PM but was still a twenty-minute program. I believe that *Zero Hour* was expanded to a seventy-five-minute program from 6:00 to 7:15 PM starting on February 1, 1944—the peak time. From April 5, 1945, *Zero Hour* was broadcast from 6:00 to 7:00 until the surrender." Short, *Film & Radio Propaganda*, 333. Circular 70-13 (Defense Exhibit G) comports with this timeline except that it has *Zero Hour* broadcasting as a 70-minute program, from 6:00 to 7:10 PM, beginning April 1, 1944. The first broadcast date of March 20, 1943 is from this same exhibit. NARA 2, Box 7.

33. Given how often Iva had to repeat her music selections, the "10,000 record collection" sounds like an exaggeration to me, but such was Mitsushio's testimony. Trial Transcript, vol. XL, 1059.

34. According to Hiroshi Saito, quoted in Meo, *Japan's Radio War on Australia*, 34.

35. To prevent confusion, I have used the name "George Mitsushio" throughout the book. Mitsushio was his correct name after 1944, and it appears most often in FBI files. His birth name was Hideo Tanabe. His father, Sanzo Tanabe, died in Japan in 1911, his mother remarried, and he was adopted by his stepfather, Kanehito Nakamoto. During his years in the United States, he was known as George Nakamoto. Iva referred to him as Nakamoto. His biological father's actual birth name was Mitsushio, but following Japanese custom, Sanzo adopted the family name of his mother (Tanabe) when that family produced no male children. When George returned to Japan, he again became Hideo Tanabe. He assumed the surname Mitsushio on July 1, 1944, when that family name was restored. Were all this not complicated enough, on Radio Tokyo Mitsushio assumed the persona of "Frank Watanabe." Worse, an actual Watanabe worked on *Zero Hour* for the Japanese military to make sure nothing favored the Allies. In summary, George Mitsushio, George Nakamoto, Hideo Tanabe, and broadcaster Frank Watanabe are the same person.

36. According to Mitsushio's testimony at trial, Shinnojo Sawada initially gave him authority to establish *Zero Hour* on March 1, 1943, telling him that the Imperial Japanese Army and Tsuneishi had requested it.

Mitsushio selected Norman Reyes, and authorized him to pick music. Sawada ordered him expand to 60 minutes in August 1943, and told Mitsushio that the order had come from Army General Staff Headquarters. This testimony contradicts the Namikawa/Defense Exhibit G timeline. See note 32. Trial Transcript, vol. XI, 1053–62.

37. Smith, *Americans from Japan*, 254.

38. Mitsushio's and Oki's condemnation of Iva at trial stemmed from the fact that they were working for, and were loyal to, the Japanese. They never disputed this fact after the war. The U.S. government did not charge them with treason for the very practical reason that it wanted them to testify on behalf of the prosecution.

39. Cousens' recollection of conversation in letter to Buck Henshaw, October 16, 1948. The program "from the South" is usually considered to be Myrtle Lipton's out of Manila, discussed in the next chapter. This, however, is impossible. Lipton did not broadcast until 1944, after *Zero Hour* and after Iva.

40. When the war began, Japanese newscasters introduced segments as "from Padang, Borneo, Lisbon, Buenos Aires, Shanghai, Manila, Rangoon, Stockholm, Berlin," etc. See transcripts, NARA 10, Box 635.

41. This paragraph represents an opportunity to discuss a problem with reference notes for primary sources that will worsen as this work continues. Every statement in the paragraph comes from trial testimony, depositions, exhibits, letters, reports, etc. Sometimes two or three witnesses affirm the sentence's truth; sometimes witnesses conflict, but one or more of them is not credible. Were I to note my warrant for every assertion, chapters would contain hundreds of references and readers would be blinded by a blizzard of little numbers. Therefore, only where there is potential controversy or confusion have I noted my source. Otherwise, readers must trust that, despite the lack of a reference note, I have not, or at least not intentionally, presented falsehoods or slanted the facts to fit my point of view. I have, of course, tried to be diligent about always citing secondary sources.

42. Letters of Margaret Kato McIntyre to Ivan Chapman, 1988, 1989, cited in *Tokyo Calling*, 154.

43. Chapman, *Tokyo Calling*, 154–55.

44. Letter, Cousens to Buck Henshaw, October 16, 1948, FBI Report, December 1, 1948. NARA 2, Box 11.

8

A New Career in Broadcasting

Zero Hour

On November 10 or 11, 1943, George Mitsushio informed Iva Toguri that she must report for a voice test.[1] Iva, taken by surprise, asked why. Mitsushio told her to follow orders. At the "test," she found Major Cousens. Cousens had sold Mitsushio on the need for a "different kind of voice" and had predetermined that Toguri would be that voice. Ted Ince didn't want a Jap on the program and worried that Iva could not be trusted. Cousens had a hunch she could. Iva read into the microphone, and Cousens informed Mitsushio that Iva's voice was fine. Iva broadcast for the first time that evening, introducing music on the new edition of the *Zero Hour*.[2]

Privately, Cousens promised her that her own part of the program, about 15 minutes of music, would never contain explicit propaganda. "Consider yourself a soldier under my command," she remembered him saying, "I write this program, I know what I'm doing, and I personally guarantee that you will never do anything against your own people."[3] He explained that the POWs intended to use the program to broadcast personal messages so that families would know their loved ones were still alive.[4] They had chosen her as a broadcaster for several reasons: they believed they could trust her; it would give them an excuse to see her regularly and learn the latest war news; the job would give Iva a pay increase; and lastly, her voice suited their larger purposes.

Iva's voice is a subject unto itself. In various documents, friends and acquaintances described her voice as "very harsh and throaty," "husky," "brassy," "like a frog," "like a WAC," "like a hacksaw," and "that awful masculine voice."[5] I myself found her voice interesting and appealing because it had a distinctive character to it. It was forceful and carried conviction. If pushed to compare Iva to a performer on the contemporary scene, I would say she sounded like Bebe Neuwirth, best known for her role on the TV show *Cheers* for playing Frazier's ex-wife, Lilith. In any case, one cannot properly describe Iva's voice—as so many GIs characterized the voice of Tokyo Rose—as soft, sexy, or traditionally feminine. In a letter to the FBI, one serviceman claimed he listened to Iva on the *Zero Hour* during the war: "Her voice was like honey and as effective as the sirens of mythology."[6] Whatever honey-voiced siren he heard, it wasn't Iva Toguri.

The scripts that Cousens prepared used "ANN" as an abbreviation for "announcer." According to Ince, Iva, completely inexperienced, actually read aloud "ANN will read the following" the first time she broadcast.[7] Immediately realizing her mistake, she ad libbed that this was Ann speaking. Cousens found "Ann," as a radio name, insipid and dull.[8] Iva remembered Harold Gray's "Orphan Annie," one of the top five cartoon strips in the United States when she left. Her loneliness and isolation in Japan caused her to identify with the title character, so she decided when she broadcast on the *Zero Hour* to refer to herself as "Orphan Ann" and to her GI listeners as "my favorite orphans." (In late 1945, Cousens claimed that he had heard that "the expression 'Orphans of the Pacific' was current in the outside world," and he chose to use it to indicate Iva was not Japanese.[9]) Throughout the war, Cousens called her Ann, not Iva, and she called him Major. It was as if they were not really themselves, merely playing parts like actors.

Iva, a practical, everyday sort of woman not given to musing about the connotative meanings of common nouns, probably gave little thought to the decision to refer to her listeners as "orphans." She should have. However affectionately she said it, the term suggested her audience was so alone and so far from home, their families were essentially dead to them. Unlike "Yankees," "cowboys," "crazy Americans," or any of a hundred other monikers she could have used, "orphans" had no positive spin. The psychological effect clearly represented an attack on morale, and was, especially in view of later events, a very poor choice of words.

Iva tried mightily to escape broadcasting. She didn't really know the managers of *Zero Hour*, Mitsushio and Oki, so she complained to her boss, Takano, that she didn't have the ability to be on the radio. Takano replied that she broadcast under Army orders "and that nothing further need be said." Ignoring this, Iva went over his head to Isamu Yamazaki, manager of the English section of the Overseas Division, and requested to be relieved of her job. Yamazaki's response was less civil than Takano's. He informed Iva that resigning was unlawful, and that if she refused to broadcast, the government would assign her to the manufacture of munitions, repairing uniforms, or gathering metal. Yamazaki noted her attitude and thereafter, whenever Iva was out sick, which she pretended to be as often as she dared, Yamazaki sent agents to fetch her.[10]

Iva essentially functioned as a disk jockey. She introduced music with light banter. She arrived just before her segment began and left the studio after her final music selection had played. News bulletins sometimes interrupted her segment, usually not. She seldom listened to the broadcast of the remainder of the hour-long program.

Cousens taught Iva to be not just an announcer but a radio personality. He sat exactly opposite her at a table with the microphone between them. As she broadcast, she looked directly into his face. Ince, who handled the music, sat at another desk with a turntable and a stack of records. Reyes took Ince's desk during his portion of the show. Everyone else—technicians, managers, guards—viewed the POWs and Iva through a glass panel from another room. Cousens taught her how to project her voice, and Iva thought it was possible she was more soft-spoken before her lessons with Cousens. He rehearsed the scripts with her, practicing every inflection, every phrasing, instructing her to change her facial expressions to change her vocal expression. "Major was like a conductor at a symphony, moving his hand up and down depending on whether I was to be light or serious." If he wanted her to be more humorous, he'd make a funny face; she wanted to laugh but knew she couldn't, so the effect was a lightness or silliness in her delivery. He later explained that "if we could make it bright and breezy, then so very much the better, for a cheerful soldier is not homesick but on the contrary, refreshed."[11] Without Cousens, Iva claimed, she would have just read her script in the flat monotone that most people use when they read aloud. Thanks to him she developed a true on-air persona and, she believed, more personality in real life.

This outcome was probably not happenstance. Although Cousens insisted after the war that he selected Iva as a broadcaster solely for her lack of appeal, it seems equally likely that Cousens recognized possibilities in her distinctive voice. Considering that *Zero Hour* became Radio Tokyo's best program, Cousens' cultivation of Iva may indicate that to some extent he succumbed to "Bridge on the River Kwai" syndrome.[12] As a radio professional, he had personal standards not easily disregarded, and therefore he at least subconsciously wanted to produce a respectable program. The development of a raw talent such as Iva Toguri undoubtedly gave him considerable pride, as Iva's memories of his strict training of her broadcast delivery suggest (Figures 8.1 and 8.2).[13]

Figure 8.2. Zero Hour *Studio 5 at Radio Tokyo.*
Courtesy of National Archives

Figure 8.1. Iva at the microphone.
Courtesy of National Archives

At Radio Tokyo, Iva met several other women, Nisei as well as Japanese nationals educated in America, who either were or would become broadcasters. They included:

Ruth Hayakawa, born in Japan but a resident of the United States from childhood through college, Hayakawa usually replaced Iva on Sundays after Iva became a broadcaster.[14]

June Suyama, previously "the nightingale of Nanking," from British Columbia; Iva recalls "she was the one with the soft, sultry voice but she mainly did the news."

Kathy (Kaoru) Moruka, a California Nisei[15] who also substituted for Iva regularly as a broadcaster; her support of the Japanese caused Iva to remark with some bitterness, "I never could figure out how she came out smelling like a rose. I never could figure that out at all."

Mary Ishii, half Japanese, half English, she spoke with a British accent as some listeners claimed Tokyo Rose did, and she too replaced Iva at various times.

Mieko Furuya, a Nisei who sometimes substituted for Iva.

Many other women, such as Margaret Kato and Katherine Fujiwara, worked at Radio Tokyo, but Iva had no recollection of meeting them. Women also broadcast from Japanese-controlled stations in other cities.

The most famous of these was Myrtle Lipton (Figure 8.3).[16] She broadcast from Manila under her own given name, but American servicemen referred to her as Manila Rose, after the more famous Tokyo Rose.

In June 1945, after the Philippines had returned to U.S. control, the 22-year-old Lipton gave an interview to Sergeant Ozzie St.

Figure 8.3. Myrtle Lipton.
Courtesy of U.S. Army, *Yank* Magazine.

George, a staff reporter for *Yank*, the Army weekly.[17] St. George lauded her "mestiza (halfbreed)" good looks (she was half-American, half-Filipina), her black eyes, black hair, and golden brown complexion, and concluded admiringly, "she has starlet's legs to go with all the rest of it." According to St. George, Lipton delivered phony news from home such as "I understand Ann finally married George; she didn't think Jim was ever coming home" and "moonlit nights in Central Park with Betty who later married a 4-F who worked at DuPont." St. George implied Lipton's behavior away from the mike was whorish. He suggested her ability to buy expensive items like cigarettes on a small salary meant "she may have had to do a little outside work for her monthly pack." When Lipton told him her Japanese boss, Omhura, was not such a bad guy, St. George added, "The rumor around Manila, where Myrtle was well known and on her way to becoming better than well known—or notorious—had it that Omhura didn't think Myrtle was so bad either." After Ken Murayama replaced Omhura, "Ken became quite a friend of Myrtle's." She had "many Jap friends," St. George suggested, because "Myrtle wasn't choosy."

This interview took place three months before any reporter would interview or even know about the existence of Iva Toguri. It is strange, therefore, that Lipton's story in *Yank* was strikingly similar to Iva's, at least as the American press reported it. Lipton applied for a job at Radio Manila primarily to obtain rations. Her program—St. George referred to it as *Memory Lane* and *Melody Lane* in the same article—broadcast in the early evenings, like *Zero Hour*. She, like Iva, was a complete novice when she auditioned. Nevertheless, she was put on the air immediately, and as a result she too made a mistake about her name on her first broadcast. Iva accidentally called herself Ann whereas Myrtle accidentally used her own name instead of Mary, her scripted pseudonym. Both stuck with their mistakes. Lipton too possessed a "low, husky voice." Lipton also disk jockeyed popular American music and considered herself an entertainer. She asserted, "My program was not a propaganda broadcast." When she tried to quit, the Japanese threatened her. They always supervised her in the studio. "There were always Japs around, civilians but they all carried guns and swords." St. George quoted Lipton as ambivalent about the war. "I'm not pro-Jap. But I'm not pro-American either. I'm pro-Filipino." Reporters would put similar ambivalent sentiments in the mouth of Iva Toguri following her initial interviews.[18]

Historians of the case[19] believe the widespread rumors among servicemen about Tokyo Rose's sexy voice, innuendo-laden patter, and taunts about faithless wives actually derived from GIs listening to Myrtle Lipton, not Iva Toguri. These allegations were serious enough that FBI agents Frederick Tillman and Nicholas Alaga investigated Lipton for treason in 1945. They found her already in the custody of an Army colonel.[20] When Lipton started to cry during their interrogation, the colonel put a stop to the questioning. According to Alaga, Tillman wrote a multipage report on the interview. It has since disappeared.

In 1949, Ken Murayama gave a lengthy deposition to defense lawyer Ted Tamba in which he stated that the purpose of the scripts he wrote for Lipton was to induce homesickness among Allied troops. "We had stories of girls having dates with men at home, while possibly their sweethearts and husbands might be fighting in the Southwest Pacific." In a separate interview, Kazumaro "Buddy" Uno told Tamba that he filled her scripts with exactly the material for which Tokyo Rose was famous. "I thought her program was wonderful; it carried a punch; it was sexy; she had everything in it."[21] Both Uno and Murayama recalled that Lipton's program opened with "Auld Lang Syne" as its theme song.[22]

The view that Myrtle Lipton was in fact the source of the Tokyo Rose broadcasts would appear to be compelling. However, nothing about the history of the Tokyo Rose legend should be taken at face value.

Yank reporter St. George went looking for a sexy propagandist at Radio Manila and found Myrtle Lipton just as, a few months later, reporters would search for a sexy propagandist at Radio Tokyo and find Iva Toguri. He, and they, went convinced the Tokyo Rose broadcasts actually happened, but as will be detailed in the next chapter, the evidence for this vanishes upon inspection of the evidence. St. George's overheated speculations about Lipton's sluttish behavior may have been nothing more than his own fantasies conjured up as a result of years of sexual deprivation. Nothing other than his interview shows that Myrtle Lipton wasn't as chaste as the next girl. She admitted she liked to smoke and drink, and lived in Shanghai for a year "seeing the town." However, at the time St. George found her, she was not living the good life with some important patron but with her mother and sister in a Manila suburb. Finally, St. George claims Omhura told Lipton to listen to Tokyo Rose to learn how to appeal to the Americans. The impossibility of following this advice, given that Tokyo Rose didn't exist, and the consequent likelihood that Omhura never gave it indicates St. George's bias. When Lipton swore she never broadcast propaganda, he dismissed her assertion as "balderdash." Iva's denials were similarly dismissed.

The depositions of Uno and Murayama are also of dubious value. In a 1945 deposition, Uno told the Army that Ince, not Cousens, chose, coached, and wrote scripts for Iva on the *Zero Hour*, which was his "baby," and that Ince only added Iva to supplement Ruth Hayakawa, whom the program "featured as 'Tokyo Rose.'"[23] Uno was so obviously and completely confused that none of this deposition could be entered into evidence at Iva's trial. By 1949, when Tamba interviewed Uno and Murayama, both had been profoundly compromised by the tremendous publicity given to the now famous Tokyo Rose and to Iva. They also conferred with each other before being deposed.

One unimpeachable source for what really happened exists. As noted in chapter 3, the Federal Broadcasting Intelligence Service (FBIS) recorded and transcribed all shortwave broadcasts from Japanese-controlled radio stations during World War II. The Philippines had three shortwave transmitters, and FBIS apparently picked up all three, especially during the evening/night when shortwave programs travel farthest.[24] The National Archives house thousands of pages of these transcripts. According to *Yank*, Myrtle Lipton broadcast from March to October 1944. According to Murayama, she only broadcast from October 1944 to January 1945. Uno didn't meet Lipton until the first week of November 1944, when she was already an announcer. Whatever is true, a thorough review of FBIS transcripts of Manila shortwave broadcasts from January 1944 through January 1945 fails to uncover any sexy patter or material about faithless wives or girlfriends. Most programming covered news of the war, as well as domestic problems such as food shortages. In addition, Manila stations broadcast addresses by President Jose Laurel and essays glorifying the nation's new independence. The programs manifested some propaganda, but it was standard Japanese fare: we never surrender; you will die trying to retake these islands; your military covers up the truth about your casualties; stop referring to Laurel as our puppet president and calling Filipinos who work with him collaborators; you must be miserable in the mud and mosquitoes; and, we destroyed this many American ships yesterday. (I stopped counting U.S. carriers sunk when the number passed 100.)

In fact, only two programs featuring popular musical selections are extant among the FBIS transcripts and neither began with "Auld Lang Syne."[25] Both broadcast from Manila in the early evening. The first, *The Philippine Republic Hour*, appeared throughout 1944. It offered lengthy diatribes, straightforward if slanted news by apparently male readers, and rather staid, often patriotic music, although now and then it featured live entertainment by singer Linda Estrella. It would not seem to be Lipton's *Memory/Melody Lane*.

The other program did contain a few taunts aimed at American invaders and appeals to the joys of life back in America. FBIS transcripts for this program are dated during November and December 1944, which comports approximately with Murayama's recollection of Myrtle Lipton's time on the air. The transcript of one of the show's openings reads like this:

> Good evening, boys down Leyte way. How are you tonight? Something tells me you're still bogged down by rain and mud. I wish I could invite you over to my apartment and give you some home-cooked food and a hot shower. Good God, why am I always wishfully thinking? Maybe I'm not the only one, eh, fellows?[26]

This chatter continued without musical interruption to announce a new Japanese plane that would soon drop bombs on the United States and to tout the value of the kamikaze. "Remember, our weapons not only have eyes and noses but also have brains." Unfortunately for our purposes, the segment concluded with the revelation that the announcer wishfully thinking about having the boys over for a hot shower and a meal was a male named Victor Campo. "And speaking of brains, if I'm smart, I'll call it a night and hurry home where my wife is waiting with dinner on the table and slippers on the floor. Good night, fellows, thanks for listening."

The program used "Baby, Won't You Please Come Home" as its theme song, not "Auld Lang Syne."

In sum, although some home sickness–inducing material does appear in 1943 and 1944, not a single transcript shows any Tokyo Rose-style sexual come-ons or taunts about faithless wives, on this program, *The Philippine Republic Hour*, or on any other Manila broadcast.

There is, however, something odd about the FBIS records. A transcript for November 28, 1944 begins, *"Preceded by Moments of Melody* . . . which continued until 7:00 AM." A transcript for the next day, November 29, concludes, "End at 6:30 AM. Followed by Moments of Melody over Radio Manila."[27] This program, "Moments of Melody," apparently broadcast between 6:30 and 7:00 AM Eastern War time, which was 7:30 to 8:00 PM Manila time.[28] It would seem a likely candidate for Myrtle Lipton's *Melody Lane*. Here's the oddity: In the last quarter of 1944 and in January 1945, the months during which every source agrees Lipton broadcast, not a single transcript exists for "Moments of Melody."

The FBIS had to receive the broadcasts. Transcripts exist for programs that began at 7:00 PM and at 8:00 PM. Second, on Wednesdays and Saturdays *The Philippine Republic Hour* broadcast during this time slot and its transcripts are available. So why for four months (October 1944 to January 1945) are there no transcripts for any program that began at 7:30 PM? A single transcript for a 7:30 PM program in Tagalog (a Filipino language) and English that featured cultural and children's segments exists for September 25.[29] Perhaps this program ran regularly in this half-hour slot, and FBIS deemed it too unimportant to transcribe. Or perhaps the 7:00 PM program, the one emceed by Victor Campo, the gentleman with the admirably firm grip on his masculinity, ran for an hour. In any case, although FBIS diligently transcribed dozens of Iva's *Zero Hour* broadcasts, no transcription of anything remotely like Myrtle Lipton's rumored program can be found today.

One explanation sure to occur to readers must be discussed. Suppose the Department of Justice (DoJ) or the FBI pulled the transcripts, either to prepare a case against Lipton or to be ready for defense claims that Lipton, not Toguri, was the real Tokyo Rose? When prosecutors and agents read the transcripts, they discovered nothing of interest and later destroyed them. Or, more malevolently, they discovered Lipton was the real source of the sexual come-ons, innuendos, and faithless wives remarks and destroyed them to cover up their perfidy in prosecuting Iva Toguri.

This explanation will appeal to conspiracy theorists, but I find it unlikely. The DoJ and FBI are huge bureaucracies. They struggle to act efficiently. They overlook documents and leave paper trails. The problem here is that not only do no transcripts exist for Lipton's program, but no memos exist that request said transcripts from FBIS, discuss their contents, weigh their import for the upcoming trial, or order them destroyed. Hundreds of related memos are extant concerning *Zero Hour* broadcasts. Second, if these agencies could effectively cover up their malicious conduct, we wouldn't know what we do today about their suborning perjury, racist profiling of the jury, withholding exculpatory evidence, and all the rest.

So, where does that leave us? Given the paucity of the evidence, the safest interpretation of the facts is that Lipton broadcast just as Iva did. Having said that, there are reasons to doubt she is the source of the Tokyo Rose material. For one, rumors of Tokyo Rose's purported taunts pre-date the end of 1944, when Lipton was on the air, by more than two years. For another, Lipton herself denied it. In the next chapter, I will argue that no announcer—Toguri, Lipton, or any of the other women on Japanese radio—broadcast Tokyo Rose's sexy material. Instead, it originated in a radio broadcast source generally overlooked by researchers.

When *Yank*'s correspondent returned to interview Myrtle Lipton a second time, she had disappeared. She's been gone ever since. What happened to her is a mystery. One rumor had it that she died shortly after the war. Another rumor asserted that the American colonel planted the death rumor and that in fact she came to live with him in America.[30] Given what happened to Iva, one can understand why Lipton went into hiding. But decades later, when the truth about Tokyo Rose came out, Myrtle Lipton, assuming she lived, missed an opportunity to tell her own story. Of course, for all anyone knows, she turned 80 in 2003 and is still alive today.[31]

After the war ended, the other women who broadcast and worked for the Japanese on the dozens of radio programs, including *Zero Hour*, also disappeared from public view. So did the many

Nisei, male and female, that Iva met at Domei, Radio Tokyo, and elsewhere in Japan. They were a sore subject with her because too many sold out their allegiance. Remembering them elicited from Iva a rare outburst of anger. "I dropped many of my Nisei friends because they would say, 'Oh, isn't it great! We're winning the war!' And I said, 'What the hell do you mean? *We* are winning? By *we*, do you mean the Japanese?' Isn't it ironic that these people came back to the U.S. without any problems as devoted United States' citizens. They deserted the victorious Japanese and now they're with the victorious Americans. I just want to spit in their faces. Some of them had the gall to write me and say how happy they were I had gotten my pardon and all that baloney—I'd use another expression if I weren't a lady. It just burns me up. Every one of those monkeys would say, 'We're winning the war!'"

This bitter complaint represents Iva's hardened attitudes late in her life. In 1948, she did not condemn her fellow Nisei so universally, writing, "In December of 1943 there were quite a few Nisei girls who started to work at Domei and . . . I felt it best to . . . get away from the Niseis who were hard to size up in their feelings towards the war. I had heard that some of them had taken Japanese citizenship and wondered why I never said anything about becoming a Japanese citizen." Her assessment of fellow broadcaster Ruth Hayakawa typifies her change over the decades. In 1987, Iva disparaged Hayakawa as "someone who's going to make damn sure she's not on the losing side." But in 1948, she wrote that Ruth "came to see me on the Sunday before I was rearrested on August 26, 1948. She offered to help in every way possible and she asked that she be called as my witness should it be necessary to do so." Hayakawa testified via deposition.[32]

~

Iva had unbounded respect and affection for Major Cousens, and he reciprocated. Yet despite almost daily interaction, they never spoke of personal matters. Iva believed neither wanted to intrude on the other's privacy, but perhaps the memories of family far away were too painful to dredge up. She unwaveringly maintained that he was not guilty of treason or even capable of it, only that he wanted to survive to go back home. Foumy Saisho, who checked the content of Cousens' scripts, made changes, and signed off on the final drafts, noted, perhaps with a little jealousy, "Iva Toguri and Cousens hit it off, and they worked marvelously as a team. He drew out her talent as no one else did. There were other female announcers, but none had a radio personality like hers."[33]

Figure 8.4. Foumy Saisho.
Courtesy of Mitchell Library, State Library of New South Wales, Australia, Papers of Ivan Chapman.

If sexy Filipina Myrtle Lipton physically embodied the legendary Tokyo Rose, Foumy Saisho (Figure 8.4) personified her mind. Fluent in English and Japanese, intelligent, shrewd, and more guileful than any modern politician, Saisho said much over the years that was untrustworthy. Shortly after the end of the war, Saisho told the Counter Intelligence Corps, "No one at Radio Tokyo ever used the name of 'Tokyo Rose.'" Earlier in the same statement, she had declared "There were three girls who used the name 'Tokyo Rose.' Toguri was the first one." In 1949, she indicated she had known Iva's broadcast name all along when she told the FBI that Iva called herself "Orphan Annie."[34] She also claimed she only worked as a translator, stating, "I do not announce." Colonel Tsuneishi, her direct superior, swore she did.[35] Asked how long she worked for Radio Tokyo, Saisho answered, "From August 1935, to 1945, September, I think." Asked less than a minute later when she quit Radio Tokyo, Saisho responded, "Around 1943."[36] A Japanese national educated at the University of Michigan,[37] she supported Japan's war effort with such fervor that Cousens believed she was an agent of the *kempeitai*. He noted that whereas the women at

Radio Tokyo were servile toward their male counterparts, Saisho bossed them around, and the men were afraid of her.[38] However much power she wielded, Saisho nonetheless referred to her government as "the Japs" when speaking to U.S. authorities.[39] Discussing Cousens' friend Margaret Kato, Saisho claimed Kato admitted to her that she was in love with Cousens and that Kato confided her plans to marry him after the war. Kato, who did in fact return to England and marry her boyfriend, labeled this "a disgusting fabrication!"[40]

Foumy Saisho's own relationship with Cousens remains the most mysterious and perhaps most duplicitous aspect of her character. After the war, Saisho described their relationship as collegial and cooperative. She also denied that his work at Radio Tokyo constituted treason, adding, "If Cousens committed a crime, it was his desire to see his family and country again, and live on somehow."[41] In 1946, Australian authorities attempted to prosecute Cousens the way American authorities prosecuted Iva Toguri. Despite her just-quoted remarks, Saisho testified against him at his hearing on treason. Years later, the prosecutor wrote in his memoirs that she was an excellent witness, able to think six questions ahead and tell lies more effectively than any man.[42] Cousens, testifying in his own defense, suggested that her testimony was payback for a spurned love. He claimed that in August 1944, Saisho sent him a letter stating, "Although we have never spoken of it, you and I know we love one another. As you know, I am a woman of much experience. I never expected to find a love like this."[43] Although Cousens lost the letter, another POW, U.S. Navy Ensign Buck Henshaw, testified that he had read it and that it was, in his words, "extremely mushy."[44] In 1987, Cousens' biographer Ivan Chapman, determined to get to the bottom of what went on between them, journeyed to Tokyo to interview Saisho in person. In her late 70s, she insisted there was no letter, no unrequited love, and that Cousens made the whole thing up.[45]

~

I asked Iva with some insistence whether she ever felt concern about her broadcasts. "Did you worry that your actions might be viewed as giving aid to the enemy? Did you consider the possibility that you might get in trouble after the war?" Her answers to me, and her actions at war's end, indicated that she was oblivious. "I never asked [Cousens] if I could get into trouble. It never crossed my mind." Did she and the POWs discuss the possibility that their actions were treasonous? "Never! The [*Zero Hour*] program, as far as I am concerned, was like any ordinary program any time of the century."

Treason consists of two elements: adherence to the enemy, and rendering him aid or comfort. Adherence means intentionally acting to strengthen the enemy or to weaken the United States.[46] In Iva's mind, neither she nor any of the POWs were guilty of treason. In her case, she asserted that she had no intention of helping Japan or harming the United States, nor did she believe that she in fact did anything to aid the enemy. She knew from her conversations with the POWs that they never gave allegiance to Japan either, and what minor acts of propaganda they committed, they did in fear of their lives. Iva Toguri broadcast on the *Zero Hour* from November 1943, until the end of the war, devoid of any pangs of conscience or sentiment of guilt.

The following is typical of Iva's cornball patter and Mitch Miller-like[47] entreaties. This is a complete script of Iva's portion of *Zero Hour*, broadcast March 9, 1944. Cousens' British spellings are retained.

Greetings Everybody!—and welcome once again to Radio Tokyo's special programme for our Friends in Australia and the South Pacific. This is your little playmate Orphan Annie, and by the way wasn't that a lousy musical programme we had last night? It was almost bad enough to be the B.B.C. or its little sister the A.B.C.—but I promise it won't happen again; and to prove it here's a presentation of Schumann . . . [plays classical music selection]

See what I mean? Now how about some [violinist] Kreisler music to follow that? Check?—alright, here's . . . [plays classical music selection]

And that brings the next item in your programme up over the horizon—in fact you can hear him [Ince] rustling papers now— the wretch!—but first we're going to have some more Kreisler, and this time it's his . . . [plays classical music selection]

And now here's your News Announcer to read the news from the A.H.F. [American Home Front]—come on in.

[Ince reads the news.]

Thank you, thank you, thank you. Now then, stand by the Orphan Choir! This is Radio Tokyo calling and presenting our special programme for listeners in Australia and the South Pacific. For the next 10 minutes we are going to listen to a superb presentation of the melodies of Stephen Foster. The performers are well known wandering minstrels, the Orphans of the South Pacific, supported by [bandleader] Nat Shilkret . . . [plays Foster music selection]

That's not bad atoll, atoll! Alright, Boys, one more lap, and then you can have your beer. What—*no beer*! Well, what sort of a war is this? Never mind, sing first, and write to [Secretary of the Interior Harold] Ickes afterwards. Maybe he'll run a pipeline for you. Sing little ones! . . . [plays Foster music selection]

Be seeing you tomorrow along about the same time. So in the meantime this is Orphan Ann reminding you GIs always to be good and . . . [plays "Good-bye Now."][48]

Excerpts from other programs, scripts, and transcriptions, indicate more of the same:

This is our special program for our Friends in Australia and the South Pacific. How's the morale this evening? Never mind, don't tell me, because I'm going to fix it for you—and if you don't feel better by the time I've finished with you, then you can go play hide and seek with the snakes. Is the Orphan Choir all ready? . . . [plays music selection]

O.K., that's a start. Now this is where we really go to town! What do you think I ran across today in my raid on the record library? Well, let me tell you. There was I, unarmed but determined. I fought off two flank attacks, plunged through a wall of Beethoven, and a terrible Wagnerian swamp—Say!—are you listening to me? Oh what's the use! Well, anyway, here's what I got for you . . .

Well, how does it [morale] feel now? Better? Sure it does. You should never let a hate like that keep festering, it poisons the whole system. Now let's enjoy some more music together.

Round number three and it's the Charioteers in a not-too-exciting number entitled, "Forget If You Can." Yes, you boneheads, forget if you can. Try and forget.

This sweet little tune comes from way back. When I remember it, I think of the times that were some of the most wonderful we have ever seen.

You are liking same? Yes or no here is Orphan Anne again to put the needle down.

Everybody comfortable? Yes, I know—but whose fault is that? You boneheads! Get as comfortable as you can then and be grateful that you've got an orphan to entertain you for awhile. All set? Orphan to orphan—over!

That Orphan Choir is a bit weak tonight. I could train a quartet of mosquitoes to do better than that! . . . [plays music selection]
    Shucks! I'm feeling all conscience-stricken over making that crack about my Orphan Family. You can't help being a bit on the Dopey side, can you Boys? Sure, that's right! Mama knows! Now where's that Orphan Choir?
    And here she is! Punctual, alert, and smiling—her radiant personality electrified all those in the studio as she addressed herself to her vast world-wide audience—what's *that* you say?—who is it?—Aw shucks! It's me of course—can't a girl give herself a little build-up when there's nobody else to do it?—you wait—you'll be sorry—In the meanwhile, you heartless wretches, here's Andre Kostelanetz . . .

Is this treason? Or is it merely a young girl bantering in a typically American way with GI listeners for whom she feels obvious affection? However one answers that question, Iva certainly should be admired for slipping in pro-Allied remarks whenever she could. This example, recorded and transcribed by monitors in the United States late in 1945, required special courage:

It was wonderful spending a few musical moments with you fighting heroes in the Pacific. So, so long orphans, and just like the Pacific war, I was never meant to go against you. So 'til tomorrow night, this is Orphan Annie.[49]

However innocuous the actual *Zero Hour*, it did have one peculiar characteristic. The announcers kept asserting that propaganda intended to undermine morale filled the broadcast. Over and over, scripts contained statements such as:

> Hello there, Enemies—how's tricks? This is Ann of Radio Tokyo, and we're just going to begin the *Zero Hour* for our Friends—I mean, our Enemies!—in Australia and the South Pacific. So be on your guard, and mind the children don't hear! All set? O.K., here's the first blow at your morale—the Boston Pops . . .

> And now while Annie arranges her dose of homesick pills, slide up and take this. [plays "I've Got Rhythm"]

> Hello, hello again, once again, to all my favorite friends. Here is Orphan Anne with some of that stuff some people label propaganda.

> Tonight we open with selections from "You're in Love," a little hate propaganda composed by . . .

> Greetings, Everybody! How are my victims this evening? All ready for a vicious assault on your morale?

> This is your favorite playmate, Orphan Ann of Radio Tokyo, the little sunbeam whose throat you'd like to cut, ready again for a vicious assault on your morale.

> Dangerous enemy propaganda, so beware? [question mark in original]

> We close up another chapter of sweet propaganda in the form of music for you, my dear little orphans wandering in the Pacific . . .

> [another announcer] That was Ann and all her vile propaganda.

Whether Cousens believed he must interject such sentiments to convince the Japanese that propaganda really did pervade *Zero Hour* or whether he intended to warn listeners that some segments of the program might contain propaganda is not clear. Whatever the reason, his explicit announcements harmed Japanese interests. In stating that the music was a "vicious assault on your morale," he undermined the likelihood that it would affect Allied servicemen's morale. Furthermore, effective cognitive propaganda depends upon an audience's believing what it hears. If one announces, "What follows is propaganda," it means that what follows cannot serve as propaganda. However, Cousens did not, and could not reasonably have been expected to, foresee that in the distant future, those already convinced of Tokyo Rose's guilt would take his claims of "vile propaganda" at face value and view them as evidence of treasonable conduct.

Iva Toguri never worked on any program other than *Zero Hour*. She never worked Sundays, and in 1945, stopped working Saturdays as well. As her POW friends disappeared, either ill or reassigned to other duties, and as the war wound down, she began to show up for work less and less. In the late Spring and Summer of 1945, we find scripts with,

> Hello to the Pacific. Yes, it's time for that sweet and languid music. And our friendly hostess, Orphan Ann, sends her regrets and says she couldn't make it this evening. But good old trooper that she is, she said the show must go on.

Anyone tuning in after this announcement might not realize the woman speaking was not Iva.

The Japanese, for their part, were too busy trying to survive in the final months of the war to keep track of absenteeism at Radio Tokyo. Police vigilance melted away under the pressure of incessant bombing. As the war neared its conclusion, Iva ceased her mandated check-ins with the police and did not bother asking their permission to travel. With respect to *Zero Hour* itself, Japanese reporter Kato summarized its trajectory in this way: "During much of the war, its producers were careful to keep it free from obvious propaganda, and it was submitted as pure entertainment, with American songs and orchestrations that could not be easily heard from any other source. The cynical theory behind the show was to play on the well-known disposition of troops to become homesick. Finally, the Army began to feel that it was a waste of time and insisted that a certain amount of obvious propaganda be introduced. It is doubtful if the program accomplished any purpose thereafter."[50] The Imperial Army's officer in charge of propaganda,

Tsuneishi, admitted under cross-examination at Iva's trial that his intention to use the program had been thwarted by Japan's unremitting series of defeats. As a result, "the opportunity did not present itself for me to present the real true propaganda broadcasts that I wished to."[51]

The entire case against Iva Toguri for treason rests upon her broadcasts. The U.S. government did not allege that any of her actions outside the studio aided the Japanese. That is not to say prosecutors did not use those actions against her. Iva's refusal to renounce her citizenship helped them greatly. Had she agreed to accept Japanese citizenship, proving a charge of treason against the United States would have been difficult, perhaps legally impossible. Fortunately for the DoJ, Iva Toguri firmly resisted pressure from Japanese Metropolitan, Special Security, and Military Police and maintained her status as an American citizen. In a terrible irony, her stubborn patriotism enabled her prosecution by U.S. authorities.

Notes

1. The date was Iva's best recollection at trial. Trial Transcript, vol. XLV, 4988.

2. Robbins asserts that "[*Zero Hour*] became notorious after the war as the inspiration for the Tokyo Rose myth (*Tokyo Calling*, 142)." Given that a female voice (Iva's) did not appear on *Zero Hour* until early November 1943, whereas Tokyo Rose was reported to broadcast shortly after the attack on Pearl Harbor, the program clearly could not be the inspiration of the myth. Robbins may mean that the Americans mistakenly believed Tokyo Rose first broadcast on *Zero Hour* due to publicity associated with Iva's arrest and prosecution. However, this too is highly unlikely. If the American public paid such close attention to the details of the case, it would not still believe today that Tokyo Rose actually existed.

3. Iva has sworn to Cousens' instructions in depositions, at trial, and in interviews, including my own. Cousens also testified that he so instructed her. Trial Transcript, vol. XXVIII, 3186; see chapter 17. On the one hand, it seems somewhat peculiar for him to make such promises, especially when he had no good reason to think he could keep them if the Japanese insisted otherwise. So, it is possible he and Iva invented the instructions later to keep her out of prison. Against this is the fact that their testimony

cohered, and yet they lost touch with each other unexpectedly after 1944, long before such testimony would have been foreseen. It seems to me more likely he made such assurances to obtain her cooperation initially so he could avoid having Foumy Saisho or some other announcer assigned to him.

4. According to Iva at trial, Cousens informed her of the POWs' clandestine plan to undermine any propaganda in the *Zero Hour* news broadcasts around Christmas 1943. Trial Transcript, vol. XLVI, 5103. This rings true. It makes sense that the POWs would be discreet with Iva initially until they were certain about her loyalties.

5. "Throaty," Phil, Trial Transcript, vol. XLIV, 4845; "husky," Namikawa in Short, *Film & Radio Propaganda*, 327; "brassy," announcer's intro on *Zero Hour*, July 10, 1945, NARA 10, Box 754; "frog," Iva, 1987 interview; "WAC," Cousens' description according to Iva, Trial Transcript, vol. XLV, 4989; "hacksaw," Tamba, Trial Transcript, vol. XXVIII, 3083; "awful masculine," Cousens, letter to Buck Henshaw, October 16, 1948, NARA 2, Box 11.

6. Handwritten letter of Kenneth Irwin, December 11, 1947. NARA 1, Box 41.

7. Ince is the only person to remember this particular story, and he recounts it in a statement given to FBI agents Tillman and Dunn. None of their transcriptions are entirely trustworthy. Iva herself says that she saw "ANN" on the script and that inspired her to choose "Orphan Ann" as her name. No one knows for certain how she came to adopt "Ann," but to me Ince's recollection has the ring of truth. See Statement of Wallace Ellwell Ince, October 19, 1948, 3. NARA 2, Box 3.

8. Robbins' claim (*Tokyo Calling*, 145) that Iva adopted the name Orphan Ann "at the suggestion of Cousens" is contradicted by Ince and Iva and not supported by Cousens in his trial testimony (vol. XXVIII, 3195–96).

9. "Statement of Major Charles Cousens" to CIC, APO343, October 28, 1945, 2. NARA 2, Box 9. I find it difficult to believe that at the same time Iva called herself Orphan Ann, Cousens coincidentally heard about this expression. His suggestion that GI listeners would infer from Iva's calling them orphans that she wasn't Japanese is preposterous. More likely, after the Tokyo Rose brouhaha exploded, Cousens recognized the name as a potential problem and made up this explanation, whereas Iva remained oblivious to the term's possible misinterpretation.

10. Iva's memories of her conversations with Takano and Yamazaki are from her Notes.

11. "Statement of Major Charles Cousens" to CIC, APO343, October 28, 1945, 1. NARA 2, Box 9.

12. In the movie, the Japanese force a British POW, Colonel Nicholson, to build a bridge across the Kwai river. Nicholson's professionalism takes hold of him to the extent that he not only builds a strong, substantial bridge but he defends it against Allied saboteurs. I do not mean to suggest that Cousens was as obsessive as Nicholson, but anyone who takes pride in his or her work understands how difficult it would be to do one's job badly, day after day. Iva's growth under his tutelage made the war more bearable for both. Although Iva's becoming a good announcer did to some extent help the Japanese, reasonable observers would not, in my opinion, believe either one's conduct constituted treason.

13. Both photos were taken after the war by U.S. photographers. Figure 8.2 is dated October 21, 1948, and "depicts exact setup as existed at time of overseas broadcasts of Zero Hour program." NARA 2, Box 7. Figure 8.1 is a posed shot of Iva, dated September 22, 1945, for the motion picture unit of the Army Signal Corps. NARA 8, Box 570, Photo #289962.

14. Sumiko Ruth Hayakawa, born November 4, 1919, in Fukuoka, Japan, was brought to the United States in 1921. According to Toguri Notes, "She was the announcer who took my place on Sundays." Hayakawa's deposition at trial comports with this. In 1987, Iva denied Hayakawa was ever on Zero Hour.

15. Born December 19, 1922, in Lemoore, Kings County, Calif. FBI Report, NARA 3, Box 6.

16. Figure 8.3, "Manila Myrtle," Yank, The Army Weekly, June 29, 1945, 9. Robbins (Tokyo Calling, 148) mistakenly states that her name was "Myrtle Lipman." Depositions of Buddy Uno and Ken Murayama use the name "Myrtle Liston," but because Yank spoke directly to Lipton, I assume that name is correct.

17. All quotations, unless otherwise noted, from Ozzie St. George, "Manila Myrtle," Yank, June 29, 1945, 9. Lipton's own quote below from same.

18. Clark Lee claimed Iva had mixed feelings about the success of the Doolittle raid and the war itself. See Lee's transcript at NARA 1, Box 42 and Trial Transcript, vol. VII, 589.

19. Gunn, Duus, and Howe; see Bibliography.

20. Masayo Duus interviewed Alaga in 1977; he did not name the colonel. I am indebted to her for the particulars of the Lipton interview. Duus, Orphan of the Pacific, 198–203.

21. Depositions of Ken Murayama and Buddy Uno, March 22, 1949, in Tokyo. NARA 2, Box 9.

These depositions are untrustworthy because they occur long after the war, when the Tokyo Rose story had been widely publicized, and because the two men discussed their recollections beforehand. For example, both men recalled Lipton used the name Sadie on the air. Uno at one point (p. 24) even snapped his fingers and exclaimed, "I know I heard her referred to as 'Sadie.'" But as noted above, Lipton told *Yank* that her scripted name was Mary but that she wound up using her own name instead.

22. Murayama claimed in his deposition (p. 4) that Lipton's program "came on with the playing of 'Auld Lang Syne.'" Uno also stated (p. 13) her program "had a regular theme song 'Waterloo Bridge' 'Auld Lang Syne.'" (The 1940 movie *Waterloo Bridge* prominently featured "Auld Lang Syne.")

23. CIC, File 80-T-5, January 19, 1945, 21. NARA 2, Box 9.

24. "The Japanese took over three of the shortwave stations in the Philippines, all in Manila. These stations were the two well-known broadcasters KZRH and KZRM, and the lesser-known KZRF." See http://www181.pair.com/otsw/Wavescan/wavescan346.html. On October 14, 1943 KZRH changed its call letters to PIAN. FBIS transcripts show reception from PIAN, PIAM, PIRM, RPRM, and RPRN. I assume transcribers simply could not hear the call letters clearly.

25. During the final quarter of 1944, when everyone agrees Lipton broadcast, only one mention of "Auld Lang Syne" appears in transcripts. The transcript of a Tagalog program from December reads, "The program started when the 'Auld Lang Syne' was about to end." NARA 10, Box 398.

26. Transcript, FBIS, Station RPRM, 6:00 AM, December 8, 1944. NARA 10, Box 398.

27. NARA 10, Box 398.

28. Manila under Japanese control used Tokyo Time. 6:00 AM EWT used by the FBIS in Portland = 7:00 PM in Manila. See chapter 15, note 86.

29. This program ends with the "Triumphal March." NARA 10, Box 397.

30. Obviously, I cannot be sure about these rumors. In truth, I'm just passing along rumors of rumors. So much of the material on Myrtle Lipton is circular, with sources quoting each other without any substantive basis. That is why the disappearance of her interview and radio transcripts is so frustrating.

31. Citing her privacy, the FBI refused to identify or allow me to read their files on Lipton unless I obtained her permission, provided them with a death certificate, or could prove she was more than 100 years old. Obviously, I could not comply.

32. Hayakawa deposition, Trial Transcript, vol. XXXV, 4001. NARA 2, Box 9. Iva quotations from Toguri Notes. See also her negative views on Chiyeko Ito in chapter 17.

33. Letter to Ivan Chapman, 1985, cited in *Tokyo Calling*, 160.

34. Saisho's remarks about the name "Tokyo Rose" are from Saisho's statement of October 4, 1945, to the U.S. Army Counter Intelligence Corps (CIC), part of HQ CIC Metropolitan Unit 80 documents of January 10, 1946. NARA 1, Box 43, also 40. Her March 31, 1949, deposition and interview with Tillman may be found in NARA 1, Box 45. Saisho at the time was an editor for *Readers Digest* in Tokyo.

35. Trial Transcript, vol. V, 368.

36. Deposition of Foumy Saisho, interview conducted by Iva's attorney, Ted Tamba. NARA 2, Box 7.

37. Saisho graduated in 1932, received a master's degree from the University of Michigan in 1933, and returned to Japan in April 1934. Deposition, March 31, 1949. NARA 1, Box 45.

38. So Cousens testified at his inquest. See Chapman, *Tokyo Calling*, 277.

39. Saisho's denial that she announced, and her use of "Japs" are from Saisho, Statement, October 4, 1945, HQ CIC Metropolitan Unit 80, January 10, 1946. NARA 1, Box 43, also 40.

40. Letter to Ivan Chapman, 1988, cited in *Tokyo Calling*, 155.

41. Letter to Ivan Chapman, 1985, cited in *Tokyo Calling*, 156.

42. Prosecutor Wilfred Robert "Bill" Dovey claimed that women in general tell lies more effectively than men and that Saisho was one of two women who were the best witnesses he ever had. From his serialized memoirs in the *Daily Mirror*, October 19, 1967. See Chapman, *Tokyo Calling*, 248.

43. The letter itself was not produced, so it remains his word against hers. The two did work closely together for years and at least feigned friendly relations. They signed their scripts "Foumy/Bill" and Cousens replied to her letter with a small gift of cigarettes. Cousens told the CIC that "I got on quite friendly terms with three or four [women at the station]" and he named Suyama, Kato, Saisho, and Toguri. CIC Interrogation, October 25, 1945, Exhibit VII in January 10, 1946 report. NARA 2, Box 9. Other POWs such as Buck Henshaw testified Cousens warned them she was a *kempei* agent, which Saisho also denied.

44. "Henshaw also remembered another letter coming from Saisho—in August 1944: 'Major Cousens laughed and when I looked up, he said, "You people think you have problems. Look at the sort of thing I have to contend with." "He gave me the letter to read. I recall it was extremely 'mushy.' (Laughter)." Chapman, *Tokyo Calling*, 298.

45. Chapman, *Tokyo Calling*, 357. Photo ML MSS 7043/7/2; the Papers of Ivan Chapman; Mitchell Library, State Library of New South Wales, Australia.

46. The elements of treason and the requirements for proving it are defined by Article III, Section 3 of the U.S. Constitution and by *Cramer v. U.S.*, U.S.N.Y., 325 U.S.1, 65 S.Ct. 918, 932, 89 L.Ed. 1441. See 18 U.S.C.A., §2381. For further discussion, see chapter 15.

47. Conductor and music producer Mitch Miller hosted a television program in the 1960s during which a choir sang popular songs as lyrics scrolled across the screen. Miller encouraged viewers to follow the bouncing ball highlighting the lyrics and sing out loud in their living rooms. "Sing along with Mitch" was hugely popular.

48. Copies of this and other quoted scripts may be found in dozens of locations. See, for example, NARA 1, Boxes 41, 46, and 47.

49. FBIS transcript, Tokyo English language broadcast of May 21, 1945, 2. NARA 10, Box 742. The words "orphans" and "war" are the best guess of the transcriber of an unclear transmission.

50. Kato, *The Lost War*, 142.

51. Trial Transcript, vol. V, 321

Figure 9.1. Milton Caniff, creator of the Dragon Lady, made this drawing in 1976 to aid the nationwide effort to obtain a pardon for Iva Toguri. It represented his "vision of the woman GIs thought of when they heard 'Tokyo Rose.'"
Courtesy of Harry Guyton for the Estate of Milton Caniff.

9

Tokyo Rose

The Legend of the Radio Siren

The origins of Japanese propagandist Tokyo Rose—the date of the first broadcast attributed to her and even her name itself—are a mystery.[1]

Reporter Clark Lee spent much of the war tracking down witnesses to those broadcasts of Tokyo Rose that announced Allied troop and ship movements and that predicted military attacks. In the end he admitted, "I never found anyone who actually had heard such broadcasts himself. It was always the guy in the next tent."[2] Trying to discover the first time anyone ever heard a broadcast by, or even the name "Tokyo Rose" is similarly frustrating.

The first book about the Tokyo Rose case appeared in 1977. The author, Rex Gunn, was a Pearl Harbor veteran and GI war correspondent for the 7th Army Air Corps picture magazine, *Brief*.[3] He attended Iva Toguri's trial and, in his book, he painted a sympathetic portrait of her and the injustice of that proceeding. In addition, Gunn tried to unravel the truth about the genesis of Tokyo Rose:

[December 8, 1941] In the wake of the shocking news, submariners cruising in U.S. submarines in the waters below the Philippines as far as the South China Seas tuned in on Radio Tokyo. They heard many announcers trumpeting the news of the Japanese victory at Pearl Harbor. The cold, hard voice of one woman in particular caught their attention. She was introduced over

shortwave as "Madame Tojo." Speaking in excellent English, she
delivered taunts about the location of the American fleet.

Early on the morning of December 11, 1941, one of those taunts
via shortwave from Radio Tokyo was picked up by a U.S. subma-
riner, and he recorded it in the ship's log. He wrote:

*"'Where is the United States fleet,' jeered Tokyo Rose . . . 'I'll tell you
where it is, boys. It's lying at the bottom of Pearl Harbor.'"*

As far as anyone has been able to learn from a review of wartime U.S. Navy logs it was the first time that the name, "Tokyo
Rose," had been recorded.[4]

In his reference notes, Gunn cites Roscoe Tanner's *United States
Submarine Operations in WWII*, published in 1949. However, an examination of Tanner's book shows only the following, reproduced
in its entirety:

> "Where is the United States Fleet?" jeered Tokyo Rose, introduced
> by a jiujitsu rendition of *It's Three O'clock in the Morning*. "I'll tell
> you where it is, boys. It's lying at the bottom of Pearl Harbor."[5]

Tanner does not mention anything about a log entry, nor does he
record a date of December 11, nor does he mention a Madame Tojo.
("Madame Tojo" is also enigmatic. Gunn believed this was the nom
de guerre of Foumy Saisho. Others think it was a generic moniker
like "Tokyo Rose" that servicemen invented to refer to any female
voice they heard on Japanese radio.) No particular submarine is
associated with this quotation in Tanner's text, and he cites no reference for it. Why Gunn believed that some researcher looking for
Tokyo Rose references had conducted a review of the radio logs of
the dozens of submarines in the Asiatic Fleet is unclear.[6]

Tanner very likely got his Tokyo Rose quotation from a book
by Gerold Frank and James D. Horan, published in 1945, on the
exploits of the submarine USS *Seawolf*. This book purports to be a
chronicle told to the authors by J. M. Eckberg, Chief Radioman of
the *Seawolf*. Eckberg remembers,

> I was alternately asleep and awake, and finally gave up alto-
> gether, wandering into [the *Seawolf*'s mess hall] in time to hear a
> tinny jazz band playing "It's Three O'Clock in the Morning." It
> was Radio Tokio, and Tokio Rose was on.[7]

Eckberg mentions no specific date in connection with this incident, although one can infer from the context that it probably was December 11, 1941. He continues,

> She was a female [traitor] who had sold out to the Japs, and she opened her program with old-fashioned sentimental songs. The idea was, I suppose, to make us homesick. She was taunting us now about Japanese victories and Allied defeats. She sunk the U.S. fleet as we listened, night after night. "Where is the great United States fleet?" she began in her phony Oxford accent. "I'll tell you where it is! It's lying at the bottom of Pearl Harbor." She went on to tell us all the details. Her voice rose hysterically:
> "Why don't you give up, you fools out there? You can't stand up against the power of the Imperial Fleet!"
> There were all sorts of stories about Tokio Rose. One was that she was an Englishwoman who'd married a Jap. We listened, amazed at the statistics she reeled off to prove we were being licked. She gave names and tonnage of the ships she said we had lost, and the dates and the places. . . . As Tokio Rose cited the destruction of the American fleet, [a fellow submariner] took down the names of the ships. "She's all wrong," he'd say mildly. "We did not have that many ships in the fleet in the first place."[8]

The first important point to make about this account is that Eckberg nowhere claims the female broadcaster herself used the name "Tokyo Rose." The U.S. government's conclusion, mentioned in chapter 3, that "there is no Tokyo Rose; the name is strictly a G.I. invention"[9] means that Eckberg heard the name later in the war, not on the radio that night. That his memories must include many later broadcasts or rumors of broadcasts is clear from his statements that "night after night" the female announcer sunk the American fleet and that she taunted them about Japanese victories and Allied defeats. Finally, the anachronistic nature of Eckberg's recollections is obvious in his remark that Tokyo Rose's purpose was to make GIs homesick. American military personnel in the Pacific in early December 1941 were not yet susceptible to homesickness. The inductees who arrived later and fought for years might have been vulnerable to homesickness, but not professional sailors like Eckberg, only a few days into the war.

In sum, Gunn's account rests on Tanner's account, which rests on Eckberg's memories. There the search for the first broadcast of Tokyo Rose reaches a dead end. As will be seen later, Eckberg could not have heard a propaganda broadcast by a woman on December 11. The radio logs of the USS *Seawolf* no longer exist. The U.S. Navy routinely destroyed them without much delay, probably before the war was over and certainly before any researcher would have thought to examine them. The War Patrol logs, which the Navy saved, contain no mention of Tokyo Rose.[10]

~

Rex Gunn and subsequent investigators have approached the Tokyo Rose phenomenon in terms of the memories of American servicemen. Suppose instead one starts from the Japanese side. The Federal Broadcasting Intelligence Service (FBIS) recorded all Japanese shortwave radio broadcasts from February 1941 through the conclusion of the war. The U.S. government lost or destroyed most of the recordings but did preserve the transcripts. Can these transcripts provide us, to some extent, with a factual basis for American memories? The short answer is no.

Legend: Shortly after Pearl Harbor, on or about December 11, 1941, Eckberg reported a radio broadcast from Tokyo. "Where is the United States fleet?" jeered Tokyo Rose. "I'll tell you where it is, boys. It's lying at the bottom of Pearl Harbor."

Factual Basis: 1) An unnamed woman broadcast on Radio Tokyo for 15 minutes on December 14, 1941, and for 15 minutes again on December 21. She said nothing about Pearl Harbor. 2) On January 5, 7, and 8, 1942, an unknown male broadcast from Tokyo the sentence, "Where is the United States fleet?"

That's the extent of the factual basis. From these two tiny seeds—a single sentence and a lone woman's voice—the entire Tokyo Rose legend grew. This outcome is so astonishing, so utterly bewildering, that it demands explanation.

The first mention of Tokyo Rose, as noted in chapter 3, appeared on March 4, 1942, in a report filed by correspondent Robert J. Casey of the *Chicago Daily News*. Casey was with the U.S. Pacific fleet when he cabled,

> With things as they are and with full cognizance of the imperfections pointed out by Tokyo Rose—the female Lord Haw Haw[11]

of the Son of Heaven—it would seem the time had arrived for an inventory of the poltergeist activities of ours. . .

It has been encouraging to one grown weary of communiques where, when and if found, to listen to Tokyo broadcasts. Save for Rose, who rumor identifies as a music student in Hawaii, voices of commentators are mostly midwestern in accent, thoroughly American in pronunciation and use of phrase. You are tempted almost to believe these boys. . . .[12]

Casey apparently assumed readers back in the States required only the briefest introduction to Tokyo Rose. In any case, we can infer from this news report that sailors considered her broadcasts routine by early 1942 and that they already were speculating about her real identity. It is also clear that Casey understood her broadcasts to be in the mode of Nazi propaganda, which predated America's entry into the war. He made no reference to Tokyo Rose's sexiness, seductive come-ons, knowledge of American military secrets, or her ability to address units and individuals by name and rank. These attributes developed later as her legend grew. Elsewhere in his report, he detailed Japanese lies about battle results, which he attributed to male commentators.

An examination of all the English-language news broadcasts from Tokyo between December 7, 1941 and March 4, 1942, shows exclusively male announcers. Transcribers in the United States were so shocked to hear a woman's voice that on the rare occasions it happened they noted, "Girl speaks. This is Radio Tokyo Shortwave station of the Broadcasting Corporation of Japan."[13] Tokyo's broadcasters usually reported on the progress of the war, recounted from the Japanese perspective. Eckberg's recollection, "As Tokio Rose cited the destruction of the American fleet, [a fellow submariner] took down the names of the ships. 'She's all wrong,' he'd say mildly. 'We did not have that many ships in the fleet in the first place,'" is an accurate reflection of Japanese propaganda, except that the newscasters who reported inflated figures for U.S. naval losses were exclusively men.

This predominance of males on Radio Tokyo is not surprising. It had nothing to do with Japan's patriarchal society. It simply represented the norm of the times. U.S. radio networks didn't feature any female newscasters either. Women might entertain, like Dinah Shore, or pass along Hollywood gossip, like Hedda Hopper, but they lacked the gravitas, the authority, to present the news, especially war news. The first female reporter on American network television, Nancy Dickerson, did not appear until 1960. One of the most prominent grievances of the Japanese against the United States was American failure to take them seriously. In view of this fact, their employing a woman to broadcast war news to the United States was unthinkable.

This same reticence applied to propaganda as well. Testimony before the Diet (the Japanese parliament) in February 1943, by Kiwai Okumura, Vice-President of the Government Information Board, explained why the Japanese did not employ women in such work.

> It has been suggested that we use women broadcasters whose sweet voices would attract listeners. Of course, women's voices are pleasant and soft, but they lack force and do not give the right impact in announcing heavy losses dealt the enemy or in driving home a strong point, and are thus not suited for propaganda directed against the enemy. At any rate, I am not using any women broadcasters for the present.[14]

American reporters and servicemen had circulated stories of Tokyo Rose's broadcasts for more than a year prior to Okumura's testimony.

Radio Tokyo also presented commentaries. Many commentators broadcast anonymously but some did not. Their names— Mathudi Nathachi, Major Yohshiro Kawakata, Masaji Nagata, Kiyoshi Nogami, Todoshi Sato, Mr. Hajurama, Chu Saito, and the "Compatriot," Ricarte Perez—indicate they too were male.[15] Some of their mangled, slang-filled remarks seem almost funny in retrospect: "What the Japanese people cannot understand and equally shared by millions of American people, is the true war aims of the United States. What in the sam-hill is America fighting for?"[16] But one important theme of these commentaries was that the Americans were disseminating propaganda that exaggerated Japanese naval losses while covering up their own. "They say that the weak dog is a good barker," taunted the Japanese.[17] Why, the commentators wondered, if the U.S. fleet remained intact, did it fail to appear to help Hong Kong, Java (Indonesia), or the Philippines?

Obviously, the Americans were either liars or cowards. It was in this context that the following comments, attributed to Tokyo Rose but in fact broadcast by men, were made:

> Where is the United States fleet? The Japanese certainly would be sorely disappointed were they to be told that the American Navy was actually frightened out of their wits.[18]

> The facts of the past month reveal that the Pacific fleet in Pearl Harbor suffered a far greater damage than what the American public was permitted to know. The American navy failed to make its appearance in defense of the Philippines. What was the U.S. navy doing?
>
> If the American navy is truly sincere in its claims, the one and only thing for them to do is to come out and fight like a man. This is war, and the Japanese navy is ready to meet you in combat.
>
> Every man on the warships of the Japanese fleet is happy that they are destined by God to kill the enemies of mankind led by Roosevelt and his warmongers. The U.S. Navy must meet the cross that God has ordained upon them. The Japanese nation requests that your navy come out and FIGHT![19]

Undoubtedly, these comments galled and infuriated U.S. sailors. But although Japanese men spoke them, American listeners attributed the remarks to Tokyo Rose.

Between December 7 and March 4 (the date of Casey's news bulletin), only one woman broadcast from Tokyo. She did not state her name or use an alias. She addressed not sailors but American women on behalf of the women of Japan. Her purposes meshed with Japanese propaganda policy but her tone sounded nothing like the sensual, belligerent Tokyo Rose.

> Here in Tokyo it is Monday morning and you are having your first Sabbath day since the start of this terrible war, surely the greatest tragedy that has fallen upon mankind. I can understand the pains that are being borne by the mothers who mourn the sudden loss of their sons. I can feel the agony of the young wife, whose husband will no longer come back to her. The same is being felt here on our side. There are many of us here in Japan who have sent our loved ones off never to see them return again.

We know that our men have gone forth with the firm determination that they are going to give their lives that this empire of ours will remain secure. We, Japanese women, find peace in that thought. [unintelligible] no matter which side we may be, our feelings are essentially the same. That feeling is the gratitude that goes out to those who go to their deaths in the defense of their nation and their people.

The address continues for 15 minutes and becomes surprisingly religious.

You, in America, are blessed with abundance; but for us in Japan, this war is a matter of life or death for our own people. Are you aware of the moral obligations of this war that has forced Japan into your enemy's camps? Can you with the honesty of your conscience, confess before the altar of Jesus Christ that this war is a righteous war on your side? Do you honestly believe that the Lord would give you support to such a war? Christ has given us the promise that he will never give up [unintelligible] when they pray to God and He never had. And yet, the great tragedy that befell at Pearl Harbor, Hong Kong, and the Philippines came to you like thunderbolts.[20]

A week later, she broadcast a similar message. No other broadcasts by women are extant in this time period.

The appeal to women, the claim of moral righteousness, the attribution of perfidy to Allied leaders (which I did not include), and the implicit suggestion that the Japanese were so committed to their cause that Americans would be crazy to try to defeat them reminds one of Axis Sally. Casey obviously understood Tokyo Rose in this way, and Japanese commentaries, although by men, would have buttressed this perception. This view of Tokyo Rose lasted into 1943, during which Tokyo Rose changed from a cognitive, Nazi-style propagandist to a sex symbol. We can track this transition through the movie, magazine serial, and book, *Destination Tokyo*.

In early 1943, Steve Fisher wrote a screenplay for the movie *Destination Tokyo*, which began production on June 21. The fictional drama starred Cary Grant as a captain who slips his submarine into Tokyo Bay in order to place American spies on the mainland. Their mission is to prepare for the Doolittle Raid. Fisher based his movie script on a few actual occurrences—a riveting scene of a pharmacist's mate performing an emergency appendectomy is based on a similar event aboard the USS *Seadragon*—as well as scuttlebutt he'd picked up while talking with submariners and other service personnel. In his script, after the sailor/spies make it to the Japanese mainland, they hide in a cave where they set up their radio.

> *Sailor*: "Picking up anything, Sparks?"
>
> *Sparks*: "Tokyo Rose giving out with that nightly guff to the USA. Listen to this."
>
> *Tokyo Rose*: "[unintelligible] have never been defeated in a war. The sooner you Americans realize that Japan is invincible, the better. So perfect is the iron ring of defense her great leaders have built around us that no American ship dares approach within 500 miles of our sacred shores. The submarine menace has been entirely removed. The American Navy is afraid to tell its people of the tremendous losses suffered at the hands of the Imperial Japanese fleet."
>
> *Sailor*: "Listen, lieutenant, if you don't need me for a while, I'll bum a ride to Tokyo and silence that dame but good." CUT to sub.[21]

When Sparks states he is listening to Tokyo Rose, the sailor doesn't reply, "Who?" Screenwriter Fisher expected the American public to recognize the name. In any event, the movie was a huge success when it broke wide January 1, 1944, and its release considerably strengthened the American public's perception that Tokyo Rose was a real person. Note that Fisher's scripted patter still sounds like Axis Sally. The vocal delivery in the film is flat, not sexy. This Tokyo Rose does not make references to faithless wives, attacks on morale, taunts, or Pidgin English mistakes in grammar; she simply states her opinions as to Japanese superiority.

Fisher also serialized a book by the same title in *Liberty* magazine between October 30 and December 11, 1943. In the text version of the story, the sailors listen to Tokyo Rose while still on the submarine:

> And that night, the ship already approaching the Japanese mainland, he stood with the men in the forward room listening to the radio broadcast of Tokyo Rose. This would make him hate

them, if anything would. He knew Tokyo Rose well. She was an English girl who had sold out to the Japanese. She had a Japanese husband, and she was quite pretty. She was broadcasting short-wave from Tokyo. In spite of the static, her voice sounded clearly through the loudspeaker.[22]

Notice that this dovetails perfectly with Radioman Eckberg's recollection that "she was an Englishwoman who'd married a Jap." The dialog that follows this passage is almost exactly the same as what appears in the movie, the script for which had to be written between March and May 1943. Thus, the view of Tokyo Rose as a political commentator who offered arguments and reasons why Japan was invincible had not changed. However, Fisher added the information that she was "quite pretty," a sexualization of Tokyo Rose that servicemen did not apply to Axis Sally.

The final iteration, the hardback book, was published immediately following the *Liberty* serialization. It appeared with the release of the movie during the Christmas/New Year's holiday season of 1943–1944. In the book, Fisher makes a crucial change to the scene above.

And that night, the ship already approaching the Japanese mainland, he stood with the men in the forward room listening to the radio broadcast of Tokyo Rose. This would make him hate them, if anything. He knew Tokyo Rose quite well. She was an English girl who had sold out to the Japanese. She had a Japanese husband, and she was quite pretty. She was a whore, of course, a nymphomaniac. Her choice of Japs in the first place had been a perverted physical attraction.

They had her tuned in. She was broadcasting shortwave from Tokyo. In spite of the static, her voice sounded clearly through the loudspeaker.[23]

Whether servicemen like Eckberg followed Fisher's lead or Fisher followed theirs is unknown. Whatever happened, it is clear that around the end of 1943, GIs began to view Tokyo Rose as a sexual fantasy in addition to being an enemy propagandist.

~

Japan's male broadcasters taunted the American Navy to come out and fight, and reported military news, considerably distorted in favor of Japan. Although it makes no logical sense to put such announcements into the mouth of Tokyo Rose, the actual broadcast of taunts presumably was the basis for that aspect of her legend. Tokyo Rose also was rumored to address GIs by name and unit. Since much Japanese programming featured POW messages that identified the POWs by name and sometimes unit, presumably those messages are the basis for that aspect of her legend. But where did the notion that she talked about unfaithful wives and girlfriends originate? Transcripts of *Zero Hour* and other Japanese programs manifest no commentaries along these lines. Did servicemen create such sentiments out of whole cloth?

We know that they thought often about the women they'd left behind, as in these memories of U.S. Marine Don Huebner:

> In 1944, Guadalcanal had evolved into a major supply base of operations with over one hundred thousand men and miles of supply dumps containing the material of war.
>
> Our communication section installed loud speakers high up in palm trees and wired in radio reception for "background" music to enhance our easy life. Armed forces radio provided most of the music and news but often we switched over to hear Tokyo Rose who had a large collection of American "big band" records.
>
> She amused us as she spoke softly to us about our sorry plight and explained how easy it would be to end our misery by simply placing a grenade beside our temple and pull the pin. Nothing but sweet peace and silence thereafter. We grinned at one another and wondered where to address a fan letter to the charming little lady.
>
> We hadn't seen a WHITE woman in many moons and this topic was foremost in all bull sessions, with favorite foods running a close second. Tropical moonlight effected [sic] all of us to the utmost and we young bucks yearned for feminine companionship during those long balmy nights [capitalization in original].[24]

The fact that GIs longed for the women back home doesn't explain why they claimed that Tokyo Rose taunted them about these women being faithless. It also doesn't explain why they believed Tokyo Rose constantly talked about sex in general. Because transcripts do not evidence salacious chit-chat and very few remarks that might be construed as sexual innuendos, it is difficult to comprehend how, by the end of the war, Tokyo Rose's taunts and sexy banter had become the predominant aspect of her fame.

An often-overlooked possibility is that the basis for her new sexual persona lay in the American music she played. As the *Zero Hour* attained greater popularity and more servicemen identified Tokyo Rose with the disk jockey Orphan Ann, the sexier the legend became. The best explanation for this is not Iva Toguri's on-air comments but the music. Iva's introductions of a musical selection took about 20 seconds. The selection might last 3 minutes. The songs, which the men knew well, stimulated their imaginations far more than the intros.

Take this example from an August 1944 *Zero Hour* broadcast of musical "requests." It features a second woman, whom I cannot identify, who sounds every bit as American as Iva does.

> *Iva*: "I see Betty's getting impatient for her request for the evening. Oh, come on, don't hold back. What do you want to hear? Don't be bashful."
> *Betty*: "Can you oblige with 'My Heart Belongs to Daddy,' Bea Wain doing the vocal of course."
> *Iva*: "Well! No sooner said than done."[25]

Elapsed time, 17 seconds. Then Bea Wain, who sang with the Larry Clinton orchestra, used almost 3 minutes for a deep-throated, sensual rendition of the song. Those familiar with its lyrics know it concerns a young woman's struggles with fidelity. She worries that "While tearing off a game of golf / I may make a play for the caddy" and "If I invite a boy some night / To dine on my fine finnan haddie / I just adore his asking for more."[26] Nonetheless, at the end of each verse she coos "my heart belongs to Daddy." One can easily imagine that Daddies who had not been home in months and years might fear the worst.

Sexual/romantic songs appeared almost every night. Iva presented "St. Louis' Blues" and Maxine Sullivan sang, "I hate to see that evening sun go down / 'Cause my lovin' baby done left this town . . . Oh, my man's got a heart like a rock cast in the sea / Or else he wouldn't have gone so far from me."[27] Even when Iva introduced an orchestral tune like Ray Noble's "Blue Moon," her orphan choir sang along, at least in their minds, "And then there suddenly appeared before me / Someone my arms could really hold / I heard you whisper 'Darling please adore me' / And when

I looked to the moon it had turned to gold / Blue moon, now I'm no longer alone."[28]

Iva did not choose the records or write the introductions. She apparently never connected in her own mind the propaganda contained in the *Zero Hour* newscasts with her segment of the program. She also seems to have been either innocently oblivious or culpably obtuse to the connection between the music and the effect of that music on her listeners. Sometimes the combination could be invidious, as for example when, as mentioned in the previous chapter, she introduced "Forget If You Can,"

> Don't you remember
> All the silly things we used to do
> The way we laughed
> When we were photographed
> As handsome hat and his ten-timing gal
> Why shouldn't we play
> More happy moments like we used to spend
> They were so perfect
> Too perfect to end
> Let your heart forget if you can.[29]

with the comment, "Yes, you boneheads, forget if you can. Try and forget."[30]

~

If the date of the first broadcast attributed to Tokyo Rose is uncertain, the origin of the name itself is a complete mystery. Various authors, including Gunn, have accepted the report of Army Air Corps Major Joseph Gervais that the name "Tokyo Rose" predated the war, that it was applied to a red-haired American captive of the Japanese on Saipan in 1937.[31] Gervais claimed this captive was the famous pilot Amelia Earhart. According to Gervais, Earhart's fabled round-the-world flight was in fact a spy mission for the United States. In his version, the Japanese spotted her plane over Saipan, forced it to land, and took her prisoner. Gervais was not the only person to have this idea. Norma Abrams, a writer for New York's *Daily News*, notified the FBI in 1944 that her husband, a lieutenant, had written her that "there was a current rumor in the Pacific and South Pacific that [Tokyo Rose] might possibly be Amelia Airhart [sic]." He had heard "that Amelia Airhart had been taken into custody by the Japanese Government and had been educated along Japanese propaganda lines."[32] Such rumors became so widespread that Earhart's husband, George Putnam, a major in Army intelligence stationed in China, snuck through Japanese-held territory to a Marine Corps receiving post on the coast so that he could hear the broadcasts of Tokyo Rose clearly and decide for himself whether the famous propagandist was in fact his wife. Whom he heard is anybody's guess, but Earhart's sister, Muriel Morrissey, recounted that, "After listening to the voice for less than a minute, GP said decisively, 'I'll stake my life that that is not Amelia's voice. It sounds to me as if the woman might have lived in New York, and of course she had been fiendishly well coached, but Amelia—never.'"[33]

Gervais interviewed a man named Kumoi who was, or claimed to be, a top police official in Saipan in 1937. He said that the captive whom everyone called "Tokyo Rosa [sic]" was not Earhart but a 25-year-old American Japanese who was born in Los Angeles.[34] This description, given years after her trial, fits Iva Toguri perfectly. Kumoi had likely confused what he learned from press accounts of the Iva's trial with the "Tokyo Rosa" rumors he had heard from others. The U.S. Army investigated these reports linking Amelia Earhart and Tokyo Rose after the war and found nothing to them.

Other explanations of the name are less fantastic. Biographer Masayo Duus speculates that the "Rose" in "Tokyo Rose" derived from its popularity at the time as a woman's name and in song titles.[35] This might be true, but "Rose" was not among the ten most popular names for girls in 1941.[36] "Rose" did appear in various song titles. But shouldn't that also explain how servicemen named Axis Sally? (She identified herself as "Midge at the Mike.")

Here's my own speculation: "Axis" ends in "s" and "Sally" continues the "sss" sound. In addition, a sally is an attack, an outburst, and a witty saying. Similarly, "Tokyo" has two long "o" vowels, so "Rose" continues the "oh" sound. Plus, since GIs knew Japan as the Land of the Rising Sun, the name works as a statement that Tokyo has risen.

I readily admit my suggestion borders on being crackpot, but I was inspired when I read the *New York Times* headline of July 28, 1941: "Chungking [China] Believes Demands of Tokyo Rose When

French Weakness Was Seen." Since this appeared pre–Pearl Harbor, I thought I had just made an important discovery about the name and this case. That is, until I realized "Rose" in the headline was a verb, not a proper noun. Still, it got me thinking.

The bottom line is that the origin of the name "Tokyo Rose" remains unknown.

~

In summary, Tokyo Rose's early broadcasts never happened and we have no idea how she got her name. The fact that GIs listened to a single female voice speaking about the pain of losing loved ones and the altar of Jesus Christ, and converted that voice into a siren and seductress, demonstrates the malleability of the aural receptors in their brains. Their wartime memories of radio broadcasts cannot be accepted at face value.

This is especially obvious when we consider what Tokyo Rose did *not* broadcast. In actual fact, Japanese radio propaganda during 1942, when the legend formed, focused almost exclusively on purported American military atrocities, the evils of American imperialism, the maltreatment of blacks, Indians, and other minorities in the United States, and the injustice of the internment camps for Japanese Americans. Transcript after transcript contains these themes. In contrast, I have read hundreds of letters from GIs about the content of Tokyo Rose's broadcasts, as well as the recollections of the servicemen who testified under oath at Iva Toguri's trial. Not one ever remembered Tokyo Rose saying anything about American atrocities, imperialism, suppression of minorities, or the injustice of the internment camps. Yet we know from the record that Japanese propaganda emphasized racism and discrimination. This discrepancy is one more proof that the overwhelmingly white American GIs created Tokyo Rose in their own minds. Since they rejected such criticisms out of hand, they never imagined/remembered her saying them. Their blindness to the possibility that U.S. society was discriminatory should come as no surprise when one considers that although 65,000 African Americans served in the U.S. Navy during World War II, in 1945, 95 percent of them still worked as food servers, cooks, or servants to officers.[37]

Therefore, although it might seem perverse, the first step in confronting the legend of Tokyo Rose is to abandon the quest for historical evidence in the form of facts and real events. We must approach Tokyo Rose as though she were a literary or fictional creation. The secret to understanding her is to expose the creative process beneath the surface of the conscious recollections of the military personnel serving in the Far East. If we can appreciate the mythology at work, we have an opportunity to see this legendary woman as she truly is.

~

The United States fought the nation of Japan upon what is ironically called the Pacific, the largest and most violent ocean on Earth. America's warships put to sea manned by sailors from Montana and marines from Kansas. Many of these men had never piloted a dinghy at an amusement park or seen a body of water larger than a swimming hole, but now they found themselves a thousand leagues from shore over an ocean depth measured in miles. The Pacific's storms produced waves that heaved and slammed their craft with such ferocity that they called their battleships, "wagons" and their destroyers, "tin cans." Whatever their bravado with one another, these men were afraid: of never holding their loved ones again, of a grave never visited, and of an unknown enemy with potentially terrible strength.

Just as a fairy tale can help children manage their fears, so too a legend can help adults manage theirs. Faced with a savage death in a lonely place far from home, the soldiers and sailors of World War II created the legend of Tokyo Rose to put a human face on a monstrous and demonic foe. The legend helped reduce their anxieties, created bonds of community with shipmates facing the same terror, and stiffened their resolve.

When people today think of legends, they often remember older stories like King Arthur and the Round Table or George Washington and the Cherry Tree. Legends, however, are not confined to distant history, nor are they the foolishness of simple folk. Therefore, lest we be too quick to smirk at those GIs who believed a radio announcer in Tokyo knew the U.S. military's every maneuver and the names of all its servicemen, we might keep in mind such contemporary phenomena as alligators in New York's sewers, flying saucers, Sasquatch, time channeling, psychics, the Bermuda triangle, plants that experience fear, poltergeists, etc. All of these are legends. This is not to say that legends are a pack of lies or that only fools give credence to them, though this may be true of the above. It is simply to remark that legends are always with us, and we ought not to denigrate their power.

Legendary stories are not history. The oft-repeated tales of broadcasts by Tokyo Rose may no more resemble what really happened than the oak resembles the acorn and the dirt. Legends are born when a group that shares beliefs and emotions interprets events they do not fully understand. The group experiences what happens to them uniquely in terms of their culture, and generally in terms of their humanity. To understand the power of Tokyo Rose to become famous throughout the Pacific theater, we must examine the memories of her broadcasts that made her legend "live."

⌒

The U.S. attacked Vella Lavella, an island in the Solomons, on August 15, 1943. The men aboard the LSTs [Landing Ship, Tank] that carried soldiers and supplies remembered uneasily "a recent boast by Tokyo Rose that no LST will be allowed to land its cargo. She may have known that the Navy Department had allotted only seven machine guns to each LST, but she did not know that, by begging and borrowing, the 'Love-Sugar-Tares' had tripled their fighting equipment for this occasion." The LSTs delivered 6,305 men and 8,626 tons of cargo to Vella Lavella and "proved that Tokyo Rose was not always a good prophet."[38]

When [Japanese] Admiral Kurita broke off action during the Battle of Leyte Gulf, "the American-born Japanese propagandist known as Tokyo Rose, putting her best face on the situation after the battle, commented, '[U.S. Admiral] Kinkaid hallooing for help in plain English showed his great anxiety.' 'She didn't know how true that was!' said the Admiral when it was all over."[39]

Sailors onboard the U.S. heavy cruiser *Indianapolis* listened to Benny Goodman and other American music playing on the ship's system. "McCoy listened as Tokyo Rose butted in over the mess hall's speakers, her mysterious voice spooking him all the way from Japan, saying 'We know you're out there, sailor boy. We know where you are. Don't you wish you could go home?'" A day later, on July 30, 1945, the *Indianapolis* was torpedoed by a Japanese submarine and sank in twelve minutes. Approximately three hundred men went down with the ship. The remaining nine hundred found themselves floating in shark-infested waters with no lifeboats and no food or water. The U.S. Navy never missed the ship, and by the time the survivors were spotted by accident four days later, only 316 men were still alive.[40]

～

When the war began in 1941, more than 80 percent of American homes had a radio.[41] Every evening, families gathered around their sets to hear entertainers like Charley McCarthy and Edgar Bergen, Bing Crosby singing on the *Kraft Music Hall*, Buck Rogers striding undaunted into the 25th century, Fred Allen's droll wit, and Rochester serving as a rock of sanity for the harried Jack Benny as he endured the antics of the loosely wired Dennis Day. Americans knew what to expect from radio. A telephone ringing by the bar would be answered with: "Duffy's Tavern, where the elite meet to eat, Archie the manager speakin', Duffy ain't here—oh, hello Duffy." When Fibber McGee reached for the door of his packed closet, listeners knew to wince, and they loved to hear The Great Gildersleeve's wicked laugh and "You're a haaaard man, McGee!" Late at night, music of the big bands inspired bobbysoxers to roll back the carpets and dance to a new rhythm they called "swing."

Radio made news and gossip available in a flash. Listeners thrilled to the staccato delivery of Walter Winchell. President Roosevelt held fireside chats and spoke personally to ordinary people in their living rooms. When radio scatterbrain Gracie Allen ran for president on the Surprise Party ticket and wrote an article for *Liberty* magazine titled "America's Next President Should Be a Woman," Americans laughed at the ditzy notion.

The other medium of mass entertainment in the 1940s, the cinema, often celebrated glamour. Movies frequently portrayed lives of impossible wealth, sophistication, heroism, beauty. By contrast, radio was regular. The fact that shows came on day after day and night after night and that the performers came right to one's home gave radio the feel of everydayness. Duffy's was a tavern just like the one down the street; Fibber Magee and Molly's farm was just like the one up the road.

Those readers who have grown up in the era of television may have difficulty appreciating the unique appeal of radio as a dramatic medium. Radio when it was new had a ghostly, haunting quality and listeners experienced it as a kind of eavesdropping. Radio told stories, but the storytellers were eerily absent. Radio forced listeners to engage their imaginations, to picture for themselves the rooms, the furnishings, the body shapes, the faces and expressions of those they heard. Listeners had to participate in radio. Shortwave broadcasts, the kind Tokyo Rose employed, heightened this participation. Listening to World War II-era shortwave over distance was like riding a roller coaster. Servicemen could hear the low-powered broadcasts perfectly for a few seconds, then the signal increased in volume until it distorted, then it was perfect again, then it dropped until it became inaudible or blanked out. The hearer had to fill in the missing words according to his own assumptions about what was likely said.

Tokyo Rose had no counterpart before or after World War II. She was, quite literally, *the* radio siren; there was and will be no other.[42] In the case of World War I, radios were rare and not available to ordinary soldiers. In the case of the Korean, Vietnam, and later wars, servicemen would have expected to see her on TV. But in the time of World War II, radio was ascendant, and American GIs huddled in little groups onboard ship or on faraway islands hoping to hear a woman's voice in the fading light. Tokyo Rose was like a dream, and every man's dream was his own. He visualized how she looked from the sound of her voice, which was intimate, brazen, and sexy, and he imagined that, when he went to sleep, she would seduce him.

～

On February 14, 1943, the *New York Times* reported on a submarine patrol: "The men often tune in on Radio Tokyo to hear the cultured, accentless English of a woman announcer they have nicknamed Tokyo Rose. Tokyo Rose pours it on so thick that the little company of Americans in a submarine far from shore who hear her usually get a lot of humor out of her broadcasts."[43]

At the end of 1943, the *New York Times* quizzed its readers about the year's events. One of the questions was "Who is Tokyo Rose?" The answer: "Tokyo Rose delivers Japanese propaganda broadcasts—in cultured English accents—directed to American fighting men in the Pacific. The men are amused by Japan's exaggeration of American losses."[44]

In April 1944, *Time* admitted, "No one knows for sure who Tokyo Rose really is. [Listeners] incline to think she is a Japanese, born on the island of Maui, Hawaii, and educated there. Her voice is cultured, with a touch of Boston.[45]

On June 25, 1944, the *New York Times* reported on a recent broadcast: "Thus spoke Tokyo Rose, in her oft-described Bostonian accent, one recent night, for the benefit of our boys in that battle area. Tokyo Rose generously fills in of [sic] a Sunday evening. And what could be more accommodating than that, save a mass hara-kiri movement on the part of the little Nips?"[46]

Radio Operator Sam Cavnar remembered nothing about her accent, only that her voice was "soft, low, and had a dreamy pitch."[47]

~

A letter of an ordinary infantryman expressed the view of legions:

"I am fighting for America. Well, then what is America? America, to me, is my wife, home, and mother. I am fighting so I can go home to my wife. She is the spirit of Americanism, of truth, purity, love, and devotion. Do you think for one minute all of us soldiers would fight for a big hunk of dirt or for some other men? You bet we wouldn't. We risk our very lives, take chances on being cripples, going blind, and laugh at death. Every dogface has a sweetheart, wife, mother, or a child that he is fighting for."[48]

Many letters home were less philosophical and more direct as soldiers pleaded for their wives to live up to this standard:

So many of the wives are doing their husbands wrong. Barbie, please be good and stick by old Charlie 'til he gets back. I trust you completely so it really must be hard on the fellows who do not trust their wives.[49]

In those cases where wives and sweethearts proved unfaithful, the soldiers felt they had nothing left to fight for and were extremely bitter:

The girls in the states aren't to be trusted. I know that from the way the girls are throwing these guys over to marry some 4-F jerk. These guys are sweating and dying for what? The one I thought was waiting on me threw me over for someone else.[50]

Two more of our boys just got word from their girl friends that they are getting married. Another three fellows from the squadron have received letters from their wives asking for a divorce. Yes sir, I sure am proud of the women back home. I don't imagine they can wear light dresses any more. The streak of yellow they have down their back would surely show through.[51]

The extent to which wives and girlfriends actually abandoned servicemen during wartime is difficult to know, but the phenomenon of the "Dear John" letter, a term coined in World War II, was sufficiently common that *Yank* magazine made printing the worst of them a feature.[52] One girlfriend informed her fiancé near the end of a long letter that she had recently married a "broadminded" sailor who "wouldn't mind you writing me occasionally." Another promised her ex- that he would like the man she married because he was "the most wonderful man in the world." Brush Off clubs sprouted in various localities that allowed men to commiserate their betrayal, or brag about how they didn't care.[53]

The concern among Allied military personnel about faithless wives and girlfriends should not be overstated. U.S. Intelligence, under the command of General Charles Willoughby, developed a monthly report on "morale, rumors, and propaganda." The Office of the Theater Censor prepared the report based on the letters of U.S. military personnel, which the censors read. The following summarizes one typical example, the survey from August 1944, in which censors processed almost 800,000 pieces of mail and analyzed what servicemen wrote to family and friends back home. With respect to morale, they discovered that the areas of greatest concern to both officers and enlisted men were, in order: 1) the failure or slowness of mail delivery, 2) lousy rations, 3) lack of recreation, 4) length of time in combat before being rotated out, 5) command stupidity, 6) poor hospital care, 7) lack of leave, 8) poor health, and, 9) miscellaneous. When servicemen wrote about these subjects, 71 percent of their opinions were unfavorable and 29 percent favorable. The issue of unfaithful wives and girlfriends was not statistically significant enough to merit a mention in the report. In addition, censors catalogued thirty-four rumors in the letters. Of these, twelve were about operational issues or troop movements. "They expect the Japs to use gas in this theater of the war very shortly." "I heard my outfit may go to China." Another twelve concerned return to the States and mail delivery. Of the ten remaining rumors, only one was about the conduct of women back home. "Many boys have told me that the girls at home are desperate for men and even women already married are marrying again." The servicemen did not attribute any rumors, military or otherwise, to the broadcasts of Tokyo Rose. All such rumors came from fellow soldiers.[54]

The later-remembered drumbeat of taunts by Tokyo Rose, given that they never happened, cannot have inspired the widespread concern about faithlessness. One actual cause of the servicemen's fear of infidelity was their own experience of its lure. To combat widespread venereal disease, the U.S. Army conducted an anonymous survey of its fighting forces in Italy in 1945. The Army found that 60 percent of married and 75 percent of unmarried servicemen had engaged in sex while overseas. For those who had been overseas for two years or more, the number jumped to 80 percent.[55] These rates were probably lower in the Pacific and Southwest Pacific theaters, but 50,000 prophylactic treatments administered each month in 1942 to patrons of the Oahu, Hawaii, brothels and the 8,000 prostitutes in the Philippines who greeted MacArthur's conquering army in 1945, along with untold numbers of other women on various isles hoping to escape poverty via an American boyfriend, no doubt kept the Pacific percentages substantial. The survey showed that those soldiers who expressed doubts as to the faithfulness of their womenfolk back home were much more likely to have had sex themselves while overseas. Blaming Tokyo Rose represented an easy way to assuage their guilty consciences.[56]

With respect to propaganda generally, servicemen both dismissed and complimented Japanese efforts. "Listened to radio Tokyo last night and they said Americans invaded Japan last October [1943] with over one hundred forty thousand men. We were annihilated. Do they think we believe that stuff? It is all so outrageous." "The programs the USA sends its men overseas are something. There was a half-hour broadcast by transcription of the actual battle of Guam. Is it any wonder 'Radio Tokyo' is so popular with US troops? Why broadcast the battle of Guam to troops that know the sounds of war from experience." The Theater Censor concluded that although 75 percent of such comments by GIs were about Japanese broadcasts and only 25 percent about the Allied, "the feeling contained in the [comments about Allied radio] is much stronger and more resentful."[57]

∽

Tokyo Rose is an example of what Freud called *overdetermination*: many needs working themselves out in one symbol.

Men crowded together on ships at sea for months or years are sexually deprived. In terms of traditional morality, they have no acceptable outlet for their desires and so they must repress them. This repression has led to the creation of a mythology with a long history.

Before the Navy allowed women to serve, sailors considered a woman on board ship bad luck. The lore of mariners holds that women are a plague to men at sea. The sea's own temptresses, mermaids and sirens, are deadly. Listening to the singing of a mermaid drives men into madness, which allows mermaids to hold them as prisoners. The songs of the sirens are irresistible; they lure sailors to their island's shore where the sirens devour them.

Both mermaids and sirens entice through singing. One might suppose their songs hold out the prospect of sexual gratification, but that is incorrect. The songs promise not sensual pleasure but knowledge. Mermaids have the gift of prophecy.[58] Odysseus strained at his ropes when he heard the Sirens' song: "For we know all things, and we know all that shall hereafter be upon the fruitful earth."[59] Men afraid on the sea lust, but they desire even more to know their fate, which is why the mistresses of the sea have only the heads and breasts of women. Their bodies—fish for mermaids, birds of prey for sirens—are ill-suited to conjugal bliss with human males.

Woman in mythology is often a symbol of knowledge. Thus, Truth usually takes the form of a woman,[60] and Socrates claimed he had an erotic passion for the truth similar to a sexual passion.[61] The sea's women offer a singular allurement: the possibility of knowing the future. The sailors never learn whether the mermaids and sirens really do foresee all things because the women seduce them, and then it is too late: Women keep the seamen for their own.

This subconscious interweaving of sexual desire and knowledge in the psyche of men burdened with fear and deprivation helps explain the legend of Tokyo Rose because Tokyo Rose was just such a temptress. She, like the other sirens, was omniscient. She knew the GIs' names, their families, their hometowns; she knew their unit's position and its battle strength. She knew the future, where their yet-to-be-received orders would take them, where they would attack.

The Tokyo Rose who predicted and then jeered at every Allied stratagem made the Japanese formidable. Enemies ought to be neither children nor gods; they must have the appearance of invincibility and yet be conquerable by a supreme effort. The all-seeing Tokyo Rose provided a daunting foe, but she also alleviated the terror of facing an adversary whose real strength was unknown. She gave a human personality to the faceless killers secreted by the tens of thousands in caves and trees and swamps and jungles. She proved them flawed. Mispronunciations, petty ignorance, reassuring mistakes, and hollow threats tarnished her storied omniscience. Tokyo Rose was, after all, only a woman.

Everyone desires to be known, by others and by oneself. This is a necessity of self-identity, and the fear of losing one's self is high in time of war. What tempts in the temptress is the promise of the fulfillment of a need in the one who is tempted. Tokyo Rose fulfilled the need to be known. Counterintelligence chief Elliott Thorpe said, "No matter how small a unit, each soldier would stoutly maintain his unit had been specifically mentioned on Radio Tokyo."[62]

Even though her listeners realized that she really did not know military secrets, she knew what was important. She knew the hearts of the men from whom she sprang, she knew they were homesick and longed to return safely to the women they loved. For this reason, the servicemen who heard her overlooked the fact that she was an illusion. Instead, they told each other tales of her exploits, and listened lovingly to her lies and songs of propaganda.

I was based aboard one of the aircraft carriers, the USS *Franklin*, and we picked up Tokyo's programs regularly, daily. The programs were part of our daily broadcast on the ship.

Q: You mean it was amplified?

Throughout the ship. We all listened to Tokyo Rose, all twenty-six hundred of us.

Q: Did you have other American broadcasts?

Oh yes, yes. We had our regular programs beamed from short wave stations in the South Pacific. Our radio operator switched in on Tokyo.

Q: Why did they switch in on Tokyo when they had . . .

We enjoyed the program so much. Many times it was taped, and re-broadcast.

Q: Did you personally think that the program was propaganda?

Oh, definitely, definitely!

Q: If you felt this, then why did you listen to it?

It was a, in a way, it was so attuned to various things that we were involved in the South Pacific, and the program was very exciting to us, and different. It was fun to hear a lady's voice during the broadcasting, and she played very unusual things and her news commentary went along with this. It was quite exciting to us.

Q: Did you listen to the program mainly out of curiosity?

We could get [American records] on our own station, but it was more fun to hear her commentary between her pronunciation of various American words. She had very good English, but of course, she had an accent. Her phrases and her sentences were rather hilarious to us, saying, "Aren't you boys very upset you're not at home, and all your girlfriends are drinking sodas with 4Fs down at the corner drugstore."

Q: Did you ever believe her when she made this kind of comment?

No, no. Her sing-song type of voice, her type of delivery made us laugh. I don't think we ever got mad at Tokyo Rose. My commanding officer wanted to fly over Tokyo and drop some flowers for her.

Q: You seem to be highly in favor of her program.

Oh, definitely! Her program was highly ineffective [as propaganda but] highly successful as entertainment. She was delightful. We waited for the program daily. That was one of the highlights of the day.[63]

The sea is not only the mother of life on our planet, it is an abundant source of metaphors and symbols for the human imagination. The legend of Tokyo Rose is especially a legend of the sea.

In its serenity, in quiet repose, the sea is beloved by all peoples. Children burst upon sandy beaches and race toward it with delight. Aphrodite, the goddess of love, was born from its foam. When men go down to the sea in ships, they leave behind a land where humanity is chaotic and boundless; onboard ship, the human is tight and self-contained. A sailor's life requires purpose and clarity, but it also offers time for reflection. On warm nights when breezes of spice and salt air dance like geishas across moonlit decks, men on ships dream and fall in love. As the Milton Caniff drawing that opened this chapter commemorates, such dreams by sailors and by marines on exotic isles is the stuff of which Tokyo Rose was made.

The sea is neither good nor evil; it is indifferent to our morality. The sea has no politics; it renders nothing unto Caesar. On land, the causes of nations ebb and flow, defined by the value of territories held. But there are no territories on the sea. Where armies have engaged, the land is scarred, cities lie in ruins, human bodies are piled in heaps. But where navies have engaged, ships and sailors die and disappear, and the surface of the sea lies undisturbed. The sea brokers no history, is an infidel to every faith, and in its depths infamy and nobility quickly fade away. Aloof and indifferent, the sea is feared by all peoples. Confronted by a mask of waves, our minds imagine what they will of the unseen abyss, and the sea cares naught. The sea tempts and seduces our creativity. She is our mother, and her womb is fertile and rich.

Tokyo Rose tempted and seduced the imaginations of American servicemen, and she cared naught. She was not motherly, not wifely, not like the girl next door. She threatened, taunted, ridiculed, and pledged death and destruction. She was both sexy and cold-hearted, and the soldiers and sailors everywhere upon the sea who created Tokyo Rose both loved and feared her.

∼

As the summer of 1945 wore on, the U.S. military, sensing victory, decided to embrace the mood of relief and elation gathering momentum throughout the nation by having some fun. Captain T.

J. O'Brien issued on behalf of the Navy Department a mock citation to Tokyo Rose:

> The men and women of the Navy, Marine Corps, and Coast Guard take pleasure in presenting this citation to Tokyo Rose of Radio Tokyo, for service as set forth in the following:
> For meritorious achievement while serving as a radio propaganda broadcaster for the Japanese. While the United States armed forces in the Pacific have been extremely busy capturing enemy-held islands, sinking Jap ships, and killing Japs and more Japs, Tokyo Rose, ever solicitous of their morale, has persistently entertained them during those long nights in fox-holes and on board ship, by bringing them excellent state-side music, laughter, and news about home. These broadcasts have reminded all our men of the things they are fighting for, which are the things America has given them. And they have inspired them to a greater determination than ever to get the war over quickly, which explains why they are now driving onward to Tokyo itself, so that soon they will be able to thank Tokyo Rose in person.
> As the Japanese Empire crumbles about her, Tokyo Rose zealously continues to bring laughter and entertainment to our men and women.
> In recognition of this meritorious service, this citation is presented and with it goes permission to broadcast soon to the United States Army of Occupation in Japan and to the ships of the United States Fleet at anchor in Yokohama Bay, the history-making scene of Admiral Halsey riding the Japanese Emperor's white horse through the streets of Tokyo.[64]

Tokyo Rose was by this time famous enough that papers carried news of the citation throughout the country. The exact identity of Tokyo Rose remained undiscovered, but due to consistent coverage in newspapers, two aspects of her legend had hardened into "fact."

First, of the thousands of reports and rumors of her broadcasts swapped as scuttlebutt among servicemen, the one every GI had heard was Tokyo Rose's taunt concerning the sinking of U.S. ships. Starting immediately after Pearl Harbor with the message mentioned at the beginning of this chapter—"Where is the United States fleet? It's lying at the bottom of Pearl Harbor!"—and continuing throughout the war, Tokyo Rose constantly predicted and celebrated the sinking of American ships. In the fall of 1944, the *New York Times* reported,

> For months after the Japanese attack on Pearl Harbor the American-educated woman announcer of Radio Tokyo, known to men of the Pacific Fleet and the marines and soldiers as "Tokyo Rose," would ask rhetorically in nearly every one of her daily broadcasts, "Where is the United States Fleet?" She has had many non-rhetorical answers since Dec. 7, 1941. She long since dropped that propaganda line. It is pertinent now to ask Rose, or whatever her right name may be, "Where is the Japanese Fleet?"[65]

Tokyo Rose may have abandoned the line about the missing U.S. fleet, but she continued to take credit for sunken ships. She even claimed that accidental losses, such as the *Mount Hood*, which sank after a munitions explosion, were the result of Japanese attacks.[66] "Hello, America! You build 'em, we sink 'em!" was a typical remark attributed to her.[67]

The second certainty about Tokyo Rose was that she announced for the *Zero Hour*. On June 19, 1943, Ira Wolfert reported for the North American Newspaper Alliance:

> Between the Tokyo radio and Japanese bombers, the nights are not always dull here. Tokyo has been beaming a program called "the zero hour" directly to the Russell Islands and Guadalcanal. The fellows like it very much because it cries over them and feels so sorry for them. It talks about the food that they miss by not being home and tells how the war workers are stealing their jobs and their girls.[68]

The report says nothing about Tokyo Rose, but the patter is obviously hers. Whoever made this announcement, it could not have been Iva Toguri. Toguri only began working as a clerk at Radio Tokyo in late August 1943, and did not broadcast until November. However, newspapers and magazines of the period reported on other occasions when we know that she was broadcasting that Tokyo Rose hosted the *Zero Hour*. Toguri had been on the air five months when, in April 1944, *Time* magazine unwittingly tagged her as Tokyo Rose:

RADIO By Any Other Name

Tokyo Rose is the darling of U.S. sailors, GIs, and Marines all over the Pacific. She is a Jap propagandist, but her broadcasts are popular among American listeners: she gives them humor, nostalgia, news, entertainment, and good U.S. dance music. In a very feminine and friendly voice she murmurs:

"Good evening again to the all-forgetting and forgotten men, the American fighting men of the South Pacific. The *Zero Hour* to the rescue once again, taking up a few vacant moments you may have to kill. And since this is Monday and therefore Old Timers' night, these few moments will be filled with music for you Old Timers who perhaps like another kind of music . . ."

Tokyo Rose's voice is wafted over the Aleutians and the South Pacific on a stronger, clearer signal than any provided by U.S. radio. She can usually be heard around 8 PM daily, Australian time, short or medium wave, on a 65-minute show designed for U.S. armed forces in the South Pacific. Her specialties, assisted by a male announcer who sounds not unlike Elmer Davis, are *News from the American Home Front* and the jazzical *Zero Hour*.

Tokyo Rose is sometimes uncomfortably close to the truth. Last Aug. 5 [1943] she announced that U.S. forces would land on Kiska on Aug. 17. The landing was Aug. 15. Her broadcasts almost never exaggerate U.S. losses. She has built a reputation on accurate broadcasts.[69]

We recognize the long quotation, "the *Zero Hour* to the rescue . . ." as being very likely a broadcast by Iva. We know the prediction of troop landings the previous August cannot be one of her broadcasts because she was a typing clerk at that time, not a radio announcer. But in a pattern of confusion that would haunt Toguri's case, *Time* linked the earlier broadcasts of Tokyo Rose to the later broadcasts of a woman on *Zero Hour*.

Ironically, on the same day that the Navy announced Tokyo Rose's citation, the U.S. Office of War Information announced the GIs themselves had invented her. The Associated Press added to their coverage of these events, "Tokyo Rose first was mentioned publicly in the spring of 1943 [we now know it was in March 1942] when newspapers carried a story from the Aleutians about a Japanese woman broadcaster known by that name to servicemen in the area." This AP report concluded:

When servicemen speak of Tokyo Rose, they refer to the mistress of ceremonies on the Zero Hour dinner-time program. She has a girlish voice and a manner described as gay and clever. Her apparent purpose is to make her listeners homesick.

The entertainer usually calls herself "Annie of Radio Tokyo," "Little Orphan Annie," or "Your favorite enemy, Annie."[70]

Notes

1. Figure 9.1, Milton Caniff, *New York Times Magazine*, December 5, 1976, used with permission of Harry Guyton for the Estate of Milton Caniff.

2. Lee, *One Last Look Around*, 91.

3. Gunn, born September 28, 1920, in Little Rock, was only a high school graduate when he covered the Tarawa, Abemama, Saipan, Tinian, and Guam campaigns. After the war, he earned a B.A. degree from the University of Oregon at Eugene and began work for the Associated Press in San Francisco on January 1, 1949. Later he received an M.A. from Stanford and a Ph.D. from the University of Southern California. For most of his career, he was an administrator at several California universities. In 1995, he returned to Oahu to marry his Hawaiian sweetheart from his pre-Pearl days. Gunn died in 1999. See http://www.authorhouse.com/BookStore/ItemDetail~bookid~5009.aspx

4. Gunn, *They Called Her Tokyo Rose*, 1.

5. Roscoe Tanner, *United States Submarine Operations in WWII* (Annapolis, Md.: U.S. Naval Institute, 1949), 32.

6. Gunn may well have had other sources—he was a war correspondent—or may have done the research himself. I had the pleasure of spending a day with him many years ago, and he was both charming and knowledgeable. Certainly his heart was in the right place, and he underwrote the cost of publishing his book to bring attention to this injustice, so I am reluctant to quibble.

7. Gerold Frank and James D. Horan with J. M. Eckberg, USS *Seawolf: Submarine Raider of the Pacific* (New York: G. P. Putnam's Sons, 1945), 33.

8. Eckberg's memories of that night are quite specific, which makes me wonder if he kept a personal diary. He recalls that the seas were rough, and the War Patrol Report substantiates this. He also recalls that when he was awakened to listen to sonar, he heard something that sounded like two ships talking to one another. The *Seawolf*'s War Patrol Report mentions that at 1126 on December 10, 1941, "Sound reported that he believed

2 ships were talking by sound on bearing 075°T but that transmission was too faint and rapid for reception." However, in Frank and Horan's book, Eckberg recalls trying to understand the sound. "Suddenly I had it. *Reef fish!* Small, green-bellied 'croakers' which emit a blubbering, bullfroglike grunting under water that can deceive the most expert ear. I reported to the Captain, feeling a little sheepish. 'Fish, Eckberg? Better go back and finish your sleep.'" But the *Seawolf's* commanding officer, Frederick Burdett Warder, makes no mention of the fish episode in his Report, instead remarking that the sounds were most likely caused by "men working in engine rooms." See M1752, War Patrol Reports, *USS* Seawolf, Fiche 919–924, NARA, College Park, Md.

9. *New York Times*, August 8, 1945.

10. On April 7, 1942, Commander Warder submitted his War Patrol Report, Track Charts (the submarine's course) and Tide and Current Charts to the submarine division of the U.S. Asiatic Fleet. All of this is standard practice. In addition, however, he included the Radio Log, which was unusual. A handwritten memo beside the radio log entry reads, "Missing. CNO." CNO? Chief of Naval Operations? Why would the CNO concern himself with a missing radio log? More important, why would Commander Warder have saved and sent it? Did it contain some mention of Tokyo Rose? The mystery lives. War Patrol Reports, *USS* Seawolf, Fiche 919–924, NARA, College Park, Md.

11. Allied service personnel in Europe dubbed various male propagandists for Germany "Lord Haw Haw," of whom the most prominent was the American-born William Joyce.

12. *Los Angeles Times*, March 29, 1942, 3. That Rose is an exception to the rule that Tokyo's propagandists are "thoroughly American in pronunciation and use of phrase" represents a view not taken a year later by the producers of *Destination Tokyo*. I assume Casey meant to describe her as a *former* "music student in Hawaii."

13. This notation concludes many scripts from this period. NARA 10, Box 634. Females also appeared as minor characters in skits before the April 1 expansion: for example, a March 10, 1942, skit with Douglas MacArthur's wife Jean and a March 17, 1942, skit with Mrs. Chiang Kai-Shek. Box 635.

14. *Asahi Evening Edition*, February 8, 1943, trans. by Kazuo Kubota. Document No. 46683, 11–12. NARA 11, Box 1.

15. Transcribers spelled the names as best they could, based on what they heard. NARA 10, Boxes 634, 635.

16. JVW, Tokyo, "The Decline of the American Way of Living," "Compatriot," March 15, 1942. NARA 10, Box 635.

17. JZI, Tokyo, March 7, 1942. NARA 10, Box 635.

18. JZJ, Tokyo, January 5, 1942. NARA 10, Box 634.

19. JZJ, Tokyo, January 7, 1942. NARA 10, Box 634.

20. JZI, Tokyo, December 14, 1941. NARA 10, Box 633.

21. *Destination Tokyo* script by Fisher, director Delmer Daves, and Albert Maltz, who would later become one of the Hollywood Ten. The film entered production in late June 1943, so a script was extant no later than April–May.

22. "Destination Tokyo," Part V, *Liberty*, November 27, 1943.

23. *Destination Tokyo* (New York: D. Appleton-Century, 1943), 130–31.

24. Don Huebner, *One Marine's Adventures in WWII* at http://www.pacificwrecks.com/people/veterans/ huebner/part6.html

25. *Zero Hour*, August 14, 1944, Tokyo Rose LP.

26. "My Heart Belongs to Daddy," Cole Porter, 1938. Finnan haddie is a Scottish haddock dish and it is unlikely lyricist Cole Porter, famous for his double entendres, was referring to her cooking.

27. "St. Louis' Blues," W. C. Handy, 1914. *Zero Hour*, June 16, 1945. NARA 10, Box 746.

28. "Blue Moon," Richard Rodgers and Lorenz Hart, 1934. *Zero Hour*, July 10, 1945. NARA 10, Box 754.

29. "Forget If You Can," Jack Manus, Ken Upham, and Leonard Joy, 1938.

30. *Zero Hour*, June 21, 1945. NARA 10, Box 747.

31. In addition to Gervais' own book, *Amelia Earhart Lives*, see Jeffrey Hart, *From This Moment On: America in 1940* (New York: Crown, 1987), 213–14. Another book arguing for Earhart's capture by the Japanese is Thomas E. Devine's *Eyewitness: The Amelia Earhart Incident* (Frederick, Colo.: Renaissance House, 1987), which contains a lengthy bibliography of Earhart related books, documents, articles, newspaper coverage, and letters.

32. Memo, Director, FBI to SAC, New York, October 3, 1944, San Francisco office files. NARA 3.

33. Muriel Earhart Morrissey, and Carol L. Osborne, *Amelia, My Courageous Sister* (Santa Clara, Calif.: Osborne Publishing Co., 1987), 266.

34. Joseph Klaas, and Joseph Gervais, *Amelia Earhart Lives: A Trip Through Intrigue to Find America's First Lady of Mystery* (New York: McGraw Hill, 1970), 129.

35 Duus, *Orphan of the Pacific*, 8–9.

36. See http://genealogy.about.com/library/blbabynames1940s.htm.

37. Technically, they worked as messmen and stewards. Gail Lumet Buckley, *American Patriots: The Story of Blacks in the Military from the Revolution* (New York: Random House, 2001), 280.

38. Morison, *History of U.S. Naval Operations*, vol. 6, 231, 238.

39. Morison, *History of U.S. Naval Operations,* vol. 12, 296.

40. Doug Stanton, *In Harm's Way* (New York: Henry Holt and Company, 2001), 83. The fictional shark hunter Quint, played by Robert Shaw in the movie *Jaws,* was a survivor of the *Indianapolis.*

41. In the 1940 census, radios could be found in 91.9 percent of urban households. Of all households, rural and urban, 82.8 percent owned a radio. U.S. Bureau of Census, 1943, vol. II, part 1, 38–39.

42. Axis Sally was a propagandist like Lord Haw Haw; she was not a siren.

43. *New York Times,* February 14, 1943, SM15.

44. *New York Times,* December 19, 1943. Questions are on E2, Answers on E7.

45. "Radio By Any Other Name," *Time,* April 10, 1944, 58–60.

46. Harry Rauch, *New York Times,* June 25, 1944, X4.

47. FBI interview, December 1947. NARA 1, Box 41.

48. For this letter as well as excellent analysis, see Ann Elizabeth Pfau, *Miss Your lovin: GIs, Gender and Domesticity during World War II* (New York: Columbia University Press, 2008), 5. Available at http://www.gutenberg-e.org/pfau/chapter1.html

49. Judy Barrett Litoff, David C. Smith, Barbara Wooddall Taylor, and Charles E. Taylor, eds., *Miss You* (Athens, Ga.: University of Georgia Press, 1990), 239.

50. "Monthly Censorship Survey of Morale, Rumors, and Propaganda," July 1945. AHEC, Willoughby Papers, Box 9.

51. "Monthly Censorship Survey of Morale, Rumors, and Propaganda," June 1943. AHEC, Willoughby Papers, Box 9.

52. For a brief discussion of the "Dear John" letter, see http://www.worldwidewords.org/qa/qa-dea5.htm.

53. Quotations and Brush Off information from *Yank,* January 13 and December 10, 1943.

54. All quotations in this section from "Monthly Censorship Survey of Morale, Rumors and Propaganda," August 1944. AHEC, Willoughby Papers, Box 9.

55. "VD Problems of White Enlisted Men in MTOUSA" and "VD Problems of Negro Enlisted Men in MTOUSA." NARA, Record Group 330, Entry 94, Box 1030. MTO is Mediterranean Theater of Operations (Italy, North Africa, Balkans), which is not the same as the European TO (Britain, France, Germany).

56. I claim the rates are "very likely" lower in the Pacific because the VD rates were so much lower. For example, gonorrhea rates (servicemen infected per 1,000) in 1944: MedTO, 73; EurTO, 22; Southwest Pacific (Philippines, Australia), 6; Pacific Ocean Areas (Hawaii, Iwo Jima, Marianas),

4. In 1945: MedTO = 73; Eur, 75; SWPac, 43; Pac, 15. See *Medical Statistics in World War II*, ed. in chief, John Lada; ed. for medical statistics, Frank A. Reister (Washington, D.C.: Office of the Surgeon General, Dept. of the Army, 1975), 570–98. This may, however, simply mean fewer Pacific women had VD. Also, deprivation homosexuality rates for heterosexuals were undoubtedly higher in the Pac and SWPac theaters. See John Costello, *Virtue under Fire: How World War II Changed Our Social and Sexual Attitudes* (Boston, Mass.: Little, Brown and Company, 1985), 117; Oahu brothels, 216; 8,000 prostitutes, 96.

57. "Monthly Censorship Survey of Morale, Rumors and Propaganda," August, 1944. AHEC, Willoughby Papers, Box 9.

58. See, for example, Hagen's encounter with the mermaids in the 25th adventure, especially 1534, of the *Nibelungenlied*.

59. Homer, *Odyssey*, trans. S. H. Butcher & A. Lang (New York: P. F. Collier & Son, 1909–1914), Harvard Classics, Book XII. I have modernized the English and shortened the passage.

60. Most famously in Boethius, *The Consolations of Philosophy*.

61. See Plato, *Symposium*, 210–12, and *Republic*, 490.

62. Elliott R. Thorpe, *East Wind, Rain* (Boston, Mass.: Gambit, 1969), 225–26.

63. From an unpublished master's thesis by Rosa Maria Fazio, "The Effects of the Broadcasts of 'Tokyo Rose' during World War II" (Penn State: December, 1968). Fazio interviewed many veterans about their memories of the broadcasts.

64. See citation in *New York Times*, August 8, 1945. This appeared one week before Japan surrendered on August 15.

65. *New York Times*, October 12, 1944, 26.

66. Edward Stafford, *Little Ship, Big War: The Saga of DE343* (New York: Jove Books, 1985), 174.

67. *New York Times*, June 23, 1943, 7.

68. *New York Times*, June 29, 1943, 8.

69. *Time*, April 10, 1944, 58–60.

70. *New York Times*, August 8, 1945.

10

Black Marketeer

The Destruction of Imperial Japan

Iva's new job as an early-evening broadcaster at Radio Tokyo combined with her job at Domei late at night left her free mornings and afternoons. Always on the lookout for ways to earn extra money for food, she immediately started to search for a day job to supplement her income. To save money, Iva never purchased the English-language newspaper *Nippon Times*; instead, she looked for it in the trash at bus and train stops. She found a copy in late December 1943 that contained an ad for general office help at the Danish legation. She was two weeks late but decided to telephone anyway. Sixteen applicants had already applied; however, the position had not been closed. Iva immediately went to the legation, where its chancellor informed her the minister had made up his mind and an interview would be pointless. Iva was indignant. She'd spent her money on transit fare, and she demanded to be interviewed. The chancellor relented and ushered her into the office of Lars Tillitse, the Danish Minister.

"The door opened and here is this *gorgeous* man," Iva remembered, "completely white haired, the bluest eyes, 6 feet 2 inches tall—the most gorgeous man I've ever seen—standing behind this huge, beautiful desk." On the desk was a photo of U.S. Ambassador Joseph Grew, Tillitse's best friend and golfing partner. He and Iva chatted informally. He said he had wanted to transit America on his way from Denmark to Tokyo but the Danish government had sent him via the trans-Siberian railway. Iva commiserated, telling him the United States was a wonderful country. They talked about their families and Iva's background. Finally Tillitse asked her the key question: Could she write formal Japanese, the honorific style used by the diplomatic service? Iva lied and said yes. When she left, she wished him well, "whatever comes." Shortly thereafter, the chancellor telephoned her at Domei and said, "I don't know why, but the minister has chosen you."

"My first thought was, 'I'm in big trouble.'"

By the end of 1943, Iva could speak enough colloquial Japanese to get by, but reading or writing formal Japanese with its thousands of Chinese-based characters far exceeded her abilities. Fortunately, due to the Japanese New Year, she did not have to report to the legation until January 8, 1944, so she resolved to use the time to study. Her friend Kimi agreed to help.

They worked diligently, sleeping only a couple of hours a night. When they got tired, they took a bath and started anew. "I worked on Japanese until it was coming out of my ears. We went through all the countries and ministries, using the Chinese characters selected for each country. I learned all the ministers and their names. On and on. I was up to here."

On the morning of January 8, Iva thanked Kimi and set off for her new job. As Minister Tillitse's executive secretary, she cleared the first hurdle, answering the phone. Her first call was in Spanish, and she knew enough Spanish from living in California to handle it. Her next call was in German; fortunately she had studied a little German in college. Calls in English, Japanese, and French followed. She had warned the minister she knew no French, so he himself took that call. Eventually, her luck ran out. They handed her a document in formal Japanese, which she was to read and write a reply. She flailed away at it using various dictionaries, but try as hard as she might, she could not make heads or tails of it.

Then came a small miracle. "This is why I say there is a reason for everything that has happened to me and the good Lord looks after me." An elderly gentleman named Mr. Iida noticed her struggles and came over to her desk. "Togurisan," he said, "you are Nisei, correct? You will probably have trouble with written Japanese." Mr. Iida, who had worked as the treasurer of the legation for 23 years, offered to write for her any correspondence with the government of Japan; she had only to copy it in her own handwriting. In return, he asked if she would please converse with him. An Englishman had taught him the English language and he desired to sound American, not British. Iva immediately accepted his proposal. The help of the generous Mr. Iida saved Iva's career in diplomacy. Mr. Iida had a peculiar style of rounding the corners of his letters, and to his considerable delight, Iva copied his Japanese exactly. Secure in her new job at the legation, Iva quit Domei, where petty jealousies and anger at her pro-Allied attitudes had poisoned the atmosphere.

Her secretarial position did not include meals. The first time she entered the kitchen, looking for tea, the chef confronted her. Who was she? Where was she from? Iva narrated her family history. The chef announced that he came from the same prefecture as Iva's father. "We Yamanashi people must look out for one another. The legation has a big ration. I will feed you some of our leftovers." He cared nothing about her American background, only that she was a woman alone and emaciated. In the United States, Iva weighed about 115 pounds; during the war, she averaged 80 to 85 pounds and, at one point, sick with dysentery, her doctor measured her weight at 72 pounds. "I was skin and bones."

Iva knew that the condition of the POWs at Bunka Camp was even more dire. They slept on thin futons amid filth and disease. Guards regularly beat them. Prisoner rations amounted to a starvation diet at Bunka. Desperate for food, they skinned, stewed, and ate stray cats.[1] Heretofore, when Iva had a little extra cash, she purchased cheap food, products the Japanese did not value such as "sunshine fruit," a bitter citrus fruit loaded with vitamin C. She ate some herself and smuggled the rest to the POWs. They in turn hid the fruit under their jackets and took it back to Bunka Camp.[2] Thanks to her new job, Iva had a chance to help her friends on a regular basis.

Besides extra food, Iva discovered the legation also had an excess of nonedible rations. The Danish legation, for reasons nobody understood, received the same rations as the much larger German embassy. The rationed items had to be purchased from the Japanese government but the official prices were artificially low, often ten to a hundred times less than the price of the same item on the black market. The legation always purchased its full ration and wound up with more cigarettes, soap, matches, bread, milk, and other items than it could use. Iva asked Tillitse if she might have these leftovers. He gave them to her without charge. She in turn used her trading skills to turn this bounty into sustenance for herself, food and supplies for the POWs, and friendships with officials in key positions.

For example, the Danish legation could buy cigarettes as part of its ration, but Tillitse hated cigarettes. He loved cigars, but these were unobtainable. Iva decided to try to help. She wrapped six loaves of excess bread in a cloth, hid the bundle in a knapsack, and called on the head of sales for the government's tobacco monopoly. They chatted. Iva sized him up. "I can get to know people pretty quickly." Before the war, Japanese mothers provided their children with daily snacks, such as cookies or cakes. By 1944, baked goods of any kind were extremely scarce. Iva inquired whether he had children. He did. Did he have difficulty obtaining snacks for his children? "Oh, yes. Nothing is available." "Suppose you were given bread. Could your children make use of it?" "Certainly. But where am I going to get bread? It's controlled." He looked at her, and she looked at him. "Suppose I could get you bread. Could you in some way help me find cigars? The diplomat I work for wants some. We will purchase the cigars, and in return I will supply you with bread." The official promised not to ask her how or where she would find bread, and she agreed he should not ask. That day, he sold Iva several boxes of cigars at the low official price, and she gave him her six loaves at no charge. For the rest of the war, Iva kept Tillitse supplied with cigars while the tobacco monopoly official became a hero to his family. Everyone was happy with the arrangement.

Iva also dealt with a man named Kobaiashi who ran the supply depot for the various foreign embassies and consulates. The Foreign Ministry informed Kobaiashi what each should receive, and on a regular schedule he would make distributions. Iva took over the job of representative for the Danish legation and dealt with him routinely when she purchased the legation's rations. One day, she found Kobaiashi smoking what he lamented was "his last cigar." Iva immediately recognized an opportunity. The supply depot featured many items such as cheese, butter, jams, jellies, and certain canned goods that Westerners liked but ordinary Japanese viewed with disdain. As a result, the items were extraordinarily cheap. Iva asked Kobaiashi what he might be willing to sell her if she could somehow obtain some cigars for him. His eyes lit up, but he said nothing. Of course, Iva went on, he would have to pay the government price for the cigars—they didn't want to do anything illegal—and she in turn would pay for whatever he would sell her. She asked only that he not disclose that she was the one supplying him. Knowing from personal experience that cigars were impossible to obtain, Kobaiashi agreed to sell her anything she wanted in the store. Shortly thereafter, Iva arrived with two boxes of cigars. Kobaiashi was shocked, but he kept his bargain. He never dared inquire about Iva's secret source.

Iva maintained these relationships for the rest of the war. She never resold any of the food. She herself ate some of the cheese and butter for the fat content. "I was almost starving, but when I had bread, butter, and jelly, I was close to heaven." She offered some to Phil D'Aquino and his mother. The rest went to the POWs. She brought foodstuffs to them in small enough quantities that they could smuggle it back to their comrades under their clothes. As "employees" of Radio Tokyo, their comings and goings were routine, so the guards never bothered to search Iva. They usually searched Cousens and Ince when they left Bunka Camp, not when they returned. Wallace Ince, who admitted after the war he never really trusted Iva, testified that she brought them eggs, noodles, rice, canned goods, salt, sugar, vegetables, and tobacco.

Iva also scrounged for medicine and clothing. She found vitamin pills, quinine, aspirin, and cod liver oil. When Cousens told her about a POW with a severe infection from a wound that left him sick with fever, and that he lay freezing uncovered at Bunka, Iva gave Cousens one of her two wool blankets to smuggle in for him. As a result, he survived.

~

Early in 1944, news reporter Matsuo Kato visited the Nakajima plane factory in a suburb of Tokyo. Nakajima's Ki43 Army Fighter ("Hayabusa" to the Japanese, "Oscar" to the Allies) was an extraordinarily beautiful aircraft but so slow, fragile, and poorly armed that those who had to fly it nicknamed it the "pilot killer." At the plant, Kato found unskilled workers including children building the plane essentially by hand.[3] Meanwhile, across the sea, vast assembly lines at American factories poured out planes, ships, guns, bombs, and every other weapon of war in seemingly limitless quantities. As a result, Americans entered battles with massive air, sea, and land superiority.

Americans brought this same business-like attitude to their style of fighting. A Japanese soldier named Kamiko Kiyoshi who fought in the battle for the Philippines noted how differently the American and Japanese military approached war. The Imperial Japanese Army (IJA) had trained for round-the-clock combat with an emphasis on night marches and night attacks. Its soldiers were expert in hand-to-hand fighting, and wore heavy uniforms to protect themselves. The Americans, he noted, treated war like a day at the office. They started attacks in the morning and quit in the afternoon. They wore light helmets and fought with comparatively lighter rifles. They destroyed their enemy at long range. Kiyoshi never saw an American soldier close up. These factors, combined with inferior food—the Japanese daily ration consisted of a small bowl of soup containing a few grains of rice—left IJA soldiers exhausted and vulnerable.[4]

Throughout 1944, Japan's military experienced disaster after disaster. The United States and other Allied forces at sea launched attacks in the Marshall, Caroline, and Mariana Islands. In each conflict, they killed tens of thousands of Japanese troops, sunk ships, and destroyed planes, all of which were irreplaceable.

On June 15, 1944, the U.S. Marines attacked the key Mariana island of Saipan. Saipan's strategic importance lay in its proximity to Japan. The 3,000 mile, 30-hour round trip to Tokyo was well within range of America's new bomber, the B-29 Superfortress. To protect Saipan, the Imperial Navy dispatched a six-carrier fleet in an attempt to destroy the American invasion forces. This engagement, the greatest carrier battle of the war, is officially known as the Battle of the Philippine Sea, but its result was so lopsided it became unofficially known as the "Marianas Turkey Shoot." The Japanese pilots were inexperienced and poorly trained, and their planes lacked speed and adequate armor. On June 19, waves of carrier-based aircraft from both sides, hundreds of planes, fought without respite for eight hours above the Philippine Sea, and on June 20, the Americans counterattacked the Japanese fleet. At the conclusion of the battle, the Japanese had damaged six U.S. ships, whereas the Americans had sunk three Japanese carriers. The Americans lost about 100 aircraft; the Imperial Navy lost more than 400.

On Saipan itself, 30,000 Japanese soldiers resisted so furiously that the battle-hardened Marines required an Army division to reinforce them. Within three weeks, the Japanese recognized their situation was hopeless. The years of ferocious propaganda that had portrayed the Americans as demons now bore its bitter fruit. Convinced that the Americans would murder the men and rape the women, Japanese civilians on the island began committing mass suicide. As American troops watched with horror, entire families jumped off cliffs. Young girls combed their hair, then calmly leapt to their deaths. Children clung to the legs and necks of parents as they drowned in the sea; mothers jumped with babies in their arms and crashed on the rocks below.[5] The remnants of the Japanese forces turned on the American invaders and made a final charge. They were annihilated. Saipan's naval commander, Vice Admiral Nagumo, leader of the attack on Pearl Harbor, committed ritual suicide.

On July 7, 1944, the Allies took control of Saipan. Guam, the largest island in the Marianas, fell to the Allies two weeks later, as did, shortly thereafter, the island of Tinian, across the channel from Saipan. The B-29s that carried the atomic bombs used on Hiroshima and Nagasaki would take off from Tinian. The battle for the Marianas cost the Japanese 46,000 fighters killed or captured; the Americans, 4,750 killed.

~

Iva's friendship with Phil D'Aquino deepened, and in May 1944, she and Phil moved from the Onarikin boarding house to Phil's mother's home in Atsugi, a country town located about thirty miles from Tokyo. Phil's father, Jose Filomino D'Aquino, lived in the Atsugi house only intermittently. A quiet and agreeable man, he had worked in the Ford plant in Yokohama before the war and for the German firm Telefunken afterward. A Portuguese born in Shanghai, China, he'd never learned to speak Japanese well. He communicated at work and with his children in English. He found the countryside too isolated, so he usually stayed in Yokohama, where his son Ted also lived. He was apolitical, and wanted his family to remain neutral as well, but he was not a forceful person and kept quiet about Phil's outspoken support for the Allies. He befriended Iva, often dropped in on her at the boarding house, and she called him "Jose" despite their age difference.

By contrast, Phil's Japanese mother, Maria,[6] was the backbone of the family. Physically small but strong in spirit, Iva described her as "a survivor." Iva admitted she recognized something of her own character in Maria D'Aquino. They never discussed the war and got along famously. Maria's mother lived even farther out in the country, and Iva and Phil would ride bicycles out to see her and scout for food.

After Iva arrived at the house in Atsugi, she noticed the D'Aquinos had no bath. Maria explained they attended a public bath. The knowledge that the bath's owner segregated men and women did nothing to allay Iva's apprehensions. "This was the first time in my life I had to be completely naked in front of other people." The bath was in a wooden building a block from the house. Bathers paid the owner for the hot water but brought their own soap and towels. "Phil's mother tried to convince me that everyone did it and that we were all the same, but I wasn't buying into the concept. Everyone else was very nonchalant, walking around naked, not thinking a thing about it. I kept my towel around me. We went into a big open room with a large hot tub about 20 feet across. Once I dipped my bucket into the tub and started washing, I had to get rid of my towel. My future mother-in-law was bathing right beside me, but at the beginning, even though I was nude, I tried to keep my arms folded in front of me and crouched so that I would not be too much exposed. My hair was long in those days, just short of my waist, so I tried to wash my hair at least once a week. I'm not sure why, but washing my hair caused me to accept public bathing without being embarrassed."

Public baths were one of the lesser disadvantages of living in Atsugi. "The Atsugi police treated me very roughly because Phil's family and myself were the only aliens living in Atsugi, and therefore the police relished giving us a bad time."[7] In addition, the commute from Atsugi to Radio Tokyo was brutal, two and a half hours each way by train, assuming fuel shortages or faulty equipment did not slow the train down. Worse, the trains were usually packed, so Iva and Phil often stood up the entire way. Although

Iva enjoyed having a companion for the ride, they could not really converse. Phil's Japanese was poor and given that *kempei* and *tokko* agents often arrested people on trains for negative thinking and disloyalty, he and Iva did not dare speak English. On one trip, Phil's hot temper almost got them into trouble. They were on a crowded train when a man standing behind Iva pushed himself against her whenever the train swayed. Phil eyed the man but said nothing. Iva thought it might be an accident, but then it happened again. "Phil wore a very heavy, solid silver ring with his family crest. The third time this man rubbed against me, Phil walloped him and the guy almost flew the length of the train." Fortunately, no police witnessed the incident.

When Iva moved to Atsugi, she requested she be freed from the obligation to travel to Tokyo on Saturdays to broadcast. Miyeko Furuya happily replaced Iva, adopting for her on-air name, "the Saturday Night Party Girl." Furuya continued on *Zero Hour* until her marriage in February 1945.

Although Iva got along well with Phil D'Aquino's family, the commute proved more than she could bear. The long hours exhausted her, limited her ability to search for extra food, and the train fares strained her budget. She decided to return to the city.

Chiyeko Ito, the young woman who traveled to Japan with Iva, had an uncle who was a "go-between," that is, a person who acted as a combination middle-man and counselor for various activities in Japanese society, including putting together landlords and renters. Iva asked him for help, and he recommended her to Mrs. Unami Kido, whose husband had been in the army in Manchuria for six years. Mrs. Kido lived near the radio station and both of her upstairs rooms were empty. On October 27, 1944, Iva rented Mrs. Kido's upstairs and moved back to Tokyo.[8] Phil returned to Tokyo as well.

∽

In 1944, war shortages drove Japanese society to unprecedented levels of privation and sacrifice. Ration coupons for clothing were worthless because there was nothing to buy. A winter clothing distribution allocated one pair of socks for every fourth person, one towel for every fifteen. Shoes had long since disappeared, and even wooden clogs were now rationed. The shoddy, ill-made clothing could not be washed because it disintegrated. The Japanese endured a Spartan diet in 1941; by 1944, their caloric intake had fallen by almost one-fifth. In contrast, American intake increased 4 percent in the same period. White rice became a luxury known as "silver rice" due to its scarcity and exorbitant cost on the black market. The government opened kitchens for workers that provided a lunch of soup using potato parts or leaves, with snail parts for meat. People began lining up at 9:00 AM. Lack of fuel for trucks meant 70 percent of Tokyo's human waste could not be removed. Children combing their hair often pulled out dozens of black lice with every stroke, but white skin lice were worse because they were harder to see. To control the lice, parents and teachers shaved children's heads, much to the shame of the girls, and used precious fuel to boil their clothes. The water turned red from the blood the lice had sucked from the children's malnourished bodies.[9]

To strengthen the war effort, the government abolished labor unions and pressed all students over the age of ten into war plants or farming on a full-time basis. Although the government had boasted shortly after Pearl Harbor that it would never conscript women for work as did the British,[10] by 1944, the government had mobilized single women between ages fourteen and twenty-five for armament factories, and Tojo had denounced those who refused to serve as a disgrace to morality.[11] Nonetheless, the recalcitrant patriarchy of Japanese society meant they were underutilized. British women made up 2.2 of 2.8 million new war workers. In the United States, where employment was voluntary, 6 million American women took jobs during the war, increasing their numbers by 50 percent. By contrast, between 1940 and 1944, the Japanese civilian workforce lost 300,000 men but gained only 1.4 million women. In 1930, women comprised 25 percent of those in manufacturing and construction; in 1944, despite desperate war needs, they comprised 24 percent. The number of female workers overall in Japan increased only 10 percent between 1940 and 1944, and the percentage of women in wartime Japanese industry actually declined.[12] For those women who did work in industry, life was brutal. Hiroko Nakamoto was typical. She toiled at night in a factory without heat. Her only meal consisted of one bowl of broth with a few noodles. When parts ran low or equipment stopped working, military superiors in charge of the plant forced her and other workers to stand for hours. They were not permitted to sit, read, or otherwise pass the time.[13]

Cultural activities practically ceased. Newspapers now had only one sheet, with text on front and back. Most magazines stopped publishing. The censors drove some, such as *Kaizo* and *Chuo Koron*, out of business because, according to an announcement from Radio Tokyo, "their policies were incompatible with the proper guidance of public thought."[14] The official position of the government was, "This is a war of survival, a war in which the vanquished will be exterminated, a war which we cannot afford to lose."[15] Stage shows, kabuki theaters, movie houses, expensive restaurants, high-end bars—all closed. The government also shut down more than 10,000 geisha houses and conscripted prostitutes as laborers for war plants.

During this period, Radio Tokyo launched a variety of programs on ancient Japanese history and cultural traditions. These proved immensely popular with a society sick of present-day reality. Japanese traditional art, Zen Buddhism, the tea ceremony, readings of literary works, and kabuki plays, one featuring 34 actors, replaced tirades on the need to sacrifice.[16]

The larger theaters were used to manufacture balloon bombs. Made from rice paper and potato glue, the balloons were fitted with bombs and released in the hope that they would float across the Pacific and detonate somewhere in the United States. Between December 1943 and March 1945, the Japanese launched 9,000 such balloon bombs.[17] A few actually made it, but they never caused any damage, exploding harmlessly in the forests of the Northwest.

In 1944, with the United States poised to begin bombing their homeland, the Japanese made the wrenching decision to protect the next generation by sending children in the third grade and above to live in the country. Voluntarily and involuntarily, hundreds of thousands were taken away from their parents and put to work on farms. School teachers journeyed with them as supervisors, but their students soon were out of hand. The children, fed only bits of sweet potato, weeds, bean husks, and licorice greens, spent most of their time scrounging for something to eat, thus causing considerable consternation among the local farmers. As the rice crop neared harvest, the children guarded it against locusts, catching them with their hands and placing them in hemp sacks. Their teachers cooked the locusts and fed them to the students as a reward.[18] However, the psychological torment of being separated from their parents, something few had ever experienced, outweighed even the pangs of starvation. An August 1944 letter from a sixth-grader named Mitsuko expressed how most children must have felt:

> Mother, please listen to Mitsuko's one great request. Mother, as soon as this letter arrives, please come to see me that very day. Please, Mother. Mother, every day Mitsuko cries. Mother, Mitsuko might die if you don't come to see me. Please bring a bowl with a little rice. I'm so hungry I can't stand it. All we ever get is pumpkin every day. Mother, please. As soon as this letter arrives, come right away. OK? By all means, come. Mitsuko[19]

Untold numbers of these children returned to the cities at the end of the war to discover they were orphans. Thousands congregated around train stations, where they slowly died of starvation and neglect.

~

Iva Toguri and the staff at Radio Tokyo first heard the name "Tokyo Rose" at the end of May 1944. After that, memories conflict.

At her trial, Iva testified that George Mitsushio, manager of the *Zero Hour*, told her that an article, "from either Lisbon or Sweden had mentioned somebody called Tokyo Rose from a Japanese source. George said it was probably referring to a program in the southern regions, either the Philippines, Java, Saigon, or could be Shanghai. He said there was no one at Radio Tokyo who could even be connected with Tokyo Rose."[20] She added that Major Cousens said it couldn't be her because the article referred to a Sunday broadcast, and Iva never broadcast on Sundays. Charles Cousens confirmed Iva's story, testifying that he had dismissed the possibility that Iva could be Tokyo Rose.[21]

In 1987, Iva recalled a rather different scenario. In this version, Cousens told her, as best she remembered, "You know, Ann, there's a strong possibility they might be referring to the 'Zero Hour.'" If Cousens did make such a remark, it seems likely both would have agreed that Iva probably was the best candidate to be the announcer the Allies had named "Tokyo Rose."

Also at her trial, manager Kenkichi Oki claimed the news item had explicitly stated "Tokyo Rose" was "Orphan Ann" and that thereafter the staff at Radio Tokyo referred to Iva as Tokyo Rose.[22] Ruth Hayakawa, however, contradicted this, claiming that Oki had told her that she, Ruth, was surely Tokyo Rose because she had a soft and appealing voice, which Iva did not, and because she did Sunday broadcasts.[23]

These contradictory recollections concern a report published in the English-language *Nippon Times* on May 28, 1944, datelined "Stockholm, May 24" and titled "Yankees in Pacific War Zone Fascinated by 'Tokyo Rose' Broadcasting from JOAK [Radio Tokyo]." Someone in Sweden had read a letter to *Time* magazine by U.S. Army First Lieutenant Caryl Weinberg of Brooklyn. Weinberg wrote in reaction to the April 10 article in *Time*, referenced in chapter 9, which mentioned *Zero Hour* and that Tokyo Rose had first broadcast to the Aleutians in August 1943. The Swedish source sent Weinberg's letter to the *Nippon Times*. Why this source sent a letter about a *Time* article instead of the article itself is anybody's guess.

The *Nippon Times* coverage introduced Weinberg's letter, in which he stated that he listened to Radio Tokyo, not some more Southern station such as Radio Manila, and he specifically named "the program called *Zero Hour*" as the source of his quotations. He cited "a lovely, warm, cultured female voice" saying, "'Hello, Big Boy, fighting man in the Pacific. Are you lonely tonight? This is Radio Tokyo bringing you your Sunday evening concert," thus lending credence to Ruth Hayakawa's memory of Oki's claim that she, not Iva, must be Tokyo Rose. On the other hand, nothing about Weinberg's letter indicated he limited his remarks to Sunday evening broadcasts, and his conclusion should have put any Tokyo Rose wannabes on their guard. "I can't get over how smart those devils are. Don't you know that this must make a hell of an impression on battle-strained minds? What a smooth Yankee voice the gal has!"[24]

Iva's willingness after the war to refer to herself as Tokyo Rose may mean that Iva herself never actually read the article. Mitsushio and Cousens told her about it, but how much of its contents they conveyed is unclear. Mitsushio probably didn't much care who

Tokyo Rose was. Iva thought that Cousens did read the article himself. Even if he did, Cousens surely did not want to testify that he, chief script writer for the *Zero Hour* and Iva Toguri's boss, had recognized thanks to this 1944 article that the Allies perceived Orphan Ann/Tokyo Rose as a "devil" attacking "battle-strained minds." Therefore, at Iva's trial, Cousens stuck to his claim that he dismissed the idea that Iva could be Tokyo Rose. His own choice was June Suyama. In a letter after the war, Cousens wrote,

> My wife told me of things she heard "that woman saying from Tokyo." Not a word of it came from Toguri. But some of it I remember was read by Hayakawa's girl friend—a thorough-going bitch of a Nisei from Canada. She was completely pro-Nip and made a great business of wearing a kimono—a thing Toguri would not do [underlining in original].[25]

The possibility that Suyama, the Canadian Nisei, was Tokyo Rose was moot. She was run over and killed by a truck just after the war ended.

Weinberg notwithstanding, the *New York Times* probably spoke for most GIs in its report titled "Tokyo Rose a Hit with U.S. Soldiers."

> If a radio popularity poll could be taken out here among American fighting forces a surprisingly large number of votes would go to "Tokyo Rose" and other of the programs beamed from the Land of the Rising Sun to the advancing American bases to the south and southwest Pacific.
>
> Tokyo is entertaining. Tokyo gives the listeners comedy and good dance music. . . . Tojo, of course, is the sponsor, and the announcer, almost always speaking smooth English, puts his product over very nicely. The boys listen but they do not buy despite the fact that sometimes there will be thirty minutes of first-class American dance music without a single interruption for the commercial plug.
>
> They do not want to hear a single program about how evil and dumb the enemy is or a single "back the attack" program. They are backing it already. They would like to hear more dance bands, light love stories, light musical comedies. . . . They will probably continue to listen to Tokyo Rose, but no one at home need worry about that.[26]

The personnel at Radio Tokyo speculated briefly about which one of them might be Tokyo Rose, but they failed to grasp the power of her legend. The thought that she was every female announcer, that all the women at Radio Tokyo were heard as a single broadcaster named Tokyo Rose, never occurred to them.

~

Rations at Bunka fell steadily as the war progressed, in part because food in Japan was increasingly difficult to obtain and also because the Japanese quartermaster at the facility stole from the rations intended for prisoners. Iva's smuggling operations could not offset the shortfall. Lack of nourishment, exposure, brutality, and psychological pressure eventually took its toll, and on June 17, 1944, Cousens collapsed. He lay in Bunka for two weeks before authorities moved him to the Shinagawa prison hospital, where they placed him in a room with a U.S. sailor who had become insane.[27]

Iva wanted very much to visit Cousens, but at Shinagawa he was kept under armed guard. So, she loitered outside the hospital and approached a couple of nurses taking a break. They chatted; Iva told them about her desire to see a friend. They thought it might be possible. Iva caught her meaning and provided the bribe. Dressed in the straw hat and baggy, staple-fiber, monpé trousers of a farmer's wife so as to hide her Nisei identity, Iva slipped into Cousens' room while one nurse kept watch for the guard. "I'll never forget that face. He was so happy to see me. 'Ann, for God's sake, how did you get in here?'" She had brought him a little fruit and she stayed for 20 minutes before the nurse became afraid. "I only visited him once. Once was enough. The whole atmosphere was too scary. I couldn't try it again. I heard they sent him back to Bunka Camp."[28]

A month after his arrival, the Japanese did in fact return Cousens to Bunka Camp, where he languished for a few days before Tsuneishi intervened on behalf of his valuable broadcaster and had him sent to Jun Tendo Hospital for civilians. Here, doctors diagnosed Cousens as suffering from cardiac problems brought on by beriberi and a nervous breakdown. The diagnosis was somewhat speculative because a shortage of batteries throughout Japan had made the hospital's battery driven electrocardiograph inoperable.[29] He remained at Jun Tendo for three months and Iva, often accompanied by Phil, visited him regularly, each time dressed in their oldest and baggiest clothes, hiding as much food as they dared.[30] Buck Henshaw, another POW, also visited and smuggled him food.

Without Major, Iva felt bereft. She still had her job at the Danish legation, which kept her moderately well supplied with food, so Iva again tried to quit broadcasting, this time claiming she could not write her own scripts. Mitsushio and Oki refused to allow her to leave. When she failed to show up for several days, they sent a man to Mrs. Kido's to fetch her.[31] Iva rearranged her old scripts to fit whatever the scheduled music and repeated the same patter. The Japanese had assigned Ince other duties earlier in 1944, and he too was no longer with *Zero Hour*.[32] Because Ince's new work took him to the same studio, Iva figured out a way to stay in contact. "One message I gave him was notice of the fall of the Philippines into the U.S. Army's hands. I often left messages between records in the record case. He would find them and take the message back to the POW camp."[33]

After his hospital stay, Cousens again returned to Bunka. He never fully recovered from this breakdown and never again worked on *Zero Hour*. Cousens did write a few essays, which were read for him on the program *Humanity Calls*, and he broadcast POW messages. Buck Henshaw consistently noted in his diary that Cousens was close to collapse and remarked on October 8, "Cousens raving about committing suicide."[34] Still, in 1945, he rallied the POWs at Bunka more than once, reinstituted discipline, and on several occasions refused direct orders to include in his essays views with which he disagreed. After the war, George Mitsushio affirmed Cousens' principled resistance.[35]

~

As the war progressed, the American navy had grown larger and stronger while the Japanese navy had grown smaller and weaker. In every clash between the two, the Americans had prevailed, usually decisively. In the fall of 1944, the Americans prepared to retake the Philippines. The Imperial Japanese Navy realized that its loss would be a calamity. To prevent the invasion, the Japanese devised a brilliant strategy and threw every fighting ship they had against the Americans, including the two great battleships, the *Yamato* and the *Musashi*, which before the war they had believed could destroy an entire American fleet before its ships could maneuver close enough to fire. The result was the Battle of Leyte Gulf, undoubtedly one of the greatest naval battles in history.

The Battle of Leyte Gulf was actually five separate engagements between October 23 and 25, 1944. The Imperial Navy executed a complicated plan of decoys and surprise attacks, which ultimately failed. A cursory glance at the strengths of the two sides as they entered the battle indicates the Japanese never really had a chance.[36]

Fighting Ships by Type	U.S.	Japan
Aircraft carriers	34	4
Carrier-based aircraft	1,500	150
Battleships	18	7
Heavy cruisers	10	13
Light cruisers	10	6
Destroyers	121	32
Submarines	29	14

In this battle, the Imperial Navy lost all its carriers, three battleships with three others damaged, six heavy cruisers with four others damaged, three light cruisers, nine destroyers, and a submarine. Destroyed by air attack, the *Musashi* went down without being able to bring her huge guns to bear on enemy ships. More than 10,000 Japanese sailors died in the battle. The United States lost only six ships, of which the largest was a light carrier. With the Japanese defeated, the Americans deployed the rest of their armada, hundreds and hundreds of landing ships, troop and tank transports, and supply and other support ships against the Philippines.

The Japanese had one last small hope. After years of intensive labor, the supercarrier *Shinano* had been completed. The largest aircraft carrier in the world, the *Shinano* was commissioned November 19, 1944, and a few days later set out for Kure, a port in Hiroshima Prefecture, to be outfitted with hull compartments and watertight doors. An American submarine, the USS *Archerfish*, put four torpedoes in her side and, on November 29, ten days after commissioning, the *Shinano* sunk. With the loss of the *Shinano*, the

Imperial Japanese Navy effectively ceased to exist as a fighting force.

~

Iva felt that of all the Japanese she met during the war, her landlady Mrs. Kido was her favorite.[37] Yet another "wiry, little" woman of indomitable spirit—one wonders how tiny these women must have been if Iva at 5 feet 2 inches described them in this way—Mrs. Kido had not seen her husband during his six years' service in Manchuria and she had grown sick of the war. She immediately warmed to Iva and her view that Japan was doomed. "I turned her pro-U.S., believe me. Had we had champagne, we'd have broken out a bottle the day Japan surrendered. She would have been right there leading the parade. I made a convert. I brainwashed that woman."

Mrs. Kido knew Iva illegally snuck into the countryside to obtain food, knew she illegally traded with various officials at ration depots, and knew she illegally smuggled supplies to the POWs. She said nothing. At this time in Japan, the Neighborhood Associations, under orders from the Army, constantly pressured members to buy war bonds; participate in air raid drills; collect cotton goods, rags, and newspapers; and plant gardens. Iva never helped the Japanese government in any of these activities and, as a result, neighbors called her a traitor. Mrs. Kido told them to mind their own business with some ferocity. "She was outspoken, got things done, and ran like a fawn. She was really something else." Mrs. Kido's brother lived next door; he stopped speaking to his sister after she defended Iva. When Iva's lawyers deposed Mrs. Kido in 1949, she confessed her brother still had not spoken to her.[38]

Unbeknownst to Iva, Mrs. Kido had another relative (not her brother) of some importance. Katsuo Okada was a Master Sergeant in the *kempeitai*. Okada often visited and conversed with Iva regularly because he said he wanted to improve his English. On what date Iva realized she was discussing the war with a *kempei* is unclear, but at some point Okada warned her that expressing the sentiment that Japan would lose was a violation of the law. "He promised to keep an eye on us and told me not to worry. He cautioned me not to be too free with my words. He said he would come if he heard of any danger and that he would take care of it."

Okada did exactly that. When two other *kempei* came to interrogate Iva, Okada told them, "She [Mrs. Kido] is a relative of mine, so leave this to me." They never came back. Iva was wary of him and kept quiet about her smuggling activities, but Okada was no fool. He knew Iva took food to the POWs because she often had Mrs. Kido buy it for her.[39]

According to Okada, Phil lived with Iva in her apartment during this period.[40] Phil himself testified that he lived at Mrs. Kido's in 1944, although he didn't exactly say he lived in Iva's apartment (Figures 10.1 and 10.2).[41] In 1987, Iva admitted that Phil moved back to Tokyo when she did but expressly denied that he lived with her.[42] Mrs. Kido in her deposition appeared to corroborate Iva's denial.[43] Given their relative poverty and the limited housing available, a condition that would worsen as Allied bombers took their toll, Okada's version is more credible. Today, persons of opposite sex sharing living quarters is so common the Census Bureau

Figure 10.1 Iva at Mrs. Kido's.
Courtesy of National Archives.

Figure 10.2. Iva at Mrs. Kido's gate. Courtesy of National Archives.

has invented an acronym for it ("posslq"), but in the 1940s this was highly improper. Even if Phil and Iva's relationship had been platonic, no lady of Iva's generation would admit to living with a man who was not her husband.[44]

The bombing of Tokyo began in November 1944, and Iva, perhaps afraid she would not live through the war, longed to celebrate Christmas as she had in America. She asked Mrs. Kido if she could put up a Christmas tree, and Mrs. Kido told her to go ahead. Iva bought a small tree—where she can't remember—and used balls of silk as ornaments as well as other items made by hand. Mrs. Kido taught Iva the art of origami, and together they created birds, animals, boxes, and other items from folded colored paper. Iva put the tree in the main room on the first floor.

"A drill was taking place one day when one of the air raid wardens opened the door and saw the Christmas tree. He threatened to have Mrs. Kido thrown out of the neighborhood. We moved the tree upstairs and celebrated just the same."[45] When neighbors learned of the tree, they harassed Mrs. Kido even more. Iva confronted the neighbors herself and told them to talk to her personally if they had problems. Both women took the position that Christianity was Iva's religion and she should be allowed to practice it. On Christmas Day, they exchanged small gifts and then took everything down. "This was my only Christmas tree. In previous years I didn't have anyone to celebrate with."[46] Before Christmas came round again, the war was over.

~

The introduction of the B-29 Superfortress sounded the death knell of Imperial Japan. A huge plane for the time, the B-29 flew 300 miles an hour at 35,000 feet, and carried ten tons of bombs plus a crew of eleven. However, before the waves of B-29s could begin their bombing runs on Japanese factories and cities, the country had to be surveilled. On November 1, 1944, the first B-29 lifted off Saipan for the longest stretch of blue-water flying ever attempted by military aviators: a total of 3,370 miles to Tokyo and back. To remain undetected, they flew so low the ocean's waves splashed their wings. In the final hour, they climbed slowly to an altitude of six miles while struggling against a 200 mile-an-hour headwind. Nineteen Japanese fighters rose to attack them but couldn't gain enough altitude. The crew photographed the Imperial Palace and downtown Tokyo. Below, Wallace Ince remembered that when the Japanese at Bunka saw the plane, they ordered the entire camp into the basement for two hours.[47] Its mission accomplished, the big B-29 turned around and, with the wind now at its tail, crossed the city a second time at great speed, leaving the fighters far behind.

The crew was jubilant as they headed back to Saipan. Unaware how they had terrified the managers of Radio Tokyo, one of them laughed, "I wonder what Tokyo Rose will say about this!" As a salute they named their B-29 after Japan's most famous broadcaster (Figure 10.3). The *Tokyo Rose* was the first American aircraft to overfly Tokyo since the Doolittle Raid of 1942. Her crew flew her unaccompanied to Japan 24 times to spy on the enemy, and she always brought them safely home.[48]

Figure 10.3. "Tokyo Rose" B-29 with her crew. Courtesy of National Archives.

Notes

1. The judge at Iva's trial did not allow this testimony but the men told the newspapers. *San Francisco Chronicle*, August 26, 1949, 5. They included Bunka's Dutch chief cook Nicolaas Schenk, his assistant Australian Kenneth Parkyns, and American sergeant Frank Fujita. See chapter 17.

2. Cousens, Ince, Reyes, and other POWs at Bunka testified at her trial and in depositions to Iva Toguri's constant supply of food, medicine, and other necessities. See chapter 17.

3. Kato, *The Lost War*, 166–67.

4. Ienaga, *The Pacific War*, 50.

5. The mass suicides are chronicled in Robert Sherrod, *On to Westward: The Battles of Saipan and Iwo Jima* (Baltimore, Md.: Nautical and Aviation Publishing, 1990).

6. That Phil's parents were named Mary and Joseph made me wonder if perhaps his mother acquired the name after the marriage, but "Maria" is her name in official records. NARA 4, Box 264.

7. Toguri Notes.

8. Iva Toguri's addresses in Tokyo during the war were, according to her sworn statement:

825 Unane-machi, Setagaya-ku, Tokyo, July 1941–June 1942

4,6-chome, Tamura-cho, Shiba-ku, Tokyo, June 1942–May 1944

2663 Haka-cho, Atsugi-machi, Aiko-gun, Kamagawa-kon, May 1944–October 1944

396 Ikejiri-machi, Setagaya-ku, Tokyo, October 1944–October 1945

See SF #61-590, Supplement to Form 213, American Consular Service, Yokohama, Japan, May 26, 1947, 20. NARA 2.

9. *Women against War*, 173.

10. Koizumi Chikahiko, Minister of Welfare, stated the government's position in February 1942: "In order to secure its work force, the enemy is drafting women but in Japan, out of consideration for the family system, we will not draft them."

11. For a complete history of female employment in Japan, see Thomas H. R. Havens, "War and Women in Japan: 1937–1945," in *American Historical Review* 80, no. 4 (October 1975): 913–34.

12. Statistics from Havens, "War and Women in Japan: 1937–1945," 916–19.

13. Hiroko Nakamoto, *My Japan* (New York: McGraw-Hill, 1970), 48–51.

14. Andrew Roth, *Dilemma in Japan* (New York: Little, Brown & Co., 1945), 158.

15. Shillony, *Politics of Wartime Japan*, 68.

16. Gordon Daniels, "Japanese Domestic Radio and Cinema Propaganda, 1937–1945: An Overview," in Short, *Film & Radio Propaganda*, 301.

17. The Japanese launched 150 per day between November 1944 and March 1945, when they ran out of supplies. *Nippon [Japan] Times*, January 16, 1946, 2.

18. *Women against War*, 154.

19. Havens, *Valley of Darkness*, 165–66.

20. Trial Transcript, vol. XLV, 5054.

21. Trial Transcript, vol. XXX, 3386–90.

22. Trial Transcript, vol. IX, 799–800, 887.

23. Hayakawa deposition. Trial Transcript, vol. XXXV, 4001. NARA 2, Box 9.

24. *Nippon Times*, May 28, 1944.

25. Letter to Wayne Collins, October 16, 1948.

26. Datelined "Espiritu Santo Atoll, March 20," *New York Times*, March 27, 1944, 4. The dateline only compounds the confusion about whom soldiers actually heard when they listened to Tokyo Rose. Espiritu Santo is part of Vanuatu, situated far south of Tokyo between Australia and Samoa. Shortwave listeners in Vanuatu would be far more likely to pick up Radio Manila than Radio Tokyo. In any case, after the war the principals did not mention the *New York Times*' article. I assume they never read it.

27. Iva wrote in her Notes, "Things were normal until spring of 1944, when Cousens had a nervous breakdown." Cousens himself, writing to Wayne Collins on October 16, 1948, referred to this incident as "my crack-up." Ivan Chapman states that Cousens had a heart attack (*Tokyo Calling*, 180).

28. I assume Iva remembered her visit to the military hospital at Shinagawa so clearly because of the stress of seeing military guards with bayoneted rifles, and her own need for a disguise, bribery, and secrecy. She essentially was involved in breaking into prison, and the experience made a much more lasting impression on her than did her later regular visits to the civilian hospital.

29. I am completely dependent on Ivan Chapman here, and he provides no reference notes concerning how he learned the details of Cousens' medical diagnosis and history. Chapman, *Tokyo Calling*, 181.

30. In her Notes from 1948, Iva seems unaware that Cousens stayed in two hospitals. She remembered bribing two nurses who helped her during multiple visits "at a private hospital." She also claimed Phil often went with her. "When I saw that the nurses were getting scared of being found out, I stopped my visits to the hospital."

31. Mrs. Kido's deposition, March 22, 1949, 7, 9–10. NARA 2, Box 9.

32. Ince told the CIC after the war that he stopped work on *Zero Hour* about February 1944. CIC, File 80-T-5, January 10, 1946. NARA 2, Box 9. At trial, he testified he was present for every broadcast through April 1944. Trial Transcript, vol. XXXI, 3483.

33. Toguri Notes.

34. George H. Henshaw, "They Made Us Slaves in Japan," *Honolulu Star-Bulletin*, 1945.

35. Statement of George Mitsushio to CIC, October 1945. NARA 1, Box 40.

36. Order of Battle statistics routinely vary. These numbers are a summary of those at http://users.swing.be/navbat/bataille/741.html

37. Iva said exactly that in her interview in 1987; I assume she had mentally excluded her husband from consideration in the category of "people I liked."

38. "Deposition of Unami Kido," March 22, 1949. NARA 2, Box 9.

39. Okada deposition, 8. Okada stated he first met Iva in October 1944. NARA 2, Box 9. For those wondering how Iva or Mrs. Kido could find food to buy, it should be remembered that Iva chose foods that ordinary Japanese disdained as inedible.

40. Okada said of Phil, "He had a house in Atsugi, and his baggage was in Atsugi, and he would commute to the Tokyo Domei from Atsugi, and there were times when he would stay at Mrs. Kido's, and times he would go directly home to Atsugi." Katsuo Okada deposition, 10. Trial Tran-

script, vol. XLII, 4687–94. NARA 2, Box 9. However, as the war wound down, train service was regularly interrupted and Allied fighters strafed trains, so it is almost certain Phil commuted less and less.

41. Trial Transcript, vol. XLIII, 4758–59. He said only that Iva lived at Mrs. Kido's, that he moved there shortly after she did and before they were married, and that they still lived at the same address.

42. Iva told me that she wasn't sure where he stayed and suggested it might have been with his brother, Ted. But when I asked if Phil stayed with her, she expressly said no.

43. "Q: Philip D'Aquino came to live in your home later [after Iva], is that right? A: Yes. Q: And he and Iva were married? A: Yes; they lived together after they were married." Deposition of Unami Kido. NARA 2, Box 9. Mrs. Kido's answer does not eliminate the possibility that they also lived together before they were married.

44. Figure 10.1, October 31, 1947, NARA 8, Box 569, Photo #289866; Figure 10.2, NARA 3, Box 1.

45. Toguri Notes.

46. At Christmas 1941, she lived with her aunt and uncle who were not Christians. In 1942 and 1943, she lived at the Onarikin boarding house. She might have celebrated Christmas with Phil in 1943 but she was under surveillance by the *kempeitai* and would not have dared put up a Christmas tree.

47. Ince specifically recalled the date of November 1, so the plane had to be the *Tokyo Rose*. "Exhibit II," 441st CIC Report, March 15, 1946, report 46, exhibit 8. NARA 9, Box 237.

48. The story of the *Tokyo Rose* and her crew, as well as facts about the B-29 from "Giants Long Gone from Tokyo Skies," *Oakland Tribune*, November 15, 1964. Figure 10.3, Photo 3A 38985, 64239. NARA 8.

11

War's End

Between late 1944 and the summer of 1945, American B-29s bombed Japan during the day and during the night. They bombed when the skies were clear, when it rained, and when it snowed. They bombed military targets and private homes. They employed percussive bombs to blow up buildings and incendiary bombs to burn them down. They flew from Saipan and Tinian, dropped their payloads, flew back, refueled, reloaded, and returned to bomb again. In a ten-day period in March 1945, B-29s dropped 2 million bombs on the Japanese. On a single day, July 10, 2,000 B-29s attacked cities across Japan. Only one-fifth of bombs dropped on Japan hit industrial targets; the rest fell on ordinary citizens.

The effect on the ground was horrific. To take just one example of thousands, the Toyokawa Naval Arsenal was an industrial facility managed by the military but staffed by female workers and students, including 50 from elementary school. When the B-29s hit it with percussive bombs, between 2,000 and 3,000 civilians died. An eyewitness described the carnage: "A girl's head hung from a tree by the road, the hair caught in the branches. A young worker with no legs, face burned black, crawled around on her hands."[1]

The worst of the conventional attacks occurred on the night of March 9–10, 1945. Before this raid, the B-29s had bombed from high altitude and usually during the day, when they could see their targets. General Curtis LeMay, head of the Twentieth Air Force,

241

realizing the Japanese would be surprised and essentially defense-less against a night attack, sent 334 B-29s at very low altitude to set fires throughout the packed district along the Sumida river of eastern Tokyo. LeMay knew the structures in the area were primarily residences and small factories, and therefore almost entirely made of wood. He used incendiary bombs to cause the greatest destruction and loss of life.

Gale force winds blew across Tokyo on the night of the bombing, which began about 11:30 PM and lasted three hours. The winds whipped fires started by the incendiaries, and the neighborhoods quickly turned into an inferno. Entire houses were reduced to a pile of ashes in less than 10 minutes. Crowds, facing a wall of flame coming toward them, ran screaming until they found themselves facing a wall of fire coming from the opposite direction. Those trying to escape trampled the old, the lame, and the children. People running from all four directions on streets slammed into each other at intersections. With nowhere to go, they burned alive. A mother ran with her infant strapped to her back, unaware the baby was on fire.[2] The fires sucked the oxygen out of the air, causing thousands to die of asphyxiation. The ash clogged their tear ducts, first making it impossible to cry and then blinding them. Some raced for the river but the B-29s had destroyed most of the bridges. The screaming masses pushed earlier arrivals into the river where they drowned. Corpses soon choked the Sumida. Other Japanese submerged themselves in the fetid waters of Tokyo's canals but they either died from smoke inhalation, carbon monoxide poisoning, or were boiled to death. Those who survived had little hope of medical help. Because of military conscription and evacuations, just nine doctors and eleven nurses remained in the entire city of Tokyo.[3]

The fires burned for four days. Only rough estimates of casualties are possible. About 100,000 people died that night, and another 125,000 were wounded. The fire bombs destroyed about 250,000 buildings and more than 1,000,000 people lost their homes.

That Iva Toguri survived this and other bombings is something of a miracle. Mrs. Kido lived farther out than the heaviest-hit districts, and her house survived the war. The Allies bombed the Danish legation but Iva was absent at the time. Radio Tokyo made it to the end. But Iva remembered the March 9 raid vividly. Because the fires had burned up the trolleys, she and Phil D'Aquino had to walk to the radio station the next morning. People had run to the Meiji Shrine believing its acres of open ground would keep them safe, but the firestorm was too intense. Phil and Iva came upon the bodies. The people had knelt in prayer before the Shrine in long rows, and now their flesh was charred black and melted together. "I couldn't tell if they were young or old, male or female. It made me so sick I just turned around and went home."

Curtis LeMay exulted. He called the attack "a diller" and used low-level incendiary bombing against other cities in the months that followed.[4] Later in the war, W. H. Lawrence, a writer on military affairs for the *New York Times*, commented that American leaders considered the March raid against Tokyo a gamble. "It marked the first all-out effort to burn down a great city, and destroy its people. The reaction at home [in America] to this wholesale slaughter of civilians might have been bad."[5] Military planners need not have worried. A Gallup poll showed that Americans generally agreed with Admiral Halsey's expressed opinion that the Japanese "monkey men" were no better than rats.[6] In late 1944, Gallup asked Americans what they thought should be done with the Japanese. The majority of respondents, 33 percent, answered that the nation of Japan should be destroyed. Another 13 percent declared that we should kill all Japanese people. Only 8 percent believed we should try to "rehabilitate and reeducate" them.[7]

Reporter Matsuo Kato's nephew Kozo was a carefree, happy child, but the incessant bombing changed his personality. He became melancholy, and when his home burned to the ground, he announced to his family with somber dignity, "We cannot defeat the B-29s." In 1945, Kozo suffered a "nervous breakdown" and died. He was nine.[8]

Kozo was right. America's B-29s flew almost 30,000 sorties against Japanese cities, destroying 40 percent of Osaka and Nagoya, 50 percent of Tokyo, Kobe, and Yokohama, and 90 percent of Aomori and other smaller cities. They reduced to ashes about 160 square miles of urban areas, leaving ten or more millions dead or homeless. The annihilation of Hiroshima and Nagasaki was yet to come.

The B-29s were so little opposed that the U.S. military felt secure enough to drop leaflets warning Japanese citizens of where it would bomb next. Japanese authorities dismissed these leaflets as disinformation, but residents of Kofu believed them, evacuated the city, and as a result relatively few died in the raid against it. (Takano, Iva's former boss and head of the radio station in Kofu, did not evacuate and was killed.) But with no official dissemination of leaflet information, rumors plagued ordinary Japanese. A rumor spread that leaflets had promised that Yokohama would not be destroyed. Tens of thousands of Tokyo residents fled there seeking safety. But the United States had made no such promise. B-29s flattened Yokohama on May 29.

~

Amid the incessant bombing, Iva and Phil decided to marry. The marriage bug hit Radio Tokyo during these perilous times. *Zero Hour* manager Ken Oki married announcer Mieko Furuya, and disk jockey Norman Reyes married announcer Kathy (Kaoru) Moruka. Iva played the piano at Reyes' wedding, accompanying Satoshi Nakamura, a professional singer who sometimes read the news on *Zero Hour*.

Why Iva got married in April 1945, is unclear. Given that it was not relevant to her case, Iva never offered an explanation in any of her depositions or pre-trial statements. She did admit after the war that, "I knew, from reading Allied news reports, that an Allied victory was near."[9] Given that an Allied victory would mean she could finally return home, the reasoning behind her decision is even more opaque. Prosecutors claimed that it was a calculated attempt to avoid treason charges by obtaining Portuguese citizenship (Phil D'Aquino was a Portuguese national). That seems unlikely. If Iva had behaved with such prescience and prudence, she would have avoided innumerable other actions that made her look guilty.

In 1987, I asked Iva about her decision. She responded to my questions in an extremely guarded manner. Unlike most women, she had no recollection of her husband's proposal (although she did remember the proposal of the diplomatic student mentioned in chapter 5). She said that when she met Phil, nothing in particular about him attracted her. She also denied she was passionately in love, claiming she felt "a general affection when you sympathize with each other." Asked why she thought this was the right time and the right man, she answered, "Well, I don't know. [long pause]

I can't put my finger on it." She continued, "Here comes someone who is genuinely concerned about you, considerate of your welfare. In all his plans, I came first. This is the thing that influenced my decision. Someone cared enough to protect me. He was always there." Her conclusion was, "I guess we all were concerned about how we would come out of the war. I guess we decided we could better meet whatever was coming together rather than by ourselves." Iva had no desire to remain in Japan where Phil had spent his life, but they never discussed where they would live after the war. In our interview, Iva alternated between claiming Phil would have happily moved to the United States and that she thought they might live in Portugal. Nor did she consider how her father would react. She and Phil also never discussed children or post-war careers.

This account comes forty years and much heartache after the fact. Perhaps their marriage was simply the result of war-related pressures to maximize experience when one's life could end at any moment. Then again, perhaps their marriage might have succeeded had the U.S. government treated Iva more fairly. Pictures of the two of them from the 1940s show a couple who seem to be in love. Iva's guardedness may represent a psychological defense against the pain of loss, more than dated recollections of how she felt about Phil during wartime. But we cannot be sure.

After they decided to marry, they visited Mr. Pinto, the Portuguese Consul in Tokyo, to ask if he would perform the marriage in the consulate. He advised them that the Portuguese government would only recognize the marriage if the Roman Catholic Church performed it. To do that, Iva would have to convert to Catholicism. Phil was not a strong Catholic, attending Church only on Easter and Christmas, but he and his family desired Iva's conversion. She agreed, and undertook studies with Father John B. Kraus, a German Jesuit priest. Iva and Father Kraus, for whom she had tremendous intellectual respect, got along well, and after two months of study, he baptized her in the Church on April 18, 1945, the day before her wedding. She remained Roman Catholic throughout the rest of her life.

The wedding itself was distinctly low key. Only a few people attended. Phil's sister Rita was Iva's maid of honor, and Mr. Pinto was Phil's best man. Her mother-in-law gave Iva her handmade lace veil, which Maria D'Aquino had worn at her own wedding. The ceremony was interrupted by an alert but no bombs fell on the church. Norman Reyes did not make it on time because of the air raid, but he did attend the reception that featured a small cake, scones, and other sweets courtesy of the Danish embassy. The honeymoon consisted of making it back to Mrs. Kido's (Figure 11.1) without being killed. Shortly after the marriage, Mr. Pinto informed them that the Portuguese government recognized the marriage and that he would register her as a dual citizen.[10]

In the winter of 1944–1945, all government-supplied fuels—oil, gasoline, charcoal, gas—faded away. To keep warm and to cook, people cut down trees and tried to burn the green wood. When the trees were gone, they burned their furniture and their books. Eventually they learned to survive by burning up whatever the bombers missed.

Figure 11.1. Phil and Iva at Mrs. Kido's.
Courtesy of National Archives

Food disappeared. During the spring of 1945, bombs destroyed more than 130,000 tons of staples. Fruits and vegetables could not be delivered from the countryside because bombing frequently disrupted transportation. Before the war, three bags of rice had cost ¥100; in 1945, the same three bags cost ¥10,000 on the black market. By way of comparison, Iva's salary at Radio Tokyo at this time was ¥120 per month after taxes. People began to eat weeds and make soup from dandelions. The Chief of Police in Osaka announced on June 21, 1945, "Due to the nationwide food shortage and the imminent invasion of the home islands, it will be necessary to kill all the infirm old people, the very young, and the sick. We cannot allow Japan to perish because of them."[11]

Iva herself faced additional hardship. Germany had invaded Denmark on April 8, 1940, and set up a puppet government. The Danes had continued to resist their occupation and on August 29, 1942, Germany arrested King Christian and placed Denmark under martial law. Martial law continued until the German troops in Denmark finally surrendered on May 4, 1945, days before Germany's total surrender on May 7. On May 17, the newly liberated government of Denmark broke off relations with Japan and instructed minister Tillitse to return home with whatever he could carry. Tillitse closed the legation, ending Iva's employment. He sold his furniture, packed his silver and other precious items, and took the trans-Siberian railway home. The Russians stripped him clean. He arrived home with the clothes on his back.[12]

The legation's closure not only cut Iva's income but it shut off her supply of hard-to-find goods that she could trade on the black market. She and Phil occasionally journeyed to the country to search for food, but this was now dangerous. More than once they had to jump off the train and flee with everyone else when American fighters strafed the railroad cars. Much to Phil's consternation, Iva insisted on carrying whatever food she had with her as she ran from the attacks. However, the resourceful Iva had prepared for the worst. In better times, Iva had shrewdly buried nonperishable food in large cans in Mrs. Kido's backyard. In 1945, at night when the neighbors could not see her, she surreptitiously dug up the cans so the three of them could eat.

In the last months of the war, more than 10 million Japanese abandoned the cities for the countryside. Almost half of these were refugees from Tokyo, about 80 percent of whom left following the March fire raid. Large portions of the major cities were reduced to rubble and devoid of people. Those fleeing tried to sell their larger possessions but there were no buyers. Only a few could find motorized transportation out. Some used bicycles, most simply walked away. Millions had no place to stay and nothing to eat.

No official, and certainly no ordinary citizen, dared to say out loud that the Japanese were beaten, but Iva knew it was true. She believed the Japanese knew it too. "You could see the war weariness in their faces. They were damn tired of the war." Iva remembered rumors in the spring of 1945. A high priest in Kyoto, according to one, had a vision of his disciples walking along a lake dressed in white carrying white lanterns. The Japanese wear white to funerals and for them, white is a symbol of death, just like the white flag is a sign of surrender for Americans. Another rumor was that a peasant had given birth to a hairy ape-child who had proclaimed that the war would end in August, after which the child died. The monkey is a symbol of wisdom and foresight to Japanese. Iva believed these and other rumors swept through Japan as a way for people to prepare themselves for the unspeakable, the first defeat in war in the nation's history.

Japan's military situation was dire. Weapons production slowed to a standstill as the Allies destroyed manufacturing plants. The Japanese had no metal to manufacture planes or ships. They had little gasoline or fuel oil to operate those that still existed. The armed forces of Japan would have to fight with whatever weapons and supplies they had left.

In Japan itself, civilians prepared for the battle of the homeland. Students pulled out stumps from forests already cut down, spurred by the claim that the gasoline that could be manufactured from "two hundred pine stumps [that] will keep a plane flying for an hour."[13] Authorities awakened civilian units at 3:00 AM for worship and then to train with bamboo spears. One wrote in his diary, "The enemy will attack with bombs and guns; it is absurd to meet them with such weapons."[14] Digging shelters became a constant activity. Iva avoided participating in such preparations.

The Japanese lost battle after battle. The Allied assault to retake the Philippines, begun in 1944, eventuated in the fall of Manila on March 3, 1945. Japanese units tried to hold out from the mountains, but American forces took complete control in mid-June.

Of greater strategic importance was the island of Iwo Jima. Iwo Jima was halfway between Saipan and Tokyo, and its capture would allow the B-29s to bomb Japan twice as frequently. Iwo Jima was a volcanic isle, and no amount of bombardment could dislodge the entrenched Japanese forces. American Marines landed on February 19, 1945. Although they were able to plant the U.S. flag on Mount Suribachi (site of the famous photograph) just four days later, they did not eliminate the last of the Japanese resistance until March 16. The fierce fighting cost the lives of 6,000 Marines and 20,000 Japanese. In the following months, thousands of B-29s used Iwo Jima as a launching point.

On January 18, 1945, Japan's Supreme Council for the Direction of the War instituted as official military policy the *kamikaze* attack. Such attacks had been made throughout the war and had become prevalent in the Battle of Leyte Gulf. Now the military concentrated what little arms production capacity still remained to create special submarines, high-speed boats, the Kaiten human torpedo, tank-destroying uniforms for Army soldiers, the Baka glider missile, and special aircraft. All these devices shared the characteristic that their operators would not survive their use. Radio Tokyo proudly broadcast stories of support for the *kamikaze*:

> Girls of high schools cut their fingers and with their blood painted rising sun flags along with poems expressing their determination to emulate the special attack corps [*kamikaze*]. "Ladies though we may be, may we humbly follow our eagles as they fall so nobly. The spirit of the special attack corps is rising in the hearts of one hundred million comrades."[15]

The desperate *kamikaze* attacks could not stem American advances. The next major Allied objective was the large strategic island of Okinawa. Okinawa had been a prefecture of Japan since the Meiji era, and it lay only 350 miles from the Japanese mainland. The assault was the bloodiest of the many Pacific island campaigns and gave the Allies a foretaste of what the invasion of the Japanese

mainland would be like. The United States had been bombing Okinawa since 1944, and the Navy had more forces concentrated for
the final battle than it had at Normandy. On April 1, 60,000 American troops landed on Okinawa to begin combat against entrenched
Imperial Army forces. The Japanese counterattacked on April 6
with hundreds of *kamikaze* raids and an assault by the battleship
Yamato. The *Yamato* set sail with only enough fuel for a one-way
trip, but American planes using bombs and torpedoes sunk it on
April 7 before it could fire on Allied ships. The *kamikaze* attacks,
however, caused the greatest number of losses the U.S. Navy has
ever suffered in a single battle.

The campaign for Okinawa lasted three grueling months. Japanese forces defended in furious, often hand-to-hand combat. The
Allies declared the campaign officially over on July 2. The United
States lost 12,000 dead, suffered 36,000 wounded, and had 34 ships
sunk and 368 damaged. More than 110,000 Japanese troops died in
the battle and after the loss, Commander Mitsuru Ushijima, most
of his officer corps, and civilian governor Akira Shimada committed ritual suicide in shame over their failure to defend the island.

The end of the war came in unimaginable horror. Early on a
warm, sunny morning, August 6, 1945, under a blue and cloudless
sky, the people of Hiroshima looked up to see a single silver B-
29 cruising high above their city. Suddenly a brilliant white light
blinded them and a shock wave knocked them backward like a
train had hit them. Everybody believed a bomb had exploded a few
feet from where they were standing.[16] In less than a second, a ther-
mal ball of several hundred thousand degrees turned Hiroshima
into an atomic inferno. The blast tore people's clothes off and then
their skin. Survivors staggered about, covered with blood, their
faces hanging from their chins and the skin of their hands dangling
from fingernails. A little girl of five recalled, "Blue-green balls of
fire were drifting around. There was a strange smell all over. I had
a terrible lonely feeling that everybody else in the world was dead
and only we were still alive."[17]

Tens of thousands died instantly but many continued to live
in excruciating pain. They vomited, bled from their eyes, ears, and
mouths, and died within hours. Eighty thousand died the first day,

but that was only the beginning. No one realized they were surrounded by an invisible killer, nuclear radiation. Radiation victims were a kind of walking dead. They developed ulcers, couldn't eat, bled uncontrollably, lost their hair, and then died. Those far enough away to survive the detonation were disfigured by scars and plagued with illness. Women unfortunate enough to be pregnant often gave birth to babies with tiny heads (microencephalitis) and other defects. The bomb also destroyed just under 100 percent of Hiroshima's structures and fried thousands of fish living in its rivers.

Yasu Takeuchi's daughter Mineko was in elementary school when the bomb detonated. Although the blast badly burned Yasu and made her bald, she searched for her child for three days without food or water until she found her lying on the hard sand floor of a lecture hall, a repository of those still alive. Mineko liked to make dolls out of leftover bits of cloth, but her hands were now swollen lumps.

> Looking at her fingers that day, she sadly said, "Mother, I won't be able to make dolls any more."
> Burns covered her whole body, bleeding and festering. The doctor would hurriedly strip away the bandages, cause the blood and pus to pour forth, exposing the raw flesh. Each time she sobbed in pain. The burns kept her in agony day and night.[18]

Mineko Takeuchi died nine days later with her mother beside her. Yasu survived, though afflicted with leukemia.

On August 9, a second atomic bomb fell on Nagasaki. Nagasaki had the largest population of Roman Catholics in Japan, about 12,000 congregants. They tended to live around the central cathedral, which was ground zero for the blast. Eighty percent of them died.[19]

The citizens of Hiroshima and Nagasaki died slowly, over weeks and months and years. To state the number of casualties of the atomic bombs is impossible due to its long-term effects. A prudent estimate is that the two bombs killed about 110,000 Japanese citizens and injured 130,000 immediately. By 1950, another 230,000 Japanese had died from injuries or radiation.[20]

The day following the second atomic attack, the *Nippon Times* wrote, "How can a human being with any claim to a sense of moral responsibility let loose an instrument of destruction which can at one stroke annihilate an appalling segment of mankind? This is not war, this is not even murder, this is pure nihilism. This is a crime against God and humanity which strikes at the very basis of moral existence."[21]

Iva broadcast for the last time on August 13. She knew peace negotiations were under way, but the station did not broadcast this information; she put on her usual program of music.[22] On August 15, 1945, Japan surrendered and the Japanese people heard the voice of their emperor for the first time. In a national radio broadcast, Emperor Hirohito commanded them "to endure what is difficult to endure, and to suffer what is difficult to suffer." The Japanese Army still had almost 5 million men in uniform; the Imperial Navy, almost 2 million. All had been trained to die rather than surrender, yet they obeyed the emperor.

The Japanese people expected the worst. They believed Allied troops would monopolize the food supply. In fact, the Americans not only brought food for themselves but food for the Japanese as well, although this did not prevent widespread starvation immediately after the war. Women who could journeyed to rural areas, fearing rape. But the Americans, despite their built-up hatred of "Japs" following years of denigrating them as rats, monkey men, yellow bastards, and the like, did not commit mass murder or mass rape as had the Japanese military in Nanking.[23] In a surprising, almost unimaginable turn of events it is difficult to imagine anyone could have predicted, American servicemen married 20,000 Japanese women and took them home to the States.

On August 28, 1945, the first American ship, the minesweeper *Revenge*, entered Tokyo Bay to prepare the way for Halsey's fleet. General Douglas MacArthur landed at Atsugi, the home of Iva's in-laws, two days later. His staff had warned him against it. The Japanese had stationed a thousand trained *kamikaze* pilots at Atsugi Air Field and 22 divisions of the Imperial Army stood ready nearby. By comparison, the U.S. Army had very few troops on the ground in Japan, and MacArthur's staff worried that the Japanese might annihilate the lot of them, including the General himself, in one last act of defiance. MacArthur landed anyway, firm in his conviction that he understood the Japanese and their code of honor.[24] As the Army drove him to Yokohama, 30,000 armed Imperial soldiers stood side by side along the route, their backs to MacArthur in a display of deference, guarding him in the same way they guarded their emperor. In the words of historian Richard Storry, "So began the most peaceful and, to outward appearance, most harmonious occupation of one great country by another that has ever been known."[25]

In the months following the surrender, the emperor, to convince the nation he was not a god but a human being, toured Japan visiting ordinary people. He wore dated clothes and spoke to farmers and workers in a shy but sincere way. As he endured what was difficult to endure, he led by example, and, as Storry puts it, "the old nationalistic phrase, the Emperor and the People are One, took on new and profounder meaning."[26]

By contrast, General MacArthur, the Supreme Commander for Allied Powers, ruled from a distance. He arrived at his office in the morning and returned to his living quarters in the U.S. Embassy in the evening on an unwavering schedule. He never dealt with ordinary Japanese. Although some American historians have criticized MacArthur for his imperiousness, traditional Japanese recognized his management style. He reminded them of a shogun, and he gained their respect. When at dawn on April 16, 1951, MacArthur retraced his route to Atsugi to leave Japan, hundreds of thousands of weeping Japanese lined the road to express their gratitude for his leadership and to say good-bye.[27]

Notes

1. Ienaga, *The Pacific War*, 200.

2. *Women against War*, 164.

3. I find this hard to believe, but Havens is usually reliable. *Valley of Darkness*, 177–79.

4. "Diller" was either LeMay's twist on "dilly" or his shortened version of "killer-diller." Both terms are slang for fabulous.

5. "Air Might Clinched Battle of Japan," *New York Times*, August 15, 1945, 11.

6. Halsey's disparagements in the *Washington Post*, August 13, 1945, 2.

7. Other responses: 28 percent believed we should "supervise and control" them; 18 percent had no opinion. Published December 20, 1944.

Survey #335, Question #2a, "What do you think we should do with Japan, as a country, after the war?" *Gallup Poll* (New York: Random House, 1971), vol. 1, 477.

8. Kato, *The Lost War*, 196.

9. Toguri Notes.

10. Figure 11.1, NARA 8, Box 625, photo 305359.

11. Ienaga, *The Pacific War*, 182.

12. I have this secondhand from Iva, who communicated with Tillitse after the war.

13. Gwen Terasaki, *Bridge to the Sun* (Chapel Hill: University of North Carolina Press, 1957), 168.

14. Isoko and Ichiro Hatano, *Mother and Son* (Boston: Houghton, Mifflin, 1962), n.p.

15. Broadcast, April 22, 1945. NARA 10, Box 737.

16. Kato, *The Lost War*, 218.

17. Mark Selden, "The United States, Japan, and the Atomic Bomb," in *Showa Japan: Political, Economic, and Social History, 1926–1989*, ed. Stephen S. Large (New York: Routledge, 1998), 142.

18. *Women against War*, 125-26.

19. See http://www.americancatholic.org/Features/WWII/feature 0283.asp.

20. Information Please Almanac at http://www.infoplease.com/spot/hiroshima1.html

21. *Nippon Times*, August 10, 1945.

22. According to Clark Lee's initial notes. NARA 2, Box 17. Since Iva recounted this date just two weeks later, I have used it. George Ozasa, a manager and technician at Radio Tokyo asserted in 1949 that Iva quit two or three weeks before the war ended. Ozasa Deposition, 7. NARA 2, Box 9.

23. For an excellent analysis of the racial aspects of the war between Japan and the United States, see John W. Dower, *War without Mercy* (New York: Pantheon Books, 1986).

24. MacArthur, *Reminiscences*, 269–70.

25. Storry, *A History of Modern Japan*, 238.

26. Storry, *A History of Modern Japan*, 248.

27. MacArthur himself put the number of well-wishers at 2 million. See *Reminiscences*, 399.

12

The Scoop

MacArthur first landed in Japan on the afternoon of August 30, 1945. Earlier that day, a planeload of war correspondents had arrived from Okinawa via B-29 to cover the event. The Army ordered these men to stay put until it had secured Tokyo. The Army believed it would be dangerous to travel unescorted in Japan and also unseemly for them to enter Tokyo ahead of MacArthur. However, the reporters had little interest in MacArthur's arrival and completely ignored these directives. After a quick breakfast, they piled into an assortment of vehicles assembled by the Japanese and, in a chase right out of *It's a Mad Mad Mad Mad World* featuring mechanical breakdowns, overheated engines, police barricades, roads whose potholes were bomb craters, and other hindrances, they made a mad dash for Tokyo.

Why the rush? A million stories awaited journalists in Japan after the war, but one towered above the others as a genuine scoop: to unmask the identity of, and then interview, Tokyo Rose. By war's end, Tokyo Rose was as famous as war minister Tojo or Emperor Hirohito, except that unlike the two men, no one knew who Tokyo Rose was. To find her and get an exclusive could make a career, to say nothing of the potential monetary rewards. Before the frenzy subsided, as many as 300 reporters fought each other for the story.[1]

A gaggle of journalists made it to Radio Tokyo by that evening; a much larger number, on the next day. They all encountered an unexpected problem. No one had ever heard of Tokyo Rose. Instead, reporters learned many women broadcast in the English language to Allied forces. The *New York Times* reported that, as of the end of August, "Tokyo Rose Identity Still Mystifies U.S."[2]

The multiplicity of female broadcasters disappointed reporters, but two working for the Hearst syndicate, Clark Lee and Harry Brundidge, decided how to resolve the problem. If they could not find *the* Tokyo Rose, they would find *a* Tokyo Rose. They contacted an old friend, Leslie Nakajima,[3] a bilingual reporter for the Domei News Agency. Lee and Brundidge believed Tokyo Rose broadcast on the *Zero Hour*[4] and, for a fee of a few hundred dollars, Nakajima agreed to help them find out about the program and its female broadcasters. Nakajima approached *Zero Hour* manager Ken Oki. Oki wanted to propose his wife, Mieko Furuya, the Saturday Night Party Girl, but instead he pointed to Iva Toguri as the best candidate because "she had originated with Cousens, Ince and Reyes."[5] The day before the *Times* reported that Tokyo Rose's identity remained a mystery, Clark Lee cabled the Hearst-owned *Los Angeles Examiner* that Iva was "propagandist Tokyo Rose No. 5."[6] Where "No. 5" came from is anybody's guess, but Lee knew that Iva was a Nisei born in Los Angeles, and the paper dug up Iva's UCLA graduation photo to run with the brief article. This was the newspaper that Jun and June Toguri saw while at the LA store on September 1.

Nakajima had visited Iva and Phil at Mrs. Kido's and informed them that Lee and Brundidge would pay $2,000 for an exclusive interview with Tokyo Rose.[7] Iva replied that she had never used the name, but Nakajima convinced her to meet with the two reporters anyway. The next morning, September 1 in Japan and August 30 in the United States, Nakajima drove Iva and Phil to the Imperial Hotel. At this important meeting, which will be discussed in detail later, Iva signed a contract for an exclusive story and gave the two reporters an account of her life, which Clark Lee jotted down in the form of typewritten notes. In the one-page contract, Iva stated that she was "the one and original 'Tokyo Rose' who broadcast from Radio Tokyo and had no feminine assistants or substitutes."[8]

To put it plainly, Iva Toguri lied.[9] She may have naively believed at that time that Tokyo Rose was only a radio personality, but she knew many women broadcast, that she was neither "one" nor "original," and that other women often substituted for her on weekends or when she was absent from the studio. Furthermore, on this occasion at least, she understood and read the contents of the document she signed.

Brundidge and Lee announced their scoop to the other reporters immediately. The next day, Dale Kramer and James Keeney of *Yank* magazine visited Iva and Phil. "Kramer told me it was unfair I gave B and L an exclusive interview without seeing the other 40 or 50 correspondents who were waiting to get some kind of story. Mr. Kramer asked me to be fair to all of them."[10] Kramer also remarked that Lee and Brundidge worked for the Hearst syndicate and only wanted scandal. Iva agreed to meet the other correspondents. On September 5, Kramer and Keeney, accompanied by Ken Oki, took Iva to the Bund Hotel in Yokohama, where she met about 50 correspondents from various news agencies from around the world (Figure 12.1). No one offered her a contract or payment for this interview. On the way, Oki lamented that he blundered in not recommending his wife as Tokyo Rose.[11]

Figure 12.1. Iva with reporters at the Bund Hotel.
Courtesy of National Archives

The press conference lasted only 30 minutes. Reporters focused primarily on learning enough about Iva so they could put together a basic biography. They did ask one or two questions about military predictions attributed to Tokyo Rose, and Iva denied having made them. The unmasking of Tokyo Rose created nationwide publicity in America. NBC claimed she had broadcast over the radio as Orphan Anne on that very day, September 5, and quoted her as saying she was "not sure she was glad she had retained her United States citizenship, since she had just undergone questioning by the military police." The United Press coverage quoted Miss Togori [sic], "I was just sitting on the fence as far as the war was concerned," which made it appear she didn't care which side won.[12]

After the news conference, the Eighth Army Counter-Intelligence Corps (CIC) picked up Iva and Phil and took them to CIC commander, Brigadier General Elliot Thorpe. Thorpe stunned Iva by yelling at her that she was guilty of treason. He immediately placed her under arrest. Upon hearing about this, Mieko Oki, Kathy Reyes, Ruth Hayakawa, and the other female broadcasters who might have had designs on fame and fortune quickly faded away, and the words of the contract came true. Iva Toguri became the one and original Tokyo Rose.[13]

~

The central question, asked from the perspective of subsequent events, is: Why in the world did Iva sign up to be Tokyo Rose?

In her 1948 memories (Toguri Notes), Iva stated more than once that she wanted to avoid being bothered by reporters, and that Lee, Brundidge, and Nakajima promised her that an exclusive would prevent this annoyance. This cannot be the reason. In the first place, she willingly and almost immediately accompanied Kramer to a press conference filled with reporters. Second, in the next few months, she signed innumerable autographs, agreed to many pictures with servicemen, made voice transcriptions for the Signal Corps, and participated in film studies of herself doing mock broadcasts. Obviously, Iva enjoyed the limelight. Nothing about her personality suggests that she was shy or retiring. She had survived Japan as an English-speaking alien "spy"; she surely believed she could easily withstand the American press.

She later stated, in 1949, that she had no interest in the $2,000. However, four years earlier she purportedly had told Kramer, "I figured someone was going to get the money, and I might as well be her."[14] In our interviews, she claimed she signed the contract solely because she wanted the money. "It was a little selfish on my part. I was looking for a way out of Japan, so when he [Nakajima] said these guys are going to offer $2,000—if you'll give them any kind of cock and bull story they'll pay you—I thought that this would take care of my transportation."

Certainly the amount of money had an appeal. When Iva left the United States in 1941, rice cost 9¢ a pound, a quart of fresh milk delivered to your doorstep was 14¢, a roast cost 27¢ per pound, movie tickets ran 35¢ for an adult, and medical care cost on average $100.80 per year.[15] To a young woman on the edge of starvation, $2,000 had to seem like a small fortune. In addition, Iva knew her family in the States must be struggling to recover and could ill afford to pay for another trans-Pacific voyage. She also very likely wanted to get home on her own to show her father how resourceful she had become during her years in Japan.

In the end, however, this explanation is also unsatisfactory. When Iva met the reporters in Yokohama, she not only voided her contract but made another "exclusive" impossible. She may have decided the additional publicity would lead to better money down the road, but as far as immediate cash for transportation out was concerned, the Hearst contract was a bird in the hand that Iva intentionally let fly away. (Iva couldn't have known it, but she wouldn't have received the $2,000 even if she had kept her bargain. Hearst voided the contract, refusing to pay money to a traitor.) She told the CIC in her initial interrogations that she had "refused the money."[16]

The most likely answer is that Iva Toguri was ambitious. She had learned through black market trading how to leverage advantage. She had shown a knack for radio announcing and very quickly had developed an appealing on-air personality. Now she realized how popular she had become with servicemen. When the tsunami of reporters hit Radio Tokyo, Iva must have hoped she could turn her entire wartime experience into profit. Iva had suffered hardship for four years, and suddenly she had the chance to make it all good, maybe even to find the career she had originally journeyed to Japan to seek. Plus, from her perspective, there was no downside. Iva did not suffer from a guilty conscience. She knew what had happened, that she was the last Nisei in Japan who could be accused of disloyalty. In fact, she was proud of how she had acted. So, with a smile on her face she told the world her amazing story.

~

General Charles Willoughby, a Prussian whose birth name was Adolf Weidenbach,[17] first met MacArthur at Fort Leavenworth in the 1930s. Something of a dandy, Willoughby wore fancy suits and, for added flair, often sported a monocle. The two men hit it off, and when MacArthur commanded the Philippines, he sent for Willoughby and made him Assistant Chief of Staff for Intelligence. Willoughby was brave—he won the Distinguished Service Cross for heroism at Buna—but his abilities in intelligence were uneven at best. When MacArthur planned an attack at Buna to cut off Japanese troops, Willoughby estimated their strength at 1,500 and assessed their capability as low. MacArthur's forces encountered instead 3,500 Japanese soldiers committed to fighting to the death. Before the Finschafen invasion in 1943, Willoughby determined the enemy had only about 350 men to defend the base. MacArthur's assault troops found 5,400 Japanese who resisted ferociously. Willoughby underestimated by half the Japanese defenders of Biak in 1944. At the end of 1944, as MacArthur attacked the Philippines, Willoughby informed him the Japanese had 137,000 troops on the island of Luzon. In fact, they had 276,000.[18]

By the conclusion of the war, when the United States moved to occupy Tokyo, Willoughby had learned his lesson. Anticipating massive resistance, he used his transport capacity to bring in combat troops and left behind counterintelligence forces. "As a result," according to reporter Frank Kluckhorn who witnessed the events, "for six weeks the Japanese Foreign Office, Radio Tokyo, and the military openly burned documents and records in the street with no counterintelligence to stop them."[19] Among the records burned were *Zero Hour* scripts, scripts from other radio programs, and Iva's employment records.[20]

~

As noted earlier, reporter Clark Lee and Iva Toguri met each other for the first time on September 1, 1945, at the Imperial Hotel. After she signed the contract, Iva recounted to Lee what really happened to her in Japan. Lee typed notes as she talked. These original notes are fragmentary but have a claim to accuracy. For example, writing in 1948, Iva remembered,

> Lee wanted to know the gist of the other fellows' parts and I told them they dealt with news in general; one of the programs, announced by Hisaghi Moriyama, discussed home life in the U.S., about the food found in the U.S., sometimes mentioning the "kamikaze." Moriyama started with the Zero Hour about June of 1944. I understand he is a graduate of College of Pacific.[21]

In the original of Lee's 1945 notes, we find somewhat similar information,

> former s. frc boy nisei thought for the day, he played lonely GI in monologue drift along saying, picked up magazine and good things eat, mama's cooking. Sure make me homesick. Power of kamikaze.[22]

However, months after this interview, Lee converted his notes into a written narrative. This new version was quite different from the original. Months after that, Lee wrote a book with a chapter devoted to Iva's story. His summary of her life story differed still further from what Iva told him at their interview. Four years later, in 1949, Lee testified at Iva's trial. By then, the facts conveyed during Iva's interview had changed considerably.

We will examine these changes in detail over the next several chapters. Here, by way of introduction, is one example. Lee's later accounts, most especially his testimony under oath at her trial, have him greeting Iva Toguri with the question, "Are you Tokyo Rose?" Iva purportedly replied, "Yes. The one and only Tokyo Rose." Next, she stated that she expected she would be arrested when Lee published his story, and she demanded a lucrative contract to make it worth her while.[23] Lee swore he had to provide it before she would talk. She did talk eventually, out of vanity. In Lee's words,

> After all, she was thinking, I am an international figure known to millions of American GIs and sailors. I have become world

famous during the war. This story will be in nearly every paper in America and in one of the biggest magazines, and my picture will be everywhere.[24]

She told him—again, according to his later accounts—how she "had sold out her country, with little regard for the consequences, for the sum of $6.66 monthly and for no other reason, motive, or reward." She admitted she had no resentment toward America, "yet, night after night, she sat down to write and broadcast a script deliberately designed to make her compatriots lose their will to go on fighting."[25] Lee testified, "She said that in her broadcasts that she told the truth, that their sweethearts were unfaithful to them, that their wives were out dancing with other men while they were fighting in the muck and jungle."[26] She further admitted that her working for Domei "was just as much treason—if I am guilty of treason—as was my later broadcasting as Tokyo Rose." Iva told him that after the Stockholm article about Tokyo Rose appeared, everyone began calling her by that name and left notes for her addressed "Tokyo Rose." However, Iva admitted, "I didn't take the name on the air because I did not want to take the responsibility of calling myself that until I had to."[27] When he asked how she felt about selling out her country for money, Iva replied, "I have no particular feeling. It was an education [learning radio technique]."[28] Finally, Lee wrote that when Iva left the interview, she "laughingly" signed an autograph, "To Harry Brundidge and Clark Lee, who may have put my neck in a noose today."[29] In Harry Brundidge's version, which he independently told to the FBI, Iva had signed, "I realize that I am placing my neck in a noose in making this statement to Mr. Brundidge."[30]

Lee's later recollections do not comport with his original interview notes, and on occasion are clearly fabrications. For example, Iva, backed up by Phil, swore that when she met Lee, she denied she was Tokyo Rose. According to them, Lee ascertained that she had in fact broadcast on *Zero Hour* and then said simply, "You will do."[31] This seems much more credible than Lee's version, especially since the *Los Angeles Examiner* had already run his story that Iva was "Tokyo Rose No. 5" and therefore Lee had a vested interest in being correct. Lee's speculation that Iva talked because she dreamed of fame and fortune may have some truth in it, but it is hard to believe she expected to be arrested for telling—confessing, in Lee's terms—her life story. Lee placed in Iva's mouth falsehoods—that she believed she "told the truth" about how wives were playing around, that her salary was $6.66 a month, that she thought her work at Domei might be treasonous—she surely never said. Lee's conversion of Iva's various salaries into the Devil's number, $6.66, is especially revealing. In 1945, Iva's broadcast salary of ¥120 would have equaled, according to the 1941 exchange rate, about $28. No exchange rate existed between 1942 and 1947, the year Lee first imagined this number. Finally, Lee's "neck in a noose" autograph story, which he wisely did not repeat at Iva's trial, is almost certainly fallacious.[32] The FBI thoroughly investigated the Brundidge version, even searching his personal effects at his apartment, and never found any such statement. In addition, the prosecution introduced Lee's actual autograph souvenir during the trial (Figure 12.2).[33]

Figure 12.2. Clark Lee's autograph.
Courtesy of National Archives

Harry Brundidge was an opportunist who drove the FBI crazy after the war with his deceptions and prevarications.[34] It is no surprise that errors and misrepresentations flaw Brundidge's version of Iva's 1945 interview, published in the *Nashville Tennessean*. But Clark Lee was a journalist of some reputation. He was neither an inveterate liar nor a hack. He had no reason to dislike Iva or want to do her harm. Iva herself in 1959 said, "Lee wasn't so bad. I might have liked him if I had known him better. I don't think he was a bad person."[35] Why then did Lee change from reasonably accurate note taker to accusatory witness for the prosecution?

One possible explanation is that Clark Lee had fallen under the spell of the legend of Tokyo Rose. Reviewing his several versions of Iva's story, one notices Lee's reporting errors continually and consistently conform the historical facts to fit what her story ought to have been if she really were Tokyo Rose. His professional reputation depended upon his finding Tokyo Rose, and, over time, he made sure he did.

In the movie *The Man Who Shot Liberty Valance*, Governor Ransom Stoddard (Jimmy Stewart) tells a group of reporters that another man, not himself as widely believed, shot Liberty Valance. However, the reporters refuse to publicize the real story. One of them explains, "When the legend becomes fact, print the legend." This clever turn of phrase obscures the reality that legends become fact because reporters print them as though they were true.

~

When the CIC placed Iva in custody on September 5, they did not take her to jail but instead sequestered Iva and Phil in the Grand Hotel in Yokohama. A military policeman (MP), after checking to make sure their room had no escape routes, and after asking for and obtaining her autograph, stood guard in the hallway all night. The next morning after breakfast, Sergeant Merritt Page of the 308th CIC Detachment questioned Iva for several hours. His six-page report, titled "Ikuko Toguri, also known as Iva Toguri, TREASON" summarized Iva's story fairly accurately and noted that she denied making anti-Allied comments on the air, denied that she made remarks about wives and girlfriends, and denied that she married in order to become a citizen of a neutral country.[36]

During this session, Sergeant Page received word that Lieutenant General Robert Eichelberger, commander of the Eighth Army's occupation forces in Japan, wanted to meet the famous Tokyo Rose. Page escorted Iva to a meeting room in the hotel and there Eichelberger gave her an entirely different reception than the accusatory confrontation she had experienced earlier with General Thorpe. She remembered, "The General [Eichelberger] shook my hand and said, 'I want to thank you for entertaining the boys with good music. Did you ever get the package of records which were addressed to you (Tokyo Rose) and dropped by one of our B-29 planes?'"[37] Iva explained that she had never used the name "Tokyo

Rose" and that she never received the records. Eichelberger had some pictures taken with her and shook hands again at the conclusion of their meeting.

Page then continued his interview and when he finished, he took Iva for fingerprinting. Afterward, Page released her into the custody of her husband. The Army drove them back to Mrs. Kido's in Tokyo. Over the next few weeks, reporters constantly visited her, as well as various soldiers who wanted autographs and photographs of themselves with her. Iva uniformly accommodated their requests.

On September 9, 1945, Vaughn Paul, a Hollywood cinematographer and former husband of actress Deanna Durbin, showed up at Mrs. Kido's along with six other servicemen. Paul had charge of a photographic group for the U.S. Navy and he wanted a newsreel of Tokyo Rose. Broadcaster Mary Ishii's husband, Ken, had referred him to Iva. Paul convinced Iva of her popularity with sailors and told her that "we wanted to make a sound motion picture which would probably be shown in the United States." Iva agreed to participate, and Paul scripted a scene in which an American serviceman asks a Japanese policeman where he can buy a kimono. The policeman doesn't understand him and Iva steps in to overcome the language barrier. Despite several takes, the acting proved to be unacceptably amateurish and Paul instead filmed a mini-scene featuring just Iva. In this scene, Iva says, "This is Orphan Ann calling for Radio Tokyo" and an anonymous questioner off-camera replies, "Well, we in the Navy know you as Tokyo Rose." After Iva states that she's glad the war is over, the voice says. "Thank you very much, Tokyo Rose, and we want you to know we appreciated your broadcasts and your music." The narrator runs down the crew credits and adds, "We've been talking to the little Jap propagandist that we've all known in the Pacific for four years."[38]

The Army Signal Corps also decided to produce a film recreating the *Zero Hour* and convinced Iva it would be helpful to her if she agreed. On September 20, the crew set up in *Zero Hour*'s Radio Tokyo studio with Iva behind one microphone and Ken Oki behind the other. Iva read from one of her scripts and Oki read from a news broadcast about Okinawa. The footage concludes with a personal interview with Iva.[39] Other minor film and photographic projects followed.[40]

For those of us who knew Iva only in her late maturity, these films are a revelation. She smiles, winks, giggles, and openly flirts with her GI interviewers. She obviously basks in their attention. In the sailor routine, the GI, who invents new lines with every take, says at one point, "I've heard you many times. You've given a great deal of—entertainment, shall we say." Iva reacts with a little guffaw, as though she knows exactly what he means. General Thorpe's charge of treason apparently meant little to her. Further, the re-created *Zero Hour* lends some credence to the theory proposed at trial by the prosecution that Iva was a draw for the propagandists. In the short, she introduces music with her usual patter, and turns the show over to the news announcer who calmly intones that an Allied attack was "not worth the sacrifice of very young men" and asks "whether [U.S.] military leaders were sane when they approved of Okinawa." Then it's back to Iva who happily introduces more music. Iva's performance suggests that this sort of scenario was routine. She seems utterly oblivious to the possibility that her popularity might cause listeners to stay tuned as the news announcer broadcast his assault on their morale.

Finally, the U.S. Treasury Department made its own Tokyo Rose mini-drama sometime in 1945 before the war ended. The film portrayed American servicemen as they listened to a female broadcaster proclaim the impossibility of dislodging the Japanese troops on Iwo Jima. She speaks unaccented English softly and seductively. She warns that "thousands of Japanese are safe in caves waiting to slaughter you. You're making this sacrifice for people 11,000 miles away, for people who've never seen a grenade burst in an American stomach." No record exists of any GI ever attributing such inflammatory rhetoric to Tokyo Rose, and the listeners look terrified. She identifies herself only with, "This is the Voice of Truth, my Yankee brothers." Next, officers shout, "OK, Yankee brothers" and order troops onto landing craft. The film ends with one GI looking into the camera to ask if there could be anything to what she said.[41] I believe the purpose of Treasury Department filmmakers in producing this mini-drama was to sell war bonds. In any event, they apparently knew enough to avoid using the name "Tokyo Rose" for their fictional broadcaster.

While Iva enjoyed her celebrity, the U.S. government stayed busy. The CIC interviewed various individuals associated with Radio Tokyo and *Zero Hour*. On October 6, 1945, Foumy Saisho informed them that three girls used the name "Tokyo Rose" and that Iva was the first and presumably most important. Later in the interview, she told them no one used the name, but apparently the CIC overlooked the discrepancy and did not question Saisho further about it.[42]

The emergence of the famous seductress also attracted the attention of the Department of Justice (DoJ). On September 14, U.S. Attorney Charles H. Carr in Los Angeles announced he wanted Iva returned to be tried for treason. On October 11, J. Edgar Hoover had a courier deliver a confidential memo to Agent Frederick Tillman in Manila about two treason suspects, Ruth Hayakawa and Iva Toguri. "The Criminal Division of the Department has expressed an interest in this case from a prosecutive standpoint and desires to be furnished all information that can be obtained as soon as possible."[43] As previously noted, Tillman would become the FBI's lead investigator on the case.

When Iva Toguri first entered Japan in the summer of 1941, the U.S. State Department refused to issue her a passport because it could not determine whether she was actually a U.S. citizen. When Iva attempted to repatriate in 1942, the U.S. State Department informed Swiss officials that her status as a U.S. citizen was doubtful. After the war ended, Iva tried to register for U.S. rations, but she could not obtain identification papers stating she was a U.S. citizen; she had to register as Portuguese. However, when the DoJ expressed a desire to prosecute Tokyo Rose, the State Department quickly determined that Iva Toguri was in fact a U.S. citizen.

On the morning of October 17, 1945, three armed CIC officers drove up to Mrs. Kido's in a jeep. The State Department had ordered the Army to arrest her, and that afternoon, Iva Toguri found herself behind bars for the first time in her life (Figure 12.3).[44] The Army interred her at the XI Corps Stockade in Yokohama. As Iva recounted the events of that day at her trial, "They asked me to go down to Yokohama to be questioned on a few matters, and at the last minute they told me that I may have to stay overnight, to take a toothbrush, which I did."[45] In 1987, she added that she had to wear the same dress for two weeks before the Army allowed Phil to send her some fresh clothes.

Military records indicate Iva's accounts at trial and in 1987 were untrue. An October 17 "Inventory of articles on or with prisoner" shows she arrived at the prison with a bag containing two blouses, skirt, sweater, jacket, stockings, pajamas, undergarments, crucifix, purse, toiletries case with two lipsticks, a silver watch, a gold watch, and ¥400. Obviously, she came prepared for a stay. Ten days later, Phil brought her another pair of shoes, two pair of slacks, two shirts, two pajama suits, a jacket, two belts, a towel, a rosary, and more cosmetics and toiletries. On November 7, Phil brought Iva another

Figure 12.3. Courtesy of National Archives

sweater, jacket, vest, gloves, a book, sewing kit, fruit, and flowers. A week later, Phil delivered more clothing including two wool sweaters, a Bible, still more cosmetics, and another suitcase to hold her belongings.[46] In mid-November, the Army moved her to Sugamo Prison in Tokyo, where it held Premier Tojo and other war criminals.[47]

Iva would remain incarcerated for more than a year. The Army did not charge her with any crime, did not allow her to speak with counsel, and effectively cut her off from the outside world. While the Army CIC and the DoJ decided what to do with her, Iva waited in a cell. She could have lived with her husband during this period, but the American military believed the fearsome Tokyo Rose "might be capable of fomenting disorder among the Japanese population, and of inciting discontent among the troops of the occupying powers."[48]

During her time at Sugamo, GIs called her "Rose" or "Rosie" with some affection and made friendly comments. Iva in turn freely gave them autographs. For example, she signed "Iva Toguri 'Tokyo Rose'" on a yen note for a young corporal of the guards, J. Richard Eisenhart. She signed this phrase many times.

In the late 1970s, biographer Masayo Duus interviewed the FBI's lead investigator on the Toguri case, Frederick Tillman. Tillman, as will be seen in later chapters, played a key role in developing, sometimes creating, evidence of Iva's treason. Tillman said of her, "She was stupid, and all her trouble came from her own stupidity."[49] In the late 1980s, journalist Russell Warren Howe interviewed Tillman and he repeated the same slur. "Toguri was sentenced because she was stupid."[50] However, the United States did not charge Iva with stupidity. Someone ought to have explained to Tillman that the American system of justice sends people to prison, not because they are insufficiently clever to escape the snares of the FBI, but because they are guilty of a crime.

Still, as Iva sat in Sugamo Prison, a penny should have dropped. She might have been confident that she had broken no laws and that her arrest was a mistake. She might not have entirely grasped the phenomenon of Tokyo Rose. Her soldier-guards might have been supportive. None of this mattered. Until she achieved greater clarity on her situation, until she comprehended the nature of this mysterious woman and what she supposedly broadcast, she should not have signed autographs, "Iva Toguri/Tokyo Rose." The fact that she signed them by the dozens does not prove, nor is it really evidence that, she was guilty of treason. But it was, to give Tillman his due, more than a little stupid.

Notes

1. Clark Lee, Trial Transcript, vol. VII, 497.

2. *New York Times*, September 1, 1945, 4.

3. This name is also spelled "Nakashima" in many case documents and by biographers Duus and Howe. Neither spelling predominates; the trial transcript uses both. *Shima* or *jima* is Japanese for "island."

4. "I told them again that I was not 'Tokyo Rose,' that I never used the name myself. They asked me if I worked on the *Zero Hour* programs. I told them yes, after which they said if I was the feminine voice on the *Zero Hour* I must be the one they were looking for." Toguri Notes.

5. Toguri Notes on her conversations with Oki shortly after the war as to how she wound up being tagged as Tokyo Rose.

6. *Los Angeles Examiner*, September 1, 1945, 1.

7. The contract offer came from *Cosmopolitan* magazine. *Cosmopolitan* at the time was a literary magazine of fiction and human-interest stories. Because the modern "Cosmo," thanks to Helen Gurley Brown, tends to focus on sex and the single girl, I have opted to refer in the text only to Hearst, the corporate owner then and now. Despite the contract, Lee did not publish his story in *Cosmopolitan* but in another Hearst publication, the *Los Angeles Examiner*.

8. Contract between *Cosmopolitan* and Iva Toguri, September 1, 1945. NARA 2.

9. Stanley Kutler concurs. He says of her contract, "Ironically, these are the only clearly provable lies d'Aquino told throughout her experience." Kutler, "Forging a Legend," 1343.

10. Toguri Notes. Also present at this meeting were George Baker, the creator of the "Sad Sack" cartoon, and David Huga, a manager at Radio Tokyo whom Iva believed worked for the Imperial Japanese Army (IJA).

11. According to Phil. Trial Transcript, vol. XLIII, 4803. Oki denied it. Vol. X, 865. In her Notes, Iva stated that Norman Reyes came to her house a few days after the Bund interview and said that "Oki had remarked to him that Oki wished he had given out his wife's name (Miyeko Oki) as the Tokyo Rose because a Norman Paige, member of the National Broadcasting Company, Blue Network, had contacted Oki to produce 'Tokyo Rose' to go on the air for the Blue Network for the salary of $2,000 per month."

12. Both quotations in *New York Times*, September 6, 1949, 2.

13. Figure 12.1, NARA 8, Box 289, Photo #211323.

14. *Yank*, October 19, 1949. I am leery of this quotation. Kramer also quotes Iva, "I figured [the people at Radio Tokyo] were trying to fix it up for me to take the rap, clearing themselves. Then this fellow from Domei came around offering money." She surely didn't realize when Lee interviewed her that there was a rap to take. Iva was not such a fool that she would sign up to be a traitor for $2,000.

15. These prices are taken from an article and photographs that appeared in *Life*, November 17, 1941, 104. *Life* wanted to illustrate the inflation of prices by comparing 1941 to 1939.

To give readers a further idea of what Iva's $2,000 could have bought in 1941, the new Hudson six-cylinder four-door touring sedan was $750.

My favorite price grabber is an ad in the *New Yorker*, May 24, 1941, that displays a photograph of a massive stone mansion in Scarsdale, New York. The description reads, "Corner Chedworth and Haddon Roads, Cotswold. Modern in every detail. Entrance hall with flagstone floor, spacious living room with stone fireplace, library, dining room, tiled kitchen and butler's pantry on main floor, also servants' rooms with bath. Large screen porch, opening on to flagstone terrace. Four large bedrooms, all with double exposures, on second floor. Price reduced to $36,000."

16. CIC, File 80-T-5, January 10, 1946, 4. NARA 2, Box 9.

17. Some sources have his name as Karl Weidenbach, born in Heidelberg, Germany, on March 8,1892, to Baron Freiherr T. Tscheppe-Weidenbach and his wife Emma from Baltimore, Maryland, whose maiden name was Willoughby. Willoughby gave the name "Adolf Charles Weidenbach" to reporter Frank Kluckhorn (see note 19) and claimed to be an orphan.

18. Campbell, Kenneth J., "Major General Charles A. Willoughby: General MacArthur's G-2—A Biographic Sketch" in *American Intelligence Journal* 18, no. 1 (1998): 87–91.

19. Frank Kluckhorn, "Heidelberg to Madrid: The Story of General Willoughby," in *The Reporter* 7, no. 4 (August 19, 1952): 28.

20. Deposition of George Ozawa, March 22, 1949. The IJA also ordered Ozawa to destroy all employment and other records of Radio Tokyo shortly before war's end. What the Army feared might be discovered in these records is not known. NARA 2, Box 9.

21. Toguri Notes.

22. Lee's note pages not numbered; about page 15. NARA 2, Box 17.

23. Lee, *One Last Look Around*, 85–86.

24. Lee, *One Last Look Around*, 86.

25. Lee, *One Last Look Around*, "$6.66 monthly" and "attacked their morale," 86.

26. Trial Transcript, vol. VII, 486.

27. "Just as much treason" and "until I had to" from Lee's typed version of his original notes (iteration #2), 10, 13. NARA 1, Box 48; also NARA 6, Box 2.

28. Trial Transcript, vol. VII, 488.

29. Lee, *One Last Look Around*, 89.

30. FBI Agent Hostetter, Teletype, January 28, 1948. NARA 1, Box 42.

31. Trial Transcript, vol. XLIII, 4975 and vol. XLVI, 5152.

32. The fact that both Lee and Brundidge used exactly the same phrasing about Iva's neck being in a noose seems to imply that either she said or wrote something of the sort, or they were in cahoots to fabricate their story. The latter seems unlikely. Lee and Brundidge had very different

personalities, were not exactly buddies, and had little contact after the war. Brundidge may have often lied, but Lee was a serious, if flamboyant, journalist. On the other hand, no such document has ever been found. A compromise explanation is that Iva laughingly said, not wrote, as she left, "I hope I didn't put my neck in a noose today."

33. Figure 12.2, NARA 2. Collins fought against the introduction of this autograph at trial, claiming it amounted to an extra-judicial confession, but he made nothing of Lee's other version from his book. Collins probably did not want to give Lee the opportunity to claim Iva merely stated her fear that her neck was now in a noose. Trial Testimony, vol. VII, 480–83. See chapter 16.

34. Brundidge's opportunism and prevarications are discussed in chapters 14 and 15.

35. Iva interview with Gunn, *They Called Her Tokyo Rose*, 108.

36. Report, October 2, 1945. NARA 2, Box 1.

37. Toguri Notes. According to the FBI, William G. Farnum in an article of August 3, 1945 in Santa Ana, California, "stated that Tokyo Rose had complained on her broadcasts to American forces that her phonograph records were scratched and she needed new ones. A rotary club in the United States purchased some records which were flown from the United States to the B-29 base on Tinian where Farnum was the Commanding Officer. Farnum stated that these records had been put aboard a Tokyo-bound Superfortress and were dropped by parachute over Tokyo. He further stated that he had heard the records played over the Tokyo radio on the following day." FBI Report, December 29, 1945. NARA 6, Box 3.

38. I have used the date given to the Vaughn Paul production by the National Archives. Since I can't find a slate on either the head or the tail, I am not sure how NARA settled on September 9.

The CIC interviewed Iva Toguri on March 25, 1948, about movies taken of her. Iva told them that at her September 5, 1945, interview reporters took "pictures without sound." This is correct, and those films still exist. She stated, "Several weeks later Paul Vaughn [sic] (husband of Deanna Durbin), made a film short" of her. The CIC agent goes on to recount the scene of the lost sailor, policeman, etc. One could understand if Iva misremembered exact dates but not that the September 5 interview and Paul film were only four days apart. Investigation Report, 441st CIC, April 7, 1948. NARA 1, Box 43.

Vaughn Paul, in an interview with the FBI on April 7, 1949, puts the production date of his short film on or about September 5. Charles A. Potts, who was present with Paul, told the FBI exactly the same story on April 13, 1949. NARA 6, Box 3; also NARA 3, Box 6. Paul remarks in his statement, "I did not tell Toguri she was under arrest." Since the CIC arrested Iva shortly after the Bund press conference, Paul may have con-fused the sailor film with the Bund Hotel film.

Sailor film short: Record Group 428, General Records of the Depart-ment of the Navy, 1941–81; Naval Photographic Center; "Interviews of Tokyo Rose," September 9, 1945; ARC Identifier 79833.

39. Film at Record Group 111, Records of the Office of the Chief Signal Officer, 1860–1982; Office of the Chief Signal Officer, 1947–1964; File: "To-kyo Rose" [moving images], September 20, 1945; ARC Identifier 19130.

40. For a complete list of films, see 441st CIC Memo of April 7, 1948. NARA 1, Box 43.

41. Record Group 56, General Records of the Department of the Trea-sury, 1789–1990; Entry: Department of the Treasury; File: "Voice of Truth" (moving images), 1945; ARC Identifier 11822. Voice quality is excellent. Therefore, it could not have been an actual shortwave broadcast; the woman's voice had to be recorded in an American studio.

42. See chapter 8. Saisho, statement, October 4, 1945, HQ CIC Metro-politan Unit 80, January 10, 1946. NARA 1, Box 43, also 40.

43. Memo, Hoover to Tillman, October 11, 1945. NARA 1, Box 39.

44. Figure 12.3, NARA 1, Box 43.

45. Trial Transcript, vol. XLVI, 5172.

46. Inventories in NARA 7, Box 58. This considerable quantity of goods presumably came from Iva's family in the United States, not her black market operations. See chapter 13, note 35.

47. Iva stayed in the Blue Section of Sugamo; Tojo and other males stayed in one of the two Red Sections. Various 1946 documents, CIC Metro Unit 60, APO 500. NARA 2, Box 9.

48. Ninth Circuit Opinion, 13–14.

49. Duus, Orphan of the Pacific, 109.

50. Howe, The Hunt for "Tokyo Rose," 125.

13

CIC and FBI Investigations

Exoneration and Release

During Iva Toguri's year in prison, U.S. authorities treated her with unnecessary severity. The State Department had certified her U.S. citizenship so that she could be investigated for treason, but the Army took the position that she was a Japanese national, which meant she could not send a letter to anyone in the United States. The Army refused to let her speak to a lawyer and allowed her one visitor, her husband, who could see her for only half an hour per month.[1] She sat in a small cell with no clear understanding of why she was there or how long she would have to remain. The lights were always on, making sleep difficult. Authorities allowed her a bath every three days. She described her experience of incarceration without charge, limit, or counsel as "worse than physical torture."[2] Neither the *kempeitai* nor the *tokkotai* treated her as badly as her own government.

∽

The Army Counter-Intelligence Corps (CIC) and the Federal Bureau of Investigation (FBI) had begun investigating Tokyo Rose before the war ended, but they increased and concentrated their efforts shortly after the press identified Iva Toguri as the famous broadcaster. The CIC regularly informed the Department of Justice (DoJ) of the results of its work but, generally speaking, the investigations of the CIC and FBI ran on separate tracks.

The CIC, in Japan immediately after the surrender, got a head start. George S. Guysi, under the direction of his executive officer James Thomas Reitz, led the investigation by the 308th CIC detachment at Yokohama.[3] He issued his first report on Iva Toguri on October 2, 1945, less than a month after her press conference. This remarkably accurate report summarized Iva's history in six single-spaced pages. Iva told Guysi and the CIC that she never broadcast news, "denied any mention of the Allies losing the war or Japan being all powerful, and denied stating that the wives and sweethearts of the American soldiers were being unfaithful." She thought of her program simply as entertainment. The CIC summed up her role:

> She introduced herself as "Orphan Ann" and sometimes it was written into the script, "your favorite playmate and enemy." She requested the boys to "sit back and relax, ignore the mosquitoes and discomforts of the jungle and imagine themselves at home enjoying their favorite recordings." She explained that she used "Orphan Ann" as her radio name, because she considered herself an orphan in Japan, and the boys to whom she broadcast were orphans in the Southwest Pacific.[4]

On December 4, 1945, after further questioning by Charles Hetrick of CIC Metropolitan Unit 80, Iva provided an affidavit to the CIC concerning her activities in Japan. About a week later, Hetrick and two other men from the CIC brought her a typed version, in which she corrected a few misspellings of Japanese names. At this meeting, the investigators told her that their main interest lay in finding "the girl who said 'damaging things' and who had access to army secrets and maneuvers." They complained that the Japanese refused to divulge information and they "repeatedly asked if I couldn't help them in locating the voice behind all this."[5] Obviously the CIC still believed in a single Tokyo Rose but had begun to doubt whether Iva was her. They "ordered," Iva's word, her to sign the document and to apply her seal. (The Japanese carry a personal stamp called a *hanko*; its imprint is placed after one's name when signing documents. Iva had a Toguri stamp made in 1941 to use with everything from bank deposits to laundry tags.) She signed and stamped the document. This affidavit is a shortened version of the interview report just quoted. In it, Iva states basic biographical information, including an innocuous paragraph on her work at Radio Tokyo, and admits to nothing treasonable.

The CIC summed up their interviews with Iva in a sidebar:

> TOGURI was very cooperative, giving information freely and answering all questions asked by this Agent. She has a deep voice, rather masculine manner, and her speech and actions are very similar to those of American women.[6]

The CIC also wanted to interview Iva's POW superiors at Radio Tokyo. After the war's conclusion, the United States placed Charles Cousens aboard the American hospital ship *Benevolence* and shortly thereafter transferred him to HMS *Speaker*, a Royal Navy aircraft carrier, which returned him to Australia in early September. Wallace Ince, the highest-ranking American POW, remained in Tokyo and, in late 1945, the CIC conducted interviews with him about the Tokyo Rose affair. Ince affirmed Iva's innocence. He admitted that when Tsuneishi ordered him to join *Zero Hour* several months before Iva, "the purpose of the program had previously been stated as an effort to break down morale among Allied troops." He told the CIC that he opposed Iva's participation because she had "a harsh unpleasant voice" and lacked experience. Her job was "to read the introductions to some three to eight musical selections." In his signed affidavit, he concluded,

> I was connected with the "Zero Hour" from the inception of the expanded program until about February, 1944 and during this time I heard her say nothing that could be considered as detrimental to the prosecution of the war by the Allied Forces. I am certain no such statements [as the taunts connected with Tokyo Rose] were made by Toguri on the "Zero Hour" prior to February, 1944. During the time I was at Radio Tokyo I saw Toguri do many things which were of help to the prisoners of war working there. She furnished us a constant supply of news . . . she gave us food from her meagre rations . . . she visited Cousens [in the hospital] on a number of occasions even though she was warned by the Japanese not to do so. At all times she was most sympathetic, denouncing the Japanese for their conduct toward the prisoners of war.[7]

The CIC also interviewed program managers George Mitsushio and Kenkichi Oki. Mitsushio told them that Iva's "only participation in broadcasting from Radio Tokyo was to the extent of introducing music on the Zero Hour." Oki agreed that Iva's "portion of the Zero Hour consisted of introducing three or four records of sweet music" and that she used "a friendly and lively manner, referring to herself as 'Orphan Ann' and to her audience as 'the Orphans of the Pacific.'" In the words of the CIC report, "Oki declared that Toguri . . . never read commentaries or news on this program. He further added that he had no knowledge of her ever broadcasting on any other program."[8]

In January 1946, an unattributed and unsigned memorandum was submitted to the CIC. This document, referenced in chapter 7, effectively debunked the Tokyo Rose myth. It laid the blame for any Allied morale problems squarely on the Allied troops themselves, who were the real source of the frightening broadcasts attributed to Tokyo Rose.

> The "Tokyo Rose" pattern is well defined. An important fact, not yet made public, is generally known in a specific area. Speculation arises whether "Tokyo Rose" will announce it. Presently this speculation turns to the subject, when "Tokyo Rose" will announce it. Finally someone, from misunderstanding or other reasons, announces that "Tokyo Rose" has announced it. After that the elaboration of what "Tokyo Rose" announced is limited only by the imaginations of the participants in this dangerous pastime [underlining in original].
>
> Tracing the source of these rumors is an exasperating job. The person most specific about the "Tokyo Rose" report never actually heard the broadcast in question himself. He always has heard the story from a friend who did the actual listening. The friend has a similar story, and the trail usually can be followed through several persons until it finally dissolves in thin air. If a person admits having heard a broadcast, he is usually vague on the details and no monitoring station can confirm what he claims to have heard.[9]

The efficient CIC quickly completed its investigation. CIC documents from the period show that no witness implicated Iva Toguri in treasonable actions or broadcasts. On April 17, 1946, the Legal Section Chief produced his summary report. The Chief reached four conclusions with respect to the Tokyo Rose case, the first two of which, given the CIC's own evidence, seem at first glance to be simply astonishing:

1] "That the facts of this case come within the definition of treason. No opinion is ventured as to the seriousness of Miss Toguri's acts and the difficulty of meeting constitutional limitations."

2] "That sufficient evidence appears to be available to warrant a charge . . . that she wilfully caused, or attempted to cause, insubordination, disloyalty, mutiny, or refusal of duty, in the military or naval forces of the United States."

3] "That Miss Toguri is not subject to trial by military authorities for any offense against military law, and that any charges ultimately determined upon, should be tried within the continental United States before a United States Civil court." [Treason is a crime and would be tried in a criminal court; the meaning of "Civil court" is a civilian, i.e. nonmilitary, court.]

4] "Inasmuch as the proper charges, if any, would be properly brought before the civil courts and the ultimate decision of whether an indictment should be sought must be made by the prosecutive authorities of the Department of Justice, no final action should be taken at this headquarters."[10]

The Legal Section may have decided, using somewhat simplistic logic, that broadcasting for the Japanese by an American was by definition treason and therefore the only legal question was whether Iva's broadcasts had sufficient "seriousness" to warrant prosecution. On the other hand, their detailed charge that she intentionally attempted to cause insubordination, disloyalty, mutiny, or refusal of duty may reflect the Section's considered assessment that when Iva addressed troops as "orphans" and "enemies," contrasted life in the jungle with life back home, played nostalgic music that reminded her listeners of what they were missing, and used patter and popular tunes to keep listeners tuned in for the deceitful news broadcasts, she served Japan's propaganda purposes even though she did not broadcast any obvious propaganda herself.

An example may help. Readers may recall the pre-war ads for the children's laxative Fletcher's Castoria mentioned in chapter

3. The ads showed story panels of mothers protecting their sons from fathers who wanted to spank them for refusing to drink the competitor's product. In these ads, Fletcher does not sell Castoria with the direct announcement, "Our laxative is better than Brand X." Instead the company expects the storyline to draw in readers, and from the story Fletcher anticipates those readers will absorb the indirect message that children so vastly prefer Castoria they are willing to be spanked rather than use another product. The CIC might have viewed Iva's friendly chitchat with the troops in a similar way, as a draw whose indirect purpose was to sell her listeners on weariness with war, nostalgia for home, and newscast falsehoods.

Having concluded its analysis, the CIC turned over its materials and findings to the DoJ for further action. On April 27, the CIC Chief of Staff recommended that Iva Toguri "be released immediately from Sugamo Prison. Legal Section approves release [and] states they have no interest in the case."[11]

∼

Dr. Lily Abegg and Iva had adjoining cells in the small women's section for war criminals at Sugamo Prison and shared meals at a common table. Abegg, a Swiss correspondent and a committed Nazi, had come to Japan due to an interest in the Far East and become the manager of a German news agency. Iva remembered her as tall and muscular, a striking contrast to the tiny Japanese women Iva knew. The Allies had locked Abegg up for writing Tokyo Rose's scripts. Iva found this rather funny because she had never met the woman before Sugamo. In talking with her during meals, Iva realized that Abegg, a Ph.D. and fluent in several languages including English, had no clue about American style and humor. She could never have written Tokyo Rose's scripts, or Iva's either for that matter. During their conversations, Abegg related her contempt for the American ignoramuses who arrested her, commenting that she felt degraded to be questioned by people of such low intelligence. Although she spoke to them in English, they asked her if she needed a translator who spoke "Swiss." When she informed her interrogators that Switzerland did not have a unique national language, the Americans wondered how the Swiss managed to talk to each other. Abegg, no doubt with considerable disdain, unraveled the mystery by explaining that the Swiss shared the French, German, and Italian languages. After her release, in April 1946, Abegg looked into the case of Tokyo Rose and sent a lengthy letter defending Iva Toguri to the American authorities.[12]

The Allies also held a few female Japanese prisoners. Iva remembers particularly a nurse who allegedly desecrated the dead bodies of downed Allied pilots. The woman screamed and fought as the soldiers tried to incarcerate her, and they asked Iva for help. Iva immediately saw the reason. They had placed her in cell No. 4. The Japanese associate four with death because their word for the number four has exactly the same pronunciation (*shi*) as their word for death. Once they assigned her to a different cell, she was fine.

Iva helped her wardens on other occasions as well. Early one morning about 3:00 AM, Major Austin L. Swanson awakened Iva with a problem. The Army had arrested a 16-year-old girl on Saipan, and she refused to be disinfected with DDT. Swanson did not want the prison contaminated with lice, but the girl spoke no English, so he asked Iva to intervene. By this time Iva had become very friendly with her jailers and she chided Swanson, saying he should be ashamed of himself for arresting a child. Swanson, who liked Iva, retorted, "Yeah, well, you haven't met her." Iva encountered a tiny little girl, about 4'8" tall and weighing less than 75 pounds, who nonetheless possessed a furious belligerence that belied her size. Her name was Keiko. Iva calmed her down and explained why the Americans wanted to de-louse her, but she still refused. She demanded to know who Iva was. Iva replied, "I'm a prisoner, just like you." That broke the ice. The girl submitted, and the two became friends. Keiko was a guerilla fighter who had lived in the mountains of Saipan with other Japanese holdouts who refused to surrender. At night, she coated herself with ashes, snuck down the mountain to the American encampment where she had dug a hole under the fence. She slipped inside and stole whatever she could—food, ammunition, weapons— and then brought them back to her comrades. She'd finally been caught. When Iva helped her to bathe, she discovered her body was a mass of scars and cuts from shrapnel. When American battleships had bombarded Saipan from both sides to soften it up, Keiko's father, her brothers, their wives, and their children had all been killed. She couldn't find her mother and assumed she had died as well. The exploding shells had torn up Keiko badly but her wounds healed, leaving the scars. The Americans had captured her once before but she escaped and rejoined the resistance in the mountains. "She was a fight-to-the-last-man type Japanese. I really respected her. She had guts. Boy, she had guts."

The "peanut guerilla," as Iva dubbed her, served one year and one day for fighting after the surrender. The U.S. Army released Keiko after it had released Iva. Her mother, who had survived along with Keiko's sisters and returned to the Japanese mainland, asked Phil and Iva for help. The family could barely feed themselves, and her mother felt they could not support Keiko as well. Phil and Iva decided to hire her to wash, iron, and sew. They didn't have much money, but it was an excuse to feed her. She turned out to have an aptitude for sewing, so they enrolled her in a designing and sewing school. Iva lost track of her after she left Japan, but during Iva's pardon effort in the mid-1970s, she learned from an article about the two of them in a Japanese magazine that Keiko had made a career for herself as a dress designer.[13]

On January 15, 1946, a group of 20 or 30 U.S. congressmen on a junket to Japan visited the prison. Naturally, they wanted to meet the famous Tokyo Rose, but officials informed them Iva was not available, that she was taking a bath. This spurred their interest even more, so they snuck into the women's area and did their best to peek into the room where a naked Iva was washing. The guards discovered them and put a stop to it. The prison chaplain was furious when he found out and promised Iva he would write a letter of complaint. Nothing ever came of it.[14]

After helping Major Swanson with other prisoners, Iva asked him for permission to contact her family in the United States. Others had previously refused her but Swanson thought no harm could come of it. He contacted Major Lounsberry, who was in charge of correspondence, and Lounsberry gave her permission. She wrote a very long letter asking for any legal aid the family could provide because months had passed and she had witnessed no progress toward resolution of her situation. The Eighth Army's Office of Civilian Information and Education returned the letter with a message stating that the Army permitted only United States citizens to send letters to the States but that, as a "Japanese national," she could mail a postcard. She immediately sent a card to her family.

~

The FBI conducted its investigation with an eye on a possible criminal prosecution. The first step in building a case against Tokyo Rose was to identify, listen to, and transcribe her broadcasts. The Foreign Broadcast Intelligence Service (FBIS) in Portland, Oregon had monitored almost all the programs broadcast by Radio Tokyo. In January 1946, the FBI learned that FBIS recorded on cylindrical wax records, kept their recordings only long enough to transcribe them or determine the programs contained nothing of interest, and then recorded over them.[15] In February, Capt. Fordyce V. Cowing, Executive Officer, Armed Forces Radio Services, reported to the FBI on what few recordings of *Zero Hour* remained: "On none of these recordings does Orphan Ann give any news broadcasts nor does she make any predictions as to American troop movements in the Pacific."[16]

During the first six months of 1946, the FBI interviewed many servicemen who claimed they heard Tokyo Rose. These interviews proved to be either unhelpful, or a little too helpful. GI Thomas Lambert, stationed in New Caledonia, heard the broadcasts of a girl known as "Ann" in March 1943.[17] Iva had not yet begun broadcasting. An FBI report in the summer of 1946, summarizing the results of these interviews, listed 24 servicemen "who swear they heard Tokyo Rose." It concluded, "Most servicemen interviewed do not recall Zero Hour programs or any woman announcer identified as Orphan Ann, and expressed the opinion Tokyo Rose was a person other than Orphan Ann of *Zero Hour*."[18]

The FBI also spoke with Iva's friends and neighbors back in the States. Two sisters, Mrs. Spendrup and Mrs. Ruiz, who had once lived near the Toguris, informed the Bureau that "the entire family [was] disloyal to the U.S." As proof they cited the high hedge that Jun Toguri had planted to prevent people from seeing his backyard and its "radio towers." The sisters claimed that the Toguris only allowed Japanese inside their house. Another neighbor, Viola Young, liked the Toguris, did not believe they were disloyal, but she wondered about Iva and Jun's trips to Seattle. After the press exposed Iva as Tokyo Rose, she thought "they might have been made for some subversive purposes." She noted that Jun Toguri was formerly a Japanese naval officer and that Iva went to Japan to study "medicine with her two uncles who were doctors." Helen Hormel claimed Iva told her that her uncle taught medicine at the

University of Tokyo.[19] In fact, Jun Toguri was never in the Japanese Navy and the uncle Iva visited was a tailor.

Several fellow students at UCLA had information to offer as well. James Kinney claimed that Iva had told him that "she had once worked in Hawaii for some pineapple or sugar company and had held a good position." Dorothy Webley told the FBI that when Iva left the United States, she said that "she was going to Hawaii to accept a position with a refrigeration and air conditioning concern and that she expected to work in the advertising department." She added that Iva hated Roosevelt. Webley had visited Iva at her home and had seen a Shinto shrine there. Dr. Clair Steggall, a zoology classmate of Iva's who had become a professor, claimed he also saw the shrine.[20] Presumably these witnesses offered the shrine as evidence that Iva was really Japanese, not American. What is odd is that not only during this period but even to the present day, few Americans know anything about Shinto. How Webley and Steggall would have recognized a Shinto shrine is a mystery. In any case, Iva's mother was a Christian, her father was not particularly religious, and the family had no such shrine.[21]

The FBI investigation took seriously the conclusion of the CIC's findings, that the evidence was sufficient to warrant a charge of treason. Special Agent Frederick Tillman led the Bureau's investigation in Japan. Iva described Tillman as "a bully." She remembered that he demanded that she treat him as the boss with herself as the underling. She also recalled his being a lot nastier than he needed to be. For Tillman, the investigation was not a disinterested exercise aimed at learning the truth. He had come to Japan from the Philippines, where he had investigated Myrtle Lipton. Now the FBI had assigned him to investigate the most famous of the female broadcasters, Tokyo Rose. Experience had taught him that criminals seldom confess, and so his intent in dealing with a traitor like Iva Toguri was to catch her in lies and pressure her into making damaging admissions.

Fans of police shows such as *Law & Order* are familiar with the scene in the sparsely furnished interrogation room where detectives grill some obviously guilty perp, but just as he is about to crack he asks to see a lawyer. Viewers groan and the detectives roll their eyes because everyone knows that's the end of any hope of a confession and an easy resolution. Frederick Tillman in the role of "bad cop" and Iva Toguri in the role of "obviously guilty perp" enacted this scene on April 29 and 30, 1946[22]—with one exception. Iva could not make him stop by asking for a lawyer. Tillman pounded on her for two solid days, aggressively questioning her for hours and hours in a little room in Sugamo Prison as MPs stood guard outside.

Iva told him her story. Tillman attacked it, asserting or implying that she was lying. For example, when Iva claimed she could not escape Japan because she could not afford the cost of a ticket, Tillman replied that she had property in the States and, if she really wanted to leave, she could have sold it. He knew this because in September 1945, the FBI had compiled a list of property in Los Angeles County owned by Iva.[23] (Considering that this perusal of the realty records of Los Angeles County came within days of Iva's presentation to the press as Tokyo Rose, one has to admire the FBI's efficiency.) The property really belonged to her father, Jun. Under California law, as noted in chapter 1, Jun could not own property so he, like many Issei, skirted the law by placing ownership in the names of his children. Iva explained to Tillman that she had talked to Japanese nationals returning from the United States in 1941 and they had told her Japanese Americans had to abandon or sell their property for next to nothing. Tillman retorted that the U.S. government did nothing illegal in requiring her family to move into a camp. Iva continued that she had also learned that relocation had forced her father to sell his business, and he had never received a single payment from the buyer. She assumed that their property was unsalable, but if it was worth something, she knew her family needed the money more than she did. Tillman derided this idea and suggested the failure to sell manifested some sort of Toguri eccentricity. He had drawn this conclusion, he informed Iva, because the FBI knew her sister, June, also owned property, yet June worked as a maid for a family in Chicago when she could have sold the property and lived off the income.[24]

And so it went. Iva mentioned that she contracted beriberi. Tillman doubted it was true. "All you needed to eat was one cranberry a day and you would not have gotten beriberi." Iva explained the various ploys the POWs used to undermine the propaganda value of Japanese broadcasts. Tillman scoffed. "You are a graduate of UCLA. Don't act dumb and tell me that you actually believed this.

You can't tell me you didn't realize the program was pure propaganda, not broadcast to defeat the purpose of the Japanese."[25] Tillman provided Iva with interpretations of the law. He asked her if anyone put a gun to her head or beat her to make her broadcast. When she said no, he explained, "Well, there were no threats."[26]

At the conclusion of the second day Tillman had Iva sign and initial every page of a 12-page "Statement."[27] Unlike the CIC affidavit, this document severely distorted the truth and represented Tillman's attempt to eliminate defenses against the charge of treason. Iva averred in the Statement that she was "never ill-treated by the Japanese police," that "no pressure was put on me by Cousens, Ince, or the Japanese to force me to take the job and no one threatened me if I did not take the job or continue in it," that the POWs had never told her they hoped to defeat the propaganda purposes of the program, and that she knew the program's aim was to lower morale. She also contradicted herself, saying, "I did not notice any broadcast which I could consider had a double meaning" and "my purpose was to give the program a double meaning."

Two weeks before Iva placed her initials on each Statement page, she had celebrated her first wedding anniversary in a prison cell. She married on April 16, 1945, and signed this document April 30, 1946. Yet the Statement reads, "In December 1943, I was married to Philip d'Aquino. . . ." No woman on earth would misremember the date of her wedding this badly. Only Tillman could make such a mistake. Either Iva was too tired to read the document coherently or too tired to read it at all. She obviously was ignorant of most of its contents.

The question remains, why did she sign? In notes to her lawyer before her trial, she described herself as "washed out," and testified at her trial that she had "no other choice" except to sign.[28] Her attorney asked Tillman, "Wasn't she so exhausted she would have signed anything just to get rid of you?" Tillman denied it.[29] In 1987, she claimed that she was anxious to expedite the legal process and did not want to sit in a jail cell forever.

When they left the interrogation room, Tillman declared to Iva, "We'll have to put you away for a couple of years." A fed-up Iva replied, "See you in jail." The MP guards in the hallway laughed out loud and said, "Good for you, Rosie! You tell him!"[30]

The FBI completed its investigation shortly after the CIC. On May 15, 1946, with all the evidence from interviews, affidavits, depositions, *Zero Hour* scripts and recordings, and analysis thereof before him, Nathan T. Elliff, the Chief of the Justice Department's Internal Security Section, summed up the results in a three-page memo to Theron L. Caudle, the Assistant Attorney General for the Criminal Division. His restatement of the case and his assessment of criminal liability are dead-on.

He began the memo with the finding that Tokyo Rose was a myth, and then added, "Assumption that subject in this case [Iva Toguri] and Tokyo Rose are identical appears to be incorrect." Furthermore, as to whether Iva's personal actions constituted treason, Elliff said what mattered was the nature of her broadcasts. In the several scripts and few recordings located and studied, Iva, he noted, only introduced music. "These introductions were accomplished in an informal, friendly manner and contained nothing whatever of propaganda, troop movements or any apparent attempts to break down the morale of the American forces." Although many servicemen claimed to have heard Tokyo Rose's broadcasts, they could not be certain whom they did hear. The three witnesses who actually watched her broadcast on a regular basis, Cousens, Ince, and Reyes, "were unanimous in stating that Toguri's broadcasts were as she herself claims, purely introductions of musical numbers." Of 12 Japanese technicians identified as witnesses of her radio work, 2 or 3 claimed the broadcasts were anti-U.S. "but can't say how." The remaining technicians either could not speak English or said she only introduced music. "It is the belief of the writer [Elliff] that the only way in which the provable broadcasts by Toguri could be considered as giving aid and comfort to the enemy is on the same theory as that which motivates sustaining programs on American commercial radio networks and that is, the maintenance of audiences for their commercials. In this case the purpose would be maintaining an audience to receive propaganda broadcasts by furnishing enjoyable programs." That is, Iva provided Allied troops with entertainment, and maybe the Japanese used her popularity to propagandize the troops on other parts of the program. His conclusion was straightforward: "Based on evidence now available as to the character of Toguri's broadcasts, it is my belief that her prosecution for treason is not warranted. However, the views of the United States Attorney for the Southern District of California are being requested. . . ."[31]

The government moved slowly but inexorably toward a just conclusion. The United States Attorney for the Southern District of California, James M. Carter, reviewed the materials early that summer and on August 6, 1946, declined prosecution.[32]

On August 23, shortly after Carter's refusal to prosecute, a brigadier general and several other officers had two MPs bring Iva to the interrogation room. They demanded to know why the Japanese didn't take control of American cities on the Pacific Coast right after Pearl Harbor. The fact that they believed Tokyo Rose would be privy to such information indicates the legend had only grown more robust. They also wanted to learn the reaction of ordinary Japanese to the war and how informed they were about its progress. Finally, they wondered if Iva had a lot of boyfriends. "I told them the Japanese were rather stoic during the war, what had to be they took. I told them I didn't know anything about why the Japanese didn't take over Pacific Coast towns soon after Pearl Harbor. I told them I didn't have so-called boyfriends, only my husband."[33]

On September 19, 1946, Elliff sent a memorandum to his superior Caudle concurring in Carter's opinion. On September 24, 1946, Caudle himself accepted the conclusion. On October 6, 1946, MacArthur's headquarters in Tokyo received a message from Washington: "Justice no longer desires Iva Toguri be retained in custody. No prosecution contemplated at present."[34] Two weeks after that, a memo from General Headquarters restating the case, complete with Tabs A through N containing exhibits, asserted that the CIC had found that Iva was not subject to military law and the DoJ did not want to prosecute her. Finally, on October 25, 1946, Iva, 15 pounds heavier[35] and carrying a bouquet of flowers,[36] walked out of Sugamo Prison and into the waiting arms of her husband (Figures 13.1 and 13.2). Colonel Creary, the prison commandant, called her "a model prisoner who had stood up remarkably" during her confinement.[37]

Hollywood had played its part in condemning Japanese Americans like Iva throughout the war. *Little Tokyo, USA* in 1942 depicted Los Angeles as a storm center of espionage and sabotage. Howard Hawks' *Air Force* in 1943 condemned the Japanese in Hawaii for similar activities. *Betrayal from the East* in 1945 told the story of a

Figure 13.1. Walking through Sugamo Prison gates.
Courtesy of National Archives

Figure 13.2. Hugging Phil.
Courtesy of National Archives

well-liked Stanford cheerleader who was in fact an agent of the Japanese Navy and a traitor to the United States.

Not long before Iva's release from prison, in June 1946, the Paramount film *Tokyo Rose*, featuring Lotus Long in the title role, opened around the country. The movie, a complete fiction, concerned a plot to kidnap Tokyo Rose. It had nothing whatsoever to do with the life of Iva Toguri, but the film led viewers to believe Tokyo Rose was an actual person, just as earlier audiences were led to believe Japanese Americans were traitors. The legend lived on.

The twin investigations of Iva Toguri had a just outcome, but the government made a huge blunder for which Iva Toguri would ultimately pay. Officials failed to publish a complete account of what they had discovered. If they had, Americans, still flush with victory, probably would have found Iva's an interesting story and quickly moved on. Perhaps she would have been hailed as a patriot for helping the POWs survive. Instead, the Justice Department's lawyers dawdled, expecting interest in the story to wane. They closed the Tokyo Rose case and released Iva without informing the press of the evidence they had gathered about Iva herself or the nature of the legend of Tokyo Rose.

~

Iva wanted to go home. Her excursion of six months had turned into five long years of freezing winters, gnawing hunger, fear of imminent death, and now, false imprisonment. After her release, she immediately contacted the U.S. consulate in Yokohama in order to obtain her citizenship papers so that she could take the next available ship to the States. Her landlady, Mrs. Kido, and her husband Phil warned against it, but she would not be swayed.[38]

One would suppose that after exhaustive investigations by two different branches of the U.S. government, the State Department would be absolutely clear about Iva Toguri's citizenship status. One would be wrong. State informed Iva that it did not consider her a U.S. citizen, and that she would have to reestablish her citizenship. This meant Iva would be subjected to the same extraordinary amount of red tape as the thousands of other Nisei applicants whom the United States had never investigated. The Consulate gave Iva a list of what they required before they would consider her for reinstatement. Among the documents she had to supply the

U.S. Consulate in Yokohama were "my birth certificate, my passport, an affidavit from the local police [as to] what registrations I fell under, a certificate from the Japanese Home Ministry that I never took out papers to become a citizen of Japan, an affidavit from the ward office that I never voted in a Japanese election,"[39] as well as a record of the schools she attended in Japan, all her residence permits, employment records detailing what type of work she did and whether the job required being a citizen of Japan, a copy of the family *koseki-tohon* (family register) to show she was not registered as Japanese, her marriage certificate issued by the Portuguese consulate in Tokyo, and a statement of her education in the States. This and more had to be submitted to the U.S. Consulate.

We today know that the CIC and FBI possessed every bit of this information and that they made it available to the State Department in several summary reports, but Iva had no way of knowing what data they had collected. For her, gathering this information would be extraordinarily difficult. For example, who was her employer at Radio Tokyo? The most direct answer was Takano, who was now deceased. In addition, the Japanese had burned her employment records. Iva, however, had no choice but to gather the information as best she could, so she started with the police station near Mrs. Kido's house, where she and Phil still lived, and began the months-long process of making appointments and gathering signatures and documents. Unable to qualify for rations as either a Japanese or an American citizen, she registered as a citizen of Portugal and obtained Portuguese ration coupons.

During this period, Iva continued to grant interviews. She told reporters of her desire to return to the United States. As a result, stories about "Tokyo Rose" appeared haphazardly in the American press. In July 1947, songwriter Abe Burrows sang a new ditty he'd recently composed on his radio show: "I'll bet you're sorry now, Tokyo Rose / Sorry for what you've done / I'll bet you're sorry that you went to work / for that old Rising Sun. / You stuck a knife into the USA / You forgot what they learned you at UCLA / I'll bet you're sorry now, Tokyo Rose / Sorry for what you've— [oriental music]—sorry for what you've done!"[40] *Stars and Stripes* ran an article about Iva on August 1, 1947, which stated she intended to write a book to clear up the confusion about herself and Tokyo Rose. In her defense, Iva's confidence that she had nothing more to fear, that the truth had won out, was eminently reasonable. The U.S. authorities had concluded their investigations and had declined prosecution. The nightmare certainly seemed to be over.

Iva probably did not realize she was pregnant when she submitted the paperwork necessary to reinstate her citizenship to the U.S. Vice-Consul in Yokohama on May 30, 1947.[41] She now found herself in line behind thousands of other Nisei involved in the same process. Months passed. On October 24, the DoJ informed the Secretary of State and the Chief of the Passport Division, "After a careful analysis of the available evidence, this Department concluded that prosecution of this individual for treason was not warranted, and we so informed the War Department. Therefore, this Department will have no objection to the issue of a passport to Mrs. D'Aquino."[42]

The State Department issued a two-paragraph press release that the Associated Press carried under the headline, "Tokyo Rose Case Dropped." The Department's terse explanation for its decision was unconvincing. Iva Toguri "occasionally broadcast programs beamed to American troops. 'But,' said United States Attorney James M. Carter in dropping the case, 'many other women in the broadcasting studio where she was employed as a stenographer also announced programs.'"[43] In other words, Tokyo Rose would get away with broadcasting propaganda because other women had done the same thing.

Few Americans took notice, but some who did were outraged.

Notes

1. Prison records include "temporary transfer of custody orders" that record each time Iva was taken out of her cell to visit the dentist (which happened six times), the hospital, and Phil. Phil visited on Christmas Day, 1945. In 1946, a visitor in January and February is noted but not named, and Phil is marked for visits on March 13, April 20, May 15, June 11, July 4 (Iva's birthday), August 6, September 4, and October 3. NARA 7, Box 58. Phil testified at trial that he had only visited Iva "on two or three occasions." Trial Transcript, vol. XLIV, 4846.

2. *Newsweek*, August 30, 1948, 20.

3. Reitz testified at trial for the prosecution on July 25, 1949. After the war, Guysi became an attorney in Oklahoma City; he supported Iva's pardon effort.

4. CIC Statement, "RE: Ikuko Toguri, also known as Iva Toguri, Treason," October 2, 1945, 4. NARA 2, Box 1.

5. Quotations, including "ordered," from Toguri Notes.

6. CIC, File 80-T-5, January 10, 1946, 4. NARA 2, Box 9.

7. Wallace E. Ince, Affidavit, January 8, 1946, 2. NARA 1.

8. All quotations in this paragraph are from the Report of HQ CIC Metropolitan Unit 80, January 10, 1946. NARA 1, Box 40.

9. Memorandum for Op-23D42 Files, January 7, 1946. See chapter 7, note 29. NARA 1, Box 43.

10. Memo from A.C.C., Col. JAGD, Chief, Legal Section, part 5, April 17, 1946. NARA 1, Box 43.

11. OCCIO, Chief of Staff, "27 Apr 46; JEA/alc." NARA 1, Box 43. According to prison records, the CIC also interrogated Iva on April 18, April 22, and May 9, 1946. Why is unclear. NARA 7, Box 58.

12. File: Letter by Lily Abegg, a Swiss citizen, formerly of Kobe, Japan, defending Tokyo Rose, (Iva Ikoku Toguri D'Aquino), April 27, 1946 (9 pp.). NARA, RG 204, Records of the Office of the Pardon Attorney, NND 009002, Box 5. In 1952, Abegg published an influential book titled *The Mind of East Asia*. Abegg was born December 7, 1901, and died July 13, 1974.

13. Memories from Iva's interviews in 1987. I have not located the magazine article.

14. Toguri Notes. Date hers. Duus states (*Orphan of the Pacific*, 98) that the guard, Sgt. Martin Pray, wrote a letter of protest to the prison commandant. I cannot find a record of it. Katherine Beebe thought she remembered testimony about it. If that testimony occurred at Iva's trial, I have not found it.

15. According to Phil K. Edwards of FBIS. FBI Report, January 9, 1946, by Cassius E. Rathburn. NARA 1, Box 40.

16. FBI Report, February 1, 1946. NARA 2, Box 1.

17. FBI Report, January 12, 1946. NARA 2, Box 1.

18. FBI Report, July 1, 1946. NARA 2, Box 1.

19. Spendrup, Ruiz, Young, and Hormel's statements from FBI Report, December 29, 1945. In a November 23 report, a Mrs. Hargett also informed the FBI that Iva's two uncles were doctors. NARA 2, Box 1. Presumably these women could have known about the doctor husbands of Iva's aunts (Fumi's deceased sisters) only if Iva told them, perhaps in connection with her interest in a career in medicine.

20. Kinney, Webley, and Steggall's statements from FBI Report, November 23, 1945. NARA 2, Box 1.

21. Testimony of June Toguri from FBI Report, November 23, 1945.

22. Prison transfer of custody orders for Iva to Tillman on these dates. NARA 7, Box 58.

23. The properties were back-to-back lots between Ruby Street and Compton Avenue, a lot on Garvey Avenue, and .628 acres located near the corner of Wilmington Avenue and Imperial Highway in Los Angeles County. Tillman probably thought Iva could have easily sold some of this because, just before she left on June 30, 1941, Iva gave full power of attorney to June. However, records also show the property secured various loans and that on June 3, 1937, the Yokohama Specie Bank had secured a judgment against Jun for $10,750 for failure to pay debt. This would be $150,000 to $300,000 today. See FBI Report, "Real Property Held by Iva Toguri in Los Angeles County," September 29, 1945. NARA 1, Box 39.

24. The report in fact does not show property owned by June but does mention "purchases and sales of personal property by Fred Toguri," which are not set out because they are irrelevant to the investigation.

25. This quotation and other memories of the interrogation are taken from Toguri Notes and my interviews with Iva. Iva was no doubt biased against Tillman, but I have chosen to believe her for several reasons. First, the signed statement that resulted from this interrogation, written by Tillman, is riddled with errors and obviously slanted toward the prosecution. Second, witnesses later confessed that "the FBI" threatened them and suborned perjury, forcing them to memorize lies. They often meant Tillman. However, I never met Tillman. Masayo Duus, who did interview him in 1976, portrays him more favorably. "Tillman probably had no particular hostility toward Iva. Questioning her was simply another job for him." Tillman brushed aside the allegation that he coached the witnesses, telling Duus, "Do you believe somebody who said that he had told a lie nearly thirty years ago?" Duus, *Orphan of the Pacific*, 101, 230.

26. Toguri's testimony as to what Tillman told her. Trial Transcript, vol. XLVIII, 5335.

27. Iva's April 30, 1946 Statement to Tillman can be found in several locations, but DeWolfe's copy, underlined and marked in his own handwriting indicating his acceptance of its accuracy, is at NARA 2, Box 12. Subsequent quotations from Statement.

28. Toguri Notes and Trial Transcript, vol. XL, 4534.

29. Trial Transcript, vol. XVI, 1604–10.

30. Toguri Notes. This is Iva's account and cannot be verified.

31. Department of Justice Memo, Elliff to Caudle, May 15, 1946. NARA 2, Box 1.

32. Report, James M. Carter, August 6, 1946. NARA 1, Box 49.

33. Toguri Notes.

34. Message, Washington WDSCA WC to CINCAFPAC. NARA 1, Box 45.

35. Iva did not lack food or clothing while she was imprisoned or afterwards. "I was getting a care package at least once a week, and I wasn't

just getting canned milk and things like that. I was getting clothing and all kinds of things. My father used to send 50 to 60 pounds to Frank, a former employee in the Army of Occupation, almost every week. And then my sisters, my brother, they used to send me care packages by the truckload."

36. These flowers are a puzzle. The *Nippon (Japan) Times* reported that Iva said they came "from my own garden" (October 27, 1946). If so, Phil had to bring them. But Phil waited for Iva outside the prison, and she already had them when the gates opened. Tamba testified her "cheap flowers" were a gift of the commandant. Trial Transcript, vol. XXXVIII, 3091. Duus offers no opinion on the bouquet's source but states it contained "cosmos flowers" (*Orphan*, 105). Admittedly, cosmos are cheap and in bloom in late October, but so are hundreds of other varieties of similarly sized flowers. If Duus identified them from the photo, her magnifying glass is way better than mine. My own analysis convinces me only that the flowers aren't roses, which is what one might have expected the commandant to give the woman that he and the guards called "Rose."

37. Quotation, *Nippon (Japan) Times*, October 27, 1946. Colonel Robert M. Hardy of Yakima, Washington, was commanding officer of Yokohama Prison when Iva was jailed there and later became commanding officer of Sugamo. Her discharge was by order of Colonel Creary. Hardy had left Japan for reassignment the previous summer. NARA 7, Box 58. Figures 13.1 and 13.2, NARA 8, Box 541, #28185, #28184.

38. Clifford Uyeda interviewed the Kidos in 1976. "Mrs. Kido stated that they, and also Felipe d'Aquino, implored Iva not to go to the United States, to remain quietly in Japan for a few more years. 'But she would not listen,' Mrs. Kido said." (Uyeda, *Report*, 55). In 1987, Iva told me, "I was determined to go back to the U.S. as soon as I could" and "No one gave me advice to the contrary." The first sentence is probably true; the second, probably false.

39. Toguri Notes.

40. *Abe Burrows Show*, July 9, 1947.

41. Statement to Harry Pfeiffer, vice-consul, May 30, 1947. NARA 2. Iva wrote to former POW Mark Streeter that she wanted her baby to be born in America so that the child's citizenship would not be in question. However, her desire to return to the United States as soon as possible predated her pregnancy.

42. Letter from T. Vincent Quinn, Assistant Attorney General, October 24, 1947.

43. *New York Times*, October 22, 1946, 14.

14

Into the Cold War

A Furor Grows

In September 1947, Andrei Zhadov, architect of the Cominform or Information Bureau of the Communist Party, announced to an international conference that the United States and the Soviet Union were locked in an epic battle for world domination. That same month, the U.S. government sent the Freedom Train containing the founding and most important documents in American history—the Declaration of Independence, the Bill of Rights, one of the thirteen original copies of the Constitution, the Emancipation Proclamation, the Gettysburg Address, the Iwo Jima flag, and more than a hundred other displays—to visit cities across America in order to encourage patriotism and to underline the differences between our system of government and that of the Soviets. Also that month, the House Un-American Activities Committee subpoenaed more than forty witnesses in its investigation of communist influence among Hollywood filmmakers. Those who failed to cooperate found themselves blacklisted.

An obsession with loyalty gripped American society in the late 1940s. On March 2, 1948, Truman issued Executive Order 9835 establishing the Federal Employee Loyalty Program. The Order created 150 loyalty boards across the United States. The FBI performed a check on 2 million federal employees in 1948, and subjected those about whom it found "derogatory information" to a full field investigation. The FBI conducted more than 27,000 such investigations between 1948 and 1958. Any employee whose loyalty was subject to reasonable doubt could be fired. The loyalty boards received the investigation results and made the determination. Employees could not appeal their dismissal, nor could they confront whatever confidential informant had accused them of disloyalty. Truman issued another executive order to prevent these investigation files from being disclosed to Congress. In June, 1948, the Department of Justice (DoJ) indicted 11 leaders of the American Communist Party. Their crime was an act of speech; they advocated the violent overthrow of the U.S. government. In August, Whittaker Chambers accused Alger Hiss, present at the Yalta Conference and one of the minor architects of the United Nations, of being a communist. In 1949, when the Soviet Union detonated its own atomic bomb, Americans read in their newspapers that turncoat spies and "fellow travelers" had supplied the communists with our atomic secrets through espionage.

These developments had a direct effect on Iva Toguri. Tokyo Rose was the quintessential disloyal American. The timing of the U.S. government's decision to issue a passport and drop the case against Tokyo Rose could hardly have been worse. In addition to an atmosphere of hyperpatriotism and paranoia, election politics increased Iva's vulnerability to prosecution.

A 1948 Gallup poll found that only 36 percent of Americans believed that Harry Truman was doing a good job as president. Professionals considered him a sure loser in the November election. A *Life* magazine cover displayed a picture of his opponent, Thomas E. Dewey, inside was a caption, "The Next President of the United States."[1] The *New York Times* speculated about President Dewey's likely cabinet, stating, "The popular view [is] that Gov. Thomas E. Dewey's election as President is a foregone conclusion."[2] Truman's unpopularity and supposed unelectability had many explanations—rising inflation, labor strife, Truman's support of civil rights—but one of the most important was the widespread perception that he was impotent before the growing strength of the Soviet Union. The loyalty tests just mentioned represented in part his response to the criticism that he lacked the will to root out the communists and other traitors from government. Dewey, by contrast, was a former prosecutor who had broken the power of the Mob in New York by obtaining convictions in 72 out of 73 cases against racketeers. Dewey, everyone knew, would not be soft on crime. Truman still had to prove himself.

~

Despite these larger societal forces, Iva Toguri might have slipped away unnoticed had it not been for Edna Copeland of South Glen Falls, New York. Mrs. Copeland was a Gold Star mother—a woman who had lost a son in the war. When she learned that the U.S. government had released Tokyo Rose, she wrote a letter of complaint. So did many others, but Copeland sent hers, not to the DoJ, but to broadcaster and columnist Walter Winchell.

Contemporary readers will barely recognize the name. Walter Winchell disappeared so precipitously and so thoroughly from public view that even Baby Boomers remember him only as the staccato voice that opened the television series, "The Untouchables." But following World War II, Walter Winchell had media power concentrated in his hands that is unimaginable today. At the height of his power, two-thirds of all adult Americans either listened to Winchell's Sunday night radio program or read his weekday newspaper column.[3]

Winchell's reporting, if it can be called that, was a jazzy combination of Hollywood gossip, muckraking journalism, society claptrap, political opinion, and sophomoric humor. He was *Entertainment Tonight*, *60 Minutes*, Rush Limbaugh, and shock radio all rolled into one. He sounded like Al Michaels on amphetamines and his wisecracking, tough-guy persona caught the spirit of America in its new role as the world's preeminent military power. Politicians kowtowed to him. In a single newspaper column in 1948, he quoted letters from J. Edgar Hoover:

> Do take good care of yourself because you are far too valuable to the country. You must really get a lot of satisfaction now when so many of your "hysterical" assertions and predictions are becoming all too real. Best wishes, John

and Lyndon Johnson

> Although you have done much for your country, you have never made a contribution equal to the one you made [on the radio]

> Sunday night. Dozens talked to me about the wisdom in your message.[4]

Society mavens and Hollywood stars feared him. Women by the dozens, including a young Marilyn Monroe, slept with him, either to boost their careers or under threat of their destruction.

Walter Winchell was a liberal who adored Roosevelt and unfailingly supported him. Following Roosevelt's death, Winchell proselytized tirelessly to preserve the New Deal and to protect FDR's personal honor from attack. But he could not abide Truman. Much of his dislike was personal. When Winchell accepted Truman's initial invitation to visit him at the White House, the story goes, Truman during their conversation offhandedly referred to *New York Post* publisher Dorothy Schiff as "that damn Jew publisher." Winchell left extremely upset, only to hear from his friend Drew Pearson a few days later that Truman had called Winchell himself a "kike" behind his back.[5] Winchell, the child of Russian Jewish immigrants whose last name had evolved from Weinschel, was livid.[6] Whatever the truth of these stories, Winchell clearly regarded Truman as a simpleton and rube, a mediocrity compared to Roosevelt. He attacked the Truman administration whenever he could.

The view of many analysts of the Tokyo Rose case that Winchell was primarily responsible for Iva's persecution is somewhat misguided. In the early summer of 1947, a few days after Iva sought reinstatement of her citizenship so she could return to the States, Winchell turned his column over to James Young, the reporter mentioned in chapter 2 whom the *kempeitai* had incarcerated and interrogated. Young noted that Iva's freedom "brought bitter comment from 30 former prisoners of war in the Philippines who think she and all other collaborator broadcast friends should get at least 15 years each."[7] Winchell himself took no further notice of the situation and effectively remained silent in the months that followed.

Iva herself unfortunately did not. On August 4, 1947, she granted an interview to Burton Crane, a correspondent with the Mutual Network, which broadcast the interview on radio.

> *Iva*: I am one of those persons who hope that we can forget the past—and I have a lot of it to forget—and concentrate on the future. Can't we let bygones be bygones?

> *Crane*: We're making a historical record, and it wouldn't be complete without the voice of Tokyo Rose.
> *Iva*: Sometimes I think that most history should be forgotten.[8]

Iva sounded as though she were reading from a prepared script, not speaking extemporaneously. Whatever the case, her remarks implied she was ashamed of her past and hoped everyone would forgive and forget her previous actions.

Later that month, the St. Louis chapter of Gold Star Mothers wrote to Truman to protest Iva's return. "Tokyo Rose, with her broadcasts to our boys, brought them much mental anguish and made the last days of some of our boys very lonely and feel forgotten [sic]."[9] In October, James F. O'Neill, National Commander of American Legion, called on the Justice Department to expedite the prosecution of Tokyo Rose.[10] In early November, the Grand Parlor Americanism Committee of the Native Sons of the Golden West publicly notified J. Edgar Hoover that it "strenuously opposed the re-entry of any disloyal citizens." Iva Toguri, in their opinion, "should be prosecuted for treasonous conduct."[11]

Winchell picked up on these protests and interjected a minor comment midway through one of his columns that "Tokyo Rose wants to come back here to live. Why not let her book passage on any of the floating hearses returning our Pacific war dead?"[12] This item apparently caused Edna Copeland to write him. Winchell read her letter over the air to millions of listeners and, probably to his surprise, it triggered an avalanche. Typical of the reaction was that of Vincent Dougherty Jr., former Chief Electrician, U.S. Navy Seabees, who wrote to the FBI, "If there is any truth to the report on Walter Winchell's program of this evening, that Tokyo Rose is to be admitted into the United States, I demand by authority of my rights as a Naval Veteran who spent twenty-three months on the Pacific Islands, that this damnable traitor be left in the country she chose to serve so well. To bring her back would be a savage injustice to the dead she helped to torture, as well as to those who outlived her torment."[13]

The DoJ might have responded to this outcry by publishing the results of its investigation. Instead, it caved to public pressure. On December 3, 1947, the FBI issued a press release that appeared in newspapers across the country. "Anyone who ever saw Iva Ikuko

Toguri D'Aquino broadcasting as 'Tokyo Rose' or recognized her voice coming over the air waves, should communicate with the Federal Bureau of Investigation," adding that the "inquiry was proceeding, and if possible the case would be presented to a grand jury."[14] In his Pearl Harbor day column on December 7, Winchell gave Copeland full credit: "News Item: Dep't of Justice to Fight Tokyo Rose. Mrs. H. W. Copeland (the Gold Star Mother whose letter was read the other Sabbath night): Take a big bow, lady!"[15]

The FBI's decision to reopen the case by launching a nationwide hunt for witnesses doomed Iva. In Los Angeles, Iva's hometown, the City Council immediately passed a resolution stating that the return of "persons of questionable loyalty or proved disloyalty would cast suspicion on the entire race of which they happened to be a member" and since loyal Japanese American citizens returning to the City have a right to live above suspicion, the Council resolved to "vigorously oppose return to this country of this person or any other person treasonably connected with the 'Tokyo Rose' wartime propaganda broadcasts."[16] In the face of these protests, the organization that represented those loyal Japanese Americans, the Japanese American Citizens League, kept quiet.

The Justice Department feared that Walter Winchell would lambast the Department for its tardiness in moving forward. He had already ripped them for failure to go after Axis Sally and other traitors. DoJ lawyers hoped to forestall Winchell's criticism by meeting with him personally to inform him of the facts, to indicate how difficult a prosecution would be, and to convince him that prosecuting Iva Toguri and losing was worse than not prosecuting her at all.

On December 4, 1947, James M. Carter, the U.S. Attorney for the Southern District of California, who had previously declined prosecution of Iva, met with Joseph Schenck, president of Twentieth-Century Fox. He took with him Charles H. Carr, his predecessor. Carr had originally called for a prosecution and then changed his mind when he learned the facts. More important, Carr was a friend of both Winchell and Schenck. Schenck took the two attorneys to meet Winchell at his office in the Fox studio complex. Thanks to a detailed four-page letter Carter wrote to Attorney General Tom Clark the next day, we know exactly what happened at that meeting.

Winchell, the attorneys learned to their displeasure, had no particular interest in Tokyo Rose. When Carter began explaining the case to him, Winchell cut him off with the dubious assertion that he was aware of the facts. Then, according to Carter, Winchell launched into an extended screed, not against Tokyo Rose but against Attorney General (AG) Tom Clark. Winchell stated that he had asked Clark at a luncheon if he was to be the new AG, and Clark had told him he didn't know. (This answer was true; at the time Clark didn't know.) Yet, Winchell noted, Truman appointed Clark to the post a few days later, thus depriving him of a scoop. Winchell griped that Clark had never properly thanked him for endorsing him for the position. Winchell also complained of libel suits and other problems of radio broadcasters, apparently intimating the Justice Department should do something to help him in this regard. Carter tried to steer the conversation back to Tokyo Rose. He complimented Winchell on his pursuit of disloyal Americans, but he "stated that as a lawyer I was not going to recommend a prosecution unless we had some kind of a case against the defendant." Charles Carr added that he had received many letters from GIs all over the world criticizing him for his announced intention of prosecuting Tokyo Rose. The GIs claimed that the "Tokyo Rose broadcasts, instead of being morale breakers were morale builders." Carter dryly noted, "Winchell replied that these people were probably communists." The three men parted amicably. Carter believed they had resolved the problem.[17]

A little more than a month before he dismissed the concerns of Carter and Carr, Walter Winchell concluded a column singing the praises of America's devotion to freedom and human rights, "So what the Freedom Train really means is that nobody in America can be railroaded."[18] Winchell then proceeded to drive the train over Iva Toguri. As will be detailed later, he harped on the case and forced the Justice Department to act. What is so terrible is that he bore Iva Toguri no animus. He simply did not care about her life. He saw in Tokyo Rose an opportunity to pursue his personal agenda. Although a champion of civil rights in the 1940s, he later abandoned his liberal principles and wholeheartedly supported Joseph McCarthy's witch hunts. Winchell deserved the contempt with which so many viewed him. He lived his final years in oblivion as a recluse in the Ambassador Hotel, home of the Cocoanut

Grove night club, in Los Angeles. He died in 1972. His daughter was the only mourner at his funeral.[19]

~

Hundreds and hundreds of servicemen replied to the Justice Department's December appeal for witnesses to Iva's broadcasts. Here's a sample:

Michael J Schulte wrote to say he heard Tokyo Rose often but said that *Zero Hour* was an entirely different program and that it had no female broadcasters.[20]

Radioman Harry Gillingham listened to both *Zero Hour* and Tokyo Rose and wrote reports. Orphan Ann was not disseminating propaganda, but the newscasters were. He noted that she had a "very feminine, high-pitched voice with a strong Japanese accent."[21]

While in the Marshall Islands, John Robert Brown "heard a woman say, 'This is Tokyo Rose calling the 100th Seabee unit in the Majuro Islands. How do you boys like our cocoanuts?' Next day she said, 'You know you Seabees are a bunch of saps; you know all your wives are having a good time in the States.' She also mentioned a time for a raid and told us not to forget it." On the day of the raid, two Japanese planes flew over but there was no attack. Tokyo Rose asked how they liked the raid.[22]

John L. Harris, a Honolulu radio engineer, reported he had recordings of Tokyo Rose broadcasting before the war as well as on *Zero Hour*.[23]

Cecil Hodson heard Tokyo Rose broadcast that his unit had been annihilated. In August 1945, he went to "Christine's Night Club" on Rijal Ave in Manila. There he saw a beautiful Japanese girl. A waiter friend told him she was Tokyo Rose. Hodson asked why she had not been picked up, and the waiter replied she was under surveillance by the authorities.[24]

Frederick Julius had Tokyo Rose pointed out to him at the Kobe subway station. She was in the company of two Japanese officers and "was very well and very expensively dressed."[25]

Henry Wagner, Colorado State Service Officer, Dept. of Veterans Affairs, listened throughout 1943 and 1944 to an hour-long program of Tokyo Rose "who sometimes mentioned the name 'Iva.'"[26]

The FBI's response to these letters was sometimes unintentionally humorous. Felix Chavez wrote to say that he could identify the voice of Tokyo Rose, but the FBI declined his help, noting in a report that it "does not believe Chavez would make a good witness, as he is of Mexican descent, and does not have too well a command of the English language."[27] Mrs. Edna R. White sent a telegram protesting the entire effort. "The FBI should let the war-weary GIs alone and should work up their own cases without bothering the citizens." This not-unreasonable advice failed to persuade the Bureau. A memo in the file stated, "It is not known whether Mrs. White is a habitual complainant or a mental case." Having exhausted the possible reasons for criticizing the FBI, the writer went on to summarize the agency's investigation of Mrs. White to determine which of the two was true.[28]

~

In January 1948, as the Winchell-fueled witch hunt gained momentum in America and the FBI began collecting evidence against her, Iva gave birth in the fairly primitive conditions of a post-war Japanese hospital. She had a long labor; the baby was born breech and died almost immediately. Iva and Phil took a long time to recover psychologically. "Phil was very quiet. We both sensed it was a big loss, but we weren't going to hammer on it. What's done is done." They expected to have more children, but they would not. Asked if she regretted not having children, Iva replied, "To be honest with you, no. I think it's just as well that I navigated by myself. Considering my years in prison, if I had any children, where would they be during that period? If you're not going to raise your child, it's just as well that you didn't have it."

~

As the FBI slowly sifted through the letters of would-be witnesses and dutifully sent field agents to interview their authors, Walter Winchell moved into overdrive. On January 4, 1948,

Winchell informed the nation via his radio program that the FBI had in its possession a "signed confession" by Tokyo Rose given to them by Clark Lee. In this confession, she admitted she was a traitor. Why, then, Winchell demanded to know, had the government failed to prosecute her?[29] The Bureau developed an internal memo the very next day to the effect that the "confession" was actually Lee's notes from his interview in 1945, that these notes and Iva's contract had been stolen at the Imperial Hotel from Harry Brundidge shortly after the interview, and that Lee had never given these materials to the FBI.[30] The day after that, January 6, Hoover wrote to his friend Winchell that the broadcast was inaccurate, that the FBI did not have the confession because it had been stolen.[31] If Hoover hoped his quick response would slow Winchell down, he was mistaken. One week later, Winchell turned the information against the FBI. He claimed the fact that her confession was mysteriously stolen in Japan proved that "Tokyo Rose has more American friends than was known." Winchell added that he possessed "sensational evidence" against her: namely, "a 35mm motion picture with sound."[32] Winchell's listeners assumed the film showed Tokyo Rose broadcasting during the war, whereas in fact it was the post-war "re-creation" by the Army Signal Corps.

Winchell's chief source for his news flashes was Harry Brundidge, the Hearst reporter who, along with Clark Lee, had designated Iva Toguri as Tokyo Rose. Brundidge now began a game of hide-and-seek with both Winchell and the FBI that made chumps of both. The FBI, which had interviewed Brundidge previously, sent an Agent Hostetter to re-interview him on January 27 in an attempt to determine what materials on Tokyo Rose he still had in his possession. Brundidge informed Hostetter that although the *contract* had been stolen, he had given a copy of the *confession* to the FBI. If the Bureau had lost it, he fortunately had the original among his personal effects.[33] He added that Iva not only signed her name to the confession but had also written, "I realize that I am placing my neck in a noose in making this statement to Mr. Brundidge."[34] In his report, Agent Hostetter expressed his opinion that Brundidge liked to brag, and Hostetter doubted he could produce the confession.[35] Meanwhile, Brundidge informed Walter Winchell the confession had not been stolen after all. Winchell announced this fact to the nation on February 1, 1948.[36]

Hoping to gain some clarity on Brundidge's story, the FBI contacted Clark Lee. Lee explained that the confession was really nothing more than his typed notes. He said that he did not give the confession to the FBI directly but instead to Brundidge, who was then to give it to an Agent Sullivan of the Bureau.[37] For his part, Sullivan said he never received the confession/notes from either Lee or Brundidge and that the latter told him the notes had been stolen.[38] Lee wrote Winchell, "It seems to me Tokyo Rose is essentially small fry, a vain and stupid girl no more guilty than the many other Nisei who worked for the enemy. It seems to me that the people to gun for are those officers who prepared Japanese propaganda against our country."[39] Winchell ignored this advice.

J. Edgar Hoover at this point was apoplectic. His hand-written notes pepper the margins of the FBI's many memos. "This is getting more confusing daily. Please get the real facts." "Get real facts tied down now." "Nail down Brundidge at once so we can get off the 'merry go-round.'"

Agents tried. They hung out at Brundidge's apartment, hoping to obtain the original of the confession. Brundidge kept inventing reasons why he couldn't access his personal belongings and turn it over. However, he did offer to fly to Tokyo and promised he could produce two overt witnesses to Iva's treason within ten days of his arrival.[40] But with Hoover breathing down their necks, agents kept after him and finally on February 11, Harry Brundidge gave the FBI "two documents, one of which purported to be the unsigned statement of the subject, and the other a narrative explanation of the unsigned statement which had been prepared by Brundidge and Clark Lee at a later time in this country."[41] The former was Lee's typewritten notes; the latter, his narrative of those notes. In short, Agent Hostetter was correct. Brundidge had lied. He had no signed confession, original or copy.

In a final twist, Attorney General Tom Clark authorized Brundidge to fly to Tokyo at Department expense "to develop evidence." The desperation on the part of Clark and the Truman administration to stop the criticism that it was soft on traitors is evident in this decision. Upon receiving the memorandum, Hoover hand-wrote at the bottom, "Well, I am left 'unspeechless.'"[42]

Harry Brundidge arrived in Tokyo in March 1948. He quickly employed his new authority as an investigator for the DoJ and had

Iva brought to General Headquarters. Iva at the time was very sick from dysentery, which had plagued her throughout the war and had now become chronic. Brundidge presented her with Clark Lee's original notes, the ones he had typed during their first meeting at the Imperial Hotel on September 1, 1945, and asked her to sign them. She signed.

She stated more than once during our interviews in 1987 that she signed because she wanted above all else to move her case along. However, at her trial, under cross-examination, Iva denied that she agreed to sign for that reason.[43] In any event, one cannot view this decision, long after she knew about Tokyo Rose and that the authorities had her in their gun sights, without wondering what in the world she was thinking. But perhaps her 1987 explanation is the simple truth. She wouldn't admit it in court, but the FBI had worn her out. Their investigation had dragged on for years with no end in sight, and she would do anything that might get her out of Japan and back home.

Shortly thereafter, Harry Brundidge announced that he had recovered the "long missing" document in which Iva Toguri admitted "in her own handwriting" that she was in fact Tokyo Rose.[44]

In April 1948, after Iva's meeting with Brundidge, two GIs in a jeep pulled up in front of Mrs. Kido's. Iva feared that she might be arrested again, but instead they wanted to take her to the General Headquarters (GHQ) building in which General MacArthur and General Willoughby, head of Intelligence, had their offices. Iva never met either officer; instead a friend of Willoughby's waited for her at GHQ. Iva remembered that a "tall, gray-haired, distinguished-looking man introduced himself as Earl Carroll. I knew his name. Everyone my age knew his night club—'through these portals pass the most beautiful girls in the world.' I'd never been to a night club but I'd read about them."

A composer and songwriter, Earl Carroll was best known as a producer of stage shows that featured comedy and scantily clad chorus girls. He made himself famous by naming everything he owned after himself. The "Earl Carroll Vanities" ran for years in New York's "Earl Carroll Theater." The show featured at various times Sophie Tucker, Milton Berle, Jack Benny, and W. C. Fields, along with a bevy of naked chorus girls. Carroll was the first person ever to show full nudity on a Broadway stage.[45] The sign Iva remembered ("through these portals . . .") hung over the entrance to his Broadway theater, as well as to the Earl Carroll Theater and Supper Club on Sunset Boulevard in Los Angeles.

Walter Winchell considered Carroll's stage extravaganzas tacky, and over the years he ridiculed him. Carroll, however, was unfailingly courteous whenever he ran into Winchell. Winchell made fun of him for that as well, telling one associate, "He turned the other cheek, which shows you what a damn fool he is."[46] Finally, Carroll had had enough. On the evening of January 30, 1932, at a huge party filled with celebrities and politicians, a somewhat inebriated Earl Carroll took control of the party's microphone and told Winchell to his face that he was not fit to be with decent people. Winchell did not speak to him for years as a result.[47]

Earl Carroll informed Iva that Willoughby had told him that, as far as he knew, the case was closed. Carroll also told her about Walter Winchell's campaign against Tokyo Rose. Iva had been unaware. He believed, perhaps unjustifiably, that he and Winchell had recently made peace, and he offered to help Iva if he could. "He never told me why he wanted to help me but the reason was obvious. He was going to use me in some commercial way. People don't do things for nothing." Exactly how Carroll imagined Iva would have fit in with the comedians and chorus girls can't be known, but whatever he intended, his plan for exploiting her wouldn't have been the screwiest. That prize belongs to Navy chaplain Father Michael Doody. Doody, who first heard Tokyo Rose broadcast during the battle of Midway in 1942, wanted to "put Tokyo Rose in a cage and take her on an exhibition tour of the United States."[48] At any rate, Carroll asked Iva to inform Winchell of the facts in a letter and promised to take it to him. She did, and he kept his promise. Winchell's reply, in a letter to Carroll, was neutral at best. He said simply that Iva would receive a fair trial.[49] Carroll subsequently promised to go to New York and speak to Winchell personally about the case, right after he attended the 1948 Republican Convention in Philadelphia. Had he succeeded, the outcry to bring Tokyo Rose to justice fueled by Winchell's tirades might have quieted. That certainly would have been the government's preference. Unfortunately, Earl Carroll died when his commercial flight to the convention crashed in Pennsylvania. Asked how she felt upon learning of Carroll's death, if she believed at that point that the die was cast, Iva said only, "I didn't hope to escape prosecution. What I wanted was, if there was any doubt in anybody's mind, go to trial, put all the cards on the table, get it cleared one way or the other."

∽

U.S. Attorney Thomas DeWolfe had been part of the Justice Department's team that successfully prosecuted Douglas Chandler and Robert H. Best, two Nazi propaganda broadcasters, for treason. Under relentless media and citizen pressure, the DoJ asked DeWolfe for an opinion about Tokyo Rose. DeWolfe responded on May 25, 1948, with a six-page "Statement of the Case."[50] In analyzing the case for his superior, Raymond Whearty, DeWolfe stated his opinion bluntly: A prosecution of Tokyo Rose would fail so thoroughly that the case would not even reach a jury. After hearing the testimony of the government's own witnesses, the judge would grant a defense motion for acquittal. "There is no available evidence upon which a reasonable mind might fairly conclude guilt beyond a reasonable doubt." DeWolfe spelled out in detail the basis for his opinion (numbering is mine):

1. Iva's POW superiors, Cousens, Ince, and Reyes, "will be the three most important witnesses against subject if an indictment should be returned against her. As Government witnesses, the Government will as a matter of law be forced to vouch for the truth of their testimony.[51] These three men have all been cleared by their respective governments of any charge of treasonous activity. They will testify that they selected subject as an announcer because she was the only woman available, white or Nisei, whom they could trust not to betray their efforts to sabotage any propaganda to the Japanese. The witnesses will likewise testify that subject on some occasions made every endeavor to see that propagandistic material was not inserted in the 'Zero Hour' program. She frequently expressed pro-American sentiments and often evinced the desire that the war should end soon and that the United States, her native land, would emerge victorious." Thus, the government's own witnesses would testify "that defendant lacked the requisite intent to betray. It must be proved that the accused acted with an inten-

tion to betray or there is no treason. Assuming the verity of the testimony of the Government witnesses, the Government's case must fail as a matter of law. The Government's witnesses, almost to a man, will testify to facts which show that subject was pro-American, wished to return to the United States and tried so to do, and beamed to American troops only the introduction to innocuous musical recordings. In other words, the testimony which the Government will offer will not make out a case sufficient as a matter of law to withstand a motion for an instructed verdict."

2. "The available evidence on the overt acts committed by subject will not from a trial standpoint show that said acts were acts in furtherance of the Japanese war effort."

3. "The statement of defendant given to Bureau Agent Tillman might not be admissible in evidence due to the fact that subject was in military custody at the time without any military or civil charges ever having been brought against her. Similar statements given to Department of Justice lawyers under similar circumstances were ruled out in recent treason trials."

4. "The type and quantum of the proof available in the case against subject is the direct antithesis of that available and utilized in the Boston litigation [against Chandler and Best]."

5. "The so-called 'confession' or 'statement against interest' given by subject to Lee and Brundidge was given only after those gentlemen offered subject $2,000." Since the methods used by the two "appear at least questionable and of doubtful propriety," its admittance would surely be challenged.

In sum, DeWolfe wrote in capital letters, "THERE IS INSUFFICIENT EVIDENCE TO MAKE OUT A PRIMA FACIE CASE." (A prima facie case has the evidence necessary to require the defendant to proceed.)

Raymond Whearty kicked DeWolfe's opinion upstairs. It continued up the chain of command until eventually T. Vincent Quinn sent it to Attorney General Tom Clark with the note, "Thought you sd. see this in light of all the publicity given to this case." Tom Clark's reply the next day was terse. "Prosecute it vigorously."[52]

DeWolfe's "Statement of the Case" marked the final chapter in the U.S. government's quest for the truth. After this, government actions were informed primarily by political expediency, the need to win at trial, and a lack of professional ethics or moral decency in securing "victory."[53]

Following Clark's directive, DeWolfe shifted the focus of government efforts from disinterested investigation to prosecution. The DoJ disregarded the fact that the hundreds of GI responses to its call for help the previous December proved that their memories were hopelessly muddled, part fact, part fiction. Instead, Justice culled the responses for witnesses whose testimony would convince a jury of Iva's guilt. If a serviceman claimed Iva's broadcasts boosted morale, he was out as a witness. As will be detailed in subsequent chapters, the FBI now reinterviewed witnesses, sometimes again and again. If they were prosecution witnesses, the task was to prepare them to testify by eliminating any recollections that might prove useful to the defense. In some cases, recollections were created.[54] If the witnesses might testify for the defense, the FBI hoped to frighten them into disappearing or, failing that, to catch them in contradictions that could be exploited during cross-examination. In general, the Bureau retained incriminating evidence and discarded exculpatory evidence.

~

In response to my question about yet another run-in with U.S. authorities in Japan, Iva sighed wearily. "This is the story of my life: Two MPs in a jeep pull up in front of my house."

On August 26, 1948, two MPs in a jeep pulled up in front of Mrs. Kido's to arrest Iva Toguri for "treasonable conduct against the United States Government."[55] The warrant ordered the Provost Marshal of the Far East Command to "make known to the person arrested, in her native language, the contents of this document." This time, at least, Iva knew what to expect. The government had announced its intentions on August 16. "Arrest of Tokyo Rose Ordered" was page-one news in the *New York Times*.[56] In explaining the arrest to the press, the DoJ admitted Iva was only one of several female broadcasters but claimed "the others were all Japanese nationals."[57] This careful phrasing covered up the fact that the others were Japanese nationals because Iva alone had accepted the hardships of being an alien and refused to renounce her American citizenship.

The MPs carried her off to Sugamo Prison, where she sat for a week awaiting return to the United States. On September 3, 1948, her husband said good-bye to her outside the gates of the prison.[58] The Army drove Iva to Yokohama, where she was taken aboard the transport ship *General H. Frank Hodges*. Iva was prone to seasickness (she once admitted to me she had become seasick watching the movie "Around the World in Eighty Days"), and her month-long voyage to America was a torment. The abdominal sickness combined with her chronic dysentery caused her to lose considerable weight from an already underweight body. In one of many small acts of kindness American service personnel showed Iva, Army Captain Katherine Stull, her guard, noticed Iva's clothes were falling off her and purchased for Iva a pair of slacks when the ship docked in Okinawa. At the trial, Iva's lawyer asked whether she had ever been repaid for the slacks. Stull answered, "I left instructions that I did not wish to be repaid."[59]

DoJ attorneys debated at length the ultimate destination of the *General Hodges*. Iva's trial would fall in the federal jurisdiction where she first touched American soil, and prosecutors wanted a jury as hostile as possible. They ruled out Hawaii with its multi-ethnic and large Nisei population. They debated the wisdom of a long voyage to the East Coast and also evaluated Los Angeles. In the end, they selected the city that had witnessed the founding of the Japanese Exclusion League and was as well home to the most rabid anti-Japanese rhetoric in American history: San Francisco.

As the *General Hodges* worked its way through various Asian ports and then slowly across the breadth of the Pacific, Iva had plenty of time to think about what would greet her when she returned to the United States. She longed to see her family again, but facing her father, the stern patriarch of the Toguri clan, must have given her concern. Jun by this time knew the seriousness of her predicament, the fact that the U.S. government considered her a traitor, and that, if convicted, she would face terrible consequences, including the possibility of a death sentence.[60] He had drummed into his children that the actions of any one of them reflected on the entire family, and that they were the only Toguris in America. Now the name "Toguri" was everywhere in the news and always associated with the word "treason." Iva had never heard her father compliment her mother or tell her that he loved her; she thought such sentiments incompatible with his character. Jun Toguri had never praised his children even when they excelled, but had been quick to chastise them when they failed. Now Iva had fallen in the mud, just as she had as a little girl, but this time the whole country believed that she had created something terrible.

When the ship docked, a row broke out between Iva and her guards over a safety pin. They wanted to confiscate it because she might use it to commit suicide. She needed it to hold her skirt up and refused to disembark without it. In the end, authorities allowed Iva to keep it and she walked down the gangplank in the custody of FBI agents (Figure 14.1).[61]

Figure 14.1. Iva disembarks followed by FBI agents Frederick Tillman and J. Eldon Dunn.

The agents immediately took her to the office of the U.S. Commissioner for arraignment. Waiting at that office was her father (Figure 14.2).

Over a period of more than two decades, I listened to Iva Toguri tell her story to me and to others many times. I can state with certainty that in her mind this was the most important and most meaningful moment in her life.

When Jun Toguri saw his daughter after seven years apart, he hugged her and said, "I'm proud of you, girl. You didn't change your stripes." Iva wept.[62]

Figure 14.2. Jun Toguri with his daughter Iva.
Courtesy of Library of Congress.

Notes

1. *Life*, March 22, 1948. Many websites claim the "Next President" caption was on the cover. This is an error; the cover had the caption "Thomas E. Dewey" only.

2. Editorial, Leo Egan, *New York Times*, October 24, 1948. A few days later, on October 29, 1948, an article by Patrick J. Beary noted that Republicans considered Dewey's election a foregone conclusion. Many websites claim the *Times* ran a headline, "Thomas E. Dewey's Election as President Is a Foregone Conclusion." This, like the mythical *Life* cover referenced in note 1, is an error.

3. Gabler, *Winchell*, xi. Gabler claims that Winchell's column was syndicated in 2,000 newspapers. Perhaps this was true in the 1950s. I searched for his column in hundreds of newspapers from two dozen states for the year 1948 and found him only in a few. However, his home paper, the *New York Mirror*, was widely read. Unless otherwise noted, the source of the information in this section about Winchell is Gabler.

4. *New York Mirror*, March 21, 1948, 10.

5. I have used the recollection of writer Herman Klurfeld, who helped Winchell with his column. See Herman Klurfeld, *Winchell: His Life and*

Times (New York: Praeger Publishers, 1976), 125. Other versions of this story exist. Winchell's producer, Paul Scheffels, claims that Truman referred in Winchell's presence to Schiff as a "damn kike." Long-time friend and lawyer Ernest Cuneo says only that after Winchell left the meeting, he overheard Truman say, "I guess we pulled the wool over that SOB's eyes." See Gabler, *Winchell*, 345–46.

6. For a rendition of the transformation from Weischel to Winschel to Winchel to Winchell, see Gabler, *Winchell*, 4–6.

7. *New York Mirror*, June 1, 1947, 10.

8. Tokyo Rose LP.

9. Letter, August 14, 1947. NARA 2, Box 1.

10. *Washington News*, October 24, 1947, 3.

11. Letter to the FBI, November 11, 1947. NARA 1, Box 41.

12. *New York Mirror*, October 19, 1947, 10. On November 12, 1947, Winchell also put Tokyo Rose on a long list of people he believed ought to be punished.

13. NARA 2, Box 1.

14. *New York Times*, December 4, 1947, 19.

15. *New York Mirror*, December 7, 1947, 10.

16. Resolution, City of Los Angeles, December 8, 1947. NARA 2.

17. Letter, James M. Carter to Tom C. Clark, December 5, 1947. NARA 2.

18. *New York Mirror*, September 26, 1947, 10.

19. Worse, Winchell's daughter Walda was mentally ill and had to be brought to the funeral. A memorial service a few weeks later, on what would have been Winchell's 75th birthday, attracted 150 guests, most of whom left early. See Gabler, *Winchell*, "Introduction."

20. Memo, December 5, 1947, SAC to FBI. NARA 1, Box 41.

21. FBI Report, December 11, 1947. NARA 1, Box 41.

22. FBI Report, December 11, 1947. NARA 1, Box 41.

23. FBI radiogram, December 5, 1947. NARA 1, Box 41.

24. FBI Report, December 15, 1947. NARA 1, Box 41.

25. FBI Report, December 29, 1947. NARA 1, Box 41.

26. FBI Report, December 11, 1947. NARA 1, Box 41.

27. Letter to the FBI, December 10, 1947. NARA 1, Box 41.

28. FBI Office Memo, December 5, 1947 re: her telegram of December 4, 1947. NARA 1, Box 41.

29. The item also appeared in his column, "In New York," *New York Daily Mirror*, January 5, 1948, 6.

30. Office Memo, January 5, 1948. NARA 1, Box 42.

31. I'm sure this letter must be archived somewhere but I haven't found it. I know Hoover sent it because he references his January 6, 1948, letter

to Winchell when he queries Tolson, "Are we completely in the clear as to the overall handling of this case?" (Undated) NARA 1, Box 41.

32. "American friends," "sensational evidence," "35mm film" are from the Jergens Journal (named after the sponsor, Jergens' Dryad Deodorant), ABC, January 11, 1948. See http://www.radiogoldindex.com/cgi-local/p2.cgi?ProgramName=The+Jergens+Journal.

33. Neither the contract nor Lee's notes were stolen. We have both today. Brundidge's claims are contained in FBI Office Memo, February 3, 1948. NARA 1, Box 42.

34. Teletype, January 28, 1948. As noted in chapter 12, the signed "my neck in a noose" statement has never been found and probably does not exist. NARA 1, Box 42.

35. Office Memo, February 3, 1948. NARA 1, Box 42.

36. *New York Daily Mirror*, February 1, 1948, 8.

37. FBI Office Memo, January 31, 1948. NARA 1, Box 42.

38. FBI Office Memo, January 30, 1948. NARA 1, Box 42.

39. Letter, Lee to Winchell, January 15, 1948. NARA 3, Box 8.

40. FBI Office Memo, February 3, 1948. NARA 1, Box 42.

41. The FBI report noted that "pages of statement numbered 1–17 with 8 and 9 missing. Given in latter part of August 1945." (Actually, it was given September 1.) Report, Joseph T. Genco, March 24, 1948, referencing additional reports for January 27; February 2, 6, 11, 14; and, March 3, 1948. NARA 1, Box 43.

42. "Develop evidence" and Hoover note from Addendum of March 9, 1948 to Criminal Division Memo, December 23, 1947. NARA 1, Box 42. Only Hoover and his grammar teacher know why he wasn't simply left speechless.

43. Trial Transcript, vol. XLVII, 5298.

44. *Nashville Tennessean*, May 2, 1948, 1.

45. See "Earl Carroll" at http://www.musicals101.com/who2.htm.

46. Gabler, *Winchell*, 143.

47. Microphone story; did not speak, from Gabler, *Winchell*, 142.

48. *Washington Post*, August 21, 1945, 2.

49. I am indebted to Masayo Duus for this letter of May 27, 1948. Duus, *Orphan of the Pacific*, 124.

50. The Clark request went through channels, but my statement summarizes the truth of the matter. Office Memorandum, to Raymond Whearty (second in command in the criminal division), from Tom De-Wolfe, "Statement of the Case," May 25, 1948. NARA 2, Box 2. Rather than separate them into individual notes, I state here that the quotations that follow all come from this document. I have edited the quotations to remove case citations and redundancy.

51. Such was the common law of the time. Today, the prosecution and defense may call adverse or hostile witnesses whose veracity they intend to impeach. This rule was important in the Tokyo Rose trial because it prevented the defense from calling Harry Brundidge; see chapter 15.

52. "Thought you sd. see this" and "Prosecute it vigorously" are handwritten on a circulating memo of AAG T. Vincent Quinn, May 27, 1948. NARA 2. I tried diligently to find an explanation of Clark's decision in the relevant archives and failed. The Truman Library and the University of Texas, the two main repositories of Clark's papers, could not help. Ramsey Clark wrote a foreword for Howe's *The Hunt for "Tokyo Rose"* He noted the decision in a single sentence without comment and without even acknowledging he was Tom Clark's son.

53. Robbins (*Tokyo Calling*, 246–47) claims, "The United States government pursued [Iva Toguri] after the end of the war in a witch-hunt for 'Tokyo Rose.' The vigour with which it did so would suggest that the Japanese radio propaganda campaign had been highly successful in demoralising American troops." This assumes that DoJ prosecuted Iva because justice demanded it, which is highly doubtful. Robbins herself indicates as much when she adds, "The evidence, however, does not seem to support the supposition that the campaign was successful." This is British understatement; the evidence refutes the supposition.

54. Notably the recollections of Mitsushio and Oki; see chapter 16.

55. Warrant of Arrest, August 26, 1948, Brigadier General W. A. Beiderlinden, Asst. Chief of Staff.

56. *New York Times*, August 16, 1948, 1.

57. *Washington Post*, August 27, 1948, 2.

58. Both Duus and Howe dramatically overstate the U.S. government's perfidy in separating Iva from her husband. Duus claims, ""No one came to see her off. Filipe had not been told when she was to be sent back to the States. He learned about her departure from the newspaper—the day after she left" (*Orphan*, 128). Howe claims, "There was a last petty act of mental torture on her final day in Japan: Felippe was not warned of her departure, and she was not allowed to call him. He learned that his wife had been shipped out of the country from the newspapers" (*Hunt*, 206).

This error may result from misreading the trial transcript. DeWolfe, in cross-examining Phil D'Aquino, wanted to show that Phil had testified to certain acts that he himself did not witness. One was his wife's departure.

DeWolfe: "Did you go to Yokohama with Iva when she boarded the transport for San Francisco?"

D'Aquino: "No, sir, I was unable to go, sir."

DeWolfe: "Well, when you say she went to Yokohama, you are telling what somebody told you, aren't you?"

D'Aquino: "Well, the last I saw her was outside the gates of Sugamo Prison stepping into—"

DeWolfe: "You weren't there at Yokohama, were you? You don't know that she was in Yokohama other than what somebody told you, do you?"

D'Aquino: "Well, from the press, sir."

Contrary to Duus and Howe, the acting Provost Marshal, Colonel Polk J. Atkinson, stated in a memo of August 30, 1948, that he wanted Phil to visit Iva at Sugamo. "Inasmuch as Mrs. D'Aquino is scheduled to depart Yokohama, Japan on September 2, 1948, it is recommended that he be allowed to visit her on at least two occasions prior to her departure in order that he may bring sufficient clothing and other necessities for the trip to San Francisco." NARA 7, Box 58.

59. Trial Transcript, vol. II, 153. At the time of trial she was Major Stull. When I asked Iva about this incident in 1987, she denied it ever happened. Presented with Stull's testimony, she said that she didn't remember it. She was confident, and Army records confirm, that she had packed up her belongings in anticipation of her arrest, that she had suitcases on the ship, and that Stull therefore would have had no reason to buy her clothing. See in this regard, chapter 13, note 35. Perhaps Stull bought slacks because the clothing Iva had with her no longer fit. At any rate, Stull comes across as having a kind heart, and Iva's lawyer Wayne Collins used her testimony to Iva's advantage at trial.

60. On the day of her conviction, the *Examiner* headlined the verdict, "Tokio Rose Found Guilty; Five Years To Death Possible." *San Francisco Examiner*, September 30, 1949, 1.

61. On February 25, 1976, the *Chicago Tribune* mistakenly reported, "A matron refused to allow her to pin up the skirt, feeling she'd commit suicide with the safety pin. Marines carried her from the ship." Several photographs, including Figure 14.1 from the *San Francisco Examiner*, September 26, 1948, show Iva walking down the gangplank under her own power. I recognize Frederick Tillman and know he personally signed to take custody of Iva. "Receipt of Prisoner," September 25, 1948, Tillman from Captain Prosnak. NARA 11, Box 1. However, I am speculating the second agent is Dunn. I have never seen a photo of him and only know he and Tillman consistently worked together on the case and continued to do so in San Francisco.

62. The story of their first meeting appeared in the *San Francisco Examiner*, September 26, 1948, 3. Figure 14.2, Collection of *The Library of*

Congress. I believe this photo, dated November 1949, shows Jun and Iva together on the train that will carry her to prison. However, my research did not indicate that Jun rode with Iva and Marshal Cole when the latter accompanied her to Alderson, nor did Iva mention her father's presence when she talked to me about the trip.

15

The Perjurers

The FBI at Work

Waiting at the Commissioner's office with Jun Toguri were Iva's sister, June, and Wayne Collins, the lawyer whose defense of Japanese Americans was detailed in chapter 6. Iva recalled, "My father had Caucasian attorneys before the war but they were all afraid to take my case.[1] I don't know whether Wayne went to my father or vice versa, but before I returned, my father had hired him to represent me. At the office, I told him that I didn't know how I was going to pay him because I had at that moment exactly two red pennies in my coin purse, which were my total assets. He said, 'Don't worry about it.'

"From the commissioner's office they took me to the San Francisco jail, where I was bathed and dressed in the jail uniform. Soon after, the matron of the jail told me two officers from the U.S. Marshal's office had come to take me out and that I should get into my street clothes. They came up in the elevator, and they took me down and were just about to put me in their car when Wayne Collins drove up. If you wanted to hear some real Irish cussing, it took place there. 'What the hell are you SOBs trying to do? Where are you taking her?' They told him the FBI wanted to talk to me, so he got right in the car with us. And he told me again not to answer anything but my name. It was quite an emotional thing for me because all of the time I had spent incarcerated, I had asked for legal representation and they had never allowed me, so I was really touched by having Wayne Collins by my side."

Iva's memories, decades after the events, were slightly more dramatic than what actually happened. (Wayne Collins filed a complete description of Iva's abduction in a letter of protest two days after the incident.) Actually, Collins was at the jail conferring with Iva when the matron came in with the order that she get Iva ready for transport. Collins knew that no court would have ordered Iva's removal on a Saturday. He telephoned prosecutor Thomas DeWolfe for an explanation, but he was not in his office. Collins refused to leave Iva when a marshal arrived, and he accompanied them down the elevator, out the backdoor, and through an alley. There he found FBI agent J. Eldon Dunn (Frederick Tillman's associate in the investigation) sitting in the back seat of a black FBI sedan. Collins jammed his way inside and no doubt some Irish cussing did ensue, although Collins does not mention it in his report. They drove to an FBI office where Tillman and a stenographer waited. The agents obviously intended to do to Iva what they had done to other witnesses; that is, interrogate her in the hope she would contradict some earlier statement. They gave up when they saw Collins. Their only excuse for taking her was that they had orders from DeWolfe. In his letter, Collins pretended that this could not be true, that no U.S. Attorney "would ever have been guilty of any such outrageous misconduct." In fact, DeWolfe had ordered the interrogation, as we now know from internal FBI memos.[2] In any case, Collins protested vehemently. "I brand such conduct as being of a nature and character we have always believed to be shunned in the United States. We are not willing to follow or adopt methods employed by Hitler's Gestapo and Stalin's Ogpu in the violation of civil liberty and constitutional right."[3] The FBI did not attempt any further interrogations of Iva.

Collins immediately petitioned for bail, but on October 14, 1948, Judge Louis E. Goodman, the same judge who had decided the renunciant's case, denied his motion. The judge did order Iva removed from the San Francisco jail to the less restrictive environment of the Immigration and Naturalization Service detention quarters.[4] Iva was in the custody of the United States Marshal. "The U.S. Marshal's office—all of them—were very good to me. I had a lot more leeway than other prisoners." Iva's father and her sister June visited her every afternoon. Still, she remained locked up until and through her trial. The United States incarcerated Iva Toguri for almost two years without having convicted her of any crime.[5]

~

On October 6, 1948, Thomas DeWolfe presented the Tokyo Rose case to a federal grand jury. The U.S. government flew witnesses from Japan and put them up in the Whitcomb Hotel at government expense. The FBI kept them under surveillance and bugged their rooms. Many chose to stay in the United States, working at various jobs until the trial, a financial bonanza.[6] DeWolfe offered seven witnesses to the Grand Jury, including Harry Brundidge and Clark Lee. Witness Hiromu Yagi[7] testified that he had personally observed Iva Toguri at Radio Tokyo during the war and heard with his own ears her propaganda broadcasts, not over the air but as she spoke into the microphone. This evidence was crucial because previous FBI interviews had demonstrated that GIs listening in the Pacific were consistently confused about what and who they heard via shortwave, and that even if they could identify Iva's voice, they had to rely on years-old memories of the specific content of her broadcasts. Yagi tied the propaganda directly to Iva.

The grand jury was as unimpressed as DeWolfe had predicted. They "insisted on the removal of all witnesses and federal prosecutors while they conferred among themselves."[8] When they allowed DeWolfe to return, they informed him that his attempted indictment was unfair. It made no sense to them that DeWolfe intended to prosecute Iva Toguri but not the American officer who commanded her, Wallace Ince. The hearing was postponed, and the next day DeWolfe came armed with a promise. "I told the grand talesmen that the case as to Colonel Ince would be presented to a Federal grand jury here in the immediate future, after an exhaustive, factual investigation of the same in the Orient had been undertaken." DeWolfe knew Ince had been thoroughly investigated, released, and recently promoted to colonel, and that no better case could be made against him than against Iva. But he had to promise to indict Ince because otherwise, as he explained to his superiors, "I believe that the grand jury would have returned a no true bill against Mrs. D'Aquino."[9] DeWolfe added, "As it was two of the grand jurors voted against an indictment. It was necessary for me to practically make a fourth of July speech in order to obtain an indictment."[10]

A month after the grand jury proceeding, the prosecution learned that Yagi's entire testimony was a lie. Yagi admitted to the FBI that Harry Brundidge had "induced him to give false information" with the promise of a free trip and fun times in the United States, and that in fact Yagi "had never witnessed a broadcast of the subject nor had any information concerning her."[11] This discovery greatly benefited the prosecution. DeWolfe knew better than to call either Yagi or Brundidge as witnesses.

Ted Tamba independently found out on his own that Yagi had lied. In a modern courtroom, the defense would have had a field day demonstrating the prosecution's case rested on perjured testimony. Unfortunately, Wayne Collins could not call either Yagi or Brundidge to the stand. Under a common law rule that governed trials at that time, which does not apply today, a lawyer could not impeach his own witness. Had Collins called Yagi, and on the stand Yagi had returned to his earlier perjury, swearing that he witnessed Iva broadcast propaganda, Collins could not have offered into evidence his subsequent statements admitting this was untrue.[12] As a result, the jury never heard from either man and only indirectly learned of the perjury that led to Iva's indictment.

Harry Brundidge also walked away from his mess unscathed. The Department of Justice (DoJ) decided not to prosecute him for suborning perjury and obstruction of justice because the attorney general worried about "the stink" it would give the whole case.[13] Prosecutors also believed that if the jury knew what happened, "it would completely destroy any chance of a conviction" of Iva Toguri.[14] FBI Director J. Edgar Hoover, whom Brundidge jauntily addressed as "Edgar,"[15] wanted nothing more to do with him. When the Justice Department asked the FBI to investigate Wallace Ince's work in Japan, Hoover balked, writing in his own hand, "We have no jurisdiction abroad and at specific direction of the President we have been told to stay out of foreign work. The Dept. has already ignored FBI in the Tokyo Rose case and sent Hogan and the 'Super-Duper' sleuth Mr. Brundidge to Tokyo. They should use this adept twosome on this case."[16] Later, when Justice asked for an FBI investigation of Brundidge, Hoover wrote in the margin of the request, "Sadd. [sic] We didn't hire Brundidge—the Dept did. Let the Special Assts [Special Assistant Attorneys General] interview him."[17]

~

After DeWolfe's Fourth of July speech, the Grand Jury endorsed a bill of indictment against Iva Toguri that she "did knowingly, wilfully, unlawfully, feloniously, intentionally, traitorously, and treasonably adhere to the enemies of the United States."[18] Jurors charged her with eight overt acts of treason. (The full text of the indictment may be found in the Appendix.) The significance of the phrase "overt acts (OAs)" is that a person cannot be found guilty of treason for thinking treasonous thoughts or intending to commit treason. The Constitution requires overt acts that put the thoughts and intentions into effect.

For modern readers, the acts are shockingly innocuous. Overt Act I charged that on an unknown day in 1944, Iva discussed participating in a radio broadcast. That is not a summary. That's the entire accusation. One could be excused for wondering how a conversation about participating in a radio broadcast could be treason. Maybe participating, but not just talking about participating. Overt Act II was much the same. It alleged she had a conversation about the nature and quality of a "proposed" radio broadcast. Treason is a capital offense. Had the jury convicted Iva Toguri on either of these first two counts, the judge in his discretion could have sentenced her to death, not for broadcasting, but for simply conversing about possible broadcasts.

Overt Act III alleged she spoke "into a microphone about the introduction of a program dealing with a motion picture involving war." The charge is vague and convoluted—speaking *about* an introduction *dealing with* a motion picture *involving* war—but the accusation concerns the American Civil War as portrayed in the motion picture *Gone with the Wind*. Readers imagining Iva Toguri in the role of the one and original Nisei Scarlett O'Hara should know the segment was more film criticism than drama and that Iva did not participate in it. What happened was this: Late in 1944, Iva attended a showing of *Gone with the Wind* at Bunka Camp along with many others, Japanese nationals and POWs alike. Shortly thereafter, personnel associated with *Zero Hour*—exactly who is disputed but the chief architect of the skit in question was an English-speaking Nisei musician named Oshidari—decided to create a pastiche of scenes from the movie along with music and commentary. Oshidari, Norman Reyes, and others attempted to produce a script for this segment, but none of them had the competence to pull it off. In addition, the movie dialogue track and music clips were of extremely poor quality. As a result, the entire enterprise was a fiasco. Iva swore she had nothing to do with it. "I did not have the ability to write so I was not included. [Norman Reyes] knows I did not contribute a word towards the script." Iva went to see the movie because "I had not seen an American film for so long and was hungry for entertainment. Because of time left over after [the segment's] broadcast, Norman and I put on a record show without a script, gave good records, and kidded in fun when putting on the records."[19]

The other Overt Acts were equally vacuous. Overt Act IV alleged she referred to enemies of Japan. What she said about them was unspecified. As far as the indictment was concerned, she might have broadcast, "Hooray for the enemies of Japan!" Overt Acts V and VII alleged she prepared a radio script. Overt Act VI claimed she spoke about "the loss of ships." Again, what she said about this loss, whose ships she spoke about—was not specified. The final OA, VIII, charged her with engaging in entertaining dialogue.

The indictment failed to charge Iva Toguri with any of the OAs traditionally associated with Tokyo Rose. None of the eight Acts made any mention of calling military units by name, predicting troop movements, or threatening dire consequences if the Allies continued to wage war against Japan. None mentioned broadcasts about wives playing around back home, war weariness, nostalgia, homesickness, or reducing morale. The indictment was as insubstantial as one would expect, given DeWolfe's assessment of the case.

The OAs so lacked specificity that readers of the previous chapters will instantly recognize that, with the possible exception of OA VI, Iva was guilty of all of them. She did have a conversation about participating in a radio broadcast and about the nature of a proposed broadcast. This happened when Cousens and Ince enlisted her for their new program. She spoke about the *Gone with the Wind* segment if only to refuse to script it. She called the GIs "my favorite enemies," so she did speak about the enemies of

Japan. She prepared radio scripts after Cousens' heart attack. She definitely engaged in entertaining dialogue. The only act of which she was not obviously guilty involved speaking about the loss of ships. Normally such an announcement would have been part of the news portion of *Zero Hour*, and Iva only introduced music. So the question for readers is not, was she guilty?—she certainly was—but instead, did the performance of these actions amount to treason?

The Austrian Franz Kafka wrote novels about people accused, tried, and found guilty without ever knowing the nature of their crime. Although Iva Toguri's trial was somewhat Kafkaesque, it is important to understand the legal and historical context of the Toguri indictment. First, modern indictments are specific. A defendant knows exactly what crime she allegedly committed as well as when, where, and how she allegedly committed it. In 1949, however, indictments were remarkably vague as to the nature of the criminal activity. Prosecutors intentionally worded charges so as to hide as much of their case as possible from defense attorneys. Iva Toguri's indictment was typical of its time but would not pass muster today. Second, treason law is unusual because the government must prove both an action—to aid the enemy—and a connected intention—to betray the United States in so doing. When the overt act is fairly innocuous, like having a conversation about participating in a radio program, the intention behind the act becomes paramount. A central issue in the Toguri trial, therefore, was the standard of proof the government had to meet to show the defendant's intentions.

Both prosecutor DeWolfe and defense attorney Collins relied on a 1945 Supreme Court decision in the treason case, *Cramer v. U.S.*[20] The *New York Times* described this case as "the first test of the treason laws in the [Supreme Court's] 150 year history."[21] The case concerned Anthony Cramer, a mechanic. Two FBI agents witnessed Cramer having drinks and talking with German saboteurs, but the agents did not overhear what the men said. Other testimony at the trial, not witnessed by two people, brought out that Cramer knew the saboteurs were Germans who were in the United States illegally, and that he aided them by, among other things, holding money for them. On November 18, 1942, Cramer was convicted of treason.[22] The Second Circuit Court of Appeals upheld the conviction. In appealing to the Supreme Court, Cramer's attorneys cited Judge Learned Hand, "Overt Acts are such acts as manifest a criminal intention and tend towards the accomplishment of the criminal object."[23] They argued that nothing about a bar conversation manifests criminal intention, and Cramer should not have been convicted.

The Supreme Court split 5–4 in its struggle to find justice. "The prisoner's contention that the act alone and on its face must manifest a traitorous intention would place on the overt act the whole burden of establishing a complete treason. On the other hand, the government's contention that it may prove by two witnesses an apparently commonplace and insignificant act and from other circumstances create an inference that the act was done with treasonable intent really is a contention that the function of the overt act in a treason prosecution is almost zero."[24] The Court sought a middle ground, and the majority concluded, "The very minimum function that an overt act must perform in a treason prosecution is that it show sufficient action by the accused, in its setting, to sustain a finding that the accused actually gave aid and comfort to the enemy."[25] The Supreme Court overturned Cramer's conviction.[26]

DeWolfe had prosecuted the first treason cases after the *Cramer* ruling's "unusually severe tests of proof." He had won both.[27] The OAs with which he charged Iva Toguri were not explicitly criminal on their face but, unlike Cramer's bar talk, they might possibly be. Since "the Court concedes that an overt act need not manifest on its face a traitorous intent,"[28] DeWolfe believed that if he could put Iva's actions in the context of morale-lowering broadcasts, he would obtain his conviction and have it upheld. He also noted that the minority dissent, written by Justice William O. Douglas, had taken a much more pro-prosecution line than had the majority.

Wayne Collins was equally confident about the meaning of *Cramer* because the Supreme Court overturned the conviction. Further, whereas testimony had brought out Cramer's mild cooperation with, and failure to report, the enemy agents, testimony in Iva's trial would bring out her cooperation with and support of the POWs and their plans to undermine the enemy.

Both attorneys realized the clause "in its setting" was crucial. The key to the verdict in Iva's case would be the context of Iva's actions. The High Court concluded in *Cramer*, "The offense is one of subtlety. The protection of the two-witness requirement, limited as it is to overt acts, may be wholly unrelated to the real controversial factors in a case."[29] The hidden setting of *United States v. Toguri*, the real controversial factor that would psychologically determine the setting of Iva's actions in the eyes of the jury, was the legend of Tokyo Rose.

~

On November 15, 1948, Wayne Collins filed a Motion to Dismiss Indictment. The first ground for dismissal was simple and straightforward and came right out of *Cramer*: "The indictment fails to state facts sufficient to constitute an offense against the United States" and the charges, "being vague, indefinite and uncertain . . . are so general" that the defendant cannot prepare a defense against them.[30] However, to ensure the court considered every possible legal argument, his Motion went on to list 31 other grounds for dismissal, the last of which contained 24 subsections. This surfeit may have overwhelmed Judge Michael J. Roche, who would preside at trial. On March 15, 1949, Roche denied the Motion without comment.

During the pretrial period, Collins also filed six other motions. He reasonably asked that subpoenas be issued for defense witnesses to be brought to the United States at government expense; he unreasonably asked for 43 such witnesses, beginning with Douglas MacArthur. He moved that parts of the trial be held in Tokyo, Hong Kong, and Sydney. Presumably he wanted Charles Cousens to testify in Sydney, although it would obviously have been far easier to bring Cousens to America than to transport judge and jury to Australia. What he expected to find in Hong Kong is anybody's guess. He moved twice again to quash the indictment. Among his grounds for dismissal were that Iva could not be tried for treason against the United States because her marriage to Phil had made her a citizen of Portugal, and that her jailing in Japan constituted double jeopardy. The government responded that Iva's marriage took place after the first six OAs and that she had not followed the proper procedures to expatriate herself. As to her imprisonment, the Army never brought charges against her, so her time in jail did not place her in jeopardy. Judge Roche denied five of the six motions.

With regard to the sixth, Roche did find that since Iva was indigent, one of Iva's lawyers could travel to Japan to take depositions of needed witnesses at government expense. (Collins asked Ted Tamba.) This ruling hardly offset the imbalance between the two sides. Whereas the defense could only take depositions to be read in court, the prosecution was able to fly nineteen of its witnesses from Japan to testify. The U.S. government not only paid for their first-class air fare but $12 a day for expenses and their time.[31] Although it seems like a small amount of money today, $12 American represented a significant windfall for Japanese nationals in 1949.

This massive advantage might have satisfied DeWolfe had he been prosecuting a guilty defendant. But Iva was innocent, so the prosecution piled on. As the court issued subpoenas for defense witnesses in San Francisco, the FBI forwarded their names to its agents in Japan and, before Tamba could depose them, Frederick Tillman, accompanied by two armed MPs, paid them a visit and had them sign an interview statement.[32] In addition, DoJ attorney Neal Story accompanied Tamba to cross-examine all his witnesses at their depositions.

Despite interference from the FBI, the Tamba name opened doors in Japan because of a well-known Japanese pottery called Tamba. Tamba's friend, J. R. Hughes, recalled,

> He used to tell me that he had no trouble getting appointments for interviews. When they heard the name Tamba, they said of course. When he showed up and here's this great big tall Swiss, they were taken by surprise and they started talking about the name. That broke the ice for him and he made lots of very, very long-lasting friends that he would go visit when he would go back to Japan.[33]

Neal Story kept close tabs on the results of Tamba's appointments. Story wrote to DeWolfe, "Mr. Tamba talked to Wayne Collins in San Francisco one day last week and explained in detail the difficulties he was having with the depositions."[34] The question arises, how could Story know this? Tamba might have mentioned he had spoken with Collins, but surely he would not have confessed he was having difficulty with the depositions or that he explained to Collins his difficulties "in detail." Today we know how Story came to be so well informed. The prosecutors received wiretaps of the defense attorneys' conversations from the U.S. Army.

Following the war, the Occupation Army's Civil Censorship Detachment (CCD) under General Willoughby wiretapped about one-quarter of all telephone calls into and from Japan.[35] The justification was national security and guarding against communism, but the transcripts now extant indicate that the government recorded first and worried about communism later. CCD files in the National Archives contain transcripts of partial conversations between Wayne Collins and Phil D'Aquino, and between Collins and Tamba. In the former, Iva's husband discusses two witnesses (Holland and Uno) he believes will be important and informs Collins that in trying to get witness statements, "I don't seem to make any headway." The single page of a transcript of a conversation between Tamba and Collins concerns Yagi. Tamba says, "I was with him until one (1) o'clock this morning and he doesn't want to commit an admission of a crime before a notary public." Collins replies, "Get a deposition anyway but he doesn't have to sign it."[36]

It is remotely, very remotely, possible that the Army bugged these two conversations accidentally and no others relevant to the Tokyo Rose case ever were. However, CCD noted on its cover sheet that the Tamba/Collins transcript was "Sensitive—attorneys for Tokyo Rose," took the trouble to locate Tamba's telephone at the Tokyo Hotel, marked the transcript "DO NOT PHOTOGRAPH," classified it "Confidential," and titled it "Intelligence: Deposition Developments in 'Tokyo Rose' Case Revealed." For an accidental wiretap, this represents a terrific amount of bureaucratic zealousness. Furthermore, the government had wiretapped Wayne Collins in the past. On more than 20 occasions between October 1945 and March 1946, the government had tapped his phone calls to Tule Lake as he worked on the renunciants' case.[37] Given this history and the government's rabid pursuit of Tokyo Rose, it seems likely that the Army intentionally transcribed and passed along all the defense's telephone conversations, and the only accident is that these few pages escaped destruction.[38]

The Army also aided the prosecution in another way. It classified Iva's various statements to the Counter-Intelligence Corps (CIC) and the results of the CIC's investigation Top Secret. This prevented her defense attorneys from introducing these generally accurate reports into evidence. Collins petitioned the Court for the records, but Judge Roche ruled that he could not compel the military to produce this material.[39]

~

When prosecutor Thomas DeWolfe prepared his "Statement of the Case" for Tom Clark, he argued that the three prisoners of war—Cousens, Ince, and Reyes—would be the key government witnesses and that all would testify in Iva Toguri's favor. After the Attorney General ignored his advice to drop the case and required him to prosecute Iva Toguri anyway, DeWolfe reversed his previous strategy. DeWolfe decided not to call the three POWs. Instead, he would allow Collins to call them as defense witnesses and leave himself free to attack them as liars and traitors covering up for Iva as well as themselves.

Of the three POWs, Charles Cousens was easily the strongest. He had stood up to the Japanese; he certainly would not falter before the Americans. Nonetheless, the FBI took a crack at him. On March 8, 1949, Colonel Longfield Lloyd, the Director of Australia's Commonwealth Investigation Service, notified his counterpart in America, J. Edgar Hoover, that "Major Charles Cousens was contemplating a visit to the United States and was leaving Australia for the purpose of giving evidence at the trial of Tokyo Rose."[40] Hoover notified DoJ's Criminal Division, and Assistant Attorney General Campbell replied, "If it is possible to locate Major Cousens upon his arrival in this country, it would be helpful to the Government's case if he could be thoroughly interviewed as to all phases of his knowledge of the defendant's activities."[41] Hoover ordered his offices to watch for Cousens. Their vigilance paid off and, on June 28, 1949, operator MDC sent a radiogram to San Francisco, "Major Charles Cousens under name C. H. Cousens, radio announcer, presently holding reservation on BC PA Air Line Flight 104-9 due to arrive at Mills Field, California at 9:30 AM on June 30 next."[42] When Cousens' plane landed, a Customs inspector buttonholed him and led him to an office where agents Tillman and Dunn waited. Also on the plane was another defense witness, Kenneth Parkyns, whom the agents took aside for interrogation as well. Frederick Tillman had just begun his interview of Cousens when Wayne Collins and Ted Tamba burst into the office. Collins denounced the agents, according to their own report, saying, "Damn you, you have no right to talk to these people. What do you think this is?"[43] Collins took his witnesses away and thus stymied FBI interference once again.

DeWolfe also hoped to undermine the testimony of Wallace "Ted" Ince. He wanted to indict Ince so that, if the defense called him to prove duress and coercion, he could suggest during cross-examination that Ince was exaggerating or lying to protect himself.[44] DeWolfe requested the FBI investigate Ince for treason,[45] but the Army blocked it. Ince received steady promotion and the DoJ never pursued him.

That left Norman Reyes. Reyes, in the eyes of prosecutors, was clearly the weak link among the POWs. After the war, he had moved to the United States to live with his mother in Nashville, attend Vanderbilt University, and complete his college education, which had been cut short by the Japanese attack on the Philippines. He was in the United States on a student visa and was, as he saw it, "half-American." Reyes knew the FBI had already twice interviewed his wife, from whom he was now separated, about her broadcasting. Still, his initial interviews in Tennessee went well. FBI Agent Winfred E. Hopton questioned him between April 8 and 12, 1948, and again between May 8 and 15, 1948. Hopton dutifully recorded what Reyes told him and as a result, his interview reports contained little that incriminated either Reyes or Iva. Then, FBI Agents Frederick Tillman and J. Eldon Dunn took control. Although Reyes had told them his story in December 1945, while still in Japan, and although he had retold it to Hopton, the two agents questioned him yet again about the same events. They worked on Reyes relentlessly for five days between October 1 and 5, 1948. They warned him that if his actions were similar to Iva Toguri's, he was just as open to the charge of treason as she was. During these sessions, Reyes had no legal counsel and was alone with the agents. The days and days of interrogation, going over and over the same events hour after hour, served no legitimate purpose. Tillman and Dunn wanted to break Reyes and conform his testimony to the needs of the prosecution. In the end, they succeeded. As per his usual practice, Tillman recast Reyes' statements using his own wording and demanded that Reyes sign the document, which he did. In Tillman's version, Reyes' story changed radically. Perhaps out of embarrassment, or because he was oblivious to the consequences, Reyes never informed Wayne Collins of his dissembling. As a result, DeWolfe successfully planted a hidden bomb in the defense that he would later use to blow it apart.[46]

For prosecutor DeWolfe to convict Iva Toguri, the Constitution required that he produce two witnesses to each of her overt acts of treason. The decision to let the POWs become defense witnesses had left a huge hole in his case. Given the years of exhaustive investigations, DeWolfe realized that the discovery of two new witnesses who could testify to Iva's traitorous actions was an unlikely prospect. Therefore, his only real choice was to compel previously neutral witnesses to lie. He decided his best chance lay with Japanese nationals and the pro-Japanese Nisei. It was a daring roll of the dice—using actual enemies of the United States and their Nisei sympathizers to convict a loyal American of treason—but he had a job to do and little choice about how to do it.

He selected the two Nisei men who were Iva's immediate superiors, George Mitsushio and Kenkichi Oki. Readers will recall from chapter 12 that Mitsushio had told CIC investigators in 1945 that Iva's "only participation in broadcasting from Radio Tokyo was to the extent of introducing music on the *Zero Hour*." The CIC also reported, "Oki declared that Toguri . . . never read commentaries or news on this program."[47] On February 19, 1948, three months before Attorney General Clark ordered DeWolfe to prosecute, Oki provided an affidavit to the FBI in which he reiterated his position that Iva only introduced music. Apparently responding to some specific questioning, Oki stated that he had a clear recollection of the evening broadcasts after the fall of Saipan and Hiroshima and that on both occasions he remembered "seeing and hearing Miss Toguri announce her portion of the program, which was as before, the announcing of the 'Jazz music.'"[48] He made no mention in this statement of Iva's broadcasting propaganda, military information, morale-reducing taunts, or news about the loss of ships.

Both Mitsushio and Oki had been born in California. They had moved to Japan before the war and registered as Japanese citizens. However, the DoJ informed them that neither had taken the necessary and somewhat complicated legal steps to expatriate, and that therefore they were as liable to a charge of treason as Iva. Were that true, and it probably was not, their acts of disloyalty would be easily proven; they had in fact supported Japan throughout the war. Oki was especially vulnerable because his wife, Mieko Furuya, the Saturday Night Party Girl, regularly replaced Iva on the *Zero Hour*. Having seen what had happened to Iva, they realized that if the U.S. government made up its mind, the same and worse could happen to them. They agreed to cooperate.

After DeWolfe made the decision to use Mitsushio and Oki, the relationship between the FBI and the two men changed. Heretofore the FBI had interviewed witnesses in order to learn what they knew. Sometimes, as for example in the case of Iva herself, the FBI distorted the witness' testimony to make statements more amenable to the government's purposes. However, in the case of Mitsushio and Oki, the FBI stopped interviewing altogether and instead simply coached them on what to say. Before the trial, the agents drilled them on their testimony day after day until they had it memorized.

This is a serious charge, but the evidence supports it. The source of this evidence is the FBI itself. Thanks to the Bureau, we even know when the transition from interview to coaching began. In late September 1948, the FBI purported to interrogate one man and then the other, interviewing the two men separately.[49] The qualifier is important. Separating witnesses is a standard practice of law enforcement, so that they cannot conform their testimony. This technique, had the FBI in fact employed it, would have prevented Mitsushio from knowing exactly what Oki said and vice versa.

Biographer Russell Warren Howe undertook an extensive and rather clever analysis of the now-available transcripts of these "separate" interviews.[50] Howe noticed the two men consistently made exactly the same mistake as to dates. They also made similar petty errors, such as claiming that Iva stood at the microphone. Employees at Radio Tokyo, including Mitsushio and Oki, knew that Iva sat when she broadcast. More important, Howe noticed that the FBI's transcription of the "individual" interviews would accidentally refer to "them" instead of "him," a mistake that makes no sense if the Bureau really interviewed only one person. Worse, someone later redacted the transcription, replacing "them" with

"him." These redactions, done before the advent of word proces-
sors, left the four spaces for the word "them" in the document.
Finally and significantly, Howe discovered that for more than
2,000 words, the two men's interviews were identical. They did not
merely conform, they were word-for-word identical, except that
whenever Mitsushio mentioned Oki, in the corresponding passage in the parallel interview, Oki mentioned Mitsushio. Take, for
example, the account of a luncheon overseen by Major Tsuneishi
and attended by about a dozen people. Iva went for the free meal
and then left early because she had no interest in the proceedings
and could not understand Tsuneishi's Japanese. Mitsushio told the
FBI,

> Shigetsugu Tsuneishi, then a Major in the Imperial Japanese
> Army and a member of the Army General Staff, gave a dinner for
> the staff of the "Zero Hour" program on Radio Tokyo in March,
> 1944 at the Tokyo Kaikan Restaurant. At this restaurant there
> were present George Mitsushio, Kenkichi Oki, Shinichi Oshidari,
> Hasashi Moriyama, and Iva Ikuko Toguri. At this luncheon Major
> Tsuneishi complimented the staff . . .

Oki "independently" told the FBI,

> Shigetsugu Tsuneishi, then a Major in the Imperial Japanese
> Army and a member of the Army General Staff, gave a dinner for
> the staff of the "Zero Hour" program on Radio Tokyo in March,
> 1944 at the Tokyo Kaikan Restaurant. At this restaurant there
> were present George Mitsushio, Kenkichi Oki, Shinichi Oshidari,
> Hasashi Moriyama, and Iva Ikuko Toguri. At this luncheon Major
> Tsuneishi complimented the staff . . .

Howe noticed that both men first called the meal a dinner and
changed their description to a luncheon, both referred to Iva by the
ungainly "Iva Ikuko Toguri" and to themselves in the third person,
and both just happened to recall the same five people in attendance
in exactly the same order. This sort of duplicity goes on for page
after page.

In early October, these sessions culminated in a series of sworn
statements by the two men concerning the OAs.[51] Their recollec-

tions, cast in the stilted language reserved for lawyers, diverged just enough to give their statements a patina of credibility. Thus, for OA VI:

> I, George Mitsushio, do hereby make the following supplemental statement to Tom DeWolfe and John. B. Hogan of the Department of Justice:
>
> On some day during the month of October, 1944, the exact date of the occurrence I am not now able to recall, the Imperial General Headquarters of the Japanese Armed Forces handed to the radio an official announcement concerning the battle of the Leyte Gulf, which announcement reflected that a great number of American ships had been sunk. I spoke to Iva Toguri about this announcement and requested her to allude to the incident in her broadcast. She stated she would do so. On said date after 6 P.M. I saw Iva Toguri at the microphone in the broadcasting studio and she stated over the microphone in substance as follows, according to the best of my recollection: "Now you fellows have lost all your ships. You really are orphans of the Pacific now. How do you think you will ever get home."

> I, Kenkichi Oki, do hereby make the following supplemental statement to Tom DeWolfe and John. B. Hogan of the Department of Justice:
>
> That on a date in October, 1944, the exact day I do not now recall, shortly after the Battle of the Leyte Gulf, Japanese Imperial Headquarters handed down an official announcement concerning the same, which announcement reflected the loss of a great number of enemy ships. I saw this announcement. After 6 P.M. on said date, I saw Iva Toguri at the microphone in the broadcasting studio and she stated in substance, to the best of my recollection, as follows: "Now you fellows have lost all your ships. You really are orphans of the Pacific, and how do you think you will ever get home."[52]

Mitsushio and Oki signed similar statements for all the other OAs, and the U.S. government had its two witnesses. DeWolfe, who was present when the two men signed and during some of their interrogation/preparation, had to know their testimony was false.

~

The stage was now set for what is arguably the most sensational treason trial in American history. Here is a brief introduction of the trial's fundamental elements—the prosecution, defense, judge, jury, and physical evidence.

Prosecution

Figure 15.1. Prosecutors James Knapp, Frank Hennessy, and Thomas DeWolfe.

Figure 15.2. Tom De-Wolfe.
Courtesy of San Francisco Chronicle.

The team of prosecutors (Figure 15.1) was led by Thomas Emory DeWolfe (Figure 15.2).[53] DeWolfe was born on July 22, 1902, in Seattle.[54] His birth name was Thomas Emory, and he was the son of Southerners. His father, G. Meade Emory, was from Georgia and had been a judge in Texas before moving into private practice in Seattle as a partner in Kelleher and Emory.[55] His mother, Josephine DeWolfe, came from North Carolina. Also living with them was Josephine's father, Frederick, a widower, who had formerly been mayor of Charlotte, North Carolina, and who now was a banker with King County Bank.[56] The Emory family was large—Thomas had five brothers and sisters—but prosperous enough to employ two live-in maids.[57] When Thomas was a child, his father died and his grandfather, Frederick, took responsibility for the financial well-being of the family. Later, in order to carry on the DeWolfe name, Thomas Emory changed his

name to Thomas Emory DeWolfe.[58] He followed in his biological
father's footsteps; in 1925, at the age of 23, he graduated from
the University of Virginia Law School[59] and, while still in his
20s, became an assistant attorney general for the United States.
He lived in Seattle, where he and his wife Carol had two sons,
the first of whom he named Frederick[60] after his grandfather and
the second, Tom, after himself. When the DoJ selected him to
prosecute the cases of Douglas Chandler and Robert Best and he
succeeded in obtaining life sentences for the two men, DeWolfe
became the obvious choice for the politically significant trial of
Tokyo Rose.

DeWolfe comes across as a combination of law professor and
Walter Matthau. News accounts of the time describe him as "a
scholarly, slow-spoken attorney" who was "solemn, dignified."[61]
Iva remembered him as "rumpled" and contrasted him with the
sharply dressed Collins. "His general appearance was poor. He was
not attractive. Wayne Collins dressed immaculately. His suits and
ties and shirts blended, whereas DeWolfe looked like he just came
off the farm. There was nothing elegant about him." Iva clearly
viewed this rumpled look as detrimental, but the jury may have
reacted differently. Iva added that trial observers would not have
considered DeWolfe a sharp lawyer. "On the contrary! He wasn't
dumb, just so-so." On this point, Iva was certainly mistaken.

DeWolfe was unfailingly polite, even fawning when it suited
his purposes. In his opening statement to the jury, he introduced,
"his Honor presiding is the Chief Federal Judge of the Northern
District of California, his Honor, Michael J. Roche" and soon again,
"his Honor, Chief Federal Judge Michael J. Roche," and consistently
referenced Roche's important role in the case.[62] Before he examined
his first witness, he solicitously asked the judge if he should remain
seated or should stand up when he questioned witnesses, and one
imagines Judge Roche practically gushed as he replied, "I have no
rigid rules here at all."[63]

When Attorney General Tom Clark ordered DeWolfe to prosecute Iva Toguri vigorously, DeWolfe faced a life-defining decision.
Tokyo Rose was one of the most recognizable names to survive the
war, and her trial would be news across the country. His career
had so worked itself out that he was the perfect prosecutor to lead
the government's efforts. If he won, he would be a hero. But if he

lost, he would be ridiculed as an incompetent, because everyone knew Tokyo Rose was guilty. By successfully prosecuting the case, DeWolfe would not only be a good soldier loyally following the directive of the attorney general, he would be serving a larger purpose in helping to elect the president.

One fly marred the ointment: DeWolfe knew the defendant was innocent. His opinion that the government could not prevail was not a "we know she's guilty but we can't quite prove it" judgment. He knew the facts, he knew Iva Toguri had not sold out, he knew she had never been disloyal, he knew he must suborn perjury to win, and we know that he knew because, unlike the defense at the time, we can read his intradepartmental assessments of the case.

Katherine Beebe[64] covered the trial for the Associated Press (AP). She stated in an interview after the events, "The United States Attorney there, whom I knew well, Frank Hennessy, had gone over the case. They'd asked him to go over all the evidence, and he had done so. He recommended against prosecuting her. But they overruled him politically in Washington and sent out a special prosecutor [DeWolfe]. Later I found that that man also was in great doubt, but he was a good soldier, so he did it."[65]

The lead investigator for the FBI was Frederick G. Tillman. Tillman was the son of Swedish immigrants, born in Butte, Montana, on November 2, 1907; his parents John and Marie Tillman, had four children. Like DeWolfe, Tillman's father died when Frederick was very young. Unlike DeWolfe's, their family was not prosperous—John Tillman had been a carpenter—and they had no well-to-do relations to fall back upon. Frederick and his older brother Axel helped their mother raise her two young daughters through hard work, Axel as a salesman and Frederick in law enforcement as a county deputy sheriff before he eventually joined the FBI.[66] Agent Tillman was assisted by Agent J. Eldon Dunn. They, like the prosecutors, knew what was up.

Defense

War correspondent Rex Gunn covered the 1949 trial of Iva Toguri and witnessed the injustice of it firsthand. He admired Wayne Col-

Figure 15.3. Clockwise from left: Wayne Collins, investigator Tetsujiro Naka-mura (standing), *George Olshausen, Iva Toguri, and Ted Tamba.*

lins for having the courage to take on her case. I once asked him what Wayne Collins was like in the courtroom. Gunn replied, "Collins was Sinn Fein. He attacked and attacked and even when there was nothing left to attack, he kept on. By the end of the trial, everybody hated him. The prosecution hated him, the judge hated him, the jury hated him, the press hated him, and the spectators hated him." On the very first day of their trial coverage, the *Chronicle* remarked that the "wiry, gray-haired San Francisco Law School graduate, is riding to a crusade. Collins is perpetually indignant."[67]

Iva Toguri, unsurprisingly, remembered Collins much more positively. "After that [the incident in which Collins forced his way into the FBI sedan and cussed out the agents], I thought, gee, now I've got someone on my side that's interested in me and my welfare. He's going to fight like hell for me, and that was a comfort after being held in prison without right to legal counsel." Iva regarded him as a defender of the Japanese in America. "He had a temper, but he was very knowledgeable in the law." Was he a moral man? "Yes!" she answered sharply. Collins was very positive before the trial. He was certain they would win because "what evidence can they have?" As for the jury not liking him, Iva conceded only a little, saying, "At times, no. At times, yes." She admitted that as a lawyer he was "pushy and demanding," but added, "Wayne Collins was 100 percent professional. It was De-Wolfe who was arrogant in the courtroom."

Wayne Collins also faced a grave decision rife with consequences. Collins had to choose between the rifle and the shotgun; that is, between two incompatible strategies for defending his client. The first possibility, the rifle, meant picking a single clear story line and holding tightly to it. The danger here was that if the jury did not buy the story, they would convict. The second possibility, the shotgun, required blasting every possible defense at the prosecution and hoping some of them would hit the mark. The hope was that if the jury felt inclined to acquit, they could pick and choose their reasons from among the many defenses.

Wayne Collins' personality disposed him to choose the latter. One problem with this course was that the various defenses appeared to contradict one another. Collins argued that Iva was a loyal American who loved her country, but also that she had voluntarily expatriated herself and become Portuguese. He argued that as a Portuguese she was safe from prosecution by the United States, but also that she had no need to be safe because she had not committed any crimes. He argued that she and the POWs conspired to blunt the effect of propaganda on the *Zero Hour*, but also that she never broadcast any propaganda. He argued that she acted under duress, but also that she had never succumbed to duress because she had never done anything wrong. He argued that she merely followed the orders of her POW superiors, but also that they never ordered her to do anything treasonous. He argued that Iva didn't know what she was doing when she signed her contract "Tokyo Rose," but also that Iva knew she wasn't Tokyo Rose. He argued that Iva had been denied access to counsel when interrogated, but also that she had said nothing incriminating. The danger with this strategy was that if the jury felt inclined to convict, they could pick and choose their reasons for that as well.

Finally, although Collins was confident no real evidence existed against Iva Toguri, he wanted to lay the groundwork for an appeal in case the verdict went against her. He knew from his previous successes in representing Japanese Americans that an appeal would require carefully crafted legal grounds that he could argue before higher courts. Some lawyers would have forced the judge to rule on difficult and carefully chosen questions of law in the hope he would make the kind of judicial error that would allow the verdict to be overturned. For Collins and the shotgun approach, it meant constant and incessant objections, objections that slowed the proceedings to a crawl and exasperated everyone in the courtroom.

Collins also convinced two other attorneys, George Olshausen and Ted Tamba, to volunteer to help with Iva's defense. Olshausen was retired and Iva remembered him as a scholarly individual in three-piece suits. Ted Tamba was an old associate of Wayne Collins. "He was a buffer. When Wayne would go off the handle and head for disaster, he would quiet him down. Wayne Collins had a very low boiling point. He'd go off at the drop of a hat." Iva and Tamba stayed in contact for years after the trial and she got to know him well. He was passionate about the rights of Japanese, though strangely intolerant of other minorities.[68] Lastly, Collins added Tetsujiro Nakamura as an investigator to the defense team (Figure 15.3).[69] Nakamura was the young Nisei food store owner and renunciant whose testimony that no one freely renounced their citizenship helped sway the lower court decision in Collins' favor.

Judge

The defense hoped to draw Judge Goodman for the trial. Goodman had not hesitated to criticize the government's handling of the renunciants, and Collins must have found considerable hope for Iva in Goodman's findings in that case that "it is shocking to the conscience that an American citizen be confined without authority, and then, while so under duress and restraint, for his government to accept from him a surrender of his constitutional heritage" and that there existed "no constitutional means by which American citizens, not charged with crime and not under martial law could be detained by administrative, military or civil officials or upon a mere administrative determination of loyalty."[70]

Instead, the defense wound up with Michael J. Roche (Figure 15.4).[71] Roche had emigrated to the United States from Ireland at age eight, had worked his way up from Justice of the Peace to California

Figure 15.4. Michael J. Roche (left) *with Earl Warren.*
Courtesy of Bancroft Library, University of California at Berkeley.

State judge to U.S. district judge.[72] He would turn 70 while presiding over the trial. Roche favored the government. Again and again, he overruled objections by the defense and sustained objections of the prosecution. By itself, of course, this pattern proves nothing. Perhaps the defense objected without grounds, whereas the prosecution did not. But we also have independent testimony of his bias.

Correspondent Katherine Beebe reported on the San Francisco legal scene, had many contacts with Judge Roche prior to the trial and knew him socially. AP assigned her exclusively to the trial, where she took dictation and prepared articles for morning and evening papers across the country. Decades later, Beebe participated in an oral history of the trial, which she remembered with amazing clarity. She said of Roche: "The judge was an old Irish Mick, a good police judge, that never should have been on the federal bench. He really didn't seem to listen to the testimony in her favor, and he later shocked me by saying, 'I always wondered what she was up to when she went to Japan.' I couldn't imagine such a thing!"[73] Because she believed that the trial was a travesty of justice, Beebe later supported Iva's quest for a pardon.

Jury

The power of the federal government when pursuing a criminal defendant can be awesome. In this case, dozens of agents devoted thousands of hours to the conquest of Tokyo Rose. A list of reports compiled in July 1948—months before Iva was indicted and the search for evidence took on real urgency—shows 9 CIC reports and 79 FBI reports issued from 34 different U.S. cities.[74] These are only the *reports*; the list does not include letters, memos, teletypes, radiograms, statements, affidavits, depositions, transcripts, and all the rest. Later, the FBI would even provide the prosecutors with a blueprint of the courtroom.[75]

This awesome federal power was especially evident in the selection of a jury. During the selection process, Tom DeWolfe used his peremptory challenges (a challenge in which no reason is stated) to exclude minorities. According to the *San Francisco Chronicle*, he "excused every dark-skinned juror. The Government [used] eight challenges which apparently hit only persons of possible Negro, Chinese or mixed blood." Afterward, DeWolfe denied

Figure 15.5. Jury and two alternates. Jury foreman John Mann is seated third from right, front row.
Courtesy of *San Francisco Chronicle*.

that race was a factor, stating that he was "not motivated by a matter of color."[76] We now know DeWolfe lied.

In a massive effort, the FBI investigated every person whose name appeared on the Master Trial Jury List—every potential juror—and compiled a brief report about each. The list contained the names of 221 people. The FBI developed credit statements, criminal records, and other information on each individual. The credit statements contained facts about race and even political affiliation. A review of DeWolfe's handwritten assessment of the jurors indicates that race was very much on his mind.[77]

DeWolfe marked almost every white juror "OK" or "Good." The few exceptions were either reasonable—two or three had criminal records—or could be considered reasonable to a prosecutor in 1949—a man whom a "confidential informant" claimed had attended a meeting of the Joint Anti-Fascist Refugee Committee, a woman who was the "Educational Director of local Communist Party," and a man who received mail from the German Embassy. One exception to this reasonableness was clearly racist—a white woman whose only flaw was that her husband was a black dentist.

By contrast, DeWolfe marked every "colored" (i.e., African American) juror "?" or "n.g." (no good).[78] Often he underlined the word "colored" in their report. Mayme Stewart also received a "?" because she was "reportedly colored." He gave Mrs. Dora Palmer a "?" even though her report says nothing derogatory about her and fails to note her race. However, her husband was a Southern Pacific Railroad chair car porter. DeWolfe figured he must be black, and that meant either she was black or unburdened by racial prejudice. DeWolfe rated anyone who was a member of the National Association for the Advancement of Colored People (NAACP) "n.g." because, according to the FBI, every Bay Area NAACP chapter was a communist front. These reports indicate the FBI surveilled the NAACP relentlessly. DeWolfe marked one potential juror "n.g." just because he had the same name as a person who attended one meeting of the Berkeley NAACP, which the FBI duly recorded "is reported to be dominated by Communist Party members."[79]

DeWolfe eliminated the other racial groups as well. Marie Sanchez received a "?" because she might be "Filipino." Francis Chinn also got a "?" even though her file contained no mention of ethnicity or derogatory information. Marguerite Sooy is marked "OK," but DeWolfe asked himself in the margin "Chinese?"; he apparently decided to make up his mind when he saw her.

As a result of DeWolfe's careful preparation, Iva Toguri was tried before an all-white jury (Figure 15.5)[80] that was selected in a little more than two hours.

Physical Evidence

The case against Tokyo Rose should have been easy to prosecute. Tokyo Rose didn't just aid the enemy, she was the enemy. If Iva Toguri was Tokyo Rose, the U.S. government had only to play recordings of the vicious propaganda in Iva's broadcasts before a jury.

When the FBI launched its investigation of Iva in 1945, the Bureau learned that the Federal Broadcasting Intelligence Service (FBIS) had failed to preserve its wax recordings of *Zero Hour*. However, FBIS turned up a few permanent recordings on acetate records, but these, according to FBIS monitors, showed that, "Her part in these broadcasts consisted only in playing recorded music and making comments. They did not contain statements of a treasonable character."[81] When Iva was freed in 1946, the FBI determined that the recordings no longer possessed probative or evidentiary value and ordered FBIS to destroy them. In February 1947, FBIS complied.[82]

After the 1948 decision to prosecute Iva anyway, the FBI recontacted FBIS in September about recordings. Here the government appeared to get lucky. FBIS had kept 31 16-inch records of Japanese broadcasts as an economy measure because they had a blank, usable side. Unfortunately, reported the FBI agent sent to listen to them, "many do not appear to contain the voice of Iva Toguri."[83] About this same time, FBIS really did destroy 42 recordings of Radio Tokyo because they were not recordings of *Zero Hour* and therefore also "not of evidentiary value." That these records might have shown other women broadcasting propaganda did not interest the DoJ. The December report of this destruction added cryptically, "Others were returned to their recording sources for the same reason."[84]

The Department further learned that in April 1948, FBIS had shipped "23 16-inch aluminum-base acetate records containing the Zero Hour Program" to the National Archives in Washington, D.C. Hoover ordered the Archives to duplicate these and send them to San Francisco.[85] However, these records were problematic as well. None had a complete *Zero Hour* program. Instead the recordings included 48 snippets that ranged from 9 to 19 minutes in length.[86] Of these, only 26 could have contained Iva's voice. The rest were from a Saturday or Sunday when Iva did not broadcast (11), were broadcast at a different time than *Zero Hour* (6), or were broadcast between August 14 and August 16, 1945, after Iva had quit Radio Tokyo (5).[87] Furthermore, the snippets were random; some came early in the program, some in the middle, and others at the end. As a result, many of them did not include Iva's segment of the broadcast.

As to other government recordings, the FBI reported that "extensive inquiry has been made in an effort to locate and obtain recordings of the radio broadcasts in which Tokyo Rose participated. Although a few records of value have been obtained, the vast majority of the records recorded by the FCC [Federal Communications Commission], Army, Navy, et cetera, have been destroyed."[88]

In short, the prosecution entered the trial phase with a paucity of relevant physical evidence. It possessed a few recordings and some scripts. None of these contained the vicious propaganda for which Tokyo Rose was famous. DeWolfe would have to make do.

Notes

1. Masayo Duus states that Jun Toguri even approached famous Hollywood attorney Jerry Geisler. Geisler had defended Errol Flynn against the charge that he had sex with an underage girl, Charlie Chaplin in a paternity suit brought by a young actress, and many other high-profile cases. But even Geisler was afraid to represent a known traitor like Tokyo Rose. See Duus, *Orphan of the Pacific*, 130.

2. Harry M. Kimball admitted in a September 28, 1948, letter to Hoover that DeWolfe ordered the FBI to question Iva when she was taken from the jail. NARA 1, Box 44.

3. Letter, Wayne M. Collins, September 27, 1948, to Attorney General Tom Clark, as well as various Department of Justice (DoJ) officials, FBI officials, U.S. Marshals, and to U.S. Commissioner Francis J. Fox. NARA 1.

4. Summary of the October 14 hearing is in a letter of October 18, 1948, from U.S. Attorney Frank J. Hennessy to Assistant Attorney General Alexander Campbell. NARA 2, Box 2.

5. Iva was first arrested in Tokyo on October 17, 1945 and released on October 25, 1946, or, as she puts it, "one year, one week, and one day." She was rearrested October 26, 1948, and remained in jail through the verdict on September 30, 1949.

6. James R. F. Woods, CID Disposition form, October 8, 1948. The witnesses received $10 per diem. "The FBI has a working agreement with the Whitcomb Hotel for billeting, and rooms with bath are priced at $2.50 per day which leaves $7.50 per day for food and incidentals." Woods added, "On two occasions the writer was lead [sic] to believe that the witnesses are under constant surveillance by agents of the FBI. In addition, it is presumed that the rooms are all wired." Tsuneishi was among those who remained in the United States; he worked at a Japanese hotel. NARA 11, Box 1.

7. Yagi's first name is anglicized Hiram, Hyram, and Hirum in various FBI documents.

8. *San Francisco Examiner*, October 7, 1948.

9. This and previous quote from a letter from DeWolfe to AAG Alexander Campbell, November 12, 1948. NARA 2.

10. Letter, DeWolfe to U.S. Attorney Raymond Whearty, November 17, 1948. NARA 1.

11. Office Memo, SAC San Francisco to Director, December 8, 1948. NARA 1, Box 44.

12. I am indebted for this analysis to Profs. Thomas Morgan and Stephen Saltzburg of George Washington University.

13. Memorandum, from D. M. Ladd to Hoover, December 7, 1948. NARA 1, Box 44.

14. Memo, Campbell to Clark, June 8, 1949. Prosecutors also believed that no white man could be convicted in California on the testimony of two Japanese. Memo, Story to Campbell, May 27, 1949.

15. See Brundidge's "Dear Edgar" letter to Hoover, December 8, 1947, in which he wondered, "What's wrong with the testimony of HTB [himself] and Clark Lee?" NARA 1, Box 41.

16. Memo, Ladd to Director, November 2, 1948. NARA 9, Box 237.

17. Incredible power rested in the hands of J. Edgar Hoover, yet his grasp of English was so infirm that he misspelled the word "sad." Telemeter, SFRAN office to Hoover, June 23, 1949. NARA 1, Box 48.

18. True bill. NARA 11, Box 1.

19. Toguri Notes.

20. *Cramer v. United States*, 325 U.S. 1 (1945), U.S. Supreme Court, decided April 23, 1945. For the full text see http://caselaw.lp.findlaw.com/scripts/getcase.pl?navby=case&court=us&vol=325&invol=1.

21. *New York Times*, April 24, 1945, 19.

22. On December 2, 1942, Cramer was sentenced to 45 years in prison and a $10,000 fine. The prosecutor had asked for the death penalty.

23. *United States v. Robinson*, D.C.S.D.N.Y. 1919, 259, F, 685, 690. The decision was followed in 1943, dismissing another indictment for treason in *United States v. Leiner*, S.D.N.Y. 1943.

24. *Cramer v. United States*, Opinion, Section III, paragraph 12.

25. *Cramer v. United States*, Opinion, Section III, paragraph 13.

26. Cramer did not go free. When the government re-indicted him for less innocuous overt acts, he accepted a plea bargain, pled guilty to two counts of treason, and was sentenced to six years in prison.

27. Cases against Robert H. Best and Douglas Chandler mentioned previously in chapter 14. Quoted phrase from the *New York Times*, January 19, 1947, E10.

28. Statement is drawn from the minority opinion. It is implied by the majority, but I do not find it explicitly stated. See Dissent, Section III, paragraph 2.

29. *Cramer v. United States*, Opinion, Section V, paragraph 2.

30. *Motion to Dismiss*, NARA 2, Box 2.

31. The *San Francisco Chronicle* reported witnesses got $10 a day, and then in the next paragraph stated they got $9 a day for subsistence and $3 a day as witnesses. *Chronicle*, July 2, 1949, 2. In her 1987 interview, Iva opined that the witnesses may have been paid much more. She claimed Oki had become a millionaire and said, "Who knows what kind of a deal they made with this government?" I found no evidence of under-the-table payments, but who knows?

32. Collins complained about Tillman's actions in his letter to Lyndon Baines Johnson, November 4, 1968, asking for a pardon of his client. LBJ did not respond.

33. Transcript of an August 10, 1979, tape-recorded interview by Iva of J. R. Hughes, in Carmel, California.

34. Letter, Story to DeWolfe, April 19, 1949, page 1. NARA 2, Box 4.

35. "External telephone calls will be monitored and recorded at the point where the call enters or leaves Japan to achieve approximately 25 percent coverage of the total number of such calls on a spot check basis." CCD Policy Regulation No. 10-300, Section VI, paragraph 5, 44. AHEC, Willoughby Papers, Box 9.

36. General Records of General Headquarters Supreme Commander for the Allied Powers, 1945–52, Civil Intelligence Section, Civil Censorship Detachment, Records Section, Press, Publications and Broadcast Division, Central File, 1945-49; Record Group 331, Entry 1803, Box 8578, Folder 25.

37. Christgau, "Wayne Collins versus the World," 13, 16.

38. This clearly undermines my assertion that Myrtle Lipton's scripts could not have been destroyed without leaving traces in the record.

39. Order denying seven motions and granting motion to take depositions overseas, March 15, 1949, NARA 2. Also, defense motions, Court's denials at NARA 4, Box 263.

40. Memorandum, Hoover to SAC San Francisco, April 18, 1949. NARA 3, Box 4.

41. Memorandum, Campbell to Hoover, April 7, 1949. NARA 1, Box 45.

42. FBI Radiogram, Honolulu to San Francisco, June 28, 1949. NARA 2.

43. Memorandum, J. Eldon Dunn to SAC, San Francisco, June 30, 1949. NARA 2.

44. Teletype, September 29, 1948. NARA 1, Box 44.

45. Teletype, October 1, 1948. NARA 1, Box 44.

46. References for Reyes' statements along with detailed analysis of same in chapter 17.

47. Report of HQ CIC Metropolitan Unit 80, January 10, 1946. NARA 1, Box 40.

48. Kenkichi Oki, Affidavit, Tokyo, February 19, 1948. NARA 1.

49. Howe (*Hunt*, 224) puts the exact date at September 24, 1948. A report was written on October 5, 1948, which strung together a series of interview summaries. The report states that Tsuneishi's interview was conducted on September 24 at the San Francisco office. The report then follows without a break to Mitsushio's. From this Howe reasons they were conducted the same day. This may be correct, but it seems to me any day up through October 4 is possible. For the original, see FBI Report, J. Eldon Dunn, "date when made" October 5, 1948, "period for which made" September 23–October 5, 1948. NARA 2, Box 8.

50. Howe, *The Hunt for "Tokyo Rose,"* 226–31. He reproduces the complete transcripts, which include quoted excerpts, in Appendix 1, 335–41. This is first-rate analysis.

51. Here, in contrast to note 49, I am the one making the assumptions. I assume that the DoJ/FBI had already settled on the scheme to make Mitsushio and Oki the two witnesses for every OA, and that the report reflected their future testimony more than actual interview statements. FBI Report, J. Eldon Dunn, October 5, 1948. NARA 2, Box 8.

52. Edited for length. For the exact language of Mitsushio's and Oki's statements, October 4 and 5, 1948, see NARA 2, Box 8.

53. Figure 15.1, NARA 1, Box 3. Figure 15.2, *San Francisco Chronicle,* July 7, 1949, 6.

54. No first name for this child of G. M. Emory [spelled "Emoryr " in the record] and Josephine DeWolfe is recorded but the closest brother, C.D., was three years older, born in 1899. "Washington Births, 1891–1907," Washington State Archives, Olympia, Washington.

55. Godfred Meade Emory told census takers in 1900 he was born in February 1869; he fathered a child in 1906, but was deceased by the 1910 U.S. Census.

56. Josephine was born in January 1873. Her father, Frederick, was born about 1836 in Tennessee. Date of death for both unknown. The 1880 U.S. Census shows him as mayor of Charlotte. One Seattle City Directory (1888–1890) indicates he worked with King County Bank and another, with C. F. Whittlesey & Co. By 1910, according to the U.S. Census, he "had his own income."

57. The 1910 Census shows Josephine DeWolfe Emory, 35, as head of household; Frederick S. DeWolfe, 74, father; and six Emory (misspelled Emery) children, Frederick DeWolfe, 12; Campbell Dallis, 10; Clara, 9; Thomas, 7; Nancy, 6; Laura, 4 with servants Berry McKenzie, 30 and Mary Moen, 22.

58. Letter of C. D. Emory, March 3, 1949, stating that Tom DeWolfe is his full brother and why his brother changed his name. NARA 2, Box 4. The reason the name change was necessary was that Frederick and his wife Laura had three daughters, Louise, Nannie, and Josephine, Tom's mother. Throughout the Trial Transcript, his name is incorrectly spelled "de Wolf."

59. Information provided by Kerry E. Graves, Assistant Director of Alumni Relations, UVA Law School Foundation.

60. The only extant record of this individual, the 1930 Census, spells the name "Fredrick." Given that his grandfather and his older brother both spelled their names "Frederick," I assume this was an error.

61. *San Francisco Chronicle,* July 7, 1949, 1.

62. Trial Transcript, vol. I, 3, 11. He also refers to Judge Roche by name on 14, and talks about the important decisions of "the Court" throughout. His opening statement runs from 3 to 32.

63. Trial Transcript, vol. I, 35.

64. Beebe is her maiden name. Iva knew her as Katherine Pinkham, and many sources refer to her as Katherine Harris. To avoid confusion with the Katherine Harris who as Secretary of State of Florida played

such a prominent role in the 2000 election, I have used "Katherine Beebe" throughout.

65. Interview with Katherine Beebe, January 3, 1991, 85.

66. John Tillman, born about 1863, emigrated from Sweden in 1905. His wife Marie, born in Sweden about 1873, emigrated in 1903. The children, Axel, Frederick, Flora, and Dorothy, were born in Montana but grew up in Idaho Falls, Idaho, where Frederick worked as a county sheriff. Information from 1920 and 1930 U.S. Census. Russell Warren Howe described him as "Montana Irish but boastful of having forced the brogue from his speech (*Hunt*, 4)." In any case, Howe interviewed him in Fresno, California, about 1988 and found him unrepentant. Frederick Tillman died June 19, 1995, in Washington, Oregon, at age 87.

67. *San Francisco Chronicle*, July 7, 1949, 1.

68. I'll let readers draw their own inferences. Iva said in our 1987 interview, "If he didn't like a group of people, he was very expressive." I asked her if she meant Tamba was strongly in favor of Japanese but prejudiced against others. "Yes, but I don't want to discuss it." Did she think such an attitude was unusual? "You mean, fight for the rights on one minority, fight for the rights of all? I don't know." I suggested a more typical example of racism would be KKK members who hate everyone who's not white. She replied, "Maybe I didn't want to think about it."

69. Figure 15.3, Bancroft Library Pictorial Collection, University of California, 1959.010, NEG, Part 2, Box 105, 77939.16: 4.

70. *Abo v. Clark*, 77 F. Supp. at 808 and 809.

71. Figure 15.4, Bancroft Library Pictorial Collection, University of California, 1959.010, NEG, Part 3, Box 52, 07-07-54.4: 6.

72. Roche was born July 21, 1878. He died July 1, 1964, in San Francisco. Information from 1910–1930 U.S. Census, 1917 Draft Registration, and California Death Index.

73. Interview with Katherine Beebe, January 3, 1991. I have conflated two sets of similar remarks from pages 86 and 144.

74. List of reports accompanied T. Vincent Quinn to Hoover Memo, July 12, 1948. NARA 1, Box 43.

75. On May 18, 1949, Harry M. Kimball, SAC, sent to Hoover "a blueprint of the courtroom of Michael J. Roche" who then forwarded it to Alexander Campbell on June 3, 1949. I like to believe this was not pure zaniness, but had to do with setting up audio equipment so that the jurors could listen to recordings. NARA 1, Box 48.

76. Quotations from the *San Francisco Chronicle*, July 6, 1949, 1 and 16.

77. FBI Report, May 13, 1949. The Master Trial Jury List was for the March (1949) term, but a new Jury Panel List was not drawn for use until

July 12; the trial began July 7. Various copies of this 10-page summary are in the Archives, but the one with DeWolfe's handwritten comments in the margin may be found in NARA 2, Box 4. The quotations that follow are from this document.

78. There is one exception: Isabelle Farnell. DeWolfe marked her "GOOD" even though her report indicated she was "colored." Given the uniformity of the other markings, I assume DeWolfe simply failed to notice her race.

79. As noted, in this report the FBI cites every NAACP chapter as a communist front. FBI Report, May 13, 1949. NARA 2, Box 4.

80. Figure 15.5, *San Francisco Chronicle*, July 6, 1949 and February 16, 1976. Jurors (left to right, back row): Aileen Catherine McNamara (alternate); Matthew J. Yerbic (a veteran of the South Pacific where GIs heard Tokyo and Manila broadcasts most clearly), Fannie Ibbotson, Adele T. Grassens, Edith Marie Scholbohm, Flora E. Covell, Robin E. Stevenson. Jurors (left to right, front row): Iva Barbara Long (alternate), Lucille Veronica Irvine, Robert Oakes, Earl M. Duckett, John Mann (an accountant; jury foreman), Robert Lee Stout, Babette F. Worts.

81. Letter, FBIS to Hoover, December 11, 1947. NARA 1, Box 41.

82. "They were destroyed in accordance with the Bureau [sic] dated February 4, 1947." Letter, FBIS to Hoover, December 11, 1947. NARA 1, Box 41.

83. Letter, R. B. Hood to Hoover, September 21, 1948. NARA 1, Box 44.

84. Letter to Hoover, December 11, 1947. NARA 1, Box 41.

85. For the FBIS list of the recordings as well as the order, see Office Memo, Guy Hottel to Hoover, September 23, 1948. NARA 1, Box 44.

86. The FBIS list can be confusing. "Time" of the snippets of the *Zero Hour* are between 0500 and 0600 hours. Thus, snippet #1 runs from "0515–0530," i.e., from 5:15 to 5:30 AM. Here's the confusion: Due to time zone differences, if it is 5:00 AM on Monday in Portland (Pacific Standard Time), it is 10:00 PM Monday in Tokyo. However, *Zero Hour* broadcast between 6:00 and 7:00 PM Tokyo time. How was it possible for FBIS in Portland to record the *Zero Hour* at 5:00 AM? The answer can be found elsewhere in written transcripts of these recordings. FBIS notations are Eastern War Time, which is 4 hours earlier than Greenwich Mean Time. Hence, 5:00 AM U.S. EWT = 4:00 AM U.S. Eastern Standard Time = 1:00 AM U.S. Pacific Standard Time = 6:00 PM Tokyo time. NARA 4, Box 268.

87. Assuming Iva left August 13, 1945. See chapter 11, note 22.

88. Office Memorandum, March 8, 1948. NARA 1, Box 42. Russell Warren Howe claims that FBIS "had recorded all the 'Zero Hour' broadcasts" and that as of June 1949, "the FBIS had a full collection of all 'Zero Hour' broadcasts." He states that the defense did not know that FBIS had such

a collection and remarks, "In retrospect, it seems regrettable that Collins did not have the clairvoyance to subpoena the head of the FBIS and ask if there were any recordings [other than those introduced into evidence at the trial] of 'Zero Hour.'"

I don't know the basis of Howe's assertion, because his book contains no reference notes. Various memos/reports, several of which (January 9, 1946; February 4, 1947; December 11, 1947; March 8, 1948) I cited, indicate the government destroyed its recordings with maddening regularity. See Howe, *The Hunt for "Tokyo Rose,"* 111, 254, 274–75.

16

The Prosecution

The United States v. Tokyo Rose

To understand the trial, readers must try to place themselves in the position of the jurors. That is, readers must now forget everything they've just read. The jurors knew absolutely nothing about Iva Toguri, her youth in America, her experiences in Imperial Japan—nothing. But they entered the jury box well informed about Tokyo Rose. Tokyo Rose was famous. She broadcast propaganda for the Japanese during the war. Jurors, who were not sequestered, knew that the United States government was prosecuting Tokyo Rose for treason because that's how the newspapers headlined it. The *San Francisco Chronicle* contained its daily coverage in a box titled "Tokyo Rose on Trial." As a result, the central question in jurors' minds was not the usual, Is this defendant guilty?, but instead, Is this woman Tokyo Rose?

The trial began July 6, 1949. Prosecutor Tom DeWolfe's "Opening Statement on Behalf of the Government" was masterful. He welcomed the jurors by introducing everyone individually, including the defendant and her defense team. Introducing himself, he admitted he had come from Washington, D.C., to try the case, but immediately added, "I am a Pacific northwesterner, and not an easterner."[1] He portrayed himself as one of their own. He explained everyone's role in the trial. He could not have been more generous toward the defendant, informing the jury that the indictment was "a mere paper charge" and that "the defendant is always clothed with the presumption of innocence, as is Mrs. D'Aquino in this case. That presumption of innocence follows her throughout the trial proceedings."[2] He graciously said he would not trouble the jurors by reading the "lengthy and verbose" indictment, although in reality it was paltry and terse.[3] After passing quickly over the actual charges of the indictment, he promised, "the proof will show that she told the troops that their sweethearts at home in the United States were unfaithful to them, that they lacked fidelity, that their wives and sweethearts were running around with 4-F's and with shipyard workers, all of whom had plenty of money in their pockets to show the wives of the soldiers a good time, and she told the boys over the air to lay down their arms, stop fighting, that the Japanese would never give up. . . ."[4] He never mentioned Tokyo Rose by name in the entire statement, but, as everyone knew, such statements came from Tokyo Rose. He was both humble and outraged as he said, "She would pick out in her broadcasts a spot familiar in the United States, to the citizenry of California. I don't know Los Angeles as well as I know San Francisco, but I have heard a little bit about it, been there a few times. She would say, 'Now how would you like to be tonight back in Los Angeles at the Cocoanut Grove dancing with your best girl?' I don't know where it is, I suppose the Ambassador Hotel, I don't know—it is a place some of you have heard about."[5] (Great guess! The Cocoanut Grove really was located at the Ambassador Hotel.) He informed the jurors he would prove Iva had not wanted to leave Japan when the war started. He disclosed her reason for marrying. Japan had lost the war by April 1945, and she needed the cover. He explained ahead of time why the government would produce so few recordings of her broadcasts. The Japanese had destroyed them all. They also destroyed her scripts, except for "a relatively few innocuous and innocent ones which she kept out for her own purposes and later showed to American conquering troops."[6]

The defense reserved its opening statement for later in the trial. This is standard practice, but in hindsight it was possibly a mistake. Jurors entered the trial with preconceived notions about Tokyo Rose and hence the defendant. As it was, DeWolfe's assertions went unchallenged.

~

Iva's father worried about the trial, but "he tried to be as cheerful as possible when he talked to me about it." If people on the outside were speaking ill of her, he never disclosed it. Iva says she herself was "concerned, but I wasn't so worried I couldn't sleep."

Each morning and evening, before and after Iva's time in court, the marshals would give her gifts of candy and flowers sent by well-wishers. "I didn't get the impression the public was on my side, but there was not 100 percent hatred." Her father wouldn't let her eat the candy, fearing it had been poisoned. Iva never cared for dessert or chocolates, so it was no loss. "I do remember an exceptionally beautiful box of chocolates from Ghirardelli's [San Francisco's famous chocolate maker]. My father told me not to touch it, but June's husband's brother happened to be there, on leave from Fort Ord. He nibbled at the corners and middles of the chocolates to check for poison and wound up eating the whole thing."

~

DeWolfe realized that the legend of Tokyo Rose was his trump card, and he played it immediately. He called as his first witness J. Richard Eisenhart, the guard at Sugamo Prison who had gotten Iva's autograph. Eisenhart presented the jury with visible proof that Iva Toguri had admitted in writing that she was in fact Tokyo Rose. It could be argued that Eisenhart won the trial for the prosecution, because DeWolfe devoted his remaining witnesses to confirming this first impression in the jury's minds. By the time the defense opened weeks later, the burden of proof had shifted from the government to the defendant.

After being released from the armed services after the war, Dick Eisenhart worked for Eastman Kodak briefly before starting a 34-year career with Gannett News Service and the Rochester, New York *Democrat and Chronicle*. He wrote in 2006, "When I went to trial, I thought she was guilty of treason and I have the same opinion today." Eisenhart was one of the hundreds of GIs who responded to the FBI's nationwide call in 1947 for witnesses. "I had heard Tokyo Rose broadcasts while in the Pacific, in the Philippines on Luzon. I contacted authorities and said I had a written self-admission by Iva Toguri that she was 'Tokyo Rose' and I thereby might help establish those who were innocent." After Japan's surrender, Eisenhart, part of the Occupation forces, wound up a corporal of the guards at Sugamo Prison. There he met Iva. "I thought of her as very quiet and unassuming. I remember the day Rose was brought in. She was wearing a jacket, skirt, saddle shoes, looking as a typical American with Japanese features. I asked for an autograph, she consented with no question nor problem, and I thanked her for it and that was it."[7]

On the stand, Eishenhart testified to his request, and the prosecution offered into evidence his souvenir yen note, which he still has today (Figure 16.1).[8]

Figure 16.1.
Courtesy of J. Richard Eisenhart.

When DeWolfe turned over Eisenhart to Wayne Collins for cross-examination, Collins faced an important decision. He could be friendly with the young corporal, perhaps asking him with a smile if GIs wanted Iva's autograph because they were fans of traitors. Collins could bring out Iva's popularity with servicemen, and the fact that she signed willingly meant she lacked a guilty conscience and was blissfully unaware of the treason of Tokyo Rose. Or, he could take the opposite approach and attack Eisenhart. Collins chose the latter. He blistered Eisenhart with questions designed to prove Iva signed out of fear. Weren't the guards at the prison armed? No, only the ones at the gates. He had a billy club, right? No. Did he tell her she had a right to refuse? Didn't she refuse at first and then he demanded she sign? Didn't the guards molest her by turning on and off the lights constantly? No to all.[9]

On and on the interrogation went. DeWolfe had asked Eisenhart just a few questions; they take up four pages of trial transcript, lengthened by Collins' objections. Collins' questions take up twenty pages. The effect on the jury cannot have been positive. Collins not only portrayed the Army as a bunch of ruffians, but his line of questioning conceded DeWolfe's implicit, if unstated, point: in signing the note, Iva had admitted something terribly damning and the defense was in a frenzy to controvert it.

Iva wore the same dress every single day of the trial, a gray plaid suit. June had sent it to her in Japan after the war so that she would have something new to wear when she got off the boat in the States. I asked Iva if this was an intentional ploy. "Neither my family nor the attorneys ever discussed how to dress or how I should look. No one ever talked about my not looking like Tokyo Rose." So why did she wear the same outfit every day? "Why bother to change? You'd have to take all that stuff into jail. You don't need a wardrobe. I never thought about this, and I never wondered what the jury thought. I had it cleaned every Friday. I didn't think I was attractive." She admitted that someone offered to buy her some clothes but that Wayne Collins refused to allow it, which may mean it was intentional on his part. If so, it worked. After the trial, one female juror "confided to a reporter that the women jurors felt 'awfully worried because that little girl didn't seem to have any other dress. We wanted to get something for her. I'd have been glad to do it myself but I suppose the prosecutors wouldn't have liked it.'"[10]

DeWolfe next sought to introduce as evidence several unremarkable documents. Wayne Collins fought him tooth and nail. When DeWolfe submitted Iva's birth certificate, Collins objected that it was a certified copy and not an authenticated copy. The wrangling continued until finally the judge overruled Collins' objections. DeWolfe sought to introduce Iva's application for a passport. He had a copy of the original certified by the State Department. Collins objected that "it is not the original document. I make the further objection it is incompetent, irrelevant and immaterial, it is not the best evidence."[11] DeWolfe read aloud the rule allowing a copy to be used to introduce such public records with proper authentication; the rule's purpose was to avoid shipping originals to individual courts and thereby to protect the record. Undaunted, Collins asserted there was no good reason not to produce the original. The judge allowed the copy. DeWolfe then asked that the last page, the State Department authentication, be removed, given that he was not offering it into evidence because Iva had not signed it. Collins objected that the record would now be incomplete. The judge allowed the last page to go out. Collins then objected that the judge had just admitted a document not authenticated by the State Department. So the judge admitted the entire document. When Collins further objected the last page was somehow incomplete, the judge cut him off. During the course of the trial, the prosecution introduced 75 exhibits. Collins fought every single one, often with multiple objections.

The legal issues here are not of interest. What matters is the effect on the judge and jury. Documents such as Iva's birth certificate, voter registration, and application for a passport could not possibly have harmed her defense. In fact, the passport application, made in Japan, manifested her desire to return to the United States. Her birth certificate and voter registration were obviously not "irrelevant and immaterial" to a treason prosecution. They proved her American citizenship; no court would have ruled them inadmissible. But suppose that Judge Roche had upheld Collins' objections and required the Government to produce the originals? DeWolfe could have done so, and they would have come in. Collins' combativeness served no purpose except to antagonize the judge and habituate his pronouncement, "The objection will be overruled." This is easily the most common sentence in the trial transcript; it appears hundreds of times. Collins' heedless attacks also gave the jury the impression that he was losing every confrontation with the prosecution and that his client must have much to hide. Wayne Collins was a moral hero for accepting Iva's case despite widespread public hatred for Tokyo Rose, but good generals choose their battles. To fight for every square inch of the battlefield means one is certain to lose the war.

On the other hand, Collins was terrific when he dealt with dissemblers and liars. His Doberman attack-dog tactics incensed everyone when he utilized them against ordinary folk, but they worked superbly to trip up the prosecution's carefully prepared witnesses. Dissembler #1 was Yukio Ikeda. A personnel manager at Radio Tokyo, Ikeda introduced his typed record of Iva's attendance and work hours; that is, her personnel record. Collins' opening salvo suggested the document had to be a forgery. "Isn't it a fact that employees of Radio Tokyo had a time card and punched a time clock?" Ikeda answered lamely that there had been a time clock but it was broken now. Wasn't it true that he had never seen Iva Toguri before that day in court? He might have seen her. Collins asked him again. This time he admitted he had never seen her previously. Weren't all of Radio Tokyo's records burned? Ikeda replied obliquely that he wasn't sure who burned them. Collins kept on, question after question, about the record burning. Ikeda, who had smiled broadly when he took the stand, never expected this. He wore down. Collins grilled him on a meeting of the Japanese Relief Society he had attended in October 1948. "Isn't it a fact that you stated to that meeting that all the records and documents at Radio Tokyo had been burned?" Reminded of the many witnesses to his statement, Ikeda fudged. "I don't remember," he said. Collins' persistence might seem yet another instance of overkill. Iva's employment at Radio Tokyo was never in dispute. But through his cross-examination, he placed in the jurors' minds the possibility that the United States government, which they trusted implicitly, might be fabricating evidence and offering untrustworthy witnesses.[12]

Next up was Major Shigetsugu Tsuneishi (Figure 16.2), the Army officer in charge of propaganda at Radio Tokyo and the POWs at Bunka Camp.[13] Tsuneishi's testimony was grueling because every question had to be

Figure 16.2. Shigetsugu Tsuneishi.
Courtesy of Library of Congress.

translated into Japanese, answered in Japanese, and then the answer translated to English. This doubled the length of his testimony.

On direct examination, Tsuneishi painted a portrait of Imperial Japan as a kingdom of sweet reason. He had requested, not ordered, Cousens, Ince, and Reyes to broadcast for the Japanese after explaining his propaganda purposes. The three POWs, in his telling, calmly considered his judicious proposal and decided of their own free will to sell out their countries. He never threatened them. The *Zero Hour*, he informed the court, was pure propaganda intended to weaken the desire of Americans to fight. He personally advised the defendant of that fact, and she too chose to broadcast of her own free will.

Tsuneishi's direct testimony was relatively brief, taking less than a day. Then for four long days, Collins lambasted him. He demanded to know the circumstances under which the three POWs had been brought to Tokyo, the threats made against them, their housing, their guards. DeWolfe objected that all this had happened prior to their meeting the defendant and had nothing to do with the case against her, but Judge Roche overruled him and allowed Tsuneishi to answer. The claim of no coercion began to crumble. Collins further attacked his assertion that *Zero Hour* was propaganda. Although at first Tsuneishi denied *Zero Hour* carried POW messages, he eventually admitted that it did, although he justified these as "one type of bait."[14] He changed from his initial "pure propaganda" statement to acknowledging that, by the time Iva appeared on the program, "the American troops were on the winning side; therefore such propaganda broadcasts from the losing side were naturally rather ineffectual,"[15] which eventually changed to his final position that "from my point of view it was satisfactory if we could produce any broadcasts that were then appealing to the GIs. I figured we would wait until the Japanese troops put up severe resistance. Until that time, it could be just a general appeal to the troops. It was unfortunate, but the opportunity did not present itself for me to present the true propaganda broadcasts that I wished to."[16] In sum, Tsuneishi moved from pure propaganda to ineffectual propaganda to no propaganda.

He continued to deny threatening the POWs. His memory of meeting Cousens, slamming his sword on the table, and shouting orders at him, remained sketchy. Collins kept after Tsuneishi. De-

Wolfe objected anew, that whatever caused Cousens to broadcast had nothing to do with Iva, and this time the judge sustained the objection. Collins kept asking him anyway. DeWolfe objected; the objection was sustained. Collins kept on asking until finally he wore out the judge. "I will allow the question in the hope that we can get through this witness. He may answer."[17] Eventually Tsuneishi began to crack. "They were not ordered, but in reply to my asking them to do so, they acted according to the circumstances."[18] Collins swung off to other topics, but then he'd return to the issue of duress. Hours later, Tsuneishi finally admitted he had told an associate at Radio Tokyo just three months before the trial that he had in fact ordered Cousens to broadcast.

Collins did more than expose Tsuneishi as a liar. He forced him to admit, name by name, the many other female broadcasters for Radio Tokyo. As the *Chronicle* summarized it, "Tokyo Roses bloomed all over Federal Court yesterday. It was a great day for the defense."[19] Tsuneishi also admitted the nine other transmitter sites. In addition, he confessed he had never spoken to Iva personally at any time about the purpose of *Zero Hour*. Collins pressured him on the duress issue until he acknowledged that any personnel at Radio Tokyo who refused to do his or her job as ordered would be subject to conscription by the Army. He even admitted he threatened through subordinates to draft Iva herself if she refused to broadcast, which meant she would work in a munitions factory or other military endeavor.[20] Tsuneishi denied up until the end that any prisoners were beaten or threatened with death, although every POW knew better.[21]

~

A poll in 1942, less than a year after the "sneak attack" on Pearl Harbor, showed that Americans most commonly described Japanese as treacherous (73 percent) and sly (63 percent).[22] Such attitudes likely still infected the jurors in 1949 and caused them to view Japanese witnesses, such as Tsuneishi, as deceitful and unreliable. Clark Lee, who followed Tsuneishi on the stand, had no such credibility problem.[23] The *San Francisco Chronicle* reported that Lee "was favored by sympathetic jury smiles."[24] Tall, handsome, employed in the glamorous career of war correspondent, Lee epitomized the American ideal of a "man's man."[25] Adding to his credibility, Lee's testimony often helped Iva. He testified that she told him of police pressure to renounce her citizenship and of her refusal to renounce. He said she had told him that to disobey orders at Radio Tokyo would have been suicide. These remarks made him come across as fair and unbiased. For these reasons, Lee's testimony against Iva harmed her immeasurably and probably did more to convict her than did the later testimony of Mitsushio and Oki, the two Japanese American witnesses to her supposed "overt acts."

As noted in chapter 12, Lee swore on the stand that when he reached Tokyo, Iva approached him claiming to be Tokyo Rose, not the other way around. He denied that she had asserted that she tried to defeat the propaganda purposes of *Zero Hour*; she only told him the program was more fun than propaganda. But far and away his most damaging testimony concerned the "loss of ships" remark alluded to in Overt Act (OA) 6. Lee swore that, in the fall of 1944, at the order of a Japanese Army major, Iva Toguri broadcast the message, "Orphans of the Pacific, you really are orphans now. How are you going to get home now that all of your ships are sunk?"[26]

Lee told Collins under cross-examination that he was confident she did confess to making the "loss of ships" comment because he had recently reviewed his notes from their interview. To assess his testimony, we must compare the various versions of this interview, also mentioned in chapter 12. We begin with the relevant section of his original interview notes, reproduced here verbatim:

> off formosa claimed sunk American fleet. they sent major from GHQ who wanted to play up great victory wiping out u.s. fleet. i get inside news. and we add up ships claimed sunk and they wouldn't add. would be suicide say truth. after this time, last year we just mouth piece of ghq. they'd bluntly suggest "you fellows all without ships. what are you going to [do] about getting home." "Orphans of the Pacific. You really are orphans now."
> about every day for past half year major come, english speaking, and tell me how to slant that day's script. when Okinawa battle, japanese took back one little place, they played it up big.[27]

Nothing in these notes proves Iva actually broadcast either the "loss of ships" message or the "you really are orphans now" taunt. The notes simply state the taunt was "bluntly suggested." By whom is unclear. (This issue will be addressed in the next chapter.)

The next version is the narrative Lee wrote some months later based on these notes and his memories of the conversation:

> The Government claimed in October, 1944, to have sunk the American fleet off Formosa. They sent a Major from GHQ who directed me to play up the great victory which wiped out the United States fleet, but I was getting inside news. We would add up the number of American ships claimed sunk and they just didn't add, but of course it would have been suicide to tell the truth. After this, at the time of the Formosa battle, we were just a mouthpiece of GHQ. For example, they directed me to say, "You fellows are all without ships. What are you going to do about getting home now?" Then I said, "Orphans of the Pacific. You really are orphans now." About every day for the past half year the Major who spoke American came to see me and told me how to slant that day's script.[28]

We can be certain that the legend of Tokyo Rose had begun to influence Lee when he created the final sentence above. Iva would never have committed such a syntax error. She knew Americans spoke English, and Lee's raw notes indicate that is what she originally said. Speaking "American" could only be a Pidgin English mistake of Tokyo Rose.[29] In this version, the Major directs Iva to broadcast the message about sunken ships and she herself comes up with the taunt "You really are orphans now." Now the final iteration, the trial testimony:

> *DeWolfe*: Do you remember any statement made by her as to the Battle of Formosa?
> *Lee*: Yes, sir.
> *DeWolfe*: Tell the Court and jury.
> *Lee*: She said that in the fall of '44, at the time that Japan claimed they had sunk a number of American ships off Formosa, a major came to her from Imperial Headquarters and bluntly suggested that she broadcast as follows: "Orphans of the Pacific, you really are orphans now. How are you going to get home now that all of your ships are sunk?"
> *DeWolfe*: Did she say whether or not she broadcast that?
> *Lee*: She said she broadcast that.[30]

Iva's alleged broadcast is now polished. The address to the GIs as orphans begins the statement; no longer is it an afterthought. She affirms positively that she did broadcast what the major bluntly suggested to her, an admission that is not part of his original notes. Lee's testimony mutates Iva's nickname for her listeners, "my favorite orphans," which she intended affectionately, into a conscious epithet of contempt.

Wayne Collins hoped to use the opportunity of Clark Lee's testifying to bring before the jury the perfidy of Harry Brundidge and the perjury of Hiram Yagi. But DeWolfe vociferously objected to each and every such foray, and the judge sustained him. Tempers flared.

> *Collins*: Now, Mr. Lee, isn't it a fact that Harry Brundidge had gone to Japan in 1948 and, while in Japan, advised Yagi to come before the Grand Jury and testify falsely in this case?
> *DeWolfe*: Object to that as assuming something not in evidence, totally improper. I ask that the jury be instructed to disregard it.
> *Collins*: We will demonstrate it to be a fact.
> *DeWolfe*: You will not. You know you won't. You are talking through your hat, and you have been for a long time.[31]

DeWolfe knew full well that Collins could demonstrate it to be a fact and would, were the Court to allow it. The Court did not. DeWolfe, needless to say, was the one talking through his hat. That Collins should appear, as the *Chronicle* charged, to be perpetually indignant is not difficult to understand. He had much to be indignant about.

∿

Kenkichi Oki and George Mitsushio (Figure 16.3),[32] Radio Tokyo's managers of *Zero Hour*, were the government's two witnesses to Iva's overt acts of treason. Although the *San Francisco Examiner* described them as "the most important prosecution witnesses to date,"[33] this was true only in a formal sense. Oki and Mitsushio gave the jury an excuse to convict. They did little to convince the jurors that they ought to convict.

However, if the jury decided that Iva was guilty, Oki and Mitsushio could serve as the two witnesses required by the Constitution and thus prevent a higher court from overturning her conviction.

Figure 16.3. George Mitsushio.
Courtesy of *San Francisco Chronicle.*

Both men were Nisei. Under the subtitle "GREAT IRONY" in bold capital letters, the *Examiner* pointed out that because they willingly deserted their American birthright, they "escaped the traitor's stigma." In contrast, Iva "did not renounce her American citizenship. If she had, she would not be on trial for treason."[34] Under cross-examination, Wayne Collins brought out that neither man renounced in a legally sufficient way, which meant the government could have charged them with treason had it been so disposed. Not much more was made of this fact at the time:

Collins: Mr. Mitsushio, did you come here voluntarily to testify in this action?
Mitsushio: No.
Collins: Were you promised immunity by anyone for coming here to testify?
Mitsushio: I do not recall.[35]

One would think he would remember such a promise, one way or the other.

Oki and Mitsushio trudged through the OAs, dutifully answering DeWolfe's questions concerning the details of each. Neither was especially credible. Oki testified first and hewed to the party line a little too closely. With respect to Iva's typing scripts, he swore that he and Mitsushio watched her do it, usually standing over her shoulder as she typed. With respect to broadcasts, he swore he and Mitsushio actually stood beside her in the studio, watching and listening as she spoke into a microphone. He even claimed no other woman ever broadcast on *Zero Hour* except Iva. Under cross-examination, he admitted he had heard that others had broadcast, but he claimed he'd never actually seen them do it. Collins undermined his highly specific memories of watching Iva type and broadcast by asking him a series of questions about other events on the same day: what he wore, what Iva wore, what he had for breakfast, for lunch, other news dispatches received that day, other news scripts prepared. Oki remembered nothing.

> *Collins*: So you really don't recall anything that you did at Radio Tokyo that day except that you read the release [about the loss of ships] concerning the battle of Leyte Gulf, is that correct?
> *Oki*: That is correct.[36]

Mitsushio was even more inept. On direct, Mitsushio clearly recalled receiving news that Americans on an island were without water. He watched Iva broadcast, "Cold water sure tastes good" as a taunt to the thirsty Americans.

> *DeWolfe*: Were you in the same studio when this broadcast was made?
> *Mitsushio*: Yes, I was in the same studio.
> *DeWolfe*: How far away from this defendant?
> *Mitsushio*: About five feet away.[37]

Mitsushio then made the dubious claim that Iva had broadcast the same taunt to this small island on two other occasions.

On cross examination, he altered his testimony:

> *Collins*: Did you see her reading [the cold water statement] from script?
> *Mitsushio*: I don't remember seeing her reading that.
> *Collins*: Were you in the broadcasting room at the time with the defendant?
> *Mitsushio*: I am not sure.
> *Collins*: You testified on direct examination that you were present at that time and that you heard that. Now, you state you are not sure that you were even in that room.
> *Mitsushio*: I heard it through the monitor.
> *Collins*: You heard her on the monitor in another office outside of the studio?
> *Mitsushio*: Yes.
> *Collins*: You were not in the room, were you, Mr. Mitsushio?
> *Mitsushio*: I don't think I was.
> *Collins*: And you heard a voice, a female voice over the monitor making a statement.

Mitsushio: Yes.
Collins: You don't know actually who was in the broadcasting room, if anyone?
Mitsushio: I did know.
Collins: You couldn't see them?
Mitsushio: I couldn't see them, but I did know who was there.
Collins: You know who was supposed to be there.
Mitsushio: Yes.
Collins: But you don't actually know who was there.
Mitsushio: No.[38]

DeWolfe must have doubted these witnesses could keep their stories straight, which is why he built redundancy into their testimony. The next day, on redirect, Mitsushio allowed as how he now remembered that he had listened on the monitor on two occasions but on the third he was actually present in the studio.[39] This sudden burst of clarity, given the testimony above, is compelling evidence that DeWolfe had grabbed his squirrelly witness the previous night and reminded him what escaping the traitor's stigma required.

Mitsushio's testimony also suffered from a lack of verbal adroitness. He kept repeating the same phrases over and over. To take one example among many, Mitsushio testified to the purposes of *Zero Hour* as follows:

> with the purpose of inducing a feeling of homesickness, nostalgia, war-weariness, discontent, and thereby lowering the morale of the American fighting forces . . . (p. 905)
>
> Which was designed to bring about nostalgia, homesickness, war-weariness, to the American fighting forces . . . (p. 909)
>
> For the purpose of bringing about homesickness, nostalgia, war-weariness, and otherwise demoralize the fighting efforts of the American forces . . . (p. 913)
>
> With the objective of bringing about a feeling of nostalgia, homesickness, war-weariness, and otherwise lowering the morale, lowering the fighting morale of these American soldiers . . . (p. 929)

As she listened to these and other witnesses against her, Iva had the same reaction as the newspaper reporters. "The thing that surprised me was the consistency of everybody's testimony. I mentioned it to Ted [Tamba] who said, 'They're just like parrots.' I was shocked and disappointed. It took the skids from under me because I thought the Japanese would certainly be truthful. I was shocked that Mary Higuchi would say she had been in the room and heard me broadcast when I had never seen the woman." The *Chronicle* summed up: "Mitsushio, the reluctant Nisei who changed to Japanese citizenship three months after the war started, remembered seven of the acts of broadcasting and scripting. He recited them gloomily and with little variance, like a schoolboy performing for visiting relatives."[40]

Given that it appeared that the witnesses had memorized their testimony, Wayne Collins pursued the issue on cross-examination. When he asked Mitsushio if he had read the indictment, Mitsushio shot a look over at DeWolfe.[41] Obviously, DeWolfe had not prepared him for this question. Collins asked him why he was looking at the prosecutor. DeWolfe blew up, and tried to confuse the issue by denying that *he* had looked at *Mitsushio*. Collins continued,

> *Collins*: Do you recall anyone having presented to you a copy of the indictment in this case?
> *Mitsushio*: No.
> *Collins*: Do you recall anyone having read to you from the indictment in this case?
> *Mitsushio*: No.[42]

As was his fashion, Collins kept circling back to this question. DeWolfe complained about the repetitiousness of the questions, that they had been asked and answered many times. One morning the judge had had enough and admonished Collins that he had to move along or the trial would last until next year. Collins brightly promised that he would be finished with Mitsushio in two hours. He was still questioning him the afternoon of the following day. But his doggedness again paid off.

> *Collins*: You read the overt acts from the indictment?
> *Mitsushio*: Yes.
> *Collins*: So that you had a copy of the indictment, didn't you, presented to you?
> *Mitsushio*: Yes.
> *Collins*: Who presented it to you?

Mitsushio: Mr. DeWolfe.

. . . .

Collins: Did anybody tell you, Mr. Mitsushio, when those acts had taken place?
Mitsushio: No.
Collins: Nobody?
Mitsushio: No.
Collins: Not a living soul told you?
Mitsushio: I told them first, and then we discussed the matter.
Collins: Then they retold you, didn't they?
Mitsushio: Yes.
Collins: And by "they," who are the persons to whom you re-fer?
Mitsushio: The Federal Bureau of Investigations [sic] and the United States Attorneys.[43]

The *Chronicle* remarked, "In the face of his letter-perfect, unchang-ing word structure, it was a damaging admission." However, the *Chronicle* immediately added, "But as the score adds up, DeWolfe has his two witnesses to seven alleged acts of treason, any one of which is enough to convict Tokyo Rose."[44]

In one of the trial's unforgettable moments, Collins elicited from Mitsushio that as a young student and Boy Scout, he had often sworn allegiance to the United States. Collins asked him to recite the Pledge of Allegiance. DeWolfe objected but Judge Roche overruled him. Mitsushio managed, "I pledge allegiance to the Flag of the United States of America and to the Republic for which it stands, one nation indivisible . . ." and then his memory failed. Judge Roche finished it for him—"with liberty and justice for all"—a small irony within the Great Irony.

～

Iva remembered Judge Roche's completion of the Pledge of Allegiance as "not mocking, not helpful—just kinda disgusted. It was the only time Roche got out of character. He was always like a piece of marble. After a couple of days, you know he's leaning toward the government. Whenever Wayne objected, it was always overruled whereas DeWolfe was always sustained." This was ob-viously not accurate, but it represented the general drift of the trial. I must add that Collins submitted ten objections for every one of

DeWolfe's and would have been more often overruled by the most impartial judge. Iva also recalled how tiresome the trial proceedings were. "I felt the jurors got bored with the case. It could have hurt me. I did think they were paying attention, though." Judge Roche was not. "Between you and me and the moon, he actually was sleeping. No one woke him, but I could see him nodding off. I never saw jurors nodding off."

~

One day during a break in the testimony of Mitsushio, prosecution witness Seizo/David Huga surreptitiously approached the defense. An associate of Oki and Mitsushio, Huga had helped newsmen identify Iva as Tokyo Rose, and was in the car when Oki regretted that he had not put forward his wife. Ted Tamba recalled the moment Huga pulled them aside during a lunch recess:

> He told us that what Oki and Mitsushio had recited from the witness stand was pure nonsense; that the events narrated had never happened; and that their testimony was downright perjury. They were friends of his, but he could not understand their conduct. Mr. Huga suggested that certain questions be asked of him on cross-examination and that he was sure the ill-founded case against Tokyo Rose would collapse.

There would be no cross-examination of David Huga.

> We were never to see Mr. Huga again. He was never called as a witness. It was learned that in the afternoon of our conversation he had been spirited away to Japan by the Department of Justice. He had apparently been followed and seen talking to us. Mr. Seizo Huga died a short time thereafter.[45]

~

The prosecution called 40 additional witnesses. Several more Japanese and Nisei employees of Radio Tokyo testified to Iva's freedom from duress, or to having seen Iva write scripts, or to having heard her make traitorous broadcasts. Iva hardly knew most of them, and some, like Mary Higuchi, she hadn't known existed. To the jury, these witnesses produced a tremendous volume of smoke.

The prosecution hoped jurors would infer there was a fire, not a smoke-making machine.

Frederick Tillman introduced Iva's 1946 statement, which the *Chronicle* thought "looked like a better document for the defense than the prosecution."[46] The seasoned FBI agent easily withstood Collins' cross-examination. No, Iva had not been under any pressure to sign the document. Yes, he had advised her of her right to counsel. Iva had read and verified the truth of every page. As to the mistaken marriage date, Tillman claimed that Iva had told him the wrong date; he had simply typed what she said. Tillman pooh-poohed Collins' suggestion that Iva's scripts contained double meanings, stating that she never told him about them and he didn't see them yet. He also dismissed Iva's contention that she was in fear of the secret police, claiming that the *kempeitai* no more oppressed the citizens of Japan than gendarmes oppressed the French.[47] However, Collins did manage through Tillman to finally get in some testimony about the Yagi affair. As the *Chronicle* reported it, when Collins brought up the subject of the bribery and perjury of Yagi, "Prosecutor Tom De Wolfe came out of his chair as though he'd been shot with a handful of carpet tacks. He was objecting while he was still bouncing."[48] Judge Roche sustained most of DeWolfe's objections, but when Collins asked Tillman, "Didn't you tell Mr. Tamba that Yagi had confessed to you that he had been bribed to come to San Francisco in the latter part of 1948 to testify falsely before the grand jury in the proceeding against the defendant?" Roche allowed the question, and Tillman answered, "Yes."[49]

Generally speaking, the remaining government witnesses were of two types: engineers and GIs. The job of the radio engineers was to connect the electronic dots. Their expertise allowed them to state that when Iva spoke into a microphone, a cable carried the signal to transmitters of a certain power and frequency that produced shortwave broadcasts that were received in different parts of the world, including Oregon, where the United States recorded them on acetate records, and so on. If ever there were witnesses to whom Wayne Collins could have given a pass, these engineers were them. Instead he exhausted and infuriated everyone, first by objecting to DeWolfe's routine questions about radio broadcasting—at one point Collins offered thirteen separate objections to a single question—and then by cross-examining the engineers as though they, out of personal malice, deployed their transmission charts as daggers to stab his client in the back. He questioned their education and their science in an attempt to defend Iva against their recordings. As the *Chronicle* put it, "In a yawning tedious tracing of the paperwork war, Defense Counsel Wayne Collins for the second day stalled off a half dozen innocuous recordings of the Tokyo Rose broadcasts to the South Pacific. He made the jury earn their $5 a day. Collins went into [the engineers'] qualifications and histories as though he intended to do a biography."[50] In the end, his questions served no purpose. The recordings came into evidence. They revealed precisely zero treasonable content.[51]

$\sim$

One U.S. marshal, Herbert Cole, walked Iva every day from the jail to the courthouse and back again at night. He became a friend, treating her with exceptional kindness. Cole told her soon after they met that he thought the whole trial was ridiculous. When the prosecution played the records of Orphan Ann's broadcasts for the jury, Iva remembered that Cole remarked to her, "You know, Iva, if they had the complete set of your programs from start to finish, you'd walk out of here tomorrow."

$\sim$

The GIs who appeared on the witness stand offered unsurprising testimony about broadcasts concerning unfaithful wives, the pleasures of being back home, the invincibility of the Japanese, and troop movements.

Sergeant Gilbert Velasquez was at Palo in the Philippines when he heard Iva say that "the Japanese were kicking hell out of the American troops at Tacloban and that by New Year's they would be in Palo."[52] Velasquez bragged to his buddies that he recognized her voice because he had patronized her father's store and talked to her three or four times a week for ten years.[53] His friends doubted him, but in fact Iva had waited on him at the store, and when her picture turned up in *Yank* magazine, it proved Velasquez right. Another witness, Army Signal Corps member Richard Henschell, was in a Philippine port when he heard Ann claim the Americans had lost all their ships.[54] Lieutenant Colonel Ted

E. Sherdeman remembered Orphan Ann saying, "Wouldn't you California boys like to be at the Cocoanut Grove tonight with your best girl? You have plenty of cocoanut groves but no best girls."[55] Jules I. Sutter, Jr. testified that on September 4, 1944, Orphan Ann announced that the Japanese had mined Saipan with high explosives and if the Americans didn't leave the island, "it would be blown sky high." In addition, he remembered her taunting them, "How would you like to be sitting down to a nice big thick steak?" On another occasion, Sutter heard Ann say, "I'm going to get my loving tonight. How about you?"[56] William Halbert Thompson recalled that Ann broadcast, "Welcome to the First Marine Division, the bloody butchers of Guadalcanal, who have just landed on Cape Gloucester, New Britain."[57] Charles F. Hall's memories were even more spectacular. He heard Tokyo Rose dedicate her program to the Jolly Rogers, the 90th Bomb Group, and she informed them they were soon to move to Dobodura, New Guinea, on December 21, 1943, and that she would have a reception committee waiting. This information, he learned, was top secret and yet sure enough, it happened exactly as she predicted. On January 17, 1944, Tokyo Rose announced they would move from Dobodura to Nadzab. This information was so highly classified even his major didn't have it, but once again Tokyo Rose turned out to be accurate to the day. She also offered 21 reasons why a man can't sleep with a redhead that revolved around the fact that no man goes to bed with a redhead in order to sleep.[58]

The simplest explanation for their recollections was that the GIs actually heard such broadcasts. No doubt the jurors accepted this explanation to some degree. It must have seemed unlikely that so many servicemen could be mistaken. Maybe they did hear them. Although no evidence exists to support it, Myrtle Lipton ("Manilla Rose") or some other woman may have broadcast such sentiments. However, as I argued in chapter 9, the perspective afforded by the passage of time suggests another solution. The primary cause of the GIs' memories was not an external source (radio broadcasts) but an internal one: namely, the needs, desires, fears, and imaginations of the GIs themselves. Consider their testimony in context:

Gilbert Velasquez was stationed at Palo just as Tokyo Rose/ Orphan Ann happened to speak about Palo. He was smarter than she was because he knew Palo was safe and smarter than his buddies because he recognized the voice. Richard Henschell also knew more than Tokyo Rose because he could actually see the American fleet when she announced the fleet was sunk. Ted Sherdeman explained his clear memory of Tokyo Rose's cocoanut remarks, "I remember that statement particularly because two nights before I left for overseas, my wife and I had gone to the Cocoanut Grove." At the time he heard the broadcast, he happened to be on the small island of Los Negros and "Los Negros was just one big cocoanut grove."[59] How amazing that Tokyo Rose, broadcasting to servicemen throughout the Pacific, would speak so personally to a California boy about that particular night club at a time when he's lonely for his wife and surrounded by cocoanut groves. Jules Sutter arrived on Saipan right before his birthday and no doubt wondered whether he would live to see another when Tokyo Rose warned he could be blown up. He also recalled, "At the time, the only meat we had had for several weeks, twice a day, was strong New Zealand mutton."[60] Tokyo Rose really hit the nail on the head when she reminded him of the pleasures of a nice steak. When Tokyo Rose welcomed the First Marine Division, the bloody butchers of Guadalcanal, to Cape Gloucester, William Halbert Thompson happened to be a member of the First Marine Division, had recently fought one of the bloodiest battles of the war at Guadalcanal, and he had just landed on Cape Gloucester. Charles F. Hall happened to be with the Air Force's 90th Bomb Group when Tokyo Rose dedicated her program to them and announced their top-secret deployments ahead of time. Finally, it requires no effort to imagine the thoughts in the minds of GIs who remembered Tokyo Rose would get her loving that night or touting the passion of redheads.

The testimony of the GIs skewed the outcome of the trial for three reasons, all of them pernicious. First, Collins could not refute their claims. How could he? The Japanese and the Americans had destroyed almost all the scripts and recordings, so no evidence existed to countervail the servicemen's recollections. Second, after the war, 10,000 soldiers and sailors would have sworn they heard a woman calling herself Tokyo Rose broadcast this and that. The Tokyo Rose legend obviously influenced GIs testifying at the trial such that they truly believed their own testimony. Their absolute sincerity helped persuade the jury, some of whose members the legend no doubt influenced as well. Third, the FBI had received hundreds of servicemen's letters but the Department of Justice had selected only those men whose memories fitted the prosecution's theory of the case. It discarded the rest. Today, the government must provide the defense with any exculpatory evidence it turns up in the investigation of a crime. That was not true in 1949. We know about the many GIs who heard Tokyo Rose broadcast when *Zero Hour* was off the air, or swore Iva's voice was not the one they heard during the war, because the FBI's confidential records are now declassified. But in 1949, prosecutors kept the defense in the dark about this evidence, and therefore they were able to give the jury the impression that the memories of its witnesses were typical, not exceptional.

These factors all came together in the testimony of Chief Bosun's Mate Marshall Hoot (Figure 16.4).[61] Marshall Hoot was the best GI witness, the best prosecution witness, and, to give the devil his due, the best witness in the entire trial. The prosecution asked Hoot a few questions and then turned him over for cross-examination. When Collins the Doberman jumped into the ring, he had no idea a Navy pit bull was waiting for him.

Figure 16.4. Marshall Hoot.
Courtesy of *San Francisco Chronicle.*

Marshall Hoot was a tough old veteran of World Wars I and II. His grammar was poor, but he had an iron grip on facts. Whereas other witnesses might refer to "sometime in early 1944," Hoot often gave an actual day and date. When asked about his boat, he typed it—"Converted Patrol Boat," specified it individually—"PTC-21000," and noted it had a keel of 75 feet and a beam of 27 feet. He accurately recalled that Naval Bomb Squadrons VB-108, known as "Tokyo Rose's Four-Engine Fighters,"[62] and VB-109 landed on Apamama Island, and that the name of the island had been changed to Abemama. Often he was mistaken,[63] but neither Collins nor the jury knew better. His testimony had the ring of authenticity.

The power of Hoot's testimony rested not just in its precision. For example, the defense at the trial, and analysts of this case over the decades, have made much of the uniformity of the testimony by servicemen as to what time of day they heard Orphan Ann's broadcasts. Several GIs stated with certitude that they had listened to *Zero Hour* between 6:00 and 7:00 PM. Prosecutors probably prepped them on the actual broadcast time of Iva's program. What DeWolfe and company forgot were time zones. The *Zero Hour* broadcast from 6:00 to 7:00 PM *Tokyo time*. GIs, however, were scattered all over the Pacific, which meant that, if they really listened between 6:00 and 7:00, they heard someone other than Iva. The defense expected to use this mistake to destroy witnesses' credibility, but Marshall Hoot dashed any hope of doing so:

> *Collins*: So you fix that program between 5:30 and, say, 6:30 PM?
> *Hoot*: Our Navy time out there. It was something in that zone there. It was only where we were. We were taking our tick from Greenwich but we had to time ourselves with the rest of the fleet. The Navy splits their time. We did not go by the hour; we run on the 24 hours. If I was in one spot today and 24 hours later in another spot, I didn't change my time like you would change if you crossed the Colorado River. We had to rendezvous with other ships, and our time stayed as much as five days at that time.[64]

The judge and jurors no doubt threw up their hands at this convoluted explanation of Navy time-keeping and as a result completely disregarded time discrepancy as an issue during the trial.

Hoot's recollections of Orphan Ann/Tokyo Rose broadcasts were nothing special. She predicted attacks. She said, "Wouldn't you like to be home dancing with the one you love in your arms?" "The boys at home are making the big money, and they can well afford to take your girl friends out and show them a good time." "If you boneheads want to go home, you better go pretty soon, or haven't you heard your navy is practically sunk?"[65] He denied that he had ever heard the voice identify herself as "Tokyo Rose," but he failed to mention he had previously told the government that she had said, "I understand that some of my Pacific listeners refer to me as the Rose of Tokyo."[66] What made Hoot unusual was that he listened to *Zero Hour* for the explicit purpose of recording the bad things Iva said. Navy Intelligence had informed him about Tokyo Rose, he testified, and he wanted to document her broadcasts. Therefore, he assigned the quartermaster to write Orphan Ann's morale-deflating remarks down in the ship's log. He knew for sure she had broadcast the remarks just repeated because he had seen them written in the log. This far exceeded the claims of any other GI.

Collins, of course, wanted to examine this log. Alas, like so many records of Tokyo Rose, it had disappeared.

> *Collins*: Where is the log book?
> *Hoot*: Some place out in the Pacific, I guess. I don't know where it is. When the war was over, I don't know where those ships went to. The one I was on was lost off the Marianas.
> *Collins*: Was the log lost with it, do you know?
> *Hoot*: I don't know whether it was or not, I was not on it at the time.
> *Collins*: When did you last see that log?
> *Hoot*: I last seen that log August the 17th, 1944.[67]

Then how, Collins wondered, could Hoot possibly remember hearing Orphan Ann predict an attack on the exact date of January 3, 1944?

> *Hoot*: I have a letter in my pocket to prove it. I wrote to my wife that day.
> *Collins*: May I see that letter?
> *Hoot*: I don't know whether you can read it or not, Mr. Collins.[68]

Hoot had thrown the stick and Collins chased it. Hoot claimed to be reluctant because his letter was personal and he had not read it in five or six years.[69] The court recessed so he could think about it. When he returned, he agreed to allow the letter to be read aloud in court. Marshall Hoot's letter to his wife, Jennie, and their two children, Biddy and Betty, damaged Iva Toguri as badly as the autographed yen note.

> Dearest Biddy and Betty:
> I received Betty's letter this a.m. Sure glad you heard from me. I know how it is to not hear, I am O.K. yet. I am just a little older today and maybe a little grayer, but we can take it, and what you

read in the papers, do not let it worry you any more than you can help. Babies, it is all bad.

I would of loved to seen mama when you gave her the letters. Yes, I wrote often to ease my loneliness, and you or mama must write every day if you can. That is the most important thing on this island, mail and more mail. Well, Charlie and his washing machine [Hoot explained this was slang for Japanese bombers] cut me off. Will finish later.

January 4th. I am still O.K. this a.m. Hope my babies are the same. We have a radio now and we get Tokyo best, they have an American Jap girl who has turned down the United States for Japan. They call her Tokyo Rose, and does she razz us fellows out here in the Pacific, telling how well Japan is getting along, and to hear her start out you would think that she was broadcasting from the U.S. and sorry that we were loosing so many men and ships, it sure makes the fellows sore. Last night before Charlie we had KNY,[70] made me so jittery I smoked half a package of cigarettes.

Dear, you must buy up some liquor and hold it if you can. I haven't had a drink in along time, now that we have a chiefs club, maybe we can order us some. Please do not fail to loan me a buck or two now and then, you see, dear, although I am thousands of miles away I still depend upon you. I would not need money for Stateside when I get that thirty-day leave, which I hope comes along soon.

Honeybabies, I must lay off for today, hope I dream of you tonight as I think of you all day. So write me anything.

Lots of love, Daddy[71]

Rereading this letter carefully, one realizes it contains nothing about Orphan Ann and no prediction of an attack. Actually, the letter indirectly exonerates Iva. The station on which Hoot claimed to have heard Tokyo Rose, KNY, did not carry *Zero Hour*. Although Collins did not know it, KNY was a shortwave repeater station that belonged to the U.S. Navy and carried war news to the Philippines and other Pacific areas.[72] If the propaganda Hoot heard on KNY made him jittery, the U.S. Navy broadcast it.

No matter. Rex Gunn told me that as he watched the jury, the men's jaws clenched and the women had tears running down their cheeks. The simple, heartfelt letter of fear and longing resonated with them. Judge Roche admitted to Katherine Beebe and Gunn after the trial,

> I think if it wasn't for the witness from Los Angeles, the reluctant witness [Hoot], I might have considered her innocent. They pressed him to tell and he produced that letter. That was the turning point. Up to the time that fellow pulled that letter out of his pocket, with all my experience, I was up in the air as to what might or might not have happened. There were so many voices.[73]

Wayne Collins counterattacked as best he could. How did Hoot know that Tokyo Rose was an American? Hoot replied that he heard it from Naval Intelligence, plus "after listening to her a while, we had her pegged then as being an American, the way she put her programs on. I don't think a Jap from Japan could have picked out the records and played them like that."[74] Collins assaulted Hoot with questions, and Hoot ate him up. Responding to Collins, Hoot described the predicted attack—"the Japs hit us both ways . . . bombs were falling within 50 yards . . . they made two direct hits"—and expressed his sorrow that "they killed two of my men and I don't know how many marines . . . one of these boys was a good friend of mine."[75] Failing to shake this story, Collins concluded in desperation, "Isn't it a fact there were no casualties?" The old seadog growled at him, "I beg your pardon. I helped bury them. I ought to know."[76]

Marshall Hoot was so good a witness that one wonders if he was somehow a ringer that DeWolfe intentionally planted. His poor verbal skills would seem to make him an unlikely accomplice of the professorial prosecutor, but it surely was not happenstance that he had a long-unread letter to his wife tucked in his pocket and that he oh-so-reluctantly allowed it to be entered into evidence. Although he managed just the right answer at every turn, Hoot probably was not a plant or a slick operator. He was a bosun's mate, nothing more, but he was the kind of guy you want to take with you when you go to war. Unfortunately for Iva, in this battle he fought for the other side.

～

On Friday, August 12, 1949, the United States rested its case, concluding with the 47th witness of a planned 71. The *San Francisco Chronicle* estimated the jurors had already heard "more than 500,000 words of testimony"[77] over six weeks and the defense had yet to present its case.

As soon as the government rested, the defense submitted a motion for a judgment of acquittal and the next day, Saturday, defense attorney George Olshausen argued the motion out of the hearing of the jury. Olshausen's presentation was both beautifully reasoned and irenic. He consistently complimented Judge Roche, even going so far as to engage in friendly banter with him, and thus tried to smooth over any hard feelings the judge might harbor from his battles with Collins. He began with *Cramer v. United States*, which "virtually states all the case law on the subject of treason."[78] He argued that since "the overt acts do not in and of themselves show treasonable intent,"[79] most of the government's evidence went to prove that intent. To determine intent, one had to consider the setting of Iva's script writing and broadcasting activities.

With respect to the setting, Olshausen proceeded exactly as De-Wolfe had predicted when he himself argued against prosecution in 1948. Olshausen turned the prosecution's own evidence against it. He quoted Tsuneishi's admission that he waited for Japanese resistance to introduce propaganda into *Zero Hour*, resistance that never materialized.[80] The witnesses who swore they stood over Iva as she broadcast proved, argued Olshausen, that she was under constant watch and that the Army had placed these people there to make sure she obeyed her orders as to what to say. "In other words, the background is, first, that the Japanese themselves were not using their program for propaganda. Second, you have a regular police state with the defendant herself under surveillance."[81]

Olshausen explained how the broadcast context of Iva's remarks was crucial to assessing their treasonable intent. He compared a fictional broadcast of "Hello, you orphans of the Pacific. You must be lonely out there" with the actual broadcast, "Hello, you orphans of the Pacific. You must be lonely out there. Let me cheer you up with some music." In a nice touch, he cited the well-known Western novel, *The Virginian*. By 1949, Hollywood had made the novel into a movie four times[82] and everyone knew its famous line, "When you call me that, smile." Olshausen argued that calling GIs "honorable boneheads" meant one thing if said in a jocular fashion and the exact opposite if said seriously. Such remarks, especially when set in the context of Iva's helping the POWs, could only be understood as the former.

Near the end of his motion, Olshausen analyzed at some length the problematic issue of when witnesses heard Iva broadcast. As noted, most swore they listened to *Zero Hour* between 6:00 and 7:00 PM. Too polite to suggest the prosecution had coached its witnesses, Olshausen instead offered the alternative theory that the witnesses had seen the notation of the broadcast time on exhibits, and he proposed that if they were that suggestible, their memories and identification of Iva's voice were open to question. Olshausen examined each serviceman's testimony one by one, emphasizing where they were stationed, and how 6:00–7:00 PM at that location did not correspond to 6:00–7:00 PM in Tokyo. He further noted that some witnesses listened to Orphan Ann as they moved across the Pacific but still managed to hear *Zero Hour* at exactly the same time. Olshausen concluded, "Not only do the witnesses get the time wrong, but they always get it wrong in the same way. They always give the Tokyo time, in whatever part of the world they happen to be."[83]

Judge Roche denied the defense's motion to dismiss without comment.[84] Olshausen informed Iva of the ruling, adding, in a tone of disbelief, "I always thought the world was round."

Notes

1. Trial Transcript, vol. I, 3.
2. Trial Transcript, vol. I, 7, 12–13.
3. Trial Transcript, vol. I, 7.
4. Trial Transcript, vol. I, 23.
5. Trial Transcript, vol. I, 23–24.
6. Trial Transcript, vol. I, 28.
7. Quotations from letters and e-mails between Eisenhart and myself during 2006.
8. I am indebted to Dick Eisenhart for providing a clean photocopy of Figure 16.1 and giving me permission to use it. The note's negatives at the National Archives are very poor in quality. The note became U.S. Exhibit

2. The FBI never returned the yen note after the trial, but Eisenhart asked about it during a tour of the FBI decades later. Amazingly, the Bureau turned it up and gave it back to him.

9. Eisenhart's direct testimony, Trial Transcript, vol. I, 34–38; cross-examination, 38–57.

10. *Washington Star*, September 30, 1949, 2.

11. Trial Transcript, vol. I, 65–76.

12. Ikeda's testimony, Trial Transcript, vol. II, 187. Newspapers covering the trial restated Collins' blunt assertion that Ikeda's records had to be forgeries. *New York Times*, July 9, 1949, 2.

13. Figure 16.2, "Tsueishi Shigetsagu" [sic], *The Library of Congress*. Tsuneishi was now a lieutenant colonel but as in previous chapters, I have decided to stay with a single military rank to avoid confusing readers.

14. Trial Transcript, vol. IV, 306.

15. Trial Transcript, vol. V, 319.

16. Trial Transcript, vol. V, 321.

17. Trial Transcript, vol. V, 337.

18. Trial Transcript, vol. V, 359.

19. *San Francisco Chronicle*, July 13, 1949, 1.

20. Trial Transcript, vol. VI, 433–34, 439.

21. On redirect, Tsuneishi returned to his initial testimony, claiming that *Zero Hour* did contain propaganda, that no one pressured Iva, etc. I assume that by this time he had lost his credibility.

22. See *Public Opinion 1935–1946*, ed. Hadley Cantril (Westport, Conn.: Greenwood Press Publishers, 1951).

23. On July 11, Special Agent Harry M. Kimball sent an urgent telegram to Hoover: "DeWolfe and Hogan have stated that they are apprehensive that Lee has been persuaded by Brundidge to testify falsely in this case and had requested agents this office interview Lee. . . . Agents this office have advised that it appears to them that Lee [a handwritten "possibly" is inserted in the typed text at this point] is not truthful in the testimony he has and it is felt that Lee should be interviewed by agents this office since DeWolfe and Hogan are reluctant to go into the matter with him. Since Defense has knowledge of attempted subordination of perjury on the part of Brundidge and are cognizant of Lee's association with Brundidge, it is possible they will be able to break Lee's testimony if he is a witness." Kimball interviewed Lee the next morning. Lee told him he was worried that it would be brought out that he had never paid Iva the money promised in their contract and this would "place him in an unfavorable light." However, Kimball determined that Brundidge had not suggested Lee's testimony. Lee testified on July 14. Teletypes, July 11, 1949 and July 12, 1949. NARA 2.

24. *San Francisco Chronicle*, July 16, 1949, 3.

25. Masayo Duus claims that "when [Lee's] book *They Call It Pacific* was made into a movie, the leading man was Clark Gable" (*Orphan of the Pacific*, 7). The Gable Centennial Tribute site also mentions the film (http://www.geocities.com/cactus_st/film/index.html). However, I can find no evidence this film actually exists. Gable did play a character named Hank Lee in *Soldier of Fortune*, but that movie, set in Hong Kong, was based on a novel of the same name by Ernest K. Gann.

In any case, Lee parlayed his good looks into a 1938 marriage to a Hawaiian pineapple heiress, Princess Liliuokalani Kawananakoa. The FBI reported that they and her three sisters split $25 million every four years, which in the 1940s was serious money. NARA 3, Box 3. Lee seems to have spent almost no time at home. He lived in Tokyo from 1938–1939, then in Shanghai. He traveled with Japanese forces in China. He was in the Philippines when Pearl Harbor was attacked and escaped with MacArthur. Lee died February 15, 1953, at age 46 of a heart attack. See his obituary, *New York Times*, February 16, 1953, 21.

26. Trial Transcript, vol. VII, 485–86.

27. Lee's raw notes, 14–15. NARA 2, Box 17.

28. Lee's narrative, 14–15. NARA 1, Box 48.

29. See chapter 3, note 27.

30. Trial Transcript, vol. VII, 486–87.

31. Trial Transcript, vol. VIII, 595–96.

32. Figure 16.3, *San Francisco Chronicle*. Witnesses generally referred to him as George Nakamoto. See chapter 7, note 35.

33. *San Francisco Examiner*, July 20, 1949, 1. Actually the *Examiner* referred to Mitsushio, but the description applies to both men.

34. *San Francisco Examiner*, July 20, 1949, 1.

35. Trial Transcript, vol. XIII, 1315.

36. Trial Transcript, vol. X, 837.

37. Trial Transcript, vol. X, 924–25.

38. Trial Transcript, vol. XII, 1140–41.

39. Trial Transcript, vol. XIII, 1322.

40. *San Francisco Chronicle*, July 21, 1949, 9.

41. Trial Transcript, vol. XII, 1168.

42. Trial Transcript, vol. XII, 1169.

43. Trial Transcript, vol. XII, 1183–84.

44. *San Francisco Chronicle*, July 21, 1949, 9.

45. From a series of Tamba recollections, "Tokyo Rose and Boobus Americanus," October 6, 1973.

46. *San Francisco Chronicle*, July 26, 1949, 1.

47. Trial Transcript, vol. XV, 1535.

48. *San Francisco Chronicle*, July 28, 1949, 6.

49. Trial Transcript, vol. XVI, 1597–98.

50. *San Francisco Chronicle*, July 29, 1949, 4.

51. *Zero Hour* scripts were Government Exhibits 22, 23, 44, 74 and Defense Exhibit R. Exhibits 16–20 were recordings made in Portland, Oregon; Exhibit 21 was made in Silver Hill, Maryland. Exhibit 25 was a transcription of 16–21. Exhibits 63 and 75 were transcriptions made by monitors in Hawaii. That is the sum of the actual broadcast evidence. None of it documents propaganda in Iva's own voice.

52. Palo was one of the landing sites for MacArthur's troops; they used it to capture Tacloban and then fought their way to Manila. Trial Transcript, vol. XVIII, 1882.

53. That he talked to Iva three or four times a week is likely an exaggeration. An FBI Report of September 15, 1949, summarizes the Agency's attempts to find neighbors or close friends of Gilbert "Veto" ("Beto" is actually the correct nickname for Gilberto) Velasquez who could establish that he knew Iva. They found eleven store customers who lived in the neighborhood. None believed he knew her, but thought she might have waited on him. The Terry family said, "Iva Toguri was far advanced as far as Veto was concerned, both in age, intelligence, and association. Because of this difference there was no fraternization between them." The age difference may also be exaggerated. Velasquez told the FBI he had met Iva in 1927 and patronized the store until she left in 1941 (FBI Report, February 9, 1948). Iva testified at trial that she worked on and off at the store from 1931 to 1941 (Transcript, 5468–69). Velasquez, born on September 9, 1922, was 9 to 19 years old during these years, just six years younger than Iva. He might have paid more attention to her than she to him. NARA 1, Box 49.

54. Trial Transcript, vol. XXVI, 2962.

55. Russell Warren Howe says, "Red Sherdeman had similarly confused memories, but he was not called as a trial witness." See *The Hunt for "Tokyo Rose,"* 243. Ted Sherdeman was called to the witness stand on August 1, 1949. His direct testimony begins at Trial Transcript, vol. XIX, 1977 and his cross-examination on 2000. My quoted remark, 1979.

56. Sutter's recollections, at Trial Transcript, vol. XX, 2027–30. What is so strange about the Saipan mines threat, as Olshausen pointed out, is that Tokyo Rose supposedly made it three months after the Americans had taken control of the island. If the Japanese really had the power to blow Saipan sky high, one would suppose they would have already done so.

57. Trial Transcript, vol. XXI, 2252.

58. Military predictions, at Trial Transcript, vol. XXVI, 2896, 2899; redhead remark, 2904.

59. Both remarks at Trial Transcript, vol. XIX, 2003.

60. Trial Transcript, vol. XX, 2030.

61. Figure 16.4, *San Francisco Chronicle.*

62. I take this from the title of an unpublished manuscript by veteran Harlan Scott, *United States Navy Bombing Squadron One Hundred Eight (Tokyo Rose's Four-Engine Fighters).* This manuscript was brought to my attention by Alan C. Carey. See http://www.alanc.carey.freeservers.com.

63. Hoot said he served on the "C-21,000," a "converted PT" (vol. XX, 2118). First, no U.S. Navy ship had a numeral designation as high as 21,000. Second, the largest beam of any PT boat in World War II was the PT-103 Class ("Elco") at 23 feet. No boat of any class had the measurements given by Hoot. Hoot claimed that his boat was lost off the Marianas after August 1944. U.S. Navy records show no boats similar to Hoot's so lost. On the other hand, Hoot correctly stated that the name of Apamama had been changed (not as he thought by the U.S. Navy during the war but in 1934) to Abemama, and that VB-108 and VB-109 had landed there. However, VB-108 landed in early December, not late. See Alan Carey's website, http://www.alanc.carey.freeservers.com.

64. Trial Transcript, vol. XXI, 2161–62.

65. Hoot's remarks appear at Trial Transcript, vol. XX, 2117, 2118, 2147.

66. FBI report of Sawtelle, April 18, 1949; "Testimony of Marshall Hoot." NARA 2, Box 15.

67. Trial Transcript, vol. XXI, 2172.

68. Trial Transcript, vol. XXI, 2174. Hoot later explained he wrote to his wife *about* that day several days later.

69. Trial Transcript, vol. XXI, 2184.

70. Hoot himself interrupted to explain that KNY "may have been some station." Trial Transcript, vol. XXI, 2204.

71. Trial Transcript, vol. XXI, 2203–4.

72. My information on the repeater station KNY comes from www.worldofradio.com/dxld2119.txt and http://radiodx.com/spdxr/ww2_california.htm.

73. They interviewed Roche together. See Gunn, *They Called Her "Tokyo Rose,"* 101–2.

74. Trial Transcript, vol. XXI, 2209.

75. Trial Transcript, vol. XXI, 2213–14.

76. Trial Transcript, vol. XXI, 2215. Hoot's account was accurate. The Japanese raided Apamama/Abemama three times, on January 2, 3, and 10, 1944. U.S. forces suffered no casualties in the latter two attacks. But concerning the air raid Hoot described at trial, the U.S. Navy announced, "Ten enemy planes bombed our installations on Abemama on the night

of January 2 with slight damage. Two men were killed." CINCPAC Press Release No. 218, January 4, 1944.

77. *San Francisco Chronicle*, August 13, 1949, 1.

78. Trial Transcript, vol. XXVII, 3006.

79. Trial Transcript, vol. XXVII, 3010.

80. Trial Transcript, vol. V, 321. That *Zero Hour* had little or no propaganda was no doubt the fact, but Tsuneishi's testimony is not quite what Olshausen claims. Tsuneishi waited for greater Japanese resistance with the idea that "from that time the propaganda would be *greatly increased*" (italics mine). Quotation below, from vol. XXVII, 3029.

81. Trial Transcript, vol. XXVII, 3029.

82. Owen Wister's 1902 novel, *The Virginian*, was produced as a movie in 1914, 1923, 1929, and 1946.

83. Trial Transcript, vol. XXVII, 3046.

84. I hope I do not give the impression that Roche's denial of the motion was unjust. In the first place, although a motion for acquittal following the prosecution's case is common, its success is extremely rare. The defense must argue for its motion using only the evidence provided by the prosecution's witnesses. Second, the same arguments offered by Olshausen were made to an appeals court after the trial and they also failed to persuade the appellate judges.

Chapter 17

The Defense

Iva Toguri v. Tokyo Rose

Attorney Ted Tamba made the opening statement for the defense. He told the jury Iva's story, and did not hesitate to embellish if he thought it might do her some good. "Coming home from work in the evenings, it was not unusual for her to walk into her room and find three or four *kempeitai* going through her personal effects, searching for things, things in the English language, harassing her, attempting to make her change her citizenship from American to Japanese."[1] Were this not bad enough, he added, "There were two metropolitan police watching her continually. She made periodical reports to the *kempeitai*. I am not particularly frightened of things, but I would hate to have four policemen follow me. I just say that offhand."[2] He contrasted the duress imposed by the Japanese police with Iva's celebration by the Americans.

> The day she was released, the guards were lined up at Sugamo Prison. Full dress. The commander of the prison escorts her through the gate, assisting her into a car, and sends her home with a cheap load of flowers, and tells the press to keep away from her. She didn't tell me that; I found out about it.[3]

Tamba also shrewdly used this opportunity to put before the jury information that the judge would never allow into evidence. For example, he told them the full story of Brundidge's bribery of Yagi. The prosecution objected, but the judge had to allow it because Tamba assured the court that he would prove the allegations. Tamba knew for a fact he could not prove any such thing, that the defense dared not call Brundidge or Yagi as witnesses, but the jury heard the tale. Tamba also informed the jury about the wretched conditions at Bunka prison camp. The POWs were so hungry they tried to fatten guinea pigs as a source of meat, but when they fed them the rations the Japanese gave the prisoners for their own food, the guinea pigs starved to death rather than eat. So the POWs ate dogs and cats to survive. All such testimony would be disallowed during the examination of witnesses because the judge deemed it irrelevant to Iva's guilt or innocence. But the jury heard it through Tamba.

Figure 17.1. Charles Cousens.
Courtesy of Mitchell Library, New South Wales, Australia

Wayne Collins called Iva's three POW superiors at Radio Tokyo as his initial witnesses. The first was Australian Major Charles Cousens (Figure 17.1).[4] After answering some preliminary questions that identified him to the jury, Cousens testified how he and his troops, after surrendering at Singapore, witnessed two horrific murders by the Japanese.

I was attracted by screams, and I saw these naked Japanese, naked except for a G-string sort of affair, and they were beating a coolie [laborer]. The word got around amongst the boys that he was starving and had tried to snatch a can of food from a Japanese soldier. They threw him to the ground and put his head under a tap so that as he drew breath and screamed, he drew water into his lungs. He got up and they proceeded to beat him again, and then put him under the tap again. Eventually I suppose he clenched his teeth because they broke his face open on the tap, turned the water on, drowned him, and threw his body away.[5]

Cousens followed this narrative with the beating of a fellow Australian with a "solid kindo stick." The Japanese beat his back until he fell, then beat his legs until he stood, then his back until he fell, and they kept this up while their compatriots kept the massed Australian troops at bay with machine guns. "Later when he didn't get up again they grunted at us, signaled to take him away. We did, and he died before we could get him on board ship."[6] At this, according to the *San Francisco Chronicle*, Cousens "was completely in tears and could not go on until the bailiff brought him water."[7] The *Chronicle*, which had noted tears in jurors' eyes when Hoot read his letter to his honeybabies, recorded no emotional reaction to Cousen's memories and breakdown.

Cousens recounted his transport to prison camps by ship, he and his fellow soldiers packed so tightly below deck they had to stand continually for two weeks. They received only a little portion of rice each day while the Japanese had so much to eat, they threw the excess overboard.[8] The Japanese degraded their prisoners. "Most of us were suffering either from dysentery or acute diarrhea, and there were no sanitary arrangements except on deck." Some of them went mad, but in general, Cousens said proudly of his fellow Australians, "They were wonderful. They maintained their love for one another and their dignity."[9]

At first, the prosecution allowed this testimony because they assumed it was preliminary, but as Wayne Collins drew from Cousens example after example of Japanese cruelty and viciousness, they realized he was undermining their entire fiction that foreigners like Cousens and Iva were under no more pressure from Japanese authorities than the French were from their own police. When the defense opened, DeWolfe shrewdly decided to give the jury a rest from his voice and turned over his duties to Attorney James Knapp. It was Knapp, therefore, who objected to Cousens' continued testimony about atrocities on the grounds that what happened to Cousens may have placed him under duress but not Iva Toguri. Collins retorted that Cousens communicated these events to the defendant. Knapp argued that even if that were true, it would not constitute a defense. Judge Roche sided with Collins. "Not in itself, it would not, but it would be hard for anyone to determine that it was not an element of coercion."[10] Knapp persisted. He claimed he could cite relevant case law if he could refresh his memory concerning the factual details of the cases. He asked for time to do some quick research, and the judge declared a recess. No one knows what happened during that recess, but when the court reconvened, the judge was now solidly on the side of the prosecution. Time and time again throughout the following weeks, Judge Roche prevented testimony of abuses to POWs. The few examples he allowed had to be tied directly to Iva and her circumstances.

These rulings forced Collins to concentrate on *Zero Hour*. Because Tsuneishi was the official in control of that program, Roche did allow Cousens to testify to his encounter with Tsuneishi and the threat of death under which he broadcast. As the *Chronicle* colorfully put it, "By the gauge of defense testimony, Shigetsugu Tsuneishi, the tough little lieutenant colonel, is a thundering liar."[11] Cousens explained his own initial distrust of Iva—"she was very friendly, so much so that we were very suspicious"[12]—and how he came to trust her with his very life. When he testified that Iva carried food and medicine to POWs, the *Chronicle* reported that "for the first time in this trial, the 33-year-old Japanese girl put her head down and wept."[13]

Charles Cousens proved to be an excellent witness for the defense. He provided every element a jury would require to reach a verdict of acquittal. He testified that Radio Tokyo was riddled with *kempei* spies and that he told Iva of what happened to anyone who crossed them. He stated that he himself chose Iva, who did not want to broadcast but did so when ordered by the Japanese. He wrote her scripts and taught her how to read them to defeat Japanese purposes. He took full responsibility for what she broadcast on *Zero Hour*.

> I said to her, "Now, listen. This is a straight out entertainment program. I have written it and I know what I am doing. All you have got to do is look on yourself as a soldier under my orders. Do exactly what you are told. Don't try to do anything for yourself and you will do nothing against your own people. I will guarantee that personally."[14]

Cousens added corroborative detail that enhanced his testimony. For example, he, not Iva, selected the word "boneheads" to address the troops. His scripts had to pass through three or four Japanese censors, and he thought that address would make it appear they were belittling Allied troops whereas in fact the term would be less offensive than "fools, idiots or suckers." He placed "honorable" in front of it and taught Iva to pronounce it "hon'able" to mock Japanese pronunciation. He stated that contrary to Japanese prosecution witnesses, Radio Tokyo had many guards. Initially armed custodians watched them, and later in the war the Japanese stationed a platoon of infantry there. When Cousens testified that Iva had brought a wool blanket for a dying POW, he added, "which was worth its weight in gold in Japan at that time." When she visited him in the hospital, he remembered she brought him another rarity, an egg. They secretly flashed each other the "V for Victory" sign at Radio Tokyo. When Iva had war news to pass along but Japanese were present, she would say, "Praise the Lord and pass the ammunition." That was a signal for a private pow-wow and a whispered sharing of her information. When Cousens testified that he informed Iva of the horrid conditions at Bunka, Knapp objected and Judge Roche tried to limit his testimony by asking him to state only what he said. Cousens replied, "I told her I discovered there was a reign of terror prevailing." Knapp objected that this must go out, that it was a conclusion of the witness, but Roche regretfully ruled, "The court asked the question. It will have to stand."[15]

As noted, Wayne Collins had considerable difficulty getting much of Cousens' evidence before the jury. Knapp constantly objected to any testimony that Iva purchased food and medicine with her own money and smuggled it into Bunka. This is a typical exchange:

> *Knapp*: Object, your Honor. I don't think it has any bearing on the question of the defendant's guilt or innocence.
> *Collins*: It goes to the question of intent, if your Honor please.
> *Knapp*: It doesn't go to the intent to commit an act of treason at all. It only shows she might be a kind-hearted person.
> *Collins*: It shows she gave aid and comfort to our own troops held prisoners of war.

> *Knapp*: That doesn't also prevent her from giving aid and comfort to the enemy, which the evidence shows she did.
> *Collins*: The evidence shows no such thing. I charge that as highly prejudicial misconduct to make such a remark in open court.
> *Court*: The jury will disregard the remarks of counsel on both sides. The objection will be sustained.[16]

Nonetheless, the jury heard about Iva's "kind-hearted" deeds through Collins' sheer tenacity.

As Collins rehearsed each of the broadcasts that prosecution witnesses had claimed they heard on *Zero Hour*, Cousens denied writing or hearing them.[17] The fact that he had left *Zero Hour* in late summer 1944, and did not return undercut his testimony. However, Cousens added helpful detail. He claimed he knew, for example, exactly where broadcasts about faithless wives and girlfriends originated. "In the German Hour. It was their standard line for a long while. 'Your girls and wives are betraying you,' in effect. Foumy Saisho, a *kempei* agent, broadcast on the German Hour."[18]

On cross-examination, James Knapp subjected Cousens to, in the words of the *Chronicle*, "a shower of sarcasm."[19] He painted Cousens as a willing collaborator who sold out in order to live a life of relative ease and pleasure in Tokyo. Had the Japanese paid him to broadcast? No, they paid him because he was an officer. Hadn't the Japanese given him two custom-made suits during the war? Yes, of wood fiber. Wasn't he housed in the number one (the literal meaning of "Dai Ichi") hotel in Tokyo? Far from it. Wasn't he provided with a room of his own and access to a bath? Yes. And wasn't this the hotel where the Japanese housed foreign collaborators? Define "collaborators." Didn't he receive butter, cheese, and extra bread? Not at first. Hadn't his Japanese superior taken him to a geisha house? Yes, once.

> *Knapp*: And he arranged a date for you, didn't he?
> *Cousens*: Will you define your terms, sir?
> *Knapp*: He introduced you to a young lady there, didn't he?
> *Cousens*: To two or three.
> *Knapp*: You spent the evening there, didn't you?
> *Cousens*: Part of it.
> *Knapp*: That is while you were a prisoner of war, wasn't it?
> *Cousens*: At the Dai Ichi Hotel.[20]

Knapp further suggested Wayne Collins bought and paid for Cousens' testimony. Cousens admitted the defense had paid his way to the United States. This was payback for Collins' similar questioning of prosecution witnesses. Knapp also suggested Cousens greatly exaggerated his starvation and the need to smuggle food. "You got a pretty good dinner [at the Dai Ichi], didn't you?" "We did not, sir." Knapp produced a sheaf of hotel restaurant receipts that Cousens had signed. Table 17.1 shows the translated version of a few of them.[21]

Collins brought out on redirect that the hotel usually served curried baby sparrows—"they were cooked complete and a little difficult to eat"—and smoked squid and octopus. However, as readers can note in the Knapp's own translations showed less exotic dishes like crab, ground meat, fruits, macaroni, and ice cream. In any case, the portions were small. Like ordinary Japanese, Cousens required additional food to supplement the meager portions. He testified that after the war ended, he stuffed himself for two weeks yet weighed only 140 pounds.[22] Unfortunately, these facts developed under redirect may have come too late to salvage Cousens in the eyes of jurors disinclined to believe him.

Cousens' restaurant receipts dated from August 1942 to March 1943.[23] During this period, Japan was still able to feed its people, and Tsuneishi wanted to encourage Cousens to fully cooperate. As the war progressed, Japan had less and less food available and

Table 17.1. Three columns of restaurant receipts entered as evidence of good treatment of POWs at the Dai Ichi hotel.

February 5		February 7		February 11	
Mince Ball	0.80				
Cod-fish	0.70	Munier	0.80	Sardine	0.60
Curry	1.00	Cheese	0.80	Munier	0.80
Tea	0.10	Spaghetti	0.80	Crab	0.90
Coffee	0.10	Cream	0.13	Cream	0.12
Fruits	0.12	Coffee	0.10	Coffee	0.10
	¥2.82		¥2.63		¥2.52
Tip	0.28	Tip	0.26	Tip	0.25
Tax	0.57	Tax	0.53	Tax	0.51
	¥3.67		¥3.42		¥3.28

POWs were the last to receive it. Tsuneishi gave up on radio propaganda and no longer cared about inspiring Cousens. His treatment worsened progressively, such that when Iva smuggled food and medicine to Cousens and other POWs, they desperately needed it in a way that they had not in 1942. Regrettably, this deterioration in treatment was not brought out with any clarity at trial.

Figure 17.2. Wallace "Ted" Ince.
Courtesy of *San Francisco Chronicle.*

Wallace Ince (Figure 17.2),[24] the defense's second witness, had lost both his parents and had no living relatives in the United States except his grandmother.[25] Shortly after the end of the war, on August 29, 1945, the Army elevated Ince from captain to major with the Fifth Infantry Division and at the time of trial, he was a lieutenant colonel in the Infantry Reserve on active duty as a major.[26] Whether he realized the Department of Justice (DoJ) hoped to prosecute him for treason is unclear. According to FBI memos, "the decision to prosecute Ince was actually reached on October 22, 1948."[27] However, on September 16, 1949, as Iva's trial wound down, Justice informed the FBI that prosecutors DeWolfe, Hennessy, and Knapp

> have agreed that . . . they believe there is little chance for a verdict of guilty should Ince be indicted for treason. The Department believes that no decision regarding the Ince case should be made pending the determination of the Toguri case.[28]

If Ince had not considered the possibility of his own prosecution, Collins set him straight. Ince initially refused to appear for the defense, but Collins got hold of Ince's attorney and reminded him that if DeWolfe ever put Ince on trial, he would want Iva to testify for him. Therefore, according to Tetsujiro Nakamura, one of Collins' investigators,

He better cooperate with us in our defense or else. If he cooperated there will be ample ammunition for his defense in the event that he be prosecuted. That was the reason we were able to get Ince's testimony.[29]

Ince hated Japs and that included Iva Toguri. When Wayne Collins asked him to recall how he had to serve them as a POW, he replied that he was "beaten, starved, subjected to indignities." Like Cousens, Ince broke down recounting his story.[30] Cousens had rebounded after the war, but the experience scarred Ince. Cousens wrote Collins in 1949 that Ince had become mentally unbalanced, that he had apparently left his wife and child without support, and was drinking heavily.[31]

Still, Ince was a good witness for Iva. He confirmed several key defense points: that she read scripts that Cousens wrote, that many other women broadcast on *Zero Hour*, that she introduced music, that the POWs had agreed to sabotage the Japanese programs whenever possible, and that Iva smuggled them food and medicine. He denied the alleged broadcasts one by one but had to admit he no longer worked on *Zero Hour* when the statement about "loss of ships" would have been broadcast.

Like Cousens, his memories were often detailed. He recalled Iva specifically informed him of the recapture of the Philippines by the Allies "because she knew I was interested in the Philippines." If she sent him news in writing, she requested "that it should be destroyed, so it couldn't be traced back to her." He remembered exactly how Iva had told him about the fall of Saipan. "I had gone up to get some records for the prisoner of war program. She whispered to me that the news was good. Who did these people think they were, referring to the Japanese. I started to make a comment in return and she warned me to look out, because Ken Oki was in the room."[32]

Ince also recalled in detail how Iva's wool blanket saved POW Larry Quille. Quille's left arm was so severely infected the Japanese almost amputated it. The Japanese took away his thin blankets after five days even though he was freezing. Cousens pleaded with them to no avail, and Iva's donation saved his life. Ince remembered that he, not Cousens, smuggled it out of Radio Tokyo because he had on a raincoat whereas Cousens did not. These and dozens of other specific memories starkly contrasted with the memories of Mitsushio and Oki who seemed only to recall specific events when they related to the indictment.

According to the *Chronicle*, "Ince was a poised and impressive witness in tailored suntans decorated with three unit citations and the ribbons of Corregidor on his Eisenhower jacket."[33] Knapp cross-examined Ince in a milder fashion than he had Cousens. As a prosecutor, he had to discredit him to some extent, but Ince was an American and therefore had to be treated with respect. Knapp brought out Ince's distrust of Iva. On direct, Ince had testified, "She constantly referred to the Japanese as 'Japs,' which was a gross insult. She was aloof. She conducted herself much more freely in the presence of prisoners of war that she did in the presence of other Japanese." But under cross, he admitted he was against her inclusion in *Zero Hour*, that he never told her of the POWs' plan to sabotage programs, and that he never completely trusted her "or any other Japanese person at the studio." At one point Knapp himself referred to Iva as Japanese. Collins thundered, "I object to that on the ground that it is highly improper. There is no evidence whatsoever that the defendant is Japanese."[34] Roche overruled Collins' objection.

Collins may have prepared Ince for questions about food at the Dai Ichi Hotel because he defended himself more convincingly than Cousens. When Knapp presented Ince with his own signed receipts, Ince stated that the portions for POWs were smaller than for Japanese nationals. Furthermore, the rations at the Dai Ichi were only one-half to three-quarters of what they got at Bunka. "We actually had more in Bunka than we had at the Dai Ichi."[35] His weight, normally 175 pounds, had dropped to 128 by the end of the war.

However, FBI Agents Tillman and Dunn had interviewed Ince over several days prior to trial and he too had signed a statement for them. His stated: "It never occurred to me that she was unquestionably loyal to the United States since apparently of her own free will she had become engaged in Japanese propaganda broadcasts." "She never mentioned that any coercion or duress had been exercised by the Japanese in forcing her to take the job, nor did I see any coercion or duress." "Cousens, Reyes and I injected into our radio scripts 'double talk.' We did not at any time, as I now recall, attempt to insert 'double talk' or hidden messages into the scripts broadcast by Toguri because should she have made a complaint concerning the same our position at Radio Tokyo might have been endangered."[36] Knapp forced Ince to reaffirm these statements in court.

~

If Marshall Hoot was the best witness at the trial, the defense's third witness, Norman Reyes (Figure 17.3), was the worst.[37] The banner headline in the *San Francisco Chronicle* said it all: WITNESS ADMITS LYING AT TRIAL OF TOKYO ROSE.[38] Reyes' testimony not only brought disrepute upon himself, it tainted if not ruined the prior testimony of Cousens and Ince, and devastated the defense of Iva Toguri as a whole. Yet the terrible tragedy of Norman Reyes is that he probably answered more truthfully on the stand than anyone, including Iva herself, and his failing was not that he lied but that he was innocent in his goodness. His lack of sophistication prevented him from ever catching on to how the world of trials and lawyers and government agents really works.

Figure 17.3. Norman Reyes.
Courtesy of *San Francisco Chronicle.*

Wayne Collins had to call him. Reyes was the only person who was with the *Zero Hour* from its first broadcast to its last. Neither Cousens nor Ince could swear that Iva had never broadcast the "loss of ships" remark. Reyes could, and did. What Collins did not know, as any modern defense attorney would, was that the FBI had broken Reyes and that he had signed statements filled with inaccuracies.

Norman Reyes, who only wanted to help Iva, wound up damning her, in part because he was not only young but immature. He was the son of a Filipino father and American mother. His childhood in the Philippines had been sheltered. He was only 19 when he became a POW. At the time of the trial, he was 27 and still living with his mom. But the deeper reason may reside in his personality. Peter Rosegg, a reporter for the *Honolulu Star-Bulletin & Advertiser*, interviewed Reyes in 1976 when he was 54. The reporter noted, "Reyes' voice does not command; it soothes and agrees. His eyes beseech, asking for cooperation and understanding; they do not contradict. Reyes is a person who seeks to smooth things over."[39] Reyes' himself admitted people could easily influence him.[40] Reyes' ability to be influenced manifested itself early on. In 1945, he told the Army Counter-Intelligence Corps (CIC) that "Tsuneishi once called Toguri 'Tokyo Rose' and we in the office sometimes called her by that name. . . . Whenever we called her 'Tokyo Rose' she did not take kindly to the appellation."[41] This cannot be true; at least two dozen witnesses swore the name was generally unknown and not applied to Iva.

Trial witnesses are most believable when they exhibit confidence and certainty, even though their testimony may actually be inaccurate. Reyes couldn't remember the month and year of certain events. For example, when DeWolfe asked him about Iva's broadcasts during the first week of July 1945, Reyes answered that he couldn't remember what she said or even whether he was at the studio that week. Reyes, testifying in 1949, could not of course be confident about Iva's words during the first week of July four years previous.[42] But most people, were they in Reyes' position and believed Iva had never broadcast such material, would be shrewd enough to obfuscate. They would answer, "Yes, I'm confident I was at the studio and that she broadcast nothing like what you claim, Mr. DeWolfe." They would realize DeWolfe couldn't offer evidence to the contrary. But Reyes wasn't that smart. He couldn't remember exactly who said what or even if he was at the station. He told the truth. Reyes, therefore, lacked credibility.

On direct examination, he did fine. He elucidated events that previously had not made much sense. Reyes explained how Iva had been able to routinely haul food into Radio Tokyo and how the POWs could smuggle it back into Bunka without being noticed, even in the summertime when no one wore coats:

> It would be left lying in a corner of the room, and when Ince came in, Iva would point to which [bag] he was supposed to pick up. On days he could pick it up and take it out, he would. Cer-

tain days he couldn't because someone was along that was particularly meticulous about searching them. Items came in small enough quantities to be put in a small metal box, about 5" by 4" by 3" deep. Butter and peanuts because of the oil content. Rice, oats, eggs. Fish liver oil and bran tablets. Never sugar but a salty bean paste. Japanese cigarettes called Kinshi.[43]

He added that the POWs needed the food because their Japanese guards stole their rations and forced them to live on supplements. "The supplements were small bits of pickled vegetable or relish, and occasional thin soup, and they certainly were not enough to sustain life."[44]

Cousens and Ince swore under oath that Iva always referred to the Japanese as "Japs."[45] They obviously hoped this would establish her in the eyes of the jury as "one of us and not one of them." Their testimony rings false. Iva's father and mother were "Japs." She knew even as a young woman from her experience in the States that it was a racist term and, as Ince put it, a gross insult. Reyes was less guileful but more honest. He admitted she sometimes said Japs but "most of the time it was 'these people.'"[46]

Reyes offered other interesting information. Iva had asked him about the treatment of the Filipino people, and he had informed her that Japanese officers kicked and stomped even little children in the Philippines when they failed to bow properly. Reyes told Iva the Japanese beat a friend to death with an iron bar in front of his friend's bride of nine days, and they whipped another man with a steel wire and he died in agony several days later. Reyes also told the court he had heard a man using the pseudonym "Reginald Hollingsworth" and three women broadcast "pernicious propaganda" in the Tokyo Rose style on *German Hour*.[47] When people at the station learned about Tokyo Rose, and gossip about who she might be started to swirl, Reyes personally put into one of Iva's scripts, "This is Orphan Ann, your Orphan Ann. Don't confuse me with anybody else." He summed up his trust of Iva, "I would have put my life in her hands."[48]

For cross-examination, Thomas DeWolfe relieved James Knapp so that the pleasure of tearing Reyes to pieces would be entirely his. Russell Warren Howe, with journalistic panache, refers to Reyes as "the colored witness."[49] DeWolfe played the race card almost immediately.

> *DeWolfe*: I believe your mother is a white lady, an American lady?
> *Reyes*: She is American.
> *DeWolfe*: And your father is a Filipino.
> *Reyes*: He is.
> *DeWolfe*: Are you married, Norman?
> *Reyes*: I am, sir.
> *DeWolfe*: Is your wife a Filipino girl?
> *Reyes*: No, sir.
> *DeWolfe*: What is she?
> *Reyes*: American, sir.
> *DeWolfe*: She is a Japanese nisei, isn't she?
> *Reyes*: Yes, a nisei.[50]

Having established the intermingling of the races in Reyes' family, DeWolfe next played the card against Ince. "Did he [Ince] marry a Filipino woman?" Collins objected strenuously, stating that "it is a deliberate attempt to prejudice this jury against witnesses." Even Judge Roche wondered, "What relation would that have to any issues in this case?" DeWolfe answered, "Well, it would have some bearing on the witnesses and their relation, and so on."[51] For that feeble reason, Roche allowed the answer. Later, on redirect, Collins asked Reyes if it wasn't true that Ince's wife and children lived in the Philippines, which the Japanese controlled during the war. With shocking disingenuousness, Judge Roche would not allow Reyes to answer, sustaining DeWolfe's objection that this information was irrelevant to any issues in the case.

DeWolfe's cross-examination was vicious. He tortured Reyes over his failure to remember minor details.

> *DeWolfe*: Who interviewed you in Nashville?
> *Reyes*: An agent of the FBI.
> *DeWolfe*: What is his name?
> *Reyes*: His name is Tipton.
> *DeWolfe*: Are you sure of that name?
> *Reyes*: It could be Tipton or Tupton.
> *DeWolfe*: It is either Tipton or Tupton. You are positive of that?
> *Reyes*: Yes, sir.
> *DeWolfe*: You are sure of that?

Reyes: Yes, sir.
DeWolfe: What is his first name?
Reyes: I do not know what his first name is.[52]

Then after grilling him for several minutes over exact times and dates of his interviews,

DeWolfe: Isn't it a matter of fact that the agent's name is Winfred, W-i-n-f-r-e-d, E. Hopton, H-o-p-t-o-n?
Reyes: It may be, sir.
DeWolfe: But you were sure it was Tipton or Tupton, right? You were sure and so testified, didn't you?[53]

Because the hapless Reyes had confused the names of interrogators Tillman and Hopton and come up with Tipton, DeWolfe made him out to be a scurrilous liar. Over Collins' objections, this sort of baiting went on for days.

The crux of the destruction of Norman Reyes lay in DeWolfe's possession of Reyes' signed statements for the FBI. As DeWolfe here sets him up, note his style of faux intimacy and repetition, as though he were questioning an unruly child:

DeWolfe: You know me, Norman?
Reyes: I do.
DeWolfe: You have told here the truth? Do you understand the question?
Reyes: Yes, sir.
DeWolfe: You told nothing but the truth, Norman, is that right? Has everything that you have testified to been truthful?
Reyes: To the best of my knowledge, sir, yes.
DeWolfe: Everything you have testified to, Norman, you are sure is the truth, right?
Reyes: To the best of my knowledge and belief, yes, sir.
DeWolfe: You know whether it is truthful or not, don't you?
Reyes: Yes, sir.
DeWolfe: And you have, haven't you?
Reyes: I have, sir.
DeWolfe: You have told the truth about the case in court under oath, haven't you?
Reyes: Yes.

> *DeWolfe*: And you told the truth about the case to special agents of the Federal Bureau of Investigation in Nashville, Tennessee, Norman, right?
> *Reyes*: Yes.
> *DeWolfe*: And you told the truth about the case, Norman, to special agents in San Francisco, California, right?
> *Reyes*: Yes.
> *DeWolfe*: The whole truth and nothing but the truth you told to agents Dunn and Tillman in San Francisco, right?
> *Reyes*: Yes, I did.[54]

From Reyes' perspective, he had told the agents the truth. They just hadn't written it down the way he said it. Reyes explained—on redirect, too late—that the agents had told him not to worry about how he said things; he could straighten them out later. "And I was told that if I did not see a thing happen, the best I could do was to say it did not happen. If I could not recall the date of the thing, I couldn't say that particular thing had taken place." The agents called his story something "rather vulgar," put words in his mouth, and "after all the arguing and shouting was over, I do not know what I finally agreed to, but this appeared in the written statement and I signed it."[55]

Reyes claimed he returned for more interrogations when the FBI summoned him out of fear. His parents had divorced, and he wanted to live with his mother in the United States. He even hoped to become an American citizen. But he was on a student visa and vulnerable to deportation. Dunn told him, "If you want to go over to the other side [the prosecution initially had Reyes as a witness], all right. I want you to know we have got a lot of stuff on you, and I will pass this on to my CIC friends in the Philippines, and you won't like it a bit."[56] He also feared that he too would be prosecuted.

> I was told I was in a highly questionable position, and nobody was going to worry about me. And I saw these people here building up a case of treason against Iva Toguri, which consisted of overt acts, overt acts, and more overt acts. And I was under the opinion, therefore, the firm opinion, that if overt acts made a treason case, certainly I, who had been working at Radio Tokyo, was as open as the defendant to the charge of treasonable collaboration with the enemy.

I signed to get rid of these people. I had had enough of it. I would sign anything to get out from under. Secondly, I was afraid. I was afraid of these two men, the atmosphere under which the questioning was conducted and of my own status.[57]

Reyes signed his various FBI statements not just with his name but with a paragraph in his own handwriting stating that "I have read the above statement and it is true to the best of my knowledge and belief."[58] His statements in Nashville to Agent Hopton were generally accurate; Hopton judiciously transcribed what Reyes told him. His statements to Tillman and Dunn, however, manifested their usual handiwork. To Hopton, Reyes said, correctly, that the Japanese had assigned Iva to the *Zero Hour* in December 1943. To Tillman and Dunn, he said, according to them, "I recall the time in August 1943, when she was first introduced to me as the woman who was to participate in the *Zero Hour* program." This was a mistake almost as bad as Iva not remembering her wedding anniversary. Everybody—the Japanese officials, Cousens, Ince, Iva, and certainly Reyes—knew *Zero Hour* had no woman associated with it until late 1943. Everybody, that is, except Tillman and Dunn. DeWolfe relied on their document almost exclusively. Some of the damaging statements to which Reyes signed his name before Tillman and Dunn included:[59]

1. "I did not trust [Iva], having gained the impression she was pro-Japanese."
2. "Toguri did not express to me any fear she had of the Japanese Government or people who supervised her work. I knew of no threats, duress, or coercion that was exercised or directed to influence her."
3. "I recall a conversation in which she stated to me that she was afraid of what might happen to her after the war because she was broadcasting Japanese propaganda."
4. "[Cousens] believed that the political problems of Asia could only be solved through the domination of this territory by a benevolent Japan. This coincided with the Japanese propaganda idea of the greater East Asia co-prosperity sphere. It is my belief that Major Cousens was induced to broadcast propaganda because he thought he would have a voice in explaining this idea to listeners of Radio Tokyo."

5. "With reference to Ince, I wish to state that never in my presence were any overt or implied threats of torture or death made to him. On the contrary, during the time that we were at Radio Tokyo the influence was one of inducements of better living quarters and more freedom."

6. "We were treated with courtesy and consideration by the officials of Radio Tokyo."

Norman Reyes was on the witness stand for four days, much of it being questioned by DeWolfe. A pattern quickly emerged. DeWolfe would ask him if such-and-such were true. Reyes would say no. DeWolfe would then read him his sworn statement to Dunn and Tillman stating exactly that. Reyes would try to explain himself without success. For example,

> *DeWolfe*: "Toguri did not at any time express to me any fear she had of the Japanese government or people who supervised her work." Is that statement true or false?
> *Reyes*: That statement is inaccurate, sir.
> *DeWolfe*: It is not true, is it?
> *Reyes*: At the time I made that statement, that was the—
> *DeWolfe*: It is not true, is it, Witness Reyes?
> *Reyes*: I answered the question. That statement is true, and I understand I am given the privilege of adding an explanation.
> *Court*: You may explain it.
> *Reyes*: I said many times to these two gentlemen of the FBI that I had heard the defendant say that she was afraid of the Japanese Army; and I was asked again and again if I could recall specific instances when she did say this, who was there, and at the time of this questioning and under the conditions and the atmosphere of this questioning, I could not recall. This was the language put into the statement not by myself, and I signed that statement.[60]

No longer addressed as "Norman," now he was "Witness Reyes."

Eventually Judge Roche could stand it no longer and took over the questioning of Reyes himself.

> *Roche*: Give me that exhibit. Is that your signature on there?
> *Reyes*: Yes, that is.
> *Roche*: Is that your writing?
> *Reyes*: That is, sir.

Roche: Read it. Read it to the jury so they may hear it.

Reyes: "I have read the above statement consisting of four pages and it is true to the best of my knowledge and belief."

Roche: And you signed that?

Reyes: I did sign it, sir.

Roche: Well, what does that indicate to you, that statement that you just read?

Reyes: It indicates what it says, sir, that I had read the statement and considered it at the time I signed to be true to the best of my knowledge and belief.[61]

Roche allowed DeWolfe to pummel Reyes a little longer before throwing out his testimony in its entirety.

Norman Reyes apologized to Iva afterward. Decades later he confessed, "I wish I had been smarter then. I should have been much more direct and repudiated the statement I made to the FBI. I should have said it was a lie and proceeded to tell the truth. It was a common situation in which the non-white feels inferior."[62] He did not participate in the effort to gain Iva a pardon. "I have never ceased to be haunted by the feeling that I did Wayne and Iva a disservice through my bad performance on the stand. I still seek forgiveness, and am convinced that the best thing I can do now—in his memory and her cause—is to remain silent."[63]

~

After Cousens, Ince, and Reyes, the defense introduced a grab bag of witnesses, including ex-Radio Tokyo employees and POWs, amateur shortwave listeners in the United States, and GI fans of *Zero Hour*. Many lived in the San Francisco area; those far away had to testify through depositions. As the *Chronicle* noted, "These are volunteer witnesses who are motivated simply by good citizenship. The defense has no investigation staff or money. Collins, Attorneys Theodore Tamba and George Olshausen are defending Iva D'Aquino without pay. They make the best they can of their volunteers."[64]

Generals Willoughby and Eichelberger did not volunteer as witnesses. As head of Intelligence, Willoughby knew firsthand the results of the CIC investigation but he chose to remain in Tokyo to work on MacArthur's reminiscences.[65] When Collins asked Eichelberger to appear as a witness for the defense, Tamba later recalled,

"This brave American General advises Mr. Collins that he has no recollection of either the incident of the records dropped from the bomber or having his picture taken with her."[66]

The Court did not treat the witnesses who did have the courage to testify on behalf of Tokyo Rose kindly. The Norman Reyes' testimony had hardened the heart of Judge Roche. Whereas previously he had allowed the defense a modest amount of leeway, now he cracked down, barring any testimony that did not directly and immediately concern Iva Toguri. Even the newspaper reporters noticed it.[67] The result was that defense witnesses would appear and disappear having testified to absolutely nothing, their every answer ruled inadmissible.

His rulings greatly diminished the testimony of former POWs anxious to explain that the image painted by the prosecution, that prisoners dined at swanky hotels, lived the good life at Bunka, and skipped to work at Radio Tokyo, was bogus. Bunka's chief cook, Nicolaas Schenck, had testified, via deposition, that the Japanese fed prisoners chicken feed and that he personally converted many dogs and cats into stew. Schenk also had witnessed Ince fall to his knees from lack of food, and that as punishment, Lieutenant Hamamoto, the Bunka commandant, beat him into unconsciousness.[68] Hamamoto knocked Schenk himself out on another occasion. Schenk's assistant, Kenneth Parkyns, had traveled from Australia with his own stories of starvation and beatings. Buck Henshaw wanted to testify they all received war news from Iva via Ince. POWs Cox and Kalbfleish tried to tell their stories of forced broadcasts and brutality. DeWolfe objected that none of them was on *Zero Hour* and therefore their testimony had nothing to do with the defendant. Roche sustained his objections. The *Chronicle* summed up, "About one-fourth or less got into the record, and the defense was particularly deprived of solid testimony to the brutalities handed out to prisoners of war who were ordered to broadcast on Radio Tokyo."[69]

The amateur shortwave monitors who volunteered to testify were genuine heroes. Throughout the war, they had listened to Japanese radio for hours and hours every day without pay in the hope of hearing POW messages. They recorded or transcribed any they heard, located the family of the serviceman, and at their own expense forwarded the message by mail or played a recording of it by long-distance telephone. Adam Welker and Mae Hagedorn each communicated as many as 4,000 such messages to families. But neither listened to *Zero Hour* because it aired at 1:00 AM on the West Coast. Therefore, Judge Roche ruled almost all of their testimony inadmissible. Collins tried to ask Hagedorn about an entry in her log dated July 25, 1943, in which she noted that "Tokyo Rose" made a specific news broadcast and that she announced her name as "Miss Ruth Somebody."[70] DeWolfe objected, and the judge did not allow her to answer.

Many GIs came to support Iva—Collins told the press more than 50 veterans had contacted him[71]—but they were ineffective witnesses. Several testified that they enjoyed *Zero Hour*, often in the company of hundreds of other servicemen. Of course this didn't prove the program did not contain propaganda, only that they didn't notice it or were immune. Others denied ever hearing the various statements attributed to Orphan Ann. But a prosecution GI testifying that he heard Ann make a particular statement was far more powerful than a defense GI testifying he never did, because the second GI might not have been listening that day. DeWolfe did not object to such testimony, but on cross he would ask questions like, "Did you ever hear Ann call GIs boneheads?" Usually they said no, but jurors had already heard Iva as Orphan Ann use this term in the government's recordings. The servicemen often failed to recognize other actual statements by her as well.

The FBI had tracked down the defense's GI witnesses and pressured most of them into making statements that DeWolfe exploited on cross-examination. Those who had refused, DeWolfe attacked with the suggestion that they had something to hide from authorities:

> *DeWolfe*: Didn't you tell Agent Christopherson on 27 or 28 April, 1949, that you were going to keep your mouth shut on the instruction of the defense attorneys?
> *Witness*: I did not speak ten words to that man, never, never in my lifetime.
> *DeWolfe*: Why didn't you?
> *Witness*: Because I was asked not to.
> *DeWolfe*: Do you do everything that some lawyer asks you to?
> *Witness*: If it is proper, yes.
> *DeWolfe*: Why were you afraid to talk to him?
> *Witness*: I am not afraid to talk to anyone.
> *DeWolfe*: Why didn't you talk to him?

Witness: Because that is my personal business.

DeWolfe: That is your personal business. Are you still in the Naval Reserve?

Witness: Yes, sir.

DeWolfe: I ask you again, why didn't you talk to the representative of the United States government?

Witness: I explained to him, "I have instructions from her attorney not to make a statement to the FBI."

DeWolfe: Because it was your own business, and you did not want to talk to anybody but the defense attorney, is that right?

Witness: That is correct, yes.

DeWolfe: Did you have anything to conceal from a government representative?

Witness: No, sir.[72]

One pleasant surprise for the defense was the appearance of Nisei Ruth Matsunaga. Matsunaga introduced records on the *German Hour*, the supposed source for many of the taunts associated with Tokyo Rose. Matsunaga explained how the Japanese forced her to work as a torpedo painter and later as a broadcaster. Not only did Matsunaga back up previous testimony, she also bore a striking resemblance to Iva. Same height, same broad nose, same lips—Ruth Matsunaga looked more like Iva than either of her two biological sisters. The defense contended that some of the prosecution witnesses who identified Iva broadcasting had in fact seen Matsunaga. Although the two women barely knew each other during the war, Iva greeted her warmly after her testimony and, according to reporters, smiled for the first time.[73]

~

Although Iva Toguri liked to view herself as a stoic who simply accepted what cannot be helped, in truth her trial for treason scarred her. The stress of the months-long trial, of watching witnesses lie, or tell the truth and be attacked for it, all the while worrying that she would be incarcerated once again, only to have her fears come true—this trauma affected her view of the world, of who were friends and who were enemies, and sabotaged her memories of what had happened to her.

During my interviews with Iva in 1987, I asked her what became of her young traveling companion, Chiyeko Ito. Iva answered that Chiyeko simply disappeared. "She must have had her good reasons never to have come forward. It's ironic that her younger sister who was not in Japan, who was here, was someone very much like myself, very outspoken. She's the one that backed me up. I think she went right to the FBI. I know she went to some branch of the government, and she just blew her stack. But Chiyeko did not come forward at all." I further inquired, "So you have really never heard from her since the war?" "No."

Given the specificity of Iva's memories of the sister's defiant attitude, it may come as a surprise to readers that Chiyeko Ito testified in person at Iva's trial for the defense. Iva obviously saw Chiyeko testify. DeWolfe specifically quizzed Iva about Chiyeko's testimony.

> *DeWolfe*: I am not asking you what you knew, Mrs. D'Aquino. I did not ask you that. I just asked you what you told Chiyeko Ito.
>
> *Iva*: I didn't tell her anything about my citizenship status [as Portuguese after Iva's marriage to Phil].
>
> *DeWolfe*: You heard her testify here that you did tell her that, didn't you?
>
> *Iva*: Yes.
>
> *DeWolfe*: She was in error, wasn't she?
>
> *Iva*: Her recollection was wrong.
>
> *DeWolfe*: Her recollection was wrong under oath?
>
> *Iva*: That is correct.[74]

Yet in 1987 Iva only remembered her former friend as another fainthearted deserter.[75]

In any case, Chiyeko Ito was a poor witness in the same way Mitsushio and Oki were poor witnesses. She testified she had seen Iva one to three times a week in Japan, yet almost the only thing she could recall of their meetings was that Iva encouraged her to maintain her U.S. citizenship. Even when Wayne Collins asked about conversations in 1945, she could only remember discussions of citizenship. This seems a highly unlikely topic of conversation. If Chiyeko hadn't renounced by 1945, she was not going to renounce. The FBI also waylaid Chiyeko prior to the trial but she gave them very little in her statement. So Chiyeko Ito was a positive if unimpressive witness.

Phil D'Aquino was the next-to-last defense witness, appearing before Iva herself. At the time of the trial, he operated a linotype for Tai Han Printing Company. The *Chronicle* described him as "self-effacing."[76] He came across as an extremely well-mannered, soft-spoken individual, not the combative firebrand who lost his temper and got into fistfights. He supported Iva's version of events insofar as he knew them personally, but one assumes the jury discounted his testimony because he was the defendant's husband.

DeWolfe immediately established that he was of mixed race but did little to damage him on cross. DeWolfe tried to turn Iva's generosity toward the POWs on its head by asking Phil if he and Iva had plenty of money, so much money that they could afford to give things away. DeWolfe also brought out that Phil could walk right in to Radio Tokyo to court his wife, which implied the place had no guards, but Wayne Collins developed on redirect that Phil had access because he wore a Domei News Agency badge. The one minor victory for DeWolfe was Phil's admission that Iva had told him she had never been ill-treated by the Japanese police.

∽

Iva Toguri followed her husband to the stand. Although contemporary news accounts describe it as "a surprising, dramatic move by the defense," Iva said all three of her lawyers agreed she should testify. She began her direct testimony on September 9, 1949, a Wednesday, and continued all day Thursday and Friday. She impressed reporters. The *Examiner* said her "answers were clear, firm and decisive. She sounded as though she was saying what she meant and meaning what she said." The *Chronicle* also assessed her testimony positively: "It is a factual, believable story that has been told before."[77]

In 1987, Iva remembered herself as being considerably braver than she had in fact been. "My father was very worried that I would collapse but I didn't." Did she ever feel on the verge of tears? "NOPE! Why would I—if I'd lived my life up until then with a bunch of lies and concocted stories?" In reality, by Friday Iva had lost control of her emotions. "It was a different Tokyo Rose on the witness stand, a girl who wept, whose radio-trained voice stumbled and dropped to a whisper."[78] Twice, the *Chronicle* reported, she burst into tears, once when she remembered Ince being led away, she assumed to be executed, and the other, when Radio Tokyo employee David Huga demanded that she cooperate with the Army and she refused. Again, no newspaper account indicated the jury had the slightest reaction to Iva's tears.

Although Iva had no previous legal training, after two months of observing witnesses and listening to objections overruled and sustained, Iva grasped how a courtroom worked. As a result, when she herself took the stand, she occasionally lied in order to protect the truth. This paradoxical expression is intended to distinguish Iva's fibs and embellishments from the outright falsehoods of various prosecution witnesses.

Here are a few examples of her testimony, what she meant by the testimony, and what the facts were:

1. Testimony: "I had a Christmas tree every year in Japan."[79] Translation: I am neither a Shintoist nor a worshiper of the Emperor but a Christian. Fact: She had a tree only once, in 1944.

2. Testimony: Iva claimed on the stand that work at Radio Tokyo interested her only because it allowed her to befriend the POWs. She denied that she preferred the shorter hours and better pay to her Domei job.[80] Translation: The truth is I did not serve Japanese interests out of a desire for self-advancement, money, or an easy life. Fact: Iva did enjoy her job, briefly had hopes for turning it into a career, needed the extra pay for food, and loved the short hours because it allowed her to work at the Danish legation and still have time to scrounge. She did admit she liked the shorter hours under cross, and also that she asked Mitsushio for a raise and got it.[81]

3. Testimony: "Immediately upon my arrival at Yokohama prison, the jailers asked me to give them an autograph. I said I wasn't going to sign anything, because I didn't know what it was all about. Mr. Eisenhart was one of the first to approach me. He said, 'Well, you will change your mind in a few days.' The jailers kept turning the lights on and off, on and off, every night for six solid nights. I hadn't slept. I signed to put a stop to that."[82] Translation: I did not confess to being Tokyo Rose. Fact: Maybe the jail had electrical problems and maybe the lights flashed. Maybe not. Iva wasn't the only prisoner in her cell block, and it's hard to imagine the prison commander putting up with a week's

worth of outcries from other inmates just so Corporal Eisenhart could have an autograph. Soldiers did not obtain Iva's myriad signatures through sleep deprivation. She later admitted in court that she signed many "Tokyo Rose" autographs because the GIs "asked me, said it was a good gesture, so I did it."[83]

These examples are straightforward. Iva's veracity is sometimes more difficult to assess, as in this key testimony:

> I found [three *kempei*] in my room when I came back from work. They had searched my room and the room was all upset. They had searched through my books and trunks, they had left the books open, and I asked them, I couldn't speak to them very well, but I asked them what was the investigation for. They said, "Oh, we are looking for English matter, things written in English." They said there had better be nothing against the Japanese government or I would be sorry.[84]

Readers will recall that in my description of these events in chapter 7, Iva was not present. Her friend Kimi, the maid at the boarding house, witnessed the *kempei* search, asked the agents what they wanted, straightened up Iva's room afterward, and then told Iva what had happened when Iva got home from work.

In my interviews, I asked Iva about this incident somewhat obliquely. I didn't quote her sworn trial testimony, but instead inquired,

> *Q*: My records show the *kempeitai* searched your room for English materials. Do you have a recollection of being searched? Did they turn your place upside down?
> *Iva*: No, they didn't turn my place upside down. I found out from one of the ladies that worked at the place.
> *Q*: So they came in when you weren't there?
> *Iva*: No, I wasn't there.

I knew about Iva's vivid description of the event at the trial, so I later returned to the subject and asked more vaguely,

> *Q*: I know they [unspecified whether *kempeitai* or some other police unit] went in at one point and looked for English materials. Was there ever a time when they turned things upside down?

> *Iva*: No, no. It's kind of strange. After I had this meeting with the police relative to my cooperating [to spy on the Soviets], things seemed to have eased up even though I didn't do a thing.

These answers are some 40 years after the fact. If she failed to remember Chiyeko Ito, perhaps she misremembered this as well. However, this incident is of a different emotional order. It is not credible that Iva could have personally confronted the dreaded *kempeitai* and then forgotten not only that they tossed her bedroom but that she was even present to witness it. She might forget one trial witness out of 40, but not 3 military policemen ransacking her belongings.

In Iva's trial testimony, she paused to note, "I couldn't speak to them very well." It's as though she recognized a hole in her story as she told it, and did a quick patch. Iva testified that she could not understand Tsuneishi at his luncheon in 1945. The 1943 *kempeitai* visit happened when her grasp of Japanese was too infirm for her to converse with them about anti-Japanese materials.[85]

My guess is that Iva twice denied in 1987 that she found her room turned upside down because she never saw it that way. Kimi cleaned it up before Iva got home. Iva knew with certainty that Kimi had told her the truth, that the *kempeitai* had searched her room. But during the trial she had watched DeWolfe time and time again prevent defense testimony, and she realized that if she said she heard about the *kempeitai* search from the maid, Judge Roche would rule the story inadmissible as hearsay. So she lied to protect the truth.[86]

After the weekend break, DeWolfe cross-examined Iva for three more days. One focus of DeWolfe's questioning was citizenship. In May 1947, when applying for repatriation to the United States, Iva had sworn she had never been naturalized by any foreign country. In May 1949, as directed by Wayne Collins, she swore that when she married Phil in 1945, she "was formally naturalized as a Portuguese national by said marriage."[87] DeWolfe asked, "Which statement under oath is true?" He asked essentially this same question for hours. Had Collins anticipated that DeWolfe would pursue this issue, he no doubt would have prepared Iva better than he did. But Judge Roche had sustained all of DeWolfe's objections to testimony from Iva as to her opinion on legal matters such as whether she had been denied the right to a speedy trial and the right to counsel. When Collins objected to DeWolfe's questions about the legal status of her citizenship—"I submit, if your honor please, that is purely argumentative. It is a simple question of law"—he expected to be sustained. Instead Judge Roche responded, "It is an important question in this case, and he has the right to cross-examine this witness within any reasonable limit, as I have given you the widest latitude on all these matters. The objection is overruled. She may answer."[88] In trying to explain why she attested to contradictory statements, Iva stumbled.

Her confusion was understandable. She traveled to Japan as an American. When she married, the Portuguese consul told her she was Portuguese. In Sugamo Prison, the Army told her she was Japanese. When she applied for a passport after prison, the American consul told her she was stateless. During her two-day interrogation by Frederick Tillman, she stated her belief that when she was in grade school, her mother "caused me to be expatriated from my Japanese nationality."[89] In response, Tillman opined that she had dual citizenship. For strategic reasons, Wayne Collins had her affirm that she was Portuguese. Iva signed the various documents in good conscience, but she couldn't be sure of her true status. Eventually, she developed this history for the record, but it came only after hours of apparent dissembling. Collins' use-every-possible-defense gambit backfired on the issue of Iva's citizenship. DeWolfe made significant progress in painting Iva as duplicitous, prepared to lie under oath, and willing to discard her American citizenship when it served her self-interest.

Another difficulty that Iva faced was a poor decision by Judge Roche about the limits of her answers:

> *DeWolfe*: Answer that yes or no, Mrs. D'Aquino, and then explain.
>
> *Collins*: Just a moment, Mrs. D'Aquino. You do not take your instructions from Mr. DeWolfe. We ask for a Court ruling on that, whether a witness has to answer yes or no.
>
> *Court*: He may propound a question to a witness and limit himself [sic] to a yes or no answer and give her a full opportunity to explain the answer.[90]

This was a formula for mischief. On the question of citizenship, for example, DeWolfe asked, "You did not state in 1947 that you were not Portuguese, did you?"[91] Say what? Try to answer that yes or no! Following this question, DeWolfe asked Iva seven times in a row if she found his questions difficult to understand. He had asked Norman Reyes the same, and obviously wanted jurors to view Iva and Reyes as birds of a feather. He concluded the series with Iva by sarcastically inquiring, "How much schooling have you had?"[92] DeWolfe took full advantage of Iva's statement to Tillman that her mother had expatriated her. "Did you ever regain your Japanese nationality since 1932?" How could Iva answer yes or no? If she answered yes, it meant she had regained her Japanese nationality. If she answered no, it meant she was originally Japanese but lost her citizenship in that country in 1932. No amount of explaining could possibly undo the confusion answering yes or no would create. DeWolfe, like most lawyers, was an expert in formulating such "Are you still beating your wife?" questions.

As with all witnesses who had been foolish enough to make sworn statements to the FBI, DeWolfe attacked Iva for her "admissions" to Agent Frederick Tillman in 1946. DeWolfe began by having her affirm that she made the statement voluntarily, read it, signed it, and, most important, he got Iva to say that it was true. This was a major mistake. In the statement she accepted Tillman's assertion, "I knew that the 'Zero Hour' was Japanese propaganda for the purpose of lowering the morale of the Allied troops. I knew all of their programs were propaganda."[93] For her to broadcast on such a program, unless she was under duress, amounted to an admission of treason.

Whether Iva herself believed she broadcast propaganda would seem an eminently predictable subject of cross-examination, but Collins apparently did not prepare Iva for it. She began her explanation of the "true" statement above by claiming that the Japanese purpose was to lower morale but not to undermine it.[94] DeWolfe didn't buy that distinction for an instant:

DeWolfe: "I knew all their programs were propaganda." You knew that, didn't you, Mrs. D'Aquino?
Iva: I am afraid those are not my words, but if it is in the statement —

> *DeWolfe*: Those are not your words. It is your signature, isn't it?
> *Iva*: Yes.
> *DeWolfe*: You read it over?
> *Iva*: Yes.
> *DeWolfe*: You certified it to be true?
> *Iva*: That is correct.
> *DeWolfe*: And it is true, isn't it?
> *Iva*: That is correct.
> *DeWolfe*: You voluntarily made that statement, didn't you?
> *Iva*: Yes, I had no choice.
> *DeWolfe*: You knew the purpose of the "Zero Hour" program was the demoralization of American troops, didn't you?
> *Iva*: I can't say yes or no to that exact statement, no.
> *DeWolfe*: You can't say yes to that?
> *Iva*: No.
> *DeWolfe*: Can you say no to that, Mrs. D'Aquino?
> *Iva*: No, I think I can't say no either.
> *DeWolfe*: You can't say no either. Let me ask you again: you can't say that you knew that the purpose of the "Zero Hour" program was the demoralization of American troops?
> *Iva*: It was the Japanese purpose, yes.
> *DeWolfe*: And you knew that the purpose of the "Zero Hour" was to undermine the morale of American troops?[95]

At this point Collins objected—one hopes, given his own conduct, with some small sense of irony—that the question had been asked and answered at least four times and that it was repetitious. Judge Roche replied, no doubt sincerely, "I do not recall it being asked."

Iva took the position that her part of the program simply provided entertainment.

> *DeWolfe*: You did not think the Japanese were paying you to get up and entertain American troops, did you?
> *Iva*: That is what they were doing.
> *DeWolfe*: That's what they were doing. You honestly and sincerely thought the Japanese were paying you money to entertain American troops, is that right?
> *Iva*: No, that is not right.
> *DeWolfe*: You didn't think the Japanese militarists were so gracious that they wanted you to make the American soldiers have a happy half hour or so, did you?

> *Iva*: I was working at the Radio Tokyo as a typist—
> *DeWolfe*: Did you think that?
> *Iva*: I do not know what you mean by that statement.[96]

DeWolfe capped off his cross-examination on the topic of knowingly broadcasting propaganda,

> *DeWolfe*: Mr. Cousens or Mr. Ince never told you directly or positively that they were trying to defeat the Japanese purpose of the program, did they, Mrs. D'Aquino?
> *Iva*: That's correct, they did not tell me positively or directly, no. But they did say it was serving their purpose, because it was an entertainment program.[97]

One could equally well say it served the Japanese purpose, which was to produce an entertaining program that drew listeners so that they could be subjected to propaganda.

The effect of this testimony was to give tremendous importance to the defense of duress. Unfortunately, Iva admitted in her Tillman statement and under DeWolfe's questioning that she had never been jailed or ill-treated by the Japanese police, never assaulted, or beaten, or whipped. She also testified, "Mr. Tillman asked me if there was any gun held against me or whether I was beaten to broadcast. I told him no. And he said, 'Well, there were not threats.'" Iva agreed there were no physical threats, but Tillman crafted her statement to read, "No pressure was put on me by Cousens, Ince, the Japanese or other persons to force me to take the job and no one threatened me if I did not take the job or continue in it."[98]

> *DeWolfe*: You told him there were no threats made against you to force you to take the job to broadcast?
> *Iva*: Yes, as a result of his conversation, yes.
> *DeWolfe*: You told him the Japanese nor any other person never made any kind of threat to make you continue in your work, didn't you?
> *Iva*: That is right; physical threats.
> *DeWolfe*: You did not say physical, did you?
> *Iva*: I told Mr. Tillman, yes.
> *DeWolfe*: You did not put it in your statement when you had a chance to correct it, did you?

> *Iva*: I was pretty tired when I signed that statement.
> *DeWolfe*: I see. You were tired. You read it all over. You were not too tired to do that, were you, Mrs. D'Aquino?
> *Iva*: That is right, I read it.
> *DeWolfe*: But you say you were threatened to take the job and threatened so that you had to continue in it, is that right?
> *Iva*: No, no, no, that is not correct.[99]

Again Iva flailed while trying to explain how her signed statement was true, but also untrue. She further admitted to DeWolfe that she had told Clark Lee "I thought I was doing wrong because I did not have enough gumption to go against army orders."[100] This was also a mistake. It implied she only had to show gumption and she could have escaped the Japanese Army's wrath. However, Iva did point out what had happened to her cousin, though she wisely didn't mention his communist beliefs. She also mentioned what the POWs had told her, even to what she had witnessed herself: Namely, that Ince had refused to broadcast something, and as a result had been punched and dragged away. Of course, none of this happened to *her*.

The subject of duress in time of war will be further explored in the next chapter. Norman Reyes gave the best description of his and Iva's position:

> Consider what it was like to live in [World War II Japan]. Escape was futile for a foreigner. Where could we have gone among the Japanese millions? You must make accommodations with life, accommodations with everything. We were handicapped by our own fear. We believed the stories of atrocities and death.[101]

Reyes might have more accurately said, "We knew the stories of atrocities and death were true."

Finally, DeWolfe wanted to hang at least one Overt Act (OA) around Iva's neck. He selected OA VI, the "loss of ships" broadcast. OA VI was the most substantive charge, and not only Mitsushio and Oki but also Satoshi Nakamura, the singer and part-time reader of the news, claimed they had witnessed it.[102] On cross, DeWolfe counted off the three witnesses one by one, asking, "His testimony was false, wasn't it?" Iva replied weakly, "I don't know whether I am in the position of saying anybody's testimony is false."[103] She reiterated that she never broadcast news. She convincingly explained how the Japanese broadcast system worked, that the military did not release war news until weeks or months after a battle, and therefore the timeline sworn to by the three men could not possibly be correct. Unfortunately, Wayne Collins reverted to interrupting with non-stop objections, which the Court routinely overruled, and jurors once again may have gotten the impression Iva had something to hide.

Collins tried to set the record straight on redirect. DeWolfe's most objective and most trustworthy witness to the statement was Clark Lee. Lee had sworn Iva told him that she had broadcast her "Orphans of the Pacific" taunt: "How will you get home now that all your ships are sunk?" Responding to Collins' questions, Iva offered her version of the event:

> *Iva*: Mr. Oki and Mr. Reyes were conversing when I went into the room. Mr. Oki stated that there had been a battle off of Formosa and Norman said, "What kind of battle?" I believe they said it was a naval battle. I was on the other side of the room typing up the script. It was almost time to go on the air. Mr. Oki said, "Why don't we say something like this?" And then he said something about mentioning the phrase "Orphans of the Pacific." Something about, "All your ships are gone, how are you going to get home?" Let's incorporate that into part of the script for today. He was talking to Norman. He wasn't talking to me.
> *DeWolfe*: Do you know whether or not he made any such broadcast?
> *Iva*: I do not know.
> *DeWolfe*: Now as a matter of fact, when you saw Clark Lee on September 2, 1945, you related that incident to him, didn't you?
> *Iva*: Yes, I think I did.[104]

~

What actually happened with respect to the taunt about the loss of the orphans' ships is the single most vexing issue in the entire case.

Iva's own testimony, cited above, only deepens the mystery. Nowhere does an Imperial Japanese Army major appear "bluntly suggesting" the remark, as she stated to Clark Lee. In her story at trial, the taunt was an impromptu idea thrown out during a bit of minor chit-chat between Oki and Reyes. If that were true, why would Iva remember it? Even if she did, she would have had absolutely no reason to mention the incident, so irrelevant to her own life story, to Lee. Iva's explanation at trial is simply not credible.

Clark Lee's trial testimony is also problematic because, as noted in the previous chapter, it was embellished and infected by the legend of Tokyo Rose.

The FBI completely compromised Mitsushio and Oki. We cannot trust them either.

Other slightly less biased witnesses existed.[105] As noted earlier, Satoshi Nakamura, the sometime master of ceremonies for the *Zero Hour*, testified at the trial about the incident. Nakamura was Canadian and presumably the FBI could not have threatened him with a treason trial. On the other hand, if Nakamura wanted to be flown from Japan and get paid for his time, he had to toe the company line. Nakamura testified that he made an announcement of the loss of American ships on the news segment of *Zero Hour*. He followed this announcement with, "So much for the war news, and here comes Orphan Ann." Iva then took the microphone and issued the famous taunt, "Orphans of the Pacific. You really are orphans now." Nakamura, however, cannot be entirely trusted because he also swore that she broadcast the remark in the fall of 1944 and that Oki and Mitsushio were present when Iva spoke. This conformed his testimony to the indictment and to theirs, but I doubt the indictment's timeline is accurate, and it is extremely unlikely that the three men stood together in the studio and watched Iva broadcast.[106]

Russell Warren Howe located Ken Ishii in the late 1980s and asked him about the "loss of ships" statement. Ishii was a news announcer on the *Zero Hour* and the husband of Mary Ishii, one of the female broadcasters. Concerning Mitsushio's testimony that he had witnessed Iva make such a remark, Ishii told Howe, "Mitsushio was lying. What he was recalling was part of a news broadcast, not Iva's patter. If headquarters had wanted a victory announced, Iva would have been their last choice as announcer."[107] Ishii assumed headquarters only wished to proclaim a victory. Perhaps general headquarters (GHQ) also wanted to taunt American listeners.

Another source, Rex Gunn, said of the orphans taunt, "It was so obviously a joke."[108] This implies Iva broadcast it but put a comic spin on it. Whether Gunn based his opinion on an early interview with Iva, or from hearing her say it over the air, or whether he simply guessed that she said it, is not known.

This paucity of trustworthy witnesses forces us to rely on Clark Lee's original notes from 1945. As Iva talked, Lee typed. At this first encounter, Lee did not have to protect his reputation against the charge that he did not find the real Tokyo Rose but simply cast Iva in the part. He no doubt expected to hear Tokyo Rose-like admissions, but his staccato sentence fragments leave the impression that Lee typed with such rapidity that such expectations played a small role in his note taking. Here again, reproduced verbatim, is the key portion of his original transcription of Iva's own words:

> off formosa claimed sunk American fleet. They sent major from GHQ who wanted to play up great victory wiping out u.s. fleet. i get inside news. and we add up ships s claimed sunk and they wouldn't add. would be suicide say truth. after this time, last year we just mouth piece of ghq. they'd bluntly suggest "you fellows all without ships. what are you going to [do] about getting home." "Orphans of the Pacific. You really are orphans now."
>
> About every day for past half year major come, english speaking, and tell me how to slant that day's script. when Okinawa battle, japanese took back one little place, they played it up big.
>
> Major GHQ stick noses in up to last day.[109]

Unless one takes the view that broadcasting for the Japanese was in and of itself treasonous, these few sentences represent the entirety of the *legitimate* case against Iva Toguri. Every phrase, every word, therefore, is crucially important.

The first question is, who is this major from GHQ who coached Iva daily on how to slant her scripts? Iva never provided his name to her lawyers. In fact, she never mentioned him to anyone except Clark Lee. According to FBI and trial transcripts, Oki, Mitsushio, and Tsuneishi never mentioned him either. Given this striking gap in the record, Masayo Duus reasons that "the 'major' who came from the General Staff could have been no one but Tsuneishi." Russell Warren Howe also understands Lee's testimony to be "an apparent reference to Tsuneishi."[110]

I consider their interpretation unlikely. Tsuneishi was in charge of *Zero Hour* from the outset. He was in place before Iva arrived at Radio Tokyo. Iva would not have claimed GHQ "sent" him in the final months of the war. Second, he did not speak English. How could he suggest changes in Iva's English-language script? Finally, Tsuneishi testified at Iva's trial that he never spoke to her personally; she was too unimportant.[111] In contrast, the recently arrived major from GHQ came every day and "tell *me* how to slant that day's script" (italics mine).[112]

If the major was not Tsuneishi, then who? I believe the answer can be found in a remark that is part of a lengthy deposition given to the Army CIC by Wallace Ince in 1945. Ince, recounting his own experiences as a POW, told the CIC that just before the end of the war Allied collaborators had supplied the Japanese with reports detailing his and Cousens' sabotage of Radio Tokyo broadcasts. As a result, Ince said, "as late as August 14, 1945"—that is, after the atomic bombs were dropped and the surrender of Japan was certain—he, Cousens, and other officers "were very nearly lined up and shot" under the orders of "Major Hifumi, who relieved Major Tsuneishi in June."[113] Consider in light of this fact that Iva stated to Clark Lee that "about every day for past half year major come." The past half year would be March through August 1945. It seems likely that Hifumi would have arrived early, before he was scheduled to officially relieve Tsuneishi, to learn the operations and personnel of Radio Tokyo. If Ince's information was correct, Hifumi must have been something of a fanatic since he considered executing Allied POWs just before the surrender. Hifumi, therefore, is the most plausible candidate to be the major sent from GHQ.[114]

The second question is, when did Iva broadcast the taunt, if in fact she did? In the first part of Lee's notes, she mentions "Formosa." The naval battle off Formosa, which is often treated as part of the large and complex battle of Leyte Gulf, occurred during October 1944. Lee, when he refashioned his notes into complete sentences, tied the taunt to the "time of the Formosa battle." The prosecution then crafted OA VI, the act in the indictment that refers to the taunt, to allude to that date, citing "an unknown day in October 1944." A swirl of contradictory trial testimony surrounds this month and this battle, with various prosecution witnesses swearing they heard Iva make the broadcast in October 1944, and defense witnesses swearing she did not. Duus and Howe side with the defense, but both accept the underlying assumption of an October broadcast.

The entirety of this debate rests, in my opinion, on a misreading. Look again at Lee's original notes: no mention of 1944 or Leyte Gulf appears. Iva located the loss of ships as "off Formosa," but the only battle she mentions is Okinawa. The losses of Allied ships during the battle of Leyte Gulf were minor, whereas during the battle of Okinawa the *kamikaze* sunk dozens of ships, more than in any other battle of the war. In the context of Okinawa, the taunt about losing ships would have had bite. The battle of Okinawa lasted from late March through June 1945, exactly the period during which Major Hifumi would have been present to suggest/demand the taunt.

My analysis must sustain several objections. 1. If Iva was actually speaking about the battle of Okinawa, why did the debate during the trial swirl around the battle of Leyte Gulf? The simple answer is that the prosecution prepared its witnesses and conformed their testimony to the indictment, which was pegged to an October 1944 broadcast date. 2. Why did Iva never mention Hifumi? The short answer is that it was not in Iva's interest to do so. *If*, and I emphasize "if," she broadcast the taunt, she was not so foolish as to name the Japanese officer who could offer direct testimony of this clearly anti-American statement. 3. Why didn't the government introduce Hifumi at trial? Here, I can only guess. Perhaps he committed ritual suicide following Japan's defeat; many diehards did. Another possibility, evidenced by the fact that no record of an investigation of Hifumi is now extant, is that the FBI overlooked Ince's brief mention of him.[115] Yet another possibility is that when Tillman found and interviewed him, Hifumi told Tillman all about the taunt, and added that he would have shot Iva on the spot if she had dared disobey his orders. This would have provided Iva with the defense of duress.[116] Or perhaps the government just wanted to keep its narrative simple. Since DeWolfe had hitched his case to the October 1944 date, the prosecution hoped the jury would assume that the major mentioned by Clark Lee was Tsuneishi. DeWolfe realized that a second Imperial Japanese Army officer, this one speaking English and overseeing the daily preparation of scripts, did not enhance the government's position.

When he coached Mitsushio and Oki on their stories, he told them to keep their mouths shut about Hifumi.

One last major question, and it is by far the most important: Did Iva actually broadcast Hifumi's "bluntly suggested" remark about sunken ships and orphaned sailors unable to get home? No definitive answer to this question is possible. No script or recording contains such a remark. We must tease the answer out of a minimum of circumstantial and contextual clues.

The initial part of the statement that Iva related to Lee, GHQ's announcement of the loss of ships, is similar to Japanese propaganda boasts throughout the war that claimed they sunk copious quantities of American warships. Given what we know about the segmented nature of *Zero Hour*, managers would treat such naval "victories" as news and therefore Mitsushio or Oki probably assigned the loss of ships statement to the news announcer for broadcast. This fits with Nakamura's recollection of events, and makes sense of the fact that Lee in his original notes separated that report from the taunt. So, it is unlikely Iva broadcast the loss of ships report.

That leaves, "you fellows all without ships. What are you going to do about getting home. Orphans of the Pacific. You really are orphans now."

The first significant point is that the term "orphans" is linked directly to Iva herself. She addressed her GI listeners as "my favorite orphans." Clark Lee surely did not conjure up "orphans" on his own at this point in the interview. Iva herself had to introduce the subject of orphans. Someone at Radio Tokyo had to connect orphans to the loss of ships to create this taunt.

Second, Iva related this event in the context of explaining how she tailored her broadcasts to the news.

> I say for instance, [in] connection [with the] news, "things are bound to become better. The world is rather upside down and get better. So lets forget the whole thing. dont think so bad of the world. lets forget with music."[117]

That is, her scripts contained comments connected to the news. Her "now you can't get home" statement would follow this pattern.

Third, the thrust of her comment that the English-speaking major came every day is that in the closing months of the war, she and other personnel were under intense, unremitting pressure to overtly propagandize the scripts. If Hifumi ordered Iva to broadcast the taunt, she would have had to comply.

However, the most salient fact about this issue is that Iva remembered the incident. It obviously meant something to her because it was the only specific broadcast with obvious propaganda content that she mentioned to Lee. It simply cannot be true that Iva would attach such importance to this incident if, as she stated at trial, Norman Reyes may or may not have broadcast something of the sort after she left the studio.

I reluctantly conclude, therefore, that the most reasonable interpretation of events is that a news commentator, probably Nakamura, announced the loss of ships and Iva followed with some version of, "Orphans of the Pacific, you really are orphans now. How will you get home now that all your ships are sunk?" She no doubt tried to burlesque her delivery, but she had no choice about broadcasting the taunt. She remembered the event because it turned her affectionate nickname for the GIs into something nasty, and she felt both guilty and ashamed when Major Hifumi forced her to follow his orders. Her admission in court that she had told Lee that she had done wrong because she lacked the gumption to go against army orders probably concerned this specific event.[118]

My conclusion in this section will irritate, if not infuriate, Iva's supporters. They believe she was not guilty of treason and was railroaded by the U.S. government. I agree completely. However, Iva's supporters presume that the absence of legal guilt must mean that Iva did not perform the act of which she was found guilty. That inference is misguided, and fails to help us understand how twelve of her peers voted to convict her.[119] Iva explained to Lee that near the end of the war, military authorities converted *Zero Hour* into their direct mouthpiece. Their propaganda, previously rather subtle and only lightly monitored by Tsuneishi, became ham-fisted under the supervision of Major Hifumi. Iva now found herself alone; she no longer had Cousens or Ince to support her. Tsuneishi had threatened to transfer recalcitrants to munitions factories, and Iva knew what American bombers did to munitions factories. Hifumi probably threatened worse. She had to obey orders, otherwise "would be suicide." She denied under oath that she ever made the taunt because she reasonably believed that if she admitted the truth, the jury would suspect her of more and worse. She no doubt feared jurors would not be allowed to take her circumstances into account. Her fears were justified. But the evidence that she did in fact broadcast the taunt is, to my mind at least, persuasive.[120]

∽

The defense concluded by calling attorney Ted Tamba. Tamba testified that when he had interviewed Mitsushio and Oki in Japan, they said they knew nothing about the OAs. The jury no doubt discounted his testimony as biased. The prosecution recalled agents Tillman and Dunn to testify that they never threatened anyone, never put words in anyone's mouth, never doctored their statements to conform to the prosecution's theory of the case. Given that Americans held the FBI in the highest esteem at the time, jurors no doubt viewed their testimony as truthful.

On September 19, 1949, the defense rested.

Notes

1. Trial Transcript, vol. XXVIII, 3079–80. Tamba has conflated the *kempeitai* and the metropolitan police. The latter nagged her about citizenship, not the former. I contend Iva never encountered *kempei* in her room, but whether I am right or wrong, it at most happened once and was not usual.

2. Trial Transcript, vol. XXVIII, 3087. Tamba's conflation, as in note 1. Iva reported to the metro police once a month. She did not have two or four policemen watching her.

3. Trial Transcript, vol. XXVIII, 3091.

4. Figure 17.1, Photo ML MSS 7043/13/2; Papers of Ivan Chapman; Mitchell Library, State Library of New South Wales, Australia.

5. Trial Transcript, vol. XXVIII, 3117–18. Edited for length.

6. Trial Transcript, vol. XXVIII, 3119.

7. *San Francisco Chronicle*, August 16, 1949, 1.

8. Cousens' testimony, Trial Transcript, vol. XXVIII, 3121. Obviously the Japanese military's food supply diminished as the war progressed.

9. Trial Transcript, vol. XXVIII, 3121. Edited for length.

10. Trial Transcript, vol. XXVIII, 3125.

11. *San Francisco Chronicle*, August 17, 1949, 9.

12. Trial Transcript, vol. XXVIII, 3158.

13. *San Francisco Chronicle*, August 17, 1949, 9.

14. Trial Transcript, vol. XXVIII, 3186.

15. "Fools, idiots," Trial Transcript, vol. XXIX, 3227; "weight in gold," 3267; "have to stand," 3291.

16. Trial Transcript, vol. XXIX, 3274.

17. The *San Francisco Chronicle* reported of Cousens' testimony, "He had written 'wouldn't you like to be dancing with your best girl at [the] Cocoanut Grove tonight,' he said." The *Chronicle* was in error. Collins read Cousens this quotation: "Hello, you boneheads out in the Pacific. This is Orphan Ann coming to you out on the mosquito-infested islands. Now, wasn't that nice? Doesn't it remind you when you were dancing with your girl at the Cocoanut Grove in Los Angeles?" Cousens answered, "No, sir. Again, the early part is—it appears to be garbled. The early part is obviously part of my script, but the Cocoanut Grove, California was something I hadn't heard of, so I don't know where that comes in." Trial Transcript, vol. XXIX, 3323.

18. Trial Transcript, vol. XXIX, 3318.

19. *San Francisco Chronicle*, August 18, 1949, 6.

20. Pay testimony, Trial Transcript, vol. XXX, 3418; suits, 3417; number one hotel, single room, bath, 3411; collaborators, 3412; extra food, 3417–18; geisha house and quotation, 3423.

21. Trial Transcript, vol. XXX, 3414. Hotel receipts, NARA 2, Box 11.

22. "Difficult to eat," Trial Transcript, vol. XXX, 3447; "140 pounds," 3343.

23. Trial Transcript, vol. XXX, 3415.

24. Figure 17.2, *San Francisco Chronicle*.

25. FBI Interview, October 16, 18, 19, 1948, 46. NARA 9, Box 237.

26. Major with Fifth Infantry from FBI Interview, October, 1948. Lieutenant Colonel, FBI Memo, November 2, 1948. Both at NARA 9, Box 237. Also Trial Transcript, vol. XXXI, 3456, 3550.

27. Memo, Ladd to Hoover, November 2, 1948. NARA 9, Box 237.

28. Memo, AAG Alexander Campbell to Hoover, September 16, 1949. NARA 9, Box 240.

29. Transcript of an August 9, 1979, tape-recorded interview by Iva of Tex Nakamura, in Los Angeles.

30. Trial Transcript, vol. XXXI, 3568. The trial transcript never takes note of emotional displays, and a reader would never realize a break of several minutes occurred as Ince wept. See the *San Francisco Chronicle*, August 19, 1949, 1.

31. Cousens' letter of April 16, 1949. As noted in chapter 5, Cousens referred to Ince's children, plural. Cousens seemed unaware that Ince and his wife had divorced. It is difficult to know whether Cousens' other information, about Ince's drinking for example, was correct.

32. Trial Transcript, vol. XXXI, "interested in the Philippines" and "be destroyed," 3508; "she whispered" and "fooling," 3510.

33. *San Francisco Chronicle*, August 19, 1949, 6.

34. "She was aloof," Trial Transcript, vol. XXXI, 3512; "at the studio," 3533; "is Japanese," 3551;

35. Trial Transcript, vol. XXXI, 3561.

36. Three quotations from Ince's Statement, October 19, 1948, 9. NARA 1, Box 51.

37. Figure 17.3, *San Francisco Chronicle*.

38. *San Francisco Chronicle*, August 23, 1949, 1.

39. *Honolulu Star-Bulletin & Advertiser*, June 27, 1976, A-4. NARA 3, Box 1.

40. Trial Transcript, vol. XXXII, 3601–64.

41. Affidavit of Norman Reyes taken in Manila, Exhibit IX, CIC, File 80-T-5, January 10, 1946. NARA 2, Box 9. Tamotsu Suzuki claimed he heard Iva called "Tokyo Rose." Foumy Saisho said three women and no women used the name. See chapter 8. Those who deny it include many mentioned elsewhere in this book as well as Sugiyama Harris, Isamu Yamazaki, Hideo Iwasaki, Kimitomo Ogimachi, Hiroa Hara, Kunio Sadamasa, Shinjiro Igarashi, Shiro Sano, Tokio Ota, Kan Mino, Naoyuki Hori, and others too numerous to mention.

42. Argument over what was said in July 1945, Trial Transcript, vol. XXXIV, 3863–67.

43. Trial Transcript, vol. XXXII, 3650 and 3653–54. Edited for length.

44. Trial Transcript, vol. XXXII, 3677.

45. Ince at Trial Transcript, vol. XXXI, 3512; Cousens at vol. XXIX, 3306.

46. Trial Transcript, vol. XXXII, 3647.

47. Trial Transcript, vol. XXXII, 3643–48. The transcript styles the name "Hollinsworth," but most sources use "Hollingsworth." Duus suggests the man's real name was Wollbauer. Duus, *Orphan*, 197.

48. "Anybody else," Trial Transcript, vol. XXXII, 3656; "in her hands," 3664.

49. Howe, *The Hunt for "Tokyo Rose,"* 279.

50. Trial Transcript, vol. XXXII, 3704.

51. This exchange from Trial Transcript, vol. XXXII, 3705.

52. Trial Transcript, vol. XXXII, 3690.

53. Trial Transcript, vol. XXXII, 3695.

54. Trial Transcript, vol. XXXII, 3685–89. Edited for length.

55. "Taken place," Trial Transcript, vol. XXXIV, 3892; "I signed it," 3893. On 3897, Reyes testified, "The word used was rather vulgar. I can't repeat it. [quoting Tillman] 'All right, Reyes, that is enough of this rubbish.'"

56. Trial Transcript, vol. XXXIV, 3897.

57. Trial Transcript, vol. XXXIV, 3896, 3891. Edited for length.

58. Trial Transcript, vol. XXXV, 3969.

59. All of the quotations listed, as well as the inaccurate date for meeting Iva, from Norman Reyes statement, October 2, 1948. Edited for length. NARA 1, Box 51.

60. Trial Transcript, vol. XXXII, 3747–48. Edited for length.

61. Trial Transcript, vol. XXXIV, 3968–69. Roche actually questioned him about two exhibits, but to avoid confusion, I changed the text to refer to one.

62. *Honolulu Star-Bulletin & Advertiser*, June 27, 1976, A-1, A-4. NARA 3, Box 1.

63. Letter, April 27, 1949.

64. *San Francisco Chronicle*, August 31, 1949, 5.

65. Tamba wrote in his papers, "All during this putative trial, General Willoughby is secluded in the Presidio in San Francisco. His presence is unknown to the defense, but is known to a certain newspaper man who never divulged this information until some 20 years later. And the cowardly General remained silent. He was living in luxury off the bounty of the American taxpayer." The magazine *Reason* stated, "The defense was guilty of one serious lapse, as attorney Tamba was to recall later, in failing to realize that Maj. Gen. Charles A. Willoughby was right in San Francisco, based at the Presidio, at the time of the trial" (February 1976, 10). The fact is that Tamba was misinformed. Willoughby was in Tokyo throughout 1949, hard at work on MacArthur's memoirs and spying on Korea. The Presidio story is false.

66. Tamba recollections, "Tokyo Rose and Boobus Americanus," October 6, 1973.

67. *San Francisco Chronicle*, August 31, 1949, 5.

68. Ince testified at trial to the brutality of Hamamoto (vol. XXXI, 3567–71) and Buck Henshaw testified that he'd watched as it happened (vol. XXXVII, 4166).

69. *San Francisco Chronicle*, August 26, 1949, 5.

70. "Ruth Somebody" = Ruth Hayakawa? Ruth Matsunaga? My understanding is that no one used their real name while broadcasting, so it seems unlikely. But then whence "Ruth"? See Trial Transcript, vol. XXXIX, second 4330–31. (The transcript page numbering system goes awry in vol. 39 and page numbers from vol. 38 are reused. Thus there is a page 4330 in vol. 38 and also in vol. 39. By vol. 40, this has been rectified.) I also note with some pettiness that Tillman's partner, J. Eldon Dunn, continued the pair's fact-mangling by spelling this witness's name "Hagedom," even

though the trial reporter and every newspaper got it right. See Dunn's synopsis of the trial, FBI Report, November 22, 1949, 15. NARA 6, Box 3.

71. *San Francisco Chronicle*, September 1, 1949, 7.

72. Trial Transcript, vol. XXXVIII, 4343–46. Edited for length.

73. *San Francisco Chronicle*, September 2, 1949, 9. Ruth Matsunaga testified under her married name, Ruth Kanzaki.

74. Trial Transcript, vol. XLVII, 5249.

75. I have been unable to independently verify the story of Chiyeko's brave sister. Some readers might wonder if Iva had confused Chiyeko with Ruth Hayakawa, but she also testified, via deposition, for the defense. I know I made it clear during my interviews that Chiyeko was our subject. However, I seldom confronted Iva with the facts, preferring to let her tell me her version of events.

76. *San Francisco Chronicle*, September 7, 1949, 6.

77. "Dramatic move," *San Francisco Chronicle*, September 8, 1949, 1; "saying what she meant," *San Francisco Examiner*, September 13, 1949, 11; "factual, believable," *San Francisco Chronicle*, September 8, 1949, 6.

78. *San Francisco Chronicle*, September 10, 1949, 4.

79. Trial Transcript, vol. XLVI, 5145. Iva told me that she did not dare have a Christmas tree at her uncle's (Christmas 1941) or at the boarding house (1942, 1943).

80. Trial Transcript, vol. XLVIII, 5356–59.

81. Trial Transcript, "shorter hours," vol. XLVIII, 5359 and "pay raise," vol. XLIX, 5407.

82. Trial Transcript, vol. XLVI, 5167–68. Edited for length.

83. Trial Transcript, vol. XLVIII, 5340.

84. Trial Transcript, vol. XLV, 4967. Edited for length.

85. Early 1943 is Iva's own date for the *kempeitai* search of her room (vol. XLV, 4967) and early 1945 is her date for the luncheon (vol. XLVIII, 5388).

86. In her Notes, Iva wrote about encountering *kempeis*, "I never came across one directly, as this was not the practice of the *Kempeitai*." This statement is technically false; she obviously knew Okada, Mrs. Kido's relative. But I think she means she never met a stranger who was part of the *kempeitai*, which supports my thesis that she was not present when the three agents searched her room. At trial Iva claimed she had found the *kempeitai* in her room a second time. (vol. XLV, 4968).

87. Affidavit in Support of Motion, May 4, 1949. Trial Transcript, vol. XLVII, 5276–81.

88. Trial Transcript, vol. XLVII, 5285.

89. Statement of April 30, 1946, 6. NARA 1, Box 40.

90. Trial Transcript, vol. XLVIII, 5329.

91. Trial Transcript, vol. XLVII, 5251.

92. DeWolfe asked the "difficult to understand" question of Norman Reyes at vol. XXXIII, 3750 and of Iva at vol. XLVII, 5251–54.

93. Statement of April 30, 1946, 7. NARA 1, Box 40.

94. Trial Transcript, vol. XLVIII, 5331.

95. Trial Transcript, vol. XLVIII, 5327–30.

96. Trial Transcript, vol. XLVII, 5310.

97. Trial Transcript, vol. XLIX, 5456–57.

98. Toguri April 30, 1946 Statement. NARA 2, Box 12.

99. Quotation and her conversation with Tillman cited here, Trial Transcript, vol. XLVIII, 5335–36.

100. Trial Transcript, vol. XLIX, 5447.

101. *Honolulu Star-Bulletin*, June 27–29, 1976. Part of my rendition is a paraphrase of Reyes' responses by the reporter, which I have treated as a direct quotation. NARA 3, Box 1.

102. One of the strongest arguments of the pro-conviction forces in the jury room was that Overt Act VI had five witnesses that testified to hearing it: the three mentioned in this sentence plus Mary Higuchi and Shinjiro Igarashi. Iva swore she had never met the latter two. Both admitted under cross they only "thought" she had made some such remark.

103. Trial Transcript, vol. XLVII, 5302.

104. Trial Transcript, vol. XLIX, 5513–15.

105. One such witness was Kiyoshi "George" Togasaki. Iva told her lawyers, "Mr. Togasaki took over the running of the *Zero Hour* program from about August of 1944 to about March 1945. He was connected with the English paper, *Nippon Times*, offices in Tokyo, Japan. He is at present English editor for the same paper. I understand he is a national of Japan, educated in the United States, speaks English very well." As a manager of *Zero Hour*, he might have been aware of the "loss of ships" broadcast. But I can find no evidence the defense or prosecution ever spoke with him. Togasaki actually was a Nisei. He was born in San Francisco and graduated from the University of California in 1920. He survived the war, ran the *Times* until 1956, was a Christian who helped missionaries in Japan, and he became president of Rotary International.

106. Nakamura's testimony, Trial Transcript, vol. XXI, 2290–2301.

107. Howe, *The Hunt for "Tokyo Rose,"* 227.

108. *Chicago Tribune*, February 15, 1976, 3.

109. Lee's original notes, n.p. NARA 2, Box 17.

110. Duus, *Orphan of the Pacific*, 163; Howe, *The Hunt for "Tokyo Rose,"* 265.

111. Trial Transcript, vol. VI, 412.

112. Another possible objection is that Tsuneishi was promoted to Lieutenant Colonel near the war's end and so Iva would not have described the 1945 propaganda editor of her scripts to Lee as a major. However, we have no evidence that Iva knew about the promotion or paid any attention to it if she did.

113. I have reproduced the name as it appears in the deposition, but we have no reason to believe Ince or the CIC knew how to spell "Hifumi." We cannot even be sure Ince heard the name correctly. Deposition, October 25, 1945, 11. NARA 9, Box 237.

114. Howe cites the Ince remark about Hifumi (*Hunt*, 175) in another context but fails to associate him with Iva's statement to Clark Lee.

115. We do know the FBI had the information about Hifumi because Ince's October 25, 1945, deposition is included in his FBI file that begins with his interview in October 1948.

116. I found no reports or interviews in the National Archives with Hifumi.

117. Lee's original notes, n.p. NARA 2, Box 17.

118. Trial Transcript, vol. XLIX, 5446–47.

119. Jury Foreman John Mann said, "The evidence against her was not conclusive. Nevertheless, the probability of guilt was such that the jury found her guilty." *San Francisco Examiner*, March 8, 1956, 27.

120. I did not ask Iva in my 1987 interviews whether she ever made the "loss of ships" taunt. Given that she was convicted of saying it, and that she believed, rightly in my opinion, that she was unjustly convicted, she obviously would have denied it. However, I must also admit that at the time I never imagined that years later the evidence itself would convince me that she did in fact make the statement.

18

The Verdict

The United States v. Iva Toguri

The *San Francisco Chronicle* summed up the treason trial of the century, "Witnesses were examined and cross-examined at such length that their testimony, at some point, will serve almost any purpose. The case of Tokyo Rose at last is headed for the jury room after 12 weeks, 800,000 words of testimony, and a $500,000 prosecution."[1] This dollar amount is often cited, but given what we now know about the massive number of background investigations, the government's costs could easily have been five or ten times that amount. Final arguments began on September 20, 1945, with Frank Hennessy speaking for the prosecution and George Olshausen for the defense. As the *Chronicle* had predicted, they quoted from the same witnesses but from different parts of their testimonies. Hennessy fulminated, "Treason is one of the most heinous, wicked and atrocious crimes known to law. It has always been so regarded by civilized people." Olshausen inveighed, "Sixteen months of monitoring by stations in Hawaii and Oregon—yet not a word introduced from such monitoring to show treasonous statements in the *Zero Hour* broadcasts."[2] DeWolfe and Olshausen delivered the closing arguments. DeWolfe sarcastically referred to Iva as "our little heroine" and described her as a "female Benedict Arnold."[3]

Before the case could go to the jury, the judge had to instruct jurors on the law. Both sides recommended language for the judge to consider in crafting his instructions. The prosecution submitted

31 such texts; the defense, 160.[4] In this trial, proposed instructions were crucially important. Only one case, *Cramer v. United States*, effectively defined the case law on treason, and therefore Judge Roche could not rely on language thoroughly tested over time, as he might have had this been a murder trial.

Judge Roche gave the jurors the weekend off and delivered his instructions to them on Monday, September 26, 1949. His instructions required two hours to deliver. Which side Judge Roche most relied upon for his text is no surprise. Olshausen had several objections to the jury instructions whereas DeWolfe had none. Thereafter the jury retired to deliberate.

Reporters covering the trial took a straw poll among themselves and voted 9–1 in favor of acquittal. Only the reporter from the *Examiner*, Francis O'Gara,[5] thought Iva would be found guilty. O'Gara explained,

> My overriding conviction is that, legalistically, she committed the crime of treason, but actually was not a traitor in the true sense. What she really was doing was playing both sides—trying to work for Japan and the U.S. at the same time.[6]

The *Chronicle* remarked that the spectators who had sat through the entire trial also "had concluded that the 33-year-old Los Angeles girl was not guilty."[7] An alternate juror, Aileen McNamara, was dismissed; when Iva later passed the U.S. Marshal's office, she saw McNamara seated inside and McNamara made an "OK" sign with her thumb and index finger, indicating she thought Iva was not guilty.[8] But not every voting juror shared that belief. According to Associated Press (AP) reporter Katherine Beebe, "There was one woman, just absolutely sure. She just didn't listen. She just had it in her mind that this was that awful siren that had plagued our boys, and they couldn't move her."[9] Initially, this woman was the only juror who stood for conviction, but the *Examiner* reported a male juror soon joined forces with her and the two of them worked to convince the others to vote for conviction.[10]

The jury began to turn, from 11–1, 10–2, and 9–3 for acquittal to an even split of 6–6 on their first formal vote Monday.[11] They debated until 11:00 PM that evening and renewed deliberations early Tuesday morning. Shortly after lunch, the jury requested and received the notes of Clark Lee from his 1945 interview.[12] At 10:04 PM that evening they reported that they were deadlocked.

Judge Roche refused to dismiss them. He explained:

> This is an important case. The trial has been long and expensive to both the prosecution and the defense. If you should fail to agree on a verdict, the case is left open and undecided. Like all cases it must be disposed of some time. There appears to be no reason to believe that another trial would not be equally long and expensive to both sides, nor does there appear any reason to believe that the case can be again tried better or more exhaustively than it has been tried on each side. Any future jury must be selected in the same manner and from the same source as you have been chosen so there appears no reason to believe that a case would ever be submitted to twelve men and women more intelligent, more impartial, or more competent to decide it, or that more or clearer evidence could be produced on behalf of either side. It is unnecessary to add that the Court does not wish any juror to surrender his or her conscientious convictions.[13]

He suggested they retire for the night, continue the next day, "and listen to each other's arguments with a disposition to re-examine your own views."

Masayo Duus faults Roche for his failure to declare a mistrial and suggests it indicated bias:

> The judge was telling the jurors how much money the trial was costing the taxpayers. Wayne Collins and the other defense attorneys were at a loss for words.[14]

Although I too believe Judge Roche was biased, I cannot fault him here. The trial really had cost a lot of money, to both sides as he noted. Perhaps jurors inferred from his remarks that they, as taxpayers, would pick up the bill for another trial. But perhaps they inferred that a second trial would be biased against the defense, which had so few resources that it couldn't even provide the defendant with a change of clothes, much less do battle a second time with the federal government.

On Wednesday, the jurors asked for clarification of two words in one of his instructions. Roche had stated, "Overt acts of an apparent incriminating nature, when judged in the light of related events, may turn out to be acts which were not of aid and comfort to the enemy."[15] The jury wanted an explication of the phrase "related events." Roche refused to elaborate, telling them to look at the instructions as a whole and not focus on any single phrase or sentence.

Russell Warren Howe criticizes Roche's refusal to clarify his instructions:

> Roche's response provided perhaps the clearest motivation of all that the judge—who could obviously see that some jurors were seeking an attenuating circumstance for Iva—was anxious that they bring in a guilty verdict.[16]

It does not seem to me amiss for Roche to direct the jury not to nitpick his instructions but to consider them as a whole.

Late in life, jury foreman John Mann buttressed the criticisms of Duus and Howe, claiming that he believed the judge essentially directed them to return a guilty verdict after they deadlocked.[17] He may have offered this interpretation to excuse his own failure of resolve.

~

Based on reporters' interviews with individual jurors after the verdict, we know the crux of the debate in the jury room. All the jurors agreed that the *Zero Hour* was a propaganda vehicle for the Japanese and that Iva aided and comforted the Japanese by making the program entertaining. They agreed the evidence indicated someone had broadcast the "loss of ships" taunt, and they eventually concluded the preponderance of the evidence indicated Iva had been that person. The jurors further agreed that the testimony proved without a doubt that Iva had helped the POWs and intercepted news broadcasts for them. The evidence had also convinced them that she tried to leave Japan, both before and after the war started.

The jurors accepted the fact that, under the judge's instructions, Iva could not claim duress. Here Judge's Roche's instructions played a significant role:

She can not avoid the consequences of her act by asserting her motive was not to aid the enemy. Motive can not negative [sic] an intent to betray. Fear of injury to one's property or of remote bodily harm do not excuse an offense. That one commits a crime merely because he or she is ordered to do so by some superior authority is, in itself, no defense. Coercion or compulsion that will excuse a criminal act must be present, immediate and pending, and of such a nature as to induce a well-grounded apprehension of death or serious bodily injury if the act is not done. The fact that the defendant may have been required to report to the Japanese police is not sufficient. Nor is it sufficient that she was under surveillance of the Kempei Tai. It is not sufficient that the defendant thought that she might be sent to a concentration camp or deprived of her food ration card. Neither is it sufficient that threats were made to other persons and that she knew of such threats. Nor is it sufficient that the defendant commenced employment and committed the acts attributed to her merely because she wanted to make a living.[18]

Judge Roche may have gone overboard in so specifically denying the elements of Iva's defense, but his instruction was well-grounded in law. The American legal definition of duress is narrow. It covers unique criminal acts. For example, Mary could claim duress if John approached her outside a bank and said, "See this gun. I'm going to follow you inside. You rob the teller or I'll shoot you." Mary probably could not claim duress if John ordered her to rob the bank but showed her no weapon. Mary definitely could not claim duress if John said, "You must rob the bank next week or else" and other people had warned Mary that bad things happened to those who disobeyed John.

This definition of duress is simply not applicable to the highly unusual circumstances of U.S. citizens trapped in foreign countries run by authoritarian regimes in time of war. Australian law is similarly confined, but the Crown realized that Charles Cousens could legitimately assert duress without every day appearing before Major Tsuneishi and being threatened anew with death unless he followed orders. Iva Toguri's failing in this regard was her practical intelligence. She had caught on to how Imperial Japan worked and how to survive there. When Takano ordered her to report or else, she reluctantly went. Had she demanded to confront Tsuneishi and forced him to slam his sword on the table and yell that she had to broadcast or die, she might have escaped conviction.

The debate in the jury room, therefore, centered on the question of intent. Here Roche's instructions favored the defense. "Where the crime charged is treason, the burden is upon the prosecution to prove beyond a reasonable doubt not only that the defendant acted voluntarily, but also that she acted with treasonable intent—intent to give aid and comfort to the enemies of the United States."[19] One side argued that her support of the POWs proved she could not have had treasonable intent. The other side argued that her kindness did not outweigh the fact that she voluntarily broadcast propaganda. As jurors cast more votes, the forces for conviction moved into the majority, 9–3. Discussion began to focus on the question of the nature of the "related events" that could render an overt act innocuous. When Judge Roche refused to clarify this instruction, the resistance collapsed and the jury returned within five minutes with their verdict.[20]

Jury Foreman John Mann was the last to capitulate. He sold himself on compromising his conscience when the nine jurors in the majority argued that a guilty verdict on just one count would be interpreted by the judge as a plea for leniency in sentencing and that Iva, who had already spent two years in jail, would be released with time served.[21]

～

At 6:04 PM on Thursday, September 29, 1949, the jury returned to the courtroom.

> *Court*: Has the jury arrived at a verdict?
> *Foreman*: We have, Your Honor.
> *Court*: Record the Verdict.
> *Clerk of the Court*: Ladies and gentlemen of the jury, hearken to your verdict as it shall now stand recorded: "We the jury find as to the defendant at the bar as follows: Guilty." So say you all? (The jurors indicated in the affirmative.)[22]

Iva remembered at the word "guilty" a whoosh went through the room as the spectators said, "Ohhhh noooo!" Both San Francisco newspapers reported an audible, "Oh!" As to her own reaction: "How do you expect someone to feel when they're convicted of a capital crime? I wasn't about to gaze around the room. It was a shock." She and the reporters agreed that she showed no emotion. "You're looking at a stoical old Japanese here." Her lawyers were stunned. The jury had found her not guilty on seven counts, guilty on one count, Overt Act VI, "that on a day during October 1944, the exact date being to the Grand Jurors unknown, defendant in the offices of the Broadcasting Corporation of Japan did speak into the microphone concerning the loss of ships."

Reporters asked jury foreman John Mann, "Did you at any time consider her not guilty." Mann replied, "If it had been possible under the Judge's instructions, we would have done it."[23]

On October 6, the day of her sentencing, Wayne Collins said on her behalf, "Her own conscience is clear. She wishes she could say the Government's witnesses' consciences were also clear."[24] Judge Roche sentenced Iva Toguri to ten years in prison and a substantial fine of $10,000 (about $100,000 in today's money[25]).

◦◦◦

The next day, the FBI patted itself on the back in an office memorandum. The Bureau was proud it had marshaled sufficient evidence for conviction even though "the Dept. of Justice indicated such could not be done. This case clearly demonstrates the outstanding quality and efficiency of the work performed by the Bureau." The memo recommended that Agents Frederick Tillman and J. Eldon Dunn "each be considered for meritorious increases in salary as a result of their outstanding work in this case."[26]

Notes

1. *San Francisco Chronicle*, September 21, 1949, 4. The *Chronicle* estimated the number of words of testimony at 800,000 on September 20 and rounded up to "nearly a million" the next day. The *Examiner* estimated the word count at 1.5 million. Just for fun, I determined the number of words on an average page of trial transcript was 170–200. In round numbers, there were 6,000 pages of testimony. That equals 1–1.2 million words, which is halfway between the two newspapers' guesses. Also, $500,000 in 1949 would be worth $4,000,000 to $24,000,000 in 2008,

depending on how one calculates it. See http://www.measuringworth. com/calculators/uscompare.

2. Hennessy, *San Francisco Chronicle*, September 21, 1949, 4. Olshausen, *Chronicle*, September 22, 1949, 4.

3. *New York Times*, September 23, 1949, 6.

4. Government's requested instructions, NARA 2, Box 5; defense's, NARA 2, Box 9.

5. Both Duus and Howe use the name "Frances Ogara." Howe adds that "Ms. Ogara" was a Nisei. See Duus, *Orphan*, 218; Howe, *Hunt*, 291. The *Examiner* covered every day of the trial and the byline always reads "Francis B. O'Gara," so this is a strange mistake for the two of them to make. I wondered if the byline might be a "George Eliot" style pseudonym required by the racism of the times. To find out, I spoke by telephone with Bill Boldenweck, a longtime reporter for the *Examiner*. He laughed when I asked him what O'Gara's sex was. "Fran and I used to get drunk together. If you'd have told that Irishman that he was a Japanese woman, you'd have been in trouble."

6. Interview by Rex Gunn, December 22, 1958. See *They Called Her "Tokyo Rose,"* 94.

7. *San Francisco Chronicle*, September 30, 1949, 1.

8. Iva told me this during a recorded 1984 telephone interview.

9. Interview with Katherine Beebe, January 3, 1991, 85. Edited for length.

10. That only one juror stood for conviction, *Reason*, February 1976, 13, apparently quoting Mann. *San Francisco Examiner*, September 30, 1949.

11. Vote of 9–3 is Mann's recollection, *San Francisco Chronicle*, February 16, 1976, 16; 6–6 at vote, *Chronicle*, September 30, 1949, 1.

12. The jury also requested the testimony of Mitsushio and Oki.

13. Trial Transcript, vol. LIV, 6009–10, including the exact time, 10:04.

14. Duus, *Orphan of the Pacific*, 217.

15. Trial Transcript, vol. LIV, 5969–70.

16. Howe, *The Hunt for "Tokyo Rose,"* 290. I think he means "indication" instead of "motivation."

17. *San Francisco, Chronicle*, February 16, 1976, 16.

18. Trial Transcript, vol. LIV, 5976–79.

19. Trial Transcript, vol. LIV, 5976.

20. The 9–3 split and judge's refusal, *San Francisco Chronicle*, September 30, 1949, 4.

21. Russell Warren Howe states that Mann confirmed this claim "much later." *Hunt for "Tokyo Rose,"* 292. I have not found this reference and do not know whether Howe spoke with Mann himself or discovered it in another source. Mann did tell the *Chronicle*, "I was surprised at the sever-

ity of the judge's sentence. I just didn't expect that much." *San Francisco Chronicle*, February 16, 1976, 16.

22. Trial Transcript, vol. LIV, 6061.

23. *San Francisco Chronicle*, September 30, 1949, 4.

24. *San Francisco Chronicle*, October 7, 1949, 5.

25. See http://www.measuringworth.com/calculators/uscompare/result.php for methods of comparing dollar values in different years. Using the Consumer Price Index, $10,000 in 1949 equals $84,528 in 2008. Using the unskilled wage comparator, it equals $141,273. See http://www.measuringworth.com/calculators/uscompare.

26. FBI Office Memo, October 7, 1949. NARA 1, Box 49.

19

Alderson Federal Reformatory

Failed Appeals

Iva Toguri left San Francisco on November 15, 1949, by train bound for the penitentiary in Alderson, West Virginia. The government granted the request of U.S. Marshal Herbert Cole that he along with his wife accompany Iva.[1] They journeyed with another prisoner, a black woman, whose name happened to be Rose. Cole quipped, "I've got two Roses instead of four," a reference to the popular whiskey "Four Roses." Iva praised the guards she had during her various prison experiences, and Cole was one of the best. "I don't know whether it was kosher or not, but he let me visit my family because we had a couple of hours layover in Chicago. His wife took the other Rose to see the city. We had a full compartment on the train. Rose and I took upper berths opposite each other, and Cole and his wife had the lower berths. I remember going up to the dome on the California Zephyr and mixing with other passengers. No one had on handcuffs. Even if they had ordered Cole, he wouldn't have done it." For his part, Herbert Cole was heartsick about the sentence. He said of his delivery of Iva to prison, "It really hurt when we had to leave her back there. It was like leaving one of our own."[2]

They arrived at the Federal Reformatory for Women on the night of November 18. Orientation Officer and former schoolteacher Adena Bass—"a wonderful woman"—took charge of "notorious offender" Iva Toguri.[3] Authorities did not force Iva to

447

undergo a cavity search, a practice they would institute a few years later, but they did strip search her. By now, this had happened to her so often she thought nothing of it. She showered but, to the best of her recollection, they did not disinfect her even though it was standard procedure at Alderson to drench new prisoners' hair with DDT and not allow them to wash it out for forty-eight hours to delouse them. Iva received clothing, which she had to re-sew to make fit, and entered quarantine. During this period, she took a battery of tests, both physical and mental. The prison staff found her to be 60½ inches tall, weighing 105½ pounds. Her vision was poor, 20/200 in both eyes, correctable to 20/40 with glasses. Tests for venereal disease and narcotics were negative. She had "superior intelligence" with an I.Q. score of 130.[4] Iva Toguri was 33 years old. She would spend the prime of her life in prison.

Today, there are many federal prisons for women in the United States, but at the time of Iva's incarceration, the Federal Reformatory at Alderson was the one and only prison for women convicted of a federal crime. Contemporary readers might have heard of Alderson because Martha Stewart served her time there, but it has held many famous prisoners over the years. Would-be presidential assassins Sara Jane Moore and Lynette "Squeaky" Fromme were incarcerated at Alderson. Blues singer Billie Holiday got out shortly before Iva moved in.[5] According to Elizabeth Gurley Flynn, a labor organizer and co-founder of the American Civil Liberties Union (ACLU), who served two years at Alderson for being a communist, Iva was among the famous inmates. "The U.S. marshals escorting us to prison said, 'You'll see Tokyo Rose and Axis Sally there!'"[6]

Alderson's prison population during Iva's stay was, to say the least, eclectic. The labor activists like Flynn, convicted under the Smith Act, were cosmopolitan, intelligent, and well educated. (The Smith Act, passed in 1940, made it a crime to advocate the violent overthrow of the U.S. government; communists were its chief targets.) The inmates who'd been chased down by revenuers for cooking liquor in homemade stills were rural, poorly educated Southern whites. Urban, impoverished blacks made up the majority of women serving time for narcotics offenses. The politicals, the moonshiners, and the addicts did share one thing in common: none believed her actions should be considered crimes. During this period, Alderson also housed several women who had murdered their husbands at overseas military bases, a woman abandoned on an Army base in Eritrea, Africa, who had killed three of her children while temporarily insane, and several American Indians incarcerated for various crimes committed on reservations, including one girl who had killed her mother and who never spoke.[7] A smattering of Puerto Rican nationalists, kidnappers, blackmailers, spies, and traitors rounded out the inmate population. Iva got to know many of these women over the years, in part because she would write letters home for those who were illiterate. It was an education in both directions. She taught the backwoods moonshiners how to use a knife and fork and explained why the prison would buy soap instead of make its own. From the heroin addicts who had usually fed their habits through selling themselves, Iva learned about the life of a prostitute. "Oh yes, yes. It was very interesting." When I asked her what they told her, she wouldn't answer.

Most readers imagine a prison as rows of iron-barred cells in vast blocks. The U.S. Bureau of Prisons had organized Alderson Reformatory in terms of relatively small two-story cottages that housed about twenty inmates, each with her own small room. However, even in Iva's time, overcrowding forced some women to sleep together in a "dormitory," a condition that has grown worse today. Dormitories were the most common scenes for rape and brutality. A cottage room consisted of a single bed, a dressing table/bureau, and a chair. If an inmate wanted a rug, she had to weave her own. The cottages also had a laundry, kitchen, dining room, bathrooms, and showers. A single warder oversaw each cottage and she locked the inmates in their rooms at night with a jar in case they had to go to the bathroom. Warders were usually local West Virginia women or ex-Women's Army Corps (WACs). The latter ran their cottages like the military. Rooms had to be dust free, floors waxed, beds made tight, everything neat. Iva resided throughout her stay at Alderson in Cottage No. 7,[8] overseen by Mabel Houchins, a 6-foot-tall former WAC whom Iva says "had a demeanor."

Typical of her positive approach to whatever life threw at her, Iva denied that anyone at the prison had it in for her. But Houchins, near the end of Iva's stay, admitted otherwise. She asked Iva to come to her office. The two of them sat in rocking chairs, and

Houchins offered her coffee. "Iva, I've been meaning to talk to you for a long time. When I first heard you were coming, I was really disturbed. I was in the Army, and I was disturbed that you had committed treason against this country. I made up my mind I was going to give you a rough time. When you were assigned to my cottage, I was elated that I could carry out this desire."[9]

After Iva's arrival and release from quarantine, Houchins had ordered her to churn ice cream for dessert. "I had to go outside in freezing weather. The ice cream maker was huge, 2 feet high. Hand cranking isn't bad at first but toward the end it takes a lot of energy. I wondered why of all people, when others were ten times bigger than me, I got this assignment. I had it four weeks in a row, but I kept quiet. I thought it was just my turn." Iva's regular cottage assignment was to clean the large second-floor bathroom. Alderson allowed no mops, forcing prisoners to scrub and wax floors on their hands and knees.[10] Iva also had to polish brass fittings and bannisters in various buildings. Her first official work assignment was the storehouse. Of all the work sites at Alderson—the dairy, piggery, farm, kitchens, bakery, garment shop, laundry, cottage painting, lawn mowing, maintenance, cleaning—the storehouse was among the most physically demanding. Workers had to stay on their feet during their shifts and lift, load, carry, and deliver heavy boxes throughout the facility. Food stuffs, paint, leather hides, metals, bolts of fabric, medical supplies, paper goods—all went through the storehouse. Iva's first jobs were as a butcher and truck driver.[11] Houchins told Iva she assigned her work in the storehouse for her safety. "They thought there might be a couple of fanatics who would resent the fact that I was there." This explanation makes no real sense. Iva would have been no safer in the storehouse than anywhere else.

Houchins concluded her litany of Iva's early assignments, "But I have to take my hat off to you. You have proved yourself a real lady. You never complained; you did your share. You have contributed to this institution. You've helped kids, counseled them when they got sad news from home. You went out of your way to help those who were sick and lonely. I've read your letters and your devotion to your father. You have hung in there. You proved that I was wrong. I want you to accept my apologies." Iva replied graciously that she did not need an apology.

Being called a "real lady" was apparently the highest compliment one could be paid at Alderson. Indeed, it was a standing joke among inmates that "they work us like a horse, feed us like a bird, treat us like a child, dress us like a man—and then expect us to act like a lady."[12] In any case, Houchins's reaction is mirrored in all of Iva's Special Progress Reports written by various prison officials. Even her Admission Summary of January 13, 1950, noted, "Her meticulous personal habits and evident experience at keeping house were shown in her ready adjustment to room training. Not just for inspection but all day long, her room was in excellent condition with clothing carefully folded and placed correctly, bed well made, and floor shining."[13]

Thomas DeWolfe still had to decide whether to honor the promise he had made to reluctant grand jurors and prosecute Iva's superior at Radio Tokyo, Wallace Ince. In September 1949, he and his fellow prosecutors agreed there was not much chance of a conviction but they postponed their decision until after the Toguri trial. However, when the jury came back with a guilty verdict against Iva, they continued to procrastinate.

A few months after the conclusion of the trial, on February 20, 1950, Ince put in a request to the War Claims Division for payment for his time as a POW. The U.S. government paid POWs $1 a day in lieu of military pay for their time spent in the hands of the enemy. Although this seems like a ludicrously small amount today, the base salary for a draftee in World War II was only $40 a month.[14] The FBI internally circulated various memos and letters about the claim but did nothing to prevent it, and Ince was eventually awarded $1,212 for his 1,212 days in captivity.[15]

Another year passed. On February 13, 1951, the Department of Justice informed the FBI that it still had made no decision on whether to present the Ince case to a grand jury but that further investigation by the FBI would not be warranted.[16] On April 10, the DoJ undertook a review of the case and determined

that the evidence was insufficient to sustain a prosecution for treason because of the lack of two witnesses to prove the majority of the incidents which might be developed as overt acts and because of the absence of evidence to prove beyond a reasonable doubt that Ince had the requisite intent to give aid and comfort to the enemy.[17]

On February 9, 1955, the Army notified the FBI that Lieutenant Colonel Ince had left the U.S. Army Reserve and it had terminated his commission. A handwritten addendum to this notification notes that on May 15, 1958, "subject's discharge has been changed to delete all security connotations and is now Honorable."[18]

To state the obvious, the fact that the U.S. government never treated Wallace Ince[19] in an adversarial manner—no imprisonment in Japan pending an investigation, no questions about his citizenship, no refusal to allow him back in the country, no trial for the treason of broadcasting for the Japanese—is persuasive evidence, if any more is needed, that the trial of Tokyo Rose was a matter of political expediency and not a quest for justice.

~

Miss Smithson managed the storehouse. Iva's initial assignment was butcher's assistant, but she quickly became invaluable in managing the flow of goods from the trucks to the various cottages. "I caught on to the work and soon was running the place." After working at the storehouse for only a few months, Iva came to work one day and discovered Smithson in a rage. "'I'm so mad I could bite nails'—that's how she talked. They were shifting me to a new project at the school building." The prospect of losing her valuable manager upset Smithson but, try as she might, she could not prevent the transfer.

Iva moved to her new assignment on April 21, 1950. The Bureau of Prisons wanted to track prisoners using the new IBM punch card computer system. Known as the Prison Census Coding Project, the work required Iva to organize and execute the transfer of large amounts of prisoner information. She found this project much more intellectually stimulating than her labors at the storehouse. In a review, prison officials said of her work on the Coding Project, "With a minimum of supervision she has used her initiative in laying the foundation for a new project which requires tedious application much beyond a cut and dried routine of performance. She has, from her first introduction to this project, plunged into her duties with the energy of a person who wants to make it a 'go,' and this attitude continues in the presence or absence of the supervisor. She not only performs the clerical work and typing required on this project, but the more important process of preparing the schedules for coding and the verifying of coded material. Her output is high and is accurate. She has volunteered for extra work when it was necessary to do final checking on 46,000 state schedules recently released for IBM punching."[20]

A year or so later, just as this job became routine, a new opportunity knocked on Iva's door in the form of the prison's Chief Medical Officer (CMO). This time when Iva came to work, she discovered her supervisor in tears. The CMO had asked for Iva, and the prison authorities allowed Iva herself to decide if she wanted to change assignments. "I can still see her, the dear soul, she was very good to me. They were all very good to me. I told her there's nothing else I can learn here. I can do it with my eyes closed. I've trained the other girls well. They can finish the coding."

On August 8, 1951, Iva transferred to the hospital and began the medical training she had dreamed about when she left the United States for Japan. She would continue in this job until her discharge. She began as the CMO's stenographer. She took dictation, typed correspondence, prepared the purchase orders, filed, coded hospital charts, maintained the venereal disease records, prepared the greater part of the monthly medical report, and answered telephone calls. Soon, she took charge of ordering medical supplies.

All these activities would normally constitute a full-time job but they were not enough to keep Iva busy. She learned to make x-rays, and ran the fluoroscope and the electrocardiogram machine. She mastered eye refraction for prescribing glasses. She learned how to draw blood. "Boy, was I good at the end! I could take the toughest junkie and find a vein even if they couldn't find it. 'Damn, I didn't know I had that vein!' They'd be just full of tracks. I found it on their legs, hands, feet, any place. Behind the knees was a good spot because they can't reach and shoot themselves back there." Eventually, she took the blood samples to the lab and ran the diagnostic tests herself. She mastered urine and basal metabolism tests as well. She scrubbed up and assisted in surgery, sterilizing instruments in the autoclave, counting sponges, handing implements, getting supplies such as sterilization packs for tracheotomies. She assisted in several births and worked in the hospital with difficult patients.

One day, the pharmacist found himself shorthanded and asked Iva if she could help him out. As a result, while she continued her work in the hospital, she became the pharmacist's assistant, aiding him with ordering, filling prescriptions, and dispensing medications.

Still it was not enough. "Her unusual resourcefulness and willingness to be of service to the institution and the inmates was well demonstrated during March of 1952 when, with all the work which she was already doing, she volunteered for the added assignment of working in the Dental Clinic. With no Dental Officer to instruct her, she proceeded to spend long hours studying on her own time until she had mastered intricate details of manufacturing artificial dentures. With a remarkable display of understanding and manual dexterity, and without professional assistance, she produced three sets of dentures for departing inmates who require artificial replacements for cosmetic and physiological reasons. The present Dental Officer, upon arrival at this institution, was amazed to see the number of girls who had been relieved of their dental suffering by temporary medicated fillings which she had performed."[21]

Dr. Alvin M. Laster, Dental Director at Alderson from 1952 to 1953, recalled her work. "On my arrival at Alderson, I entered the dental clinic to find a small person with her back to me, administering a dental treatment to an inmate in the dental chair. A text book was on the bracket tray, and Iva was referring to it as she proceeded. In the laboratory, I found evidences of her work on dentures. I couldn't imagine how a lay person could accomplish those things."[22]

The administration at Alderson realized it would need four people to replace Iva in her various jobs after her release. She trained them before she left. If life as an enemy alien in Imperial Japan tested Iva's mettle, her imprisonment after the war demonstrated her character. Iva did not serve time at Alderson; she mastered it. Not one minute went to waste.

~

On October 7, 1949, the day after Judge Roche sentenced Iva Toguri to ten years in prison and a $10,000 fine, Wayne Collins served notice of appeal and petitioned for admission to bail such that Iva could be released from prison during the appeals process.[23] Roche denied the petition on October 10, but Collins appealed that decision as well. On February 6, 1950, Supreme Court Justice William O. Douglas granted Iva Toguri's application for bail, setting the amount at $50,000 and writing that he considered it "fairly debatable" whether she had received a proper trial.[24] Wayne Collins announced that she would be released within a few days, even if he had to post the $50,000 bail himself.[25] Iva, however, no longer had confidence that the system of American justice would do right by her, and so she decided to remain in prison during the appeals process rather than get out for a year or two only to be forced to return to serve her full sentence.

Wayne Collins appealed Iva's conviction to the Ninth Circuit Court of Appeals. Here, he expected his continuous objections and legal arguments that so taxed the jury to pay off. On September 13, 1950, he served U.S. Attorney Frank Hennessy with the Appellant's Brief.[26] It was 262 pages long, augmented by a 106-page appendix. George Olshausen explained in an affidavit that the brief was lengthy because the trial record "consists of 6,020 typewritten pages, 871 printed pages and 147 exhibits and exhibits for identification. The trial lasted 54 days and over 90 witnesses were called by both sides."[27]

Opening arguments before the Ninth Circuit began on March 16, 1951. Collins blasted the court with every shotgun shell in his arsenal and then threw the gun at them for good measure. In his Appellant's Brief, Collins divided his argument for overturning Iva's conviction into ten general categories, which he further subdivided into a couple dozen subcategories and further still into an equal number of sub-subcategories. He offered hundreds of arguments against the government and the trial judge. He and his defense team cited about 250 cases, dozens of federal statutes and rules of criminal and civil procedure, and additional documents; these included such diverse authorities as the War Department's Basic Field Manual, *Foster's Crown Cases* of 1776, and *Rhode Island Recreation Center v. Aetna Casualty and Surety*. Balancing the Brief for Appellant was the 150-page Brief for Appellee from government attorneys Hennessy, DeWolfe, Knapp, and James M. McInerney.[28] Various motions and memoranda added to the record. The clerk of the Ninth Circuit estimated that the cost of printing the entire transcript of record[29] would amount to $12,000.[30] In short, the three appellate judges would search for justice while blinded by a blizzard of paper.

The appeals process is often misunderstood. Many people believe that appellate courts exist to give losing litigants the legal equivalent of a second opinion, a top-to-bottom review of what the judge and jury decided at trial. It is true that if an appeals court thinks the trial judge misinterpreted the law in ways that changed the outcome of the trial, it will reverse the trial court decision. But appellate courts accept no new evidence, and reverse only if they decide that the trial court's factual determinations, including guilt, were unreasonable and not supported by the evidence introduced at trial. Appeals courts almost never, for example, declare that a witness who the trial judge or jury believed told the truth was actually lying.

To comply with the special requirements of the appeals court process, Wayne Collins offered rather technical arguments on behalf of Iva Toguri. In the following summary, these technical grounds have been elided where possible. I have tried to state the more important miscarriages of justice, as Collins understood them, in a way that readers who are not lawyers, as I myself am not, can grasp. His grounds for asking that Iva be granted a new trial or outright release included:[31]

1. Iva Toguri's arrest and imprisonment in Tokyo and subsequent rearrest and imprisonment in the United States constituted double jeopardy and the denial of the right to a speedy trial.

2. Iva's various statements to agents of the U.S. government in Japan violated the McNabb Rule. The McNabb Rule requires reasonable promptness in taking a prisoner before a judge. Otherwise, any confession obtained is inadmissible. The Army had held Iva for more than a year without taking her before a judge. Therefore, her FBI statements and the interview notes that Brundidge had her sign should have been ruled inadmissible.

3. Eisenhart's yen note amounted to a confession by Iva that she was Tokyo Rose. The judge should not have admitted it into evidence because it too violated the McNabb Rule.

4. The Court did not allow the defense to subpoena witnesses in Japan, nor did it require the government to pay for their travel expenses.
5. The government lost or destroyed its recordings of Iva's broadcasts. They would have shown what the few recordings introduced at her trial showed—that her broadcasts were innocuous—and she would have been acquitted.
6. The Court wrongly prevented testimony that Harry Brundidge committed fraud on behalf of the government when he attempted to bribe witnesses.
7. Iva's program simply entertained Allied troops and therefore did not manifest treasonable intent. Further, the Court wrongly excluded evidence such as the Navy's Citation that her broadcasts actually boosted morale.
8. Her many acts of kindness and support for the POWs proved that she lacked the intent to betray her country.
9. Iva clearly acted under duress. The POWs informed her of the brutalities they witnessed, Takano warned her what would happen if she failed to follow orders, and the *kempeitai* and police constantly harassed her.
10. The United States unjustly prosecuted and convicted Iva because she maintained her citizenship. Had she renounced it, she could have done the same acts with impunity.

Wayne Collins did not complain about the worst miscarriage of justice, the prosecution's subornation of perjury by witnesses such as Mitsushio and Oki whom the government had bullied and threatened. He didn't complain because he didn't know. Their falsehoods remained a secret of the government.

~

At Alderson, inmates left their assigned jobs and returned to their cottages at set hours of the day. This meant that Iva had time on her hands during evenings and weekends. She did not let her free time go to waste either.

One favorite activity of hers, according to a prison report, was reading. "She rarely comes to the living room in the evenings, but prefers to be locked in her room to read. She reads both fiction and non-fiction as well as *Time* magazine and daily newspapers [most especially, the *Chicago Tribune* to which she subscribed]. She seems deeply interested in present-day world affairs."[32] After she started working in the hospital, doctors provided her with medical texts on biology, physiology, and laboratory techniques.

She played baseball, or tried to. "I didn't get to play much. The girls were bottled up all winter. They'd go out to play and boom, they'd knock each other down. I spent a lot of my time helping the doctor set the bones they broke while playing."

She took up weaving, learning the craft from a narcotics addict from Texas who was "a great weaver. We'd set up the loom together and weave up a storm." She wove rugs for her room. For her family, she wove rugs, napkins, and place mats. Iva still used some of these in her home late in life.

She learned to knit and crochet. She studied silversmithery and made silver picture frames for her room, placing in the first a photo of herself and her father in Oakland. She completed the course work in journalism, perhaps trying to discover whether truth carried any weight in the field. She started music appreciation but left it to join the farm group in the evenings. She decorated the tables, especially at Thanksgiving. She was prolocutor (narrator) for the Christmas pageant. She attended movies once a week and Catholic services twice a week. Father Ballinger[33] asked her to read the responses during Mass, and Iva learned enough Latin to become his mid-thirties "altar girl."

She studied leather craft. She hand-made key cases, napkin rings, picture frames, secretary cases, and a missal cover (Figure 19.1). She sent her first wallet to her father "He used it for years. One day, long after I'd

Figure 19.1. Iva's handmade missal cover.
Photograph taken by the author.

come home, he said to me, 'See if that 100 dollar bill is in my wallet.' I made the wallet with a secret compartment. He kept a hundred dollar bill in it for an emergency. I always used soft calf leather and the inside of the compartment was unfinished. Because the bill had been there so long, the imprint of Benjamin Franklin was on the leather."

Iva's craft work impressed the prison staff and so, in May 1952, they encouraged her to enter the West Virginia State Fair. As an anonymous numbered inmate at Alderson, she submitted four items, one woven, two of leather, and one of silver. Iva won three blue and one red ribbon for her entries. As a result, citizens began ordering wallets, purses, and other items from her, unaware their orders helped the infamous Tokyo Rose make money. "Strangers would call the prison and ask if the person who won the blue ribbon would make them a leather bag. I could sell purses for $25 because they were hand tooled. I was darn good at it. I ordered leather by the hide. I could make a bag in one day, and $25 is $25."

Her craft work was so prolific that Iva stood out. "When officials from the Bureau of Prisons would come for inspection, guess whose room they came to first? The officers wanted to show what could be done if an inmate wanted to make her room as attractive as possible. The woman before me left her drapes, but I wove my own rugs and made a lot of things of leather and silver to decorate." When authorities released Iva, she left her drapes, rugs, and many other decorations for the woman who followed her.[34]

~

The opinion handed down by the Ninth Circuit Court of Appeals was peevish. The Court complained that counsel for the appellant, Wayne Collins and associates, had ignored the Court's requirements on the proper form for the specification of errors. This meant the judges had to reorganize the "very lengthy" briefs submitted, which "added materially to the task of the court." The Court reorganized the defense arguments into twenty-three general contentions with many lesser arguments subsumed under each. In assessing these, the judges referred to the "trivial character of some of the complaints." They characterized the defense's objections to the judge's instructions as the "wholesale blanket method." They noted sarcastically "appellant rather bitterly complains," and described various arguments as "obviously without any basis whatsoever" and "wholly without merit." The judges backhanded the defense's own florid attack on the trial judge for allowing a "torrent of improper questions" by noting that the section of the defense's brief stating said impropriety contained "some of the most flagrant failures to comply with the rule relating to specification of errors, and the appellant has here wrapped up in a small bundle a very long list of complaints which have been dumped into the lap of the court."[35]

Obviously, the heft of the Appellant's Brief did not please the justices of the Ninth Circuit. They apparently believed the defense could have substantially reduced the sheer number of its arguments without deleterious effect. It is also likely that the length, expense, and complexity of the trial carried weight with the justices. They did not intend to order a new trial on the basis of a sound but trivial complaint. Only a serious miscarriage of justice would suffice to overturn the trial court's decision.

Juries, invaluable though they may be, are composed of lay people who sometimes fail to pay attention to testimony and who can be swayed by emotion, ignorance of the law, prejudice, or other factors. In theory, appellate court justices cannot be so swayed. For this reason, their judicial analysis is valuable because it represents the opinions of thoughtful professionals. Here is how the Ninth Circuit Court of Appeals assessed the merits of Iva's arguments:

1. The U.S. Army detained Iva Toguri as an enemy combatant who "might constitute a threat to the security of the military forces occupying Japan."[36] It neither charged nor prosecuted her for a crime. Therefore, her incarceration did not constitute double jeopardy. Following her arrest in August 1948, the DoJ did bring her to trial in a timely fashion.

2. The McNabb Rule "applies to civil officers making arrests for criminal offenses." The McNabb Rule "could have no application to the conduct of the military."[37] The FBI interrogation of her, therefore, was not the fruit of unlawful detention and was admissible. The Court admitted a procedural burden on the military similar to McNabb, but held that Iva was not a person serving with the Japanese Army and so was not subject to the Articles of War.

3. In perhaps its most dubious piece of analysis, the Court of Appeals ruled that the prosecution had introduced Eisenhart's yen note only "for the purpose of proving the appellant's signature" and not to show she had admitted being Tokyo Rose. Apparently, in the Court's view, it was simply happenstance that of all the documents Iva had signed, the prosecution opened the trial with this particular example of her signature. The Court pressed on, compounding its folly: "There was no attempt at the trial to identify the appellant as 'Tokyo Rose.' The inclusion of the reference to Tokyo Rose in the signature on the yen note could under no circumstances be regarded as prejudicial to the appellant."[38]

4. The Court noted that substantially all the witnesses sought by the defense were not U.S. citizens and their attendance could not have been compelled. Payment of fees and expenses of defense witnesses is within the discretion of the trial court. The justices failed to note the fact that the prosecution's witnesses, who also were not U.S. citizens, testified that when the Army of Occupation ordered them to go to the United States, they believed they had to comply. Even if that were not true, the payment of travel expenses and fees sufficiently encouraged all of them to appear, and presumably would have encouraged defense witnesses in a similar manner.

5. The defense had no basis for claiming the missing scripts and recordings would have favored Iva because the scripts introduced at trial did not in fact show her broadcasts were innocuous. As proof, the Court cited one script's lengthy section about casualties at Okinawa that were part of a *Zero Hour* news commentary. "While this conclusion was not read by appellant, the evidence shows she did participate in the same broadcast at an earlier stage."[39] In other words, Iva was guilty of anything broadcast on *Zero Hour*, whether she said it or not.

6. The DoJ asked Harry Brundidge to travel to Japan to find witnesses and paid his expenses, but he was not a DoJ agent because he did not have express or implied authority to speak on behalf of the U.S. government. Therefore, whatever frauds he committed, he did as a private citizen.

7. The Navy's press release praising Tokyo Rose was "plainly inadmissible as hearsay containing incompetent conclusions." That is, the Navy was not competent to discern whether Tokyo Rose's broadcasts boosted the morale of its sailors or not. Further, that commanding officers never ordered servicemen not to listen to *Zero Hour* only indicates their personal opinion of the program, which was also incompetent. In any case, the fact that Iva's broadcasts did nothing more than entertain the troops proved nothing. The government introduced evidence that showed she knew the program's objective was to cause Allied troops to become homesick. Although Toguri's version of events contradicted this evidence, which witnesses should be believed was a question for the jury. The Court supported the prosecution's version. "Insofar as it is contended that the program was merely one to entertain American troops, such a version of the evidence would, we have no doubt, tax the credulity of a jury who would be hard put to imagine the Japanese military spending time and money solely for that purpose." In any case, even if *Zero Hour* only entertained and did not reduce morale, it didn't matter. "That a traitorous plan does not have the desired effect is immaterial."[40]

8. Iva's smuggling of food, medicine, a blanket, and war news did not, in the Court's view, constitute evidence that she was not in the service of the Japanese. "A general treasonable intent to betray the United States might well accompany a particular feeling of compassion toward individual prisoners and sympathy for the plight in which they found themselves. We think that the question of the effects of these acts of kindness upon appellant's intent was one for the jury."[41]

9. Judge Roche properly instructed the jury that, under American law, duress can excuse a criminal act only if one acts "under the apprehension of immediate and impending death or of serious and immediate bodily harm."[42] Iva Toguri, in the Court's opinion, was not under immediate threat.

10. As to the claim that the United States punished Iva for maintaining her allegiance to it, the Court soberly admitted that she was. Under the Nationality Act of 1940, she presumably could have renounced her citizenship and served

Japan with impunity. She did not. Therefore, she owed allegiance to the United States, which rightfully convicted her of treason. The Court, not wishing to be accused of judicial activism, graciously allowed, "Whether the provisions of the Nationality Act which appellant thinks work unfairly represent a wise or sound legislative policy is a problem for Congress, not for us."[43]

On October 10, 1951, the Ninth Circuit Court of Appeals declined to grant Iva either acquittal or a new trial. "Since we find no prejudicial error in the record the judgement is affirmed."[44]

Wayne Collins petitioned the Ninth Circuit to reconsider. The Court believed that Collins' petition "discloses some misapprehension as to what we endeavored to say in the opinion" and on December 17, 1951, it issued a three-page clarification while refusing to rehear the case.[45] Collins appealed to the Supreme Court. The Supreme Court refused to hear the case. If William O. Douglas still had qualms about the trial,[46] he failed to convince his fellow justices. Among those justices who were confident that the case should not be heard was the man who had decided to indict Iva in the first place, former Attorney General Tom C. Clark. Truman had appointed him to the Supreme Court in 1949.[47] Collins petitioned the High Court to reconsider. On May 26, 1952, the Supreme Court declined. The appeals process came to an end. Iva's presentiment that she would not prevail on appeal and that she should remain in prison had proven to be correct.

～

Despite losing in the various courts of appeal, Iva might still have been released from prison via early parole. The Justice Department requested that Tom DeWolfe prepare a parole report and on May 6, 1953, he wrote to the Criminal Division, "I personally feel that no objection should be interposed to subject's application for parole, and I am inclined to recommend that the same be granted." He cited as his reason that she helped the POWs and that credible evidence showed she had to work to eat and this was the only job available. However, he added that Judge Roche had not made a recommendation "as is his usual practice" and, more important, "I believe that my trial colleague James W. Knapp would oppose the grant of parole."[48] Knapp did oppose—why is not known—and parole was denied.

~

Inmates often crowded into Iva's room. Because she was older than average, and because she helped with medical care, writing letters, and teaching crafts, the young inmates would come to Iva to fix her hair and talk about their lives. Iva heard the stories of people that she otherwise would have never met, and as a result she became much more sympathetic to those accused of crimes. "I'm on the other side of justice. I'm afraid if I serve on a jury I would be inclined not to convict. I didn't get the feeling that many of the women were innocent. But there were circumstances, like abuse by parents or husbands. I don't think I met a bad criminal there."

One prisoner Iva helped was a 16-year-old Southern girl whose teeth were horribly discolored, twisted, or missing. The dentist had never seen such bad teeth in a girl so young, and he decided he should manufacture for her a "Hollywood splint," a prosthetic device popular among actors. A Hollywood splint was essentially a complete row of teeth that was cemented into place and replaced the real teeth. Iva, working from impressions of the girl's real teeth, made the upper and lower sets out of acrylic enamel. Iva said with some pride, "She cried when she saw herself in the mirror. Her teeth looked gorgeous."

Iva's one and only reprimand during her prison stay resulted from helping another inmate. The dentist had just departed to attend a three-day conference when Iva's assistant, Roxie Shelton—"I would have trusted Roxie with my life"—brought her a black woman in terrible pain from an abscessed tooth. Iva gave her oil of cloves, but that didn't help. The woman was in agony. She sobbed that she couldn't stand another night of pain, and begged Iva to pull the tooth. Roxie encouraged Iva to do it, swearing the three of them could keep it secret. Iva realized the matrons would notice the woman's sudden improvement and figure out what had happened, but she felt she couldn't let the woman suffer. So, she injected her with Xylocaine, pulled the tooth, packed it with sponges, and instructed the woman how to change the sponges to avoid a dry socket. "It was done kosher. The dentist admitted it was a good job." News of Iva's act of kindness lit up the prison grapevine, sending her stock even higher among the inmates, but it also brought her into conflict with the authorities. The punishment board summoned her to appear even though the dentist declined to testify against her. "I could tell that it tickled them that I did this on my own. I told them I just didn't want the woman to suffer anymore, and I knew I could pull the tooth. I could see them smiling." The board disallowed her meritorious days that month, causing Iva to spend an extra two days in prison.

The other famous traitor at Alderson, mentioned in chapter 3, was Mildred Gillars, "Axis Sally." Gillars had traveled to Germany before the war and fallen under the spell of a German professor who made her his mistress but never married her. When the American public learned her story, they found Gillars' love life much more titillating than Iva's. Gillars had been lost among millions of refugees following the end of the war but the U.S. Army eventually found her. The Army arrested and held her in Germany for a year before bringing her to Washington, D.C., in 1948. The United States charged Gillars with eight counts of treason, the same number as Iva. In March 1949, a jury found her guilty on one count, again the same number of which Iva was convicted. However, unlike Iva, Gillars swore allegiance to the Nazi regime and willingly broadcast propaganda, which the U.S. government recorded and maintained. Gillars never helped Allied POWs; rather they testified that she had masqueraded as a Red Cross worker and tried to coerce them into broadcasting. The court no doubt found her anti-Semitic rants and accusations of Roosevelt's homosexuality pernicious. She received a much harsher sentence than Iva. Iva served six years at Alderson; Gillars, twelve. The sentence could have been even harsher, but the judge took into account that others had written her scripts.

According to Iva, Gillars was well educated and somewhat haughty. She considered herself above the common rabble. Nonetheless, inmates respected her for being scrupulously fair in her administration of the kiln and photography lab. One day, Gillars, who lived across the hall from Iva, approached her about playing contract bridge. Iva knew nothing about the game or cards in general but agreed to learn. Under Gillars' tutelage, she studied diligently and soon was qualified to play. Iva and Gillars teamed up against two inmates, Bloomberg and Frankenstein, convicted

under the Smith Act. One need seek no further for a more fe-
licitous portrait of Alderson's egalitarianism than this scene of
the Japanese and Nazi propagandists playing bridge against two
Jewish communists. "Mildred looked down her nose at those who
couldn't read or write, but not at the communists. She gave the
devil her due. We all got along fabulously. Everyone handled the
situation with kid gloves, and never brought up subjects we knew
were taboo."

One of the Smith Act convicts with whom they did not play
bridge, Elizabeth Gurley Flynn, met Iva under different circumstances during her first days at Alderson. "The bright spot in my
first visit to the clinic was when an inmate aide leaned over while
taking a blood specimen and said, 'Dorothy sends you her love.'
The message was from Mrs. Dorothy Rose Blumberg, who was
serving a Smith Act sentence of three years. The woman who gave
me the welcome message was Iva Toguri."[49]

Inmates commonly passed messages to one another, but unlike
this example, they usually intended more than a friendly greeting. Lesbianism was endemic at Alderson. Flynn viewed it much
more insidiously than did Iva. Flynn reported "husbands" forcing
"wives" to tear up pictures of real-life husbands and children, and
extorting money and services from their prison mates. Jealousy
resulted in fights and brutal assaults, and actual rapes occurred in
out-of-the-way places. Women kissed during movies, made out in
secluded places, and had sex in their rooms while others kept the
officers distracted downstairs. Flynn blamed this on the complete
cessation of the women's sex lives and a lack of self-control on the
part of addicts, prostitutes, and "perverts." She reported, "One
woman, who worked beside me at the sewing table remarked, 'I
had all the sex I wanted outside and I'm going to get all I want in
here.'"[50]

Perhaps in the same way she had denied witnessing racism in
Southern California, Iva claimed she never saw Alderson's darker
side. She remembered no violence, no assaults, no gangs, no hate-
ful officers, no attempts to escape, and denied she feared anyone.
As for lesbianism, "I can truthfully say that the women who were
involved would have never been were they on the outside. It was
a smart aleck, cute thing to do. It was prestigious to have a lover at
another cottage. They'd send notes and so forth, but it was a game

and a drama, and they were no more homosexual than I was." She doubted any actual sex took place, but admitted, "I might be way off." She herself most often encountered attempts at liaisons at the hospital. Two women would pretend to be sick, but "after you've been there awhile, you could tell. The hospital was a ward, so they hoped to sneak around after 'lights out.' But the nurses were real sharp. They'd call the guards right away."

~

On June 7, 1954, Ted Tamba applied on Iva's behalf to President Eisenhower for a pardon, executive clemency, commutation of sentence, and remission of fine. In October, the Justice Department's Internal Security Division asked DeWolfe for his recommendation. This application represented the final opportunity for the defense to free Iva Toguri and the final opportunity for DeWolfe to do right by her. Iva had by this time served seven years in various prisons. DeWolfe knew what he and the FBI had done behind closed doors to convict her. He had proved his mettle, been a good soldier, and won the case he had privately assessed as unwinnable. The Tamba application gave DeWolfe the opportunity to be magnanimous.

He was not. In a six-page analysis, he informed the attorneys at Justice, most of whom only knew of the case secondhand, that Iva stayed in Tokyo because she didn't want to return to America, "enjoyed her work at Radio Tokyo immensely," knew her program contained "much flagrant and propagandistic broadcasting," "had many opportunities to quit the service of the enemy but never sought to do so," and was under no duress. He explained her treason with the novel theory that "she may have been torn between her loyalty to the United States of America, which nurtured and educated her in her youth, and her devotion to her parents." He concluded that "to grant the relief would do away with the judgment and sentence and punishment. The trial was long and protracted and appellant has had a fair trial and has had her day in court."[51]

Eisenhower never responded to Tamba's application.

~

Throughout Iva's incarceration her father, now in his seventies, regularly visited her, often enlisting her brother or sisters to drive him. They met in a small living room in the cottage set aside for such purposes. Asked if her father was sad to see her in prison, Iva replied, "No, and I think he deliberately tried not to be. They all were upbeat, to keep my morale up." Nor were they angry about what had happened to her. "This is Japanese stoicism. Just live with it. It's a great philosophy—'It can't be helped.'"

On one visit near the end of her sentence, Jun noticed that Iva had lost weight and that her dress was soaked through with sweat even though the temperature was quite cool. He began to question her closely, and she finally had to confess that she was seriously ill. As she had anticipated, he was extremely worried. Prison doctors had diagnosed Iva with hyperthyroidism, an excessive activity of the thyroid gland that causes an increase in basal metabolism. Iva's hyperactive work schedule probably masked the onset of the condition, but at the time of her diagnosis her heart rate had accelerated to 136–142 beats per minute (a normal rate is 60–100) and her weight was dropping three to seven pounds per week. She went from her usual 105 pounds to 85, then down to 70. The prison medical staff fought the loss with a 5,000 calorie per day diet. "They fed me milkshakes made with pure cream. Bacon, meat. They woke me up at 3:00 AM with a milkshake. Still I burned up everything they gave me." Fortunately, her release date was near, and after she was freed, her father immediately put her into the nuclear medicine facility at the University of Chicago for treatment with radioactive iodine, a new management technique developed during the war. Iva eventually recovered, although she had complications late in life due to residual effects of the iodine.

The day before Iva's scheduled release from prison, warden Kinzella summoned Iva to her office. There, two men from the Immigration and Naturalization Service (INS) informed her that she must leave the United States voluntarily or face expulsion as an undesirable alien. "I was more shocked at that than the day I was indicted because it made less sense." Actually the decision made perfect sense. At the time, the government's power to strip citizens of their citizenship was well established. Under the Nationality Act of 1940, U.S. citizens could be forcibly expatriated on many grounds, including treason. The 1952 Immigration and Nationality Act explicitly listed being convicted of treason as a ground for loss of citizenship.[52]

Fortunately, the men did not intend to take Iva directly to some ship. They explained deportation proceedings would follow, and they only wanted her to sign a receipt for the order. Iva had finally learned her lesson. Before she signed, she telephoned Wayne Collins from the warden's office. The INS had not notified him. "Wayne was furious. 'The goddamn SOBs! They blow hot and cold to suit their own fancies!'" Collins' displeasure was nothing compared to that of the INS agent. Mary Cottrile, Iva's parole officer, remembered, "He was so angry because we had permitted you to contact an attorney. The cords of his neck stuck up until I thought that man would have a stroke."[53] Collins told Iva the receipt meant nothing. "Sign it. I just want you to get out of prison." This new litigation ruined Iva's joy at being released because now she feared she could wind up in Portugal, Japan, or some other country. The

Figure 19.2. Iva with reporters.
Courtesy of Library of Congress.

INS had not specified the nation to which it intended to deport her.

Iva Toguri walked out of Alderson prison on Saturday, January 28, 1956 (Figure 19.2). She was 39 years old. She had hoped to return quietly to the obscurity of private life in Chicago with her family, but "Tokyo Rose" continued to captivate the American imagination. Thirty reporters, their microphones and still cameras, plus two television trucks, awaited.[54] Asked about her future, she answered, "I'm going out into the darkness."[55] She added, "I'd like a chance to get back on my feet. I'd like to show I'm a good American if I am given the chance." As to her husband, she said only that they corresponded but "we have no plans right now."[56]

Jun, Fred, and Inez Toguri had driven from Chicago in the family's black Chrysler, arriving the previous Friday. Jun had shrewdly convinced the police in Chicago to send two detectives with him in a separate car. One, whom Iva only knew as Zip, was the single Japanese American detective on the Chicago police force. The other was local precinct captain Tony Campioni. After the impromptu news conference, Zip and Tony hustled Iva out of the sight of the crowd of reporters, and then roared out of the prison in their car. The reporters, assuming they had Iva with them, tore after them. Iva, however, drove off later with her family. The two groups intended to meet for breakfast in Charleston, West Virginia, 100 miles away. They were confident the reporters would have given up by then, but when they stopped at a diner, the relentless reporters piled in. Here, the two policemen identified themselves and intervened, and asked them to give Iva a break. In that very different time, the reporters complied.

Two days later in Chicago, when Iva reported to Ben S. Meeker, chief U.S. probation and parole officer, she again found reporters waiting with more questions: Are you going to fight deportation? Why were you in Japan during the war? Do you plan to get back together with your husband? What are your immediate plans? To the latter she again said, "I'm just going out into the unknown. I don't know what to expect or what I'll find."[57] Her photo appeared in newspapers across the country, typically captioned, "Tokyo Rose is on probation. The honey-voiced Japanese radio broadcaster of World War II leaves the Federal probation office. . . ."[58] She had to report once a month, could not leave northern Illinois without permission, had to abstain from narcotics and liquor, and had to answer truthfully questions put to her by probation officers.

Wayne Collins saw she was under assault yet again and wrote a letter of encouragement. "Inasmuch as you, I believe, are the most courageous woman I know and have suffered immeasurably for some 10 years for wrongs of which you were guiltless and survived the ordeal, you are not likely to break at this late stage. You should take pride in the fact that although the government betrayed you, you never betrayed your government or country."[59]

After the Chicago office of the INS issued an order for her deportation, Wayne Collins had the negotiations transferred to San Francisco, where he knew the local INS official personally. The proceedings forced Iva to leave her father once again. She moved in April 1956, to live with the Collins family in Oakland. During this period, she met the younger Wayne Collins, who would represent her after his father's death. Wayne was eleven at the time, and Iva helped him with his algebra. To keep busy, she worked as the receptionist, typist, and office manager at the law office. She returned to Chicago for Inez' wedding in June 1957. The deportation case dragged on for two and a half years.

In March 1958, the Supreme Court decided *Trop v. Dulles* in favor of Trop. Trop was a World War II soldier who had deserted for one day, thought better of it, and returned voluntarily to his post. Because desertion was also a ground for forcible expatriation, the State Department sought to strip him of his citizenship.[60] Trop argued that to do so was, under the Eighth Amendment "cruel and unusual punishment." Chief Justice Earl Warren held that the "Amendment's phrase must draw its meaning from the evolving standards of decency that mark the progress of a maturing society." Although it was not a capital case, *Trop v. Dulles* continues to be recognized as a milestone in the ongoing debate about capital punishment. The Court's decision made it clear that the federal government would not succeed in its effort to strip Iva Toguri of her citizenship.[61] It required four months for the message to sink in, but on July 10, 1958, Director Bruce Barber announced that the INS would drop its effort "to deport Tokyo Rose."[62]

Iva's battles with the U.S. government were almost at an end. There remained only the matter of the unpaid fine for her treason, $10,000.

Iva maintained friendships with her former guards for the rest of her life. "Marshal Cole and his wife sent me Christmas and birthday cards even after I got out of prison." She kept in contact with Orientation Officer Adena Bass and Alderson Parole Officer Mary Cottrile in their retirement in Bradenton, Florida. Storehouse manager Smithson "wrote me a very nice letter after the pardon from Albuquerque." Chief Medical Officer Catherine Harold stayed in touch with Iva after she moved to Indiana, as did Chicago Probation officer Ben Meeker. "He was an absolutely wonderful person. Even to this day, I hear from him and his daughter." Her probation case worker, Marcella Frost, "made adjusting back to life very easy. She and I would go out to lunch, and she was just as nice as she could be." Frost too remained a friend after she left law enforcement to join the Salvation Army.

For decades after her release, from the 1960s through the 1990s, Iva visited her former guards in their retirement in Florida, New Mexico, and other places. Every year, she would spend several days with each, sightseeing, reminiscing, and enjoying each other's company. Death slowly reduced the ranks of the officers she knew at Alderson and elsewhere, and then poor health slowed her own travels. But Iva had proven herself to be "a real lady," and her warm relationships with these individuals testify to her good will, and theirs.

$\sim$

On June 19, 1959, Thomas DeWolfe shot himself to death in a Seattle hotel room. He was only 56. He left a note for the coroner that he had been in ill health. His son Tom had drowned the previous year, but his wife and son Frederick were still alive.[63]

No one can know what was in DeWolfe's heart when he committed suicide. Given the current context, it is tempting to speculate that his death had something to do with this case. But no one can know that.

Few biographical materials and no firsthand accounts of DeWolfe's life exist. His true character remains in doubt. Tom DeWolfe may have been an amoral opportunist. He received his orders to prosecute Iva Toguri, and he went to work. He knew he had no case, so he fabricated one. He prosecuted it ruthlessly. He threatened people until they capitulated and then dictated their lies to them. He sabotaged the defense by intimidating its witnesses. He himself lied about what he knew to be true and covered up those lies. He picked the jury by racist profiling. He biased the trial with the help of a complicit judge. In short, on this view, he framed an innocent woman out of political expediency and personal arrogance, and never thought twice about it.

We read about individuals like this in positions of power in the newspaper almost every day, and Tom DeWolfe may well have had such a character. But we should also consider the possibility that DeWolfe was an honorable man who succumbed to temptation. When the attorney general awarded him the plum assignment of prosecuting the most famous American traitor of the century, he faced a grave moral crisis. One can imagine DeWolfe struggling with his conscience. On the one hand, he would be doing his job, performing the duties of the office he had sworn to uphold; he could serve the interests of the president; he could send a message to all potential traitors that the United States would not tolerate their treachery; and, he could respond to the outcries from servicemen and Gold Star Mothers that Tokyo Rose be punished. He had spent his entire life preparing for this one momentous trial and now he had it in his hands. If he refused to prosecute, he knew he could expect to be demoted or even fired. The evidence against her was iffy, but there might be enough. He could win. On the other hand, weighing heavy in the scales of justice, Iva was innocent, and DeWolfe knew it.

Iva Toguri stood alone before the intimidating forces of Imperial Japan and remained true to herself. Tom DeWolfe, by contrast, failed his test of character. Had he steadfastly refused to prosecute, perhaps his superiors might not have persevered. But he knuckled under and accepted his moment in the sun, which was easy, instead of maintaining his professional integrity and accepting the consequences, which was hard. Once the trial process was under way, the need for a successful prosecution required him to make more and more ethical compromises. After he heard the verdict announced and his colleagues crowded around offering congratulations, he must have realized, if he were an honorable man, that his great victory was ashes in his mouth.

DeWolfe never tried another case. In 1956, when Iva Toguri got out of prison, he retired. In the end, he could not live with himself. Why, no one can know.

Notes

1. Iva remembered only Cole and his wife. The AP reported that "with her were two matrons and another woman prisoner." *New York Times*, November 16, 1949, 17. A contemporary photo shows Iva with matrons Ruth Berliner and Mrs. Mildred R. Cole. I assume Iva is correct about Mr. Cole and the press is correct about the second matron.

2. Interview with Rex Gunn, December 23, 1958. *They Called Her "Tokyo Rose,"* 100.

3. On January 8, 1980, Iva Toguri and her friend, Mary Coday, journeyed to Bradenton, Florida, where they taped an interview with Mary Cottrile and Adena "Dina" Bass. Iva gave me a transcript of this tape. Many recollections in this chapter come from it.

4. In our interviews in 1987, Iva remembered "a Washington paper" reported her IQ as the highest ever recorded at Alderson, at least to that time. I have verified that the report was not in the *Washington Post* but cannot swear such an item did not appear elsewhere. However, she also recalled her scores on two separate IQ tests were 150 and 160. Prison records do not substantiate this. Her records are on the Internet thanks to Dafydd Neal Dyar at http://www.dyarstraights.com/orphan_ann/alderson.html.

5. Billie Holiday served a year and a day in 1947–1948 for narcotics.

6. Flynn, *Alderson Story*, 145.

7. Flynn, *Alderson Story*, 172–73, 137.

8. One would suppose, given the years she lived there, that Iva would remember this number, but she told me in 1987 she lived in No. 8. She told Cottrile and Bass the same in 1980 and neither corrected her. Prison records, however, indicate her cottage was No. 7. It's a toss-up.

9. This is Iva's 1987 memory of what Houchins said. Obviously it is a paraphrase.

10. Flynn cites this as one of many unnecessary cruelties at Alderson. See *Alderson Story*, 33.

11. Special Progress Report, August 31, 1950, states her "regular assignment" at the storehouse was butcher; Cottrile on tape remembers her first assignment was truck driver.

12. Flynn, *Alderson Story*, 159.

13. Iva continued this meticulousness into her old age. During the many years she visited me at my home, I marveled at the fact that she packed her suitcase like a parachutist. She perfectly arranged every item and used tissue paper to separate and protect each garment.

14. Base pay does not include housing allowance. For E-1, $40; E-2, $46; E-3, $64; E-4, $70. See "Military Compensation Background Papers," Department of Defense, Under Secretary of Defense for Personnel and Readiness.

15. "Application for Living Ex-Prisoner of War Benefits." FBI letters of April 25, 1950; May 19, 1950; September 28, 1950; October 16, 1951. Benefits awarded July 24, 1951. NARA 9, Box 240.

16. Memo, AAG James McInerney to Hoover, February 13, 1951. NARA 9, Box 238.

17. Reference in letter to unnamed agency, July 13, 1954. NARA 9, Box 240.

18. Letter, J. E. Stearns, Department of the Army to Hoover, February 16, 1955. NARA 9, Box 240.

19. Wallace Ellwell Ince died in McMinnville, Oregon, on September 4, 1996, at age 84. He was succeeded in death by his wife, Dorothy Ursula Ince, who died on January 18, 2000. Oregon Death Index, 1903–1998. Oregon State Archives and Records Center, Salem.

20. Special Progress Report, August 31, 1950.

21. Special Progress Report, September 18, 1952.

22. From a March 20, 2000 letter to Dafydd Neal Dyar. See http://www.dyarstraights.com/orphan_ann/ alderson.html.

23. *New York Times*, October 8, 1949, 3.

24. *180 F.2d 271*. See *Washington Post*, February 7, 1950, 12.

25. *Oakland Tribune*, February 7, 1950.

26. Complete *Appellant's Brief* at NARA 5, Box 4960. Service, other materials at NARA 2, Box 5.

27. *Affidavit on Behalf of Extra Pages in Appellant's Opening Brief*, September 11, 1950. NARA 5, Box 4959.

28. *Brief for Appellee*. NARA 5, Box 4960.

29. "Transcript of record" refers to "the proceedings and pleadings necessary for the appellate court to review the history of the case." See *Black's Law Dictionary*, 1497.

30. Letter from Paul O'Brien to Henry Chandler, Director, Administrative Office of the U.S. Courts, November 21, 1949. NARA 5, Box 4959.

31. In case there is any confusion, the points that follow are my summary of the central arguments made in the *Appellant's Brief*.

32. Special Progress Report, August 31, 1950.

33. I am unsure how to spell many names in this chapter. I am transcribing Iva's spoken pronunciation and have no independent source. So it could be Father Ballinger or Balenger. I have "Mary Cottrile" in Iva's handwriting but cannot be sure if the last letter is an 'e' or a second 'l'.

34. Photo taken by author.

35. *Opinion*, U.S. Court of Appeals for the Ninth Circuit, *Iva Ikuko Toguri D'Aquino v. United States of America*, No. 12,383, October 10, 1951; 31, 17, 48, 5, 32, and 40–41, respectively. NARA 5, Box 4960; also NARA 2, Box 2. (Hereafter "Ninth Circuit *Opinion*.")

36. Ninth Circuit *Opinion*, 4.

37. Ninth Circuit *Opinion*, 12–13.

38. Ninth Circuit *Opinion*, 14.

39. Ninth Circuit *Opinion*, 7, footnote.

40. Ninth Circuit *Opinion*, 46, footnote, 11, and 46, respectively.

41. Ninth Circuit *Opinion*, 11.

42. Ninth Circuit *Opinion*, 19, citing Judge Roche's jury instructions.

43. Ninth Circuit *Opinion*, 3–4.

44. Original spelling, Ninth Circuit *Opinion*, 51.

45. *On Appellant's Petition for Rehearing*, U.S. Court of Appeals for the Ninth Circuit, December 17, 1951, 1. NARA 6, Box 2.

46. Douglas may not have. One biographer has noted that his judicial behavior in loyalty and treason cases "clearly evidences manifestations of Douglas's penchant for backing off or changing positions originally taken by him in important cases and controversies." In the view of another, Douglas was "emotionally divided between his own self-image as judicial champion of the underdog and his equally powerful loathing for Communists—and those who betray their country." Douglas's autobiography does not mention the Toguri case. The first citation is Howard Ball, "Loyalty, Treason and the State," in *He Shall Not Pass This Way Again*, Stephen L. Wasby, ed. (Pittsburgh, Pa.: University of Pittsburgh Press, 1990), 25. The second citation is Michael E. Parrish, "Justice Douglas and the Rosenberg Case: A Rejoinder," in *Cornell Law Review* 70 (1985), 1054.

47. Truman appointed Tom Campbell Clark on August 24, 1949. He was among four conservative (at least in comparison to the Roosevelt liberals like Douglas) justices appointed by Truman including Harold Burton, Sherman Minton, and Chief Justice Fred Vinson.

48. Letter, Thomas DeWolfe to William A. Paisley, Chief, Trial Section, Criminal Division, May 6, 1953. NARA 2, Box 6.

49. Flynn, *Alderson Story*, 31–32.

50. Flynn, *Alderson Story*, 158–62. "All the sex," 163.

51. Letter, Thomas DeWolfe to William F. Tompkins, AAG, Internal Security Division, Department of Justice, November 17, 1954. NARA 2, Box 6.

52. For an overview of this issue, see http://supreme.paxtv.findlaw.com/constitution/article01/36.html, especially footnote 1191. The relevant sections of the U.S. Code are 8 U.S.C. Sec. 1481–89.

53. Iva's 1980 interview transcript. See note 3.

54. Older New Yorkers may remember columnist Dorothy Kilgallen and older Americans generally may remember her from the TV series, "What's My Line?" Her father, James Kilgallen of INS, was among the reporters at Alderson that morning. He outsmarted all the other reporters at the boarding house by graciously agreeing to stay in a tiny anteroom, which happened to contain the only telephone.

55. This quote, other details of Iva's release at *Editor and Publisher* 89 (February 4, 1956): 16.

56. *Chicago Daily News*, January 30, 1956, 1. Photo from Library of Congress.

57. *Chicago Daily News*, January 30, 1956, 1.

58. *Washington Star*, January 31, 1956.

59. Letter sent in 1956; published in *San Francisco Examiner*, February 23, 1976.

60. The State Department strips citizens of their citizenship (hence *Trop v. Dulles*, i.e., John Foster Dulles, Secretary of State) and the INS then deports them. To avoid confusion, I refer to the INS only.

61. Congress deleted a clause about loss of citizenship as a penalty for affiliation with a terrorist organization from the Patriot Act.

62. *San Francisco Chronicle*, July 11, 1958.

63. *New York Times*, June 20, 1959, 43.

20

The Quest for a Pardon

After the U.S. government abandoned its attempt to deport her, Iva Toguri returned to private life. Except for rare press coverage, she managed to stay out of the newspaper for almost two decades. Individuals associated with her life in Japan or with the trial dispersed, returning to their own lives as well. Her husband, Phil, was among them.

Phil (Felipe) d'Aquino had journeyed to the United States to participate in the trial. He arrived in Seattle on Northwest Orient Airlines Flight 800 from Tokyo via Anchorage, Alaska, on June 5, 1949, along with fellow passengers Ted Tamba and defense team investigator Tetsujiro Nakamura.[1] U.S. Immigration had its eye on him. Edwin C. Stevens, the officer in charge in Anchorage, wrote on the passenger manifest,

> [D'Aquino] referred to Seattle for further investigation, inasmuch as he appears to be an immigrant rather than a visitor. He is destined to his wife who is a U.S. citizen on trial for treason; he is in possession of an affidavit of support showing he is coming to the United States for permanent residence. . . . He informed me he would like to stay in the United States permanently; but was informed by the U.S. Consul in Japan that he could not obtain an immigration visa, so he secured a visitor's "visa as the next best thing." It appears to me that if not IANIV he should probably be required to post departure bond.[2]

479

Stevens also issued a "Notice to Deliver, Detain on Board, or Remove Aliens" with instructions "Imm. Detention Quarters 815 Airport Way." When Phil was detained, Ted Tamba contacted Wayne Collins, who raised hell with Washington officials. Washington telephoned Seattle, and they released Phil after an overnight stay. Iva understood that agents told Phil, "Boy, you've got some high-priced lawyers to swing you overnight." Phil himself recalled, "When I told them I had come to testify, they said I would not be allowed to unless I signed a paper saying I would never return to the U.S."[3]

Phil bid Iva farewell the day before she left for prison and returned to Japan. Iva recalled, "Felipe was even more angry at the verdict than I was. He said, 'The lying bastards put you in jail.'" His treatment by immigration officials and the injustice of the trial destroyed Phil's sentimental attachment to the United States and its values. He corresponded with Iva in prison, but authorities censored his letters. When Iva was released in 1956, Japanese newspapers contacted Phil, now a newspaperman himself in Yokohama. The title of one article read, "Husband of 'Tokyo Rose' Implies He Still Loves Her."[4] But Iva, fighting with immigration officials and on parole, couldn't leave the United States and Phil couldn't enter it. They lost touch with each other. In 1976, Iva had tears in her eyes as she read an interview with him. "Poor guy," she said at the time, "He went through hell, too. What happened to him was unfair to him—more even than to me in a way."[5] Iva and Phil never saw each other again. They divorced in 1980.[6]

In 1987, as noted in chapter 11, Iva described her love affair with Phil using decidedly cool rhetoric. Asked whether she missed him, she replied, "I don't have any particular feelings," but added that she wouldn't see him even if she had the opportunity. As their correspondence wound down, she wrote to him that "he had his whole life ahead of him and he should get married and have a family. I sensed he knew that my love for my father was stronger than my love for him. I really did encourage him to think about a divorce. But he said he would still be married in the eyes of the church. That kind of started turning me off." According to Iva during our interviews, Jun went to Japan on business several times after the war. He visited Iva's former landlady Mrs. Kido on every trip until her death, but never Phil. When asked why, Iva replied dismissively, "What was there to see him about? She was more responsible for protecting me than he was."

Iva's account is no more trustworthy than her tale of the disloyalty of Chiyeko Ito. Perhaps Jun never visited Phil, but Iva's reason, that Mrs. Kido helped her more, is nonsense. Even if that were true, which it isn't, so what? Phil supported Iva unfailingly. Perhaps Jun's personality clashed with Phil's when they met in 1949, and so he never visited him later on. Perhaps Jun couldn't find him. However, it's entirely possible that Jun visited Phil on every trip but that Iva, having added Phil to her enemies list along with so many others, misremembered what happened in a way that maintained her father's unwavering fidelity to her.

How Phil became persona non grata to Iva is as much a mystery as why she married him in the first place. Phil had fought for her at work, his family had taken her into their home, he had testified for her in person at trial, and he had never said a word against her. His remarks to Immigration Agent Stevens that he intended to permanently reside in the United States indicate a firm intention at least on his part to preserve their marriage and to leave his family for Iva. Given this devotion, Iva's attitude toward Phil later in life comes across as uncharitable at best, mean-spirited at worst. Did Iva view him as merely a wartime convenience—a helper, a second income, and a sexual partner? One can understand that she would not dare leave the States after getting out of prison, especially since the U.S. government so much wanted her to do so, because without citizenship or a passport she could never expect to return. In addition, her memories of Japan overall were so negative that she told me in another context, "I don't ever want to go back to Japan." Since her failure to return to Phil needs little explanation, Iva could have declared that Phil was a terrific guy whom she loved but circumstances forced them apart. Instead, she denied any affection for him, explaining that Phil knew she loved her father more than him, which seems a gratuitous rationalization.

Iva's skewed perceptions of Phil are complicated by the fact that, while she was in prison, her father remarried.[7] Jun chose a Japanese woman 16 years his junior who had children of her own. Iva despised his new wife. In 1987, she described her as "greedy," "quite a little actress," "selfish, grabby," and "not a decent person."[8] Iva socialized so little with the two of them that she couldn't say whether their marriage was happy or not. The marriage clearly disappointed Iva, who saw in this woman not only a replacement of her mother but in some ways a replacement of herself. One might speculate that this relationship soured Iva on men and marriage, hardened her defenses against emotional vulnerability, and infected her memories of her own marriage to Phil.

~

Ted Tamba had filed a petition for executive clemency in the summer of 1954, but President Eisenhower had ignored it. On November 4, 1968, the day before the election of Richard Nixon, Wayne Collins filed a petition for a presidential pardon. He wanted to give outgoing President Lyndon Johnson an opportunity to grant the pardon without making the request a campaign issue. The Attorney General at the time was Ramsey Clark, the son of Tom Clark, the Attorney General who had directed DeWolfe to prosecute. Johnson denied the request. The Johnson administration, however, did confiscate in 1968 the cash value of two of Iva's life insurance policies as partial payment of her $10,000 fine. This small matter nevertheless made national news and again thrust Iva into the public spotlight, stimulating the uninformed to send her hate mail:

> Why aren't you living in Japan? What are you doing in the U.S.? You tried to help Japan enslave us. Shame. How can you face anyone? Go to Japan and stay there. Americans despise you.[9]

In 1971, the Nixon administration summoned her into court and demanded payment of the remainder. Wayne Collins was incredulous:

> They must have billions in fines they never collect and never try to collect. They know now that the whole case was trumped up. This is just another form of persecution. They have done enough of that. She didn't do anything. I don't know who's pushing this. All the people who hounded her then are now dead—the prosecuting attorneys, the judge, and most of the witnesses. Today, a court would dismiss the case out of hand. The war is a long way off. I believe that girl was innocent absolutely. I have never had any doubt in my mind.[10]

As Collins himself indicated, the government officials seeking payment probably knew nothing about the trial or Iva's guilt or innocence. They saw she owed a fine, and they tried to collect it.

~

Six people about whom Iva cared deeply died during these years. Iva's brother, the kindhearted Fred, had not only inherited his mother's sweet disposition but her frail health. In early 1959, doctors diagnosed Fred with bilateral uremia (toxicity in the bloodstream due to kidney failure) and told him he had one month to live. The news devastated Jun Toguri. Fred himself became despondent. Iva admitted, "Many times he attempted suicide because the thought of not being able to live long enough to see his kids grow up was very depressing." Iva installed him in Inez' house where they could watch him, put him on a strict diet, and went over every morning to inject him with insulin. Under Iva's care, Fred lasted a year. He succumbed in January 1960; he was only 49. In 1964, Charles Cousens died of a heart attack at age 60. Iva remembered him as the most perfect gentlemen she had ever met.[11] Her youngest sister, Inez, died in 1972 at age 47.[12] In the winter of 1973, Ted Tamba suffered heart failure at age 74, and the next summer, on July 16, 1974, Wayne Collins, also 74, died of a heart attack aboard a Pan Am flight from Honolulu to San Francisco. He had stopped in Hawaii for a brief vacation after representing a client in Hong Kong. The Japanese American community mourned Wayne Collins as their greatest champion. Iva attended both of her attorneys' funerals in San Francisco.

Upon his death, his son, also Wayne Collins, took over his father's law practice and Iva's representation. Although Iva affectionately referred to him as "Wayne Junior," he is not actually Wayne Collins, Jr., as some newspaper accounts have it. The father was Wayne Mortimer Collins and the son, Wayne Merrill Collins. Together, the two Wayne M. Collins represented Iva Toguri for 60 years. Neither ever charged Iva or her father for their services.

~

As noted in chapter 6, Jun Toguri functioned as a principal architect of the migration of Japanese Americans to Chicago. In addition to helping internees find housing and jobs, he sponsored and underwrote the education of many Japanese students at American universities, as well as sending hundreds of books and packages of educational supplies to schools in Japan after the war. Iva recalled, "One day a big box came full of letters from students at a grammar school. They were spectacular letters, all illustrated, thanking my father for these books. He sat there and tears were coming out of his eyes. One little boy said, 'I used to wait for the school bell so I could run home to play, but now I run to the library to read about America.'"

Near the occasion of Jun's 88th birthday, an important milestone to Japanese, the emperor of Japan recognized his efforts with a medal. Jun Toguri traveled to Japan to accept this honor under the assumption the proceedings would be low-key. "When the newspapers caught the name 'Toguri' they knew there was only one Toguri and they knew that he had to be my father. He was staying at the Imperial Hotel and so many reporters came to the hotel, he couldn't leave his room. My father almost had cardiac arrest. It had been years—he didn't think [the case] was newsworthy." Eventually, he agreed to be interviewed on a television program. Among those watching were the children of his mother from her Tokyo remarriage. Immediately after the program aired, "his half-brothers came flocking to the Imperial Hotel. 'Ah, the long-lost half-brother, the one that went to the United States!' This is the first we [his children] knew of it. I don't know why my father never mentioned—well, yes I do. My father was a very proud man. He was very, very conscious of the fact that he came from a broken home. I have a feeling this is why he left." On his actual birthday, Iva and June threw him a large birthday party similar to those he had thrown for the neighborhood when Iva was a child. They invited 350 guests, and his 2 youngest half-brothers flew over from Japan.

On June 24, 1972, Jun Toguri died of a massive stroke at age 90. Friends from Chicago and Japan sent thousands of dollars worth of flowers, which Iva considered a waste. Although Iva hoped for a simple ceremony, "it was a monstrosity. Every Buddhist priest in the city participated in the service," even though Jun did not wish to be cremated in Buddhist tradition. The family buried him in Chicago, beside Iva's mother and brother. (Jun had removed Fumi's ashes from Tulare and placed them in Fred's grave.)

The knowledge that her father died believing that the Tokyo Rose scandal would forever taint the family name heightened Iva's grief. "He said, 'Oh, it had to happen to you. It couldn't have been Yamada or Yamashita. It had to be Toguri, the only one in this country.'"[13] Iva had slowly paid down her fine, but to finally put an end to Iva's persecution, Jun Toguri made a provision in his will that the remainder of the $10,000 fine be paid from his estate.[14] "Wayne Collins said not to pay it. I can't explain why [my father] left money in his will. We never talked about it, and we never talked about the effect of the case on my life. He just accepted what had happened and built the future without looking back."

~

The quest for a pardon for Iva Toguri began with an obscure and unlikely event: a Boston pediatrician who had never heard of

Tokyo Rose read a master's thesis in history submitted to the University of San Francisco by a retired lieutenant colonel of the U.S. Army. The retired officer was John Hada, and his thesis concerned the indictment and trial of Iva Toguri/Tokyo Rose. The pediatrician, Dr. Clifford Uyeda (pronounced *wed duh*; Figure 20.1[15]), had been immersed in his residency at Massachusetts General at the time of the trial and took no notice of it.[16] Shortly thereafter, he decided to practice medicine in San Francisco. How Dr. Uyeda learned of Hada's thesis in the summer of 1973, even

Figure 20.1. Clifford Uyeda.
Courtesy of National Japanese Historical Society.

he wasn't sure. In any event, his discovery was serendipitous for Iva. Clifford Uyeda was a methodical and serious-minded person who throughout his career translated theoretical knowledge into action.[17] He read everything he could find about the case. When he finished, "the enormity of the injustice perpetrated against this single unfortunate woman was overwhelming."[18] He resolved to do something about it.

Uyeda enlisted Hada in his cause, and the two of them somewhat naively contacted the Japanese American Citizens League, the JACL, or, as the elder Wayne Collins derisively called them, the jackals. JACL had offered no support whatsoever during the postwar years when Iva needed it, and Collins never forgave them. JACL had belatedly passed a resolution in the summer of 1974 offering assistance to Iva if she desired it, but nothing had come of their gesture. Unconvinced of their sincerity, Iva's reaction was, "Why now, after thirty years?"[19] Uyeda persuaded David Ushio, JACL's National Executive Director, to form an action committee. Nine people showed up at Uyeda's apartment on the night of April 2, 1975. Despite considerable foot dragging and even roadblocks set up by JACL,[20] this small group created in short order a national movement to obtain a pardon for Iva Toguri and the reinstatement of her citizenship.

～

Uyeda believed the times were propitious. President Gerald Ford had pardoned draft dodgers after Vietnam and Richard Nixon after Watergate. Why should he not pardon Iva Toguri? (Figure 20.2).[21] The committee contacted the younger Wayne Collins, and Uyeda wrote to Iva herself. She was polite, thanked him for his interest, but replied that she had no real hope they would be successful. Iva did not tell the committee at that time that she feared a national effort. Whenever a story about her or Tokyo Rose appeared in the paper, she received crank calls and hate

Figure 20.2. Campaign button.
Photograph taken by the author.

mail. Despite her reluctance, the committee and Collins prepared a game plan. They agreed to present the effort as the committee's work on behalf of Iva without her involvement; to avoid publicity for JACL or committee members; to garner support from individuals, organizations, the press, politicians, and finally intimates of the president; and, to delay filing of the pardon application until just before the election, so that Gerald Ford would not have to take a position or act on the application during the campaign.

The committee prepared a background piece for the press. Titled "Victim of a Legend," this little booklet summarized the case and argued that a full and unconditional pardon was the only just resolution. Masayo Umezawa Duus aided the committee by sharing her research on the subject. Duus was preparing *Orphan of the Pacific*, the first book-length treatment of the case in English. Later on, she helped ensure the prominent reporting of Iva's story in Japan. The committee members printed their booklet at their own expense and distributed it initially to friends.

In retrospect, the American press and public took surprisingly little time to appropriate the novel idea that Tokyo Rose was innocent. The prevarications of Vietnam and the Watergate cover-up had undermined Americans' faith in the honesty of their government. The committee sent out the first few booklets in November 1975. On January 8, 1976, the *Denver Post* published an editorial titled "Clemency Due in 'Tokyo Rose' Case." Shortly thereafter, similar editorials and favorable articles appeared in the *Wall Street Journal*; *Washington Post* and *Star*; *San Francisco Examiner, Chronicle*, and *Bay Guardian*; *Los Angeles Times* and *Herald-Examiner*; *Chicago Tribune, Sun-Times*, and *Daily News*; *Christian Science Monitor*; *Newsweek*; and other outlets. Edwin McDowell's op-ed in the *Wall Street Journal* was typical: "Convicted of treason 20 years ago, she still maintains her innocence. And she's probably right. A presidential pardon would be tacit acknowledgment that the government was punishing a legend rather than a human being who stood in the dock of justice."[22] Individuals such as George R. Ariyoshi, governor of Hawaii, and John Mann, jury foreman at the 1949 trial, joined the chorus of support in the early days. John Gildersleeve, one of only two grand jurors to vote against Iva's indictment in 1948, sent the committee a check to help defray its costs.

Not everyone was kindly disposed, however. A poll of readers by the *Detroit Free Press* showed 72 percent disapproved of a pardon.[23] The national Commander of the Veterans of Foreign

Wars declared on NBC's *Today* show that he and presumably his organization opposed a pardon.[24] However, the Uyeda committee believed such opinions resulted merely from ignorance of the facts of the case, and redoubled their efforts to get the truth out.

～

The laurels for opening the floodgates of support for the pardon effort belong to the *Chicago Tribune* and reporter Ronald Yates. Yates was the *Tribune*'s correspondent in Tokyo. He located and interviewed trial witnesses Kenkichi Oki and George Mitsushio. Safe now from American justice, they confessed the truth of what had happened.

Yates clearly disdained Oki and Mitsushio, who by 1976 were wealthy businessmen. In one paragraph, he noted that "former government witnesses who were interviewed asked not to be identified for fear of 'harmful repercussions,'" adding that they were Iva's superiors at Radio Tokyo. In the very next paragraph, he named Oki and Mitsushio as Iva's superiors. Readers immediately figured out that they were the source of the quotes in the article, but Yates literally kept his promise of anonymity by never making clear which one of them said what. They were Tweedledum and Tweedledee at the trial and maintained the symmetry in their confession:

> U.S. Occupation Army police came and told me I had no choice but to testify against Iva, or else.
>
> We were told if we didn't cooperate, Uncle Sam might arrange a trial for us too. All of us could see how easy it was for a mammoth country like the United States to crucify a Japanese American—all we had to do was look at Iva.
>
> After I was flown to San Francisco, we were told what to say and what not to say two hours every morning for a month before the trial started.
>
> Even though I was a government witness against her, I can say today that Iva Toguri was innocent—she never broadcast anything treasonable.
>
> Iva never made a treasonable broadcast in her life. She got a raw deal—she was railroaded into jail.[25]

Yates also found Shigetsugu Tsuneishi, the IJA major who had been head of Japanese propaganda, living in retirement on the island of Shikoku. Tsuneishi said he intended *Zero Hour* to be soft propaganda but, "ironically we discovered that the show was so popular among American soldiers that it was having just the opposite effect. It was actually building the enemy's morale instead of destroying it."[26] Noting that more than 200 Japanese Americans worked on propaganda during the war and none were prosecuted, Tsuneishi told Yates, "It was very surprising to me when she was arrested and put on trial. Very surprising, indeed." Nonetheless, he wished it understood that he was not like Oki and Mitsushio. "My conscience is clear. I told the truth at her trial." Tsuneishi had apparently forgotten his many lies; for example, that he never threatened anyone, and that the truth about his propaganda broadcasts that he now so freely admitted was dragged out of him at trial only after days of pounding by Wayne Collins.

Yates also managed to locate Teruo Ozasa. Ozasa had heard more of Iva on the radio than any other person. A Nisei born in Salt Lake City, he had moved to Japan in 1940 and taken Japanese citizenship because "it was impossible to get a job if you weren't Japanese."[27] During the war, Ozasa worked as the sound engineer for *Zero Hour* and listened to about 80 percent of Iva's broadcasts. He had testified for the defense via deposition at the trial, but his statements were lost in the welter of testimony. "A lot of people who testified against Iva did it to save their own necks," Ozasa told Yates. "I never heard Iva make any treasonable statements while broadcasting. All she did was play records and make small talk."[28] Ozasa also confirmed General Eichelberger's statement that a B-29 had dropped a box of new records for Tokyo Rose a few days after Iva apologized for playing the same ones over and over, but Ozasa explained that a hard landing had broken most of the records.[29]

On the morning of March 22, 1976, the day the *Tribune* broke its story, Iva frantically telephoned Clifford Uyeda in San Francisco. "There's a huge crowd gathered outside my store. Reporters and cameramen are all over the place. I'm not stepping outside my office."[30] Iva Toguri was suddenly back in the news in a big way. She couldn't hide much longer.

∼

Almost a decade earlier, Bill Kurtis, best known today as the host of the Discovery channel's *Biography* series, met Iva Toguri on a routine news assignment. By 1976, he was the anchor of Chicago's CBS news broadcast. Kurtis had gained Iva's trust over the years. He strongly believed in her innocence before it became fashionable, and as a result he was the person locally that Iva called for help on March 22. Kurtis hurried to the store and found Iva hiding in her upstairs office. Kurtis immediately telephoned Walter Cronkite, and they did a brief piece that night on the *CBS Evening News*. Cronkite recognized a good story, and told Kurtis to arrange for *60 Minutes* to do a segment on the case. Iva, fearing Mike Wallace would replace Brundidge in her pantheon of media tormentors, refused. Kurtis called Uyeda and Collins, who convinced her that Gerald Ford watched the program regularly. Iva eventually agreed, and correspondent Morley Safer treated her with kindness during the shoot in April. On June 20, 1976, the American public got their first good look at the woman convicted of being the venomous traitor Tokyo Rose. Fifty-nine years old, short, round-faced, wearing spectacles, Iva Toguri didn't appear to be that scary. Clifford Uyeda and his committee felt the effects immediately:

> The impact of the *60 Minutes* [broadcast] was tremendous. Editorials across the nation came to her support. Letters poured in. Two weeks later on July 4th, the country's 200th and also Iva's 60th birthday, Iva's store looked like a florist shop. Brilliant colored carnations, gladiolas, birds-of-paradise, and potted plants of all shapes and sizes were delivered to her store. Some came from those she knew, but many were from total strangers. "I can't believe it, she said. It's 180 degrees from twenty-seven years ago."[31]

The California State Assembly passed a resolution supporting Iva 60–0; the State Senate, 22–0. The San Francisco Board of Supervisors adopted a pardon resolution and became the first city to officially support the effort. Shortly thereafter, the city of Los Angeles rescinded its 1947 resolution urging the U.S. government to force Iva to remain in Japan and passed a new resolution endorsing a pardon.

The backing of GIs gratified Iva even more. Asked who should shoulder most of the culpability for the injustices perpetrated against her, Iva answered that she considered the government and the media equally to blame, but added, "the government does not include the Army." Typical of Army support was the 41st Infantry Division, which declared in their publication *The Jungleer*:

> If it were in the power of the 41sters, Mrs. D'Aquino—"Tokyo Rose"—would be pardoned as promptly as Washington's bureaucratic tape would allow. In fact, there isn't a single man in the 41st Infantry Division who thinks she should have been tried and punished in the first place. The case is considered a travesty on justice and a blot on our postwar behavior.[32]

A few Nisei veterans groups endorsed the effort, but most, especially the decorated 442nd Regimental Combat Team, remained silent.

Four days after the *60 Minutes* broadcast, the *New York Times* ran an article entitled, "Tokyo Rose Pardon Viewed as Unlikely." The *Times* reported that "White House officials know of no plans by President Ford to grant Tokyo Rose a pardon despite reports from the director general of the Japanese Prime Minister's office."[33]

On November 17, 1976, Wayne Collins, Clifford Uyeda, and Iva announced the filing of an official request for pardon at a press conference on the steps of the federal courthouse where she had been convicted (Figure 20.3).[34] The building had since become a Post Office, and reporters took pictures of Iva with the postmaster mailing her petition for pardon. They asked, "How did you manage to survive all these years as a convicted person if you are innocent?" Iva answered, "My conscience is clear. I can sleep nights."

The next day, David Brinkley of NBC used the movie

Figure 20.3. Wayne Merrill Collins and Iva.
Courtesy of *San Francisco Chronicle*.

short produced by the Army Signal Corps in 1945 in which the Corps re-created Iva's broadcasts in her Radio Tokyo studio to inform listeners that she wanted a pardon because she was old. Later, he defended his remarks. "We offered no grounds for Mrs. Toguri's appeal for a pardon because there were no grounds, beyond the fact that she simply wants a pardon." UPI also quoted Iva as saying, "I am not asking for exoneration, only a pardon."[35] She never made such a statement.[36]

~

When Jun Toguri emigrated to Canada at the turn of the century, he made friends of other Japanese from Yamanashi Prefecture who also chose Canada because they were barred from U.S. citizenship. Many of these friends, like Jun, journeyed back and forth between Japan, Canada, and the United States on business. Most also selected brides from their native country. Jun married Fumi in Japan and their first child, Fred, was born in Japan before Jun brought Fumi and Fred to live with him in the United States. One of his Yamanashi friends brought his bride to Canada while she was still pregnant. Canadian immigration authorities, however, ruled her papers were not in order and denied her entry into the country. Jun interceded on their behalf. Canadian immigration relented and thereby spared the pregnant wife the rigors of a return trip to Japan. She gave birth shortly thereafter.

Iva's application for clemency arrived, as planned, too late to be an issue in the 1976 campaign. Gerald Ford, in part because he had been so liberal with pardons, lost the election to Jimmy Carter. Iva desperately needed someone close to Ford, a personal friend, to convince the president to grant her pardon before his administration concluded. Here, Jun Toguri's generosity paid off for his daughter. The newborn whom Jun had saved from birth on a ship sailing back to Japan was S. I. Hayakawa. Hayakawa had grown up to be U.S. Senator from California and an intimate of Gerald Ford.[37]

Hayakawa called on Ford in early December, shortly after the election, to argue Iva's case. He warned Uyeda to keep his visit confidential, which Uyeda did. Ford was noncommittal, but shortly thereafter FBI agents visited Iva and each person she had named as a character reference in her application. The agents told those they interviewed that they were under orders to submit their findings by mid-December. This boded well for a Christmas decision, a traditional time for pardons. But Christmas came and went. Hayakawa pressed the issue. On January 3, Uyeda sent a telegram to the White House indicating how wonderful it would be if a pardon could be announced at the "Wayne Collins Appreciation Dinner" to be held January 8, 1977. January 8 passed with no response to the telegram.

Jimmy Carter would be sworn in on January 20, 1977. As the date neared, Iva believed the pardon effort had failed. Still she sat by her phone at home, too nervous to go to work. After three days of waiting, she couldn't tolerate sitting around any longer. On January 19, "I said 'to heck with it' and I went back to work. The store was packed with media, reporters just milling about waiting for news." Bill Kurtis knocked at the back door. He informed her the pardon had come through. When Iva remained incredulous, Kurtis called the presidential pardon attorney, Lawrence M. Traylor. "Traylor was not in the office, so Bill spoke to another attorney. I heard [Bill] say, 'Would you please tell this woman what you just told me?' He handed me the phone and the man said he had the papers before him granting an unconditional pardon. Of course, then all hell broke loose." Amid the cheers and shouts of congratulations, Iva found her sister June. The two of them wept together, partly in joy for the pardon and partly in sorrow that their father had not lived to witness his daughter's vindication.

In San Francisco, at JACL headquarters, Clifford Uyeda hung up the phone he had kept open to Iva at the store.

> I linked my fingers behind my neck and closed my eyes to gather my thoughts. So it had finally happened. Thirty years of waiting were over for Iva Toguri. Nothing could restore or change those thirty miserable years, but at last the President had recognized the injustice of the ordeal she had undergone. The dignity with which she suffered in silence, the indestructible loyalty she held toward the United States—it was remarkable. If Wayne Mortimer Collins and Theodore Tamba were still alive, I thought, how they would have rejoiced this day.[38]

Iva wrote a letter to Gerald Ford thanking him for the pardon and affirming that she "prized her American citizenship above everything I ever possessed." Among the joys of citizenship is the ability to vote and possibility of traveling overseas. "I think I'll get a passport now. Before, I was always afraid that if I left the country I'd start World War III," she told me in 1987. But she never left.

~

Iva Toguri died September 26, 2006, at age 90, of a massive stroke, exactly as her father had. She still lived in the apartment building her father bought with the proceeds from her mother's life insurance policy.

In the years following her pardon, she actively supported various causes, especially the White Crane Senior Citizen Health Center. She held season tickets to the Chicago Opera Company and the Goodman Theater. "I'm the first one in line whenever the tickets to a ballet go on sale." Her sister June had passed away in 1996,[39] but Iva had many friends who kept her busy. She slowly weaned herself from J. Toguri Mercantile, which is now managed by her nephew. Following a mild stroke in 2002, she ceased her annual travel to friends throughout the United States.

In 1987, I asked her what in her life made her happiest. "Trying to keep alive what my father left in my care, the business. I've enjoyed it, and I have proven that I could do it." Years after her father's death, Iva learned that the Toguri patriarch had stubbornly held onto his traditional beliefs about women and business while at the same time acknowledging his admiration for her abilities. She discovered this fact late one night when she entertained his lawyers at a favorite restaurant. Fueled by cocktails, they confessed that Jun had once opined, "Unfortunately, I wish my son had been my daughter and my daughter had been my son. My number one should have been my number two and vice versa." Jun never expected that Iva, not Fred, would take his place as manager of the family business and succeed so handsomely. But, "He knew me. He knew me well enough." Every week, she visited the grave of this "grand old man" whom she missed more than anyone else.

Although she described her later life as tranquil, the war still haunted her. A visitor snooping around Iva's apartment in Chicago would have found cupboards and freezers filled with several months' worth of canned goods, frozen meats and vegetables, powdered milk, and other foodstuffs. She slowly rotated them, opening and eating the oldest and buying replacements to put at the back of the shelf. Every so often, she made a large donation to a food kitchen for the poor and then immediately replenished her supplies. Her father often made fun of her for keeping enough food to feed a small army, but she could not break herself of the habit. Stockpiling was her only psychological defense against the fear of starvation and the memory of going for days with only water to drink.

Looking back on her experiences, Iva drew a somber conclusion: She believed she came into the world burdened with a melancholy destiny. "I guess I'm a fatalist. Had I not gone through these years of hardship and deprivation, I would probably have had a chronic illness with which I would have had to cope all my life. And if not that, some other disaster."

This philosophy protected her from regret. "I have resigned myself to what I've said and done and what I've subjected my family to. Had I done something different, there would have been something else." She was convinced that she, and none of the other women who broadcast, had to be Tokyo Rose. "I was the only one the POWs trusted. I was the one they recruited. I retained my American citizenship, and if you go from there, I was the logical candidate because everyone else was either a Canadian citizen or born in Japan or married to a Japanese. No one was in the same situation that I was."

Bitterness never overtook her, and she remembered the counsel of her champion, the elder Wayne Collins, who said to her near the end of his life, "It's true you have had it tough. But most of us grow up, get a job, get married, have kids, and we die. That's it. What's so exciting about that? Whereas you've met all of these famous people, and criminals and prostitutes, too. You've been exposed to an environment the rest of us have never experienced. Your world has a lot of little honeycombs, and it's much more colorful than the drab life that we've lived."

Iva's world seems to have been more catacombs than honeycombs, but in any case, had Iva never gone to Japan, her father's traditionalist views of business and the sexes would have probably forced her into conformity with the life of her sister June: marriage, children, and a secondary role in the family store. Instead, the war came, and Iva Toguri had to battle her way through foreign conflicts and domestic intrigues. Handed a life that she did not intend, she acted as she thought best, although her own ambition and myopia about the larger political forces at work clouded her judgment. Over time, as events hammered her with adversity, humiliation, and finally catastrophe, she developed her character. Iva Toguri did not merely endure her history. In the end, she prevailed over it and became, not a person of perfect virtue, not an individual without flaws, but who she ought to be.

~

Finally, a word on this work's second biographical subject, Tokyo Rose. When Iva Toguri died, Brian Williams on the *NBC Evening News* offered this obituary:

> The men and women who served this nation in World War II came to know her voice instantly. She was the voice of propaganda, the voice of the enemy. Tonight Tokyo Rose is dead. Her real name, it turns out, was Iva Toguri. She was a first-generation Japanese American who was stranded in Japan at the start of the war, and soon went on the air for Radio Tokyo, notoriously telling U.S. servicemen in the Pacific that their cause was lost and their sweethearts back home were betraying them. Luckily, military power won out over propaganda. The right team won. Tokyo Rose was convicted of treason. But interestingly, she was later pardoned by President Gerald Ford, who once served in the South Pacific in the Navy. In later years, she lived a quiet life in Chicago where she died Tuesday at the age of ninety.[40]

From Brinkley to Williams, NBC's record of ignorance on this subject remains unblemished. Despite its research department, NBC never learned that Iva Toguri and Tokyo Rose were not one and the same, and that Tokyo Rose was a legend, not a real person.

Hollywood, as might be expected, has followed its own dictum, "When the legend becomes fact, print the legend." Despite the nationwide publicity surrounding Iva's 1949 trial, which included the information that she broadcast under the name "Orphan Ann," the submariners in the 1958 film *Run Silent, Run Deep* crowd around the radio to listen to "Tokyo Rose." That same year, the sailors in

South Pacific sing, "We get speeches from our skipper and advice from Tokyo Rose," as they lament that "there ain't nothin' like a dame."[41] In 1959, a shortage of paint forces the sailors in *Operation Petticoat* to use a mixture of red and white on their submarine. Within hours, Tokyo Rose recommends that the "pink submarine" begin the New Year (1942) by surrendering. As usual, she is much better informed than the U.S. Navy, which, fearing a Japanese trick, orders that "any unidentified submarine, pink or otherwise, is to be sunk on sight."[42] In *Bridge to the Sun* (1961), which is set in Japan, a svelte and sexy Tokyo Rose herself appears on screen clad in a kimono; "Tokyo Rose is in rare form tonight," remarks one character concerning her broadcast.

The references to Tokyo Rose in movies continue through the decades. As the pardon effort that brought nationwide attention to the fact that Tokyo Rose did not exist reached its zenith in 1976, that summer the movie *Midway* featured a scene of three pilots discussing the whereabouts of the Japanese fleet. "He gets his dope straight from Tokyo Rose," one kids another. Even after Iva won her pardon in 1977, the boss in the 1980 movie *Nine to Five* growls at his resigning secretary, "Tokyo Rose and now you." However, screenwriters eventually became aware that no one broadcast as Tokyo Rose. In 2001's *Pearl Harbor*, the radio siren to whom servicemen listen does identify herself as Orphan Ann. Unfortunately, she's broadcasting before the Doolittle raid. Doolittle bombed Tokyo in April 1942; Iva/Orphan Ann did not appear on the radio until late in 1943. In Clint Eastwood's 2006 film *Flags of Our Fathers*, the servicemen hear Orphan Ann shortly before they attack Iwo Jima, which is at least chronologically possible. However, Eastwood's incarnation speaks with a sensuously soft and seductive voice, has a Japanese accent, struggles with English, is informed about upcoming military operations, and taunts GIs with the traditional Tokyo Rose patter:

Welcome, all marines off Iwo Jima. We have a long time wait for you. Poor marines, so far from home for no good reason. Think of your girls back home waiting for you. But a girl cannot stay home every night. Who do you think they're with tonight? And will she let him kiss her? And will he comfort her at your funeral? (Laughs) This sweet music is to make you think of your girls back home who are missing you. This is Orphan Ann. I'll see you tomorrow night.[43]

No matter. Contrary to the pronouncement of Brian Williams, despite the name change in Hollywood films, Tokyo Rose is not dead. Axis Sally is long forgotten, but Tokyo Rose remains young and vibrant. Her legend thrives because journalists, ad copywriters, composers, novelists, and politicians can expect their audience to recognize her name.

The contours of the legend, however, have changed somewhat. Entering the term "Tokyo Rose" into an Internet search engine returns 340,000 hits, only a small percentage of which refer to the Iva Toguri case. A month before the presidential election in 1991, southern California Congressman Duke Cunningham attacked Democratic nominee Bill Clinton for having protested the Vietnam War, saying, "This is an issue that will kill Clinton when people realize what a traitor he is to this country. Tokyo Rose had nothing over Clinton."[44] (In 2005, Cunningham pled guilty to federal charges of conspiracy to commit bribery, mail fraud, wire fraud, and tax evasion.) Before the 2004 election, a partisan of John Kerry complained about the coverage of the Associated Press. "And who is leading the charge? The reprehensible Repug [sic] operative-posing-as-journalist, Nedra 'Tokyo Rose' Pickler. She is the WORST of the anti-Kerry propagandists."[45] Former Secretary of Defense Donald Rumsfeld attacked the news media for its coverage of the war in Iraq by comparing their misinformation to "the infamous radio broadcasts of 'Tokyo Rose' during World War II."[46] *Washington Monthly* criticized CNN's decision to use a background graphic of an American flag for its coverage of the Patriot Act. The headline claims "it's a 'controversial' measure, but judging from the picture you'd have to be Tokyo Rose to oppose it."[47] Editorialist Clint Willis described Rush Limbaugh as "the male 'Tokyo Rose' for the Bushevik oligarchy."[48] In 2006, the blogosphere was filled with hundreds of iterations of the following rant:

> During World War II, our enemies developed a method specifically designed to demoralize our troops fighting for the future of the Free World. These experts produced scripts that were provided to a famous broadcaster who, everyday, would package

three main points in different ways while the core message remained the same:

1. Your president is lying to you
2. This war is illegal
3. You cannot win this war

The famous broadcaster was "Tokyo Rose." Each day her goal was clear. Do everything she could do to impact the fighting men in hopes of one day breaking their morale and ultimately causing them to give up. She failed. The American GI was focused on the mission. Honor was the highest calling, not scoring points in the media. Listen closely to the words coming from the Democrats and you will hear, verbatim, the same words used by "Tokyo Rose" with one slight difference. Reid and Pelosi claim to support our troops before they demoralize them. Hey, wait a minute. "Tokyo Rose" told our soldiers she was on their side just like the Democrats are telling our troops today. I guess there is no difference.

"Tokyo Rose" had one radio station to spew her message to the troops. Ted Kennedy and company have ABC, CBS, NBC, cable news outlets and any of the liberal newspapers to propagate their hate speech. But I have news for them all. Just as "Tokyo Rose" underestimated the resolve and strength of the American fighting men, so have the Democrats underestimated the resolve of the American people.[49]

Tokyo Rose survived the defeat of Imperial Japan and the hunt for subversives during the Cold War. She survived the trial, the pardon effort, and now the death of Iva Toguri. Again and again, newspapers reported the truth about her mythical existence, and yet she survives. Even as the soldiers and sailors who created her fade away, Tokyo Rose lives on.

The contemporary Tokyo Rose has lost her sexual desirability and has thus become a somewhat paler creature. She now simply represents disloyalty, especially political disloyalty. Those who apply the label "Tokyo Rose" to their adversaries do not view them as people much like themselves whose political opinions differ from their own. Tokyo Rose is the Other, the enemy whom they fear and hate. They warn their fellow patriots against the attractions of her siren's song. They are the true Americans and she, the false, the deceitful, the traitorous. In this lies the danger, for the more passionately we embrace her legend, the more it will demoralize us by undermining our trust in one another.

The sirens lured sailors with the promise of knowledge, most especially knowledge of the future. They tempt us still. We long for certainty where there can be no certainty. We imagine ourselves as part of a vanguard of the brave and special few who do battle against treasonous neighbors and maniacal enemies of every color and persuasion. We should renounce such pretensions. Instead, we must be vigilant against ourselves, against our irrational fears and shallow hatreds, because if we are not careful, the Tokyo Rose whose presence endures in the darkness of our own subconscious needs and desires will seduce and eventually devour us.

Notes

1. In an interview with the *Chicago Tribune* on March 23, 1976, Phil stated, "I arrived in Seattle aboard a ship and immediately I was taken into custody by the FBI and immigration authorities." However, Iva told me in a 1984 telephone interview that Phil and Ted Tamba flew together to Seattle. She even remembered their carrier was Northwest Airlines. Since Phil had lived it and Iva's information was secondhand—she was in jail at the time—his version of the story would seem to be definitive. How could he forget what would have been his first plane ride? But the record is clear. Phil flew on a Douglas DC-4, aircraft N95421; Tamba was passenger No. 4, Nakamura No. 12, and Phil No. 13 on Flight 800's Airline Passenger Manifest. However, when Phil left the States following the trial, he traveled by ship with a stopover in Honolulu. This probably was the source of his confusion.

2. Airline Passenger Manifest, "Passenger and Crew Lists of Airplanes Arriving at Seattle, Washington, March 1947–November 1954." Records of the Immigration and Naturalization Service, 1891–1957, Record Group 85, Micropublication M1386. NARA, Washington, D.C. The acronym IA-NIV is no longer utilized and, given that INS now uses IV to abbreviate immigration visa, investigation, and independent verification, its meaning is unclear. "Notice to Deliver," same source.

3. *Chicago Tribune*, March 23, 1976, 3. I assume the deportation bond is the document to which he referred.

4. *Tokyo Mainichi*, January 31, 1956.

5. *Chicago Tribune*, March 24, 1976.

6. The 1980 date is from http://www.dyarstraights.com/orphan_ann/rosemyth.html.

7. I have not been able to independently verify the date of this marriage. An FBI report dates the marriage as February 2, 1966. NARA 2, Box 6. However, the same report states the wife's age was 54. On February 2, 1966, she would have been 67. Iva told me that they married while she was in prison, and I have assumed she remembered the unhappy event.

8. This woman and her children, whose names I have intentionally omitted, contested Jun's will following his death. When she died, the children continued the suit. In 1987, Iva told me, "I have a letter from the attorney of her three children. I've often thought if I ever wrote a book I might end with this letter." The attorney did a complete search of the family's holdings, including Jun's properties in Japan, and the children made demands. "They said if we didn't agree, they would have a trial that was more sensational than the one I had in 1949. I kept the letter just for this purpose." Eventually Iva settled out of court.

9. Unsigned letter postmarked April 26, 1969.

10. Richard M. Harnett, Report on UPI story, March 21, 1971. NARA 1, Box 52.

11. Chapman, *Tokyo Calling*, 342.

12. Inez Toguri Yasukawa died October 2, 1972 in Ventura, California.

13. Iva believed her father's statement throughout her life. On July 27, 1996, Iva wrote to me about the death of her sister June, "She is sorely missed. I am [the] last of the original U.S. Toguris." Although Jun's claim struck me initially as unlikely, considerable research has confirmed his statement. There were several Toguris in Hawaii but it was not admitted to statehood until 1959. As noted previously, a large and prominent Toguri family resides in Canada. My examination of census and other records for the period from 1900 to 1940 developed only Toguris associated with Jun's family.

14. The contest over Jun's will (see note 8) caused Iva to seek relief in November 1972 from DoJ agents who were garnishing her wages in order to collect the $5,255 she still owed on her fine. Her request for a hearing was denied. *Reason* (February 1976): 15.

15. Figure 20.1, courtesy of the National Japanese Historical Society.

16. Uyeda, *Report*, 5. His claim may seem surprising for a Japanese American, but national news coverage was uneven, and the Boston papers may not have highlighted the case. Uyeda claimed he was on duty from 6:30 AM until at least 7:00 PM, often had night duty, and never read the newspaper.

17. It was my pleasure to know Clifford Uyeda over many years, and the description of his character is my own. I met him in 1980, after he

had become National Executive Director of JACL. He was not shy with his opinions. I once watched him hassle a Japanese American business-man who had committed the sin of displaying little Japanese flags in his store's front window. "We work every day to be accepted by white Americans and you do this!" On another occasion, I took him to visit a film lab where he interrogated editors about the proper disposal of their used chemicals. I have also observed his softer side. At one dinner he wept over the fate of elderly Issei abandoned by their children. With him, Iva finally got lucky. Had she launched her own pardon campaign and selected her own director, she could not have found a finer human being to lead it than Clifford Uyeda. Dr. Uyeda died of cancer at age 87 on July 30, 2004. See http://www.sfgate.com/cgi-bin/article.cgi?file= /chronicle/archive/2004/08/06/BAGT383 DQM1.DTL

18. Uyeda, *Report*, 6.

19. Uyeda, *Report*, 14.

20. Uyeda details complaints of roadblocks in his *Report*, 57, 59, and 82.

21. Figure 20.2 by author.

22. *Wall Street Journal*, February 6, 1976.

23. *Detroit Free Press*, March 18, 1976.

24. *Today Show*, June 14, 1976, interview by Jim Cummins.

25. Quotations in this paragraph from *Chicago Tribune*, March 22, 1976, Section 1, 15.

26. Quotations in this paragraph from *Chicago Tribune*, March 29, 1976.

27. From "George" Ozasa's deposition. Ozasa's deposition was also compromised by the efforts of Frederick Tillman, who had him swear to statements he later denied were his own or true. He also said, erro-neously, that Charles Cousens was still with *Zero Hour* in August 1945. NARA 2, Box 9.

28. *Chicago Tribune*, March 22, 1976.

29. Ozasa was 84 when he placed the dates of Iva's apology and the drop of a box of records a few days apart and suggested they were cause and effect. He also said, "That was the first indication Iva had as to how popular she was—it made her feel real good." Iva denied ever knowing about the box. Since Ozasa knew of the drop, someone must have deliv-ered the unbroken records to Radio Tokyo and told him where they came from. I can imagine no one passed the story on to Iva since no one at the station believed she was Tokyo Rose. I can also imagine that Iva did not want to admit she was delighted to receive records addressed to Tokyo Rose. Both possibilities seem equally likely to me.

30. Uyeda, *Report*, 38.

31. Uyeda, *Report*, 42–43.

32. *Jungleer* XXVII, no. 2 (July 1976): 1.

33. *New York Times*, June 24, 1976, section 1, 29.

34. Figure 20.3, *San Francisco Chronicle*.

35. Uyeda, *Report*, Brinkley explanation and statement, 66; UPI, 67.

36. According to Clifford Uyeda who attended the press conference. See Uyeda, *Report*, 67.

37. This remarkable story from Uyeda, *Report*, 79.

38. Uyeda, *Report*, 74–75.

39. June Toguri Hori died July 6, 1996, in Anaheim, California.

40. Transcribed from broadcast, *NBC Evening News*, September 27, 2006.

41. Lyrics by Oscar Hammerstein II, music by Richard Rogers.

42. Plot summary at http://www.spiritus-temporis.com/operation-petticoat.

43. If viewers of *Flags of Our Fathers* turn on the English subtitles, they will discover the line "This is Orphan Ann" is rendered "This is all for now." I'm unclear why an English-language movie would have English-language subtitles, but I surmise that subtitlers believed hearers would quickly pass over the identification whereas readers would pull up short wondering, who is Orphan Ann?

This scene reminds me of the U.S. Treasury Department film, "The Voice of Truth" mentioned in chapter 12. See also the Charlie Chan section in chapter 3.

44. *Los Angeles Times*, October 9, 1992.

45. See http://archive.democrats.com/preview.cfm?term=propaganda.

46. *Wall Street Journal*, July 18, 2005.

47. Kevin Drum, "Political Animal." See http://www.washingtonmonthly.com/archives/individual/2006_03/008372.php

48. See http://www.buzzflash.com/reviews/05/rev05075.html. Edited for length.

49. Craig Smith, "Democrats: Today's 'Tokyo Rose.'" See http://www.worldnetdaily.com/news/article.asp?ARTICLE_ID=50412. Edited for length.

Epilogue

Plutarch explained how he crafted his seminal work of biography, the *Parallel Lives*:

> My design is not to write histories, but lives. And the most glorious exploits do not always furnish us with the clearest discoveries of virtue or vice. So I must be allowed to give my more particular attention to the marks and indications of people's souls. *Lives*, 540d–541.

History, Plutarch believed, describes what people do, whereas biography reveals who they are, most especially, their moral character. His interest in writing biography was explicitly ethical. He expected readers to learn from the valor and weakness of his subjects, and to use this knowledge to forge more honorable lives themselves.

Plutarch and other traditional biographers surely would have appreciated how the fates escalated a small flaw in Iva Toguri's character, an excess of ambition, into tragedy. Ancient Greeks and Romans would have viewed Iva's story as a cautionary tale and drawn from it moral lessons. Today, however, Plutarch's interest in discovering virtue and vice in order to illuminate his subject's soul has gone out of style. No modern author would dare presume to offer readers of his biography advice on moral conduct and improvement. Nevertheless, I want to return in this Epilogue to the classical style, which I believe has much to recommend it. I hope readers will not take offense at the moral lesson I propose, especially since it applies every bit as much to myself as it does to them.

Iva Toguri was an ordinary person. She did not plan her life to be a moment in world history. She did not seek out a role as Heroine or Scoundrel. No one would have written her biography were she not identified with an infamous Other. A book about Iva Toguri is worth reading, and her life is worth caring about, because we Americans can learn from her something about ourselves. We can witness a chapter in American history in which our society did unto the least of its citizens what could in the future, if we are not careful, be done unto any of us.

The quest to identify Tokyo Rose grew in intensity throughout World War II until it became a virtual tornado. Iva Toguri once stood where the tornado touched down. Her sudden elevation from obscurity to worldwide fame and disgrace destroyed much of what she had, but she lived through it. Although Iva paid a great price for her notoriety in the evening papers of America, she did not lose her way. After the American judicial system had done its worst, after she had served her time in prison, and after journalists had moved on to other stories, she picked herself up and began the sober task of rebuilding her life. Although the reader, like the author, may applaud Iva's bravery and determination, he or she must not lose sight of the fact that a place in history sometimes comes very dear.

Tokyo Rose will abide defiantly in the spotlight of public memory as one of history's great villains. Iva Toguri has returned to obscurity, her name an artifact of historical trivia. Neither rich, beautiful, brilliant, nor saintly, she was in essence you and me. This biography belongs to her, but also to every individual who must confront the blindness of state and cultural institutions, the ignorance of crowds, and the treachery of powerful but morally weak officials.

Plutarch's *Parallel Lives* served as my model for this dual treatment of Iva Toguri and Tokyo Rose, and I now close with an endorsement of his antiquated yet venerable philosophy of biography: the primacy of character in understanding the life. Iva

Toguri's character determined in the end who she was. Trapped in the authoritarian regime of Imperial Japan, she did not sell out her citizenship to serve her own interests. If her every action during the war did not achieve an ideal of perfect patriotism, it was only because she needed to survive. Unfairly hated by the American public and unjustly persecuted by the American government, she never turned against her country. She made mistakes, some rather foolish, but when it counted, Iva didn't change her stripes.

Iva Toguri can serve, therefore, as a moral example for all of us who may be called upon, perhaps when we least expect it, to stand firm against the ofttimes vicious forces of history. We have one hope of emerging from such a trial with our moral character intact, and that is to be resolute, grounded in our most precious possession, our own integrity.

Appendix

The Indictment

That said defendant committed each and every one of the overt acts herein described with treasonable intent and for the purpose of, and with the intent in her to adhere to and give aid and comfort to the Imperial Japanese Government.

Overt Act I

Between March 1, 1944 and May 1, 1944, the exact date being to the Grand Jurors unknown, defendant in the offices of the Broadcasting Corporation of Japan discussed with another person the proposed participation of defendant in the radio broadcasting program.

Overt Act II

Between March 1, 1944 and May 1, 1944, the exact date being to the Grand Jurors unknown, defendant in the offices of the Broadcasting Corporation of Japan did discuss with employees of the said corporation the nature and quality of a specific proposed radio broadcast.

Overt Act III

Between March 1, 1944 and May 1, 1944, the exact date being to the Grand Jurors unknown, defendant in the offices of the Broadcasting Corporation of Japan did speak into a microphone regarding the introduction of a program dealing with a motion picture involving war.

Overt Act IV

Between March 1, 1944 and May 1, 1944, the exact date being to the Grand Jurors unknown, defendant in the offices of the Broadcasting Corporation of Japan did speak into a microphone referring to enemies of Japan.

Overt Act V

Between March 1, 1944 and May 1, 1944, the exact date being to the Grand Jurors unknown, defendant in the offices of the Broadcasting Corporation of Japan did prepare a script for subsequent radio broadcast concerning the loss of ships.

Overt Act VI

That on a day during October 1944, the exact date being to the Grand Jurors unknown, the defendant in the offices of the Broadcasting Corporation of Japan did speak into a microphone concerning the loss of ships.

Overt Act VII

That on or about May 23, 1945, the defendant in the offices of the Broadcasting Corporation of Japan did prepare a radio script for subsequent broadcast.

Overt Act VIII

That on a day between May 1, 1945 and July 31, 1945, the exact date being to the Grand Jurors unknown, defendant in the offices of the Broadcasting Corporation of Japan did engage in an entertainment dialogue with an employee of the Broadcasting Corporation of Japan for radio broadcast purposes.

Bibliography

Government Documents

U.S. National Archives and Research Administration (NARA)

NARA 1. College Park, Maryland. Series: Headquarters Files from Classification 61 (Treason) Released Under the Nazi War Crimes and Japanese Imperial Government Disclosure Acts, March 22, 1935–April 9, 1984. Record Group 65: Records of the Federal Bureau of Investigation. Entry: A1-136L. File Number: 61-11000. Boxes 39–52.

NARA 2. College Park, Maryland. Series: Select Subject Files Relating to the Treasonable Utterances of Iva Toguri D'Aquino (a.k.a. Tokyo Rose) Released Under the Nazi War Crimes and Japanese Imperial Government Disclosure Acts, 1942–1967. Record Group 60: General Records of the Department of Justice. Entry: A1-1082. File number: 146-28-1941. Boxes 1–18.

NARA 3. College Park, Maryland. Series: Select Field Office Case Files From Classification 61 (Treason) Released Under the Nazi War Crimes and Japanese Imperial Government Disclosure Acts, 1942–2004. Record Group 65 (above). Entry A1-149. Boxes: 1–11.

NARA 4. San Bruno, California. Series: Records of the District Courts of the United States, Northern District of California, San Francisco Criminal Case Files, 1936–1949. Record Group 21: Records of the District Courts of the United States, 1685–1991. Boxes 263–270.

511

NARA 5. San Bruno, California. Series: Ninth Circuit Court of Appeals, Case #12383 ("Tokyo Rose"), 12381–83. Record Group 276: Records of the U.S. Courts of Appeals. Boxes 4959–4961.

NARA 6. San Bruno, California. Series: Records of the U.S. Attorneys, Northern District of California, Records Related to Criminal Case 31712, *U.S. vs. Iva Ikuko Toguri D'Aquino*, 1943–1969. Record Group 118: Records of U.S. Attorneys, 1821–1980. Boxes 1–3.

NARA 7. College Park, Maryland. Series: Sugamo Prison Records (1945–1952), Released Prisoner 201 Files. Record Group 554: Records of General Headquarters, Far East Command, Supreme Commander Allied Powers, and United Nations Command. Box 58.

NARA 8. College Park, Maryland. Series: Army Signal Corps, "Tokyo Rose." Record Group 111: Records of the Office of the Chief Signal Officer, 1860–1982. Still and moving images, Special Media Archives Services Division. Other non-Signal Corps. images also included.

NARA 9. College Park, Maryland. Series: Wallace Ellwell Ince. Record Group 65 (above). Boxes 237–241.

NARA 10. College Park, Maryland. Series: Transcripts of Broadcasts from Tokyo and Manila. Record Group 262: Records of the Foreign Broadcast Intelligence Service, 1940–1947. Boxes 730–754 and 392–398.

NARA 11. College Park, Maryland. Series: Provost Division. RG 389: Records of the Office of the Provost Marshal General, Tokyo Rose Investigative File, 1947–1955. Box 1.

Army Heritage and Education Center Collection (AHEC). Carlisle, Pennsylvania. The Charles A. Willoughby Papers, 1941–1972. Operations of Military and Civil Censorship, Volume X, Intelligence Series, Documentary Appendices I and II. Boxes 1–13.

Books and Articles Cited More Than Once (in alphabetical order by author's last name)

Asahi Shimbum staff. *The Pacific Rivals.* (New York: Weatherhill/Asahi, 1972).

Chapman, Ivan. *Tokyo Calling: The Charles Cousens Case.* (Sydney: Hale & Iremonger, 1990).

Christgau, John. "Wayne Collins versus the World: The Fight to Restore Citizenship to Japanese American Renunciants of World War II." *Pacific Historical Review* 54, no. 1 (February 1985): 1–31.

Duus, Masayo. *Tokyo Rose: Orphan of the Pacific.* (Tokyo: Kodansha International, 1979).

Gabler, Neal. *Winchell: Gossip, Power and the Culture of Celebrity.* (New York: Alfred A. Knopf, 1995).

Goodman, Jack, ed. *While You Were Gone.* (New York: Simon and Schuster, 1946).

Gunn, Rex. *They Called Her Tokyo Rose.* (Self-published, 1977).

Havens, Thomas H. R. *Valley of Darkness: The Japanese People and World War Two.* (New York: W. W. Norton & Company, 1978).

Howe, Russell Warren. *The Hunt for "Tokyo Rose."* (New York: Madison Books, 1990).

Ienaga, Saburo, trans. Frank Baldwin. *The Pacific War: World War II and the Japanese, 1931–1945.* (New York: Pantheon Books, 1978).

Kato, Masuo. *The Lost War: A Japanese Reporter's Inside Story.* (New York: A.A. Knopf, 1946).

Kutler, Stanley "Forging A Legend." *Wisconsin Law Review* 1980, no. 6 (1980): 1341–82.

Lee, Clark. *One Last Look Around.* (New York: Duell, Sloan and Pierce, 1947).

MacArthur, Douglas. *Reminiscences.* (New York: McGraw-Hill, 1964).

McWilliams, Carey. *Prejudice: Japanese-Americans: Symbol of Racial Intolerance.* (Boston: Little, Brown and Company, 1944).

Meo, Lucy D. *Japan's Radio War on Australia.* (New York: Cambridge University Press, 1968).

Modell, John. *The Economics and Politics of Racial Accommodation: The Japanese of Los Angeles, 1900–1942.* (Urbana: University of Illinois Press, 1977).

Morison, Samuel Eliot. *History of United States Naval Operations in World War II.* (Boston: Little, Brown & Co., 1957).

O'Brien, David J. and Stephen S. Fugita. *The Japanese American Experience.* (Bloomington: Indiana University Press, 1991).

Robbins, Jane. *Tokyo Calling: Japanese Overseas Radio Broadcasting, 1937–1945.* (Florence, Italy: European Press Academic Publishing, 2001).

Shillony, Ben-Ami. *Politics and Culture in Wartime Japan.* (Oxford: Clarendon Press, 1981).

Short, K. R. M., ed. *Film & Radio Propaganda in World War II.* (Knoxville: University of Tennessee Press, 1983).

Smith, Bradford. *Americans from Japan.* (New York: J. B. Lippincott, 1948).

Storry, Richard. *A History of Modern Japan.* (Baltimore: Penguin Books, 1960).

Thorne, Christopher. *Allies of a Kind.* (New York: Oxford University Press, 1978).

Tolischus, Otto D. *Tokyo Record.* (New York: Reynal & Hitchcock, 1943).

Uyeda, Clifford I. *The Pardoning of "Tokyo Rose": The presidential pardon and the restoration of American citizenship to Iva Ikuko Toguri D'Aquino: A Report.* Seattle: University of Washington. *Asian American Studies Program Occasional Monographs Series,* no. 1 (1980). (Note: This report is generally difficult to find, but Uyeda presented it along with seven volumes of committee reports and other memorabilia to the Bancroft Library at the University of California at Berkeley.)

Women against War, compiled by Women's Division of Soka Gakkai and trans. Richard L. Gage. (New York: Kodansha International, 1986).

Other References

Beebe Interview. Katherine Beebe was interviewed as part of an oral history series by Shirley Biagi. www.npc.press.org/wpforal/beebe3.htm (January 3, 1991).

Toguri Notes. Iva Toguri gave me a copy of notes she had typed years earlier for use in writing this book. They appear to be her memories of people and events typed before her trial, but I cannot be sure of that. There are more than 80 pages, but many pages have no numbers and those that do follow no particular order. Thus, page 5 is about a reporter she met after the war, on page 5C she denies she knows anyone named Namikawa, pages 8 to 11 do not exist, etc. Therefore, I have not bothered with page numbers.

Toguri Memories of 2000. In 2000, during Iva Toguri's annual visit to my home, I encouraged her to put into writing personal memories that only she would know. To show her what I had in mind, we sat together at the computer, and I typed her stories as she told them to me during the week.

Tokyo Rose LP. "Tokyo Rose," Long Playing 33 1/3 vinyl record, MR-1076, Actuality Series No. 2, Release No. 76, produced by the Radiola Company, 1977.

Index

Axis Sally (Mildred Gillars), 45–46,
64n13, 64n15, 188–190, 194,
213n42, 302, 465–466, 498

Beebe, Katherine (also Pinkham,
Harris), 293n14, 340, 344,
352n64, 383, 438

Chapman, Ivan, 104n38, 150n19,
168, 238n27, 238n29
Churchill, Winston, 36, 91
Clark, Tom, 109, 115, 302–303, 307,
311–312, 318n52, 332, 334, 339,
463, 476n47, 482
Collins (the elder), Wayne
Mortimer, 101n9, 102n19,
112–115, 128n15, 128n17,
272n33, 319n59, 321–324,
327–334, 339, *341*, 341–343,
350n32, 354n88, 360–366,
368–384, 386n12, 392–401, 404–
405, 409–414, 417–420, 423, 439,
443, 454–457, 459, 463, 469–470,
480, 482–483, 485–486, 489,
492–493, 495

Collins (the younger), Wayne
Merrill, 471–483, 486, 490–491,
491
communism: Japan, 72–74, 89,
100n1; United States, xvi, 10,
297–298, 303, 331, 346, 422, 448,
466, 476n46
Cousens, Charles, 95–98, 100,
104n38, 106n44, 141, 146–148,
150n19, 151n21, 153n39,
155–158, 162, 166–169, 172–173,
174n3, 175n4, 175n8–9, 176n12,
178n43–44, 219, 226–230, 236n2,
238n27, 238n29–30, 256, 277,
286–287, 310, 326–327, 329, 332,
364–365, *392*, 392–401, 403, 407,
421, 426, 429, 431n17, 431n31,
441, 483, 502n27

D'Aquino, Phil (Felipe), 92–93,
134–136, 144, 149n5, 219,
221–223, 230, 233, 238n30,
238n40, 239n41–43, 239n46, 242–
247, *246*, 256–258, 262, 264, 268,
282, 286, *289*, 290–291, 292n1,

295n36, 305, 318n58, 329, 331,
414, 479–482, 500n1
D'Aquino family, 92–93, 134–135,
219, 221–223, 236n6
DeWitt, John L., 108–109, 113–114
DeWolfe, Thomas E., 149n5,
294n27, 310–312, 318n58,
322–340, *338*, 345–348, 348n2,
352n54, 352n58, 353n77, 354n78,
357–375, 380, 383, 386n23, 393,
398, 402–414, 417–423, 427, 437,
451, 455, 463, 467, 472–473
Domei News Agency, 90–92,
100, 102n19, 103n21, 134–136,
140–141, 144, 150n16, 166, 215,
239n40, 256, 262–263, 270n14,
414–415
Doolittle raid, 88–89, 101n17,
102n18–19, 176n18, 188, 235, 497
Douglas, William O., 112–113, 328,
455, 463, 476n46–47
Dunn, J. Eldon, 175n7, *314*, 319n61,
322, 332–333, 340, 400, 406–408,
430, 433n70, 443
Duus, Masayo, 22n13, 23n15,
115, 129n27, 176n20, 194, 269,
293n14, 294n25, 295n36, 318n49,
318n58, 348n1, 387n25, 425–426,
432n47, 439–440, 444n5, 487

Earhart, Amelia, 193–194
Eisenhart, J. Richard, 269, 359–361,
385n8, 415, 456, 461

Furuya Company, 4–5, 18, 21n10,
117
Furuya Oki, Mieko, 159, 223, 244,
256, 335

Gillars, Mildred, *see* Axis Sally
Great East Asia Co-Prosperity
Sphere, 31, 94, 139, 407

Hattori family, 67–76, 79n2, 79n9,
80n17, 83, 85, 89–90, 94, 100n1,
102n19, 239n46
Hayakawa, Ruth, 150n18–19, 159,
162, 166, 176n14, 227, 258, 267,
433n70, 434n75
Hayakawa, S.I., 492
Hearst, William Randolph and
Hearst syndicate, 107, 256–259,
270n7, 306
Hennessy, Frank, 112, *338*, 340,
398, 437, 455
Hoover, J. Edgar, 267, 299, 301,
306–307, 317n31, 317n42, 324,
332, 348, 349n17, 386n23
Howe, Russell Warren, 115, 269,
318n58, 335–336, 351n49–50,
353n66, 354n88, 388n55, 403,
424–426, 436n114, 440, 444n5,
444n21

Ince, Wallace "Ted," 99–100,
106n44, 106n49, 141, 146–147,
151n20–21, 155–157, 162,
169–170, 175n7–8, 219, 230, 235,
236n2, 238n32, 239n47, 256,
277, 286–287, 310, 323–324, 326,
332–333, 364, *398*, 398–404,
407–410, 414, 421–422,
426–427, 429, 431n30–31,
433n68, 436n113–115, 451–452,
475n19
internment camps, *see* Japanese
Americans
Ishii, Ken and Mary, 159, 424
Ito, Chiyeko, 35–37, 38n18, 70,
80n25, 84–85, 88–89, 101n17,
223, 412–413, 417, 434n75, 481

Japan: emperor, 5, 21n8, 74, 77–8,
137, 140, 207, 252–253, 255,
415, 484; Metropolitan Police,

70–71, 83–86, 89, 93–94, 101n2, 102n19, 103n20, 104n38, 134, 136, 173–174, 222–223, 247, 265, 286, 291, 366, 384, 391, 414, 417, 421, 430n1–2, 441, 457; military (Imperial Army and Navy), 28, 31, 46, 76–78, 87–88, 91–92, 95, 99–100, 133–134, 144, 219–221, 230–232, 248–250, 252–253, Military Police, *Kempeitai*, 73–74, 83, 96–100, 136, 141, 148, 150n19, 167, 178n43, 223, 232–233, 239n46, 275, 300, 375, 391, 394, 396, 416–417, 430n1, 434n85–86, 441, 457; racial attitudes, 88–89, 94–96, 138; radio / propaganda, 34, 95–100, 104n32, 104n37, 142–148, 184–188, 190–191, 195; rationing, 35, 69, 71, 84–85, 87, 90, 134–135, 137, 139, 217–218, 220, 223–226; Thought Police, *Tokkotai*, 30, 72–73, 83, 86, 93–94, 101n2, 136–137, 223, 275; war with China, 28–29, 31–32, 71–73, 77, 96

Japanese American Citizens League, xvi, 107, 302, 486–487, 493, 501n17

Japanese Americans (*Issei* and *Nisei*), 3–4, 11, 16, 24n23, 112–115, 331; prejudice against, 9–13, 16, 24n22–23, 27–28, 107–109, 123–125, 243, 288, 290, 313; internment, 108–115, 118, 124–126, 128n13, 195; Japan, support for, 118, 136, 166

kamikaze, *see* suicide

Kato, Margaret, 148, 159, 168, 153n42, 178n43

Kato, Matsuo, 36, 173, 219

Lee, Clark, 63n2, 102n18, 131n48, 176n18, 181, 256–258, 261–264, 270n7, 270n14, 271n32–33, 306–307, 311, 323, 349n15, 365–368, 386n23, 387n25, 422–429, 436n112, 439

Lipton, Myrtle, 153n39, 159–165, 167, 176n16, 176n21, 177n22, 177n25, 177n30–31, 284, 351n38, 377

Manila Rose, 159, 227, 237n26, 304, 354n80. *See also* Myrtle Lipton

Matsumiya Japanese Cultural School, 75, 80n22, 89–91, 102n19, 140

Mitsushio, George, 146–147, 150n18, 152n31, 152n33, 152n35–36, 153n38, 155, 157, 226–227, 230, 278, 318n54, 334–337, 351n49, 351n51, 366, 368–374, *369*, 387n33, 400, 413, 415, 422–425, 428, 430, 444n12, 457, 488–489

Moruka Reyes, Kathy, 159, 244, 258, 404

movies relevant to Tokyo Rose (various), xiv, 49–50, 63n2, 188–190, 211n12, 266, 273n41, 290, 496–497, 403n43,

Mutsu, Ian, 103n21, 135–136

Nakamura, Satoshi, 244, 422, 424, 428–429

Nakamura, Tetsujiro, 115. *341*, 343, 398–399, 479

Namikawa, Ryo, 97, 104n38, 152n32, 152n36, 514

Native Sons of the Golden West, 10, 24n22, 301

Neighborhood Associations, 84–85, 134, 140, 232

Oki, Kenkichi, 146, 153n38, 157, 227, 230, 244, 256–257, 265, 270n5, 270n11, 278, 318n54, 334–337, 350n31, 351n51, 366, 368–370, 374, 399–400, 413, 422–425, 428, 430, 444n12, 457, 488–489

Plutarch, xiii, xv, 505–506

Reyes, Norman, 87–88, 99–100, 106n45, 106n48–49, 141–142, 146–147, 152n36, 157, 236n2, 244, 246, 256, 270n11, 287, 310, 326, 332–334, 364, 400–410, *401*, 419, 422–423, 429, 432n55, 435n92
Roosevelt, Franklin Delano and Eleanor, 30–36, 45, 97, 108, 111, 128n3, 142, 187, 198, 284, 300, 465

Saisho, Foumy, 97–98, 104n38, 105n39, 150n19, 166–168, 174n3, 178n33, 178n37, 178n42–44, 182, 267, 396, 432n41
Sugamo Prison, 102n19, 268–269, 273n47, 275, 280–282, 285–286, 288, *289*, 292n1, 294n35, 295n36–37, 312, 318n58, 341, 359–361, 391, 415, 418, 456
suicide/kamikaze, xiii, 23, 31, 41, 88, 97, 100, 140, 163, 221, 230, 249–252, 261, 314, 319n61, 366–367, 425, 427, 429, 472–473, 483
Suyama, June, 159, 178n43, 228

Tillman, Frederick, 102n19, 161, 175n7, 178n33, 267, 269, 284–286, 294n23, 294n25–27, 311, *314*, 319n61, 322, 330, 332–333, 340, 350n32, 353n66,

375, 400, 405–408, 418–421, 427, 430, 432n55, 433n70, 443, 502n27
Toguri, Fred Koichiro, 1, 5, *6*, 22n14–15, 7–8, 18, 22n14, 23n15, 27, 35, 38n16, 110–111, 117, 124–125, *126*, 130n39, 131n47, 294n24, 469, 483, 492, 494
Toguri, Fumi Iimuro, 1–5, *6*, 7–8, 14–18, 20n6, 22n12–14, 23n15, 33–36, 75, 105n39, 110, 117, 120, 125, 129n27, 284, 293n19, 313, 403, 418–419, 482–484, 493
Toguri, Inez Hisako, 1, 5, *6*, 7–8, 23n15, 38n16, 110–111, 124, 469, 471, 483, 501n12
Toguri, Iva, *xviii*, *6*; ability to speak Japanese, 34–35, 37, 38n16, 72, 75–76, 90–91, 140, 216–217, 265. *See also* Matsumiya Japanese Cultural School; analysis of treasonous taunt, 423–430; citizenship and passport, xvi, 36, 70, 83, 85–86, 90, 94, 103n20, 104n26, 141, 166, 174, 244, 246, 258, 264, 267, 275, 282, 290–292, 295n41, 300, 312, 329, 342, 362, 366, 369, 391, 413, 417–419, 430n1, 457, 462–463, 468, 471, 479, 481, 486, 493, 495, 507; education, 2–3, 8–9, 15, 17–18, 24n31, 27. *See also* Matsumiya Japanese Cultural School; illness, 2, 18, 69, 135–136, 468, 493; jobs, 27, 90–91, 102n19, 103n22, 140–141, 150n16, 155–158, 215–219, 415, 450, 452–454, 458–459, 464–465, 494; ration cards, xiii, 90, 103n20, 134, 232, 291, 441; residences, 24n31, 79n2, 236n8, 449, 474n8, 493; romance and marriage, 16,

18, 27–28, 89, 244–246, 291, 329,
    375, 417, 481–482
Toguri, Jun Mamoru, xvi, 1–5,
    6, 7–11, 13–19, 20n4, 20n6–9,
    22n13, 24, 27–28, 33–37, 69–70,
    75–76, 79n8, 80n24, 107,
    109–112, 116–121, *121*, 124–127,
    129n25–26, 129n28, 129n31,
    130n39, 141, 217, 245, 256, 259,
    283–285, 294n23, 294n35, 313,
    315, 320n62, 321–322, 348n1,
    358–359, 403, 414, 450, 458,
    467–470, 480–485, 492–494
Toguri, June Mizue, xvii, 1–5, *6*,
    9–11, 20n5, 23n15–16, 34, 38n16,
    110–111, 115, 124–127, *126*,
    128n12, 130n39, 131n46–47, 256,
    285, 293n21, 294n23–24, 321,
    323, 361, 484, 493–495, 501n13,
    503n39
Toguri, Makoto, 115–122, *120*, *121*,
    129n26–28, 129n31
Tojo, Premier, 72, 77, 88
Tokyo Rose, vii, xiii–xvi, 1, 16,
    41–62, 63n2, 63n4, 100, 115, 127,
    144–145, 151n29, 156, 159–167,
    174n2, 175n9, 176n21, 178n33,
    180–210, 211n10, 211n12,
    226–229, 235, 237n26, 255–258,
    261–266, 269, 270n4–5, 270n11,
    272n37, 275–285, 290–292,
    298–312, 316n12, 318n53, 326,
    329, 331–332, 339–342, 347–348,
    348n1, 357–362, 367, 374,
    377–383, 402–403, 411–412, 415,
    425, 432n41, 461–462, 485–487,
    489, 495–500, 502n29, 506

Tolishchus, Otto, 30, 67–68, 86
treason, 153n38, 161, 166, 168–174,
    176n12, 179n46, 244, 258,
    262–269, 275, 277–279, 284–287,
    292, 301–302, 307, 310–313,
    325–329, 333–335, 338, 342, 347,
    350n26, 357–360, 362, 368–369,
    373, 376, 384–385, 395, 398, 406,
    419, 437–438, 442, 450–452, 457,
    462–471, 476n46, 479, 488–489,
    496, 500, 509–510
Truman, Harry, xiv, xvi, 115,
    297–303, 307, 316n5, 463, 476n47

Uyeda, Clifford, xvi, 295n38, *485*,
    485–493, 501n16–17, 502n20

Warren, Earl, 109, *344*, 471

Yamamoto, Admiral, 77, 144
Yamato, battleship, 31, 230, 250
Young, James, 30, 300

Zero Hour, 146–147, 152n31–32,
    152n35–36, 153n39, 155–166,
    169–173, 174n2, 175n4,
    176n13–14, 191–193, 208–210,
    223, 226–230, 238n32, 244, 256,
    260–262, 265–267, 270n4,
    277–278, 283, 287, 304, 310,
    325–327, 334–336, 342, 347–348,
    354n86, 354n88, 364–371,
    379–382, 384–385, 386n21,
    388n51, 390n80, 394–396,
    399–401, 407–411, 419–429,
    435n105, 437, 440, 461–462, 489,
    502n27

About the Author

Frederick P. Close has a background in public broadcasting and education. As a founder of the non-profit Southwest Center for Educational Television, Close spearheaded the production of 76 ethnographic documentaries produced throughout the United States, Mexico, and Puerto Rico and broadcast in four season-long series by the Public Broadcasting Service (PBS) and National Public Radio (NPR), as well as selected commercial television, radio, and cable channels in the United States, Canada, and Latin America. The award-winning documentaries, highlighting ethnic American communities, addressed a series of issues including social history, culture, ethnicity and race, immigration, unemployment, and the problems faced by disaffected inner-city youths. His seminal documentary, *The End of the Race*, examining the dilemma faced by the long-distance runners of the Pueblo Indians of New Mexico, whose striving for individual success is at odds with aspects of their culture, was included in the Corporation for Public Broadcasting's Independent Anthology Series on PBS and is exhibited in the collection of the Smithsonian's National Museum of the American Indian. A writer, lecturer, and consultant on the subjects of ethics and morality, Close was one of the founders of the Character Education Partnership, based in Washington, D.C., an umbrella organization of educators, teachers' groups, youth organizations, and corporations with an interest in character education. Close has a B.A. degree from Stanford University, graduating with departmental honors, and M.A. and Ph.D. degrees from the University of Texas at Austin.